HISTORY OF THE CHURCH

I

HISTORY OF THE CHURCH

Edited by
HUBERT JEDIN
and
JOHN DOLAN

Volume I

FROM THE
APOSTOLIC COMMUNITY
TO CONSTANTINE

by

KARL BAUS

With a

General Introduction to Church History

by

HUBERT JEDIN

A Crossroad Book
THE SEABURY PRESS · NEW YORK

1980

The Seabury Press

815 Second Avenue

New York, N.Y. 10017

Translated from the *Handbuch der Kirchengeschichte*, edited by Hubert Jedin

Vol. I: *Von der Urgemeinde zur frühchristlichen Grosskirche*, 3rd ed.

© Verlag Herder KG Freiburg im Breisgau 1962

English translation © 1965 Herder KG

Printed in the United States of America

Library of Congress Cataloging in Publication Data

Jedin, Hubert, 1900-   ed.

History of the church.

Translation of Handbuch der Kirchengenschichte..

"A Crossroad book."

Vols. 1, 3, and 4 previously issued under title:

Handbook of church history.

Includes bibliographies and indexes.

CONTENTS: [etc.]—v. 5. Iserloh, E., Glazik, J. and

Jedin, H. Reformation and counter reformation.

1. Church history. I. Dolan, John Patrick. II. Title.

BR145.2.J413   1980 v. 1   270   79-29649

ISBN 0-8164-1038-0 (v. 1)

CONTENTS

PART TWO: THE GREAT CHURCH OF EARLY CHRISTIAN TIMES
(c. A.D. 180–324)

CONTENTS

CONTENTS

PREFACE

As any historical work of this kind must do, the handbook seeks first of all
to give a reliable account of the principal events and leading figures in
Church history. In the second place — and here it is distinguished from
most previous manuals — it examines not only the Church's external career
in the world but also her inner life, the development of her doctrine and
preaching, her ritual and devotion. Our presentation does not follow the
usual lines but attempts to evoke the fruitful plenitude of the mystery
which is the Church by shedding light on the interaction between her
outward vicissitudes and her inner life. With this end in view (and in
order to avoid duplication as far as possible) the collaborators drew up
a complete table of contents in 1958, and at their last meeting in Trier, in
1960, submitted specimen chapters which indicated the arrangement and
orientation of the book. We discovered in the course of this work how
difficult it is to give the most comprehensive possible account of the facts
in a readable style. Each collaborator has had to wrestle with this problem;
with what success, we must leave the critics to judge.

No less difficult was the problem of sources and literature. The handbook
must after all provide an introduction to these if it is to be useful not
only at university level but also for religious instruction in secondary
schools and for adult education. Now bibliographies of every sort abound.
But who is in a position to collect the material there cited — scattered as
it is all over the world —, to read it, and to sift the important information
from the unimportant? We had to content ourselves with a limited bibliography relevant to our purpose and selected on the following principles:
we must indicate the most important sources and such of the older literature
as is still indispensable, and cite the most recent books and articles in
which further bibliography can be found. The Bibliography at the back
of the book contains a section for each chapter. Reference to sources and
literature on special subjects, as well as some biographical material in the

sections on modern times, are given in the footnotes, which we have purposely kept to a minimum.

The chief editor, Professor Jedin, has attempted in the General Introduction to Church History to point out the basic method of this discipline and to show in more detail than has been done hitherto how the Church's consciousness of her history evolved into an academic study. It is a first attempt and the writer is by no means unaware of its shortcomings.

The author of this volume on the pre-Constantinian Church, Professor Baus, was only entrusted with his task in 1958. Some of his decisions regarding choice of material and the scope of particular chapters were taken in view of the following considerations: The apostolic age might have been given much fuller treatment on the basis of the history of New Testament times, but the volume would then have far exceeded the size proposed. The author has therefore tried to summarize those features of the early Church which continue to characterize her during her subsequent history. The bibliography for this period sufficiently indicates his indebtedness to special studies. In contrast with most textbooks, considerable space is here devoted to the development of Christian literature, a factor of such importance for the Church's inner life that its neglect would seriously distort the general picture. Finally, the special aims of the handbook made it necessary to include comparatively detailed chapters on the growth of early Christian liturgy, on the sacrament of penance, and on the life of the Christian community, which in certain respects — for example the spirituality of baptism and martyrdom — are still an almost untouched field.

In the course of preparing this volume the author received help from many quarters, help which was most welcome when it took the form of criticism. He is indebted in the first place to the other collaborators, but particularly so to the general editor, Hubert Jedin, to his former teacher J. A. Jungmann, and to Oskar Köhler, head of the Lexicographical Institute at the publishing house of Herder. A special word of thanks is also due to the staff of the library of the Theological Faculty at Trier, who showed such zeal in finding important literature.

This first volume of the handbook appears during the deliberations of the Second Vatican Council. The authors hope that their work may contribute in some measure to a deeper understanding of the Church and a greater love for her.

Hubert Jedin, Karl Baus

PREFACE TO THE ENGLISH EDITION

It is sincerely hoped that the appearance of the English version of the *Handbuch der Kirchengeschichte* so soon after the original German edition will fill a long neglected need in this area of study. Over half a century, unparalleled in productive historical research, has passed since the publication in English of Funk's *Manual of Church History*. Similar works available in translation have, for the most part, failed to utilize much of the post-war scholarship in scriptural and patristical studies. Unlike traditional manuals of this type, with their skeletal outlines and perfunctory narrative, the present work combines a wealth of current and scholarly research with an accompanying text that is equally scholarly in presentation and interpretation. The *Handbuch* not only offers the student precise information on the important events and personalities in the history of the Church, it also focuses considerable attention on all that expresses or reflects its internal life — the development of dogma, liturgy, ecclesiastical organization, the spiritual and moral life, and the literary activity of the Christian communities.

The ample treatment given the Dead Sea scrolls and the discoveries at Nag Hammadi is extremely relevant as theologians continue to rethink the attitude of the primitive Church toward Judaism and to examine the syncretistic aspects of early Christianity and its reaction to the ancient mythological image of the world. The international and non-sectarian composition of the secondary source material gives the book an ecumenical dimension, while the objective treatment of such problems as the Vatican excavations and the political turn of Constantine to Christianity are representative of its avoidance of the polemic and confessional partisanship often latent in Church histories.

Professor Jedin's masterful introductory essay on the historical development of Church history from Christian antiquity to the present day is a forthright declaration of the serious academic nature of ecclesiastical history and may well prove a literary landmark in the final emancipation of that discipline from the lingering effects of the rationalistic attack on the theological interpretation of history. It confronts the anti-historical mentality, so dominant since Trent — with its tendency to isolate dogma from the living fabric of history —, with a bold affirmation of the need for examining the Church in its concrete and contingent development. The neglect of the study of Church history in seminaries and the curious lack of chairs of ecclesiastical history in Catholic universities point only too clearly to a need for some kind of reappraisal.

Above all the *Handbuch* aims at implementing the conviction that theology is an activity within the historic organism of the Church, and that Church history must not only provide the necessary framework and documentary material for this activity, it must also communicate the life and the mind of the Church as well.

John P. Dolan

LIST OF ABBREVIATIONS

AAB *Abhandlungen der Deutschen* (till 1944: *Preussischen*) *Akademie der Wissenschaften zu Berlin*. Phil.-hist. Klasse, Berlin 1815 seqq.

AAG *Abhandlungen der Akademie der Wissenschaften in Göttingen* (down to Series III, 26, 1940: *AGG*), Göttingen 1949 seqq.

AAH *Abhandlungen der Heidelberger Akademie der Wissenschaften*, Phil.-hist. Klasse, Heidelberg 1913 seqq.

AAM *Abhandlungen der Bayerischen Akademie der Wissenschaften*, Phil.-hist. Klasse, Munich 1835 seqq.

Abel HP F.-M. Abel, *Histoire de la Palestine depuis la conquête d'Alexandre jusqu'à l'invasion arabe*, I–II, Paris 1952.

ACO *Acta Conciliorum Oecumenicorum*, ed. by E. Schwartz, Berlin 1914 seqq.

ActaSS *Acta Sanctorum*, ed. Bollandus etc. (Antwerp, Brussels, Tongerloo) Paris 1643 seqq., Venice 1734 seqq., Paris 1863 seqq.

ACW *Ancient Christian Writers*, ed. by J. Quasten and J. C. Plumpe, Westminster, Md. – London 1946 seqq.

ADipl *Archiv für Diplomatik, Schriftgeschichte, Siegel- und Wappenkunde*, Münster – Cologne 1955 seqq.

Aegyptus *Aegyptus, Rivista Italiana di Egittologia e Papirologia*, Milan 1920 seqq.

AElsKG *Archiv für elsässische Kirchengeschichte*, publ. by the Gesellschaft für elsässische Kirchengeschichte, ed. by J. Brauner, Rixheim im Oberelsass 1926 seqq.; since 1946 ed. by A. M. Burg, Strasbourg.

AGG *Abhandlungen der Gesellschaft der Wissenschaften zu Göttingen* (after Series III, 27, 1942: *AAG*), Göttingen 1843 seqq.

AH *Analecta Hymnica*, ed. by G. Dreves and C. Blume, 55 vols., Leipzig 1886–1922.

AHVNrh *Annalen des Historischen Vereins für den Niederrhein, insbesondere das alte Erzbistum Köln*, Cologne 1855 seqq.

AkathKR *Archiv für katholisches Kirchenrecht*, (Innsbruck) Mainz 1857 seqq.

AKG *Archiv für Kulturgeschichte*, (Leipzig) Münster and Cologne 1903 seqq.

Altaner B. Altaner, *Patrology*, Freiburg – London – New York, 2nd imp. 1960.

ALW *Archiv für Liturgiewissenschaft* (formerly *JLW*), Regensburg 1950 seqq.

AnBoll *Analecta Bollandiana*, Brussels 1882 seqq.

ANF *Ante-Nicene Fathers* (Buffalo Collection) 1804–86.

AnGr *Analecta Gregoriana cura Pontificiae Universitatis Gregorianae edita*, Rome 1930 seqq.

ANL   *Ante-Nicene Christian Library* (Edinburgh Collection) 1866–72.

AnzAW   *Anzeiger der Oesterreichischen Akademie der Wissenschaften*, Vienna 1864 seqq.

AÖG   *Archiv für österreichische Geschichte*, Vienna 1865 seqq.

APhilHistOS   *Annuaire de l'Institut de Philologie et d'Histoire Orientales et Slaves*, Brussels 1932 seqq.

APraem   *Analecta Praemonstratensia*, Tongerloo 1925 seqq.

ArSKG   *Archiv für schlesische Kirchengeschichte*, publ. by K. Englebert, I–VI, Breslau 1936–41, VII ff., Hildesheim 1949 seqq.

ARW   *Archiv für Religionswissenschaft* (Freiburg i. Br., Tübingen), Leipzig 1898 seqq.

AST   *Analecta Sacra Tarraconensia*, Barcelona 1925 seqq.

ATh   *L'année théologique*, Paris 1940 seqq.

AttiPontAc   *Atti della Pontificia Accademia Romana di Archeologia*, Rome 1923 seqq.

AuC   F. J. Dölger, *Antike und Christentum*, I–VI and supplementary vol., Münster 1929–50.

AUF   *Archiv für Urkundenforschung*, Berlin 1908 seqq.

Augustiniana   *Augustiniana. Tijdschrift vor de studie van Sint Augustinus en de Augustijneorde*, Louvain 1951 seqq.

AZ   *Archivalische Zeitschrift*, Munich 1876 seqq.

BA   *The Biblical Archaeologist*, New Haven, Conn. 1938 seqq.

BAC   *Biblioteca de Autores Cristianos*, Madrid 1945 seqq. (138 vols. so far issued).

Bächtold-Stäubli   H. Bächtold-Stäubli, *Handwörterbuch des deutschen Aberglaubens*, 10 vols., Berlin–Leipzig 1927 seqq.

Bardenhewer   O. Bardenhewer, *Geschichte der altkirchlichen Literatur*, 5 vols., Freiburg i. Br. 1902 seqq.

Bauer   W. Bauer, *Griechisch-Deutsches Wörterbuch zu den Schriften des Neuen Testaments und der übrigen urchristlichen Literatur*, Berlin, 5th ed. 1957.

Bauerreiss   R. Bauerreiss, *Kirchengeschichte Bayerns*, I–V, St. Ottilien 1949–55.

Baumstark   A. Baumstark, *Geschichte der syrischen Literatur mit Ausschluß der christlich-palästinensischen Texte*, Bonn 1922.

BECh   *Bibliothèque de l'École des Chartres*, Paris 1839 seqq.

Beck   H.-G. Beck, *Kirche und theologische Literatur im Byzantinischen Reich,* Munich 1959.

Bedjan   *Acta Martyrum et Sanctorum* (syriace), ed. by P. Bedjan, 7 vols., Paris 1890–7.

BHG   *Bibliotheca hagiographica graeca*, ed. socii Bollandiani, Brussels, 3rd ed. 1957.

BHL   *Bibliotheca hagiographica latina antiquae et mediae aetatis*, ed. socii Bollandiani, 2 vols., Brussels 1898–1901; Suppl. editio altera, Brussels 1911.

BHO   *Bibliotheca hagiographica orientalis*, ed. by P. Peeters, Brussels 1910.

Bibl   *Biblica*, Rome 1920 seqq.

BIFAO   *Bulletin de l'Institut français d'Archéologie Orientale*, Cairo 1901 seqq.

Bijdragen   *Bijdragen. Tijdschrift voor Filosofie en Theologie*, Nijmegen 1938 seqq.

BJ   *Bursians Jahresbericht über die Fortschritte der klassischen Altertumswissenschaft*, Leipzig 1873 seqq.

BJRL   *The Bulletin of the John Rylands Library*, Manchester 1903 seqq.

BKV   *Bibliothek der Kirchenväter*, ed. by O. Bardenhewer, T. Schermann (after vol. 35, J. Zellinger) and C. Weymann, 83 vols., Kempten 1911 seqq.

BLE   *Bulletin de littérature ecclésiastique*, Toulouse 1899 seqq.

BollAC   *Bollettino di archeologia cristiana*, ed. by G. B. de Rossi, Rome 1863–94.

Bréhier	L. Bréhier, *Le monde byzantin*, I–III, Paris 1947–50.
BThAM	*Bulletin de Théologie Ancienne et Médiévale*, Louvain 1929 seqq.
ByZ	*Byzantinische Zeitschrift*, Leipzig – Munich 1892 seqq.
Byz(B)	*Byzantion*, Brussels 1924 seqq.
ByzNGrJb	*Byzantinische-Neugriechische Jahrbücher*, Athens – Berlin 1920 seqq.
BZ	*Biblische Zeitschrift*, Freiburg i. Br. 1903–24; Paderborn 1931–9, 1957 seqq.
BZThS	*Bonner Zeitschrift für Theologie u. Seelsorge*, Düsseldorf 1924–31.
CahArch	*Cahiers Archéologiques. Fin de l'Antiquité et Moyen-âge*, Paris 1945 seqq.
Cath	*Catholica. Jahrbuch für Kontroverstheologie*, (Paderborn) Münster 1932 seqq.
CathEnc	*The Catholic Encyclopedia*, ed. by C. Herbermann et al. 15 vols., New York 1907–12; index vol. 1914, supplementary vol. 1922.
Catholicisme	*Catholicisme, Hier — Aujourd'hui — Demain*, ed. by G. Jacquemet, Paris 1948 seqq.
CBQ	*The Catholic Biblical Quarterly*, Washington 1939 seqq.
CChr	*Corpus Christianorum, seu nova Patrum collectio*, Turnhout – Paris 1953 seqq.
CH	*Church History*, New York – Chicago 1932 seqq.
Chalkedon	*Das Konzil von Chalkedon. Geschichte u. Gegenwart*, ed. by A. Grillmeier and H. Bacht, I–III, Würzburg 1951–4.
ChQR	*The Church Quarterly Review*, London 1875 seqq.
CHR	*The Catholic Historical Review*, Washington 1915 seqq.
CIG	*Corpus Inscriptionum Graecarum*, begun by A. Boeckh, continued by J. Franz, E. Curtius and A. Kirchhoff, 4 vols., Berlin 1825–77.
CIL	*Corpus Inscriptionum Latinarum*, ed. by the Berlin Academy, Berlin 1863 seqq.
CivCatt	*La Civiltà Cattolica*, Rome 1850 seqq. (1871–87 Florence).
ClP	*Clavis Patrum Latinorum*, ed. by E. Dekkers, Steenbrugge, 2nd ed. 1961.
COH	*Het Christelijk Oosten en Hereniging*, Nijmegen 1949 seqq.
CSCO	*Corpus scriptorum christianorum orientalium*, Paris 1903 seqq.
CSEL	*Corpus scriptorum ecclesiasticorum latinorum*, Vienna 1866 seqq.
CSL	*Corpus scriptorum latinorum Paravianum*, Turin.
CT	*Concilium Tridentinum*. Diariorum, Actorum, Epistularum, Tractatuum nova Collectio, edidit Societas Goerresiana promovendis inter Catholicos Germaniae Litterarum Studiis, 13 vols. so far, Freiburg i. Br. 1901 seqq.
Denzinger	H. Denzinger, *Enchiridion Symbolorum, Definitionum et Declarationum de rebus fidei et morum*, Freiburg i. Br., 31st ed. 1960.
DA	*Deutsches Archiv für Erforschung des Mittelalters* (1937–43: *für Geschichte des Mittelalters*, Weimar), Cologne – Graz 1950 seqq. (cf. *NA*).
DACL	*Dictionnaire d'archéologie chrétienne et de liturgie*, ed. by F. Cabrol and H. Leclercq, Paris 1924 seqq.
DBS	*Dictionnaire de la Bible, Supplément*, ed. by L. Pirot, cont. by A. Robert, Paris 1928 seqq.
DDC	*Dictionnaire de droit canonique*, ed. by R. Naz, Paris 1935 seqq.
Delehaye OC	H. Delehaye, *Les origines du culte des martyrs*, Brussels, 2nd ed. 1933.
Delehaye PM	H. Delehaye, *Les passions des martyrs et les genres littéraires*, Brussels 1921.
Delehaye S	H. Delehaye, *Sanctus. Essai sur le culte des saints dans l'antiquité*, Brussels, 2nd ed. 1954.
DHGE	*Dictionnaire d'histoire et de géographie ecclésiastiques*, ed. by A. Baudrillart et al., Paris 1912 seqq.

Diehl   E. Diehl, *Inscriptiones christianae latinae veteres*, 3 vols., Berlin, 2nd ed. 1961.

Dölger Reg   *Corpus der griechischen Urkunden des Mittelalters und der neueren Zeit. Reihe A, Abt. 1: Regesten der Kaiserurkunden des oströmischen Reiches*, ed. by F. Dölger.

DomSt   *Dominican Studies*, Oxford 1948 seqq.

DOP   *Dumbarton Oaks Papers*, ed. Harvard University, Cambridge, Mass. 1941 seqq.

DSAM   *Dictionnaire de Spiritualité ascétique et mystique. Doctrine et Histoire*, ed. by M. Viller, Paris 1932 seqq.

DTh   *Divus Thomas* (before 1914: *Jahrbuch für Philosophie und spekulative Theologie*; from 1954 *Freiburger Zeitschrift für Theologie und Philosophie*), Fribourg.

DThC   *Dictionnaire de théologie catholique*, ed. by A. Vacant and E. Mangenot, cont. by E. Amann, Paris 1930 seqq.

Duchesne LP   *Liber Pontificalis*, ed. by L. Duchesne, 2 vols., Paris 1886–92.

DVfLG   *Deutsche Vierteljahresschrift für Literaturwissenschaft und Geistesgeschichte*, Halle 1923 seqq.

ECatt   *Enciclopedia Cattolica*, Rome 1949 seqq.

EE   *Estudios ecclesiásticos*, Madrid 1922–36, 1942 seqq.

Ehrhard   A. Ehrhard, *Überlieferung und Bestand der hagiographischen und homiletischen Literatur der griechischen Kirche von den Anfängen bis zum Ende des 16. Jh.* (*TU* 50–52), I–III, Leipzig 1937–52.

ELit   *Ephemerides Liturgicae*, Rome 1887 seqq.

EO   *Échos d'Orient*, Paris 1897 seqq. (from 1946 *RÉB*).

Eranos   *Eranos-Jahrbuch*, Zürich 1933 seqq.

EstB   *Estudios Bíblicos*, Madrid 1941 seqq.

EtB   *Études Bibliques*, Paris 1907 seqq.

EThL   *Ephemerides Theologicae Lovanienses*, Bruges 1924 seqq.

Euseb. HE   Eusebius, *Historia Ecclesiastica* (to 324) ed. by E. Schwartz (*GCS* 9, 1–3) Berlin 1903–9.

Evagrius HE   Evagrius Scholasticus, *Historia Ecclesiastica* (431–594), ed. by J. Bidez and L. Parmentier, London 1898.

FC   *The Fathers of the Church*, New York 1947 seqq.

FF   *Forschungen und Fortschritte*, Berlin 1925 seqq.

FKDG   *Forschungen zu Kirchen- und Dogmengeschichte*, Göttingen 1953 seqq.

Fliche – Martin   *Histoire de l'eglise depuis les origines jusqu'à nos jours*, ed. A. Fliche and V. Martin, Paris 1935 seqq.

FlorPatr   *Florilegium Patristicum*, ed. by J. Zellinger und B. Geyer, Bonn 1904 seqq.

Gams   P. Gams, *Series episcoporum ecclesiae catholicae*, Regensburg 1873; supplement ibid. 1879–86.

García–Villada   Z. García–Villada, *Historia eclesiástica de España*, 2 vols., Madrid 1929.

GCS   *Die griechischen christlichen Schriftsteller der ersten drei Jahrhunderte*, Leipzig 1897 seqq.

Gelas.HE   Gelasius, *Historia Ecclesiastica*, ed. by G. Loeschke und M. Heinemann (*GCS* 28) Berlin 1918.

GhellinckP   J. de Ghellinck, *Patristique et Moyen Age. Études d'histoire littéraire et doctrinale*, I, Paris, 2nd ed. 1949, II–III, Brussels 1947–8.

Gn	*Gnomon. Kritische Zeitschrift für die gesamte klassische Altertumswissenschaft* (Berlin) Munich 1925 seqq.
Gr	*Gregorianum,* Rome 1920 seqq.
Grumel Reg	V. Grumel, *Les Regestes des actes du patriarcat de Constantinople,* Kadiköi– Bucharest I/1 1932, I/2 1936, I/3 1947.
GuL	*Geist und Leben. Zeitschrift für Aszese und Mystik* (to 1947, *ZAM*), Würzburg 1947 seqq.
Hanssens	J. M. Hanssens, *Institutiones liturgicae de Ritibus Orientalibus,* I–V, Rome 1930 seqq.
Harnack DG	A. von Harnack, *Lehrbuch der Dogmengeschichte,* 3 vols., Tübingen, 4th ed. 1909 seq. (photographic reprint, Tübingen, 5th ed. 1931 seq.).
Harnack Lit	A. von Harnack, *Geschichte der altchristlichen Literatur,* 3 vols., Leipzig 1893–1904.
Harnack Miss	A. von Harnack, *Die Mission u. Ausbreitung des Christentums in den ersten drei Jahrhunderten,* 2 vols., Leipzig, 4th ed. 1924.
Hauck	A. Hauck, *Kirchengeschichte Deutschlands,* I–IV, Leipzig 1906–14, V 1929, I–V, Berlin–Leipzig 8th ed. 1954.
HAW	*Handbuch der Altertumswissenschaft,* founded by I. von Müller, newly ed. by W. Otto, Munich 1929 seqq.; new ed. 1955 seqq.
HDG	*Handbuch der Dogmengeschichte,* ed. by M. Schmaus, J. Geiselmann, A. Grillmeier, Freiburg i. Br. 1951 seqq.
HE	*Historia Ecclesiastica.*
Hefele–Leclercq	*Histoire des Conciles d'après les documents originaux,* by C. J. Hefele, translated by H. Leclercq, I–IX, Paris 1907 seqq.
Hennecke–Schneemelcher	*Neutestamentliche Apokryphen in deutscher Übersetzung,* Founded by E. Hennecke, ed. by W. Schneemelcher, I–II, Tübingen, 3rd ed. 1959–64.
Hermes	*Hermes. Zeitschrift für klassische Philologie,* Berlin 1866 seqq.
HJ	*Historisches Jahrbuch der Görres-Gesellschaft* (Cologne 1880 seqq.), Munich 1950 seqq.
HNT	*Handbuch zum Neuen Testament,* founded by H. Lietzmann (now ed. by G. Bornkamm), 23 parts, Tübingen 1906 seqq.
HO	*Handbuch der Orientalistik,* ed. by B. Spuler, Leiden 1948 seqq.
HThR	*The Harvard Theological Review,* Cambridge, Mass. 1908 seqq.
HZ	*Historische Zeitschrift,* Munich 1859 seqq.
IER	*The Irish Ecclesiastical Record,* Dublin 1864 seqq.
IKZ	*Internationale Kirchliche Zeitschrift,* Berne 1911 seqq.
IThQ	*The Irish Theological Quarterly,* Dublin 1864 seqq.
JA	*Journal Asiatique,* Paris 1822 seqq.
JbAC	*Jahrbuch für Antike und Christentum,* Münster 1858 seqq.
JBL	*Journal of Biblical Literature,* published by the Society of Biblical Literature and Exegesis, Boston 1881 seqq.
JdI	*Jahrbuch des Deutschen Archäologischen Instituts,* Berlin 1886 seqq.
JEH	*The Journal of Ecclesiastical History,* London 1950 seqq.
Jerphanion	G. de Jerphanion, *La voix des monuments,* I–II, Paris 1932–8.
JLH	*Jahrbuch für Liturgik und Hymnologie,* Kassel 1955 seqq.
JLW	*Jahrbuch für Liturgiewissenschaft,* Münster 1921–41 (now *ALW*).
JÖByzG	*Jahrbuch der österreichischen Byzantinischen Gesellschaft,* Vienna 1951 seqq.

JQR   *The Jewish Quarterly Review,* Philadelphia 1888 seqq.

JRS   *The Journal of Roman Studies,* London 1910 seqq.

JSOR *Journal of the Society of Oriental Research,* Chicago 1917–32.

JThS   *The Journal of Theological Studies,* London 1899 seqq.

Jugie   M. Jugie, *Theologia dogmatica Christianorum orientalium ab ecclesia cath-*
olica dissidentium, I–V, Paris 1926–35.

K   C. Kirch–L. Ueding, *Enchiridion fontium historiae ecclesiasticae antiquae,*
Freiburg i. Br., 8th ed. 1960.

Karst G J. Karst, *Littérature géorgienne chrétienne,* Paris 1934.

Katholik *Der Katholik,* Mainz 1821 seqq. (General index for 1821–89).

KlT   *Kleine Texte,* ed. by H. Lietzmann, Berlin 1902 seqq.

König H *Christus u. die Religionen der Erde. Handbuch der Religionsgeschichte,* ed.
by F. König, I–III, Vienna, 2nd ed. 1956.

Kraus RE F. X. Kraus, *Real-Encyclopädie der Christlichen Altertümer,* 2 vols., Freiburg i. Br. 1882–6.

Krumbacher K. Krumbacher, *Geschichte der byzantischen Literatur,* Munich 1890; 2nd
ed. by A. Ehrhard and H. Gelzer, Munich 1897.

KuD   *Kerygma und Dogma,* Göttingen 1955 seqq.

Künstle K. Künstle, *Ikonographie der christlichen Kunst,* I, Freiburg i. Br. 1928; II,
Freiburg i. Br. 1926.

Lanzoni F. Lanzoni, *Le Diocesi d'Italia dalle origini al principio del secolo VII,*
2 vols., Faenza, 2nd ed. 1927.

Lebreton J. Lebreton, *Histoire du dogme de la Trinité,* I–II, Paris, 4th ed. 1928.

Lietzmann H. Lietzmann, *Geschichte der alten Kirche,* I, Berlin 2nd ed. 1937 (3rd ed.
1953), II–IV 1936–44 (2nd ed. 1953).

LJ   *Liturgisches Jahrbuch,* Münster 1951 seqq.

LNPF *A Select Library of Nicene and Post-Nicene Fathers* (Buffalo and New York
1886–90).

LQ   *Liturgiegeschichtliche Quellen,* Münster 1918 seqq.

LThK   *Lexikon für Theologie und Kirche,* ed. by J. Höfer and K. Rahner, Freiburg i. Br., 2nd ed. 1957 seqq.

LuM   *Liturgie und Mönchtum. Laacher Hefte,* (Freiburg i. Br.) Maria Laach 1948
seqq.

MAH   *Mélanges d'archéologie et d'histoire,* Paris 1880 seqq.

Mai B   *Nova Patrum bibliotheca,* I–VII by A. Mai, Rome 1852–7; VIII–X by
J. Cozza-Luzi, Rome 1871–1905.

Mai C   A. Mai, *Scriptorum veterum nova collectio e vaticanis codicibus edita,* 10
vols., Rome 1815–38.

Mai S   A. Mai, *Spicilegium Romanum,* 10 vols., Rome 1839–44.

MAMA *Monumenta Asiae Minoris Antiqua.* Publications of the American Society
for Archeological Research in Asia Minor, 7 vols., Manchester 1928–56.

Manitius M. Manitius, *Geschichte der lateinischen Literatur des Mittelalters,* Munich,
I 1911, II 1923, III 1931.

Mansi   J. D. Mansi, *Sacrorum conciliorum nova et amplissima collectio,* 31 vols.,
Florence–Venice 1757–98; new impression and continuation ed. by L. Petit
and J. B. Martin in 60 vols., Paris 1899—1927.

MartHieron *Martyrologium Hieronymianum,* ed. by H. Quentin and H. Delehaye
(*ActaSS* Nov. II, 2), Brussels 1931.

MartRom	*Martyrologium Romanum*, ed. by H. Delehaye, Brussels 1940.
MCom	*Miscelánea Comillas*, Comillas–Santander 1943 seqq.
MD	*Maison-Dieu*, Paris 1945 seqq.
MF	*Miscellanea francescana*, Rome 1886 seqq.
MG	*Monumenta Germaniae Historica inde ab a. C. 500 usque ad a. 1500;* indexes by O. Holder-Egger and K. Zeumer, Hanover–Berlin 1826 seqq. Sections:
MGAuctant	*Auctores antiquissimi.*
MGSS	*Scriptores.*
MiscMercati	*Miscellanea Giovanni Mercati*, 6 vols., Rome 1946.
MiscMohlberg	*Miscellanea Liturgica in honorem L. Cuniberti Mohlberg*, Rome 1948.
Moricca	U. Moricca, *Storia della Letteratura latina cristiana*, 3 vols. in 5 tomes, Turin 1924–34.
MSR	*Mélanges de science religieuse*, Lille 1944 seqq.
MThZ	*Münchener theologische Zeitschrift*, Munich 1950 seqq.
Muratori	L. A. Muratori, *Rerum italicarum scriptores ab anno aerae christianae 500 ad 1500*, 28 vols., Milan 1723–51; continuation by Tartini 1748–70. and N. G. Mittarelli 1771; new ed. by G. Carducci and V. Fiorini, Città di Castello 1900 seqq.
Muséon	*Le Muséon*, Louvain 1881 seqq.
NA	*Neues Archiv der Gesellschaft für ältere deutsche Geschichtskunde zur Beförderung einer Gesamtausgabe der Quellenschriften deutscher Geschichte des Mittelalters*, Hanover 1876 seqq. (from 1937, *DA*).
NAG	*Nachrichten von der Akademie der Wissenschaften in Göttingen* (till 1940, *NGG*), Göttingen 1941 seqq.
NBollAC	*Nuovo Bollettino di archeologia cristiana*, Rome 1895–1923 (Continuation of *BollAC*).
NC	*Nouvelle Clio. Revue mensuelle de la découverte historique*, Brussels 1947 seqq.
Nilles	N. Nilles, *Kalendarium manuale utriusque ecclesiae orientalis et occidentalis*, 2 vols., Innsbruck, 2nd ed. 1896 seq.
NovT	*Novum Testamentum*, Leiden 1956 seqq.
NRTh	*Nouvelle Revue Théologique*, Tournai–Louvain–Paris, 1879 seqq.
NTS	*New Testament Studies*, Cambridge–Washington 1954 seqq.
NZSTh	*Neue Zeitschrift für Systematische Theologie*, Berlin 1959 seqq.
OrChr	*Oriens Christianus*, (Leipzig) Wiesbaden 1901 seqq.
OrChrA	*Orientalia Christiana (Analecta)*, Rome (1923–34: *Orientalia Christiana;* 1935 seqq: *Orientalia Christiana Analecta*).
OrChrP	*Orientalia Christiana Periodica*, Rome 1935 seqq.
OrSyr	*L'Orient Syrien*, Paris 1956 seqq.
OstKSt	*Ostkirchliche Studien*, Würzburg 1951 seqq.
OxP	*The Oxyrhynchos Papyri*, London 1898 seqq.
Pauly-Wissowa	*Paulys Realencyklopädie der klassischen Altertumswissenschaft*, new ed. by G. Wissowa and W. Kroll (with K. Mittelhaus), Stuttgart 1893 seqq.
PG	*Patrologia Graeca*, ed by J.-P. Migne, 161 vols., Paris 1857–66.
Philostorgius HE	Philostorgius, *Church History* (down to 425), ed. by J. Bidez (*GCS* 2), Berlin 1913.

PhJ   *Philosophisches Jahrbuch der Görres-Gesellschaft*, Fulda 1888 seqq.
Pitra A   J. B. Pitra, *Analecta sacra Spicilegio Solesmensi parata*, 8 vols., Paris 1876–91.
Pitra S   J. B. Pitra, *Spicilegium Solesmense*, 4 vols., Paris 1852–8.
PL   *Patrologia Latina*, ed. by J.-P. Migne, 217 vols. and 4 index vols., Paris 1878–90.
POR   *Patrologia Orientalis*, ed. by J. Graffin and F. Nau, Paris 1903 seqq.
PrOrChr   *Le Proche-Orient chrétien*, Jerusalem 1951 seqq.
PS   *Patrologia Syriaca*, ed. by R. Graffin, 3 vols., Paris 1894–1926.
PSI   *Papiri greci e latini della Società Italiana*, Florence 1912 seqq.

QFIAB   *Quellen und Forschungen aus italienischen Archiven und Bibliotheken*, Rome 1897 seqq.
Quasten P   J. Quasten, *Patrology*, Utrecht–Brussels, I 1950, II 1953, III 1960.

R   M. J. Rouët de Journel, *Enchiridion Patristicum*, Freiburg i. Br., 19th ed.
Raby Chr   F. J. E. Raby, *A History of Christian Latin Poetry*, Oxford, 2nd ed. 1953.
RAC   *Reallexikon für Antike und Christentum*, ed. by T. Klauser, Stuttgart 1941 (1950) seqq.
RAM   *Revue d'ascétique et de mystique*, Toulouse 1920 seqq.
RB   *Revue biblique*, Paris 1892 seqq.; new series since 1914.
RBén   *Revue bénédictine*, Maredsous 1884 seqq.
RD   M. J. Rouët de Journal and J. Dutilleul, *Enchiridion asceticum*, Freiburg i. Br., 5th ed. 1958.
RÉA   *Revue des Études Anciennes*, Bordeaux 1899 seqq.
RÉB   *Revue des Études byzantines* (Continuation of *ÉO*), Paris 1946 seqq.
RÉG   *Revue des Études Grecques*, Paris 1888 seqq.
RÉL   *Revue des Études latines*, Paris 1923 seqq.
RET   *Revista Española de teología*, Madrid 1941 seqq.
RevÉAug   *Revue des Études Augustiniennes* (Continuation of *L'Année Théologique Augustinienne*), Paris 1955 seqq.
RevSR   *Revue des Sciences Religieuses*, Strasbourg 1921 seqq.
RGG   *Die Religion in Geschichte und Gegenwart*, Tübingen 1909–13; 2nd ed. 1927–32; 3rd ed. 1956 seqq.
RH   *Revue historique*, Paris 1876 seqq.
RHE   *Revue d'histoire ecclésiastique*, Louvain 1900 seqq.
RHEF   *Revue d'histoire de l'église de France*, Paris 1910 seqq.
RHLR   *Revue d'histoire et de littérature religieuses*, Paris 1896–1907.
RhMus   *Rheinisches Museum für Philologie*, Bonn 1833 seqq.
RHPhR   *Revue d'histoire et de philosophie religieuses*, Strasbourg 1921 seqq.
RHR   *Revue de l'histoire des religions*, Paris 1880 seqq.
RicRel   *Ricerche Religiose*, Rome 1925 seqq.
Righetti   M. Righetti, *Manuale di storia liturgica*, Milan, I: Introduzione generale, 2nd ed. 1950; II: L'anno liturgico. Il Breviario, 2nd ed. 1955; III: L'Eucaristica sacrificio e sacramento, 1949; IV: Sacramenti — Sacramentali, 1953.
RivAC   *Rivista di archeologia cristiana*, Rome 1924 seqq.
RM   *Mitteilungen des Deutschen Archäelogischen Instituts, Römische Abteilung*, Rome 1886.
ROC   *Revue de l'Orient chrétien*, Paris 1896 seqq.
RPAA   *Rendiconti della Pontificia Accademia Romana di Archeologia*, Rome 1923 seqq.

RQ   *Römische Quartalschrift für christliche Altertumskunde und für Kirchen-*
            geschichte, Freiburg i. Br. 1887 seqq.
RQum   *Revue de Qumran,* Paris 1958 seqq.
RSO   *Rivista degli studi orientali,* Rome 1908 seqq.
RSPhTh   *Revue de sciences philosophiques et théologiques,* Paris 1907 seqq.
RSR   *Recherches de science religieuse,* Paris 1910 seqq.
RSTI   *Rivista della storia della chiesa in Italia,* Rome 1947 seqq.
RThAM   *Recherches de Théologie anciennne et médiévale,* Louvain 1929 seqq.
Rufin. HE   Rufinus of Aquileia, Translation of Eusebius's *Church History,* ed. by T.
            Mommsen in GCS 9, Berlin 1909.

SA   *Studia Anselmiana,* Rome 1933 seqq.
SAB   *Sitzungsberichte der Deutschen* (till 1944: *Preussischen*) *Akademie der*
            Wissenschaften zu Berlin. Phil.-hist. Klasse, Berlin 1882 seqq.
Saeculum   *Saeculum. Jahrbuch für Universalgeschichte,* Freiburg i. Br. 1950 seqq.
SAH   *Sitzungsberichte der Heidelberger Akademie der Wissenschaften.* Phil.-hist.
            Klasse, Heidelberg 1910 seqq.
SAM   *Sitzungsberichte der Bayerischen Akademie der Wissenschaften.* Phil.-hist.
            Abt., Munich 1871 seqq.
SAW   *Sitzungsberichte der* (after 225, 1, 1947: *Österreichischen*) *Akademie der*
            Wissenschaften in Wien, Vienna 1831 seqq.
SC   *Scuola Cattolica,* Milan 1873 seqq.
SCpr   *Scriptores christiani primaevi,* The Hague 1946 seqq.
SE   *Sacris Eruditi. Jaarboek voor Godsdienstwetenschapen,* Bruges 1948 seqq.
Seeberg   R. Seeberg, *Lehrbuch der Dogmengeschichte,* Leipzig, I–II, 3rd ed. 1922
            seqq.; III, 4th ed. 1930; IV, 1, 4th ed. 1933; IV, 2, 3rd ed. 1920 (I–IV
            new impression, Basle 1953–4).
SO   *Symbolae Osloenses,* ed. by the Societas Graeco-Latina, Oslo 1922 seqq.
Socrates HE Socrates, *Historia Ecclesiastica* (305–439), ed. by R. Hussey, 3 vols., Oxford
            1853.
SourcesChr *Sources chrétiennes,* ed. by H. de Lubac and J. Daniélou, Paris 1941 seqq.
Sozom. HE   Sozomen, *Historia Ecclesiastica* (324–425), ed. by J. Bidez and G. C. Hansen
            in GCS 50, Berlin 1960.
Speculum   *Speculum. A Journal of Medieval Studies,* Cambridge, Mass. 1926 seqq.
SQS   *Sammlung ausgewählter Kirchen- und dogmengeschichtlicher Quellen-*
            schriften, Tübingen 1893 seqq.
StC   *Studia Catholica,* Roermund 1924 seqq.
SteT   *Studi e Testi,* Rome 1900 seqq.
StrP   *Stromata Patristica et Medievalia,* ed. by C. Mohrmann and J. Quasten,
            Utrecht 1950 seqq.
StTh   *Studia Theologica, cura Ordinum Theologicorum Scandinavicorum edita,*
            Lund 1948 seqq.
StudiBiz   *Studi Bizantini e Neoellenici,* Rome 1925 seqq.
StudGen   *Studium Generale. Zeitschrift für die Einheit der Wissenschaften im*
            Zusammenhang ihrer Begriffsbildung und Forschungsmethoden, Berlin–
            Göttingen–Heidelberg 1948 seqq.
Sulp.Sev.Chron Sulpicius Severus, *World Chronicle* (to 400), ed. by C. Halm (CSEL 1),
            Vienna 1866.

TD   *Textus et Documenta, Series Theologica,* Rome 1933–5.
ThBl   *Theologische Blätter,* Leipzig 1922 seqq.

Theodoret HE   Theodoret, *Historia Ecclesiastica*, ed. by L. Parmentier, 2nd ed. by
F. Scheidweiler *GCS* 44 (19) Berlin 1954.

ThJ   *Theologische Jahrbücher*, Leipzig 1842 seqq.

ThLL   *Thesaurus Linguae Latinae*, Leipzig 1900 seqq.

ThLz   *Theologische Literaturzeitung*, Leipzig 1878 seqq.

ThQ   *Theologische Quartalschrift*, Tübingen 1819 seqq.; Stuttgart 1946 seqq.

ThR   *Theologische Rundschau*, Tübingen 1897 seqq.

ThRv   *Theologische Revue*, Münster 1902 seqq.

ThSt   *Theological Studies*, Baltimore 1940 seqq.

ThW   *Theologisches Wörterbuch zum Neuen Testament*, ed. by G. Kittel, cont.
by G. Friedrich, Stuttgart 1933 seqq.

ThZ   *Theologische Zeitschrift*, Basle 1945 seqq.

Tixeront   L. J. Tixeront, *Histoire des dogmes dans l'antiquité chrétienne*, 3 vols., Paris,
11th ed. 1930.

Tr   *Traditio*, New York 1943 seqq.

TSt   *Texts and Studies*, ed. Armitage Robinson, Cambridge 1891.

TThZ   *Trierer Theologische Zeitschrift* (till 1944: *Pastor Bonus*), Trier 1888 seqq.

TU   *Texte und Untersuchungen zur Geschichte der altchristlichen Literatur.
Archiv für die griechisch-christlichen Schriftsteller der ersten drei Jahrhunderte*, Leipzig–Berlin 1882 seqq.

Tüchle   H. Tüchle, *Kirchengeschichte Schwabens*, I–II, Stuttgart 1950–4.

Ueberweg   F. Ueberweg, *Grundriss der Geschichte der Philosophie*, Berlin, I, 12th ed.
1926 by K. Praechter; II, 11th ed. 1928 by B. Geyer; III, 12th ed. 1924 by
M. Frischeisen-Köhler and W. Moog; IV, 12th ed. by K. Österreich 1923; V,
12th ed. by K. Oesterreich 1928.

VigChr   *Vigiliae Christianae*, Amsterdam 1947 seqq.

ViVr   Βυζαντινὰ Χρονικά. *Vizantiyskiy Vremennik*, St Petersburg 1894 seqq.

VS   *La Vie Spirituelle*, (Ligué, Juvisy) Paris 1869 seqq.

Wattenbach–Levison   W. Wattenbach, *Deutschlands Geschichtsquellen im Mittelalter,
Vorzeit und Karolinger*, vols. I–III ed. by W. Levison and H. Löwe,
Weimar 1952–7.

Wilpert   G. Wilpert, *I Sarcofagi cristiani antichi*, 3 vols., Rome 1929–36.

Zacharias Rhetor   Zacharias Rhetor, *Church History* (*circa* 450–540), ed. by E. W. Brooks,
CSCO 83–84, Paris 1919–21.

ZAM   *Zeitschrift für Aszese und Mystik* (from 1947 *GuL*), (Innsbruck, Munich)
Würzburg 1926 seqq.

ZBlB   *Zentralblatt für Bibliothekswesen*, Leipzig 1884 seqq.

ZBLG   *Zeitschrift für Bayerische Landgeschichte*, Munich 1928 seqq.

ZDMG   *Zeitschrift der deutschen morgenländischen Gesellschaft*, Leipzig 1847 seqq.

ZDPV   *Zeitschrift des deutschen Palästina-Vereins*, Leipzig 1878 seqq.

ZKG   *Zeitschrift für Kirchengeschichte*, (Gotha) Stuttgart 1878 seqq.

ZKTh   *Zeitschrift für Katholische Theologie*, (Innsbruck) Vienna 1877 seqq.

ZMR   *Zeitschrift für Missionswissenschaft und Religionswissenschaft*, vols. 34 ff.
Münster 1950 seqq. (*Zeitschrift für Missionswissenschaft*, 1–17, Münster
1911–27; *Zeitschrift für Missionswissenschaft und Religionswissenschaft*,
18–25, Münster 1928–35; *Zeitschrift für Missionswissenschaft*, 26–27, Münster
1935–7; *Missionswissenschaft und Religionswissenschaft*, 28–33, Münster
1938–41, 1947–9).

ZMkRd *Zeitschrift für Missionskunde und Religionswissenschaft*, Berlin 1884 seqq.

ZNW *Zeitschrift für die neutestamentliche Wissenschaft und die Kunde der älteren Kirche*, Giessen 1900 seqq., Berlin 1934 seqq.

ZRGG *Zeitschrift für Religions- und Geistesgeschichte*, Marburg 1948 seqq.

ZSavRGkan *Zeitschrift der Savigny-Stiftung für Rechtsgeschichte, Kanonistische Abteilung*, Weimar 1911 seqq.

ZSavRGrom *Zeitschrift der Savigny-Stiftung für Rechtsgeschichte, Romanistische Abteilung*, Weimar 1880 seqq.

ZSKG *Zeitschrift für Schweizer Kirchengeschichte*, Fribourg 1907 seqq.

ZThK *Zeitschrift für Theologie und Kirche*, Tübingen 1891 seqq.

GENERAL INTRODUCTION
TO CHURCH HISTORY

*I. The Subject Matter, Methods, Ancillary Sciences, and Divisions
of Church History, and its Relevance for Today*

The Subject Matter

CHURCH history treats of the growth in time and space of the Church
founded by Christ. Inasmuch as its subject matter is derived from and
rooted in the Faith, it is a theological discipline; and in this respect it
differs from a history of Christianity. Its theological point of departure,
the idea of the Church, must not however be understood as though it were
based on the structure of the Church as revealed in her dogma: a kind
of preconceived pattern which history must follow and demonstrate,
limiting or hindering the empirical establishment of facts based on
historical sources. It refers solely to the Church's divine origin through
Jesus Christ, to the hierarchic and sacramental order founded by Him,
to the promised assistance of the Holy Spirit and to the eschatological
consummation at the end of the world: the very elements, in fact, in
which her essential identity consists, namely her continuity in spite of
changing outward forms. The image of the "ship of the Church", sailing
fully rigged and unchanged over the ocean of the centuries, is less apt
than the comparison made by Vincent of Lerins wherein he compares it
with the growth of the human body and of the seed which is sown, a
growth "which involves no injury to its peculiar qualities nor alteration
of its being" (*Commonitorium*, c. 29). As the grain of wheat germinates
and sprouts, produces stalk and ear, yet always remains wheat, so does
the Church's nature manifest itself in changing forms during the course
of history, but remains always true to itself.

The historical character of the Church rests ultimately on the Incarnation of the Logos and Its entry into human history. It rests, above all,
on the fact that Christ willed his Church to be a society of human

1

beings, the "people of God" under the leadership of men: the apostolic college, the episcopate and the papacy. Thus He made her dependent on human actions and human weakness; but He has not left her entirely to her own devices. Her suprahistorical, transcendent entelechy is the Holy Spirit, who preserves her from error, produces and maintains holiness within her, and can testify to His presence by the performance of miracles. His presence and working in the Church, like those of grace in the individual soul, can be inferred from historically comprehensible effects, but belief in them is also necessary; and it is in the co-operation of these divine and human factors in time and space that Church history has its origin.

The understanding and interpretation of Church history depend then ultimately on the notion which a writer holds of the Church. To the philosophers of the Enlightenment, the Church appeared as a "natural society which exists alongside many others in the State";[1] according to their view the Church is indeed "founded by God, but God's spirit did not dwell in her": rather is she dominated by men. J. Möhler[2] opposed this anthropocentric conception with his own theocentric view, and defined Church history as "the series of developments of the principle of light and life imparted to men by Christ, in order to unite them once more with God and to make them fit to glorify him". Later, at the close of the nineteenth century, the fashion in historical writing required that Church history should be merged in secular history, that the ecclesiastical historian should become a profane historian,[3] and Albert Ehrhard then introduced the term "historical theology". He defined the task of the general Church historian as "the investigation and presentation of the actual course of the history of Christianity, in its organized manifestation as a Church, through all the centuries of its past, in the whole of its duration in time and in all aspects of its life".[4]

The beginning and end of Church history rest on a theological basis. It does not begin with the Incarnation, or even the choosing and sending forth of the apostles, but with the descent of the Holy Spirit on the primitive community at the first Pentecost;[5] and it ends with the Second Coming of our Lord. Within these chronological limits it has for its subject all the manifestations of the Church's life. These may be divided into external and internal factors: the former being the spread of the Church

---

[1] E. Säger, *Die Vertretung der Kirchengeschichte in Freiburg* (Freiburg i. Br. 1952), 68.

[2] J. A. Möhler, *Ges. Schriften und Aufsätze*, ed. J. J. I. Döllinger, II (Regensburg 1840), 272.

[3] R. Fester, "Die Säkularisation der Historie", *HV* 11 (1908), 441–59.

[4] *Festschrift S. Merkle* (Düsseldorf 1922), 122.

[5] H. Zimmermann, "Über das Anfangsdatum der Kirchengeschichte" in *AKG* 41 (1959), 1–34.

through the whole world, her relations with the non-Christian religions and the separated Christian communions and her relations with the State and society; the latter being the development and establishing of her dogma in the struggle against heresy, aided by the science of theology, the proclaiming of the Faith by preaching and teaching. To these internal activities must be added the fulfilling of her sacramental nature by the celebration of the liturgy and the administration of the sacraments, together with the preparation for these by pastoral care and their effect in works of Christian charity. Finally, there is the development of the Church's organization as a supporting framework for the fulfilment of the offices of priest and teacher, as well as the irradiation by the Church's work of every sphere of cultural and social life.

That the conception of the Church is fundamental for the definition of the subject and purpose of Church history is clear if we compare the notions of the Church as defined by non-Catholic ecclesiastical historians. Church history cannot be conceived in the Hegelian sense as the dialectical movement of an idea (F. C. Baur), for the Church is not only a divine idea but also an historical fact. Its subject is not merely the "Church of the Word" (W. von Loewenich), the "history of the interpretation of Holy Scripture" (G. Ebeling), "the history of the Gospel and its effects in the world" (H. Bornkamm), or the Church as we find it in the New Testament (W. Delius): all these definitions being derived from the Protestant idea of the Church. Of the more recent definitions by Protestant historians the nearest to ours are those of K. D. Schmidt, for whom the Church is "Christ continuing to work in the world, His Body which is led by the Holy Spirit to all truth and whose history is wholly God's work, but also wholly man's", and of J. Chambon, who speaks of "the history of the Kingdom of God on earth". These later definitions safeguard the character in Church history as a theological discipline, but they are still influenced by the underlying Protestant conception of the Church, inasmuch as this is determined in the case of Schmidt by the writings of Luther, and in that of Chambon by the Calvinist doctrine of the Church.

The Methods of Church History

In fulfilling its task, Church history makes use of the historical method, whose application to the subject as defined above, namely the Church of faith which is also the visible Church, suffers no limitations arising from the subject itself. But it can sometimes lead to tensions between faith or theological postulates (which are identified with faith), on the one hand, and positively or apparently established historical fact, on the other; and this may confront the ecclesiastical historian with difficult decisions. The scientific honesty of Church history is not thereby affected: it is both theology and historical science in the strict sense; and the application of the historical method to it is carried out in three stages.

Firstly, like all history, Church history is bound by its sources. It can reveal about events and conditions in the past only what it finds in its sources, correctly interpreted: so much and no more. The sources (monumental and written remains, literary sources) must be sought out, tested for their genuineness, edited in accurate texts and investigated for their historical content. The first object of historical research thus conducted is the establishment of dates and facts which form the framework of all history. Without the knowledge of these, every further step (the tracing of origins, the determining of intellectual relationships and the evaluation of information) becomes unreliable or sinks to the level of mere conjecture. Only through the accessibility of the sources and by their critical study has Church history since the seventeenth century developed into a science. On this level of research, Church history is indebted for many important results to scholars outside the Church who do not acknowledge its character as a theological discipline. Even the denominational point of view is hardly noticeable here.

But, in the second stage, the causal connexion of the facts related, research into the motives of individuals and consequent judgments on ecclesiastical personalities, the assessment of spiritual and religious movements and of whole periods: all these go beyond the mere establishment of facts, and are based on presuppositions and standards of value which cannot be derived from history itself, yet cannot be separated from it. The recognition of human freedom of decision prevents the creation of determinist historical laws. Historical causality must remain open to the intervention and co-operation of transcendent factors; the possibility of extraordinary phenomena (such as mystical phenomena and miracles) must not be excluded *a priori*. The concepts which Church history has created or adopted for grouping together facts and religious or intellectual currents are based on judgments of value, especially when terms such as "Golden Age", "Decline", "Abuse" or "Reform" are used. The standards for judging persons and events must not be those of our own time, but must be adapted to the period in the Church's historical development with which we are dealing. Human failure and human sin are not in this way made relative, nor is human responsibility removed. There are historical guilt and historical merit; but the judgment of history is not a sentence pronounced upon the Church's past.

The historian's philosophical and religious point of view will demand respect at this second stage, that of historical presentation, if he is at pains to achieve the highest degree of objectivity and impartiality. Conflicts with philosophical systems, such as historical materialism, Spengler's biological view of history, or sociological schools of historical writing, are not part of the Church historian's task. It is, however, inevitable that these will influence not only judgments but also the selection of material and the literary form. The forms of presentation most frequently used today are the biography, the monograph and the essay. The biography seeks to understand a person of historical significance both as an individual and as a point of intersection of the forces at work in his period; if it is to achieve anything more than a statement of the bare facts and dates, personal utterances must also be included, derived from such sources as letters and diaries. The monograph, confined to a particular time and place, may deal with a period (as Duchesne and Lietzmann treated of the primitive Church, and H. von Schubert of the early Middle Ages), a single country (as Hauck wrote on the Church history of Germany, G. Villada on that of Spain, and Tomek on that of Austria) or a diocese; with institutions such as the papacy and the religious orders, events such as the General Councils, or religious and intellectual movements (as Borst wrote on the Cathari, and Maass on Josephinism). Alongside the strictly scientific monograph, the essay has in recent times become of increasing importance. It aims in the most concise and perfect literary form to interpret the essential character of historical persons and events, and to make this knowledge available to a wider reading public, but dispenses with sources and bibliographical references.

Yet, in the third and final stage, Church history as a whole can be understood only as the history of salvation: its ultimate meaning can be apprehended only by the eye of faith. It is the abiding presence of the Logos in the world and the fulfilment, in the "people of God", of Christ's community, in which ministry and grace work together. It is the growth of the Body of Christ: not a continuous falling away from the ideal of the early Church, as some would have us believe; nor yet a continuous progress, as the men of the Enlightenment imagined. The growth of the Church is sometimes hindered through internal or external causes; she suffers sickness, and experiences both reverses and periods of renewed vitality. She does not appear as the Bride without spot or stain, as those who believe in a purely "spiritual" Church in all ages have fondly thought her to be, but covered with the dust of centuries, suffering through the failures of men and persecuted by her enemies. Church history is therefore the theology of the Cross. Without injury to her essential holiness, the Church is not perfect: *semper reformanda,* she is in constant need of renewal. Although she is never to be superseded in the world of space and time by a "spiritual" church, she retains a provisional character and awaits perfection. When that goal is attained, in the Parousia, the path she has travelled during the course of history will be fully illuminated, the true meaning of all events will be understood and the finally valid judgments of human guilt and merit will be made. Only at the end of the world will the history of the Church, profane history and the history of salvation merge into one.

Ancillary Sciences of Church History

Church history makes use of the same ancillary sciences as general history, just as it makes use of the same methods. Chronology, epigraphy, palaeography, diplomatics, the use of archives and libraries, heraldry: all these are of practical importance; and so too in a wider sense are geography, cartography, and statistics. For a detailed treatment of these sciences, see the bibliography at the back of the book.

The Divisions of Church History

The divisions of Church history cannot be based on abstract historico-philosophical categories, any more than on the divine plan of salvation, whose details remain unknown, though its outlines are given in Revelation. They cannot be dependent on the relationship between the Church and her milieu, for "the Catholic Church is not identified with any civilization".[6] Any division into periods which corresponds with the facts and facilitates our understanding of them must take into consideration this truth: the inward and outward growth of the Church, brought about by the Holy Spirit in co-operation with human free will, is achieved by her constantly coming to terms with civilization. In her spreading over the whole earth and in her penetration of mankind and civilizations, peoples and societies, the Church makes use of the historical circumstances and she adapts herself to them: Church history is something midway between universal history and history of salvation.[7]

Division into periods became a problem only when the patterns of medieval historiography and the annalistic method of the Centuriators and Baronius had been superseded. The usual threefold division into Antiquity, the Middle Ages, and Modern Times, popularized since the seventeenth century by Cellarius (Christoph Keller), was adopted comparatively recently, by Möhler,[8] and has never become universal. A division that is convincing in all respects and generally accepted has not yet been found. If one considers primarily the unity of the Church and regards as epoch-making the breaking away of sects which followed the councils of the fifth century, the Greek Schism, and the Protestant Reformation, one

---

[6] "The Catholic Church does not identify herself with any civilization": Pius XII in his address to the Tenth International Congress of Historians on 7 September 1955.

[7] O. Köhler in *HJ* 77 (1958), 257.

[8] K. Heussi, *Altertum, Mittelalter und Neuzeit in der Kirchengeschichte* (Tübingen 1921), 18 f.

ignores no less important events inside the Church, her expansion and her relations with civilization. The end of the old Canon Law (discussed by R. Sohm) and the rise of the papacy after the eleventh century are, from the constitutional point of view, the great dividing line; but all other viewpoints cannot be left out of account. The fourfold division adopted in this book seems to embrace the whole phenomenon of the Church throughout the changing ages, and to take into consideration both internal and external factors of development.

1. The expansion and formation of the Church in the Hellenistic Roman world.

Growing outward from her native Jewish soil, the Church spread within the area of Hellenistic-Roman civilization over the whole Roman Empire and beyond its frontiers in the East, officially unrecognized and repeatedly persecuted until the time of Constantine, and then during the fourth century as the Church of the Empire. Her hierarchical system of government was organized with reference to the divisions of the Empire, the ecumenical councils were imperial councils; the primacy of the bishop of Rome did not infringe the extensive autonomy of the eastern patriarchates. After the rise of the Greek apologists in the second century, Christianity came to terms with the culture and religion of the East and the Hellenistic world, made use of Greek philosophy at the first four councils in the formulation of her trinitarian and christological dogmas, and employed forms of expression taken from Antiquity in her worship and art. As a consequence of the christological disputes, the national churches beyond the eastern frontiers of the Empire separated themselves from the imperial Byzantine church, while Germanic Christian kingdoms of both Arian (Ostrogothic and Visigothic) and Roman (Frankish) observance were formed in the western Empire. The rise of the specifically Roman Church of Gregory the Great and the Arab invasions of the seventh century marked the turning-point: the flourishing churches of North Africa and Syria withered away, and the Germano-Roman West became estranged from Byzantium.

2. The Church as the entelechy of the Christian nations of the West: A.D. 700–1300.

While the Greek church concentrated on the preservation of the traditions of primitive Christianity, the acceptance of the Catholic faith of the Roman Church by the Franks and the Anglo-Saxons, the consequent "germanizing" of Christianity and the alliance of the papacy with the Frankish empire in the eighth century created the only possibility of permeating with the Christian spirit the Germano-Roman nations (to the community of which were now added the converted western Slavs), encircled as they were by Islam and only loosely connected with Byzantium, and of passing on to them the treasures of ancient civilization.

The prevailing form of government in the feudal structure of society, which the Church found already existing and did not itself create, was the theocratic kingship of the renewed Western Empire, until, from the mid-eleventh century, the papacy, revitalized by the Gregorian reforms, rose through repeated conflicts with the secular power (most notably in the Investiture Controversy and in the struggles with the Hohenstaufen emperors Frederick I and Frederick II) to a position of dominating power and arbiter of the West, creating the Roman Curia as the instrument of the Church's central government. But the Church, as a result, became increasingly involved in power-politics and thus entangled with "the World". A more individual and highly subjective piety drove liturgical, objective devotion into the background; scholastic philosophy and Canon Law projected a Christian system of thought and order, not uniform indeed, but complete in its main outlines, which was developed at the universities. The mendicant orders of the thirteenth century took up the idea of poverty and devoted themselves principally to pastoral work in towns. Russia's attachment to Byzantium, as well as the Eastern Schism, increased the isolation of the West; the Crusades enlarged its horizons; the Mongol invasion made possible a temporary breach in the encircling wall of Islam and missionary attempts in the Far East. Boniface VIII, in conflict with Philip the Fair, formulated a theory of the papacy that was conditioned by the times, but was defeated by the catastrophe of Anagni.

3. The break-up of the western Christian world; reforms and Reformation; the transition to world-wide missionary activity.

The universalism of the two highest powers faded before the rise of the national states of western Europe. The unity of the Church, threatened by the Schism, was restored at the Council of Constance. Philosophical unity was lost through Nominalism, and the Church's monopoly of education through the spread of Humanism. Within the feudal social order the bourgeois culture of the cities and the beginnings of Capitalism confronted the Church with new problems which were never satisfactorily solved. The Church, so much in need of reform, became herself a problem, as the writings of Marsiglio of Padua and Wycliffe and the Conciliar Movement bear witness. The "Reformers", Luther, Zwingli, and Calvin, claimed to bring at last the long-demanded reform, and separated all northern Europe and part of central Europe from the papacy. After the Council of Trent the Church opposed the Protestant Reformation with a Catholic Reform, renewed her religious life and was even able in the Counter-Reformation to win back lost territory. Missions in newly-discovered America and Asia enlarged the sphere of her activities. With the dying-down of denominational conflicts the secularization of the

European mind began; the papacy was unable to assert itself against the absolutist states. Western thought was no longer guided by the Church in the period of the so-called Enlightenment; and Revolution and secularization broke the external forms inherited from feudal times.

4. The world-wide Church in the industrial age.

The development of the Church in the nineteenth and twentieth centuries shows three recognizable tendencies. One trend involves the separation of the Church from the laicized State, the accentuation of the contrast between Christian and modern thought, together with an evolution to constitutional and democratic forms of government, the encouragement of lay activity at all social levels by means of modern methods of influencing the masses (as through trades-unionism and the press) and the taking up of the social question by the Church. A further tendency is seen in the intensification of religious life by means of the liturgical movement, the lay apostolate and new forms of pastoral work, and new religious orders. And, in a third context, the definitions of the First Vatican Council concerning the primatial power of the pope assured the latter's position within the Church, while the loss of the Temporal Power marked the beginning of an increase in his religious and moral authority over the Church's members. Through the world-wide missionary activity, which in the nineteenth century followed colonial expansion and in the twentieth began to detach itself from colonialism and European connexions, the Church became in fact a world religion and was forced to come to terms with the others (most notably with Buddhism, Hinduism, and Islam) and with atheistic Communism. At the same time she began to encourage efforts towards the re-establishment of Christian unity.

The Relevance of Church History for Today

Church history is not the Church's cabinet of antiquities; it is her understanding of herself and therefore an integral part of ecclesiology. He who studies the development and growth of the Church in the light of faith enters into her divine-human nature, understands her as she is, not as she ought to be, learns to know the laws by which she lives and himself gains a clear view of her from within; his *sentire Ecclesiam* becomes *sentire cum Ecclesia,* and he will stand fast in every crisis. A prerequisite of this pragmatic way of writing Church history must of course be a strictly scientific investigation and an impartial presentation of the facts. If these tasks are carried out, Church history can and must draw conclusions that will be important for the understanding of the present day and modern problems. The history of the general councils throws light upon the present council, for this is but the most recent link in a long chain. The student of earlier attempts at reunion gains a view of ecumenical strivings which is balanced and free from illusions. The history of religious orders is more than the history of individual orders: these are branches on the tree of the Church, witnesses to the element of grace that is active within her and responses to the questions that face her in every age. When missionary history is concerned with the problems of adaptation and europeanization, it is making an important contribution towards a definition of the relations between civilization and the Church. Church history makes clear the original meaning of ecclesiastical institutions and opens the eyes to the need for reform: the question of the liturgy is an example of this.

In any case: "We cannot understand the Church at the present day if we have not first understood the *whole* of the Christian past."[9] To limit Church history to what is at present alive in the Church, or what is thought to be so, would be a form of pragmatism which, though indispensable as a principle of teaching, is unacceptable as a foundation for research and for the presentation of facts, inasmuch as it would endanger the scientific character of historical writing. Nevertheless, Church history is constantly being faced with the problems of the present day, as in the discussions about an ecumenical council or in the questions raised by the ecumenical movement. The value of Church history for religious education lies in the fact that it opens up the rich possibilities of the Christian life, and faces squarely the problems of the human element in the Church, of power, of sin and failure. But it can only achieve its object if it is presented in its entirety, not merely in summaries of religious history or in extracts of an apologetic nature. In its completeness it is the Church's most effective apologia; without it a purified love of the visible Church is hardly conceivable.

The ecclesiastical historian must have not only, like every historian, "a love of history" (J. G. Droysen), he must also bring to his task "Christian feeling and a Christian spirit";[10] that is, he must first have the Faith in order to explain it, and then he becomes "the interpreter of the working of the Holy Ghost upon earth".[11] He does not passively let the Church's past move before his eyes like a cinema film, because he is conscious that, as its interpreter, he is taking an active part in it. His relation to Church history is determined by his point of view within the Church; his faith is not prejudicial to his inner freedom in the search for truth and his will to judge impartially men and events. His metahistorical standard excludes relativist writing, but not the writing of true history.

[9] J. A. Möhler, *op. cit.* II, 287.   [10] J. A. Möhler, *op. cit.* II, 282.
[11] J. Spörl, *Grundformen hochmittelalterlicher Geschichtsanschauungen* (Munich 1935), 20.

II. The Writing and Study of Church History

The Writing of Church History: its Beginning in Antiquity

"THE sense of history, which was comparatively active when the Gospels and the Acts of the Apostles described the work of Christ and his apostles, remained almost without expression in the period when the Church was developing out of Christ's revelation and was acquiring its historical character, in the midst of struggles and persecutions" (Altaner). Amid a flood of apocryphal writings and legends, the genuine and ancient Acts of the Martyrs bear witness to this historical sense, in such sources as the *Martyrium Polycarpi*, the Acts of St Justin Martyr and of the Scillitani. So also do the historical accounts which the apologists, like Hegesippus and Irenaeus, inserted to support their proofs of Christianity. Somewhat later, attempts were made in the "World Chronicles" of Sextus Julius Africanus[1] († post 240) and Hippolytus of Rome[2] († 235) to fit the historical facts of the Incarnation and the rise and growth of the Church into profane and Old Testament history. The *World Chronicle* of Eusebius of Caesarea († 339), published in 303, was, in the free Latin version by Jerome, to set the pattern of this type of Christian historiography for more than a thousand years.

But it was Eusebius's *Ecclesiastical History* ('Εκκλησιαστικὴ ἱστορία) which made him the "Father of Church History". Published in its original form in seven books before the Diocletian persecution, it was afterwards continued down to 324 to include later events and enlarged to ten books. At the outset the author states his plan as follows: "I have decided to give an account in writing of the successors of the holy apostles and of the times that have gone by from the days of our Redeemer to ours; of the great and numerous events in the history of the Church, of all the excellent leaders and heads of the most respected congregations, of all those who have served the Word of God whether by speaking or writing; of the number and the times of those persons who, out of a desire for novelty, have allowed themselves to be led astray by the worst of errors, and have then proclaimed themselves as guides to a new wisdom which is no wisdom, like ravening wolves who rush without pity on Christ's flock; furthermore, of the fate that befell the Jewish people after their crime against our Saviour, and of the numerous grievous attacks to which the Word of God was exposed at the hands of the pagans; of the heroes who again and again fought for the Faith amid tortures and bloodshed, and

---

[1] The surviving fragments are in *PG* 10, 63–94.
[2] The World Chronicle has been ed. by A. Bauer and R. Helm (Berlin, 2nd ed. 1955) *GCS* 46; cf. *LThK* V, 379 f.

11

finally of the witnesses to the Faith in our own days and of the ever-gracious, ever-loving mercy of our Redeemer."

In accordance with this programme (and making use also of the uncanonical sources Philo and Flavius Josephus), Eusebius describes in roughly chronological order the activities of Jesus and the apostles as well as the post-apostolic period: these matters are dealt with in Books I–III. Following these, Books IV—VII contain lists of bishops of the apostolic churches of Rome, Antioch and Jerusalem; but they also give an account of the heresies that arose, of the great ecclesiastical writers, and of persecutions by Jews and pagans. Books VIII and IX are devoted to "the persecution of our days"; and Book X to the victory of Christianity under Constantine. This last part has a supplementary account of the martyrs of Palestine and the laudatory life of Constantine by the same author. Eusebius in his history of the Church was "still unable to give an account that showed clearly the relation of cause and effect" (Altaner). However, by getting away from the eschatological viewpoint, he was the first to venture on a "solitary and untrodden path", to demonstrate in the history of Christ's chosen "people of God" the victory of God over the Devil and to "edify his readers" (III, 24). Because of his transcription of numerous documents and the excerpts he gives from writings now lost (such as those of Papias), Eusebius's work is by far the most important historical source for the first three centuries. The documents and the lists of bishops are fitted into the chronological framework of the emperors' reigns; the literary form follows the example of profane history, but it is written with "no mean skill" (E. Schwartz); its original contribution is its metaphysical basis.

Eusebius was followed by three continuators who all treat more or less of a common period. Socrates († 439), a lawyer of Constantinople, groups the ecclesiastical events of the years 305–439 around the great emperors; he uses good sources, is less involved than his predecessor in theological conflicts, and is therefore more impartial; above all, he is more lenient towards heretics. Sozomen, who was also a lawyer of Constantinople and who knew Socrates, was superior to the latter in literary skill but not in reliability or critical powers; in his presentation of events in the period 324–425 (dealt with in detail only to 421), his own point of view is kept entirely in the background. Theodoret of Cyrus, on the other hand, writes as a supporter of the Antiochian school and is often silent about the defects of his heroes; but, a versatile writer, he could describe events perceptively and vividly. In his account of the years 323–428 he has included many synodal decisions and letters, as well as other documents, though he is sometimes cursory and inexact in his chronology. Evagrius Scholasticus († 600), with his *Ecclesiastical History*, is the successor to the three continuators of Eusebius already mentioned.

He relates from a strictly orthodox but truthloving point of view the christological disputes of the period 432–594.

The three continuations in Greek of Eusebius's History were put together and extended to 527 by Theodorus Lector, whose work, however, only survives in an epitome. The later Byzantine chroniclers (such as Theophanes Confessor and Xantopulos) borrowed from his work. The chronicle written by the Monophysite John of Nikiu is important for the seventh century; it is written in Coptic but survives only in Ethiopian. The later Byzantine historiographers, although in the first place treating of State history, also recorded the theological disputes, particularly Georgios Pachymeres († 1310) and Nikephoros Gregoras († 1359–60).

The Latin Church meanwhile took over from the Greek historians. A Latin version of Eusebius's *Ecclesiastical History* was made in 403 by Rufinus of Aquileia, who added two more books, for which perhaps (according to Heseler) the lost history of the Church by Gelasius of Caesarea served as a pattern. Cassiodorus arranged for the monk Epiphanius to translate into Latin the three continuators of Eusebius and, on the model of an already-existing Greek work by Theodorus Lector, to combine them into an *Historia tripartita*. Rufinus's version and the *Historia tripartita* became the basic ecclesiastical histories of the Middle Ages. The various subjects dealt with by Eusebius soon came to be treated separately. Between 374 and 377 Epiphanius of Salamis collected together eighty heresies in his "Medicine Chest" (Πανάριον).[3] In 392 Jerome published the first catalogue of Christian writers, comprising 135 names, which was augmented *c.* 480 by the semi-Pelagian Gennadius, and in the seventh century by Isidore of Seville and Ildefonsus of Toledo.[4] In the fourth century, lists of bishops began to be compiled, not with traditional dates but with regnal years worked out by reckoning backwards: such were the list of bishops of Jerusalem given by Epiphanius (66, 19 f.) and the catalogue of Roman bishops in the chronicle of 354;[5] the earliest version of the *Liber Pontificalis* (down to Felix IV, 526–30) dates from the sixth century.

In both East and West the collecting of synodal canons concerning ecclesiastical discipline began in the second half of the fourth century. The oldest extant Greek collection is the systematically arranged collection of Johannes Scholasticus, compiled *c.* 550. In the West, that of Dionysius Exiguus dates from 500, and was the first of a long series of similar

[3] Ed. K. Holl, 3 vols. (Berlin 1915, 1921, 1933) GCS 25, 31, 37; *Altaner* 367 f.

[4] *De viris illustribus*, PL, 23, 631–760; the new ed. by G. Herding (Leipzig 1924) also contains the continuation of Gennadius. For Isidore of Seville, see *PL*, 83, 1081–106; for Ildephonsus of Toledo, PL, 96, 195–206; cf. *Altaner* 10.

[5] Ed. by T. Mommsen, *MGAuctant* IX, 13–196; for list of Roman bishops, ibid., 73–76; cf. *RAC* II, 407–15 (L. Koep).

collections.[6] The oldest Acts of an ecumenical council to be preserved are those of Ephesus (431). Optatus of Mileve, between 330 and 347, collected documents to serve as a history of the Donatist heresy; and in 417 Augustine edited an account of the origins of the Pelagian dispute. To the second half of the sixth century belongs a collection made at Rome of letters of popes and emperors, which is known as the *Collectio Avellana* from the place where it was found.

Christian biography of the pre-Constantinian period was aimed primarily at edification. Examples of this kind are the Life of Cyprian by Pontius, that of Antony by Athanasius, that of Macrina by Gregory of Nyssa, the *Vita Ambrosii* by Paulinus and the *Vita Augustini* by Possidius. In the monastic biographies of Palladius which appeared in the East and in the *Historia Lausiaca,* the historical account is overshadowed by demonism and miracle seeking.

The influence which Eusebius' *Ecclesiastical History* exercised on later histories of the Church through Rufinus' version and the *Historia tripartita* has been noted above. In a similar fashion Eusebius' *World Chronicle,* in Jerome's version, influenced later histories of the world and of salvation. Of less worth were the short "World Chronicles" of Sulpicius Severus (down to 400) and Prosper of Aquitaine (to 455); the *Chronicon* of Isidore of Seville (to 615) attained a higher reputation. But far more important for the historical thought of the Middle Ages than these collections was Augustine's *De civitate Dei* in twenty-four books, written in the period 413–26. Herein, the City of God, equated with the Church as a sacramental fellowship, is in incessant conflict with the *Civitas terrena,* which is not identified with any particular State, not even the Roman. The struggle between faith and disbelief is in this context the main theme of world history, conceived as the history of man's salvation. Like Augustine's *De civitate Dei,* the almost contemporaneous *Historiae adversus paganos* of Paulus Orosius provide an apologia for Christianity; he seeks to prove that Christianity is not responsible for the disasters of the age.

The history of the world and of salvation is usually divided according to one of two basic plans, though these show many variations. With reference to Psalm 89:4, which says that a thousand years are as a day in God's sight, and by analogy with the six days of Creation, history had been divided in Jewish Messianic writings into six millenia, which the Messianic kingdom was to follow as the seventh. Justin Martyr and Irenaeus had taken over this division and interpreted it chiliastically: the

---

[6] *PL,* 67, 139–316; for all older collections, C. Turner's *Ecclesiae occidentalis monumenta juris antiquissimi,* 3 vols. (Oxford 1899–1913) is still fundamental; cf. also E. Schwartz, "Die Kanonessammlungen der alten Reichskirche" in *ZSavRGkan* 25 (1936), 1–114.

world will be consummated in as many "days" as were spent in its creation; after the year 6000 the thousand-year reign of Christ on earth will follow. Hippolytus and Lactantius converted the eschatological schema into a chronological one, which forms the basis of Jerome's *World Chronicle* and was also known to Augustine. Here, moreover, we find a parallel with the six ages of man (*infantia, pueritia, adolescentia, juventus, gravitas,* and *senectus*) and the threefold division from the viewpoint of human salvation: *ante legem, sub lege,* and *sub gratia.* The doctrine of the six ages of the world (*aetates mundi*) was bequeathed to the Middle Ages by Jerome and Augustine via Isidore of Seville and Bede's *De sex aetatibus mundi.*

The second schema divides world history according to the four empires: the Assyrian-Babylonian, the Persian, the empire of Alexander and the Roman Empire. This schema also is of non-Christian origin (it was used in the time of Augustus by Pompeius Trogus); but it was incorporated into Christian thought by Jerome with reference to the prophet Daniel (2:36 ff.): the christianized Roman Empire will, as the last of the world-empires, remain until the end of the world. Sleidan clung to this view as late as the sixteenth century.

The Writing of History in the Middle Ages: Christian History, not Church History

Eusebius's *Ecclesiastical History* found no imitators throughout the Middle Ages, even though the expression "Church history" occurs occasionally from the twelfth century onwards. During the transitional period the subjects of Christian historical writings are not the Church as such, but the christianized Germanic peoples and, later, monasteries, bishoprics, and saints. The medieval chronicler and annalist, in so far as he is not continuing the chronicle of Jerome, usually augments his account of contemporary events with information taken over uncritically from earlier authors, intended to serve as general historical background. He is concerned with world history and religious history, but not Church history. Three historians of the transitional period stand out: the Roman Gregory of Tours († 594) with his *History of the Franks* (to which is appended a short history of the bishops of Tours), the history of that people being regarded as the victory of the True Faith;[7] the Visigoth Isidore of Seville († 636),[8] with his *Chronica Majora* down to 615 (and in a second version to 625), famous also for his literary history, the

---

[7] *Historiarum libri X,* ed. R. Buchner, 2 vols. (Darmstadt 1955); *Wattenbach–Levison,* I, 99–108.

[8] *MG Auctant* XI, 391–506; *Wattenbach–Levison,* I, 86 ff.

Etymologies, and his *History of the Visigoths;* the Anglo-Saxon Bede the Venerable († 735) with his *Historia Ecclesiastica gentis Anglorum,* in which he shows how his people "became the Church of Christ".[9] Through his *De sex aetatibus mundi* and his method of calculating Easter, Bede became "the teacher of the whole of the Middle Ages" (Levison).

The "Christian era" established by Dionysius Exiguus in the Easter table of 532, which fixed Christ's birth in the year 754 *ab urbe condita* as the central point of time, marks in the field of chronology the triumph of the school which saw human history as the history of salvation. World history begins with man's creation by God, follows the human race in its God-directed course under the Old and New Covenants, and finally relates the history of the Kingdom of Christ on earth, in which the Christian State and the Church form one body containing both good and evil men, until at the end of time the Lord will separate the former from the latter and the New Jerusalem will become a reality. The amalgamation of the concept of the Kingdom of God with the Church had for its result that the Middle Ages did indeed produce Christian history, but not Church history in the modern sense of the term: "Ecclesiastical historiography takes up the whole historical field" (Zimmermann). By the climax of the Middle Ages this kind of historical writing had developed three literary forms: the world chronicle, annals, and biography.

The numerous world chronicles not only draw their material about early periods from the chronicles of Eusebius and Jerome, and their continuators, but also retain the view of history established in the post-Constantinian "imperial" Church: the regnal years of the emperors form the chronological framework into which the succession of popes and other secular or ecclesiastical events are fitted. The closer they come to the author's own period, the more frequent are the events narrated from personal knowledge and the higher the value of the chronicles as sources. The *Chronicon* of Regino of Prüm provides a typical example:[10] starting from the birth of Christ, it is a mere compilation to the reign of Louis the Pious; but from there till its conclusion in 906 it becomes a good source for the late Carolingian period. The *Chronicon Augiense* of Hermann the Lame of Reichenau († 1054),[11] which reflects the many-sided knowledge

[9] Ed. C. Plummer, 2 vols. (Oxford 1896), I, 73: "nostrum gentem ... Christi fecit Ecclesiam"; W. Levison: "Bede as Historian" in *Aus rheinischer und fränkischer Frühzeit* (Düsseldorf 1948), 347–82.

[10] Ed. F. Kurze (Hanover 1890); H. Löwe, "Regino von Prüm und das historische Weltbild der Karolingerzeit" in *Rhein. Vierteljahresblätter* 17 (1952), 151–79, new offprint in Lammers (ed.), *Ausgewählte Aufsätze und Arbeiten aus den Jahren 1933–1959* (Darmstadt 1961), 91–134.

[11] *MGSS* V, 67–133; R. Buchner, "Geschichtsbild und Reichsbegriff bei H. von R. in *AKG* 42 (1960), 27–60.

of its author, is pre-eminent for its careful use of older models; and in its later part it develops into a history of the Empire. Sigebert of Gembloux takes pains in his prosaic and summary chronicle (finished before 1105) to arrange the events of imperial and ecclesiastical history in correct chronological order, and bases his work on a wealth of source material.[12] Frutolf of Michelsberg and Ekkehard of Aura make use of him in their chronicle, one of the masterpieces of medieval historiography, which extends to 1106 and 1125, and contains valuable information on the Investiture Dispute. Otto of Freising († 1185), the greatest German historian of the Middle Ages, does indeed indicate in the title of his work[13] that Augustine, not Eusebius through Jerome, was his master. For him the Empire is only "the shadow of a great name"; he believes in the realization of the *Civitas Dei* in a Christian empire, and addresses himself with his eschatological outlook more to the religious reader than to the enquiring historian.[14]

The primary concern of the annalists, when they were not officially employed in writing State annals, was the recording of events, whether known by tradition or from personal experience, which affected their own diocese or abbey. If through family or personal relationships they were involved in matters of more general importance, their range of vision was widened, as in the case of Thietmar of Merseburg († 1018). Diocesan annals were compiled in episcopal cities which, through their schools, took part in the flourishing intellectual life of the age of the Saxon and Salian emperors, as did Hildesheim, Magdeburg, Liège, and Trier. But few of these can be ranked as histories, save perhaps the history of the church of Rheims by Flodoard († *c.* 966) and the *Gesta Hammaburgensis ecclesiae pontificum* by Adam of Bremen († 1081), the best part of which is the biography of Archbishop Adalbert of Bremen.[15] Obit books and necrologies, in which dates of death are noted in the calendar,

---

[12] *MGSS* VI, 300–74; *Manitius* III, 344 ff.

[13] *Chronicon sive Historia de duabus civitatibus*, ed. A. Hofmeister (Hanover-Berlin, 2nd ed. 1912); *Manitius* III, 376–88; H. M. Klinkenberg, "Der Sinn der Chronik Ottos von Freising", *Festschrift G. Kallen* (Bonn 1957), 63–76; E. Meuthen, "Der ethische Charakter der civitates bei Augustinus und ihre platonische Fehldeutung", ibid., 43–62; J. Koch, "Die Grundlagen der Geschichtsphilosophie Ottos von Freising" in *MThZ* 4 (1953), 79–94, reprinted in Lammers, *op. cit.* 321–49; *O. von Fr., Gedenkgabe zu seinem 800. Todesjahr* (Freiburg i. Br. 1958), with contributions by J. Spörl, J. Staber etc.

[14] "Sic de utraque dicere proposuimus, ut tenorem hystoriae non omittamus, quatinus et religiosus auditor, quid in mundanis rebus ob innumeras mutationum miserias abhorrendum sit, animadvertat ac studiosus seu curiosus indagator non confusam rerum preteritarum seriem inveniat": Hofmeister's ed., 9.

[15] Flodoard, *MGSS* XIII, 404–599. Adam of Bremen: B. Schmeidler (Hanover–Berlin, 3rd ed. 1917); there is a rather unsatisfactory interpretation in M. Misch, *Geschichte der Autobiographie* (Frankfurt 1955–62), III, 1, 251–61.

owe their origin to the desire to include founders and benefactors in the community of prayer and sacrifice; and the lists kept in many monasteries, such as Fulda and St Blasien, show a continuous record of the deaths of inmates and benefactors.

In the *Vita* or biography, which is usually but not invariably the life of a saint, the main purpose is edification. The *Vitae* of extraordinary men are designed to serve as examples of virtue, and their nearness to God is demonstrated by miracles. Virtues and miracles are therefore their main theme. This tendency, together with the use made of classical or Christian models (including Suetonius, Sallust, and Sulpicius Severus), by no means excludes concrete facts with definite literary intentions. Ruotger, in his Life of Bruno of Cologne (written in 967–9), portrays a bishop of the Empire as he ought to be;[16] abbot Norbert of Iburg, in his Life of Bishop Benno of Osnabrück (written between 1090 and 1108), does not conceal his subject's human weaknesses, so that the reader may therefore pray for the soul of the abbey's founder. The Life of Anselm of Canterbury by Eadmer (composed soon after the saint's death in 1109) is based on information supplied by Anselm himself and on an intimate knowledge of his personality: his holiness is illustrated not by miracles, but by his constant fidelity to the monastic ideal. From the thirteenth century, hagiographical literature came under the influence of the collections of *exempla* compiled with a view to preaching. Such is the Life of Engelbert of Cologne by the Cistercian Caesarius of Heisterbach, which shows a clear relationship with the same author's collections of *exempla*.[17] The *Vitae* of the great founders of orders, such as St Francis of Assisi, owe their origin to the desire of the orders to possess a model picture of their founders.

The reform movement of the eleventh century and the Investiture Dispute seem to have provided a new impulse to the writing of Church history, perhaps even to mark a turning-point. The struggle for the independence of the spiritual power, against lay domination, once more made the Church as such a subject for historiography. In the literature of reform the primitive Church appears as the ideal towards which the Church of the present, her clergy and monks, must strive: that is, not

[16] Ed. I. Ott (Weimar 1951, new impression 1958); F. Lotter, *Die Vita Brunonis des Ruotger* (Bonn 1958). A new impression of H. Bresslau's ed. of the genuine *Vita Bennonis* (1902) also appeared in 1956. For Eadmer see M. Misch, *Geschichte der Autobiographie*, (Frankfurt 1955–62), III, 1, 215–61.

[17] The old ed. of the *Dialogus miraculorum* by J. Strange (2 vols., Cologne 1851) has been supplied with an index in the new impression (1922), but has not been replaced by a new ed.; the Life of Engelbert has been edited by F. Zschaeck: *Die Wundergeschichten des Caesarius von Heisterbach*, III (Bonn 1937), 225–328. For a general survey of medieval exempla literature, see A. Hilka, ibid., I (Bonn 1933).

merely the primitive Church of apostolic times, but the "ancient Church"; and even the phrase "Church history" reappears. In the prologue to his *Historia ecclesiastica,* the second version of which was finished in 1110, Hugh of Fleury promises to lead the reader to the hidden secrets of the Church concealed in history; but his title hides merely a further compilation of sacred and profane history.[18] Neither does the work of Ordericus Vitalis, bearing the same title and ending with the year 1141, by any means fulfill its author's claims, in spite of its originality: *Ecclesia Dei* means for him both the whole Church and individual churches; the *gesta Dei* happen in her and to her, not through her.[19] For John of Salisbury († 1180), the keenly observant secretary of Thomas Becket and later Bishop of Chartres, the history of the Church, whose beginnings are related in the Acts of the Apostles and whose growth Eusebius has described, is already a history of the priesthood and thus of the papacy,[20] as it was also for the Dominican Bartholomew of Lucca († 1326) writing two centuries later. The latter's *Historia ecclesiastica nova*[21] identifies the kingdom of Christ with the reign of the Roman pontiffs: for the contemporary of Boniface VIII and John XXII the dualism of the two kingdoms no longer existed. But Bartholomew's work, again, was no real Church history.

The germ of a new method of writing Church history which appeared in the creative twelfth century never in fact developed. On the contrary, the Church became at that time the subject of "historical theology". Rupert of Deutz († 1129) associates creation, redemption, and sanctification with the three persons of the Trinity; sanctification occurs through the seven gifts of the Holy Spirit, who works in the Church.[22] Like Rupert, Gerhoh of Reichersperg, who followed in his wake, is not interested in reporting

---

[18] *MGSS* IX, 349–64 (little more than the prologues); *PL,* 163, 821–54; cf. *Manitius* III, 518 ff. The words referred to in the Prologue are: "Praeterea hujus historiae liber nimis profunda latenter continet ecclesiae sacramenta" (350).

[19] *PL* 188, 15–984. In the Prologue, Ordericus justifies this title: he writes "de rebus ecclesiasticis ut simplex ecclesiae filius ... unde praesens opusculum ecclesiasticam historiam appellari affecto" (16). Cf. H. Wolter, *Ordericus Vitalis. Ein Beitrag zur kluniazensischen Geschichtsschreibung* (Wiesbaden 1955); see also T. Schieffer, *ZKG* 62 (1955–6), 336 ff.

[20] *Historia Pontificalis,* ed. M. Chibnall (London 1956); H. Hohenleutner, "John of Salisbury in der Literatur der letzten zehn Jahre" in *HJ* 77 (1958), 493 ff. A history of the popes preserved in a MS at the abbey of Zwettl also dates from the twelfth century: cf. K. Ross, *Die Historia Pontificum Romanorum aus Zwettl* (Greifswald 1932).

[21] *Muratori* XI, 753–1216: cf. M. Grabmann, *Mittelalterliches Geistesleben* I, 354 ff.

[22] *PL,* 167–170. For the critical ed. now in preparation, cf. R. Haacke, "Die Überlieferung der Rupertus-Schriften" in *DA* 16 (1960), 397–436; W. Kahles, *Geschichte als Liturgie. Die Geschichtstheologie des Rupertus von Deutz* (Münster 1960): the attitude is unhistorical.

facts but in interpreting them and finding their symbolic relationships.[23] Anselm of Havelberg († 1158) developed an interpretation of the Apocalypse which he found already existing. He divided the history of the Church into seven parts: the white horse of the Apocalypse is the primitive Church, the red horse the age of persecutions, the black horse the attacks of heretics, the pale horse signifies the false brethren, rendered harmless by the monks; the subsequent periods belong to the final age which will precede the end of the world. The Holy Spirit renews the world by means of the monks. He is the principle of progress in the Church.[24] From Anselm it is but a step to Joachim of Floris († 1202), the Calabrian Cistercian abbot, who in his commentary on the Apocalypse divides the history of salvation into three periods: the age of the Father, or the Old Testament, in which the Law ruled; the age of the Son, or the New Testament, in which faith and grace rule, and the imperfections of which will be removed in the third age: the approaching age of the Holy Spirit, who will bring the fullness of grace and the dominion of love. Instead of the present, imperfect, Petrine Church there will appear at a time which can be calculated from Holy Scripture (about the year 1260) the perfect Johannine Church of the Spirit, in which the eternal gospel will be proclaimed.[25] The Church of the present is not the final form of Christ's Church; it can and will be superseded by a church of the Spirit.

Joachim's view of history determined not only the historical interpretation of the Franciscan spiritual writers such as Ubertino of Casale and Peter John Olivi,[26] who saw in Francis of Assisi the proclaimer or at least the precursor of the "eternal gospel"; his influence is traceable even in such a lively historian as Salimbene of Parma. And for Bonaventure himself the actual purpose of studying history is "not the understanding of the past, but prophecy about what is to come".[27] Late medieval

---

[23] *PL*, 193 and 194; *Opera inedita*, ed. P. Classen, I (Rome 1955); E. Meuthen, *Kirche und Heilsgeschehen bei G. von R.* (Cologne 1959); P. Classen, *G. von R., Eine Biographie* (Wiesbaden 1960); H. Hürten in *HJ* 80 (1961), 265–9.

[24] *PL* 188, W. Kamlah, *Apokalypse und Geschichtstheologie* (Berlin 1935); K. Fina, "Anselm von Havelberg", *APraem* 32 (1956), 69–101 and 193–227; W. Berges, *Jahrbuch für Geschichte Mittel- und Ostdeutschlands* 5 (1956), 39 ff.

[25] The collected ed. by E. Buonaiuti, for the *Fonti per la storia d'Italia*, is not yet complete. Cf. H. Grundmann, *Studien über J. von F.* (Leipzig 1927); idem, *Neue Forschungen über J. von F.* (Marburg 1950); M. W. Bloomfield, "J. of F., a Critical Survey" in *Tr* 13 (1957), 249–311.

[26] R. Manselli, *La Lectura super apocalypsim di P. G. Olivi* (Rome 1955); also important is Alexander Minorita, *Expositio in Apocalypsim*, ed. A. Wachtel (Weimar 1955).

[27] J. Ratzinger, *Die Geschichtstheologie des hl. Bonaventura* (Munich 1959), 22; Salimbene's *Chronica*, ed. F. Bernini, 2 vols. (Bari 1942); N. Scivoletto, *Fra Salimbene da Parma e la storia politica e religiosa del secolo XIII* (Bari 1950).

studies of the Apocalypse frequently follow Joachim's lines of thought.[28] Nicholas of Cusa draws a parallel between the historical life of Jesus and that of His mystical body the Church: to every year of our Lord's life corresponds a period of fifty years in the history of the Church. As the Precursor appeared in Jesus's twenty-ninth year, so will the Holy Spirit awake in the Church about the year 1450, and the kingdom of God will be spread by saints throughout the world; but then, corresponding to the thirtieth year of our Lord's age, will begin the passion of the Church and her persecution by Antichrist.

These systems of historical theology had their origin in the unsatisfactory condition of the Church of the time, which was so much in need of reform; and, with the Church's past in mind, they developed into the so-called theory of decadence: namely, that the history of the Church is that of a continuous falling away from the ideal state of the primitive Church.[29] Sometimes this theory is expressed in the form of a division into periods: the Golden Age of the martyrs was succeeded by the Silver Age of the great Fathers of the Church, the Bronze Age of the monks and finally by the contemporary Iron Age, in which moral decay provokes the judgment of God. The theory of decadence does not, like the theologies of history and the apocalyptic interpretations, involve the undervaluing of historical facts; apart from reforming works, it is to be found in the writings of such important historians as Dietrich of Niem and Thomas Ebendorfer.[30] But knowledge of the Church's historical past was hardly increased between the thirteenth century and the end of the fifteenth. Writers were content to recapitulate what already existed, as did Vincent of Beauvais († 1264) in his *Speculum historiale*,[31] or to reduce it to synoptic form, as did Martin of Troppau († 1278) in his tabular chronicle of emperors and popes, which had many continuators and was translated into several languages.[32] These two, as well as Bernard Gui

---

[28] J. Rohr's "Die Prophetie im letzten Jahrhundert vor der Reformation als Geschichtsquelle und Geschichtsfaktor" in *HJ* 19 (1898), 22–56 and 447–66, has not yet been superseded; cf. ibid., 32 f., concerning the work *De eversione Europae*, falsely ascribed to St Vincent Ferrer; N. Cohn, *The Pursuit of the Millenium* (London 1957), concerns mainly the earlier Middle Ages. For the Franciscan J. Hilten (c. 1500) and his commentary on Daniel and the Apocalypse, see H. Volz in *ZKG* 67 (1955–6), 111–15.

[29] No thorough research on this subject has yet been done; cf. E. Seeberg, *Gottfried Arnold* (Meerane 1923), 285 ff.

[30] Thomas Ebendorfer's *Schismentraktat*, ed. H. Zimmermann in *AÖG* 120 (1954), 45–147; A. Lhotsky, *T. Ebendorfer* (Stuttgart 1957), 109 f. and 125 f..

[31] Cf. K. Young, "The Speculum Majus of V. of B.", *The Yale University Library Gazette* 5 (1930), 1–13; B. L. Ullmann, "A Project for a new Edition of V. of B.", *Speculum* 8 (1933), 212–26.

[32] *MGSS* XXII, 377–475. For continuations, see H. Schmidinger, "Das Papstbild in der Geschichtsschreibung des späten Mittelalters", *Röm. Hist. Mitteilungen* 1 (1958), 106–29

(† 1331)[33] and Antoninus of Florence († 1459), belonged to the Dominican order. The latter's chronicle had for its purpose the promotion of virtuous actions by historical examples.[34] The numerous compendia of papal history show new and individual characteristics specifically for the popes of the period.[35] The strong nationalistic tones, already audible in Matthew Paris[36] and Alexander of Roes[37] grow louder in the French biographies of the popes of the Avignon epoch and the years of the Great Schism. Catalogues of bishops and abbots were compiled, and the great orders wrote their chronicles.

The literary history of the Church, whose ancient standard works (by Jerome, Gennadius and Isidore of Seville) had been continued in the twelfth century by Sigebert of Gembloux and Honorius of Autun, was little advanced by the catalogue of Henry of Brussels (formerly ascribed to Henry of Ghent) or by that of Arnold Geylhoven of Rotterdam († 1442) more than a century later, or by other works of that kind.[38] Only the list of writers compiled by the Benedictine abbot Johannes Trithemius († 1516) is based on extensive researches, but it is disfigured by many errors and confusions.[39]

---

esp. 113 f. and 120. One of the few critical editions of late medieval papal and imperial chronicles is that of Andreas of Regensburg: *Chronica Pontificum et Imperatorum Romanorum,* ed. G. Leidinger (Munich 1903).

[33] For Gui's *Flores chronicorum,* the *Catalogus brevis Pont. Rom. et Imperatorum* and the *Tractatus de temporibus et annis generalium et particularium conciliorum,* all written in the second decade of the fourteenth century, cf. *HistLittFrance* XXXV, 139–232; *DHGE* VIII, 667 ff. (G. Mollat).

[34] R. Morçay, *St Antonin* (Tours-Paris 1914), 322 ff.; B. Walker, *The Chronicles of St Antonin* (Washington 1933).

[35] Excerpts from the *Actus Romanorum Pontificum* of Amalricus Augerii are in Baluze and Mollat, *Vitae paparum Avenionensium,* I 89 ff., 183 ff., and 405 ff.; for Ebendorfer's *Chronica Pont. Rom.,* see Lhotsky, *op. cit.* 59 ff.

[36] *Chronica Majora,* ed. H. R. Luard, 7 vols. (London 1872–84); R. Vaughan, *Matthew of Paris* (Cambridge 1958).

[37] A. von R., *Schriften* ed. and trans., H. Grundmann and H. Heimpel (Weimar 1949); Heimpel, "A. von R. und das deutsche Selbstbewußtsein des 13. Jh." in *AKG* 26 (1935), 19 ff.; idem, "Über den Pavo des A. von R." in *DA* 13 (1957), 171–227, reprinted in Lammers, *op. cit.* 350–417.

[38] P. Lehmann, "Literaturgeschichte im Mittelalter", *Erforschung des MA* I, (Stuttgart 1941), 82 ff.; F. Pelster, "Der Heinrich von Gent zugeschriebene Catalogus Virorum Illustrium und sein wirklicher Verfasser" in *HJ* 39 (1919), 234–64; Lehmann, "Der Schriftstellerkatalog des A. G. von Rotterdam" in *Erforschung des MA* (Stuttgart 1961), 216–36; A. Auer, *Ein neugefundener Katalog der Dominikanerschriftsteller* (Paris 1933); T. F. Bonmann, *Die literaturkundlichen Quellen des Franziskanerordens im MA* (Fulda 1937).

[39] *De scriptoribus ecclesiasticis,* completed in 1494 and printed in the same year at Mainz; for the sources, see I. Silbernagl, *J. Trithemius* (Regensburg 1885), 61 ff.; H. Jedin, "Fra contemporanei del Tritemio" in *Benedictina* (1948), 231–6.

The great events of ecclesiastical history did of course find their historians. Dietrich of Niem, Ludolf of Sagan, and Martin of Alpartil wrote of the Schism[40] and John of Segovia of the Council of Basle.[41] But for the period after the thirteenth century the scope and value of their work are swallowed up by the rapidly swelling stream of documents, letters, deeds, and other records of the most varied kinds, as well as liturgical books and rubrics. The papal registers have been preserved from 1198 onwards, albeit with some gaps; the register of petitions, which begins with Clement VI, comprises 7,365 volumes, down to the pontificate of Leo XIII. The collections of documents and *regesta* of the German bishoprics and provinces, as well as of the cities that were ever increasing in importance, became more and more extensive,[42] and are augmented by lists of property, copies of deeds, account-books, and tax-lists. Letters and collections of letters make possible the writing of genuine, vivid biographies; and the admittedly still sporadic reports of ambassadors (like those of the Aragonese ambassadors at the Curia and of the participants in the Councils of Basle and Constance), and the acts of the councils and imperial diets give us a glimpse into the conduct of ecclesiastical affairs.

The Flowering of Church History from the Sixteenth to the Eighteenth Century

The contribution of Humanism to the revival of Church history was the result of the Humanists' cry: "Ad fontes!" By making the sources (and first of all those for the history of the early Church) flow again, they broke the drought of the late medieval compendia. As regards the earlier period, the papal biographies of Bartolomeo Platina († 1481) were no more than a stylistic rewriting of the *Liber Pontificalis*.[43] Lorenzo Valla's criticism of the Donation of Constantine[44] marked a new beginning, which

---

[40] Dietrich of Niem, *De Schismate*, ed. G. Erler (Leipzig 1890); cf. Heimpel, *Dietrich von Niem* (Münster 1932), 181–268; Ludolf of Sagan: *De Longevo Schismate*, ed. G. Loserth in *AÖG* 60 (1880), 411 ff.; Martin of Alpartil: *Chronica actitatorum temporibus D. Benedicti XIII*, ed. by F. Ehrle (Paderborn 1906).

[41] *Historia gestorum generalis synodi Basiliensis*, in *Monumenta Conc. gen. saeculi XV*, II–IV (Vienna-Basle 1873–1935); cf. U. Fromherz, *Johann von Segovia als Geschichtsschreiber des Konzils von Basel* (Basle 1960).

[42] For a general survey of narrative sources for the history of German bishoprics and cities, see Jacob and Weden, *Quellenkunde der deutschen Geschichte im MA* (5th ed. Berlin 1952), III, 128–142. The marked lack of information on sources for Church history from this time forward has been partly remedied for Germany by G. Wolf in *Quellenkunde der deutschen Reformationsgeschichte*, 2 vols. (Gotha 1915–22).

[43] The *Liber de vita Christi et pontificum* (Venice 1479) ends at 1474, but numerous later editions and continuations take it beyond that date.

[44] L. Valla, *De falso credita et ementita Constantini donatione declamatio*, written 1440,

could however be further developed only when the art of printing had begun not only to multiply single works by the Fathers and by later ecclesiastical writers, but also to produce collected editions. In the preliminary work of this kind questions of authenticity arose, the feeling for literary form was awakened, authors began to enter into the language and spirit of the early Church and learnt to know her institutions. Although Erasmus was by nature a philologist, not an historian, we cannot leave him out of account in connexion with the revival of the historical sense. It was from his circle that the earliest editions of the ancient Christian histories issued. Beatus Rhenanus edited in 1523 the Latin version of Eusebius's *Ecclesiastical History* and the *Historia tripartita;*[45] in 1544 the works of Eusebius and Theodoret were published in the original Greek. About the same time there appeared the still very imperfect editions of the councils by Merlin and Crabbe. Sources which had hitherto been employed only in derivative form and at second hand (such as Gratian's *Decretum*) were now directly accessible. That they were used for the writing of a history of the Church was, it must be admitted, a result of the Reformation.

Luther's historical view of the Church was determined by his conviction that the true, biblical, doctrine of salvation had been falsified through the guilt of the papacy and by Aristotelean scholasticism, and that a thorough reform of the Church was possible only by a return to that doctrine of salvation and a laying aside of "human ordinances". This view, which gave quite a new turn to the theory of decadence, demanded a Church history that would justify it. The *Historia ecclesiastica,*[46] written by the strict Lutheran Matthias Flacius (actually Vlačich, 1520–75) with the help of Johannes Wigand and other collaborators, and generally known because of its divisions and place of origin as the *Magdeburg Centuries,* sought to prove by a wealth of systematically arranged references to sources that Lutheranism, and not the papal Church, was in agreement with the doctrine of the early Church. In 1556 this work was preceded by a catalogue of witnesses to evangelical truth in papal times. This powerful attack at once provoked a series of replies, partly inadequate

---

ed. W. Schwalm (Leipzig 1928). For later medieval discussions of its authenticity, see D. Laehr, "Die Konstantinische Schenkung in der abendländischen Literatur des ausgehenden MA" in *QFIAB* 23 (1931–2), 120–81; Jedin, *Studien über Domenico de Domenichi* (Wiesbaden 1958), 264–8.

[45] *Auctores historiae ecclesiasticae* (Basle 1523) contains only the Latin versions of Eusebius' Church History by Rufinus, the *Historia Tripartita* and texts from Theodoret; a new and improved ed. was published at Basle in 1544.

[46] Fourteen vols. (Basle 1559–74): the last, incomplete, ed. was published at Nuremberg 1757–65; W. Preger, *M. Flacius Illyricus und seine Zeit,* 2 vols. (Erlangen 1859–61); P. Polman, "Flacius Illyricus, Historien de l'Eglise" in *RHE* 27 (1931), 27–73; M. Mirkovič, *Matia Vlačič Ilirik* (Zagreb 1960).

and partly unfinished, (by Conrad Braun, Wilhelm Eisengrein and Peter Canisius);[47] then came Bigne's systematically arranged collection of early ecclesiastical writers,[48] and finally the epoch-making *Annales ecclesiastici* of the Oratorian Caesar Baronius († 1607), based on lectures delivered by him in the Oratory of Philip Neri, and giving in twelve volumes the history of the Church down to Innocent III. He makes use of a vast amount of source material, some of it quoted verbatim, but makes no attempt at a division into periods.[49] Baronius was fully aware that he was producing something new; he wrote his *Annales* with an apologetic purpose: "in defence of the antiquity of hallowed traditions and of the authority of the Holy Roman Church, especially against the innovators of our time".[50] His work was continued down to Pius V by the Pole Abraham Bzovius († 1637), further and better continued by the Oratorians Odoricus Raynaldus († 1671) and Jacob Laderchi († 1738), and remained till the nineteenth century the standard text of Catholic ecclesiastical history, which somewhat unjustly overshadowed other not less important achievements in the field of historical research.

A decisive factor in dissociating Church history from profane and from purely religious history was the disruption of Christian unity, which led to a more sharply defined understanding of the idea of the Church. The true Church of Christ, recognizable by certain signs, was opposed by a false church;[51] but she must be historically proved to be the true Church. The apostolicity of her doctrine, the continuity of her teaching office and

---

[47] On C. Braun, *Admonitio Catholica* (Dillingen 1565), see N. Paulus in *HJ* 14 (1893) 544 f. On W. Eisengrein, *Descriptionis rerum in orthodoxa et apostolica Christi ecclesia gestarum* (Ingolstadt 1566), see L. Pfleger, "W. Eisengrein, ein Gegner des Flacius Illyr.", *HJ* 25 (1904), 774–92; the commission of the Jesuit General Borgia to Canisius is in his *Epistolae et Acta*, ed. O. Braunsberger, V (Freiburg i. Br. 1910) 480 f. (31 March 1567).
[48] *Bibliotheca veterum Patrum et antiquorum scriptorum ecclesiasticorum*, 9 vols. (Paris 1575–9).
[49] Vols. I–XII (Rome 1588–1605); Vols. XIII–XXI (Rome 1646–77), by O. Raynaldus, to 1564; Vols. XXII—XXIV (Rome 1728–37), by J. Laderchi, to 1571; for the continuation by A. Theiner (Rome 1856) and other eds., see *LThK* I, 1271 f. An unsatisfactory but still unsuperseded biography is G. Calenzio's *La vita e gli scritti del Card. C. Baronio* (Rome 1907); G. Mercati, "Per la storia della Biblioteca Vaticana, bibliotecario C. B.", *Opere minori*, III (Vatican City 1937) 201–74; A. Walz, *Studi historiografici* (Rome 1940), 5–27: the bibliography given there is enlarged in the new imp. by G. De Luca of A. Roncalli's, *Il Card. C. Baronio* (Rome 1961), 47 ff.
[50] In the Preface addressed to Sixtus V: "Praesertim contra novatores nostri temporis, pro sacrarum traditionum antiquitate ac S. Romanae Ecclesiae potestate."
[51] Thus Michael Buchinger's *Historia ecclesiastica nova* (Mainz 1560) was significantly a revised version of the work *De ecclesia* which appeared in 1556. Cf. Paulus, "M. B., ein Colmarer Schriftsteller und Prediger des 16. Jh." in *AElsKG* 5 (1930), 199 ff. For the doctrine of the marks of the true Church, see G. Thils, *Les notes de l'église dans l'apologétique catholique depuis la Réforme* (Gembloux 1937).

the antiquity of her institutions must be demonstrated by reference to genuine sources. Thus, controversial theology had from the beginning an emphasis on tradition and history.[52] Evidence was sought and found in the Fathers and in the ancient liturgies for the sacrifice of the Mass and the Real Presence, for the papal primacy and the authority of councils; original texts were published, sometimes for the first time, with a definitely apologetic purpose.[53] Guglielmo Sirleto († 1584) provided the legates at the Council of Trent, Cervini and Seripando, with patristic material to serve as a basis for the Tridentine definitions,[54] the Augustinian Hermit, Onofrio Panvinio († 1569) collected material for the history of the popes, the college of cardinals and the churches of Rome.[55] After the rediscovery of the catacombs in the pontificate of Gregory XIII, Antonio Bosio († 1629) founded Christian archaeology.[56] The need for information about theological writers of ancient and modern times gave a new impetus to the study of ecclesiastical literary history. The printing of the ancient catalogues of authors by Suffridus Petri (1580) was followed at short intervals by the *Epitome* of Angelo Rocca (1594), the comprehensive *Apparatus sacer* of Antonio Possevino (1606) and Bellarmine's booklet *De scriptoribus ecclesiasticis* (1613), destined to serve practical ends; the Belgian Albert le Mire († 1640) extended the catalogue of Trithemius. At the end of the seventeenth century the Jansenist Louis-Ellies du Pin produced the *Nouvelle bibliothèque des auteurs ecclésiastiques* (1684–91), which with its continuations formed by far the most complete work of reference for the history of ecclesiastical literature; the *Histoire générale des auteurs sacrés et ecclésiastiques* (23 vols., 1729–33) by the Benedictine Remi Ceillier concludes with the thirteenth century.

Although the predominantly apologetic tendency of the period sometimes prevented the acceptance even of results definitely established by

[52] P. Polman, *L'élément historique* 284 ff. Melchior Cano states *(De locis theologicis, XI 2)*: Quod autem in dissertatione adversum fidei Christianae inimicos rerum gestarum monumenta theologo peropportuna sint, clarissimorum virorum usus aperte confirmat. G. Gieraths, "M. Cano und die Geschichtswissenschaft" in *FZThPh* 9 (1962), 3–29.

[53] Thus the controversial theologian J. Cochlaeus prepared eds. of Cyprian, Optatus of Mileve, Gregory Nazianzen and Chrysostom, and in 1525 published the decrees of the ancient councils: cf. bibliography in M. Spahn, *J. Cochlaeus* (Berlin 1898), 341–72. In 1546 Georg Witzel edited the *Liturgia S. Basilii nuper e tenebris eruta;* and Franciscus Torres published the Apostolic Constitutions for the first time in 1563.

[54] Excerpts from the letters to Cervini (1545–7) are in *CT* X, 929–55; cf. S. Merkel, "Ein patristischer Gewährsmann des Tridentinums," in *Festgabe A. Ehrhard* (Bonn 1922), 342–58. The letters to Seripando (1562–43) have not yet been published; cf. Jedin, *G. Seripando*, II (Würzburg 1937) 300 ff.

[55] D. A. Perini, *O. Panvinio e le sue opere* (Rome 1899); there is no adequate modern biography.

[56] *Pastor*, IX, 194 ff., Eng. tr. vol. XIX, 269 ff.

Protestant criticism (as with the proof adduced by Blondel of the forgery of the *Pseudo-Isidore*), the publication of extensive groups of sources led inevitably to the improvement of the historico-critical method, and so to the establishment of Church history as a science. The earlier histories of the councils had already taken their material from sources anterior to the medieval collections of canons, and now the *Editio Romana* (1608–12) for the first time published Greek texts. Subsequently the Jesuit Hardouin († 1729) produced the best, and J. D. Mansi († 1769) the most comprehensive, edition of the general and many provincial councils. These works were paralleled by the collections of national councils made by Sirmond for France, Aguirre for Spain, Hartzheim for Germany, and Wilkins for England.[57]

The collections of saints' Lives, the publication of which was intended to stimulate and defend the worship of saints, followed a comparable line of development from an initially uncritical accumulation of material to a critical outlook. Luigi Lippomani († 1559), supported by G. Hervet and G. Sirleto, wrote a preliminary compilation; and the Carthusian Laurentius Surius († 1578), basing his work on this but far surpassing it, published "authenticated lives of the saints";[58] then the Jesuit Heribert Rosweyde drew up in 1607 a project of publishing the ancient *Vitae Sanctorum* in their authentic texts, not as rewritten by the Humanists, nor based on manuscripts accidentally discovered but on manuscripts systematically sought out. In spite of Bellarmine's warning, Rosweyde's fellow-Jesuits Johannes Bolland († 1665) and Gottfried Henskens († 1681) began to carry out this plan in 1643, arranging the *Acta Sanctorum* according to the calendar.[59] Against literary attacks and the Spanish Inquisition,

---

[57] Details of the great eds. of the councils are in Quentin, *J.-D. Mansi et les grandes collections conciliaires* (Paris 1960); see also S. Kuttner, *L'Édition romaine des conciles généraux et les actes du premier Concile de Lyon* (Rome 1940). The most important national collections are: *Concilia antiqua Galliae*, ed. J. Sermond, 3 vols. (Paris 1629), with supplement by P. Dalande (Paris 1666); *Collectio maxima conciliorum omnium Hispaniae et novi orbis*, ed. J. Sáenz de Aguirre, 4 vols. (Rome 1693): 2nd ed., J. Catalanus, 6 vols. (Rome 1753–5); *Concilia Magnae Britanniae et Hiberniae*, ed. D. Wilkins, 4 vols. (London 1737); *Concilia Germaniae*, ed. J. F. Schannat and J. Hartzheim, 11 vols. (Cologne 1759–90). For the collection of decrees and canons of the general and provincial councils ed. by the Augustinian C. de Wulf, of Louvain (Louvain 1665, Brussels 1673), cf. A. Legrand and L. Ceyssens *Augustiniana* 8 (1958), 200–36 and 328–55.

[58] P. Holt, "Die Sammlung von Heiligenleben des L. Surius" in *NA* 44 (1922), 341–64.

[59] The first two vols. of the *Acta Sanctorum*, covering the month of January, bore the title: "Acta Sanctorum, quotquot toto orbe coluntur vel a catholicis scriptoribus celebrantur, quae ex antiquis monumentis latinis, graecis aliarumque gentium collegit, digessit, notis illustravit Johannes Bollandus; operam et studium contulit Godefridus Henschenius." For the whole work, cf. Peeters, *L'Œuvre des Bollandistes* (Brussels, 2nd ed. 1961).

Daniel Papebroch († 1714), Bolland's outstanding successor, defended the method employed by the Bollandists in his *Responsia* of 1696–7. Fifty-two folio volumes issued from the Museum Bollandianum in Antwerp down to the time of its suppression in 1788.

Working concurrently with the Bollandists as critical investigators of ecclesiastical sources were the Maurists: the Benedictines of the French congregation of St Maur. They also continued what had been begun in the sixteenth century: replacing the editions of the Fathers, which had become largely a Protestant monopoly, with Catholic editions printed at Rome, Louvain, and elsewhere. [60] After the turn of the century there followed at short intervals bilingual editions of the Greek Fathers, mostly printed at Paris. [61] The Jesuit Dionysius Petavius (Denis Petau, † 1652), himself the editor of Epiphanius of Salamis, opened the way to historical proof in systematic theology, and was the founder of scientific chronolgy. [62] These not insignificant achievements were however far surpassed by the Maurist editions, the fruit of exemplary co-operation: especially the edition of Augustine by Thomas Blampin († 1710) and Pierre Coustant (1721), which appeared in the years 1679–1700; and that of Chrysostom by Bernard Montfaucon († 1741), which had been preceded in 1667 by an edition of the works of Bernard of Clairvaux by the greatest of the Maurist scholars and the founder of palaeography, Jean Mabillon († 1707). Mabillon and his pupil Edmond Martène († 1739) became the initiators of the scientific study of the liturgy with their *De antiquis ecclesiae ritibus* (1700–2). The extensive journeys undertaken by the Maurists to visit libraries in France, Belgium, Germany, and Italy led to the discovery of numerous hitherto unpublished sources. [63]

To the Bollandists and Maurists Church history owes the principle that every historical statement must be based upon authentic sources, edited according to the strict rules of philological criticism. All historical research stands upon their shoulders, and the texts which they produced are to some extent still in use. They share this distinction with the great editions of early texts made by Italian scholars of the eighteenth century, such as L. A. Muratori († 1750), the incomparable editor of medieval Italian sources, and the brothers Pietro and Girolamo Ballerini. Besides these

[60] An ed. of Augustine appeared at Louvain in 1577, of Jerome at Rome in 1565–72, and of Ambrose also at Rome in 1579–87.

[61] Basil the Great, Gregory Nazianzen, Gregory of Nyssa, Epiphanius of Salamis, and Chrysostom; further details will be given later, in Volume IV.

[62] P. di Rosa, *"Denis Petau e la cronologia"* in *AHSI* 29 (1960), 3–54.

[63] The first of these collections of unpublished works, so characteristic of the period, was J.-L. d'Achéry's *Spicilegium* (Paris 1655–77). This was followed by the Martène-Durand *Thesaurus anecdotorum* (Paris 1717) and *Amplissima collectio* (Paris 1724–33). Equally excellent were the accounts of journeys: e.g., Montfaucon's *Diarium Italicum* (Paris 1702; new imp. 1962).

there are the authors of the great statistical works on papal and diocesan history and on that of the religious orders, which appeared in the seventeenth and eighteenth centuries. The Dominican Alphonse Chacon (Giaconius, † 1599) in his posthumously printed *Vitae et res gestae Pontificum Romanorum et S. R. E. Cardinalium* (1601–2) created the first reference work on papal history, subsequently continued by Agostino Oldoini.[64] The *Italia sacra* of the Cistercian Ferdinando Ughelli († 1670), a collection of lists of bishops of the Italian dioceses,[65] admittedly uncritical as regards the earlier period, was the model for the *Gallia Christiana* of the brothers St Marthe, which far surpassed it. Martène and his collaborators were commissioned by the assembly of the French clergy in 1710 to revise this work,[66] which in turn encouraged the Spanish Augustinian Enrico Flórez to compile his *España Sagrada*,[67] the Jesuit Farlati to compile his *Illyricum sacrum*,[68] and abbot Gerbert of St Blasien to resume earlier projects for a *Germania Sacra*.[69] Like the latter, the project of an *Orbis christianus*, embracing the whole ecclesiastical hierarchy, conceived by the prefect of the Vatican Archives, Giuseppe Garampi († 1792), did not get beyond the preliminary stages.[70]

More perhaps was done for the history of the religious orders. The *Annales ordinis Minorum* of the Irish Franciscan Luke Wadding († 1657),[71] and the supplementary catalogue of Franciscan authors prompted other orders to bring out similar comprehensive historical works,[72] foremost among them being Mabillon's *Annales OSB*, which were preceded by the *Acta Sanctorum OSB*. The Dominicans received from the hands of J. Quétif and J. Echard the best catalogue of their authors, and from P. Ripoll and A. Brémond the most comprehensive bullarium. The Franciscan Helyot attempted for the first time a general history of the religious orders.[73] When one further considers that at the same time

---

[64] The 3rd ed., prepared by Oldoini, comprised 4 vols.; the 4th (1751), 6 vols.

[65] Nine vols. (Rome 1643–62); the 2nd ed., by N. Coleti, was in 10 vols. (Venice 1717–22).

[66] *Gallia Christiana (nova)*, 13 vols. (Paris 1715–85); cf. *LThK* IV, 497.

[67] *España Sagrada. Teatro geográfico-histórico de la Iglesia de la España*, 51 vols. (Madrid 1754–1879).

[68] Eight vols.; V–VIII by J. Coleti (Venice 1751–1819).

[69] G. Pfeilschifter, *Die St Blasianische Germania Sacra* (Munich 1921); for the extraordinarily interesting ed. of Gerbert's correspondence by Pfeilschifter and W. Müller, see *LThK* IV, 710 f.

[70] P. Dengel, "Sull' Orbis christianus di G. Garampi", *Atti del II Congresso Nazionale di Studi Romani* (Rome 1931), 497 ff.

[71] *Father Luke Wadding: Commemorative Volume* (Dublin 1957); for the "Wadding Papers 1614–38", ed. B. Jennings (Dublin 1953), cf. *Irish Historical Studies* 10 (1956), 228–36 (F. X. Martin); C. Mooney, "The Letters of L. W." in *IER* 88 (1957), 396–409.

[72] F. Roth, "Augustinian Historians of the XVIIth Century" in *Augustiniana* 6 (1956), 635–58.

[73] For further details see my article: "Ordensgeschichte" in *LThK* VII, 1201–4.

many dioceses and monasteries were producing well-documented histories,[74] and that reference works, excellent in many respects, were being written, especially in Italy,[75] as a contribution to the biography of ecclesiastical personages, one cannot but ask the question: what use did historiography make of all these sources and aids to historical research which were accumulated during the course of two centuries?

Writers of Church history were not in a position to keep pace with this widening horizon and improvement in methods of research. The attitude which regarded Church history as equivalent to the history of man's salvation, which still persisted and found its last classic expression in Bossuet's *Discours*,[76] need not have been an impediment. On the other hand, it is undeniable that on the Protestant side the separation of ecclesiastical from profane history, first made by Melanchthon, unintentionally promoted its secularization while contributing to its independence. The Pietist viewpoint represented in Gottfried Arnold's *Unpar007heyische Kirchen- und Ketzerhistorie* (2 vols., 1699–1700), namely that personal piety, not dogmas and institutions, was the real subject of Church history, seems hardly to have any effect on Catholic writing. Even after the end of the wars of religion, when eirenic tendencies were gaining ground, the dispute with Protestantism went on: the monographs of the Jesuit Louis Maimbourg provide an example of this tradition.[77] The history of the Council of Trent by the Servite Paolo Sarpi attracted far more attention than any controversial work, because under the appearance of a sober, factual account it was a large-scale attack on the post-Tridentine papacy. The reply of the Jesuit Pietro Sforza Pallavicino, based on far better sources and skilfully written, was intended as an historical apologia.[78]

The impulse to comprehend and organize Church history as a whole was lacking in the education of the time. The same Jesuit general Aquaviva, who in 1609 was considering a plan [79] to establish courses for advanced students in ecclesiastical history, especially the history of the

---

[74] E.g., N. Hontheim, *Historia Trevirensis*, 3 vols. (Augsburg 1750); S. H. Würdtwein, *Dioecesis Moguntia*, 5 vols. (Mannheim 1768–90); also the letters published by H. Raab in *AHVNrh* 153–4 (1953), 170–200.

[75] E.g., the index of authors published by G. Fantuzzi for Bologna: by G. Agnostini for Venice; and, surpassing all others, Tiraboschi's classic *Storia della letteratura Italiana*.

[76] In the *Discours sur l'histoire universelle* (1618), as W. Kaegi and others have shown, the old outlook is permeated and transformed by new ideas; cf. O. Brunner in Lammers *op. cit.* 444 f.

[77] *Histoire du Grand Schisme d'Occident* (Paris 1676); *Histoire du Luthéranisme* (Paris 1680); *Histoire du Calvinisme* (Paris 1682); the first two have indexes.

[78] Jedin, *Der Quellenapparat der Konzilsgeschichte Pallavicinos* (Rome 1940); followed by a general survey, 61–118.

[79] P. de Leturia, "L'insegnamento della storia ecclesiastica nella Roma dell'Umanesimo e del Barocco" in *CivCatt* (1945), IV 393–402.

councils, had excluded the subject from the normal curriculum in his *Ratio Studiorum,* which dominated higher education for two hundred years. At Rome, Church history was indeed studied in private circles,[80] but only in 1714 was a chair of ecclesiastical history founded at the Roman College.[81] The works dealing with the subject which had been appearing since the middle of the seventeenth century in France, the dominating country at that time in intellectual matters, were not the product of instruction: They served more or less to justify Gallican ideas of the Church. By far the best achievement were the *Selecta historiae ecclesiasticae capita et ... dissertationes,* by the Dominican Alexander Natalis († 1724): a collection of 230 topics, mainly on points of doctrine and arranged according to centuries.[82] These were placed on the Index on account of their Gallican views, but were nevertheless republished in 1699 without significant corrections, under the title *Historia ecclesiastica veteris novique Testamenti,* and there were eight subsequent editions. The *Mémoires* of L. S. Lenain de Tillemont († 1698), pieced together like a mosaic of selections from early sources, were confined to Church history down to the year 513; Claude Fleury († 1723) brought his twenty-volume *Histoire ecclésiastique* (1691–1720) down to the Council of Constance.[83] Its critical acumen and pleasing style assured the success of the work, but its Gallican tendencies called forth a reply from the Dominican G. A. Orsi, whose *Istoria ecclesiastica* (1747–62) covered only the first six centuries. Nevertheless, it had many continuators and was still being reprinted in the nineteenth century.[84] To these many-volumed works the *Breviarium historiae ecclesiasticae usibus academicis accommodatum* by the Augustinian Gianlorenzo Berti († 1766) formed a modest exception: yet it marks a turning-point because it was intended for instruction.[85]

[80] P. Paschini, "La Conferenza dei Concili a Propaganda Fide" in *RSTI* 14 (1960), 371–82.

[81] P. de Leturia, "El P. Filippo Bebei y la fundación de la cátedra de historia eclesiástica en el Colegio Romano 1741" in *Gr* 30 (1949), 158–92. The chair of ecclesiastical history founded by Alexander VII in 1657 at the Roman Sapienza had no influence on the education of the clergy; those established after 1725 at Madrid, Barcelona, and Calatayud, were in colleges conducted by the Jesuits for the nobility.

[82] Twenty six vols. (Paris 1676–86); there is a list of later eds. in A. Hänggi, *Der Kirchenhistoriker Natalis Alexander* (Fribourg 1955), 189. According to its preface, the work was intended "for the benefit and advantage of those who study sacred antiquity and positive theology".

[83] F. Gaquère, *La vie et les œuvres de C. Fleury* (Paris 1925).

[84] Fifty vols. (Rome 1838).

[85] B. van Luijk, "Gianlorenzo Berti Agostiniano" in *RSTI* 14 (1960), 235–62 and 383–410.

Church History as a Theological Discipline

The introduction of Church history into the curriculum of the universities had begun in Protestant Germany. During the period of reconstruction after the Thirty Years' War, the University of Helmstedt had received its own chair of ecclesiastical history in 1650, and nearly all the other Protestant universities of Germany had followed suit. In the numerous textbooks of Church history written for academic instruction, [86] biblical history, especially that of the Old Testament, was gradually superseded by specifically Church history. Slowly, too, the division into centuries yielded to one based on periods. The pedagogic aim and the polemic attitude remained: the latter found expression mainly in dealing with and passing judgments on the Middle Ages. The *Compendium Gothanum*, designed for instruction at the grammer school (or Gymnasium) in Gotha, was published in 1666 by Veit Ludwig von Seckendorff, who, like his later continuators E. S. Cyprian and C. W. F. Walch, was outstanding as an historian of the Reformation. One-third of this work was still devoted to the Old Testament, and the division by centuries was likewise retained; but the beginnings of a division into periods is also discernible: the Primitive Church is treated as one period, and further divisions are made at the times of Constantine, Charlemagne, and Luther. The *Summarium historiae ecclesiasticae* (1697) of the Leipzig professor Adam Rechenberg distinguished five periods corresponding with phases of the Church: *Ecclesia plantata*, from the first to the third century; *Ecclesia libertate gaudens*, from the fourth to the sixth century; *Ecclesia pressa et obscurata*, from the seventh to the tenth century; *Ecclesia gemens et lamentans*, from the eleventh to the fifteenth century; and *Ecclesia repurgata et liberata*, of the sixteenth and seventeenth centuries.

But it was Johann Lorenz Mosheim († 1755), the "father of Protestant Church history", [87] who paved the way for a scientific view of Church history as a whole. In his *Institutiones historiae ecclesiasticae antiquioris* (1737), he defined it as "the careful and true narration of all external and internal events in the society of men which takes its name from Christ, for the purpose of recognizing the workings of Divine Providence through the connexion of cause and effect in its foundation and preservation, in order that we may learn piety and wisdom". Without excluding God's action in the history of the Church, man is placed at its centre, and the Church is examined in its development as a human community, according to laws valid for history in general. Mosheim's view of history and his

---

[86] The titles of the works mentioned here are in E. C. Scherer, *Geschichte und Kirchengeschichte an den deutschen Universitäten* (Freiburg 1927), 493–9.

[87] K. Heussi, *Johann Lorenz Mosheim* (Tübingen 1906); for more recent discussion, cf. *RGG*, 3rd ed. IV, 1157 f. (M. Schmidt).

marked pragmatism lead on to the Enlightenment, which makes its appearance in the *Historia religionis et ecclesiae Christianae* (1777) by his pupil Johann Schröckh.[88] And in this "enlightened" form Church history was transplanted to the Catholic universities, after the mid-eighteenth century, firstly to those in the Habsburg empire.

The curriculum prescribed by the empress Maria Theresa in 1752, which had been drawn up by the Jesuit Gerhard van Swieten, regarded "spiritual history" as a compulsory subject. In what spirit instruction was to be imparted appears from the directive to teachers inspired by abbot Rautenstrauch (1775): it was to be pragmatical, that is "useful and profitable for practical application"; it was to show "the true limits of the spiritual and temporal powers" (in a sense, of course, that gave supremacy to the State), and to deal mainly with the early centuries and with more recent times (but not with the Middle Ages); the teacher was to "discuss" ecclesiastical matters, in order thus to sharpen his pupils' judgment and to influence them morally.[89]

Other German Catholic universities followed the Austrian example: Ingolstadt, Heidelberg, Mainz, and Bonn. Since Berti's *Breviarium* did not follow the prevailing autocratic tendency, anti-Roman and "enlightened," Joseph II introduced the Protestant textbook by Schröckh. Later, after Archbishop Magazzi of Vienna had protested, this was replaced in 1788 by the *Institutiones historiae ecclesiasticae Novi Testamenti* by the Swabian Matthias Dannenmayr which appeared in a German edition as *Leitfaden in der Kirchengeschichte* (4 vols., 1790). Dannenmayr's book was moderately "enlightened", but decidedly anti-Roman. It divided Church history into five epochs, the divisions being made at the reigns of Constantine, Charlemagne, and Gregory VII, and at the time of Luther, and dealt with each according to a uniform scheme: expansion, organization, authors, doctrine, heresies, liturgy, discipline, and councils. If one ignores the basic attitude due to Schröckh's influence, the author's attempt at an intellectual mastery of the subject and the boldness of his frequently quite acute judgment must be acknowledged. Similar "guides" and "introductions" for students were produced under different titles by Alioz (1791), Aschenbrenner (1789), Batz (1797), Becker (1782), Gmeiner (1787), Gollowitz (1791), Jung (1776), Lumper (1788), Pelka (1793), Pronat (1779), Sappel (1783), Schmalfuß (1792–3), Schneller (1777), Wiesner (1788) and Wolf (1793–1803). The *Christliche Religions- und Kirchengeschichte* (4 vols., 1789–95) by Kaspar Royko and the *Geschichte der Christlichen Religion und Kirche* (2 vols., 1792–3) by Milbiller, the

---

[88] Schröckh's principal work is the intolerably prolix *Christliche Kirchengeschichte*, 45 vols. (Leipzig 1768–1813); see *RGG*, 3rd ed. V. 1545 ff.

[89] E. C. Scherer, *op. cit.* 400 ff.; for Dannenmayr, cf. ibid. 408–15.

latter of which appeared anonymously, were decidedly rationalistic. More moderate successors with an "enlightened" point of view continued to write in the nineteenth century: thus, *Die großen Kirchenversammlungen des 15. und 16. Jahrhunderts* by J. H. von Wessenberg appeared as late as 1840. In England J. Milner and in America the Unitarian J. A. Priestley turned away from the Enlightenment history, the former with his *History of the Church of Christ* (1794–1809), the latter in his *General History of the Christian Church* (1802–3).

However dangerous the intrusion of the Enlightenment was, and even of Rationalism, the introduction of Church History into theological instruction and the consequent need of many new textbooks contributed to the opening up of a new view of Church history, under new auspices indeed and on a different basis. In marked reaction against the Enlightenment with its delight in passing judgments, its Caesaro-papism and its contempt for the Middle Ages, Romantic writers strove to feel their way lovingly and with faith into the Church's great past, especially in the hitherto-despised Middle Ages, and they discovered the greatness of the papacy. Chateaubriand's *Génie du Christianisme* (1802), and Joseph de Maistre's *Du Pape* (1819), however uncritical they were in their reporting of facts,[90] opened the eyes of contemporaries to the great religious tradition and the cultural achievements of the Church, to which Rationalism and the anti-Romanism of the age of Enlightenment had blinded them. In England Sharon Turner in his *History of England from the Norman Conquest to 1509* (1814) could speak of the Middle Ages as that period "in which our religion, literature, language, manners, laws, and constitution have been chiefly formed". Friedrich Leopold, Count Stolberg († 1819), in his *Geschichte der Religion Jesu Christi* (15 vols., 1806–18) revived the opinions of Augustine and Bossuet, to whom the history of the Church meant that of man's salvation. He even returned to pure chronography, renouncing any division into periods: he was writing a history of the religion of Christ, not of the Church. But since he recognized its ultimate significance to be the "firmer grounding of the Faith by the help of history",[91] his book became "an epoch-making work for the reawakening of the serious study of Church history and especially for the revival of Christian feeling" (Janssen). Stolberg's basic religious attitude was shared by Theodor Katerkamp, a member of the Münster circle, in his *Kirchengeschichte* (5 vols., 1823–4); but he had more regard than the former for the natural causes of events. The historical writers

[90] S. Merkle, "Die Anfänge französischer Laientheologie im 19. Jh.", *Festgabe Karl Muth* (Munich 1927), 325–57.
[91] L. Scheffczyk, *F. L. zu Stolbergs Geschichte der Religion Jesu Christi* (Munich 1952), 133.

of the Enlightenment had looked upon the Church as an institution useful to the State in raising the standard of morality and popular education; now her transcendent, supernatural essence, her independence from the State and her universality were being rediscovered.

Church History as an Historical and Theological Science in the Nineteenth and Twentieth Centuries

The re-establishment of Church history as a theological and historical science was the work of Johann Adam Möhler (1796–1838). Under the influence of the "pectoral theologian" Neander in Berlin, and even more under that of Johann Sebastian Drey († 1853), the dogmatician of the Tübingen school, and in opposition to the German idealism of such writers as Hegel and F. C. Baur, Möhler discovered the essential historicity of Christianity as an organic development from supernatural revelation. He forsook the "spiritual" idea of the Church expressed in his early work *Die Einheit der Kirche* (1825); and by his definition of the Church (discussed in Section I, above), he restored to Church history its universality,which it had lost through the Enlightenment and Josephinism. The scientific work of this author, who died so young, was certainly fragmentary; but his successor at Tübingen, Carl Joseph Hefele (1809–93), completed in his *Conciliengeschichte* (7 vols., 1855–74) the most lasting achievement of German historical science in the ecclesiastical field. Though now outdated in many details, Hefele's work has not yet been superseded;[92] and his successor, F. X. Funk († 1907), showed himself by his researches into early Church history to be the keenest critic produced by the Tübingen school.[93]

Whereas Möhler had treated of the general history of the Church only in lectures, published posthumously by P. Grams in 1867–8, Johann Joseph Döllinger (1799–1890) made three attempts to write a general Church history: the first was his version of Hortig's *Handbuch der Christlichen Kirchengeschichte* (1828); the second a *Lehrbuch* (1836) of his own conception; and the third his two large-scale monographs, *Heidentum und Judentum als Vorhalle des Christentums* (1857) and *Christentum und Kirche in den ersten drei Jahrhunderten* (1860): but neither of these were finished. Denominational differences, which had been blurred by the Enlightenment and more sharply emphasized again in Möhler's *Symbolik*, inspired Döllinger's *Reformation* (1846–8). At the height of his activity

---

[92] S. Lösch, *ThQ* 119 (1939), 3–59; A. Hagen, *Gestalten aus dem schwäbischen Katholizismus* II, 7–58.

[93] *Kirchengeschichtliche Abhandlungen und Untersuchungen*, 3 vols. (Paderborn 1897 to 1907).

he was indisputably the most learned ecclesiastical historian of his time, surpassed in depth of thought only by John Henry Newman. The influence of his school at Munich reached beyond Germany to France and England (to such as Lord Acton); but he came into conflict both with neo-Scholasticism and with the Roman Curia: first on the question of the Temporal Power, and then on the doctrine of Infallibility. Failing to submit on this issue to the Vatican Council, he was excommunicated.

This catastrophe resulted in a severe setback for historical studies in Germany, but it could not in the long run prevent their further progress. The theological foundations were laid, and constructive work continued with the opening up of new sources and with specialized research, both closely connected with the mighty flowering of historical science in the nineteenth century. The first step was to make the great editorial achievements of the seventeenth and eighteenth centuries more accessible. The enterprising abbé Migne († 1875) reproduced in his two patrological series only the texts already available at the time; A. Tomasetti's new edition of the *Bullarium Romanum* (named *Taurinense* after Turin, its place of publication, 1857–72) was but a re-impression of Cocqueline's work (1739–44). The Viennese Academy of Sciences in the *Corpus scriptorum ecclesiasticorum latinorum* (from 1860) and the Berlin Academy in *Griechische Christliche Schriftsteller der ersten drei Jahrhunderte* (from 1897) produced new texts of the Fathers on improved philological principles. The editing of medieval and more recent historical sources in the best texts attainable, a task recognized and promoted as a national obligation, was to the advantage of Church historians. In the *Monumenta Germaniae Historica* (founded in 1819 and taken over by the Imperial goverment in 1874) there appeared such important documents as the Letters of Gregory the Great and St Boniface, the *Libri Carolini,* the Register of Gregory VII and the Chronicle of Otto of Freising. Textual and literary criticism, initiated by the Bollandists and the Maurists, were vastly improved by the collaborators in the *Monumenta.* In documentary research Theodor Sickel took over and improved the methods of Delisle and his *École des chartes;* M. Tangl, E. von Ottenthal and Paul Kehr, above all the last named, applied them to the study of papal documents.

For more recent times there was an enormous increase of source-material from the great national collections, as a result of the opening of state archives following the July and March revolutions: the *Collection des Documents inédits sur l'histoire de France* (from 1835), the *Colección de documentos inéditos* (from 1842) and the *Calendar of State Papers* (from 1856). At the same time the Vatican archivist Augustin Theiner († 1874) began to edit, in extensive *Monumenta,* sources for the history of the Papal States, Ireland, and the western and southern Slavonic peoples; and the convert Hugo Laemmer († 1918) gave some idea of the riches of the

Roman archives and libraries for the history of the Reformation and the Counter-Reformation.[94] The throwing open of the Vatican archives for research, by Pope Leo XIII (in the *Regolamento* of 1 May 1884), marked a new epoch and led to the foundation of numerous national institutes of history at Rome.[95] It also made possible such large-scale undertakings as the publishing of nuncios' reports from the sixteenth and seventeenth centuries, the *Concilium Tridentinum* of the Görres Society, the pioneering researches of the Dominican H. Denifle († 1905)[96] and the Jesuit Franz Ehrle († 1934),[97] and finally the *Geschichte der Päpste* of Ludwig von Pastor († 1928), the most detailed work of Church history produced in the past century.[98] Like the *Geschichte des Deutschen Volkes* by his teacher Johann Janssen († 1891), Pastor's work was the outcome of the defensive attitude into which German Catholicism had been driven since the outbreak of the Kulturkampf.

The rapid increase of source material, the constant improvement in methods and aids, and the growing number of scientific monographs and separate investigations did not discourage the work of synthesis in the nineteenth century, as they had in the seventeenth and eighteenth centuries, if only because academic instruction required textbooks and manuals of Church history.

The many-volumed *Histoire universelle de l'Église catholique* by R. F. Rohrbacher (29 vols., 1842–9) was intended for a wider public, but the academic historians were obliged both to keep pace with research and to compete with the numerous and in some respects excellent Protestant works of this kind: the Church histories of J. K. L. Gieseler (5 vols., 1824–57), F. C. Baur (5 vols., 1853–63), K. R. Hagenbach (7 vols., 1869–72), and W. Möller and G. Kawerau (3 vols., 1889–1907). The earlier editions of the *Handbuch* of J. J. Ritter († 1857) were still composed under the influence of G. Hermes (3 vols., 1826–35); the leading work of the middle of the century, Johann Alzog's († 1878) *Universalgeschichte der Christlichen Kirche*, was based on Möhler's lectures. After the first Vatican Council Alzog's study was superseded by the *Handbuch der*

[94] For A. Theiner and the authors Ritter and Alzog of textbooks mentioned below, see Jedin, "Kirchenhistoriker aus Schlesien in der Ferne" in *ArSKG* 11 (1953), 243–59; for Laemmer, see J. Schweter, *H. Laemmer* (Glaz 1926): an inadequate study; for principal works, *LThK* VI, 767 f.

[95] K. A. Fink, *Das Vatikanische Archiv* (Rome, 2nd ed. 1951), 155–67.

[96] A. Walz, *Analecta Denifleana* (Rome 1955); for principal works in *LThK* III, 227.

[97] Obituaries by H. Finke, *HJ* 54 (1934), 289–93; K. Christ, *ZblB* 52 (1935), 1–47; M. Grabmann, *PhJ* 56 (1946), 9–26; bibliography in *Miscellanea F. Ehrle*, I (Rome 1924), 17–28.

[98] Diaries, letters and memoirs, ed. W. Wühr (Heidelberg 1950); also A. Schnütgen, *AHVNrh* 151–2 (1952), 435–45; A. Pelzer in *RHE* 46 (1951), 192–201; obituary by P. Dengel, *HJ* 49 (1929), 1–32.

Allgemeinen Kirchengeschichte by Joseph Hergenröther († 1890), who was raised to the cardinalate in 1879. Passing through several revisions, the last complete edition being published by J. P. Kirsch (4 vols., 1911–17), this work survived into the twentieth century. Specially written for academic use were the textbooks, first published in 1872–5, of F. X. Kraus,[99] who was also important as an art historian and archaeologist, and of Alois Knöpfler (1895), and F. X. Funk (1866). Both these scholars were of the Tübingen school, though the former taught in Munich. Their books went through many editions and were the most useful textbooks of their time; but they were very insistent in a critico-positivist way on the exact reporting of facts. In this respect the instructional works of Heinrich Brück (1874), of the Mainz school, and of Jacob Marx (1903), a professor at Trier, show a marked contrast in their strict ecclesiasticism. At present, the *Kirchengeschichte* (3 vols., 12th ed. 1951, 1948, and 1956) of Karl Bihlmeyer († 1942), based on Funk and revised since his death by H. Tüchle, is the best general account of moderate size, distinguished by its concise formulation and its wealth of bibliographies. There is also an Italian edition by J. Rogger in four volumes. The second volume in English appeared in 1963 translated by V. Mills and F. Muller. Like most of the preceding textbooks, Bihlmeyer's work took over from profane history the customary threefold division into Antiquity, the Middle Ages, and the Modern Age, although this in comparison with many textbooks of the Enlightenment represents a backward step. *Die Katholische Kirche im Wandel der Zeiten und Völker* by A. Ehrhard[100] and W. Neuss (4 vols., 1959) and the *Geschichte der Kirche in ideengeschichtlicher Betrachtung* by J. Lortz (21st ed., 1962–4) are aimed at a wider public. The *Geschichte der Päpste* (6 vols., 2nd ed., by G. Schwaiger since 1954) by F. X. Seppelt spans the whole of Church history, as does the same author's one-volume *Papstgeschichte*.

Only after the turn of the century, when Church history in France had received a new impetus, especially from the fundamental researches and publications of Louis Duchesne († 1922) and Pierre Batiffol († 1929) on Christian antiquity, did there appear in that country also textbooks on the German model, such as those of L. Marion and V. Lacombe (1905) and of C. Poulet (1926), and comprehensive manuals, like F. Mourret's *Histoire générale de l'Église* (9 vols. 1909 21) or the *Histoire de l'Église* under the editorship of A. Fliche and V. Martin, planned in twenty-four volumes but not yet completed (since 1935). An Italian version of this

---

[99] F. X. Kraus, *Tagebücher,* ed. H. Schiel (Cologne 1957); with a remarkably complete bibliography, 765–88.
[100] A. Dempf, *Albert Ehrhard* (Colmar 1944); J. M. Hoeck, "Der Nachlaß Albert Ehrhards und seine Bedeutung für die Byzantinistik" in *ByZ* 21 (1951), 171–8.

project was begun in 1938. The English version is published in four volumes (1942–8). In Italy textbooks have been written by L. Todesco (6 vols., 1922–30), A. Saba (3 vols., 1938–43), and P. Paschini (3 vols., 1931); and in England by Philip Hughes (3 vols., 1934–47).

In the many textbooks and general accounts, which it would be both impossible and unnecessary to enumerate in full, we can see that the idea of the Church's historical character has been generally accepted and that Church history has been recognized as a theological discipline. Having become a science, it is subject to those tendencies which are commonly observable in the science of our time. The pre-eminence of research has led to the founding of numerous periodicals and series of publications dealing with ecclesiastical history, to the collecting of the results of work in institutes and the training in seminars of future researchers. Progressive specialization has resulted in the separation of large fields of study from general Church history and in their becoming independent. As a reaction against specialization and also against the positivism of the nineteenth century, there has been since the second world war a marked tendency towards a theology of history and ecclesiology.

The upsurge of research made the foundation of special periodicals and series of publications necessary.[101] The *Zeitschrift für Kirchengeschichte*, founded by the Protestant theologian T. Brieger in 1876, which at first concerned itself mainly with researches on the Reformation period, was joined in 1887 by the *Römische Quartalschrift für Christliche Archäologie und Kirchengeschichte*, which published work on Roman archaeology and newly-discovered source-material in the Vatican archives, under the direction of Anton de Waal († 1917), H. Finke and S. Ehses. The *Historisches Jahrbuch* of the Görres Society also contained numerous contributions to Church History. The *Revue d'histoire ecclésiastique*, founded at Louvain by Alfred Cauchie in 1900, became an indispensable organ of research, since, besides containing essays and critiques, it also published a complete bibliography of all the works important for the study of Church history. In Italy, in spite of the collaboration of such eminent scholars as G. Mercati and P. Franchi de' Cavalieri, the *Miscellanea di Storia Ecclesiastica* (1902) and the *Rivista storico-critica delle Scienze teologiche* (1904) had to close down as a consequence of the Modernist Dispute. On the other hand, the *Zeitschrift für Schweizerische Kirchengeschichte* (1907) and the *Revue d'histoire de l'Église de France* (1910) continued to appear, playing an influential part in the growth of historical studies of the Church in Switzerland and France. In North America, P. Guilday, who had been trained at Louvain, founded the

---

[101] R. Aubert, "Un demi-siècle de revues d'histoire ecclésiastique" in *RSTI* 14 (1960), 173–202.

Catholic Historical Review (1917); and Holland had possessed the *Nederlands Archief voor Kerkgeschiedenis* since 1900. Periodicals for diocesan history had been established in Germany since the nineteenth century, like the *Annalen des Historischen Vereins für den Niederrhein, bes. das alte Erzbistum Köln* (1855) and the *Freiburger Diözesanarchiv* (1865); and the number of these increased in the twentieth century, as by the *Archiv für Elsässische Kirchengeschichte* (1926), the *Archiv für Schlesische Kirchengeschichte* (1936) and the *Archiv für Mittelrheinische Kirchengeschichte* (1949). Even before the first world war, several of the greatest orders had started periodicals for the study of their own history: Among these were the *Studien und Mitteilungen aus dem Benediktiner- und Zisterzienserorden* (1880), the *Revue Mabillon* and the *Analectes de l'ordre de Prémontré* (both 1905), the *Archivum Franciscanum historicum* (1908), and the *Archivo Ibero-Americano* (1914).

The results of research which were too extensive for the periodicals were published in series: H. Schrörs and M. Sdralek had been editing their *Kirchengeschichtliche Studien* since 1891; and from these Sdralek branched out into his *Kirchengeschichtliche Abhandlungen*. The *Veröffentlichungen des Kirchenhistorischen Seminars München* (1899) and the *Forschungen zur Christlichen Literatur- und Dogmengeschichte* (1900), edited by A. Knöpfler, were of a similar character; the latter included A. Ehrhard as one of its editors. The preponderance of Reformation history at that time found simultaneous expression in the founding of three series of publications: *Erläuterungen und Ergänzungen zu Janssens Geschichte des Deutschen Volkes* (1898) by L. Pastor, *Vorreformationsgeschichtliche Forschungen* (1900) by H. Finke, and *Reformationsgeschichtliche Studien und Texte* (1905) by J. Greving. [102] These had been preceded by Harnack's *Texte und Untersuchungen zur Geschichte der Altchristlichen Literatur* (1882). In addition to the periodicals, numerous series of publications edited by ecclesiastical universities, faculties and religious orders assembled the results of research in the field of Church history.

These developments were made easier by the steady improvement of scientific aids. While the *Series episcoporum* (1873) of the Benedictine B. Gams was based only on printed sources, the *Hierarchia catholica* (from 1898) of the Franciscan Conrad Eubel and his successors drew upon the newly opened Vatican archives for their historical statistics of the episcopate. [103] The *Nomenclator litterarius* of the Jesuit Hugo Hurter (5 vols., 3rd ed., 1903–13) was unable to replace the old lexica of writers of the religious orders, but went beyond du Pin and Ceillier. Works of

---

[102] Jedin, *Joseph Greving* (Münster 1954).
[103] Jedin, "Die Hierarchia Catholica als universalgeschichtliche Aufgabe", in *Saeculum* 12 (1961), 169–80.

such exhaustive learning as U. Chevalier's *Répertoire* (first published 1877–86), his *Topo-Bibliographie* (1894–1903) and P. Jaffe's *Regesta pontificum Romanorum* (1851, 2nd ed. 1885–8) had not been at the disposal of earlier generations of students. Excellent bibliographies, such as Dahlmann-Waitz's *Quellenkunde der Deutschen Geschichte* (9th ed., 1931) for Germany, made information about early works readily available. The historical content of theological encyclopedias was continually being augmented, as can be seen if we compare the second edition of Wetzer and Welte's *Kirchenlexikon* (1822–1901) with M. Buchberger's *Kirchliches Handlexikon* (1904–12) and the *Lexikon für Theologie und Kirche* (1930–8, 2nd ed. from 1957). On the Protestant side, the copiousness and completeness of the *Realencyclopädie für Protestantische Theologie und Kirche* (3rd ed. by A. Hauck, 1896–1913) have not been surpassed, even by the excellent but differently planned *Religion in Geschichte und Gegenwart* (3rd ed. from 1957). The *Dictionnaire de théologie catholique* (1902–50) has been joined by the *Dictionnaire d'archéologie chrétienne et de liturgie* (1924–53) and the *Dictionnaire d'histoire et de géographie ecclésiastique* (begun in 1912 but not yet completed).

The rise of Modernism and the circumstances of the first world war hindered but did not interrupt the growth of historical enquiry. Hitherto, Germany, France, and Belgium had been the foremost countries in promoting its advance; now the reorganization of ecclesiastical studies by Pope Pius XI was of great importance in extending its influence beyond their frontiers. The constitution *Deus Scientiarum Dominus* of 24 May 1931 enjoined theological faculties and ecclesiastical colleges to establish seminars for the provision of methodical training. [104] At the Gregorian University a faculty of Church history was set up in 1934 to train teachers and archivists, especially for Italy, Spain, and Latin America. About the same time the Jesuits, Dominicans, Augustinians, and Capuchins established institutes for the study of the history of their orders, to which were entrusted the editing of sources and the publication of periodicals. Several new periodicals have appeared during and since the end of the second world war: *Traditio* (from 1943) in America; the *Rivista di storia della Chiesa in Italia* (from 1947) in Italy; *Hispania Sacra* (from 1948) in Spain; and the interdenominational *Journal of Ecclesiastical History* (from 1950) in England. [105]

The specialization of research has led to the independence of certain disciplines and their separation from general Church history, as is shown

[104] *AAS* 29 (1931), 254.
[105] Jedin, "Drei neue Zeitschriften für Kirschengeschichte in Italien, Spanien, und England" in *ZKG* 63 (1950–1), 201–4. K. Aland, "Der Stand der patristischen Forschung in Deutschland", *Misc. hist. eccl.* (Louvain 1961), 119–36.

by the establishment of special professional chairs and periodicals and the writing of specialized textbooks. History of ecclesiastical literature, which had been incorporated in the theological curriculum along with Church history in the eighteenth century, has been deepened in method and narrowed down in time to patrology, in the study of which the German Protestant school, represented by Adolf von Harnack's *Texte und Untersuchungen zur Geschichte der Altchristlichen Literatur* (from 1882), has distinguished itself, the results of its work being collected in textbooks and manuals. In Germany the lead was taken by Otto Bardenhewer's *Geschichte der Altkirchlichen Literatur* (5 vols., 1913–32) and B. Altaner's *Patrologie* (6th ed. 1960, Eng. tr. *Patrology,* 1960); in France by the *Patrologie* of F. Cayre (3 vols., 3rd ed. 1945–55), to which is attached a history of theology (Eng. tr. *A Manual of Patrology*), and in the English-speaking world by J. Quasten's *Patrology* (3 vols., 1950–60). The *Bulletin d'ancienne littérature* of the *Revue bénédictine* gave information about new publications, as from 1959 onwards did the *Bibliographia patristica,* based on international co-operation; the *Vigiliae Christianae* (from 1947) are devoted mainly to linguistic research. The history of medieval theological literature became partly the province of Middle Latin philology (as in the work of L. Traube, M. Manitius, P. Lehmann, and E. R. Curtius) and partly that of Scholastic research, flourishing since the turn of the century (as exemplified in the work of H. Denifle, F. Ehrle, C. Baeumker, M. Grabmann, B. Geyer, and A. Landgraf). For such extensive fields as that of medieval biblical interpretation and the history of preaching, research is still only at the beginning; and for this aspect the contribution of F. Stegmüller should be noted. A concise but comprehensive *Geschichte der Theologie seit der Väterzeit* (1933) has been written by M. Grabmann.

By a process similar to that which has taken place in the case of history of Christian Literature, Christian archaeology has detached itself from classical archeology. Gianbattista de Rossi († 1894) raised it to the rank of a science and made it his object to render monuments, inscriptions, and patristic texts available to students of early Christian life. At first the area of interest of this kind was exclusively Roman, as in the extensive and important works of Joseph Wilpert († 1940) on the paintings in the Catacombs and on Christian sarcophagi and mosaics. But the situation has now been remedied as a result of excavations in the Christian East by J. Strzygowski, C. M. Kaufmann, and others, and by a detailed study of the relations between Classical antiquitiy and Christianity, in the work of F. J. Dölger († 1940)[106] and T. Klauser's *Reallexikon für Antike und*

---

[106] T. Klauser, *F. J. Dölger, Leben und Werk* (Münster 1956); with bibliography by K. Baus.

Christentum (from 1941). The *Bollettino di archeologia cristiana,* founded by de Rossi in 1863, became in 1924 the *Rivista di archeologia cristiana.* At the same time Pius XI established the Pontifical Institute for Christian Archaeology, of which J. P. Kirsch († 1941) became the first director.

The College of Bollandists, refounded in 1837, flourished again under three outstanding directors: Charles de Smedt († 1911), Hippolyte Delehaye († 1941) and Paul Peeters († 1950). Hagiography acquired its leading periodical in the three "libraries": the *Bibliotheca hagiographica: graeca, latina,* and *orientalis.*[107]

Patrology, Christian archaeology, and hagiography were the offspring of ecclesiastical history. A number of other special disciplines arose through reciprocal action with other sciences, especially when these had an historical orientation and therefore concerned themselves with certain spheres of the Church's activity. On the Catholic side, the history of dogma has been least able to detach itself from dogmatic theology. The incomplete essays of H. Klee, J. Schwane, and J. Bach in the nineteenth century have indeed been followed by many not insignificant individual researches and in 1905–12 by a history of dogma in the ancient Church by L. J. Tixeront; but there has been no general account comparable to the Protestant histories of dogma by A. von Harnack, R. Seeberg, and F. Loofs. The *Handbuch der Dogmengeschichte* of M. Schmaus and A. Grillmeier (from 1951, Eng. tr. *Herder History of Dogma,* from 1964) is concerned with the history of individual dogmas only.

In the study of Greek Orthodox literature and liturgy, Leo Allatius († 1669), Joseph Assemani († 1768) and his nephew of the same name, followed in the nineteenth century by cardinals Angelo Mai († 1854) and J. B. Pitra († 1889), all did meritorious work. But only after Karl Krumbacher († 1909) had established Byzantine studies as an independent discipline did Albert Ehrhard write, at Krumbacher's instigation, the first history of theological literature in the Byzantine Empire (1897); and this was superseded only in 1959 by H. G. Beck's *Kirche und Theologische Literatur im Byzantinischen Reich.* During the pontificate of Leo XIII, who was himself interested in questions concerning the Eastern Church, were founded the first periodicals dealing with the history of other Eastern churches as well as the Byzantine: the *Revue de l'Orient chrétien* (1896), *Echos d'Orient* (1897) and *Oriens Christianus* (1901). The latter was founded by Anton Baumstark († 1948), whose *Geschichte der Syrischen Literatur* (1922) together with the *Geschichte der Christlichen Arabischen Literatur* (5 vols., 1944–53) by Georg Graf became the standard works on Eastern Christian studies. The Pontifical Oriental Institute established

---

[107] Peeters, *L'Œuvre des Bollandistes,* 77–208; R. Aigrain, *L'Hagiographie, ses sources, ses methodes, son histoire* (Paris 1953).

in 1917 has been publishing *Orientalia Christiana periodica* since 1935; and since 1951 the *Ostkirchliche Studien* have been appearing in Würzburg.

In liturgical studies, the publication of sources by E. Martène, Eusebius Renaudot's *Collectio liturgiarum Orientalium* (1716), and L. A. Muratori's *Liturgia Romana vetus* (1748) had paved the way towards overcoming the symbolic explanation of the liturgy. The Enlightenment's desire for liturgical reform was unfavourable to liturgical history; even more so was the nineteenth-century degeneration of liturgical study to that of mere rubrics. Only by the pioneering researches of L. Duchesne, P. Batiffol, S. Baeumer, E. Bishop, A. Franz, J. Braun, C. Mohlberg, and J. Jungmann did the historical view of the liturgy prevail, while at the same time the source-material was extended by the Bradshaw Society (from 1890), the *Analecta hymnica* (from 1886) of M. Dreves and C. Blume, which were later followed by the editions of the *Ordines Romani* and the *Pontificale Romanum* by M. Andrieu († 1956), and the survey of the French liturgical manuscripts by V. M. Leroquais († 1946). The *Jahrbuch für Liturgiewissenschaft* founded in 1291 by Odo Casel, and renamed the *Archiv für Liturgiewissenschaft* since 1950, gave its annual reports an almost complete survey of new works in this field. At the University of Notre Dame a programme of liturgical studies was introduced in 1947 which has produced a series of scholarly volumes entitled *Liturgical Studies* to which L. Bouyer, J. Daniélou, and J. Jungmann have contributed. In other liturgical periodicals, such as *Ephemerides liturgicae* (from 1887), the historical viewpoint now dominates. This has had considerable influence on the development of the liturgical movement, in consequence of which liturgical science has now become an independent theological discipline.

In the study of Canon Law history, development was otherwise. This subject could build on the great achievements by Thomassin and Benedict XIV; in the nineteenth century it was aided by the school of legal history and reached its peak in the Protestant canonist Paul Hinschius († 1889) and his pupil Ulrich Stutz († 1938), who founded in 1908 the leading organ of the history of canon law: the canonistic section of the *Zeitschrift der Savigny-Stiftung für Rechtsgeschichte*. For the history of the sources and literature of canon law Johann Friedrich von Schulte († 1914) wrote what is still in spite of many defects an indispensable work of reference: *Die Geschichte der Quellen und Literatur des canonischen Rechts* (3 vols., 1875–80). This branch of study was promoted at the same time by Friedrich Maassen († 1900), later by Paul Fournier († 1935), and most recently by Stephen Kuttner, who founded an institute for the history of medieval Church law at Washington in 1955. Among systematic studies of canon law, besides the classic *Kirchenrecht* (6 vols., 1869–97; new impression, Graz, 1959) by Hinschius, the textbook by the Tübingen canonist

J. B. Sägmüller († 1942) is noteworthy for its painstaking regard for legal history: the final complete version of this work was the third edition in 1914; the fourth edition remained unfinished after the promulgation of the new *Codex Juris Canonici*. Still unsurpassed is the *Verfassungsgeschichte der Deutschen Kirche im Mittelalter* by Albert Werminghoff (2nd ed., 1913). The outlines by A. M. Königer (1926), I. Zeiger (1940–7), and Bertrand Kurtscheid (1941–3) were intended for academic instruction; the best general accounts in German are by H. E. Feine, a pupil of Stutz, (4th ed., 1964) and W. M. Plöchl (Vienna, I 2nd ed., 1960; II 2nd ed., Vienna 1962; III 1st ed., Vienna 1959).

The history of Missions became an independent study only after missionary science had been born. In Protestant Germany the way was prepared by Gustav Warneck († 1910). The first occupant of a Catholic chair for missionary science (1914) was the Church historian Joseph Schmidlin († 1944), who occupied himself from the beginning with missionary history in the *Zeitschrift für Missionswissenschaft* (1911) and in the series *Missionswissenschaftliche Abhandlungen und Texte*, which he founded. His *Katholische Missionsgeschichte* (1925) was the first convenient textbook on the subject. The establishment of further chairs and of a missiological faculty at the Gregorian University in 1932 by Pius XI was followed by the appearance of other textbooks: by P. Lesourd (1937), F. J. Montalbán (2nd ed. 1952), T. Ohm's *Wichtige Daten der Missionsgeschichte* (2nd ed. 1961), and A. Mulders's *Missionsgeschichte* (1960); and by longer works: the *Histoire universelle des Missions catholiques* (4 vols., *s. d.*), edited by S. Delacroix, and K. S. Latourette's *A History of the Expansion of Christianity* (7 vols., 1937–47). In the *Bibliotheca Missionum* (22 vols. so far since 1916), founded by R. Streit, missionary history received an almost complete bibliography, which has been supplemented since 1935 by the current *Bibliografia missionaria* of J. Rommerskirchen and others. Numerous periodicals, such as the *Revue d'historie des Missions* (1924) and the *Neue Zeitschrift für Missionswissenschaft* (1946), and series of publications like the *Studia missionalia* (1943) of the Gregorian University, all these help research, which is always facing new problems arising from missionary methods: baptismal practice, the question of the vernacular, adaptation to native customs, and a native clergy.

How important the introduction of a new discipline into the theological curriculum can be for the development of a special science related to Church history is demonstrated by the history of asceticism and mysticism which has been built up during recent decades. Ascetic and mystical theology was made a subject on instruction by the constitution *Deus Scientiarum Dominus* (1931); a corresponding chair at the Gregorian University had already been established in 1919. In the meantime there had appeared H. Brémond's *Histoire littéraire du sentiment religieux en France* (12 vols., 1916–38) and P. Pourrat's *La spiritualité chrétienne* (4 vols., 1918–28). Periodicals treating the subject from an historical angle were founded: such as the *Revue d'ascétique et de mystique* (1920) and the *Zeitschrift für Aszese und Mystik* (1926; since 1947 under the title *Geist und Leben);* from their beginnings, such periodicals as these dealt with the subject historically, but other and older publications to an increasing degree treated the subject in a similar way: an example of this kind is the *Etudes carmélitaines* (from 1913). The *Dictionnaire de spiritualité* has been since 1937 an excellent work of reference. The great religious orders are working on their own traditions of asceticism, producing editions of their classics such as the writings of Ignatius or Teresa of Avila, publishing these works both in monographs and in general accounts, as in J. de Guibert's *La spiritualité de la Compagnie de Jésus* (1953). Much preliminary work has to be done towards carrying out the task of writing a general history of Catholic piety; in this connexion may be mentioned the study of religious folklore by L. A. Veit († 1939), G. Schreiber, and others.

Although the specialized sciences mentioned above have become independent and belong at the same time both to neighbouring theological disciplines and to other branches of learning (as do also the history of Christian art and that of Church music, which we have not touched upon), dogma, law, liturgy, and Missions belong particularly to the realm of general Church history. The latter must continue to study and write about these if it is to fulfill its task. It is the mother-science; they the daughters; together they constitute historical theology.

As in all branches of science, the progress of knowledge in Church history is effected by special research, which has become so extensive that no scholar is in a position to survey the whole field. General accounts such as that in the Fliche and Martin series and in the present manual had therefore to be shared out among several authors. If we talk about a "reaction" to this development, we do not mean that special research could or should be abandoned. The "reaction" is not directed against research, but aims beyond it. It seeks to escape from the practical positivism which predominated at the turn of the century, and to offer more than merely an exact exposition and interrelation of facts. It tends towards pragmatism inasmuch as it judges events ecclesiologically, as by Y. Congar, H. Lubac, J. Daniélou, and K. and H. Rahner, or ecumenically as by J. Lortz. It tends towards a theology of history inasmuch as it relates the history of the Church to that of man's salvation, and thus leads back to the attitude which prevailed till the seventeenth century, but has since been pushed into the background by research into sources and narration of the course of history. Finally, it discusses the problems in the writing of history which have been raised by E. Troeltsch and F. Meinecke and the historicity of the Church as such. Only the future will tell if, and how much, these new ways of looking at things broaden and deepen our knowledge of the history of the Church.

Church History in England and America in the Nineteenth and Twentieth Centuries[108]

In England as on the continent the status of ecclesiastical history in the nineteenth century was largely determined by the reactions of the Romantic movement to the rationalism of the Enlightenment. Enlightened historians of the eighteenth century, Hume, Robertson, and Gibbon, studied and wrote history because they found it a useful teacher of private virtue and correct public policy. Hume in *The History of England from the Invasion of Julius Caesar to the Revolution of 1688* (1761) conceived the medieval Church as a corrupt political monolith, and consequently interpreted the dissolution of the Church in the sixteenth century as something politically and economically advantageous to the State. Gibbon regarded his classic *The Decline and Fall of the Roman Empire* (1776–88) as a chronicle of the triumph of superstition and barbarism and described the Church as the great obstacle to progress and the advance of learning during the Middle Ages. Yet in spite of his rationalism he was the first of the English historians to appreciate fully the importance of the element of continuity in history.

The romantic historians, on the other hand, cultivated an appreciation for the Church's past by approaching its history in unprejudiced fashion and attempting to judge it according to its own standards. As a result their work was characterized by an enthusiasm for the past and a concern for historical continuity. By seeking the roots for the social organization of modern England, they succeeded in making the Middle Ages a respectable period of investigation and thus prepared the way for the scientific study of ecclesiastical history. The publication of source material was supported by Parliament. In the late eighteenth century the House of Commons established the Records Commission to calendar, restore, and publish manuscripts. In 1822, under the editorship of Henry Petrie, keeper of the records in the Tower of London, work began on the *Monumenta Britannica Historica* which was to collect the medieval sources of national history but the first volumes did not appear until 1848. Nine years later the Treasury approved the Master of the Roll's proposal to publish critical editions of the rare and valuable sources of British history from the invasion of the Romans to the reign of Henry VIII.

---

[108] Additional part written by the editor of the English edition.

Probably the most widely read ecclesiastical history in the first half of the nineteenth century was Joseph Milner's (1744–97) *History of the Church of Christ* (1794–1809). Newman said in his *Apologia pro vita sua* that reading Milner's Church history awakened his interest in patristic Christianity. Milner's intention was to provide an antidote for histories of the Church like Mosheim's which he thought too much concerned with recording its failures, heresies, and disputes. "The terms 'church' and 'Christian,'" said Milner, "in their natural sense respect only good men. Such a succession of pious men in all ages existed, and it will be no contemptible use of such a history as this if it proves that in every age there have been *real* followers of Christ." The Bible, which gave man a glimpse of himself as he really is—a creature fallen but retaining elements of his original glory—opened the meaning of history for Milner. As an Evangelical vicar he knew through the experience of conversion what the Fall and Redemption meant, and, consequently, he could appreciate the significance of continued failure in the world. If the Fall of man was apparent in secular history, the Redemption of man was equally apparent in Church history: God is operative among His people. The guide-line which enabled Milner to cut neatly through Christian Church history was the fact that he wrote about no special institution, but about the invisible collectivity of believers which Evangelicals recognized as the Church. Milner's principle of including only those believers who accepted the doctrine of justification by faith alone as Evangelicals understood it turned the book into a polemical rewriting of ecclesiastical history. But although the *History of the Church of Christ* was intended to provide an interpretation satisfactory to Evangelicals, Milner was not averse to praising good in the Roman Church when he saw it.

Joseph Strutt (1749–1802) is typical of the growing interest in ecclesiastical history that was fostered by romanticism and nationalism. More interested in social antiquities than political theories, he delved into the Anglo-Saxon medieval past, examining in great detail the religious and cultural aspects of early English ecclesiastical history. His *The Regal and Ecclesiastical Antiquities of England from Edward the Confessor to Henry the Eighth* provided a font of information that was to stimulate a more critical interest among later historians. During the 1830's and 1840's this interest bore fruit in the appearance of the Caxton Society, the English Historical Society, and the Camden Society. At Cambridge the work of the "Ecclesiologists" gave an impetus to the study of church architecture and hymnology and laid the groundwork for the English liturgical revival. The publication of *The Symbolism of Churches and Church Ornaments* by J. Neale and W. Webb in 1843, a translation in part of the *Rationale Divinorum Officiorum* of William Durandus with selections from Hugh of Saint Victor, was a milestone in the increasing interest in the history of the liturgy. Neale was also the first English historian to produce important works on the eastern churches.

August Pugin (1812–52), a convert to Catholicism, was probably the most well known of the gothic revivalists. In 1850 as Professor of Architecture and Ecclesiastical Antiquities at Oscott College, he published *An Earnest Appeal for the Revival of Ancient Plain Song* which voiced an appeal for a return to historical sources similar to the works of Chateaubriand and Görres. He constantly berated his co-religionists for their lack of historical perspective and was appalled by the parodies of the liturgy he witnessed in Rome and Cologne. An interest in the historical origins of the liturgy continued throughout the nineteenth century in the editions of Feltoe, Wilson, and Bradshaw.

Easily the most significant English Church historian in the first half of the nineteenth century was John Lingard (1771–1851). The *Antiquities of the Anglo-Saxon Church* (1806), which Lingard intended to be an apologia for the Roman Catholic Church in England, was a pioneer accomplishment in scientific history. It was the product of extensive research in and careful exegesis of Latin and Anglo-Saxon sources, a remarkable achievement in itself, since neither the Rolls Series nor any other printed collections were then in existence. Lingard recounted the birth of Christianity in Britain, gave a detailed survey of the life and practices of the Anglo-Saxon Church, and concluded with an account of the Danish invasions, the consequent decay and later revival of Church discipline, and a final, somewhat unsatisfactory section of the Anglo-Saxon missions. In order not to offend non-Catholics, Lingard avoided direct reference to the Mass, referred to the Pope as the Bishop of Rome and to priests as presbyters. Throughout he dismissed evidences of the miraculous in the Anglo-Saxon Church as lately-acquired popularizations and he refrained from canonizing anyone.

In 1819, when the first three volumes of Lingard's *History of England* were published, many Protestants were attracted to this Roman Catholic priest who could write history with such candour and truth. Lingard did not share the romantic fervour of his co-religionists for things medieval and was hardly of a "pro-Catholic" predisposition. As could be expected, Catholics rankled when they read about St Joan of Arc's "mental delusion".

His treatment of the Reformation was aimed at dispelling misconceptions and commonly accepted misstatements. He admitted the need for reform in head and members during the fifteenth century and made no apologies for the wordly popes of the Renaissance. He frankly stated in his interpretation of the Reformation, founded on a careful examination of the sources, that it was a revolution based in contemporary political upheaval. The secular power in England triumphed over the spiritual power at the expense of civil liberties. Because Lingard found the roots of the Reformation more directly in Luther and Calvin than in a calm reading of Scripture and Church history, he asserted that it had broken the historical tradition of English institutions.

Although Newman (1801–90) cannot be strictly regarded as an historian, he, nevertheless, as the greatest figure in the Oxford Movement, contributed to the study of ecclesiastical history in England. He found the neglect of ecclesiastical history in England, even among Anglican divines, a sign that Protestants must realize that they were not representative of the Christianity of History. "It is a melancholy to say it", he wrote, "but the chief, perhaps the only English writer who has any claim to be considered an ecclesiastical historian, is the unbeliever Gibbon." [109] He spoke equally well of the Romanticist, Walter Scott, as a writer who "has contributed by his works in prose and verse, to prepare men for some closer and more practical approximation to Catholic truth." The subject of ecclesiastical history was in fact a field that in a certain sense projected him into the public eye in England. Patristical studies, especially the Alexandrians, formed the background of all his theological thinking. His first important work was to have been a history of the councils. But he "lost himself in a task for which a lifetime had been insufficient". The result of this effort was his *Arians of the Fourth Century* (1833) which however gives sparse notice to the councils. Yet the main thesis of the work, that Antioch rather than Alexandria was the source of Arianism and that its underlying philosophy was Aristotelian rather than Platonic, evoked the praise of Döllinger. He reached conclusions through conjecture and without critical apparatus that were later arrived at by continental scholars, notably Neander.

Newman's contribution to the *Library of the Fathers,* a pioneering effort in patristics, was the *Select Treatise of St Athanasius* and has been described as among the richest treatises of English patristic literature. He also published in the *British Magazine* between 1833 and 1836 a series of essays entitled *Church of the Fathers* which appeared in 1840 as a one-volume work. It was a most effective instrument in the propagation of Tractarian opinions. A further historical project that was never completed was a series of essays on the three periods of Christian education, ancient medieval, and modern, represented by the three great founders of religious orders, Benedict, Dominic, and Ignatius, and subtitled the poetic, the scientific, and the practical eras. It was, however, in his famous *Essay on the Development of Christian Doctrine* (1845) that Newman presented his theory of antecedent probability and confirmed his philosophy of history as an attempt to grasp the sacred meaning of

[109] J. Newman, *An Essay on the Development of Christian Doctrine* (London 1846), 5.

the promise of Christ "I am with you all the days even to the consummation of the world."

Henry Hart Milman (1791–1868) gave nineteenth century Englishmen their best look at the medieval history of the Church. *The History of Christianity under the Empire* (1840), which cautious clergymen made it a point to ignore, served as an introduction to Milman's later compact survey of the medieval Church from Theodosius down to the eve of the Reformation. *The History of Latin Christianity down to the death of Pope Nicholas V* (1854–5) is a masterpiece of Victorian literature. The author traces the modifications of Christianity, by which it accommodated itself to the spirit of successive ages and portrays the genius of the Christianity of each successive age, demonstrating the reciprocal influence of civilization. The same attitude through which Milman de-emphasized the miraculous in his *History of the Jews* (1829) led him to focus attention on the secular activity and life of the Church in his later works. He was not interested in theological controversy, and as a consequence he avoided the anti-Catholic polemic so common among Protestant scholars of his time. Froude termed the *History of Latin Christianity* "the finest historical work in the English language" and Gooch praised him as an historian who did not write for the edification of his readers but portrayed the Church as an institution rather than as an influence.[110]

Along with Milman, William Stubbs (1825–1901) is accredited with the introduction of German historical methodology in England. He made his first important contribution to the study of Church history in the *Registrum Sacrum Anglicanum* which traced the succession of bishops through the centuries. In 1863 Stubbs, who had criticized the Records Commission for publishing too many sources of only secondary importance, was commissioned as an editor for the Rolls series. Through the magnificent contributions he made during the next twenty-five years, he inaugurated the critical study of medieval sources in England. His classic, the *Constitutional History of England down to 1485* (1873–8) had a wider range than the title indicated. It was, in effect, a history of England from Julius Caesar down to the accession of the Tudors.

In 1866 Stubbs became professor of Modern History at Oxford. His inaugural lecture indicates his efforts to emanicipate "the history of the Church as a whole" from its theological heritage. By this Stubbs meant that Church history was beginning to be considered as a discipline independent from theology. Ecclesiastical history was broadened to a more universal study, and freed from its former restriction to the first Christian centuries and the general councils. It became 'the study of the Church as a whole ... as the life of the Christian Church itself, the whole history

---

[110] G. P. Gooch, *History and Historians in the Nineteenth Century* (Boston 1962), 499.

of the body of which the modern nations claim in their spiritual character to be members". Stubbs considered this study of universal Church history as one with the study of Modern History:

"The study of Modern History is, next to theology itself ... the most thoroughly religious training the mind can receive. It is no paradox to say that Modern History, including Medieval History in the term, is co-extensive in its field of view, in its habits of criticism, in the persons of its most famous students, with Ecclesiastical History. We may call them sister studies, but if they are not really one and the same, they are twin sisters, so much alike that there is no distinguishing between them."[111]

Lord Acton (1834–1902), the first Catholic to hold the chair of Modern History at Cambridge, with Stubbs would not separate ecclesiastical and profane history, but for different reasons. Acton perceived that the only unifying element in history was the conception of freedom and his fondest plan, which he never realized, was to write a universal history of human liberty. The Church, in Acton's vision of world history, cannot withdraw from the confusion of modern politics with the excuse that its kingdom is not of this world. The Church is incarnate in the temporal, political order, so that its history is a part of this world's experience. "Religion", wrote Acton, "had to transform the public as well as the private life of nations, to effect a system of public right corresponding with private morality and without which it is imperfect and insecure." The Church's role in history binds her to work on and influence temporal order, and as a consequence, her history has universal significance.

In Acton's political theory the Church is a guardian of free conscience and a barrier against political despotism in any shape, whether it be absolute monarchy or rationalist democracy. The Church was the only force powerful enough to ensure human freedom against the rise of omnipotent States. Acton was critical of the Reformation and the establishment of Protestant States because it weakened the institution whose mission included the preservation of human freedom.

The other side of the coin — the tendency of churchmen in authority to curtail freedom of conscience — was impressed upon Acton through bitter personal experience. In 1859 at the age of twenty-five Acton became the editor of the *Rambler,* a liberal Catholic journal which insisted thematically in every issue that scientific truth could not but vindicate the true religion. If unsavoury truths in the history of the Church are covered up, Acton said, the authority of the Church confuses its heavenly goal with a perverse attachment to earthly power and property. When it became apparent thet the *Rambler* was about to be suppressed, in 1862

---

[111] B. W. Stubbs, *Seventeen Lectures on the Study of Medieval and Modern History* (Oxford 1887), 10.

Acton began publishing it under a new name, *The Home and Foreign Review*, but he did not change the editorial policy. The journal collided head on with the hierarchy in 1863 by supporting Döllinger, Acton's mentor, in his plea made at a Munich Catholic Congress for the Church to end its hostility to historical criticism. The Pope's response was a demand for prior censorship of Catholic writing in Germany. With disaster portending for the *Home and Foreign Review*, Acton closed it in April, 1864, rather than provoke a showdown with the hierarchy in which he would either have to suspend his principles or disobey authority.

Acton never wrote his *History of Liberty* or any other complete, systematic work, but his vision of history in general and his appreciation of truth and free conscience in particular commend themselves as standards to the writer of ecclesiastical history. "It is the duty of the historian", wrote Acton in an appendix to a letter to Mandell Creighton, "to extricate himself from the influence of social groups, political parties, Church, and the like, which tend to interfere with conscience." This is an accurate summary of Acton's opinion on his own situation. The condemnation of the final heresy by Pius IX in the *Syllabus of Errors*, reads like a declaration of Acton's principles: "The Roman Pontiff can and ought to reconcile himself to, and agree with, progress, liberalism, and recent civilization."

The attitude towards the historical interpretation of the papacy was the point of difference between Acton and Mandell Creighton (1843–1901). As a curate of Bishop Lightfoot in the Northumberland village of Embleton, he began to write *A History of the Papacy from the Great Schism to the Sack of Rome* (1887–94). "It would fill a void", said Creighton of his book, "between Milman, which becomes very scrappy towards its close, and Ranke's 'Popes', and my object is to combine the picturesqueness of the one with the broad political views of the other." [112] Creighton's interest in political and diplomatic technique gave the *History of the Papacy* a broader scope than the title indicates, for he used the papacy as a focal point to study the changes in European history during the sixteenth century. On Creighton's request Lord Acton reviewed the first two volumes which appeared in 1882 and praised Creighton for his "sovereign impartiality". What Acton found lacking was concern for the force of ideas in history, and what he objected most to was the favourable verdict on conciliarism. Creighton finished the next two volumes in 1887, three years after he was appointed first Dixie Professor of Ecclesiastical History at Cambridge and two years after he became the first editor of the *English Historical Review*. Again he requested Acton's review and when Acton responded with a severe critique, naked of all the usual, softening academic amenities, he found himself in the unenviable position

112 Quoted in Gooch, *op. cit.* pp. 349, 350.

of an editor who requested, received, and was about to publish a condemnation of his own work. Acton's objections were two. In the first place he criticized Creighton's evading moral judgments on the papacy, and secondly, he thought Creighton's attention to life and action was a superficial substitute for thought and law. He was also critical of Creighton's remarks in the preface, indicating his willingness to explain away the questionable activities of the popes. Neither Acton nor Creighton were surprised with evil when they found it in history, but Creighton was more tolerant of weakness and less quick to judge. For example, he did not cover up the vices of Pope Alexander VI, but he salvaged what he could of the Pope's reputation by praising him for not adding hypocrisy to his sins. Acton would not yield his stand that the office could not absolve the man; the exchange of letters between him and Creighton concerning Acton's review occasioned Acton's famous dictum "Power tends to corrupt, and absolute power corrupts absolutely." Acton toned down the language but did not alter the content of his article.

Downside Abbey has given England a number of ecclesiastical historians. William Bernard Ullathorne (1806–89), monk of Downside and Bishop of Birmingham for thirty-eight years, wrote a small octavo *History of the Restoration of the English Hierarchy* which he published in 1871. The first of several abbots of Downside who made significant contributions to the study of Church history was Francis Neil Gasquet (1846–1929). Gasquet was forty years old when he began to research the history of monasticism in England during the Tudor period. He was the first scholar to treat the papers of Cromwell methodically and the first to use the records of the Court of Augmentations and the pension list of Cardinal Pole. Working seven or eight hours daily in the British Museum, the Public Records Office, and with private collections, in three years he produced *Henry VIII and the English Monasteries*. *Edward VI and the Book of Common Prayer* followed in 1890.

In 1900 Gasquet published *The Eve of the Reformation* which grew out of the article he had submitted to Lord Acton for the *Cambridge Modern History*. Acton returned the article because Gasquet's standard of impartiality was somewhat different from his and the difference was never settled. Although he was a gifted antiquary credited with many discoveries and with recognizing the value of wills, library records, inventories, and bishops' registers for historical interpretation, Gasquet was not only a careless scholar, but he also lacked the fidelity demanded of an editor. "Towards the end of his life, indeed," observed David Knowles, "Gasquet's capacity for carelessness amounted almost to genius." "In his transcription of the Acton correspondence . . . Gasquet consistently omitted or even altered without indication passages of phrases which might . . . cause personal offence or exhibit Acton's critical or petulant attitude toward venerable ecclesiastics. Thus he would print 'Newman' where Acton had written 'old Noggs', and the forthright remark 'Pius IV was an ass' appears in the anodyne form 'Pius IV was no good'."[113]

Because of his friendship with Gasquet, Edmund Bishop (1846–1917), although not one of its sons, will always have his name associated with Downside Abbey. Before Bishop became a Catholic in 1867 he had served a year as literary secretary to Thomas Carlyle (1864). He demonstrated his gift for scholarship in his discovery, transcription, and analysis of the *Collectio Britannica* which consisted in some three hundred papal briefs from the fifth to the twelfth centuries previously unknown. Bishop, unable to have them published in England, edited them for the *Monumenta Germanica Historica* and won praise from Mommsen himself. He was a student of early and medieval Church history and his knowledge of the western liturgies far surpassed that of any of his contemporaries. His interest in liturgical studies went beyond the textual and ritual to a much broader dimension. He was, in effect, an historian of Christian social and religious life. His natural equipment for research, especially his vast memory, helped him make his works a treasure-house for other scholars, including his friend Gasquet. Some of these works were collected and published in 1918 under the title *Liturgica Historica*.

In 1919, Dom Cuthbert Butler, another abbot of Downside, published *Benedictine Monachism*, which was not merely a history, but a fully appreciative mystical, ascetical and constitutional study of the Benedictine spirit. In his discussion on Cassian's *Conference on Prayer* and the chapter "Is Benedictine Life Contemplative?", he raised the question which became the topic for his next book, *Western Mysticism* which appeared in 1922. In 1930 Butler published the *History of the Vatican Council* which has not made so favourable an impression. The book's weakness has two sources. On one hand, it grew out of Ullathorne's letters, which are not of first importance because the Bishop, not one for theological or diplomatic warfare, was not attuned to subtle undertones or overtones in the council wrangling. Moreover, he was not by training an historian of political and intellectual life and could not deal adequately with the complex cross-currents of the mid-nineteenth century. It remains, however, the only satisfactory history of the Council in English.

Dom David Knowles, former Professor of Medieval and Modern History at Cambridge is the finest scholar of Downside. *The Monastic Order in England* which he published in 1940 begins amid the tenth century, because it was then that St Dunstan founded anew Anglo-Saxon monasticism which disappeared during the Danish invasions. In the first half of the book Knowles studies the influence of various continental

---

[113] D. Knowles, *The Historian and Character* (Cambridge 1963), 256.

houses on monastic foundations and reforms in England, noting especially the distinctions between Cluniac attitudes of withdrawal from the world and the tendency of Norman monasticism to fit itself into society. The second half studied the internal life and structure of the monasteries. In the first two volumes of the *Religious Orders of England* Knowles continued the history of the Benedictine revival down to the end of the Wars of the Roses. Volume III, *The Tudor Age*, appeared in 1959, thirty years after he began his initial research. It is the history of the decline and deep-rooted decay of monasticism in England before the destruction by Henry VIII. Mention must also be made of two other contemporary English Church historians, H. O. Evenett, whose study on Charles Guise, *The Cardinal of Lorraine and the Council of Trent* is a substantial contribution to the Counter-Reformation period, and Philip Hughes. The latter's *History of the Church*, 3 vols. (1934–47) and his *The Reformation in England*, 3 vols. (1950–4) are standard works in English-speaking lands.

The first history of the Church to be written and published in the United States was the six-volume *A General History of the Christian Church* (1802–3) by the Unitarian J. A. Priestley. The author held high regard for Fleury whom he used extensively and for Mosheim although he criticized the latter for his "artificial and unnatural" division by centuries. He particularly deplored the artful insinuations of Gibbon. Milner and Mosheim continued to be read by American Protestants but were gradually replaced by translations of Gieseler and Neander. P. Schaff's *History of the Christian Church* (1882–1910) is typical of the strong German influence on American Protestant historiography during the later nineteenth century.

The layman, John G. Shea (1824–92), may be regarded as the foremost Catholic Church historian of the nineteenth century in America. Although lacking in formal professional training, he nevertheless produced work of a highly scientific nature. His four-volume *History of the Catholic Church in America* (1886–92) was the first comprehensive work of this kind. Since most of the documentary material relating to the early Church in America, deposited in the archives of the Propaganda de Fide, has not been utilized, there is as yet no adequate "History of the Church in America". Peter Guilday (1884–1947), who studied under A. Cauchie at Louvain, directed most of his research into the colonial period. The *Life and Times of John Carroll Archbishop of Baltimore* (1922) set the pattern for subsequent Catholic historians in America who have concentrated for the most part in writing biographies of the hierarchy. Guilday's *An Introduction to Church History* (1925) and *Church Historians* (1926), the latter a collection of essays on Eusebius, Orosius, Möhler, Lingard, Pastor, and others, were the first attempts to stimulate an interest in the serious study of ecclesiastical history among American Catholics.

PART ONE

The Beginnings

Jewish Christianity

CHAPTER 1

Judaism in the Time of Jesus

THE New Testament account of salvation history tells us that Jesus Christ came into this world "when the fullness of time was come" (Gal 4:4, Mk 1:14). A longing for the promised Messiah was certainly alive in Jewry at that time, but it was more generally rooted in the political distress of the people than in religious motives. For more than half a century the Jewish people had lived under Roman domination, which was all the more hated because it was exercised by a man who had deeply offended their most sacred national and religious feelings. Herod the Great, the son of Caesar's friend Antipater — an Idumaean and therefore a foreigner — had contrived to obtain from the Roman Senate the title of King of the Jews, in return for which he had to pledge himself to protect Roman interests in the politically important Near East, especially against the dangerous Parthians.

He had first to conquer his kingdom by force of arms, and from the moment that he first trod upon Palestinian soil he was met by the hatred of the people, who under the leadership of the Hasmonaean prince Antigonus offered violent resistance to him. Herod overcame this with Roman assistance and took Jerusalem in 37 B.C. He ruthlessly exterminated the Hasmonaean dynasty, which more than a century earlier, under Judas Maccabaeus and his brothers, had defended Jewish religious freedom in an heroic struggle against Syrian overlordship. Herod managed to hold in check the seething fury of the people, but in his efforts to win the hearts of his subjects by rebuilding the Temple, founding new cities, and promoting the economic and cultural life of his kingdom, he failed. In his will he divided the kingdom among his three younger sons: the central part, Judaea, with Samaria and Idumaea, was left to Archelaus, who was also to inherit the royal title. The adjacent territory to the north went to Herod Antipas, the provinces of Batanaea, Trachonitis, and Auranitis in the north-east, to Philip.

However, the change of ruler led in Judaea to serious disturbances, which could be put down only with the help of the Roman army. The Romans, seeing that Archelaus was unable to guarantee peace and security, deposed him in 6 B.C. Augustus gave the country a new administration in the person of a Roman procurator who had Caesarea as his official residence and who was responsible, in association with the Roman governor in Syria, for the military security and economic control of the region, while the Sanhedrin, a purely Jewish body under the presidency of the high priest, was made competent for Jewish internal affairs. But even this arrangement failed to bring the awaited civil peace. For the Jews, it was a grave affront to their national consciousness that a Roman cohort was always stationed in Jerusalem and that their taxes were fixed by Romans. Many a procurator overplayed his role as representative of the Roman master-race with too much emphasis and so fed the flames of hatred against foreign domination. The root cause of the continued strained relations between political overlords and subject people is, however, to be found in the latter's unique intellectual and spiritual character, for which a Roman could hardly have had much understanding.

The Religious Situation among Palestinian Jewry

The Jewish people was, in the eyes of surrounding nations, characterized above all by the peculiarity of its religious convictions, which it sought to defend in the midst of utterly different currents of thought and forms of worship. While not avoiding contact with this surrounding world in every-day life, the Jews had held fast to the essential features of their faith and religious life with remarkable persistence, even when it cost them heavy sacrifices and resulted in isolation from other peoples. The central point of the Jewish religion was its monotheism; the Jews were conscious of being led, throughout all the phases of their history, by the one true God, Jahweh, for he had often revealed himself to them as their only Lord by his immediate intervention or by the word of his prophets. This belief in the guidance of a just and faithful God might, indeed, waver in its degree of intensity and immediacy, and it might in later times be exposed through the speculations of many rabbis to the danger of a certain rigidity, yet the people never lost it. The pious Jew planned his daily life out of his belief in God's faithful and merciful guidance: the people as a whole knew themselves to have been chosen before all the nations of the world by the Covenant which he had made with them, so that one day salvation for all men might go forth from them. This faith was nourished by the hope in a future Saviour and Redeemer, whom the prophets had unwearyingly proclaimed as the Messiah. This hope constantly raised up again both individuals and people. The Messiah was to spring from among them and to establish in Israel the kingdom of God, thus raising Israel above all the kingdoms of the world, and he was to be king over them.

This expectation of the Messiah and of the kingdom of God was, in times of grave peril for the religious and political freedom of the people, their chief source of strength. With merging of religious and political life, the idea of the Messiah easily took on an all too earthly tinge, coloured by the daily distresses of the Jewish people, so that many saw in the Messiah predominantly the saviour from worldly tribulations, or later, quite concretely, the liberator from the hated Roman yoke.

But there were also in contemporary Jewry circles which did not lose sight of the essentially religious mission of the Messiah, as foretold by the prophets, and who awaited in him the king of David's stock who would make Jerusalem all pure and holy, who would tolerate no injustice, no evil, who would reign over a holy people in a holy kingdom (cf. Dan 7:9, 13, 27). Out of such a glowing hope were born those religious canticles which are called the psalms of Solomon,[1] and which, following the pattern of the biblical psalms, express in living and convincing accents the longing for the promised Saviour, as for instance the seventeenth psalm: "Behold, O Lord, and raise up unto them their king, the son of David, at the time in the which Thou seest, O God, that he may reign over Israel Thy servant. Gird him with strength, that he may cast down the lord of wickedness; cleanse Jerusalem from the heathen who so pitifully oppress her ... Then shall he gather together a holy people which he shall rule with justice, and he shall raise up the tribes of the people which the Lord his God hath blessed ... He shall keep the Gentiles under his yoke, that they may serve him; he shall glorify the Lord before all the world. He shall make Jerusalem all holy and all pure, as it was in the beginning ... Injustice shall be done no more among them in his time, for all shall be holy and the Lord's anointed shall now be their king ... Blessed is he who shall live in those days! O God, let his grace soon appear over Israel: let him save us from defilement by unholy enemies. The Lord is Himself our king for ever and ever."

Besides belief in one God and the expectation of the Messiah, the Law was of decisive importance in Judaism at that time. To observe the Law was the daily task of every pious Jew, and its fulfilment was his most serious endeavour; if he transgressed against it, even unwittingly, he must make atonement. His fidelity to the Law had its reward, even in this life, in those blessings of modest well-being which the Lord gives; but its true reward would come when the Last Judgment confirmed that upon earth he had been just and could enter into eternal life. The Law was given to every Jew in the Holy Scriptures, into the spirit of which he was initiated

---

[1] Eighteen of these psalms have been preserved in a Greek translation; text in A. Rahlfs, *Septuaginta*, II, 471–89; English translation in Charles, *The Apocrypha and Pseudepigrapha of the Old Testament* (Oxford 1913), II, 631–52,

in early childhood by his parents and which he was later taught in special schools. Participation in divine worship in the Temple, or in a synagogue such as were to be found in all the principal towns of Palestine, kept alive his knowledge of the Scriptures which were expounded there in sermons. As the Law did not provide ready-made answers that covered every situation in life, its interpretation was entrusted to special scholars (known as Scribes) who became an important institution in the religious life of the Jews.

In their fundamental reverence for the Law all Jews were agreed; yet the Law itself became the occasion of a division of the people into several parties, based upon the differing degrees of importance that they attached to its influence on the whole of life. Even before the beginning of the Maccabaean wars there had arisen the movement of the Hassidim or Hasideans, a community of serious-minded men who, for their religious life, sought the ultimate will of God that lay behind the Law. This will of God seemed to them so sublime that they wanted to build "a fence around the Law", so as to make every transgression, even involuntary, impossible.[2] They wished to serve the Law with an unconditional obedience even unto death, and thus they helped to create that attitude of heroic sacrifice which distinguished the people in the time of the Maccabees. The Hasideans, however, did not gain a universal following; in particular, the noble families and the leading priests held aloof from them. These were the circles which are called Sadducees in the New Testament; they subscribed to a sort of rationalism which rejected belief in angels and spirits and ridiculed the idea of the resurrection of the dead. For them, the five books of Moses, the *Tora* proper, were the principal authority. In political questions they inclined towards an opportunistic attitude in dealing with their overlords. They were a minority, though an influential one.[3]

The most considerable religious party at the beginning of the first Christian century, not in numbers but in the esteem in which it was held by the people, was that of the Pharisees. Although their name signifies "the separated ones", they sought consciously to influence the whole people and to spread their opinions, an attempt in which they largely succeeded. They regarded themselves as the representatives of orthodox Judaism, and their conception of the Law and its observance was at that time the typical expression of Jewish religion. They took over from the Hasideans the basic idea of the overriding importance of the Law in the life of the individual as well as of the people as a whole, and in this respect the Pharisees may be regarded as their successors. But they made the "fence

[2] Cf. W. Foerster, *Neutestamentliche Zeitgeschichte*, I, 2 (Hamburg 1956), 45 ff.
[3] E. M. Smallwood, "High Priests and Politics in Roman Palestine" in *JTS* 13 (1962), 13–34.

around the Law" even more impenetrable in as much as they wished to lay down the line of conduct required by the Law for every situation in life. This detailed interpretation of the Law found expression in the *Mishna* and the *Talmud,* in which great importance was attached to the opinions of earlier teachers, so that, in succeeding times, tradition played a predominant part in the study of the Law. The attempt to apply the Law to every conceivable situation of daily life led to an exegesis in which every particle was of great moment, and which could draw the most abstruse conclusions from incidentals.

More fateful was the consequent casuistic attitude in all moral questions, which either rendered free moral decision on the part of the individual impossible or gave it a spurious basis. At the same time the Pharisaic Scribes were induced in particular cases to make concessions which contradicted their own principles, since they had after all to make decisions which could be followed by the whole people. With such a casuistic attitude, differences of opinion among the Scribes were unavoidable, and schools of interpretation grew up as for example the school of Shammai or the school of Hillel. In public life the Pharisees were at pains to serve as living models for the fulfilment of the Law, and accepted certain honours in return, such as the title Rabbi or the first places in the synagogues. Sometimes there is traceable, even in their personal piety, a vain self-complacency on account of their fidelity to the Law, which looked down with a mixure of pity and contempt on sinners and on "the multitude that knoweth not the Law" (Jn 7:49). In the face of such an attitude, the great fundamental idea of the God of Israel as the Lord of History, to whose will men had to bow down in humility and trust and whose mercy they might implore in hopeful prayers, receded into the background.

The Pharisees did not, however, succeed in permeating the whole of contemporary Judaism with their religious opinions. The group known as the Zealots likewise wished to observe the Law faithfully, but their attitude was markedly warlike, ready for martyrdom. They actively rejected all that was pagan and refused to pay tribute to Caesar; they even called for open resistance to heathen domination, because they considered that obedience to the Law demanded such a holy war.[4]

The Qumran Community

Fidelity to the Law and zeal for its complete and pure fulfilment drove another group of the Jewish people, the Essenes, out of public life into the

---

[4] M. Hengel, *Die Zeloten, Untersuchungen zur jüdischen Freiheitsbewegung in der Zeit von Herodes I bis 70 n. Chr.* (Leiden - Cologne 1961), esp. 235–92; N. Oswald, "Grundgedanken zu einer pharisäischen rabbinischen Theologie" in *Kairos* 5 (1963), 40–59.

wilderness. The numerous literary and archaeological discoveries which have been made since 1947 among the ruins of Hirbet Qumran, west of the Dead Sea (a centre of this sect), have greatly enriched the picture which Pliny[5] and Flavius Josephus drew of them. Their beginnings go back to the time of the Maccabees and they flourished about the year 100 B.C.

The Essenes believed that Belial, as Satan was usually called in Qumran, had spread three nets over Israel: unchastity, ill-gotten riches, and pollution of the Temple.[6] They meant by this the enrichment of the leaders of the people with heathen booty and the very lax way in which some of them interpreted the marriage laws (Lev 18:13). To the Essenes it seemed that the service of the Temple could no longer be carried out without defilement by priests holding such lax views; and, when their representations were not followed by removal of the evil, they ceased to attend the Temple or to take part in its services, renouncing all communion with "the men of corruption". In practice this meant a schism of the Hasideans into the party of the Pharisees and the numerically smaller group of the Essenes, who now felt themselves to be the "holy remnant" of the true Israel. Their leadership was assumed by a person who, in the Qumran texts, is called the "Teacher of Righteousness" and to whom the first organization of their community is attributed. This teacher proclaimed a new interpretation of the Law which consisted in the total fulfilment of the will of God, as expressed in it. Here there were no half-measures: one could only love God entirely or reject him utterly, walk in his ways or consciously persist in the obstinacy of one's own heart. He who did not join the Essenes in their unconditional obedience to the Law as understood by them was of necessity godless. The will to observe the Law completely led to such concrete results as the reform by the Essenes of the Jewish calendar, so that the feasts might be kept annually on the same day of the week.

The Teacher of Righteousness further proclaimed a new interpretation of the Old Testament prophecies. The last age foretold by them had already begun; the final struggle between the sons of light and the children of darkness was at hand, and its outcome would bring, for the sons of light, the Essenes, the commencement of an eternity of peace and salvation. Two Messiahs were to play a part in this final combat, the high priest of the last age, the "*Anointed of Aaron*", and the prince of the last age, the "*Anointed of Israel*". The Essenes' consciousness of being specially chosen went with a reverent recognition of the divine omnipotence, which had sorted men out through a kind of predestination; some were given to the spirit of truth and light, some to the spirit of darkness and wickedness. The salvation of the children of light was an unmerited grace.

[5] J.-P. Audet, "Qumran et la notice de Pline sur les esséniens" in *RB* 68 (1961), 346–87.
[6] W. Foerster, *op. cit.* 58 f.

This radical doctrine and the practice based upon it led to an organized union of the Essenes, which, in the Qumran group, took on the character of a religious order. Here the community of God developed into a quasi-monastic brotherhood into which a man was received as a full member after a period of probation, a novitiate, whereupon he swore an oath to observe the rules of the order. The property of a new member became the property of the brotherhood. Meals and consultations in common brought the members together. On these occasions a rigid order of precedence prevailed, the priests taking a higher position. Special regulations governing ritual cleanliness required numerous and repeated washings; the brotherhood in Qumran was celibate, but in the neighbourhood of the settlement there lived married followers, and there must have been individual Essenes all over Palestine. There was no pity for the godless man; he was regarded with merciless hatred and the wrath of God was called down upon him.

The non-biblical writings which have been found at least in fragmentary form at Hirbet Qumran show the strong interest of the group in the so-called apocalyptic literature, the themes of which are the great events which are to take place at the end of the world: the final victory over evil, the resurrection of the dead, the Last Judgment and the glory of the ever-lasting age of salvation. Fragments of works of this kind already known, such as the Book of Jubilees, the Book of Enoch, and the Jewish prototype of the Testament of the Twelve Patriarchs, suggest with great probability the Essene origin of those writings. Other fragments, such as that of a Book of Noah, a Book of Mysteries, and a manuscript on the New Jerusalem, confirm the supposition that the number of "apocalypses" was much larger than what now survives. Certain features of this apocalyptic literature of the Essenes indicate that a change took place in the community's views during the course of time. A more merciful attitude towards the godless and towards sinners appears; the hate theme recedes into the background and the duty of loving one's neighbour embraces those who do not belong to the community, even the enemy and the sinner. The age of salvation came later to be understood as a kind of return of Paradise on earth; no more than the Qumran texts of the earlier period do the apocalyptic texts point to a clearly defined Messiah-figure.

The literature so far known permits no complete reconstruction of the Essene movement. Only Josephus, writing after the destruction of Jerusalem[7] goes into detail. According to him, there was no far-reaching inner development among them; they maintained unshaken their demand for heroic fidelity to the Law, and Josephus also describes their charitable assistance even to non-members, though the duty of hating the godless remained. Whether the Essenes also took part in the fight against the Romans

---

[7] Josephus, *Antiquitates*, 20, 5, 4, sect. 113–17.

during the rebellion of A.D. 66–70, is not definitely stated, but it appears probable, since that conflict might easily have been interpreted by them as the final battle of the sons of light against those of darkness. Josephus is quite silent about their Messianic ideas at that time; he mentions neither John the Baptist nor Jesus of Nazareth in this connexion, so the most faithful to the Law of all Jewish groups probably knew hardly anything about the latter. Nor can a close relationship with or dependence of Jesus on the Qumran sect be proved.[8]

The monastic centre of Qumran was destroyed by the Romans in A.D. 68; the remnant of the community was probably so decimated in the Bar Cochba rebellion (A.D. 132–5) that reorganization was impossible. The Essene movement has no importance in the subsequent history of the Jewish religion; the leading role passed to their great opponents, the Pharisees.

The Jewish Diaspora

Outside Palestine there dwelt large numbers of Jews who were to have a decisive influence on the expansion of Christianity in the Hellenistic world. Since the eighth century B.C. they had spread in repeated waves, of forced settlement or of voluntary emigration, over the Near East and the whole Mediterranean basin, and at the beginning of the Christian era they considerably outnumbered the inhabitants of Palestine. The great centres of Hellenistic culture had a special attraction for them; thus, for instance there were powerful Jewish colonies at Antioch, Rome, and especially Alexandria, where two of the five districts of the city were allotted to them. Their fellow-citizens saw in their strong community feeling an especially striking characteristic. Wherever their numbers allowed, they organized themselves into congregations, of which about one hundred and fifty are known to have existed in the coastal areas of the Mediterranean when the apostles first began their mission. The centre of each congregation was the synagogue, presided over by an archisynagogus as leader of their prayer-meetings, while a council of elders, with an archon at its head, concerned itself with civil matters.

The bond which held the Diaspora Jews together was their religious faith. It was this principally which prevented them from being contaminated in greater numbers by their pagan surroundings. They had skilfully contrived to win from the city or State authorities a great deal of special consideration, a number of exceptions and privileges which respected their religious opinions and manner of worship. This only emphasized all the more their peculiarity and their unique position in public life. They belonged mostly to the middle class; in Asia Minor and Egypt many of

[8] J. Carmignac, *Le docteur de justice et Jésus-Christ* (Paris 1955).

them were engaged in agriculture as workers on the land or as tenant farmers, but some were independent farmers or estate-owners. One trade had a special attraction for them, that of weaving and clothmaking. Inscriptions also mention the occupations of tax-collector, judge, even officer in the army, although such examples are rare. In the great city of Alexandria they early played a considerable role in banking; but here they did not enjoy the unqualified approval of their pagan neighbours.

Their new milieu had in many respects exercised its influence on the Jews of the Diaspora without leading to actual infringement of the Law. Like all immigrants they gave up their mother-tongue after a while and adopted the international Greek language, the *koinê*, a fact which led to the use of this language in the worship of the synagogue. Here Egyptian Jewry had shown the way when it translated over a long period the individual books of the Old Testament into Greek and thus created the Septuagint, which was used throughout the Diaspora in the first century A.D. as the recognized translation of the Bible. The reading of the Scriptures in Greek was followed by prayers in Greek, of which some have been adopted by the Christian Church. It was even more necessary that the explanatory sermon should be in the new tongue. The use of Greek in the religious sphere inevitably exposed the Jews to the cultural influences of Hellenism in a wider sense, and in a narrower sense to the effect of Hellenistic religious currents.

Such influence was strongest in Alexandria, intellectually the most active centre of the Diaspora. This city was the home of the Jew Philo († *c.* 40 A.D.), whose extensive writings seem like the final echo of those inner conflicts which the intellectual world of Hellenism might have caused in the mind of an educated and intellectually alert Diaspora Jew. In his work, preserved for posterity by Christianity, we feel the effects of the different philosophical tendencies of his time. From the Stoics the Jews took over the allegorical method of scriptural interpretation which apparently was taught at a special school of exegetics for Jews in Alexandria. Without giving up the literal sense of the biblical description of events in the great Jewish past, the new teachers found a deeper secret meaning beneath it, which saw in Adam for instance the symbol of human reason, in Eve that of sensuality, and in the tree of life that of virtue. Paradise itself was an allegory of the wisdom of God, and the four rivers that flowed from it were the cardinal virtues. More even than the Stoics, the "most holy Plato" influenced the intellectual world of Philo, who took from him not only his philosophical terminology but also his high esteem for the intellect and his longing for a spiritualized life, as well as his idea of the imperfection of the material world. Philo's doctrine of creation has also a Platonic colouring, especially his notion of the "middle powers" which exist between a perfect God and the imperfect world; they are called "thoughts of God", and the highest of them is the Logos, Reason itself, which was to play such an important part in the theology of the first Christian centuries. Philo also explained the ritual laws of the Jews in an allegorical sense and developed from them, using the philosophical terminology of Hellenism, ethical principles, culminating in the demand for ascetic control of the life of instinct; only thus could the soul free itself from the prison of the body and become capable of that mystical rapture which unites it with God in "sober intoxication" and loving surrender.

Despite this enthusiasm for the Hellenistic philosophy of his time, Philo remained a convinced Jew by religion. What he took over from Hellenistic philosophy was after all, he believed, only an earlier gift from the Jews to the pagans, whose teacher, unknown to them, had been Moses. His God remains the eternal God of the Old Testament, whose name men cannot utter, to whose mercy and goodness they owe all, and on whose grace they depend. He is to be honoured by observance of the Sabbath and by the other precepts of the Law, upon which Israel's former greatness was based. Philo remained inwardly and outwardly united with the Jewish people; he shared their belief in a Messiah who would bring them victory over all the nations of the earth and give them a new Paradise.

If the faith of a Jew so receptive to Greek ideas as Philo, was not endangered in its innermost citadel, the loyalty of the average Diaspora Jew to the faith of his Fathers was even more secure. An essential part of it was the spiritual and practical attachment to the Palestinian homeland which he unwaveringly maintained. Jerusalem and its Temple were the focus of this attachment. In the consciousness of every adult Diaspora Jew the Temple was the supreme symbol of his religious origin, and with great conscientiousness he made his annual financial sacrifice, the Temple tax; it was his earnest desire to pray there one day with his Palestinian co-religionists at the time of the Pasch. A further support for his faith was the aforementioned close association of all the Diaspora Jews, which led to an exclusiveness often criticized by their pagan neighbours, and which played its part in causing those recurrent waves of anti-Semitism that swept over the Roman Empire.

But all the mockery and scorn, all the slights and persecutions which from time to time were the lot of the Diaspora Jews did not prevent them from carrying out enterprising and methodical propaganda for their convictions and their religion which met with considerable success. This propaganda was served by a not inconsiderable body of writings which, adapting itself to the literary tastes of the Hellenistic reader, sought to inform the latter that the orginal source of all culture, including religious culture, was to be found in Moses and his people. To this literature belonged, for example, the so-called Letter to Aristeas,[9] which by its skilfully told legend of the origin of the Septuagint directed the reader's interest to the sacred scriptures of the Jews and included an attractive description of Jerusalem, its temple and worship, and of the Jewish priesthood. Books Three to Five of the *Oracula Sibyllina* are also an advertisement for the Jewish religion. These praise monotheism and draw from the fulfilment of ancient prophecies in the history of the Jewish people an allegorical interpretation of history as a whole; with the prophecy of an approaching Last Judgment they endeavour to persuade the pagans to embrace the Jewish religion. Josephus's book *Contra Apionem* was openly apologetic in tone, painting an impressive picture of the history of the Jewish people with all its vicissitudes and describing in enthusiastic terms its great leaders, prophets and martyrs, religious laws and customs, with a view to winning converts to the Jewish faith. Its representation of Jewish theocracy, based upon unconditional monotheism, and its references to the undeniable effects of Jewish piety and ethics on the life of the people could not fail to make an impression on many a Hellenistic reader in search of religious truth.

The success of this propaganda, supplemented no doubt by the spoken word, is shown by the great number of pagans who entered into closer relations with the Jewish religion. Those who formally went over to the Jewish faith and by circumcision, ritual bath, and offering of sacrifice, became fully-fledged Jews, were known as proselytes and undertook all the obligations of the Jewish Law. Considerably larger was the number of the "God-fearing", who would not indeed accept circumcision — painful to pagan sensibilities — but could not resist the attraction of monotheistic belief and the services of the synagogue. They joined in the celebration of the Sabbath and many other religious exercises; their children usually took the final step of formal conversion. The sources give no information as to the precise numbers of either group, but they were no doubt represented in most Jewish congregations of the Diaspora.

The Jewish Diaspora has a significance for the early Christian Missions which cannot be overlooked. It performed an important preliminary work in this connexion, firstly by preparing the Septuagint, which at once became the Bible of the early Christians, secondly by preaching monotheism and the Commandments of Moses, which were also the foundation of Christian morality. Since the synagogues were often the starting-place of Christian missionaries, the latter found there, above all among the God-fearing and the proselytes, hearts ready to receive their message. In the conflict which

---

[9] Edition of the Greek text with French translation by A. Pelletier, *Sources chrétiennes* 84 (Paris 1962); English translation in Charles, *op. cit.* II, 83 ff. See also A. Pelletier, *Flavius Josèphe, Adaptateur de la lettre d'Aristée* (1962).

soon ensued between Christian preachers and Diaspora Jews, the struggle to win the souls of these two groups was — along with the doctrinal differences — an essential factor. That the Christian met with greater success is shown not least by the reaction of the born Diaspora Jews, who now gave up the Septuagint and made other translations to replace it, because they saw their former Bible being employed so successfully by the Christians. They rejected too the allegorical method of writers like Philo, as the Christians had taken it over and used it in particular to dispute the claim of the Mosaic Law to continued validity. A rigid emphasis was placed on the *Tora,* the strict rabbinical interpretation of which now prevailed even among the Jews of the Diaspora. On the other hand, many features of the developing Christian liturgy, much in the worship and preaching of the primitive Christians, in early Christian literature, and in the text of prayers, is an inheritance from the world of the Diaspora, an inheritance which was sometimes taken over directly by the Christians to serve the purposes of anti-Jewish propaganda.

CHAPTER 2

Jesus of Nazareth and the Church

THE history of the Church has its roots in Jesus of Nazareth, who was born into the intellectual and religious world of Palestinian Jewry which has just been described. His life and work, by which the Church was founded, are therefore a necessary preliminary to a history of the latter.

The sources which tell us of that life and its significance for the Church are of a quite exceptional nature. Apart from a few references in pagan and Jewish works, which are valuable because they place beyond discussion any attempt to deny the historical existence of Jesus, the main sources are the writings of the New Testament, especially the first three gospels, the Acts of the Apostles and some of the letters of St Paul. None of these was intended to be an historical biography of Jesus of Nazareth, to tell the story of his life from beginning to end with all the details we would like to know. The three synoptic gospels are the outcome of the apostolic preaching about Jesus and accordingly give the image of him which remained vivid in the minds and hearts of his first disciples when they proclaimed him after his ascension as the crucified and risen Messiah. That image is shaped by the requirements of the apostles' preaching and the faith which supported it. We are not on that account forced to adopt an attitude of radical scepticism when faced with the question whether such sources can ever lead us to a true picture of the "historical" Jesus.

True, an actual "Life of Jesus" cannot be obtained from them. But these New Testament writings are always going back to that Life, giving prominence to single facts and events, to actions and words of Jesus in his earthly life which have a special significance for the proclamation of the apostolic message, bearing witness to them at the same time as important historical facts of his life. The preaching of the apostles was expressly intended to prove that the earthly Jesus of Nazareth was the same Christ that they proclaimed, from whom came salvation for all men. Thus a series of individual facts and characteristics can, with all the scrupulous care that historical criticism demands, be built up from these sources and presented as a kind of outline of the life of Jesus.

Four or five years before the beginning of our era, Jesus of Nazareth was born in Bethlehem of the Virgin Mary. Forty days after circumcision the child was presented to the Lord in the Temple as a first-born son, in accordance with Jewish Law, on which occasion two pious Israelites, Simeon and Anna, spoke prophetically of his Messianic mission. Dangers which threatened the infant from King Herod forced his mother and his foster-father Joseph to sojourn for a long period in Egypt, until, after Herod's death, the family was able to settle at Nazareth in Galilee. The boy grew up in this quiet village, perhaps without ever attending a rabbinical school. Only once did something of his future greatness shine forth, when at twelve years of age he spoke with the Scribes in the Temple about religious questions, showing knowledge superior to theirs and excusing himself to his parents with the words: "I must be about my Father's business" (Lk 2:49).

About thirty years after his birth Jesus left his parental home and began his work among the people of his homeland. First he took a remarkable step, seeking out the great preacher of penance, John the Baptist[10] by the Jordan and accepting baptism from him, whereby God "anointed him with the Holy Spirit", who descended upon him in the form of a dove while the voice of the Father bore witness from Heaven that this was his "beloved Son" (Mt 3:13 f.). Conscious of his Messianic mission and his divine sonship, which he was able to confirm by numerous miracles, Jesus now proclaimed in word and deed that the kingdom of God was come, and that all men, not only Israelites, were called to the kingdom, provided they served God with true piety. The supreme law of the religion he preached was the unconditional love of God and a love of one's neighbour that embraced men of all nations. In clearly recognizable opposition to

---

[10] E. Lohmeyer, *Das Urchristentum, I: Johannes der Täufer* (Göttingen 1932); C. H. Kraeling, *John the Baptist* (New York 1951); H. W. Brownlee, "John the Baptist in the New Light of the Ancient Scrolls" in *Interpretation* 9 (1955), 71–90; J. Steinmann, *St John the Baptist and the Desert Tradition* (New York 1963).

pharisaical practice[11] with its outwardly correct observance of the Law, he declared purity of mind and intention to be the basis of moral behaviour, thus giving to the individual conscience the decisive role in the sphere of religion. Jesus furthermore re-established the true priority of obligations, derived from that life of inward union with the Father which he preached as the ideal: more important than scrupulous observance of the Sabbath is a helpful action performed for our neighbour — of more value than the prescribed prayers recited in the Temple is silent converse with the Father in the solitude of one's own room. Shocking for many was his message that publicans and sinners, the poor and infirm, whom God seemed so obviously to have punished, had the first right to expect a welcome in the house of the Father. The self-righteousness of the Pharisees was deeply shaken by the news that there is more joy in Heaven over one sinner who does penance than over ninety-nine just men; they did not understand that in the coming kingdom of God all human actions count for nothing, that only he is just to whom the Father graciously grants it. The poor were called blessed, because they were free from earthly cares about possessions and riches, which all too easily take up in men's hearts the place that belongs to God alone.

But consoling though his message was for those who had hitherto been despised and lowly among the people, great though the effects of his miraculous powers were upon those marked by lameness, blindness, leprosy, and spiritual diseases, no less strict were the conditions which Jesus imposed upon those who would enter the kingdom of God. The whole man was called upon to follow him without regard for previous friendships, family ties, or possessions; he who set his hand to the plough and looked back was unworthy of the kingdom (Lk 9:62). Such demands dispel any idea of a peaceful family idyll; his words cut like a sword through all existing social and familiar bonds. But the new and unique thing in his teaching was this above all: no man could come to the Father except through Jesus. He demanded a discipleship that was quite impossible without painful self-denial; the man who would truly be his disciple must be able to lay aside his own life (Lk 14:26).

All those, however, who made up their minds to follow him and were thus called to the kingdom formed a new community. Jesus' words and deeds tend unmistakably towards the creation and development of such a community. He proclaimed no kind of only individual piety or religion, but a message which binds together those who hear it and are filled by it as brothers in a religious family that prays together to the Father for the forgiveness of its sins. Jesus himself on one occasion called this community his Church, and he claimed that he was establishing it by his

[11] W. Beilner, *Christus und die Pharisäer* (Vienna 1959).

work (Mt 16:18). He carefully prepared the ground for the foundation of this religious society. If, at times, because of his miracles, great multitudes greeted him with loud acclamations, it was but a minority of the people who accepted to become his disciples. From this group he selected twelve men,[12] who occupied a special position among his followers; they were the object of his special attention: with them he discussed the special tasks for which he intended them in the community that was to be. They were to take up and continue the mission which the Father in Heaven had entrusted to him; "As the Father has sent me, even so I send you" (Jn 20:21). The Gospels emphasize again and again with unmistakable clarity the special position of the Twelve, who received the name of apostles, envoys.[13] The content of their mission was the proclamation of the kingdom of God; to fulfill it, the apostles were expressly appointed as teachers, whose word the nations must believe and trust like that of Jesus himself (Lk 10:16; Mt 28:20), to whose judgment they must submit as if it were a verdict of the Lord (Mt 18:18). Finally, to the Twelve, who were to carry out his own office of High Priest in the new community, Jesus gave priestly powers (Jn 17:19; Mt 20:28). They were to nourish and sanctify its members through a mysterious, sacramental life of grace. From the group Jesus chose Peter for a special task: he was appointed to be the rock foundation on which his Church should stand. With a singular form of words he was given the mission to feed the sheep and the lambs and to strengthen his brothers. (Mt 16:18; Jn 21:15).

Thus the foundation prepared by Jesus before his resurrection received an organic framework, perceptible even from without, which would now grow in space and time, according to laws of growth implanted in it by its founder. Its purely supernatural basis lies indeed elsewhere: it is ultimately founded on the death of Jesus, through which alone salvation can be newly given to men, from which alone the new structure of the salvation community of the redeemed receives its mysterious life. With his death, which completed the work of atonement and redemption, and his resurrection, which gloriously confirmed that work, the founding of the

---

[12] B. Rigaux, "Die 'Zwölf' in Geschichte und Kerygma" in H. Ristow and K. Matthiae, *Der historische Jesus und der kerygmatische Christus* (Berlin 1960), 468–86; G. Klein, *Die zwölf Apostel, Ursprung und Gehalt einer Idee* (Göttingen 1961).

[13] K.H. Rengstorf in *ThW* IV, 406–46; Eng. tr.: K.H. Rengstorf, *Apostleship, Bible Key Words* 6 (London 1962); H. v. Campenhausen, "Der urchristliche Apostelbegriff" in *StTh* 1 (1947), 96– 130; E. M. Kredel, "Der Apostelbegriff in der neueren Exegese" in *ZKTh* 78 (1956), 169–93, 257–305; K. H. Schelkle, *Jüngerschaft und Apostelamt* (Freiburg i. Br. 1957); J. Dupont, "Le nom d'apôtre a-t-il été donné aux Douze par Jésus?" in *OrSyr* 1 (1956), 267–90, 466–80; W. Schmithals, *Das kirchliche Apostelamt* (Göttingen 1961); P. Bläser, "Zum Problem des urchristlichen Apostolats: Unio-Christianorum" in *Festschrift L. Jaeger* (Paderborn 1962), 92–107.

Church was complete, and her historical existence began with the descent of the Spirit.

Jesus had to go to his death because the majority of his people closed their ears to his message. The religious leaders of Jewry decisively rejected his Messianic claims and persecuted him as a sedition-monger with ever-increasing hatred, which finally led them to plan his violent death. The Roman procurator allowed himself, albeit unwillingly, to be won over and he delivered Jesus into their hands to be crucified. The crucifixion took place on the fourteenth or fifteenth day of Nisan in a year between 30 and 33 of the Christian era.

So the labours of Jesus among his own people come to a sudden end, which in the eyes of those who did not believe in his mission meant too the end of the kingdom which he announced. But after three days he rose again from the dead as he had foretold, and during a period of forty days appeared to his disciples on many occasions, until he was taken up into heaven. Belief in his second coming, which was promised to the disciples by two angels at the time of his ascension, was one of the main supports of the young Church's now growing structure.

CHAPTER 3

The Primitive Church at Jerusalem

The External Events and Early Environment

THE most important source for the fortunes of the primitive Church immediately after the ascension of our Lord is the account given in the first seven chapters of the Acts of the Apostles. This does not indeed give a complete picture of events, because the author chose for his subject only what served his purpose, which was to show that the tidings of the Kingdom, though first addressed to the Jews, were then, in accordance with God's will, to be delivered to the Gentiles, and that the Jewish Christian Paul, with the approval of the apostles and commissioned by them, had become the legitimate missionary to the Gentiles. Therefore only about the first fifteen years of the origin and growth of the community are described; of its later history mention is made only in occasional references to Jerusalem.

It was the fact, at first hardly comprehensible, of the resurrection of the Crucified One that brought together the scattered disciples and united them in a community sharing the same belief and profession of faith. When the story of the Acts begins, a group of 120 believers has re-assembled. Firm in their belief that their Lord who has ascended into heaven will return, they are determined to carry out the instructions he gave them during the forty days between his resurrection and his ascension. First of all under Peter's leadership they hold an election to complete the apostolic college, the number twelve being considered as sacrosanct; the candidate must, like the others, be a reliable witness to the life and work of the Lord. The result of the election is entrusted in prayer to God, who makes his will known when the lot falls upon Matthias. [14]

The events of the first Pentecost, [15] when the promised Holy Spirit, to the accompaniment of extraordinary phenomena — a mighty wind and tongues of fire — descended upon the assembled believers, gave them a great access of strength and courage to bear witness in public. The enthusiasm of that day caused Peter to preach a sermon before the people in which he proclaimed the crucified and risen Jesus as the true Messiah. The external growth of the community reflected its inward strengthening: as a result of Peter's preaching about three thousand Jews professed their faith in Jesus. The healing of a man born lame by Peter and John, and another sermon by the former, brought further successes. Soon the number of members of the community had risen to five thousand (Acts 3–4:4).

Such success disturbed the Jewish authorities, who sent for the apostles to examine them. Peter was their spokesman, and here too he boldly proclaimed the message of the Crucified. A threatening warning to the apostles to keep silent for the future was rejected in the name of Jesus (Acts 4:5–22). When fresh miracles and repeated preaching further increased the number of the faithful, all the apostles were again arrested, whereupon they dared to say before the Sanhedrin that God must be obeyed rather than men (Acts 5:29). A first scourging with rods, to which the leaders of the Church at Jerusalem were sentenced, and renewed prohibition to speak in the name of Jesus, were preliminaries to the first persecution.

As the tasks to be carried out in the community increased with the number of members, some organization became necessary; the apostles must remain free to preach, and therefore seven men were appointed to serve the tables, to care for the poor and to help the apostles in their pastoral activities (Acts 6: 1–6). These were ordained for their work with prayer and the laying on of hands. The Greek names of these men indicate that the number of Hellenistic Jews from the Diaspora was not inconsiderable in the community. It is clear that tension arose between them and the Palestinian Jewish Christians. Among the Hellenistic Christians Stephen [16]

---

[14] K. H. Rengstorf, "Die Zuwahl des Matthias" in *StTh* 15 (1961), 35–67.

[15] N. Adler, *Das erste christliche Pfingstfest* (Münster 1938); E. Lohse in *ThW* VI, 44–53; G. Kretschmar, "Himmelfahrt und Pfingsten" in *ZKG* 66 (1954), 209–53.

[16] Besides the commentaries on the Acts of the Apostles, cf. F. Büchsel in *ZNW* 30 (1931), 202 f., 33 (1934), 84–87; M. Simon, *St. Stephen and the Hellenists in the Primitive Church* (London 1958); J. Bihler, "Der Stephanusbericht" in *BZ* 3 (1959), 252–70.

was especially distinguished for his courage and skill in debate; but he suffered a martyr's death by stoning when he was bold enough to say to the Jews that through Christ's work the Old Testament had been superseded. The death of Stephen was the signal for a persecution, which fell most heavily upon the Hellenistic members of the Jerusalem community. While the apostles themselves remained in Jerusalem, many Christians evaded persecution by flight. However, they now took to preaching the Gospel in the countryside, especially in Judaea and Samaria.[17] The Samaritan mission of the Hellenist Philip was particularly successful.

This spread of the faith outside the capital was the occasion for a journey of inspection by the apostles Peter and John to the newly won Christians in Samaria, upon whom they laid their hands that they might receive the Holy Spirit. The two apostles were also active as missionaries on this journey and preached in many places in Samaria. Later Peter paid another visit to the brethren outside Jerusalem — "the saints" as the Acts call them — and the presence of Jewish Christians in cities like Joppa and Lydda shows how strong the movement had become in the more remote parts of Palestine.

The peace that had followed the persecution was again threatened by Herod Agrippa, who caused the arrest of the leading apostles, Peter and James the Elder, and the execution of the latter (A.D. 42 or 43), in order to please the Jews of the capital (Acts 12:2).[18] Perhaps Peter would have shared the same fate if he had not then finally left Jerusalem and betaken himself to "another place" (Acts 12:17). The leadership of the congregation then passed to James the Younger.

The sudden death of Herod in 44 again brought more peaceful times for the Church and made possible a more widespread preaching of the Word. For about twenty years James was able to work in Jerusalem, surrounded by his congregation and highly respected by the other apostles — Paul calls him, together with Peter and John one of the "pillars" of the primitive Church (Gal 2:9). His strictly ascetic life and his loyalty to Jewish traditions earned him the name of "the Just". He was, however, also concerned for the Jewish Christian congregations outside the capital, to whom he wrote a letter which has been accepted into the canon of the New Testament.[19] His authority carried great weight at the so-called Council of the Apostles,[20] where he played the part of mediator (Acts

---

[17] O. Cullman, *Samaria and the Origins of the Christian Mission in the Early Church* (London 1956), 185–92.

[18] J. Blinzler, "Rechtsgeschichtliches zur Hinrichtung des Zebedaiden Jakobus" (Acts 12:2) in *NovT* 5 (1962), 191–206.

[19] H. v. Campenhausen, "Die Nachfolge des Jakobus" in *ZKG* 63 (1950), 133–44; P. Gächter, "Jakobus von Jerusalem" in *ZKTh* 76 (1954), 129–69.

[20] A. Lemmonyer, *DBS* II, 113–20; S. Giet in *Mél. Lebreton*, I (Paris 1951), 201–20;

15:13–21). He too met a martyr's death in 62, when the high priest Ananus was able to vent his hatred upon him, the post of Roman procurator being vacant owing to the death of Festus. They cast the old man from the pinnacle of the Temple, and, while he still lived, they stoned him and beat him to death. Following the example of his Lord he prayed for his enemies as he lay dying.

A few years later the independence of the Jerusalem congregation came to an end, when the rebellion against the Romans turned into a catastrophe for the whole nation. The Jewish Christians obviously did not wish to take part in this struggle and emigrated in 66–67 to the land east of the Jordan, where some of them settled in the city of Pella. The fortunes of the young Church took a new turn. Under Peter's leadership in Palestine there had already been individual conversions from paganism. Now Philip received the chamberlain of Queen Candace of Ethiopia into the Church by baptism, and Peter himself, by the reception of the pagan captain Cornelius, made it clear that the message of the Gospel was not for the Jews alone. Even while the original community was still in Jerusalem, a considerable number of former pagans had formed a Christian congregation in the Syrian capital of Antioch,[21] the care of which was entrusted to the Cypriot levite Barnabas. Here the designation Χριστιανοί was first applied to the followers of the new faith, although it is an open question as to whether this term was introduced by the local pagan authorities, was a popular slang word, or, which seems more likely, was an expression used by the Christians to distinguish themselves from official Judaism and from Jewish sects (see Acts 1:6–8 and Peter 4:16).[22]

The future of the young Church after the destruction of Jerusalem lay with the pagan nations of the eastern Mediterranean area, whose evangelization had already been successfully begun by the Jewish Christian Paul.

Organization, Belief, and Piety

"Sect of the Nazarenes", ἡ τῶν Ναζωραίων αἵρεσις, their Jewish opponents called the disciples of Jesus (Acts 24:5), who had formed themselves into a special community; "congregation, assembly", ἐκκλησία, is the name that the Jewish Christians had for this community of theirs

---

P. Gächter in ZKTh 76 (1954), 139–46; V. Kerich: St Vladimir's Quarterly 6 (1962), 108–17; P. Gächter in ZKTh 85 (1963), 339–54; T. Fahy in IThQ 30 (1963), 232–61.

[21] J. Kollwitz in RAC I, 461–9; H. Dieckmann, Antiochien ein Mittelpunkt christlicher Missionstätigkeit (Aachen 1920).

[22] E. Peterson, "Christianus" in MiscMercati, I (Rome 1946), 355–72; H. B. Mattingly "The Origin of the Name Christiani" in JThS NS 9 (1958), 26–37; B. Lifschitz, "L'origine du nom des chrétiens" in VigChr 16 (1962), 65–70.

(Acts 5:11; 8:1 etc.) [23] They were therefore not merely a group of Jews, who shared the conviction that Jesus was the true Messiah, but who otherwise led their own individual religious lives; rather did that conviction bring them together and cause them to organize themselves as a religious community.

This community was, from the beginning (as a glance at the Acts of the Apostles clearly shows), an hierarchically ordered society, in which not all were of equal rank. There were in it persons and groups of persons to whom special tasks and functions in the life of the community were assigned by higher authority. The first of such groups was the college of the apostles, disinguished in a unique way from all other members of the community; by them were carried out the special tasks which Jesus had given to the chosen Twelve before his ascension and for which he had trained them. The community felt the number twelve to be sacred, so that after the departure of Judas the complement had to be made up by an election at which Matthias was chosen. This election had, however, a purely religious character; it was begun with prayer, and God himself made the decision by means of lots, so that it became unequivocally clear that a man could be called to the office of an apostle only by the supreme authority of God. The principal task of an apostle was to bear witness to the life, death, and resurrection of Christ. Linked with this was the duty of leading the community in the solemnities of the cult, when it met together united in faith: to administer the baptism by which a man became a member of the community, to preside at the religious meal which symbolically expressed the sense of belonging together, to undertake the laying on of hands by which members were consecrated for special tasks — in a word, to be mediators between Christ and his Church through the exercise of priestly functions. Christ himself gave the apostles power to work signs and wonders in his name (Acts 2:42; 5:12). Bound up with that power was the right to rule with authority in the community, to ensure discipline and order and to found new congregations of believers (Acts 8:14 f.; 15:2). Nevertheless, the apostle was not so much lord as rather servant and shepherd in the Church, which was firmly based upon the apostolic office (Mt 16:18; 24: 45; Acts 20:28). [24]

Among those holding the office of apostle, Peter displayed an activity which shows that he, in this turn, occupied a leading place among the Twelve, which could have been given him only by a higher authority. The

---

[23] K. L. Schmidt in *ThW* III, 502–39; M. Goguel, *The Primitive Church* (London-New York 1964); J. M. Nielen, "Zur Grundlegung einer neutestamentlichen Ekklesiologie" in *Festschrift F. Tillmann* (Düsseldorf 1950), 370–97; H. Schlier, *Die Zeit der Kirche* (Freiburg i. Br., 3rd ed. 1962).

[24] See above, note 13 and E. M. Farrer, "The Ministry in the New Testament" in K. B. Kirk, *The Apostolic Ministry* (London, 2nd ed. 1957), 119–83.

account of the fortunes of the primitive Church clearly shows this special position: Peter conducts the election to the college of apostles, he composes the prayer recited on that occasion and he is the spokesman of the disciples at the first Pentecost (Acts 2:15 ff.). He preaches after the healing of the man born lame (Acts 3:1). He is again the spokesman of the apostles before the Scribes and Elders (Acts 4:8). as well as before the Sanhedrin (Acts 5:20). He appears with judicial authority in the episodes of Ananias and Sapphira (Acts 5:3) and with Simon Magus (Acts 8:19). His visits to the "saints" outside Jerusalem have the character of a visitation (Acts 9:32). His decision to admit the pagan Cornelius to baptism was of great significance for the future, because it authoritatively proclaimed that the Gospel was not addressed exclusively to "those of the circumcision" but also to the Gentiles and thus had a universal character. This step did indeed lead to a dispute with some of the Jewish Christians, but by that very fact it shows Peter to have been the responsible leader of the primitive Church.

The picture which the author of the Acts draws of Peter's position is significantly confirmed by Paul. The latter, after his flight from Damascus, went to Jerusalem "to visit Cephas" (Gal 1:18); obviously Paul's recognition by the community depended on him. Even though James, as local leader of the Jerusalem congregation, presided at the Council of the Apostles, Paul clearly gives us to understand that Peter's attitude was the deciding factor in the dispute as to whether the Gentile Christians were subject to the Mosaic Law or not. It cannot be objected that Peter on another occasion appears not to act with authority towards James; this was rather due to his hesitant character than to his official position. The whole of his work in the primitive Church up to the time when he finally left Jerusalem to engage actively in the mission to the Gentiles can be rightly understood only if one regards it as the fulfilment of the task given to him by his Master, of which not only Matthew but also Luke and John tell us when they write that Peter was called by the Lord to strengthen the brethren and to feed Christ's flock. [25]

There was another office in the primitive Church of which we learn from Acts 6:1–7. It was that of the above-mentioned seven men who were to assist the apostles in their labours and to take over the service of the tables among the poor of the community. The appointment of these seven did not take the form of an election, but it was done with prayer and laying on of hands by the apostles. In the Acts the work of the seven is repeatedly mentioned, and the accounts make it clear that it went far beyond purely charitable activities. One of them, Stephen, played a leading role in the theological dispute with the Jews about the mission of Christ and the

[25] E. Stauffer, "Petrus und Jakobus in Jerusalem" in Festschrift O. Karrer (Frankfurt a. M., 2nd ed. 1960), 361–72.

validity of the old Law (Acts 6:8 ff.). and Philip was an active missionary; he preached among the Samaritans and in many other places (Acts 21:8). No special name is given to this group in the Acts of the Apostles, but their work is described by the verb "to serve" διακονεῖν (Acts 6:2). Whether they can be regarded as precursors of the deacons in the Pauline congregations is difficult to decide, for the work of the latter is not easily discernible. The duties of the seven were determined by the needs of the Church. [26]

The sphere of activity of a third group, whom the Acts call "Elders", πρεσβύτεροι, is not so clearly defined as that of the seven (Acts 11:30). The name was not newly coined by the Christians, for there had long been Elders, heads of Jewish patrician families, in the Sanhedrin at Jerusalem, and Elders of the synagogues in the Jewish communities of Palestine. In the primitive Church of Jerusalem these "Elders" are always to be found in the company of the apostles or of James as leader of the congregation; they take part in the decisions of the apostolic Council (Acts 15:2 ff.). They were therefore assistants to the apostles or to the pastor of Jerusalem in the administration of the community. [27]

Only once in connexion with the Jerusalem community are "prophets" mentioned (Acts 15:32); these were Judas Barsabas and Silas, who were chosen and sent to Antioch that they might inform the Christians there of the decisions of the Council. Their task was not therefore one that belonged to a permanent office; they were selected because of their special gifts to carry out such a commission and to encourage and strengthen the brethren in Antioch.

The existence of such office-holders, the apostles, the Elders and the seven, shows clearly that there was already in the primitive Church a division among the members into groups, consecrated by a religious ceremony for special tasks, apart from the main body of the faithful. Even at that time, therefore, there existed clergy and laity, the division between whom, however, was not felt to be a separating gulf, because the Jews in the community were already familiar with an official priesthood which was highly respected, especially by the pious Jews who eagerly awaited the Messiah.

The new and revolutionary event that brought about the formation of the followers of Jesus into a community, the resurrection of the Lord, had been experienced as a fact by all those who had witnessed one of the appearances of the risen Christ. But it was also one of the fundamental

[26] T. Klauser in *RAC* III, 888–909; P. Gächter, *Petrus und seine Zeit* (Innsbruck 1958), 105–54; H. Zimmermann, "Die Wahl der Sieben" in *Festschrift für Kard. J. Frings* (Cologne 1960), 364–78.

[27] W. Michaelis, *Das Ältestenamt der christlichen Gemeinde im Lichte der Hl. Schrift* (Berne 1958), and P. Gächter in *ZKTh* 76 (1954), 226–31; H. v. Campenhausen, *Kirchliches Amt und geistliche Vollmacht in den ersten drei Jahrhunderten* (Tübingen 1953).

elements of the religious faith by which the primitive Church lived, and it was the pivot upon which the apostolic message hinged.[28] It had therefore to be accepted by all who wished to follow the Gospel. Both as an historical event and as part of the faith the fact of the resurrection was confirmed by the descent of the Spirit at the first Pentecost (Acts 2:1 ff.), which gave its final clarity and direction to the apostolic message. From then on the apostles, in their preaching, emphasized the new element which separated them in their belief from their Jewish brethren. This was primarily the conviction that the Risen One whom they proclaimed was none other than the earthly Jesus of Nazareth, and from this identification all that Jesus taught by word and deed before his death derived its validity and its claim to be preached by them. Therefore they bore witness that it was Almighty God who had raised Jesus from the dead, as he had wrought miracles through him during his life on earth.

Equally radical and new when compared with the beliefs till then held by the Jews was the conviction of the Christians that Jesus was the true and promised Messiah. That their Master was the Messiah could not be proved more clearly and compellingly to the apostles than by his resurrection. The belief that in Jesus they possessed the Messiah expressed itself in the various titles which the preaching of the apostles and the piety of the faithful bestowed on him. More and more he came to be called "the Christ", a designation that was used as a kind of surname to Jesus. The apostles preached "the Gospel of Jesus Christ" (Acts 5:42); it was "Jesus Christ" who healed through the apostles (Acts 9:34). Because Jesus was the Messiah he was called the *Kyrios*,[29] which he had been called by God himself (Acts 2:36); he belonged therefore at the right hand of God, and the title of *Kyrios* could be given to him as properly as to God (Acts 1:21; 7:59; 9:1, 10ff., 42; 11:17). So the Church addressed the *Kyrios* in prayer with all confidence; from its midst came the cry *"Marana-tha"* Come, O Lord!" (1 Cor 16:22), a prayer preserved for us by Paul. To Stephen it was so natural to pray to "the Lord Jesus" that even in the hour of death the words came spontaneously to his lips (Acts 7:59). Other titles likewise place the risen Jesus close to God; in Acts 10:42 he is the

---

[28] J. Gewiess, *Die urapostolische Heilsverkündung nach der Apostelgeschichte* (Breslau 1939); M. Meinertz, *Theologie des Neuen Testaments* I (Münster 1950), 212–47; J. Schmitt, *Jésus resuscité dans la prédication apostolique* (Paris 1949), 175–248; F. X. Durwell, *La résurrection de Jésus* (Paris 1954); J. Sint, "Die Auferstehung Jesu in der Verkündigung der Urgemeinde" in *ZKTh* 84 (1962), 129–51; H. Grass, *Ostergeschehen und Osterberichte* (Göttingen, 2nd ed. 1962).

[29] W. Foerster, *ThW* III, 1038–98; J. Gewiess, *op. cit.* 57–70; I. Hermann, *Kyrios und Pneuma* (Munich 1960); S. Schulz, Maranatha und Kyrios Jesus" in *ZNW* 53 (1962), 125 to 144; F. Hahn, *Christologische Hoheitstitel im Neuen Testament* (Göttingen 1963); W. Kramer, *Christos, Kyrios, Gottessohn* (Zürich 1963).

judge of the living and the dead who now reigns in heaven but will come again at the end of the world (Acts 1:11; 3:20 ff.). He is furthermore "the Holy and Righteous One" (Acts 3:14), the ἀρχηγός of life, who brings life and is the origin of life. The designation "Servant of God", familiar from its use in the Old Testament, was used by the early Christians in a connexion which suggests an increase and elevation of the dignity of the Messiah, for this Servant was, according to Peter (Acts 3:13), glorified by God and sent by him with the authority of a Messiah in order to bring redemption. He was "thy holy servant Jesus" against whom his enemies had banded together (Acts 4:27); the community hoped that miracles performed "in the name of thy holy Servant" would give, as it were, letters of credence to the ambassadors of the Gospel in their mission (Acts 4:30).

Finally, the risen Jesus was the Saviour, Σωτήρ, called by God to bring salvation to men (Acts 5:31); the Christians believed that without him men could not attain salvation, and so their faith in him included all that had been given to mankind by redemption through Jesus Christ. The tidings of salvation were, following the example set by Jesus, called by the apostles in their preaching *evangelium* ("good news," "Gospel") (Acts 15:7; 20:24); the preaching of salvation is usually referred to with the verb εὐαγγελίζεσθαι. The content of their message is either simply "Jesus Christ" (Acts 5:42; 8:35; 11:20) or "the Word of the Lord" (15:35), "peace by Jesus Christ" (10:36), "the promise" (13:32) or "the Kingdom of God in the name of Jesus Christ" (8:12).

The belief of the first Christians in salvation through Jesus Christ was expressed in the most exclusive terms: "And there is salvation in no one else, for there is no other name under heaven given among men, by which we must be saved" (Acts 4:12). Circumcision could not save, but only the grace of the Lord (15:1 11). The Gospel showed the way to this salvation, but a man could accept it or reject it; therefore Peter adjures his audience: "Save yourselves!" (2:40). The first step to salvation through Jesus was the forgiveness of sins which he had brought (2:38; 5:31; 10:43; 13:38); he was sent to turn men away from sin (3:26). Penance and inner conversion were of course necessary for the removal of sins (3:19).

The reception of the Holy Spirit was for the primitive Church proof and confirmation that salvation had already begun for its members. After the first Pentecost the descent of the Spirit was continually repeated whenever new brethren professed faith in the living Christ, as in Samaria (Acts 8:1 ff.), at the baptism of Cornelius (10:44 ff.), and even when the community gathered together for prayer (4:31). It was the Holy Spirit who according to their conviction gave that inner, supernatural strength which was effective in the individual believer (2:33), and was also the cause of the missionary zeal of the apostles and the other early messengers of the Gospel. They were "filled with the Holy Spirit", therefore they stepped forth boldly (4:8;

4:31). Stephen especially possessed this gift and so did Philip (6:5; 8:29), and it showed itself too in Barnabas and Paul (11:24; 16:6 ff.). A man like Simon Magus misunderstood its essential nature (8:20); unbelief resisted it (7:51).

Other gifts which redemption by Jesus Christ brought to the faithful were (eternal) life and membership of the kingdom of God. The apostles, in their preaching, spoke of this life (Acts 5:20), which would be shared by pagans who professed belief in the risen Christ, whereas the Jews by their rejection of the Messiah rendered themselves unworthy of eternal life (13:46 48). The kingdom of God is a theme which constantly recurs in the preaching of the apostles, just as after the resurrection it was the subject of Jesus' conversation with them. The kingdom of God and eternal life, the community knew, were not yet fully realized; their realization would come only when the Lord came again, and therefore the first Christians were filled with an ardent hope in the approaching *parousia* of their master. This would bring about "the restitution of all things"; only with it would come "the times of refreshment" (3:20 ff.). But they believed that the final age had already begun, they already possessed "peace by Jesus Christ" (10:36), they already partook of grace (4:33; 6:8; 15:11) and therefore lived "rejoicing" (5:41; 8:8; 13:48) in "gladness and simplicity of heart" (2:46).

The religious life of the community was based upon these convictions. Its members indeed lived wholly in the presence of the risen Lord, but they did not therefore feel that they had to give up their inherited forms of piety. So the first Christians, including their leaders Peter and John, continued to attend prayers in the Temple (Acts 2:46; 3:1). The Jewish hours of prayer were retained, as well as the gestures of worship and the customary forms of words, which were used in their common prayer together, especially the Psalms (3:1; 9:10; 9:40). Like James the Younger, the Jewish Christians of Palestine felt themselves bound to follow the religious and liturgical usages of their fathers. To the converts of the Diaspora these things obviously meant less, as Stephen's attitude makes clear. The discussions at the apostolic Council show that a universally held opinion as to the binding character of the Old Law did not exist in the primitive Church. The demands of the group that affirmed its obligatory force upon all believers were rejected; but in the so-called clauses of James a certain consideration was accorded to this group, to facilitate harmony in mixed congregations. It is noteworthy, however, that, in the preaching of the apostles, obedience to the Law as a condition of salvation is not stressed. Nevertheless, there was not in the primitive Church of Jerusalem any complete breaking away from the liturgical practices of Palestinian Jewry as a whole.

We can, however, observe certain tendencies that were later to lead to independent forms of piety and ritual. Such a new liturgical act was baptism itself,[30] which was the basis of membership in the community. It was by no means merely a matter of taking over the baptism of John, for the baptism of the Christians was unequivocally carried out "in the name of Jesus Christ, for the forgiveness of your sins" (Acts 2:38). Jesus as a person was thus the centre of this liturgical act; from him it got its supernatural efficacy, namely the forgiveness of sins and entry into the community of the faithful. The reception of the Holy Spirit was also in some way bound up with baptism, although the connexion of ideas is not quite clear. Baptism was often followed by a laying on of hands, which was the means of imparting the Spirit; this rite could also take place at a later time, but baptism was felt to be a prerequisite for the reception of the Holy Spirit.

The author of the Acts of the Apostles says in his description of the life of the Jerusalem Christians that they were persevering in "the breaking of bread" (Acts 2:42). Although absolute certainty is hardly possible, many commentators[31] think this refers to the liturgical celebration in memory of the Last Supper of the Lord, and they see in the expression "breaking of bread" a designation that had already become a technical term for the eucharistic celebration, which could take place only in the houses of the faithful. This view is supported by a passage from Paul which is certainly impressive. In his description of the Lord's Supper he says that he is drawing on the tradition of the Jerusalem community. His reference to "the bread that we break" (1 Cor 10:16) is in a clearly eucharistic sense. Thus, such a semantic development of the expression "breaking of bread" is at least probable. The Acts later relate (20:7) how the Christians met "on the first day of the week" to break bread. The special mention of the day on which this celebration was held clearly indicates that the Lord's Supper is here referred to; a day was chosen which had no special significance in the worship of the Jews. In this case too, we note a liturgical development among the first Christians which marks a new departure; Sunday was the day on which the young community assembled for its own form of worship. Why Sunday was chosen it is not difficult to see, for it was the day of the Lord's resurrection, and with this fact was linked the expectation that he would come again on the same day of the week. In view of the growing tension between the early Church and the Jews, Sunday, as the special festival of the Christians, continually rose in importance as opposed to the Sabbath.[32]

Some new Christian religious practices are also indicated by the choice

---

[30] G. Schille, "Zur urchristlichen Tauflehre" in *ZNW* 49 (1958), 31–52; G. R. B. Murray, *Baptism in the New Testament* (London 1962).

[31] Cf. e. g. C. Callewaert, "La synaxe eucharistique à Jérusalem" in *EThL* 15 (1938), 34–73; M. Meinertz, *op. cit.* 131 f.

[32] W. Rordorf, *Der Sonntag. Geschichte des Ruhe- und Gottesdiensttages im ältesten Christentum* (Zürich 1962).

of new fast days, different from the Jewish ones held on Monday and Thursday. That the Christians preferred Friday is easily understood; it was the day on which the Lord died. The choice of Wednesday as the second fast day of the week follows the same line of thought; for it was on a Wednesday that he was taken prisoner and his Passion began. Already therefore the development of a liturgical week based upon Christian ways of thinking is apparent, emphasizing the growing contrast with Jewish practice.

The letter of James speaks of another Christian practice, the anointing of the sick, which was entrusted to the elders: "Is any one among you sick? Let him call for the elders (presbyters) of the Church and let them pray over him, anointing him with oil in the name of the Lord; and the prayer of faith will save the sick man, and the Lord will raise him up; and if he has committed sins, he will be forgiven" (James 5:14 ff.). Even if the letter was addressed to the Jewish Christians of the Diaspora, James would hardly have recommended to them a religious custom unknown to his own congregation.

The whole religious attitude of the primitive Church was rooted in a courageous enthusiasm, prepared for sacrifice, which manifested itself above all in works of active charity: "Now the company of those who believed were of one heart and soul, and no one said that any of the things which he possessed was his own, but they had everything in common" (Acts 4:32). The brotherly love engendered by the enthusiasm of the new faith made the individual believer easily and gladly renounce his private property in order to help the poor of the community. The voluntary principle makes it impossible to regard this early Christian community of goods as in any way equivalent to modern Communism. Such enthusiasm was no doubt largely nourished by the expectation among the Christians of the *parousia*[33] to which reference has already been made. The generous indifference to the goods of this world which it brought made them inwardly free, unselfish, and therefore capable of great deeds. This moral and religious strength, born of the faith and the eschatological outlook of the primitive Church, also gave its members the strength not to give up when the *parousia* failed to arrive, but instead, to open the way for Christianity into a greater future.

---

[33] J. Gewiess, *op. cit.* 31–38; O. Cullmann, "Parusie und Urchristentum" in *ThLZ* 83 (1958), 1–12; E. Käsemann, "Zum Thema der urchristlichen Apokalyptik" in *ZThK* 59 (1962), 257–84; R. Schnackenburg, *Eschatologische Heilsgemeinde — Mysterium der Kirche* I (Salzburg 1962), 138–42.

The Way into the Pagan World

CHAPTER 4

The Religious Situation in the Graeco-Roman World at the Time of its Encounter with Christianity

IN contrast with the political and cultural unity which prevailed in the Mediterranean area at the beginning of the Christian era, we are presented in the religious sphere, with a multiplicity of religions. In all her political conquests Rome had never sought to impose on subject peoples a single religious faith and a single form of worship, rather was it a principle of Roman policy to leave undisturbed all the religious convictions and practices of the tribes and nations included in the empire. A brief survey of the manifold religious currents at the end of the pre-Christian period of Hellenism will enable us to see clearly and to estimate the task with which Christianity was faced when it undertook to win the Graeco-Roman world for Christ.

Decline of the Ancient Greek and Roman Religions

The first characteristic of the general religious situation in the Hellenistic world of the first century B.C. is the decline both of the ancient Greek polytheism and of the old Roman religion. The causes for this development are various and differ for each. In Greece itself, rationalistic criticism of the gods, which had prevailed in the philosophical schools, and especially among Stoics and Epicurians, had had an adverse effect on traditional beliefs. In these circles belief in the Homeric gods had long since been given up. The monistic doctrine of the Stoics, which offered the doctrine of a divine providence (πρόνοια) and of the Logos as world-reason pervading and ordering the universe, did not lead to the acceptance of a personal, super-natural God; for even the Stoic world-reason was subject to the iron law of *Heimarmenē*, which watches over the course of earthly events as they revolve in an eternal circle, and thus deprives the Logos of freedom of action. Epicurus, for his part, did indeed reject the existence of such an inalterable fate, but his view of the world, following Democritus' doctrine of atomic laws, led only to a physically determined universe and likewise left no room for the mythical world of the gods or for a personal God directing all things. The attempt of the Greek Euhemeros to explain belief in the gods historically (Euhemerism), by saying that the gods were outstanding personalities of the past to whom, when glorified in the memory of men, divine honours had gradually come to be paid, only contributed further to the decay of the Greek belief in the gods. Those who held such ideas were indeed to be found at first only in "enlightened" upper-class circles, but their subsequent popularization through the writings of the Cynics and Stoics had a destructive effect on the faith of larger sections of the people.

Political developments in the eastern Mediterranean area also played their part in furthering the decline of the classical Greek religion. The period of the rule of the Diadochs involved in Greece itself the final dissolution of the old city-states, and this in turn was a death-blow to the religious cults which had been maintained by them or their associations of noble families. The newly founded Hellenistic cities in the East, with their commercial possibilities, enticed many Greeks to emigrate, so that the homeland grew poorer and many ancient sanctuaries fell into ruin. Of much more far-reaching effect was the exchange of religious ideas and their liturgical forms of expression, which was brought about by the hellenization of the East, an exchange in which the gods of Greece and the Orient were to a great extent assimilated to one another but lost many of their original attributes in the process. After a manner, of course, the religion of ancient Greece extended its influence; together with the externals of the way of life of the Greek *polis*, its forms of worship also reached the colonies of the East, and so there soon arose in them magnificent monuments of religious art in its characteristic Hellenistic form. But the spirit of the old religion was not to be found in them. On the other hand, oriental cults streamed into Greece and beyond to the western parts of the empire, effecting there a decline of old beliefs and, even in spite of new forms, a loss of religious content.

The ancient Roman religion was also subjected to the same process of dissolution. Since the Second Punic War there had been a steadily growing hellenization of Roman religion, which expressed itself in the erection in increasing numbers of temples and statues of Greek gods on Roman territory. While the Hellenistic gods were introduced mainly by way of the Greek cities of southern Italy and Sicily, it was the direct influence of Greek literature on the beginnings of Latin literature which very largely promoted the hellenization of religion. The stage, with its Latin versions of Greek comedies and other poetical works, also made the people familiar with the world of the Greek gods and mythology. In the face of such an invasion, the ancient gods and their festivals receded into the background, and this, in turn, led to a decline in influence of the colleges of priests who maintained the worship of the old Roman gods. When towards the end of the Second Punic War the Sibylline books demanded the introduction of the cult of Cybele from Asia Minor, the gods of the East began their triumphal entry into Rome and contributed to the disintegration of the ancient Roman faith. All attempts to stem the invasion on the part of the Senate and of those circles in Rome which viewed these developments with anxiety were in the long run unsuccessful.

The military conquests of the last century of the Republic made the Roman troops familiar with the cult of Mithras, and increasing contact with oriental civilization at last opened the gates of the capital to the worship of the Cappadocian Bellona and the Egyptian Isis. Even less could the penetration of Hellenistic philosophical ideas be prevented among the Roman upper class, to whom Stoic thought made a strong appeal; but with them came also a critical attitude towards the gods and a deterministic view of the universe. Especially in Rome itself the sceptical attitude of the leaders of society towards belief in the gods and the State religion could not remain concealed, and so the private family religion of the citizens was infected. The Roman populace still took a keen interest in the games, which were of religious origin; but they were a poor substitute, since their connexion with any religious function was no longer consciously felt.

Augustus on attaining the supreme power had attempted to call a halt to the threatened religious and moral breakdown of the people and introduced a comprehensive reconstruction of the State religion and of belief in it. It was this last that he could no longer recreate. The old colleges of priests were indeed reorganized, shrines were restored, forgotten feasts revived, and members of the leading families once more assumed religious offices and functions. But the inner spiritual content was already too little for the renewed cult to be performed with any real participation of the heart. This is especially apparent in Horace, whose *Carmen Saeculare*, written in 17 B.C. to celebrate the dawn of a new epoch in Rome, reflects his own scepticism by its lack of deep religious feeling. Even the fact that in 12 B.C. Augustus himself assumed the title of *pontifex maximus* and linked it for ever with the principate could not change the course of events.

The Emperor Cult

One feature of Augustus's religious policy was to have far-reaching consequences and to be of special significance when it encountered the growing power of Christianity, namely the adoption of the oriental cult of the ruler and the attempt to include it in his reorganization of the State religion under the modified form of the emperor cult. Religious veneration of the ruler had its origin in the East, where royal power was early regarded as having a religious basis. Alexander and his successors were able to build on this foundation when they added to it elements of Greek hero cult and Stoic ideas about the superiority of the wise man, and thus succeeded in introducing the religious cult of Hellenistic kingship. The first to adopt it were the diadochs of the Near East, and after them, without any special difficulty, the Ptolemies of Egypt, for in that country there already existed a willing priesthood. The example of the Ptolemies was soon followed by the Seleucides. The Hellenistic sovereigns received from the Greek cities of Asia Minor in return for favours and benefits, the title *Soter,* to which others of a religious character, such as *Epiphanes* and *Kyrios,* were later added. The idea increasingly prevailed that in the reigning king God visibly manifested himself. When the kingdoms of the diadochs were replaced by the Roman power, it was natural to transfer the cult of the ruler to those who embodied that power and to pay religious honours to them too. As the Roman Republic lacked a monarch, temples and statues were erected to Roma herself as a personification of Roman power. Even individual Roman generals, such as Anthony, permitted themselves without hesitation to be accorded divine honours when in the East.

It was easy for Augustus to take advantage of this veneration of the ruler in the eastern provinces of the empire, by having temples and shrines to himself set up alongside those of the goddess Roma and by not refusing religious honours, the offering of which was the responsibility of the municipal authorities or the provincial governments. To Augustus personally such honours were most willingly granted, because the *pax Augusta* had brought lasting peace to those territories, and he thus enjoyed unparalleled popularity.

In Rome and Italy the cult of the ruler had to be introduced more discreetly. There the Senate decided only after the emperor's death whether *consecratio,* inclusion among the gods, should be accorded to him because of his services to the State. In fact, the Senate had already placed Caesar as *Divus Julius* among the immortals, established a special cult for him with its own priesthood and thus introduced religious veneration of the Julian house. No doubt Eastern influences were at work here too. Octavian was able to assume the title Augustus, which was of a religious nature. Private citizens were to sacrifice to the *genius* of the emperor in their houses, for in him the divine was made manifest; men swore by the *genius* of the emperor, and the breaking of such an oath was regarded as high treason. When Vergil sings in his fourth Eclogue that in Augustus an old Etruscan prophecy has clearly been fulfilled, according to which a saviour should come into the world as a child and inaugurate a new Golden Age, we discern the same idea, namely the ascription of divine origin to the ruler.

In the course of the first century A.D. some of the Roman emperors gave up the prudent restraint of Augustus and demanded divine honours in Rome during their lifetime,[1] although their way of life and their performance as rulers of the empire hardly recommended them for deification; this had the effect of somewhat cheapening the emperor cult in Rome. Nevertheless there were even in the West private organizations which devoted themselves to promoting this cult. Since the cult of the Emperor was intimately linked with the power of the State, special importance was inevitably attached to it when Christianity, which rejected any form of divine honours paid to men, sooner or later came into conflict with that State.

The Eastern Mystery Cults

While the cult of the emperor as part of the State religion was becoming of universal significance both in East and West, though graduated in intensity in different parts of the empire, the oriental mystery-cults always retained their original private character, albeit their influence on all classes was considerable. The chief reason for their attraction is to be found in their claim to be able to give the individual a liberating answer to his questions about his fate in the next world. They claimed to show him how, by ordering his way of life in this world, he could assure his survival in the next; in a word, how he could find his eternal salvation, σωτηρία.

The oriental mystery-cults could begin their conquest of the East after Alexander's campaigns provided the opportunity. At first they groped their way slowly, gaining gradually a more certain foothold in the commercial and cultural centres, until by imperial times they reached the zenith of their influence. The Greeks on the coast of Asia Minor were the readiest to accept this new world of religious experience; and they were the principal means of its spreading to the West.

These cults were not strictly exclusive, but adopted from time to time elements of existing religious systems, permeated them, mingled characteristics of related divinities with those of their own objects of worship, and thus contributed to that religious syncretism which is typical of the Hellenistic age. Three oriental civilizations were the sources from which the new cults flowed into the Hellenistic world: those of Egypt, Asia Minor and Syria, to which may be added that of Iran, whence came the cult of Mithras which was of a rather different type.

In the centre of the Egyptian cult stood first of all the figures of Isis and Osiris, who are well known from the official religion of Egypt. The goddess Isis was honoured every year by a solemn procession, in which the outlandish and bizarre parade of shaven-headed, white-clad priests, of noisy musicians and other strange participants was the most noticeable

[1] K. Scott, *The Imperial Cult under the Flavians* (Stuttgart 1936).

feature. In the course of a long development, Isis had become a universal goddess who was believed to have brought morality and civilization to mankind. She was regarded as the inventor of agriculture and writing, as goddess of seafarers, as foundress of law and civil order, a protectress of the persecuted and liberator from every kind of distress.

In the secret cult of Isis, Osiris figured as her husband. He was the ancient Egyptian god of vegetation, who died and rose again, as the annual sowing and growth of the crops symbolically signify. His death was mourned by his worshippers, his resurrection celebrated with joy. In his dying, man saw his own death expressed; but like Osiris he would rise again to new life. That is the basic idea of these mysteries, to which the goddess Isis, in a dream, would herself call him who was found worthy. An impressive initiation ceremony[2] consecrated the chosen one to the service of the goddess; he had previously prepared himself by a bath of purification and a ten days' fast, and he was now led by the priest into the sanctuary of the temple of Isis, crossed the threshold of death, passed through all the elements and adored the sun and the gods. Clothed with the "mantle of Heaven", with a torch in his hand and a wreath on his head, he was then presented to the congregation as an image of the sun-god, celebrating the day on which he was born to a new life. Before the statue of the goddess he spoke an enthusiastic prayer of thanksgiving, pledging himself constantly to keep in mind her divine countenance and her holiness.

In the Ptolemaic period Osiris was pushed into the background by the new Egyptian god Sarapis (Serapis), a creation of Ptolemy I, who wished in this way to unite the Egyptians and the Greeks of his kingdom. Therefore Sarapis combined in himself features which appealed to all the king's subjects: he too is associated with Isis as a god of life and death, earth-god and sun-god. Not only did his image, with its Hellenistic beauty, radiate sublime tenderness and helpful humanity, reminding one of Zeus and Asclepios; but his whole being made him widely honoured as a helper in material and spiritual needs. He was the Lord of Fate who led the soul safely into the next world. Zealous propaganda spread his cult from his main sanctuary, the Sarapeion at Alexandria, over the whole Mediterranean world as far as Rome; everywhere resounded the cry of praise: "Sarapis is conqueror!" (Νικᾷ ὁ Σάραπις). It was he whom Emperor Julian was to praise in words which reveal the monotheistic tendency of the cult: "One is Zeus and Hades and Helios, One is Sarapis."[3]

Asia Minor was the home of the cult of the Great Mother, the fertility

---

[2] Cf. the description of the ritual in Apuleius, *Metam.* XI; see W. Wittmann, *Das Isisbuch des Apuleius von Madaura* (Stuttgart 1938).

[3] Julian, *Orat.* 4, 136 A.

goddess Cybele, who was early known to the Greeks. In the Hellenistic age her worship spread quickly beyond her homeland and was introduced into Rome as early as 204 B.C. She too was connected with a male divinity, the Nature hero Attis, her lover. According to the myth (of which more than one version exists), Attis was unfaithful to her, wherefore he was cast into a frenzy, from the consequences of which he died. He was awakened to new life and reunited with the Great Mother. This myth became the basis of a wild and strange mystery cult, served by a special college of priests, the Galli. These, by ecstatic dancing and flagellation, brought on their own "mystical" frenzy, in which they were driven even to self-castration. In the rite of initiation, the candidate or *mysta* symbolically relived the fate of his god in death and resurrection; he was sprinkled with the blood of a bull and then entered the "bridal chamber", which he left as one reborn. At a sacred meal he made his profession as a *mysta* of Attis, and a priest proclaimed to the initiated the joyful tidings: "Be comforted, ye *mystae!* Salvation came to the god. So also shall we be partakers of salvation after tribulation."[4] Here, too, the promise of salvation was the deciding motive for joining the cult, the orgiastic features of which were not altogether foreign to a Greek, if he remembered the ways in which Dionysus had formerly been worshipped by his countrymen. The excesses of self-mutilation attendant upon the cult could, indeed, hardly have had much attraction for him; and Greek comedy did not spare with its mockery the itinerant priests of Cybele who travelled through the land propagating their religion.

A cult which originated at Byblos on the Syrian coast was marked by similar ecstatic features. Its divinities were the Mistress of Nature, Atargatis, akin to Cybele, and the beautiful youth Adonis, her husband. The latter was also a god of vegetation who died and rose again. According to the myth he was wounded by a boar while hunting and died of his wounds, but in the spring he would rise once more, a radiant god. The centre of the mystical celebration was the annual commemoration of Adonis' death, at which the women of Byblos abandoned themselves to unrestrained mourning, and interred an image of the youthful god amid loud lamentations. After a short time their mourning was turned to gladness, and the worshippers of the god joyfully proclaimed: "Adonis lives!" The symbolism of this cult, too, expressing sorrow at premature death and longing for a rejuvenating resurrection, was able to attract many people in the later Hellenistic period.

The three mystery cults have, in spite of differences of detail, one basic idea in common. The death and constant renewal observed in Nature were

---

[4] Firmicus Maternus, *De Errore Prof. Rel.* 22: Θαρρεῖτε, μύσται, τοῦ Θεοῦ σεσωσμένου· ἔσται γὰρ ἡμῖν ἐκ πόνων σωτηρία.

symbolically crystallized in the myth of a young god of vegetation, who is torn from the side of the goddess by a tragic death but rises again to new life. By this is represented the fate of man, whose strange and sometimes incomprehensibly tragic death weighed like a dark burden upon the thought and feeling of Antiquity. Should there not be for him also, as for the god in the myth, a resurrection into a mysterious hereafter? The mere possibility, hinted at in the myth, of such an eschatological hope was bound to appeal to Hellenistic man. Precisely because the old religions of Greece and Rome knew no encouraging answer to this exciting question, people turned to these new forms of religious faith, whose attraction was increased by the mysterious and outlandish nature of the initiation ceremonies, which seemed like an echo from beyond the grave. The hymns and prayers, with their intensity of feeling, caught in their spell many an anxious and excitable mind.

The mystery cult of Mithras came also to be dominated by ideas of a future life, though indeed these did not come to the fore until Christianity was both inwardly and outwardly well established. This cult had its origins in the Iranian world, was developed, as to its outward form, mainly in Cappadocia, and then spread from East to West. At first it met with little success in the central provinces of Asia Minor and Egypt and found hardly any response in Greece, but it was all the more successful in the western parts of the empire, where Rome and its surroundings — in Ostia alone about fifteen sanctuaries of Mithras are known to have existed — and the northern frontier on the Rhine were the regions in which it was most prevalent. It was essentially a masculine cult, having most of its devotees among the soldiers of the Roman army. Its main figure was the Persian god Mithras, who stole a bull belonging to the moon and slew it on the orders of Apollo; the representation of this event is the central motif of the image which was set up in all Mithraic temples. The blood of a bull was sprinkled over the believers, who were thus initiated and became entitled to expect salvation. The candidate for initiation prepared himself by undergoing various tests of courage and ritual washings; after his reception he proceeded through seven grades to that of a full disciple of Mithras. As Mithras was taken up by the sun-god Helios in the chariot of the sun, so did the disciple hope to be raised up in glory in the next world. The members of the cult were also united in a sacred meal, which prefigured, to those who partook of it, a happy life together in the hereafter.

Our sources give no precise data enabling us to state the number of devotees of all these cults. Their expansion throughout the Hellenistic world and their relative density in the larger centres of population leads us to suppose that their membership was not inconsiderable. The educated upper classes were, no doubt, least represented; these rather sought fulfilment of their religious needs in the philosophical schools of the time.[5] All the more did the mystery cults appeal to the middle classes, whose religious feelings were not yet stifled by the material brilliance of Hellenistic civilization; they longed for actual contact with the divine and to find in rites appealing to the senses, an interpretation of life and a palpable guarantee of a better lot in the next world.

Popular Religion

Emperor cult and mystery religions did not, however, appeal to everyone in the Mediterranean world. The former was relatively seldom in evidence and it had moreover little contact with the rural population. As for the mystery cults, their esoteric character made them difficult of approach for many. The great mass of simple folk, therefore, turned towards the lower kinds of superstition, which in Hellenistic times especially were very widespread in numerous forms.

Chief of these, no doubt, was the belief in astrology, which ascribed to the stars a decisive influence on human destiny. The Graeco-Roman world first became more closely acquainted with it when Berossos, a priest of Baal from Babylon, the home of all astrology, set up a school on the island of Cos in 280 B.C. In the second century B.C. the priest Petosiris in Egypt wrote the fundamental astrological work on which later astrological literature repeatedly drew. A decisive factor was that Stoic philosophy was on the side of astrology, because it found therein confirmation of its doctrine that all things in this world were determined by the laws of destiny. The rejection of astrology by the Academic Carneades was far outweighed by the authority of Poseidonios, who gave to belief in astrology the appearance of a scientifically based system and gained for it such a degree of consideration that Roman emperors like Tiberius kept their own court astrologers, while others such as Marcus Aurelius and Septimius Severus erected, for the seven planetary gods, special buildings, the *septizonia*, which became centres of astrological activity. An extensive literature spread astrological knowledge among high and low and provided its readers with a belief in fate founded upon the stars; not only for important undertakings, but even in the simple and commonplace affairs of everyday life, they consulted the stars with an almost slavish fear. Whether one should go on a journey, accept an invitation to a party, take a bath — such matters depended on the words of an astrologer, who invariably found numerous believers in his wisdom. He was consulted especially to find out the position of the stars at the hour of birth, for that determined the whole of a person's life — whether he were destined for success or failure, sickness

[5] W. Nestle, *Griechische Religiosität*, III (Berlin 1934), 86–98.

or health, above all for long life or early death. This particular question concerning the hour of death, the darkest of all hours in the life of man in Antiquity, drove him constantly into the arms of astrology. Even when its adherents asserted that through information obtained from astrologers, they had achieved certainty and so were delivered from care and anxiety, they deceived themselves and sooner or later fell victims to a gloomy fatalism, which found expression in many an epitaph of the time. If life was so inevitably subject to the fatal power of the stars, there was no point in praying to the gods, and so faith in the old religions fell into greater neglect than ever among devotees of astrology.

Magic offered an escape from the iron compulsion of astrological fate. It undertook by secret practices to bring into the service of man both the power of the stars and all the good and evil forces of the universe. This form of superstition had likewise made its way from the ancient East to the West and, especially in Egypt, had reached alarming depths of religious confusion during the Hellenistic period. The magical books of Antiquity and numerous magical papyri which have survived give an instructive glimpse into that world, in which primitive human instincts, fear of the obscure and incomprehensible in Nature and in human events, hatred of fellow-men, delight in sensation, the thrill of the uncanny all find unrestrained expression. Belief in magic presupposes that mighty fear of demons which, from the fourth century B.C. onwards in ever more fantastic forms, had spread in the imagination of Hellenistic man. According to this belief, the whole world was filled with δαίμονες, δυνάμεις, κυριότητες and ἄρχοντες, strange beings halfway between men and gods. Greater and greater became the number of evil demons who could and would harm mankind, but whose power could be held in check by magic. But in order that magic rites and magic words might be effective, one must first of all know the secret name of the god or demon and employ exactly the prescribed formula, however senseless its text might appear.

The professional magician, who was master of this secret science, could make the weather, set free captives, heal or induce sicknesses, calm the sea, sunder lovers or assure one of the love of another, deliver from diabolical possession, call up the dead and make them appear. The influence of such magic was supported and confirmed by certain philosophical currents, such as neo-Pythagoreanism and the neo-Platonic school, which, with their highly developed doctrine of demons, contributed largely to the extensive demonization of Hellenistic religion. A certain influence on contemporary magical literature must be ascribed to Judaism, in which magical practices and conjuring of spirits were quite usual (Acts 8:9–13).

Connected with magic were the belief in the secret meaning of dreams and the art of interpreting them which consequently developed. The latter was particulary successful in Egypt; special dream-books informed credulous readers about the meaning and import of things seen in dreams, and even the most bizarre interpretation found believers. No wonder that the ancient faith in the wisdom of oracles survived into Hellenistic times, only that, in this case too, a descent from a higher level to one of mere charlatanism is observable. Though the Delphic oracle of Apollo and that of the Egyptian Ammon were less respected, others gained in popularity, such as the oracle of Apollo near Miletus, that of Glycon at Abunoteichos in northern Asia Minor (which uttered about 60,000 pronouncements annually), or the oracle of Fortuna at Praeneste, to consult which the Romans made pilgrimages into the Campagna. At popular festivals professional soothsayers were regularly to be found, who with their oracular mirrors and sacred cocks were at the disposal of all classes of the population. A higher form of oracular soothsaying is exemplified by the Sibylline books, collections of which were numerous. [6]

Finally, the strong belief in miracles characteristic of the Hellenistic age belonged mainly to popular religion, even though it was shared by many among the educated classes. The miracle that was most ardently longed for was the restoration of lost health. For this, men prayed to the god Asclepios, who in the Hellenistic period was worshipped more than ever before. Originally a physician and demigod who healed the sick, he became the helper of mankind in distress, the "saviour of all". Where his principal temples stood, there soon developed places of pilgrimage, to which pilgrims streamed from far and near, in order that they might, after preparatory washings, be healed during sleep in or near the sanctuary, or that they might learn of the medicine that would take away their sickness. The great sanctuary of Asclepios (dating from the fourth century B.C.) at Epidauros in the Peloponnese was overshadowed in Hellenistic times by the magnificently laid out temple of the god at Pergamon, [7] this, in its turn, became the mother-house of numerous new foundations, of which about two hundred are now known to have existed.

Men expected of the saviour Asclepios that he would make the blind see, restore to the lame the use of their limbs and to the dumb their speech, and that he would heal lung diseases and dropsy. If the miraculous cure succeeded, thanks to the god were expressed by costly votive gifts, which often took the form of gold or silver images of the healed member, thus proclaiming to all who visited the temple the wonder-working power of Asclepios. In the second century A.D. the rhetor Aelius Aristides became the enthusiastic prophet of this saviour; and the emperor Julian in the fourth century sought to set him up again as the saviour of mankind in opposition

---

[6] A. Kurfess, *Sibyllinische Weissagungen* (Munich 1951).
[7] K. Kerényi, *Der göttliche Arzt. Studien über Asklepios und seine Kultstätte* (Basle, 2nd ed. 1952).

to the Saviour of the Christians. Christianity itself waged a long and hard campaign against Asclepios' claim to be a saviour, the beginnings of which are already apparent in the New Testament writings of John, and which lasted into the fourth century. [8]

When one considers the general religious situation in the Hellenistic world at the beginning of the Christian era, the first impression is discouraging, if the missionary task of the early Church is seen in relation to it. The cult of the emperor was bound to prove a great obstacle to the peaceful expansion of the new faith, if only because the tidings of a Redeemer who had been executed upon the cross like a criminal were not likely to be readily accepted by a superficial society which had before its eyes the sacred figure on the imperial throne, surrounded by all the trappings of earthly glory. Moreover, the State could set all the machinery of power in motion if the adherents of the Gospel dared to disdain or attack this State cult, were it only with words alone. A further factor that would seem to prevent the acceptance of Christianity was the extreme licentiousness of the oriental mystery cults, the orgiastic features of which often led to serious moral deterioration. The reliance of these cults on outward demonstrations, calculated to affect the senses, was frequently due to a religious superficiality that was part of Hellenistic civilization, which was itself becoming more and more lacking in depth and inner feeling. The contemporary bold and disrespectful criticism of the gods, with its contempt for the beliefs and worship of the old religions, was another unfavourable factor, undermining as it did all reverence for what was sacred. The mocking irony with which educated circles greeted the preaching of Paul at Athens shows clearly what attitude the Christian missionary had to overcome there.

But, in opposition to these negative tendencies, we may discern also some positive features in the general picture of Hellenistic religion which may be regarded as starting-points for the preaching of the new faith. There was, for instance, the feeling of emptiness which had undeniably arisen among men of more thoughtful nature on account of the failure of the ancient religions. It was not too difficult to fill this emptiness with a message that proclaimed a high ideal of morality and thus appealed particularly to those who felt disgusted with their own previous lives. Certain features of the mystery cults show the presence of a deep desire of redemption in the men of that time which was bound to be quickened when eternal salvation was offered by a Saviour who, while stripped of all earthly greatness, was for that very reason superior to a helper who would bring only salvation in

[8] F. J. Dölger, "Der Heiland" in *AuC*, VI (1950), 241–72; K. H. Rengstorf, *Die Anfänge der Auseinandersetzung zwischen Christusglaube und Asklepiosfrömmigkeit* (Münster 1953).

this world. Finally, the strong tendency to monotheism, so apparent in the religions of the Hellenistic period,[9] provided the Christian missionaries with an ideal bridgehead in the pagan lands, for the peoples of which — as for the Jews — " the fullness of time was come" (Gal 4:4).

CHAPTER 5

The Apostle Paul and the Structure of the Pauline Congregations

ONLY through a series of shocks could Jewish Christianity arrive at the knowledge that it was under an obligation to carry the tidings of redemption through Jesus Christ into the Gentile world also; the after-effects of the Israelites' consciousness of being the Chosen People were too strong. The first reception of a pagan into the community of the faithful, the baptism of the Ethiopian chamberlain by Philip (Acts 8:26–39), appears to have given no cause for a fundamental change of attitude. All the more powerful was the effect created by the baptism of the pagan captain Cornelius of Caesarea and his family (Acts 10:1–11:18). Peter, who was responsible for this step, was formally called to account by the disturbed community, and only his reference to the commission given to him directly by God in a vision was able to reconcile the Jewish Christians in some measure to his action. However significant this was in principle, it had at first no immediate consequences in the way of increased missionary activity among the Gentiles.

The impulse which started such activity came from a group of Hellenistic Jewish Christians from Cyprus and Cyrenaica, who had had to leave Jerusalem after the persecution of Stephen and had first settled in Antioch. Here they "spoke to the Greeks also, preaching the Lord Jesus" and "a great number that believed, turned to the Lord" (Acts 11:19 ff.). Thus, the first numerically significant group of pagans that accepted Christianity came from the world of Hellenistic civilization, which showed that there the Christian faith need not expect to meet with uncompromising rejection. The success of this missionary expedition caused the Jerusalem congregation to send one of its members, the former levite Barnabas,[10] to Antioch, in order to appraise the situation. Barnabas, who himself came from the Jewish Diaspora in Cyprus, was sufficiently unprejudiced to be able to appreciate the importance of the events at Antioch. He approved the reception of the

---

[9] W. Weber, *Die Vereinheitlichung der religiösen Welt: Probleme der Spätantike* (Stuttgart 1930), 67–100.
[10] H. Bruns, *Barnabas* (Berlin 1937); J. B. Bruger, *Museum Helveticum* 3 (1946), 180–93.

Greeks into the Church and at the same time saw clearly what was to be of vast consequence for the history of the world: that for the preaching of the new faith in this place there were needed the courage and spirit of the man who, after his own remarkable conversion to Christ, had withdrawn to his Cilician home town: Paul (or Saul) of Tarsus. Barnabas succeeded in persuading him to work in the Syrian city, and after a year's labouring together, the existence of the first large Gentile community was assured. It was at Antioch that its members first received the name of "Christians" (Acts 11:22–26).

The Religious History of the Apostle Paul

Like his earliest collaborator, Barnabas, Paul also came from the Diaspora; his birthplace was Tarsus in Cilicia, where his father carried on the trade of saddler which the son also learnt. When the family settled there is uncertain; according to a late account, his ancestors came from Galilee. His father already possessed hereditary Roman citizenship, the privileges of which Paul could later invoke with effect in his trial before the Roman governor. It was a fortunate circumstance for Paul's missionary work in the great centres of Hellenistic culture that he had in his youth[11] become acquainted with all the manifold aspects of that culture in the fair-sized city of Tarsus with its lively transit traffic. Of even more consequence was the fact that the Greek *koinê*, the common tongue of the Mediterranean region, had become as familiar to him as his native Aramaic. His family had, with that firm loyalty often to be found in a Diaspora situation, remained true to the convictions and traditions of Judaism, all the more so as it followed the Pharisaic school in its strict observance of the Law.

It was probably not until after the death of Jesus that Paul went to Jerusalem to be trained as a teacher of the Law in the school of the Pharisee Gamaliel (Acts 22:3). When the disciples of Jesus began to attract the attention of the Jewish authorities, Paul joined zealously in persecuting them, especially after the martyrdom of the deacon Stephen (Acts 7:58; 8:3). The account in the Acts of the Apostles is impressively confirmed by his own witness: "I persecuted the Church of God violently and tried to destroy it; and I advanced in Judaism beyond many of my own age among my people, so extremely zealous was I for the traditions of my fathers" (Gal 1:13 f.; cf. 1 Cor 15:9).

The lightning and radical change which made the persecutor into an ardent disciple of Jesus and his Gospel was, according to the Acts (9:3–18;

---

[11] Cf. W. C. van Unnik, "Tarsus of Jerusalem de Stad van Paulus' Jeugd", *Mededelingen Koninkl. Nederl. Akad. Wetenschappen, Afd. Letterkunde NR* 15, 5 (1952), 141–89; Eng. tr. *Tarsus or Jerusalem, the City of Paul's Youth* (London 1962).

22:3–16; 26:12–30), brought about by a direct apparition of Jesus which Paul encountered when he was on his way to Damascus to persecute the Christians there. Paul refers to this event only in restrained terms in his letters (cf. Gal 1:15; 1 Cor 15:9; Phil 3:4), but he makes it clear that in the apparition of the Lord he saw the supernatural call of grace that, by calling him to be an apostle, gave his life the final purpose which he was never to give up and in which he was never to falter.

Soon after being baptized and during a short stay in Nabataean Arabia, Paul began to proclaim in the synagogues of Damascus and later in Jerusalem the message of his life, that Jesus was "the Messiah and the Son of God" (Acts 9:20, 22, 26—29). At both places he met with such strong opposition that his life was in danger; he therefore withdrew to his native city of Tarsus (Acts 9:30); and here, no doubt, while he may have engaged in local missionary activity on a small scale, he attained certainty about the scope of his mission and the forms which his preaching of the Gospel was to take. When, after several years' silence, he resumed work in Antioch, he knew that he was to concern himself with the pagan world which, no less than the Jews, could find its salvation only in Jesus Christ (Gal 1:16; Rom 15:15 f.).

The Mission of Paul

Once Paul knew that he was called to preach to the pagans, the Roman Empire presented itself as the appointed mission field. Within its frontiers dwelt those to whom his message must be addressed; they shared the same civilization and (in the cities at least) the same language, the koinê. However much he felt himself to be immediately guided, even in detail, by the Spirit of God, it is nevertheless possible to speak of a plan to which he adhered. His journeys were mapped out at a kind of mission-base. For his first missionary period, up to the Apostolic Council at Jerusalem, his base was the Syrian capital, Antioch. The Gentile Christian congregation, which had grown up there, was at once spur and bridle for the first large missionary undertaking that Paul began with two companions, Barnabas and the latter's kinsman, John Mark. The account of it which the Acts give us clearly shows the special character of Paul's method.

The starting-points for his missionary work were the synagogues of the cities in the Mediterranean provinces; here the Diaspora Jews held their religious meetings, and here were to be found former pagans who had joined the Jewish community as proselytes or "God-fearing ones". The missionaries first went to Cyprus, where they worked in the city of Salamis. From there the way led to the mainland of Asia Minor, where the cities of Antioch in Pisidia, Iconium, Lystra and Derbe in the province of Lycaonia, and Perge in Pamphylia were the scene of their labours. Everywhere Paul's preaching was addressed to both groups, Diaspora Jews and former pagans. Both discussed his sermons and in both he met with acceptance and rejection; it is possible that the discussions reached the ears of the occasional pagan, who then joined the band of disciples (cf. Acts 13:49).

The Acts leave us no room to doubt that the majority of the Diaspora Jews decidedly rejected the message of Paul. In many places, as for example at Antioch in Pisidia, Iconium, and Lystra, excited discussions developed into tumults, in the course of which the missionaries were driven out, sometimes mishandled. The initiative on these occasions lay with the Jews, who occasionally goaded their pagan fellow-citizens into using violence — a characteristic trait which can be observed in many subsequent persecutions. Nevertheless the preaching of Paul and his assistants generally found some receptive hearts, especially among the former pagans, "God-fearing ones" and proselytes, and thus there arose in most cities visited on this first journey Christian congregations, to which suitable leaders were appointed. In this way there were established a number of cells of the faith amid pagan surroundings which became centres of further activity.[12] Clearly this was Paul's real object, for he never stayed very long in one place to work in depth, but aimed rather at making the Gospel known in as many places as possible in Asia Minor, leaving its further propagation to the newly-won disciples of Jesus. Paul certainly regarded the result of this first undertaking as a success, for his report to the congregation at the mission-base of Antioch reaches its culmination when he says how God "had opened the door of faith to the Gentiles" (Acts 14:26).

Paul, in conformity with his own conviction that belief in Christ implied the end of obligations under the Old Law, had not imposed either circumcision or the observance of other Jewish ritual prescriptions upon the Gentile Christian congregations of Asia Minor. This freedom from the Law for new converts, a central point of his message, was soon after his return decisively rejected by the extreme wing of Palestinian Jewish Christians, the so-called Judaizers, who demanded circumcision as an essential condition for attaining salvation (Acts 15:1–5). This was the occasion of that dispute between Paul and the Judaizers in the primitive Church, which reached its climax and its theoretical resolution at the Council of Jerusalem, but which was to hinder Paul's missionary work for a long time and compel him again and again to engage in a determined battle for his convictions.

The dispute began at Antioch, when "some from Judaea" demanded circumcision of the Gentile Christians in the local congregation. It was

---

[12] F. J. Schierse, *Zellen und Gruppenbildung im Urchristentum: Die Zelle in Kirche und Welt* (Graz-Vienna-Cologne 1960), 111–28.

decided to send a delegation with Paul and Barnabas to Jerusalem to settle the question. Consultation led to the recognition in principle of the Pauline thesis that the Mosaic Law could have no binding force for Gentile Christians, and so the independence of the Pauline mission was acknowledged by the original apostles. Paul also undertook the task of collecting money in the congregations of his mission field for the poor of the Jerusalem community, symbolically testifying by this charitable act to the mutual bond between Gentile and Jewish Christians (Gal 2:1–10).[13]

The Acts also tell of the resolution to "lay no further burden" upon the newly converted pagans; nevertheless James proposed that they should be required to "abstain from things sacrificed to idols and from blood and from things strangled and from fornication" (Acts 15:28 f.). Perhaps James intended this concession to Judaism to facilitate the living together in one community of Jewish and Gentile Christians. It is hard to reconcile this account with that of Paul in his letter to the Galatians; one is led to suppose that this point was only later brought into harmony with the resolutions of the assembly at Jerusalem. How difficult it was in practice to carry out the latter appears from the incident between Peter and Paul at Antioch mentioned in Galatians 2:14. Peter came to Syria probably soon after the Council of Jerusalem and took part in the communal meals of the congregation there; but he gave up doing so, "fearing them who were of the circumcision", Jewish Christians belonging to James' circle who had appeared in Antioch. His action signified a disparagement, if not a betrayal of the Gentile Christians by a leading personality of the primitive Church, which was in direct contradiction to the resolutions of the Council. Paul publicly criticized the inconsistent and cowardly behaviour of Peter and passionately proclaimed his conviction that "man is not justified by the works of the Law, but by faith in Jesus Christ" (Gal 2:16). Paul did not, however, succeed in winning over the Judaizers to his opinion; even though they no longer opposed him directly, they intrigued fanatically against him and tried to alienate his congregations from him, especially in Galatia.

The second phase of Paul's missionary work took him into a new field of activity, comprising principally the provinces of Macedonia, Achaea, and proconsular Asia. He was now in the very centre of Hellenistic civilization. The missionaries, who now included the cultivated Silas (instead of Barnabas) and later Timothy, made their way at first through Cilicia and Lycaonia — where no doubt they visited the congregations Paul had earlier founded — to the districts of Asia Minor whose cities offered possibilities of preaching. The Acts give no precise details of the length of their stay and the measure of their success; but the congregation to which the letter to

[13] G. Klein, "Gal 2:6–9 und die Geschichte der Jerusalemer Urgemeinde" in *ZThK* 57 (1960), 275–95; W. Schmithals, *Paulus und Jakobus* (Göttingen 1963).

the Galatians was addressed was probably founded at this time. They reached the coast in northern Troas, where Paul was called in a nocturnal vision to go to Macedonia (Acts 16:9). In Philippi the missionaries soon found adherents, who formed the nucleus of what was later to be a flourishing community (Acts 16:11–40).[14] In Greece, the cities were the centres of Paul's activity, which in essentials followed his previous methods. In Thessalonica, Beroea, Athens and Corinth, the synagogues were the scene of his preaching; in them he proclaimed Jesus as the Messiah (Acts 17:1–10). In the first two of these cities congregations were formed which consisted of Jews and Gentiles. The majority of the Jews there, however, rejected the message of the Kingdom and bitterly persecuted the missionaries. In Athens success was small; in Corinth only a few Jews accepted the Gospel (Acts 17:34; 18:8), but many pagans listened to it. Paul therefore stayed eighteen months in that city, which thus became one of his main centres.

Only after the missionaries had laboured for some time did opposition arise on the part of the Jews, who accused the apostle before the Roman proconsul Gallio (Acts 18:12–17). A dated inscription bearing the latter's name and containing a message from the emperor Claudius to the city of Delphi allows us to date fairly accurately Paul's sojourn at Corinth and to place it in the years A.D. 51–52 or 52–53.[15] Gallio refused to listen to the Jews' accusation, and soon afterwards Paul, with the Jewish couple Aquila and Priscilla, who had greatly promoted his work in Corinth, betook himself to Ephesus in Asia Minor. There he began no intensive missionary labours, but shortly after returned to Palestine by sea.

Ephesus was nevertheless soon to become, as Paul no doubt had long intended, the centre of missionary activity on the west coast of Asia Minor. This began probably in the summer of 54. Setting out from Antioch, Paul had visited the Galatian and Phrygian congregations on the way (Acts 18:23). Paul's work in Ephesus, which lasted about two years, was filled with successes but also with difficulties and worries which were almost unavoidable in such a city (Acts 19). His zealous proclamation of the Gospel soon caused a congregation to grow up which detached itself from the synagogue; but its members had yet to be weaned from many remarkable superstitious ideas and customs. Difficulties came not only from the Jews but also from the pagans, as when Demetrius, owner of a business that made small silver models of the temple of Diana, saw his profits threatened by Paul's preaching and staged a demonstration against the missionaries.

The apostle's concern for his earlier foundations, especially those at Corinth and in Galatia, found expression in letters (letter to the Galatians and first letter to the Corinthians) which were written in Ephesus. About the

[14] O. Glombitza, "Der Schritt nach Europa" in ZNW 53 (1962), 77–82.
[15] L. Hennequin in DBS, II (1934), 355–73 (with bibliography).

autumn of 57 Paul left the city to go to Macedonia and Greece. After a short stay in Troas he visited Corinth again for a few months; here originated his letter to the Christian community of Rome, still personally unknown to him. In this he announced his intention of coming himself to the imperial capital before going to work in Spain (Rom 15:24 29). For the return journey to Jerusalem, Paul chose first the land route through Macedonia, where he celebrated the Pasch with his congregation in Philippi. Then he sailed to Troas and afterwards to Miletus, whither he had summoned the elders of the Ephesian congregation (Acts 20:1–17). In spite of his own dark forebodings, he felt obliged to return soon to Jerusalem, to hand over the money he had collected for the poor of the congregation there. After taking a sorrowful farewell of the elders of Ephesus, he travelled on with his companions through Tyre, Ptolemais, and Caesarea, visiting the Christians in each place and reaching Jerusalem about the time of Pentecost (Acts 21:1–17).

In Jerusalem Paul's missionary work, in the form it had hitherto taken, came to an end. On a visit to the Temple he was recognized by some Diaspora Jews from Asia Minor. These tried to cause his death at the hands of the people. The Roman guard, however, took him into protective custody, and their commander sent him to the governor at Caesarea (Acts 21:27–23:35). From there a military escort took him to Rome, because Paul, to avoid a trial before the Jewish Sanhedrin, had appealed to the Emperor, so that the case had to be heard in the capital (Acts 27–28). As the lenient conditions of his custody permitted intercourse with the outside world, he resumed his missionary work in the only form possible; he addressed himself to the representatives of the Jewish community of Rome, "testifying to the kingdom of God and trying to convince them about Jesus ... And some were convinced by what he said, while others disbelieved" (Acts 28:23 f.). With the statement that "this salvation of God has been sent to the Gentiles; they will listen" (Acts 28:28), Luke concludes the last Pauline sermon in his book. And with it, too, the author's task is accomplished, namely to describe how the Gospel made its way from Jerusalem to the capital of the Roman Empire.

The Acts of the Apostles are silent about the subsequent events of Paul's life. There is much evidence that the trial ended with an acquittal and that he afterwards carried out his planned journey to Spain[16] and also visited the Hellenistic East once more. This hyphothesis alone can explain the pastoral letters which tell of events and situations that can only be fitted into such a final period of his life.[17] On this last missionary journey Paul was specially

---

[16] This is suggested by 1 *Clem* 5:7. See E. Dubowy, *Klemens von Rom über die Reise Pauli nach Spanien* (Münster 1914).

[17] On the question of authenticity, cf. C. Spicq, *Les épîtres pastorales* (Paris 1947),

concerned with giving directions for the organization of his congregations and with warning them against the menace of false doctrines. A second imprisonment at Rome led to his martyrdom, which took place in the reign of Nero, even though it cannot with certainty be attributed to the actual Neronian persecution.

Organization of the Pauline Congregations

Every attempt to provide from historical sources an answer to the question of the organization or "constitution" of the Pauline congregations must reckon with the peculiar nature of those sources, which makes it impossible to give a picture that conveys all the facts. Not a single piece of writing originating in one of those congregations offers a description of its daily life or a clue to its organization. The Acts fail to give such a description, preferring to keep to their central theme, the route followed by Paul on his missionary journeys. The letters discuss matters of organization only on given occasions and therefore afford only casual indications, never principles or a complete system. Nevertheless, even these occasional utterances make it quite clear that an organization existed which regulated and established the congregations' religious life. It is indeed a special kind of organization, not to be compared, for instance, with the rules of a secular body, which are purely the work of man, based on human counsel and human judgment and therefore subject to alteration. But the organization of which we speak rests on a supernatural foundation, the same as that on which the Church herself is based, her Lord, who guides his Church through his Holy Spirit. The same Spirit which caused the young Church to grow (Acts 2:47; 6:7), directed Paul's missionary travels (Acts 16:9; 19:21) and crowned his work with success (Acts 19:11; 1 Cor 2:3 ff.; Rom 15:17 ff.), also created this organization for the life of the community (1 Cor 3:9 ff; 2 Cor 12:19; Eph 4:12–16).[18] When, therefore, members of the community were appointed to special tasks in the service of that organization, they were called by the Holy Spirit, whose organs they were (1 Cor 12:4 f.). Those who were called thus knew themselves to be in the service of the Lord and fulfilled their tasks in and for the community in a spirit of love such as Jesus had required from his disciples (Mark 10:42–45). So this organization was willingly accepted by the congregation and not felt to be in opposition to the free working of the Spirit in those charismatically gifted, for it was the same Spirit who called all.

introduction; H. Schlier, *Festschrift Gogarten* (Giessen 1948), 36–60; A. Wikenhauser, *New Testament Introduction* (Freiburg-New York-London, 3rd ed. 1963), 445–52.
[18] Cf. O. Michel in *ThW* V, 142—5; J. Pfammater, *Die Kirche als Bau. Zur Ekklesiologie der Paulusbriefe* (Rome 1960); K. H. Schelkle, "Kirche als Elite und Elite in der Kirche nach dem Neuen Testament" in *ThQ* 142 (1962), 257–82.

In the organization of the congregations their founder Paul occupied a unique place, ultimately based upon his direct vocation to be the Apostle of the Gentiles. He, indeed, felt himself to be the least of the servants of Jesus Christ and as such due to suffer every tribulation and humiliation (1 Cor 4:9–13; 2 Cor 6:4–10; Phil 2:17). But he was likewise fully persuaded that his office gave him full power and the authority he required for the "edification" or building up of his congregations (2 Cor 10:8; 13:10; 1 Cor 4:21). Conscious of this, he made decisions binding on them, as for instance when he cast out the incestuous adulterer from the congregation at Corinth (1 Cor 5:3 ff.), or gave directions for the worship of God (1 Cor 7:17; Tit 1:5) or for the moral behaviour of the faithful (1 Thess 4:11). Paul was, then, for all his congregations not only the highest teaching authority but also the chief judge and lawgiver, the apex of an hierarchical order.

In the individual congregations, other men were called to be members of this hierarchical order, particular tasks being assigned to them, care for the poor and the conducting of religious worship. For the exercise of their functions they had a right to give directions, to which the faithful according to Paul's explicit order had to submit (1 Cor 16:15 f.; 1 Thess 5:12; Rom 12:6 ff.). Paul stood behind these office-holders with his authority, their powers being similar but subordinate to and limited by his. Those entrusted with such duties were called (Acts 14:23) πρεσβύτεροι, presbyters or elders, whom Paul ordained with laying on of hands and prayer during his first missionary journey in Lystra, Iconium and Pisidian Antioch, before he left those cities to continue on his travels. One may assume that the elders of the congregation of Ephesus were called in a similar way; to them Paul said that the Holy Spirit had appointed them overseers (ἐπίσκοποι) to rule the Church of God as shepherds their sheep. Here it is obvious that the terms "presbyters" and "episcops" indicate the same group of persons, that the two expressions could be used for holders of the same office. At the beginning of the letter to the Philippians "deacons" are mentioned alongside "episcops" as having special duties in the congregation. The later pastoral letters make it clear that the sphere of activity allotted to them was distinct from that of the "presbyters" and "episcops" (1 Tim 1:1–10; 5:17 19; Tit 1:5–11). That the pastoral letters should give a clearer picture of the circumstances is due to the quite understandable development which brought the functions of those who had received ordination into greater prominence as the number of the faithful increased.[19] From the nature of things it is obvious that the office-holders were attached to local congregations; overseer-elders and deacons did not, like Paul and his closest collaborators,

---

[19] H. Schlier, "Die Ordnung der Kirche nach den Pastoralbriefen" in *Die Zeit der Kirche* (Freiburg i. Br., 3rd ed. 1962), 129–47; H. W. Bartsch, *Die Anfänge urchristlicher Kirchenordnung in den Pastoralbriefen* (1963).

travel from city to city and province to province, but fulfilled their tasks within the framework of a particular congregation, from which of course further missionary activity might be carried on in the immediate vicinity. Their vocation can only be understood as a permanent one, if the work begun by Paul in each place was to endure; Paul knew himself to be called, like the other apostles, to continue the work of Jesus of Nazareth and to prepare the community of the final age. In this task those who by God's will occupied the lower rungs of the hierarchical ladder had to play their appointed part.

Besides the holders of authority, there were in the Pauline congregations the charismatically gifted, whose function was essentially different.[20] Their gifts, above all prophecy and the gift of tongues (glossolaly), came direct from the Holy Spirit, who imparted them to each as he wished; they were not therefore attached permanently to particular persons and were not necessary for the existence of the community. The charismatics appeared when the faithful assembled for worship, and, by their prophetic utterances and stirring prayer of thanksgiving, kept alive the lofty enthusiasm of the new faith; they were not guardians and guarantors of order. Here and there, indeed, order was endangered because of them, since the extraordinary and mysterious nature of their performances led many members of the congregation to overestimate their gifts — a danger against which Paul had to issue an admonition (1 Cor 14).

Finally, it was an essential feature of the structure of the congregations established by Paul that they did not regard themselves as independent communities which could go their own individual religious way. There was of course already a certain bond between them in the person of their founder who, even after his departure, remained for them the highest teaching and guiding authority. Paul had, besides, implanted in them a strong consciousness that they were closely linked with the community of Jerusalem, whence had gone forth the tidings of the Messiah and of the salvation wrought by him. To this connexion was due their charitable assistance to the poor of Jerusalem; Paul, in his letter to the Galatians, emphasized the duty of caring for "those who are of the household of faith" (Gal 6:10). By preaching unwearyingly that Christians of all congregations served one Lord (1 Cor 8:6), that they were members of one body (1 Cor 12:27), he kept alive the consciousness that all the baptized were "the Israel of God" (Gal 6:16), the Church of both Jews and Gentiles (Eph 2:13–17).[21] From

---

[20] See J. Brosch, *Charismen und Ämter in der Urkirche* (Bonn 1951) and the commentaries on 1 Cor 12 and 14, e. g. E. B. Allo (Paris 1934), 317—86.

[21] Cf. E. Peterson, *Die Kirche aus Juden und Heiden* (Salzburg 1933), and the commentary on Ephesians by H. Schlier (Düsseldorf, 2nd ed. 1959); idem, *Zeit der Kirche* (Freiburg i. Br., 3rd ed. 1962), 159–86, 287–307.

the point of view of Church history, it was one of the greatest achievements of the Apostle of the Gentiles that this consciousness of being one Church which he awakened and encouraged in his congregations made possible the spread of Christianity in the pagan world. Otherwise the believers in Christ might have split into two separate communities, one of Jewish and one of pagan origin, so that, even by the end of the apostolic age two Christian "denominations" might have come into being. [22]

Religious Life in the Pauline Congregations

The religious life of the Pauline congregations was centred on belief in the risen Lord, which gave a decisive character both to its worship and to its everyday life. This was in accordance with the preaching of Paul, in the centre of which Christ stands and must stand; for this reason he could endure that during his imprisonment others should seek to supplant him, "only that in every way ... Christ is proclaimed" (Phil 1:18). The message of Christ, Paul leaves us in no doubt, must be accepted with real faith: because "if you confess with your lips that Jesus is Lord and believe in your heart that God raised him from the dead, you will be saved" (Rom 10:9). This belief in the Kyrios, the Lord raised up and glorified after the humiliation of the Cross (cf. Phil 2 5:11),[23] included the conviction that in him dwelt the fullness of deity (Col 2:9f.), that he therefore as Son of God possessed the divine nature together with the Father and was himself "the power and the wisdom of God" (1 Cor 1:24).

Admission to the community of the faithful was to be gained by baptism, which for Paul, as for the original apostles, represented no mere external act of worship but made effective the death of Jesus, which he underwent for our sins (1 Cor 15:3). In his preaching, Paul was above all at pains to bring his hearers to the knowledge that baptism stands in a real relationship to Christ's death on the cross and to his resurrection. Only because the Christian is buried with Christ and so lets his former self ("the old man") die, does he, like Christ, rise from the dead to new life (Rom 6:2–8); through baptism and only through baptism can he win a share in salvation.[24] The profound conviction of the Pauline congregations that by baptism they were not only symbolically but in reality "born again"[25] to a new life, that

---

[22] R. Schnackenburg, *Die Kirche im Neuen Testament* (Freiburg i. Br. 1961), 71–77, Eng. tr. *The Church in the New Testament* (Freiburg-New York-London 1965).

[23] M. Meinertz, "Zum Verständnis des Christushymnus Phil 2:5–11" in *TThZ* 61 (1952), 186–92 and G. Strecker in *ZNW* 55 (1964), 63–78.

[24] R. Schnackenburg, *Das Heilsgeschehen bei der Taufe nach dem Apostel Paulus* (Munich 1950); E. Klaar, *Die Taufe nach paulinischem Verständnis* (Munich 1961). H. Schlier, *Zeit der Kirche* 47–56, 107–29.

[25] Cf. J. Dey, *Palingenesia* (Münster 1937).

would one day become one life with Christ's, gave this sacrament its pre-eminent rank in the religion of Pauline Christianity.

The worship of the congregations fitted into the larger framework of the assemblies at which the faithful regularly met together "on the first day of the week" (Acts 20:7). Even though no religious reason for the choice of this day and its preference over the other days of the week had been adduced, the giving up of the Sabbath clearly marked the beginning of a break with Jewish religion. Well-to-do members of the congregation placed their private houses at the disposal of the faithful for their communal act of worship (1 Cor 16–19; Rom 16:4; Col 4:15). Songs of praise, hymns and psalms introduced the celebration; these were to thank the Father for all things in the name of the Lord Jesus Christ (Eph 5:18 ff.; Col 3:16).

The central point and climax of the service was the eucharistic celebration, the Lord's Supper.[26] Details of the way it was conducted are hardly to be found in Paul's writings. It was associated with a meal, no doubt intended to strengthen the solidarity of the faithful, but at which social distinctions among members were sometimes too much in evidence (1 Cor 11:17–27). Even more evident, however, is Paul's striving to convey a deeper theological understanding of the eucharistic act. The "breaking of bread" is unequivocally represented as a real participation in the body and blood of the Lord; this sacrifice is incomparably greater than those of the Old Law and quite different from those of the pagans: "The cup of blessing which we bless, is it not a participation in the blood of Christ? The bread which we break, is it not a participation in the body of Christ? ... You cannot partake of the table of the Lord and of the table of demons" (1 Cor 10:16 21). Because the blood and body of the Lord are truly received in wine and bread, whoever partakes unworthily of this fraternal eating and drinking makes himself guilty of betraying the Lord (1 Cor 11:27). Participation in this meal confirmed to the believer again and again his direct bond with the heavenly Lord. Therefore the congregation was filled with joy and thanks (Eph 5:20); it was a pledge of that final community with him which his second coming would bring about. Longing for this final consummation was expressed in the cry of the congregation at the eucharistic meal: "*Marana-tha* — Come, Lord Jesus!" (1 Cor 16:22; Apoc 22:30).[27] For the Pauline congregation the eucharistic celebration was the source which nourished and constantly reaffirmed its inner unity; as all its members had a share in the same bread, which was the body of Christ, all of them formed one body, the community of God (1 Cor 10:17). This sacramentally based

[26] P. Neuenzeit, *Das Herrenmahl. Studien zur paulinischen Eucharistieauffassung* (Munich 1960).
[27] K. G. Kuhn in *ThW* IV, 470–5; O. Cullmann, *Christologie des Neuen Testaments* (Tübingen 1958), 214–22, Eng. tr. *The Christology of the New Testament* (London 1959).

unity must however show itself in self-sacrificing regard for all, that the kiss of brotherhood given in the assembly (1 Cor 16:20) might not be meaningless.

The assembly of the congregation was also the place where "salvation was preached"; for not only was it the task of the travelling missionaries to proclaim the Gospel (Acts 20:7–11; Cor 1:17; 9:16f.), the congregation must continue to hear from its permanently appointed preacher "the message of reconciliation" with God (2 Cor 5:18–21). The sermon was an instruction in the apostles' doctrine of the crucified and risen Saviour; it referred to the passages in Scripture dealing with salvation and derived from them belief in Christ. In doing so, it stressed the duty of the faithful to praise the Father, to await with courage and good cheer the coming of the Lord and to serve one another in brotherly love (Acts 14:22; 1 Thess 2:2–12; 2 Cor 6:1–2; Phil 2:1–11). Preaching, as the proclamation of the Word, had therefore its assured place in the Pauline congregation and was of prime importance. Finally in the worship of the congregation the speeches of the "prophets" also had a part; they were confirmed by the "Amen" of the assembly (1 Cor 14:16).

The realization of the new religious ideal in everyday life faced the Gentile Christian communities of Paul's missionary field with no inconsiderable difficulties. The surrounding pagan world, with its customs, deep-rooted in family and business life and often utterly opposed to the demands of Christian morality, demanded of them a far greater effort at good conduct and self-discipline than was required of the original community at Jerusalem, whom monotheism and the Jewish moral law had raised to a considerably higher level. Paul's preaching incessantly emphasizes, not without grounds, the sharp contrast which Christianity had set up between Christ and Belial, light and darkness, spirit and flesh, between the "old man" of sin and the "new man" of freedom and truth. That there were in individual congregations members who failed to live up to this high ideal may be inferred from the apostle's unwearying admonitions, even though such glaring examples as that of the incestuous adulterer of Corinth may have been exceptional (1 Cor 5:1 9–13). Frequent references to the spirit of unity and peace among the brethren indicate offences against the commandment of brotherly love (1 Cor 1:10; Eph 4:2f.; 1 Thess 5:13). As is usually so in such cases, the lapses stand out more than the faithful observance of the moral law. In many congregations no doubt the light prevailed over the shadows. When the apostle could say of the Christians in Philippi and Thessalonica that they were his "joy and crown" (Phil 4:1; 1 Thess 2:19), such unreserved praise was assuredly to be highly valued. Those Christians were numerous whose help and selfless labours in the service of the saints Paul could remember with gratitude.

The strongest proof of the moral strength which the Gospel had developed in the Pauline mission field is to be seen in the continuance of his congregations in post-apostolic times and later. The seed that he had sown in his sermons about the power of God's grace and the happiness of being children of God in a pagan world, had sprung up marvellously. At the apostle's death the Hellenistic world was covered with a network of Christian cells, the viability of which ensured the further expansion of the Christian faith in the time to follow.

CHAPTER 6

Peter's Missionary Activity and his Sojourn and Death in Rome

Extra-Pauline Gentile Christianity

COMPARED with Paul's mission, which both in extent and depth was the most successful, the work of the other apostles who were active in the eastern or western parts of the empire is much less easy to follow. Paul himself is witness to the existence of such activity when he asserts that he made a point of not preaching the Gospel where the name of Christ was already known: he would not, as he says, "build on another man's foundation" (Rom 15:19–20). The existence of Gentile-Christian communities, whose origin was due to other missionaries, was therefore known to him; but he does not mention the names of the cities and provinces in which such communities had developed. The Acts of the Apostles refer only casually to extra-Pauline missions, as when it is stated that Barnabas, after his departure from Paul, travelled to Cyprus (Acts 15:40), clearly in order to do missionary work there. In another passage, the existence of a Christian congregation on Italian soil at Puteoli, near Naples, is taken for granted, when the Acts relate that Paul on his way to Rome met "brethren" at the port there who invited him to stay with them (Acts 28:14). Similarly, members of the Roman congregation came to meet him, being already informed of his arrival (Acts 18:15). The name of a Roman missionary is not mentioned. A reference to extra-Pauline mission fields may be found also in the opening of Peter's first letter, which is addressed to the Christians of Pontus, Galatia, Cappadocia, Asia, and Bithynia. If, as is probable, the Roman provinces of the East are here meant, three are named that did not actually belong to the area covered by the Apostle of the Gentiles: Pontus, Cappadocia, and Bithynia. As the Acts (2:9 ff.) number Jews from Cappadocia and Pontus among those present at the first Christian Pentecost at Jerusalem, these may well be regarded as the earliest missionaries in those regions. That the new adherents of the

Christian faith in these provinces had formerly been pagans is quite clear from many passages in the First Epistle of Peter.[28]

The fragmentary nature of our sources for the history of early Christianity is especially apparent when one inquires about the labours or even the lives of the other apostles (with the exception of Peter, John, and James the Younger). It might be expected that their missionary activities would have been confined mainly to Palestine and the surrounding areas, but all the reliable sources are silent. Only in the second and third centuries did the so-called apocryphal "Acts of the Apostles" seek to fill these gaps,[29] giving more or less detailed accounts of the lives and deaths of several apostles. From a literary point of view these writings are related to the ancient novels and travel-books, the heroes of which are portrayed according to the models of profane aretology.[30]

In so far as they proceed from heretical, Gnostic circles, they were intended to procure increased respect for the doctrines of that sect by the use of a revered name. The apocryphal acts of non-heretical provenance or rewritten in orthodox versions rely upon the strong interest shown by the common people in picturesque detail from the lives of great figures of the Christian past, and to this they owed their success. Their value as sources lies in the glimpses they give of the world of religious ideas in the age that produced them; their information about the missionary activity and manner of death of the apostles, or about the places where they laboured, is quite incapable of being checked.[31] At the most it is conceivable that what these works relate of the countries or provinces where the apostles are said to have preached may be based upon genuine traditions; for curiously enough the mission field of the apostle Paul is hardly ever included. The persons named in the apocryphal acts as companions or assistants of the apostles can certainly be regarded as imaginary. Only for three leading members of the apostolic college, James, Peter and John, have we reliable sources of information which make it possible for us to know some facts about their activities. The last two will now be dealt with in more detail.

Sojourn and Death of the Apostle Peter in Rome

The Acts of the Apostles conclude their account of Peter's activity in the primitive Church of Jerusalem with the mysterious words: "He went to

---

[28] Cf. K. H. Schelkle, *Die Petrusbriefe. Der Judasbrief. Herders theologischer Kommentar zum Neuen Testament* (Freiburg-Basle-Vienna 1961), 2.

[29] See the account (with bibliography) in *Quasten P*, I 128–43 and *Altaner* 72–79; J. Michl in *LThK* I, 747–54.

[30] L. Hertling, "Literarisches zu den apokryphen Apostelakten" in *ZKTh* 49 (1925), 219–43.

[31] E. v. d. Goltz, "Apostelgeschichten als Geschichtsquellen" in *Harnack-Ehrung* (Leipzig 1921), 149–58.

another place" (Acts 12:17). The motive for his departure is not known, nor is it apparent where he intended to go. The attempt to see in this vague form of expression a reliable piece of evidence for the apostle's early death[32] is as misleading as the thesis that Paul, in the Epistle to the Galatians, (2:6–19) bears incontrovertible witness that Peter was already dead when the chapter was written.[33] The tradition of Peter's sojourn at Rome and his martyrdom there is too strong to be brushed aside by such weakly grounded hypotheses. The route he followed to Rome, the time of his arrival in the imperial capital and the length of his stay (with interruptions perhaps) are matters on which no definite statement is possible. It is certain that Peter was present at the Council of Jerusalem, which must have taken place about the middle of the century, and that shortly afterwords he was staying at Antioch (Acts 15:7; Gal 2:11–14).

The basis of the Roman tradition concerning Peter is formed by three pieces of evidence, chronologically close to one another and forming together a statement so positive as practically to amount to historical certainty. The first is of Roman origin and is to be found in a letter written to Corinth by Clement in the name of his congregation. Therein he refers to cases in the recent past in which Christians had suffered ill-treatment and death "because of intrigues". Among them Peter and Paul stand out: "Peter, who because of unjust envy suffered tribulations not once or twice but many times, and thus became a witness and passed on to the place of glory which was his due."[34] With him a great number died a martyr's death, among them female Christians, who were executed dressed up as Danaïdes and Dirces. This points to the persecution of the Christians under Nero, to be described later,[35] and permits us to connect Peter's death with it and to date the latter event about the middle of the sixties. Clement says nothing of the manner and place of Peter's martyrdom; his omission of such details clearly presupposes in his readers a knowledge of the events; to himself they were no doubt known at first hand, having taken place in the city where he dwelt and within his own time.

The essential part of this evidence occurs again in a letter from the East addressed, about twenty years later, to the Roman congregation. The bishop of the Gentile Christian community that possessed the most traditions and which was most likely to be informed about the careers of the two leading

---

[32] Thus D. F. Robinson in *JBL* 64 (1945), 255–67, and W. M. Schmaltz in *JBL* 71 (1952), 211–16.

[33] Especially K. Heussi, *Die römische Petrustradition in kritischer Sicht* (Tübingen 1955), 1-10; H. Katzmann also favours 55 as the year of Peter's death, *IKZ* 29 (1939), 85–93. Against such early estimates see esp. O. Cullmann, *Petrus, Jünger–Apostel–Märtyrer*, (Zurich, 2nd ed. 1960), 35f., Eng. tr. *Peter, Disciple–Apostle–Martyr* (London 1953), and K. Aland, *Kirchengeschichtliche Entwürfe* (Gütersloh 1960), 49–54.

[34] 1 *Clem* 5:1–4; 6:1–2.

[35] See below, chapter 8.

apostles, Ignatius of Antioch, begs the Christians of Rome not to rob him of the martyr's crown he expected to receive there, by interceding with the pagan authorities. He qualifies his request with the respectful words: "I do not command you as Peter and Paul did."[36] These two, therefore, stood in a special relationship to the Roman congregation, which had given them a position of authority; that is, they had stayed there for a lengthy period as active members of the community, not temporarily as chance visitors. The weight of this evidence lies in the fact that the knowledge of the Roman congregation about the sojourn of Peter in their midst is unequivocally confirmed by a statement emanating from the distant Christian East.

The third document may be placed alongside Ignatius' letter. Its value as evidence for Peter's residence and martyrdom at Rome has only recently been emphasized.[37] The *Ascensio Isaiae* (4:2–3), which in its Christian version dates from about the year 100,[38] says, in the style of prophecy, that the community founded by the twelve apostles will be persecuted by Belial, the murderer of his mother [Nero], and that one of the Twelve will be delivered into his hands. This prophetic statement is illuminated by a fragment of the "Apocalypse of Peter", which can also be ascribed to the beginning of the second century. Here it says: "See, Peter, to thee have I revealed and explained all things. Go then into the city of fornication and drink the chalice that I have foretold to thee.[39]

This combined text, with its knowledge of Peter's martyrdom at Rome under Nero, confirms and underlines the reliability of the Roman tradition considerably. To these three basic statements two further references can be added which complete the picture given by the tradition. The author of the last chapter of John's Gospel clearly alludes to Peter's death as a martyr and obviously knows of his execution upon the cross (Jn 21:18–19), but is silent about the place of his martyrdom. On the other hand, Rome is indicated as his place of abode in the final verses of the first epistle of Peter, which is stated to have been written at "Babylon"; this is most probably to be understood as meaning Rome, which corresponds to the equation of Babylon with Rome in the Apocalypse (14:8; 16 ff.) and in Jewish apocalyptic and rabbinical literature.[40]

The tradition of Peter's residence at Rome continued unchallenged through the second century and was further confirmed by evidence from

---

[36] Ignatius, *Rom.* 4, 3.
[37] Cf. E. Peterson, "Das Martyrium des hl. Petrus nach der Petrusapokalypse" in *Miscellanea Belvederi* (Rome 1954–5), 181–5, reprinted in *Frühkirche, Judentum und Gnosis* (Freiburg i. Br. 1959), 88–91, where the texts are also given.
[38] E. Peterson in *ByZ* 47 (1954), 70 f.
[39] Greek text in *JThS* 32 (1931), 270.
[40] Cf. K. H. Schelkle, *op. cit.* 135.

the most distant regions in which Christianity had been established, for instance by Bishop Dionysius of Corinth[41] in the East, by Irenaeus of Lyons[42] in the West, by Tertullian[43] in Africa. Even more important is the fact that this tradition was neither claimed for itself by any other Christian community nor opposed nor doubted by any contemporary voice. This almost amazing lack of any rival tradition is without doubt to be regarded as a deciding factor in the critical examination of the Roman tradition.[44]

The Tomb of Peter

However positive the answer to the question of Peter's last residence and place of death may sound, the situation becomes surprisingly complicated when our inquiry has to do with the place of his burial and with the form it took. Here the literary evidence is joined by the weightier testimony of archaeological discovery. Both the excavations and the examination of the literary sources make it clear that in Rome itself the tradition concerning the location of Peter's tomb became divided in course of time. That the Vatican hill was the place of Peter's execution, as is implied by Tacitus' account[45] of Nero's persecution read in conjunction with Clement's first epistle, is confirmed and amplified by the testimony of Gaius, an educated and active member of the Roman congregation under Bishop Zephyrinus (199–217). Gaius was involved in a controversy with the leader of the Montanists in Rome, Proclus, which was concerned with proving the possession of apostolic graves as evidence for the authenticity of apostolic traditions. Just as, earlier, Bishop Polycrates of Ephesus[46] had asserted, in discussing the question of the date of Easter, that the tombs of apostles and bishops in Asia Minor guaranteed indisputably the eastern custom, so Proclus argued that the graves of the apostle Philip and his charismatically gifted daughters in Hierapolis proved the truth of Montanist opinions. Gaius outdid his opponent with the counter-argument: "But I can show you the *tropaia* of the apostles; for if you will go to the Vatican or on the road to Ostia, there you will find the triumphal tombs of those who founded this congregation."[47] So about the year 200 the conviction was held at Rome that Peter's tomb was on the Vatican hill; Gaius gives no indication that this conviction was not shared by the whole Roman community.

---

[41] *Euseb. HE* 2, 25, 8.

[42] Irenaeus, *Adv. haer.* 3, 1–3.

[43] Tertullian, *Praescr. haer.* 36, 3.

[44] Thus, following H. Lietzmannn, *Petrus und Paulus in Rom* (Berlin, 2nd ed. 1927), T. Klauser, *Die römische Petrustradition im Lichte der neuen Ausgrabungen unter der Peterskirche* (Cologne-Opladen 1956), 16.

[45] Tacitus, *Annal.* 15, 44, 5.

[46] *Euseb. HE* 5, 1–8.

[47] Ibid, 2, 25, 7. See T. Klauser, *op. cit.* 20 f.

As opposed to this, an entry in the Roman liturgical calendar of 354, supplemented by the so-called *Martyrologium Hieronymianum* (after 431), states that in 258, on June 29th, the memory of Peter was celebrated at the Vatican, that of Paul on the road to Ostia, and of both *in catacumbas;* there was therefore about the year 260 a shrine of the two princes of the apostles on the Via Appia under the basilica later known as St Sebastian's, which in the fourth century was still called *ecclesia apostolorum.*[48] An epitaph composed by Pope Damasus says that the two apostles had once "dwelt" there, which probably means that their bodies had once been buried there.[49] Excavations in 1917 proved the existence of such a shrine about the year 260, in which both apostles were honoured by *refrigeria,* memorial services, as the numerous *graffiti* on the walls testify. In these, visitors to the shrine invoke the intercession of the two apostles.[50]

Although the excavations brought to light no grave which could be regarded as the burial-place of the apostles, certain of the *graffiti* force us to the conclusion that the Christian visitors were convinced that here were the tombs of Peter and Paul. The discovery gave rise to a number of hypotheses, of which none has as yet decisively prevailed. Whereas the excavators maintained the view that the actual burial-place of both apostles was on the Via Appia, their bodies having been translated to Constantine's basilicas only after these were built,[51] others held that the relics had been brought to St Sebastian's for safety during Valerian's persecution and had remained there until their translation to the new basilicas.[52] A third opinion denies the possibility of such a translation to the Appian Way, in view of the Roman burial laws which strictly forbade the opening of graves; a substitute shrine may well have been set up here when the persecution of Valerian made visits to the real tombs impossible.[53] Or again, there may have been on the Appian Way a centre of veneration of the apostles belonging to some schismatic group, perhaps the Novatians,[54] who living in Rome itself, could not desist from such veneration.

Finally, it is said that the existence of two places in which the tomb of Peter was supposed to be proves that the Roman congregation in the third

---

[48] J. P. Kirsch, *Der stadtrömische christliche Festkalender* (Münster 1924), 20 ff.

[49] A. Ferrua, *Epigrammata Damasiana* (Rome 1942), 142.

[50] A. von Gerkan in H. Lietzmann, *op. cit.* 248–301; most recently in F. Tolotti, *Memorie degli apostoli in Catacumbas* (Vatican City 1953).

[51] P. Styger, *Römische Märtyrergrüfte* (Berlin 1935), 48.

[52] H. Lietzmann, *op. cit.* 122; E. Kirschbaum, *Die Gräber der Apostelfürsten* (Frankfurt, 2nd ed. 1959), 202 f., Eng. tr. The Tombs of SS. Peter and Paul (New York 1959); A. v. Gerkan, *Bonner Jahrbücher* 158 (1958), 99.

[53] Esp. *Delehaye OC* 267 f.

[54] C. Mohlberg, "Historisch-kritische Bemerkungen zum Ursprung der sogenannten memoria apostolorum an der Appischen Straße" in *Colligere Fragmenta, Festschrift A. Dold* (Beuron 1952), 52–74.

century no longer possessed any certain knowledge of the actual burial-place of the apostles; one group, represented by Gaius, thought Peter's grave was under the *tropaion* on the Vatican hill, another was convinced that it was on the Via Appia. The leaders of the congregation had to tolerate this double tradition till after the time of Constantine, for he himself erected basilicas in both places — on the Vatican hill that of Peter and on the Appian Way the *ecclesia apostolorum*, which only later received the title of St Sebastian's.[55] The date of June 29th given in the Calendar is usually linked with an early liturgical celebration on the Appian Way.

The highly important excavations of 1940–9 under the Petrine basilica[56] led first to the discovery of a vast necropolis reached by a street of tombs ascending to the west, from which one arrived at numerous mausolea, many of them richly adorned. Among them there is one that is purely Christian, possessing very ancient mosaics which include a representation of Christ-Helios, a very valuable piece of early Christian iconography.[57] The mausolea were built in the period 130–200; but as the necropolis was only part of a larger cemetery, it is probable that graves were made there, especially towards the east, at an earlier date.

The ground immediately below and in front of the *confessio* of St Peter, where one might have expected to find evidence of Gaius' *tropaion*, proved to be a cemetery, unroofed before the building of Constantine's basilica and measuring approximately 7 × 4 metres (called P by the excavators), bounded on the west by a red wall erected about the year 160. In the east side of this wall there is a double niche (whether contemporary or later is uncertain), flanked by two small projecting columns, of which one was found *in situ*. It is not difficult to recognize this as an *aedicula* or tomb, not exceptionally ornate, which was regarded by the builders of Constantine's basilica as the monument in relation to which the new church, in spite of all the work involved — such as filling in the mausolea and difficulties caused by the ground level — had to be orientated. We are compelled to assume that they regarded the *aedicula*, built probably about 160, as the *tropaion* of Gaius with the tomb of Peter beneath.

In front of the lower niche a flat stone covered a space about 60 cm square, but set at an angle (approximately 11° less than a right angle) to the red wall. In the earth beneath this there were no actual remains of a grave, such as tiles; but there was here also a niche let into the lower edge of the red wall in which lay a little heap of bones from the skeleton of an elderly man. It is noteworthy that around this asymmetrically placed square four later graves (γ,η,ϑ,ι) were so arranged that they would not encroach upon it; one of them (ϑ) can be dated by a tile as being of the

[55] T. Klauser, *op. cit.* 73–75.
[56] The factual details are taken mainly from E. Kirschbaum, *op. cit.*
[57] See also O. Perler, *Die Mosaiken der Juliergruft im Vatikan* (Freiburg i. Br. 1953).

117

time of Vespasian. This leads us to presume that an already existing grave was intentionally left intact. As all the other graves of the area P show only earth burials, the excavators concluded that it contained none but Christian graves, although no other indications prove their Christian character. The carefully preserved square under the stone of the aedicula is, say the excavators, the place where Peter was buried, and they think that the grave was shortened when the red wall or the *aedicula* was built. The absence of anything that might identify the tomb can be explained by the conditions of emergency, in which Peter had to be buried; its defective state may be due to interference either at the time of a possible removal or on some other occasion of which we can know nothing.

The assumption that Peter's tomb has been found must of course rest upon clues, the worth of which as evidence can be variously assessed. Their power to convince depends on how far they can explain the difficulties which still remain. Thus it does not appear to be proved that all the graves around the square under the stone of the *tropaion* are Christian; in the case of the child's grave (γ) with its libation vessels, the possibility, in the second century, seems to be excluded. Moreover, grave η does in fact encroach upon the alleged tomb of Peter, the situation of which would therefore appear not to have been exactly known when that grave was made. The "newly opened" tomb is not big enough for the burial of a man, and the hypotheses necessary to explain the shortening of the original grave are rather unconvincing. What remains regrettably unexplained is why the existing bones were not carefully placed in security either when the *aedicula* was built, or on the occasion of a translation, or after violation of the tomb. Finally, since all reliable information about the place of Peter's execution and burial is lacking, the possibilities concerning it continue to remain as so many open questions. The body might have been burnt or mutilated after execution, or buried in a common grave; or the authorities might have refused to hand it over to the Christians.

These difficulties taken together have not as yet been satisfactorily cleared up; they therefore make it impossible for the present to agree with the opinion that the excavations have with certainty brought to light the tomb of Peter or its original site. They have, however, led without doubt to some very important discoveries. The remains of the *tropaion* of Gaius have most probably been found; the Christians who had it erected certainly believed the apostle's burial-place to be on the Vatican hill. This conviction, shared by the builders of Constantine's basilica, excludes the likelihood of a translation of the bones into the new basilica, for then there would have been opportunities for reconstructing the tomb and orientating the new church which would surely not have been missed. In spite of all hypotheses, the shrine of the apostles on the Appian Way remains a great riddle, to be the subject of further researches in the future.

CHAPTER 7

The Christianity of the Johannine Writings

TOWARDS the end of the first century we encounter a group of Christian writings which tradition early ascribed — not entirely with one voice — to the apostle John, son of Zebedee and younger brother of James the elder. In these Johannine writings, which comprise a Gospel, a fairly long admonitory letter, two short letters and an apocalypse, we see a general picture of Christianity which unmistakably represents a unique stage in its development, in many respects more advanced than the primitive Church of Jerusalem and the Christianity of the Pauline congregations. Here we must note especially those features which are relevant from the point of view of Church history, those which emphasize features in the development of Christian belief and ecclesiastical life that shaped the future history of Christianity. Two in particular stand out: the image of Christ, which is projected in the fourth gospel especially, and the image of the Church, which in the Apocalypse acquires new characteristics.

Even if no generally accepted solution to the question of the authorship of the Johannine writings has been found — if, in particular, the assumption that the Gospel and the Apocalypse in their present form are the work of the same author involves serious difficulties — nevertheless, they can be dated to the end of the first century, and it can be stated with a high degree of probability that they originated among the Christian communities of the west coast of Asia Minor.[58] But there, at that period, the apostle John was the outstanding figure, so that the scriptures that bear his name come also from his spirit, even though they may have received their final form from his disciples.[59] The Gospel of John must have existed at the turn of the century, for Ignatius of Antioch very probably knew it,[60] and a papyrus fragment of a codex written in Egypt about 130[61] containing John 18:31 ff. presupposes such a date of origin. Evidence for an approximately contemporaneous origin for the first letter of John is the use made of it by Papias[62] and the fact that Polycarp of Smyrna quotes it in his letter to the Philippians (7:1). The Apocalypse, too, must have been written, as Irenaeus states,[63] in the last years of Domitian's reign, for the letters it

---

[58] Besides the introductions to the N. T. see F.-M. Braun, *Jean le théologien* (Paris 1959), 301–64.

[59] J. Bonsirven, *Commentaire de l'Apocalypse* (Paris 1951), 69–75.

[60] C. Maurer, *Ignatius von Antiochien und das Johannesevangelium* (Zurich 1949).

[61] This is P 52, ed. by C. H. Roberts, *An Unpublished Fragment of the Fourth Gospel* (Manchester 1935); see also *RB* 45 (1936), 269–72.

[62] *Euseb. HE* 3, 39, 17.

[63] Irenaeus, *Adv. haer.* 5, 30, 3.

contains to Asiatic churches imply a development of ecclesiastical life which had not taken place before the year 70. Its clear references to a clash between the Church and the State cult of the emperor, especially in the thirteenth chapter, are most easily understood if the work received its final form towards the end of the reign of Domitian.

The purpose which guided John when he wrote his Gospel is thus expressed by him at the end of the book: "But these [signs] are written, that you may believe that Jesus is the Christ, the Son of God, and that believing you may have life in his name" (20:31). If the readers here addressed were all Christians, the Gospel was intended to confirm and deepen their faith in the Messiah and the divine sonship of Christ. Indeed, chapters 13–17 could have been written only for those whose belief in Jesus as the Messiah and Son of God was subject to no doubt. But we cannot exclude from the number of the evangelist's readers or hearers those groups who disputed or doubted Christ's claims. The author of the Gospel, writing in Greek, must have had in mind Jews of the Diaspora who were opposed to such ideas.[64] Not without asperity does he attack them, since they had not only denied that Jesus was the Son of God and of divine origin (John 5:18; 8:40–59), but also cast out of their synagogues those who believed in him (9:22; 12:42).[65] He wished to make clear to them that, with Jesus, the Jewish Law had lost its validity (2:1–22; 4:21 ff.), that grace and truth had come into the world with him (1:17), and that the Old Testament scriptures bore witness that he was the Messiah. In Ephesus itself a group of Jews was seeking to destroy belief in the true Messiah, because they considered he had already come in the person of John the Baptist.[66] To these disciples of John the fourth Gospel opposes the testimony of John himself, when it emphatically quotes him as saying that he was not the Messiah, nor the Prophet, nor the Light, but only a witness (1:6 ff. 20 ff.), only the friend of the bridegroom (3:28 ff.), only he who pointed to the Lamb who takes away the sins of the world (1:29).

The evangelist seeks to impart to his readers, believers as well as Jews, an understanding of Christ unique in its depth and grandeur, when he proclaims him as the Logos who has existed from all eternity, being himself divine, and who, when he took flesh, came into this world out of his pre-existence. This is the content of that majestic exordium of the Gospel which serves as a prologue. There is much to support the view that the evangelist was here making use of an already extant hymn to the Logos. It was not, however, the hymn of a Gnostic group in praise of John the Baptist, for John's disciples never worshipped him as the Logos. It may have originated

[64] Cf. esp. W. C. van Unnik in *Studia Evangelica* (Berlin 1959), 406–10.
[65] See K. L. Caroll in *BJRL* 40 (1957), 334–49.
[66] R. Schnackenburg in *HJ* 77 (1958), 24 f.

in a Christian congregation of Asia Minor.[67] The idea of the Logos had already found there its inalterable and specifically Christian character, which the prologue endeavours to protect from misunderstanding by the insertion of certain phrases. However widespread the Logos-idea then was in different circles — it was known even to early Greek philosophers, to Philo, for whom the Logos was a middle being between God and the world, and to the Gnostics, for whom he was a redeemer, while Jewish wisdom speculation moved in a world of ideas related to that of the Logos — the very attributes given to the Logos by John — divine essence, personal subsistence and the Incarnation based thereon — are lacking in previous conceptions of it. The specifically Christian achievement consists in having taken over an idea already existing in many variations and in having given it an unmistakably Christian stamp.

The author of the prologue recognized with a sure instinct the significance of this christianized idea of the Logos and, by putting it into the fourth Gospel, he assured for it an effect that cannot easily be estimated. Wherever Jews or pagans met the Logos as represented in John's Gospel, they encountered the person of Jesus interpreted in a way that left no doubt as to his real Godhead. It was a formulation that was essentially in agreement with Pauline christology, but which, by its conceptual formulation, opened to the Gospel new spheres of influence. In spite of the fact that the evangelist was deeply rooted in Jewish thought, as the Qumran texts have again emphasized,[68] he was able, by taking over the idea of the Logos, to create an image of Christ which, without affecting the essential uniqueness of the message of the Gospel, created fresh possibilities of missionary expansion in the Graeco-Roman world.

To this image of Christ the evangelist joins a clear consciousness of the universal mission of Christianity and of its character as a world religion. This Logos is the light of men; with him came into the world the true light "that enlightens every man" (Jn 1:9); he is "the Lamb of God, who takes away the sin of the world" (1:29); he was sent that the world might be saved through him, so that every man that believed in him might have eternal life (3:16f.). He gave his flesh for the life of the world, and he went to his death that he might unite the scattered children of God into one community (6:51; 11:52). This image of the divine Logos, who brings light and life and therewith salvation to all mankind, is John's bequest at the end of the first century to the next generation of Christians. In making this bequest John performed an act of first-class importance in the history of the Church.

[67] Idem in *BZ* 1 (1957), 69–109, esp. 90–101, with which P.-H. Menoud, *L'évangile de Jean* (Paris 1958), 17, agrees.
[68] Cf. e.g. F.-M. Braun, "L'arrière-fond du quatrième évangile" in *L'évangile de Jean*, 179–96.

Beside this concept of Christ there appears in the Johannine writings an image of the Church which also shows a new aspect. [69] The ecclesiological content of John's Gospel has indeed often been misunderstood because critics allowed themselves to be too much influenced by a phraseology which seems to imply an individualistic concept of the salvation process (3:16; 5:24; 6:56; 15:5). It was believed that he showed a lack of interest in active missionary and pastoral work, characteristics of a community conscious of being a church. [70] In reality the author of the Johannine writings possessed a highly individual, deeply thought out concept of the Church, which he over and over again sought to impart to his readers.

John's Gospel leaves no doubt that men are received by a sacramental act into the community of those who by faith in Jesus attain eternal life: "Unless one is born of water and the Spirit, he cannot enter into the kingdom of God." (3:5) The Spirit that the risen Lord will send effects this new birth and gives the new, divine life. The baptized form the community of believers, cleansed from all sin by the blood of Jesus (1 Jn 1:7). The "anti-Christs" are separated from their fellowship, because they do not hold steadfastly to the true faith of Christ and to brotherly love (1 Jn 2:19–20; 5:1–2; 4:2–3; 2:9–10), and so lose their divine sonship. [71] Only within this community does one become a partaker in the other source of that life, given, as in baptism, by the Spirit: namely, the Eucharist. Participation in the eucharistic meal, at which the faithful receive the real flesh and blood of the risen Lord (Jn 6: 53–58), unites them most intimately with him and with one another and strengthens the bonds of their fellowship as nothing else can.

The evangelist seeks to explain and interpret the reality of this fellowship by words and images employed by Jesus, which have always had an ecclesiological significance. The image of the one shepherd and one flock (Jn 10) illustrates above all the inner unity and compactness of the Church, but also her universality; for all men, Jew as well as Gentile, will one day be members of her flock (11:52; 17:20 ff.). [72] The transfer to Peter of the office of shepherd will ensure the unity of the Church in the future as well. The secret inner life of the Church shines forth in the figure of the vine and its branches. Only in close and permanent attachment to the true vine, Christ, do the members of the Church possess life; only if they remain in

---

[69] For what follows cf. esp. R. Schnackenburg, *Die Kirche im Neuen Testament* (Freiburg i. Br. 1961) 93–106, Eng. tr. *The Church in the New Testament* (Freiburg-New York-London 1965).

[70] E. Schweizer, "Der johanneische Kirchenbegriff" in *Studia Evangelica* (Berlin 1959), 363–81, esp. 379.

[71] R. Schnackenburg, *Die Johannesbriefe* (Freiburg i. Br. 1953), 155–62.

[72] For the origin of the supplementary chapter from Johannine tradition, cf. M.-E. Boismard, "Le chapitre 21 de S. Jean" in *RB* 54 (1947), 473–501.

this community do they remain also in him and be capable of bringing forth fruit.

According to the evangelist's view, the Church is called to bear witness, in the midst of a hostile world, to the risen Christ and to the salvation brought by him. (15:26–27). This leads to conflict with the world and so inevitably to actual martyrdom: the Church becomes a church of martyrs. It is a theme to which the Apocalypse constantly returns, whether the Church be regarded under the image of the heavenly woman[73] who has to fight and overcome the dragon (Rev. 12), or whether she be represented as those who follow the Lamb (14:1–5; 13:7–10). The fellowship of the followers of the Lamb here on earth is strengthened in its constancy by the sight of the perfect brethren who have already conquered, "for they loved not their lives, even unto death" (12:11), and have overcome Satan "by the blood of the Lamb and the word of their testimony" (ibid.). Thus is completed the bridge between the heavenly and the earthly Church, who, as the bride of the Lamb, is on the way to her marriage, to her own perfecting. When she reaches the goal of her journey, she will live on as the new Jerusalem in the kingdom of God at the end of the world.

This majestic view of the perfected Church was proclaimed, as a message of comfort and encouragement, to the actual Church of the late first century, oppressed by the persecution of Domitian.[74] In the fortifying possession of such a vision, she strode out boldly towards her objective. Out of these riches she was able to renew her steadfastness in the faith, whenever she was called upon to give further concrete witness to it.

[73] Cf. J. Sickenberger, "Die Messiasmutter im 12. Kapitel der Apokalypse" in *ThQ* 126 (1946), 357–427.

[74] R. Schütz, *Die Offenbarung des Johannes und Kaiser Domitian* (Göttingen 1933).

The Post-Apostolic Age

WITH the death of the last of the apostles the young Church lost the last leading figure who could be invoked as an eye-witness to the life, death and resurrection of the Lord. Her destinies were now entrusted to a new generation which was, however, conscious of being in a unique way pledged to maintain the traditions of the apostles. Therefore the post-apostolic age represents a phase in the history of the Church which can be regarded as a direct development of what was already begun. In points of detail, the Church of that period did indeed display characteristics which mark her off from the apostolic Church in the strict sense. Her mission field remained essentially the same as in the previous generation, which, starting out from Antioch, had taken a decisive step by addressing her preaching to the world of Hellenistic civilization. Missionary successes had evidently not been revolutionary either in numbers or in the social rank of the new adherents, even though a numerical increase, especially in the big cities of the empire, was clearly perceptible. Because of this, Christianity was to an increasing degree awakening the interest of its pagan surroundings; local persecutions occurred, usually caused by the antipathy of the local population, whereas the pagan State had as yet no definite policy in its relationship to the new religion. The chief development in the post-apostolic age was within the Church, and for our knowledge of it, the primary sources are the writings of the apostolic Fathers which began to appear at this time.

One can hardly speak of a deeper understanding or development of the central themes of Pauline theology. The favourite subject of theological discussion remained the controversy with Judaism, carried on however in a form so steeped in Jewish ideas that at first it might rather be called a theology of Jewish Christianity. Only in the works of the apologists do we perceive a Christianity more strongly affected by the religious philosophy of Hellenism; conflict with this and with Gnosticism (now a keen rival), necessitated a further theological development and represents a new phase in the history of the early Church.

The religious practice of the post-apostolic age remained, both in the narrower sacramental sphere of baptism and Eucharist and in its daily expression in prayer and asceticism, largely that established by apostolic tradition. Only in the question of discipline did the Church seek solutions for new problems which arose from the lapses of individual Christians during times of persecution. The greatest progress is probably to be seen in the further development of ecclesiastical organization, which gave each congregation a monarchical episcopate, whose jurisdiction was clearly defined. This arrangement became general. At the same time a growing consciousness of the underlying union of all Christian congregations with one another is apparent, expressing itself in cordial relations between them, in personal visits, in correspondence and in solicitude for the welfare of other congregations; in this respect, the church of Rome felt itself obliged by a higher degree of responsibility for all the others. The unity of all who confessed Christ in the Roman Empire was believed to be what the founder of the Church demanded. They also believed that in the episcopate set up by him and based on the apostolic succession they possessed a guarantee of that unity.

CHAPTER 8

The Conflict between Christianity and the Roman State Power

The Beginnings of the Conflict

THE Christian communities which sprang up in the cities of the Roman Empire at the beginning of the Church's missionary activity were bound, sooner or later, to attract the attention of their pagan neighbours on account of their marked aversion from everything connected with pagan worship. From the beginning this interest had a hostile tendency, all the more remarkable inasmuch as such a reaction on the part of the pagan masses towards new religious cults from the East (except for a few outbreaks against the Jews) was otherwise unusual. Besides, these non-Christian oriental cults generally conducted a lively propaganda, which in places met with considerable success. The cause of this hostile attitude on the pagan side towards the adherents of the Christian religion must, therefore, be sought in the latter itself. It lay ultimately in the claim to absolute truth with which the Christian faith entered the world, a claim which evidently could not be tolerant towards any other religion and was bound to involve the Church in a conflict of principles with the Roman State religion. There now appeared in the Roman Empire, for the first time, a religious movement which did not look upon its God merely as a special divinity, but as the only true God and Redeemer of the world, beside the worship of whom none other might exist. As the Christians also drew the practical conclusion from their convictions in daily life and cut themselves off absolutely from their pagan surroundings, they gradually came to appear to the latter as declared enemies of classical culture, permeated as it was by religion.

The hostile atmosphere thus created was demonstrably nourished by the Jews of the Diaspora, who could not forgive the Jewish Christians for their apostasy from the faith of their fathers. The way the Christians shunned contact with the outside world continually provided fresh fuel for and an appearance of credibility to those dark rumours which accused them of sexual immorality at their nocturnal meetings, and revolting practices in their religious worship. All this formed the soil from which grew that general opinion of the Christians as a low rabble who had only too much reason to avoid the light of publicity. A trifling occasion was therefore often sufficient for the mistrust and stored-up resentment of the pagan population to vent themselves in outbreaks of persecution. Sometimes during these, adherents of the new faith were deprived by mob justice of goods or life, or dragged before the civil authorities with loud demands for punishment.

The Christians themselves always felt such proceedings to be unjust persecution and showed little understanding of the fact that their religious exclusiveness offered some grounds for them. For this reason, the sources of our knowledge of the conflict between Christianity and paganism in pre-Constantinian times are of a peculiar nature and need careful consideration. Both separate descriptions and general accounts of the so-called persecutions were nearly all the products of Christian pens; a detailed history of them from the pagan point of view does not exist. In later Christian historical writing, the Christian attitude towards the events has understandably prevailed, showing on one side only the brutal persecutor who was later stricken down by well-merited divine punishment, and on the other the elect and the just, who by their steadfast witness deserved an imperishable heavenly crown. The view of writers like Lactantius and Eusebius have determined the image of the persecutions right down to modern times. The number of them was said to have been ten, because by mystical anticipation they were thought to have been prefigured in the ten plagues of Egypt.

With the abandonment of this traditional scheme, a more objective estimate of the question has become possible which has led us to recognize two important points: first, that it will not do to look upon every Roman emperor or provincial governor, under whose rule or administration Christians were put to death, as a man who persecuted them in blind rage solely because of their faith. The causes in individual cases differed widely and must be separately assessed. Moreover, the initiative for reprisals against the Christians did not come primarily from the State authorities; it was contrary to the principles of Roman religious policy to proceed with the power of the State against the adherents of a religious movement solely because of their beliefs. No doubt, the close connexion between the Roman religion and the State was regarded as one of the main supports of the empire. If, in Republican times, the invasion of foreign cults from the East was looked on with mistrust, and if, in 186 B.C. on the occasion of the famous affair of the Bacchanalia, certain counter-measures were taken, these were not primarily directed against the religious convictions of the adherents of a new cult, so much as against the immoral excesses which it brought in its train, making it a danger to Roman morality and therefore, indirectly, to the public good. The same motives later prompted the Roman authorities to take proceedings against soothsayers, astrologers and charlatans who caused political unrest by their horoscopes and prophecies.[1]

This policy was continued during the first century of the empire. The cult of the emperor, as it developed into divine worship such as Augustus received in the eastern provinces, did indeed become a new and essential component of the State religion. But its external form, its ritual, developed only slowly, so that the conscious rejection of emperor worship on the part of the Christians, could but seldom, in the first century, have been the motive for proceedings against them by the State. Only on isolated occasions did emperors like Nero and Domitian press certain prerogatives of the emperor cult and thus provoke conflicts which, however, did not affect the Christians exclusively.

The pagan State power first began to notice the special character of the new religious movement only because of the disturbances that occurred between Christians and Jews or pagans, and then it had to step in, in order to get these tumults under control. Only then, did the authorities gradually become convinced that the religious peace which had reigned hitherto, was being disturbed by the Christians and that the latter in fact constituted a threat to the customary religious policy of the empire. Only after closer observation did it become clear that the Christians also rejected the Roman State religion on principle and thus, in the opinion of the government, jeopardized the State itself. So the pagan State power can be mentioned only with certain limitations when we list the factors to which the persecution of the Christians is to be attributed. The primary cause was rather the claim to absoluteness made by the Christian religion itself; a secondary cause was the hostile attitude of the pagan population. Only in the third century did the conflict between Christianity and the pagan State become one of principle, when the latter thought it saw in the new religion a power that threatened its own existence.

[1] Cf. J. Moreau, *La persécution du christianisme dans l'empire romain* (Paris 1956), 15–19.

Such a view of the circumstances in no way precludes unrestricted admiration for the attitude of the Christian martyrs, who professed their religious convictions with exemplary heroism and defended, for all time, freedom of conscience in the face of all earthly power.

The Persecutions under Nero and Domitian

The first case that can be verified with certainty in which a Roman State authority was closely concerned with a Christian has hitherto been thought to have been that of the apostle Paul who, invoking his right as a Roman citizen, appealed to Caesar when brought before the procurator Porcius Festus in 59 and was, therefore, taken to Rome. The proceedings apparently ended, as we have already mentioned, with an acquittal. Paul's religion was evidently not regarded as offending against the existing laws or public order. Recently, however, it has been claimed that indications have been found of an anti-Christian attitude on the part of the Roman State which may be dated to the beginning of Claudius's reign. This emperor, in a letter discovered in 1920,[2] was answering the complaints which had been brought to him by a Jewish (and Greek?) delegation from Alexandria which simultaneously conveyed a congratulatory address on his accession. The emperor specifically forbade the Jews of the Egyptian capital to invite thither fellow-countrymen from Syria or Egypt; if they disobeyed in this matter he would be compelled "to proceed against them with every means, since they would spread, as it were, a kind of pestilence over the whole world."[3] This "pestilence" has been understood as the Christian religion, which was then being propagated by its missionaries in Egypt and elsewhere in the Roman Empire. The text of Claudius' letter does not, however, force us to such an interpretation; its wording can without difficulty be understood as referring to the continual quarrels of the Jewish inhabitants of Alexandria among themselves and with the Greek population, which had repeatedly led to bloodshed. It is, moreover, against all probability that the Jews, in order to strengthen their position, should admit into the Egyptian capital precisely those Jews who had become converts to Christianity.

Another action of the same emperor can, with much greater justification be connected with Christian missionary work in Rome; it is mentioned by Dio Cassius and Suetonius. Claudius expelled the Jews from Rome

[2] This is the London Papyrus 1912, published by J. Idris Bell, *Jews and Christians in Egypt* (London 1924); see also S. Lösch, *Epistula Claudiana* (Rottenburg 1930); H. Janne, "La lettre de Claude aux Alexandrins et le christianisme" in *APhilHistOS* 4 (1936), 273–95; H. Idris Bell, *Cults and Creeds in Greco-Roman Egypt* (Liverpool 1954), 78 ff.; F. F. Bruce, "Christianity under Claudius" in *BJRL* 44 (1961–2), 309–26.
[3] *Pap. Lond. 1912*, 98–100.

because they were continually in conflict among themselves, the conflict being provoked by a man called Chrestos. [4]

An identification of this Chrestos with Christ positively obtrudes itself; and we may here be seeing the first effects of the Christian message among the Jewish community of Rome. The married couple Aquila and Priscilla, were also affected by the emperor's expulsion order, and they thereupon took up residence at Corinth, where they gave hospitality to Paul when he was preaching there about the years 49–50 (Acts 18:2–4). It may be assumed that the Jewish couple had already embraced Christianity, but were included in the imperial order simply because they belonged to the Jewish race. The emperor's action is, therefore, not yet to be regarded as anti-Christian; it was merely intended to put an end to a centre of unrest among the Roman population.

The earliest example of adherents of the Christian faith being persecuted by Roman authorities remains therefore the events which befell the Christian community at Rome after the burning of the city under Nero in the year 64. The account which Tacitus gives in his Annals provides valuable information about the background to these occurrences. [5] A remarkably persistent rumour was circulating among the people that Nero himself was responsible for the conflagration which on 16 July 64 destroyed several districts of the city completely and others in part. To get rid of this suspicion, the emperor (Tacitus reports) diverted it onto the Christians, "who on account of their misdeeds were hated". Some men, who had been arrested and charged, were bribed to denounce the Christians as the actual culprits. The latter were then seized in large numbers (ingens multitudo) and executed in the ways reserved for arsonists: some of the Christians were sewn into the skins of animals and thrown to wild dogs, others were clothed in inflammable materials and used as living torches after dark in Nero's gardens, which he threw open to the public for the spectacle. Tacitus had no doubt that the Christians were unjustly accused of arson, even though he believed that they deserved the severest punishments on account of their other crimes. He did not, therefore, share the compassion which was shown towards them at the time "because they were sacrificed to gratify the cruel whim of one man". Tacitus' description, no doubt correct in essentials, shows us that the Christian community at Rome in the seventh decade of the first century had a considerable number of members, for *ingens multitudo* certainly implies more than a handful. Furthermore, it is clear that the motive of the persecution by Nero was not his belief that the new religion constituted a threat to the State. In carrying out his plan he made unscrupulous use of the hostile attitude of the population towards the

---

[4] Suetonis, *Claud.* 25, 4: "Judaeos impulsore Chresto assidue tumultuantis Roma expulit."
[5] On the interpretation of Tacitus' account (*Annal.* 14, 44) cf. esp. H. Fuchs, *VigChr* 4 (1950), 65–93, and K. Büchner, *Humanitas Romana* (Heidelberg 1957), 229–39.

Christians, but he was not aiming at the Christian faith as such. Later Christian apologists, of course, generally regarded him as the first Roman emperor who persecuted Christianity from religious motives; according to Lactantius, Nero's proceedings had as their objective the complete extirpation of Christianity.

The statements about a persecution of the Christians which Clement of Rome made in his letter to the congregation of Corinth before the end of the century no doubt also refer to the events under Nero. He is the first Christian writer to mention them. Without naming Nero directly, he says that not only did Peter and Paul suffer a violent death, but also "a great number of the elect", among them women, had died after cruel tortures. [6] The reference to the great number and the manner of execution hardly admits room for doubt that we are here reading of the same events that Tacitus describes.

Lactantius is the only author who states that the Roman persecution under Nero was not confined to the capital but included the whole empire. This is improbable, for the other sources are silent on this matter and Lactantius possesses in other respects no exact knowledge of the events in Nero's reign. It would, besides, imply that the measures taken in 64 were not due to a passing caprice, but were based upon a law valid for the empire as a whole. Tertullian indeed says, when telling of the persecution under Nero, that all the proceedings of that cruel emperor were subsequently declared null and void, with one exception: the proscription by him of the Christian name was the only *institutum Neronianum* that was not removed by his *damnatio memoriae*. [7] Many modern historians quote this statement, assuming from it that a general edict of persecution was issued by Nero. [8]

The following considerations, however, are decisively against such an assumption. An edict of that kind must have had effects in the whole empire, and therefore in the East also; but all the sources, and, in particular, those for the East, say nothing of it. Moreover, at the beginning of the sixties, Christianity was hardly of such importance to the Roman Government that the latter should have had any occasion to take legal measures against it. What speaks most strongly against the existence of a Neronian edict of persecution, is the fact that never in later times did the Roman authorities base their attitude towards the Christian problem on such a decree. So Tacitus' account possesses in this matter also a greater degree

---

[6] Clement, *Ep. ad Cor.* 6.

[7] Tertullian, *Ad. nat.* 1, 7, 9: "et tamen mansit erasis omnibus hoc solum institutum Neronianum."

[8] E.g. J. Zeiller in *Fliche-Martin* I, 292; H. Grégoire, *Les persécutions dans l'empire romain* (Brussels 1951), 25 ff.; J. Beaujeu, *La religion romaine à l'apogée de l'empire I* (Paris 1955), 107.

of credibility; Nero's action against the Christians had no legal foundation, but sprang from the arbitrary will of the ruler, who thereby hoped to cleanse himself from the suspicion of arson. Nevertheless, public opinion regarding the Christians was certainly influenced by Nero's persecution of them; and Tertullian's words are no doubt to be understood in this sense. The vague feeling in the mind of the pagan masses that the Christians were a suspect lot, capable of dark crimes, was, as it were, sanctioned by their execution. From that time on, to be a Christian was to be an outlaw in the eyes of the people; what Nero had begun (id quod a Nerone institutum est), the moral proscription of the name of Christian, persisted for a long time. In the future, the Roman authorities could always find support from public opinion whenever the circumstances obliged them, in any particular case, to face the question whether the State should take action against the Christians or tolerate them. It is not hard to understand how this view of Christianity should gradually acquire the force of a principle of law by which the legal position of the Christians in the empire was largely determined.

The sources tell us far less about the persecution which the Christians endured under the emperor Domitian, though there is no doubt that it took place. There is first the clear and unequivocal statement of Melito of Sardes, who was fairly close in time to the event. He, in his apologia for the emperor Marcus Aurelius, mentions Domitian alongside Nero as an opponent of Christianity.[9] The remarks of the Roman Bishop Clement in his letter to the Corinthians (1:1), saying that the perils and tribulations which had suddenly fallen upon the Christians had prevented his writing sooner, can, moreover, hardly be interpreted otherwise than as a reference to measures taken by that emperor against the Christians.[10] Some statements of non-Christian authors can also be understood in this sense. Epictetus' reproach to the Christians that they went foolishly and thoughtlessly to their death,[11] implies that they were being persecuted, as does the remark of the elder Pliny, in his letter to Trajan,[12] that certain alleged Christians had asserted in court the fact of their renunciation of Christianity twenty years before.

Special importance seems due to the statement of Dio Cassius[13] to the effect that the consul Flavius Clemens and his wife Domitilla had been accused and condemned on account of "godlessness" (ἀθεότης), and with them "many others, who favoured Jewish practices". As Dio Cassius a little later calls the crime of these persons ἀσέβεια, it becomes clear that here is meant the *crimen laesae majestatis*, the crime of which the Christians

---

[9] *Euseb. HE* 4, 26, 9.
[10] J. Vogt, "Christenverfolgungen" (historical) in *RAC* II (1954), 1168.
[11] Epictetus, *Diss.* 4, 7, 6.
[12] Pliny the Younger, *Ep.* 10, 96, 6.
[13] Dio Cassius, 67, 14, 1–2.

were said to be guilty when, in the second century, they were accused of atheism. If the author here refers, as he evidently does, to Christians — he never mentions them by that name anywhere in his work — the accusation of godlessness makes intelligible the motive behind Domitian's action: it was the emperor's claim to absoluteness for his own person, expressed in the demands of a cult that knew no limitations. Certain references in the Apocalypse also fit in with this view of the facts if one accepts that it was written, at least in its present form, in the last years of the first century, as there are strong grounds for supposing. [14] According to the Apocalypse, the persecution of the Church which the author saw approaching, had, for its cause, the clash between emperor-worship on Domitian's pattern and the Christian idea of God. To the congregations of Asia Minor especially, Domitian's claim to divine honours must have been a heavy blow, because the flourishing imperial cult in that region hardly permitted any avoidance of the conflict. The pretext for the persecution in the eastern provinces was, therefore, based solely on the accusation of *lèse-majesté* which rejection of emperor-worship involved.

The sources make few concrete statements about the extent of the persecution and the number of its victims. We may believe the words of Dio Cassius that in Rome, besides the above-named consular pair, "many others" were implicated. That the consul for the year 91, Acilius Glabrio, likewise condemned to death by Domitian, was also executed for his Christian belief, cannot be proved, but the possibility is not to be excluded. In any case we must not try to support this view by reference to an archaeological discovery which has often been adduced as proof: the so-called crypt of the Acilii in the catacomb of Priscilla is not of earlier date than the middle of the second century. [15] Nor can the nucleus of the present catacomb of Domitilla on the Via Ardeatina be proved to be a burial place founded by the Roman lady put to death by Domitian, even though inscriptions suggest that Domitilla had connexions with the district where it lies. [16] As Dio Cassius states, the emperor Nerva did not accept the accusations of godlessness and Jewish practices and so the persecution ceased.

The Court Trials of Christians under Trajan and Hadrian

Of the legal position of the Christians during the reign of Trajan (98–117) and of the proceedings of the authorities in Asia Minor, in particular, we should know nothing if we had only Christian sources to rely on. The

[14] See above, chapter 7.
[15] Cf. A. M. Schneider, *Festschr. Akad. Wiss. Göttingen* 2 (1951), 182–90.
[16] L. Hertling and E. Kirschbaum, *Die römischen Katakomben und ihre Märtyrer* (Vienna, 2nd ed. 1955), 44–46.

official question addressed to the emperor by a governor of Bithynia, as to what principle he should follow in certain border-line cases when dealing with Christians, shows clearly that in that Asiatic province numerous persons were denounced to the authorities as Christians, tried and examined, and, if they remained true to their faith, executed. Together with the answer, which the emperor personally sent to the governor in the form of a rescript, this correspondence between Pliny the younger and his imperial master[17] gives us an opportunity to study the attitude which the Government of the empire adopted towards Christianity at the beginning of the second century.

Pliny, who took office in 111 or 112, gives us welcome information about the situation of the Christian religion as he found it in his province. It had already found many adherents outside the towns among people of all classes and ages. The reason why the governor was concerned with the Christian community was the fact that many of its members did not obey the imperial decree banning the *hetairies,* associations unrecognized by the State. These Christians were denounced to the governor, sometimes even anonymously. Pliny first established by examination that they were Christians and then ordered them, with threats of the death penalty, to give up their religion. Only when they obstinately persisted in it did he have them put to death, with the exception of those who were Roman citizens; these were, in accordance with the law, kept apart from the others that they might be transported to Rome for their cases to be heard.

Various occurrences during the trials, however, caused doubts to arise in the mind of the governor as to whether the method employed was legally correct; it sometimes came out at the hearings that many denunciations were made solely from motives of spite; in a long list of names of alleged Christians the accusers were anonymous. Many of those denounced asserted that they had never been Christians; they confirmed this by calling on the gods or by sacrificing before their images or before that of the emperor. Others claimed that they had long since renounced Christianity and likewise sacrificed to the gods and the emperor; they even emphasized their recantation by reviling the God of the Christians. The examination of those who confessed themselves Christians before the governor disclosed no crime against the existing laws, even when torture was applied.

Pliny formulated his scruples in a few precise questions addressed to the emperor. Must the age of the accused be taken into consideration? May one grant pardon if one of them recants? Is it the name alone (of Christian) which is to be punished, even when there are no other crimes? Are only those crimes to be punished which are associated with the name of Christian? Finally, Pliny tried to suggest an answer to the emperor which would

[17] Both documents are in Pliny the Younger, *Ep.* 10, 96, 97.

enable him to proceed with leniency: if he were indulgent towards the penitent, he might expect to win back a large number to paganism.

One thing appears clearly from Pliny's letter: the governor of Bithynia was unaware of any law or decree of the State which might serve as a norm in proceedings against adherents of the Christian faith. He does not at all ask how this or that formulation of a law should be interpreted or amplified. His dilemma is simply this: does the mere name of Christian suffice as grounds for persecution, or must other crimes be proved?

Trajan's answer confirms equally unmistakably that there was no general law regulating proceedings against Christians; the situation was still in the emperor's opinion such that he could establish no universally valid norm. He gave Pliny certain directives intended to lighten his difficulties — Christians were not to be sought out, anonymous accusations were to be ignored. A man denounced as a Christian was to be examined; if he denied his Christianity and confirmed his denial by invoking the Roman gods, he was not to be punished even if he had formerly been a Christian. Only he who on examination confessed himself to be a Christian and persisted in his confession was to be punished. Proof of crimes against other laws was therefore not to be demanded; the mere fact of being a Christian sufficed for condemnation.

The rescript of Trajan does not in any way attempt to give a reason for or to justify these principles; they were clearly self-evident and familiar to the emperor as an expression of the current public opinion about the Christians. The estimate of them which had grown up since Nero's time had become firmly established and was so general that even the Roman authorities could make this maxim their own: to be a Christian is something which is not allowed. That such a maxim was in contradiction to the acknowledged principles of Roman law shows the inconsistencies which the rescript contains. Although to be a Christian was already an offence, the authorities were not on their own initiative to seek out Christians. He who had made himself guilty of this crime could nevertheless escape punishment if he renounced his religion. It is noteworthy that even after this rescript the State authorities in the provinces were given wide freedom of action; according to the degree of the Roman official's independence from the pressure of pagan opinion, persecution could flare up in individual provinces and take extreme forms, or complete peace might reign. One positive advantage the Christians might feel they had gained, arose from the emperor's directive that no consideration was to be given to anonymous accusers; they were thereby protected from many vexations and might with the exercise of a little prudence expect to live in anyway relative security.

The sources give little information about the effects of Trajan's rescript. Thus we know no names of Christians who lost their lives in Bithynia, nor do we learn the fate of those who as Roman citizens were kept apart in order to be tried at Rome. Whether the references to persecutions in Polycarp's letter to the congregation of Philippi[18] apply to the reign of Trajan cannot be determined. There are only two martyrs whose names have been handed down that can with any certainty be attributed to this period. Bishop Simeon of Jerusalem, successor of James, met death by crucifixion at the age of 120 years.[19] Ignatius of Antioch was brought to Rome, probably being a Roman citizen, and was executed there while Trajan was still emperor, as Eusebius relates[20] on the authority of Irenaeus, without giving the exact date of his death. Reports of other martyrdoms under Trajan in later Acts are of such doubtful value that we can learn little from them.

Under Trajan's successor Hadrian (117–38) a governor again applied to the emperor for directions in his dealings with the Christians. The letter of the proconsul of the province of Asia Proconsularis, Getulius Serennius Granianus, to Hadrian is lost, but the emperor's answer to his successor in office, Minucius Fundanus, has been preserved by Justin, who included it in his *Apologia*.[21] Even more decisively than Trajan, Hadrian condemned anonymous denunciations of Christians and demands made by the mob for their punishment. Only when someone vouched with his name for the accusations was a Christian to be brought to trial, and only when it could be proved that the accused "had offended against the laws" was the governor to pronounce sentence "according to the gravity of the offence".

This rescript of Hadrian has been regarded as nothing more than a reaffirmation of the norms which Trajan had established.[22] In this view, the proof which the accuser had to produce would then be nothing more than evidence that the person named was a Christian. The proconsul, however, was to punish "according to the gravity of the offence". It is hard to see how in the mere fact of being Christian there could be any differences of degree in the eyes of the judge. The interpretation which Justin gives of the rescript is therefore more probable. According to him, Hadrian's attitude meant a relief for the Christians which went far beyond the norms fixed by Trajan; Christians could be punished only if they could be proved to have committed crimes against the existing laws of the State. Hadrian does not indeed exclude the possibility of prosecution for merely being a Christian, but he appears to have demanded proof that the accused had offended against Roman law. Be that as it may, the rescript was only giving guidance to a proconsul on how to act in his own province. Elsewhere

---

[18] Polycarp, *Phil.* 9, 12.
[19] *Euseb. HE* 3, 32, 3, 6 according to Hegesippus.
[20] *Euseb. HE* 3, 36, 3; Irenaeus, *Adv. haer.* 5, 28, 4.
[21] Justin, *Apol.* 68, 5–10; *Euseb. HE* 4, 9.
[22] W. Schmid, *Maja 7* (1955), 5–13; J. Moreau, *op. cit.* 48.

a Roman administrator could well follow the maxim that the *nomen Christianum* in itself was worthy of punishment.

There is every indication that Hadrian's rescript perceptibly ameliorated the position of the Christians. No document mentions an actual or even an alleged martyrdom in the province of Asia Proconsularis, nor can executions of Christians in other parts of the empire be attributed with certainty to the reign of Hadrian.

The principle that the mere fact of being a Christian was punishable remained the general norm during the rest of the second century, as is proved by several martyrdoms under Hadrian's successor Antoninus Pius (138–61). Justin adds to the appendix of his *Apologia* an account which relates, obviously with an exact knowledge of the details, the execution of three Christians at Rome,[23] who because of their steadfast profession of faith were condemned to death by the prefect of the city. The *Shepherd* of Hermas, with its remarks about Christians who remained constant or relapsed, likewise presupposes proceedings against them under Antoninus Pius.[24] The part played by the pagan populace in the carrying out of legal procedure against a Christian is made very clear in the report which the congregation of Smyrna gave on the death of their Bishop Polycarp.[25] In the form of a letter to the Christian community of Philomelion, the Christians of Smyrna relate how the pagans of the city, making a tumult, demanded of the magistrates that the bishop, who had fled, should be sought out and brought to judgment. As he refused to deny Christ he was condemned to death at the stake and burnt in the theatre. Fixing the date of this martyrdom does indeed involve some difficulties; but placing it in the reign of Marcus Aurelius, as Eusebius does, demands such a number of weakly-based hypotheses that the traditional view that Polycarp died under Antoninus Pius seems to be preferable.[26]

This survey of the persecutions of Christians in the Roman Empire from the time of Nero to the middle of the second century leads us to the following conclusions. There was no general law that governed the attitude of the State towards the Christians. Out of the hostile feeling of the pagan population there developed an opinion that regarded being a Christian as incompatible with the Roman way of life; from this arose a kind of legal maxim that made it possible for the authorities to punish adherence to Christianity as a crime in itself. The persecutions that resulted were only local, occurred only sporadically and were directed against individual

[23] Justin, *Apol. append.* 2.
[24] Hermas, *Past. Vis.* 2, 2–3; 3, 6–7; 4, 2, 5.
[25] *Martyr. Polycarp.* 3, 2.
[26] Cf. H. Grégoire, "La date du martyre de Polycarpe" in *AnBoll* 69 (1951), 1–38; E. Griffe in *BLE* 52 (1951), 170–7; 54 (1953), 178–81; H.-I. Marrou in *AnBoll* 71 (1953), 5–20.

Christians. They were generally sparked off by popular disturbances, and only because of these did the State authorities intervene. The number of victims was relatively small.

CHAPTER 9

The Religious World of the Post-Apostolic Age as
Mirrored in its Writings

IF we turn from the letters of the New Testament to the writings of the post-apostolic age, we are immediately struck by the vast difference in form and content between the latter and the former. The writers of this period are but epigones of the great figures of the apostolic era. They took up the pen almost hesitantly in order to discuss questions concerning the Christian interpretation and ordering of life. In so far as we can clearly identify individual personalities among these writers, they have been given the honorary title of "Apostolic Fathers," to express the fact that they were conscious of being close to the time and world of the apostles. They felt themselves to be only followers of those great men, whose stature they did not in any way reach. Even Ignatius of Antioch, pre-eminent emong them for his lively religious sense, knew that he could not at all compare himself with them,[27] and Clement of Rome saw in "the excellent apostles" the unattainable ideal for his own generation.[28]

The regard in which the apostles were held remained undiminished, as is shown by those apocryphal writings which soon appeared, seeking to gain a heightened interest for themselves by the use of titles such as *Letter of the Apostles, Missionary Sermon of Peter, Letter of Barnabas, Acts of Paul, Acts of John,* etc.[29] Post-apostolic writings were largely nourished by the legacy of the apostles; what the apostolic fathers had to say was the echo and result of apostolic tradition. The pictures they paint of the religious life and thought of their time is for that very reason deserving of special attention.

The series of apostolic fathers begins with Clement of Rome, who is held to be the author of a lengthy letter addressed by the Roman congregation to the church of Corinth shortly before the end of the first century. Clement evidently wrote the letter in his capacity as leader of the Roman congregation, as is asserted by the most ancient tradition,[30] even though his

---

[27] Ignatius, *Rom.* 4, 3.
[28] 1 *Clem* 5:2.
[29] Some of them belong to the first half of the second century, cf. *Altaner,* 72–83.
[30] Thus Hermas, *Past. Vis.* 2, 4, 3; Irenaeus, *Adv. haer.* 3, 3, 3. Above all there is the tradition of Corinth itself, maintained by Bishop Dionysius in a letter to Pope Soter: *Euseb. HE* 4, 23, 11.

position in the list of Roman bishops cannot be determined with certainty. The occasion of this letter was the report of a regrettable schism within the Corinthian church, which led to the removal from office of presbyters of proved worth by a group of younger members of the community. The Roman Christians felt themselves bound to their brethren in Corinth by strong ties of solidarity, because of which they earnestly admonished them to restore the unity of the Church.

In language and style, as well as in his handling of the subject, Clement shows his formal education no less than his religious and theological originality. Hellenistic philosophy, especially in its Stoic form,[31] was not unfamiliar to him, and he was highly receptive towards Hellenistic culture as a whole; but he stood closer to the world of the Old Testament and Jewish ways of thought, so that some have seen in Clement a convert from the Judaism of the Diaspora.[32] Especially informative about the personal piety of the author are those parts of the letter (chs. 59–61, 64) in which, as a Christian preacher, he addresses the congregation of Corinth and begs them to praise God in a prayer composed by him, just as he may often have concluded his homilies at religious assemblies in Rome. The letter also gives valuable information about office-holders in the early Church.

The most sharply defined figure among the apostolic Fathers is the bishop of a large Christian community in the East, Ignatius of Antioch, who during a wave of persecution was condemned to be thrown to wild beasts and suffered martyrdom at Rome in the last years of Trajan's reign (98–117). On the journey to the capital he wrote from the seaport town of Smyrna seven letters, three of which were addressed to the churches of Ephesus, Magnesia, and Tralles, members of which had come to Smyrna to visit the highly respected Bishop of Antioch. At Smyrna too he composed his epistle to the Roman Christians, whereas those to the Philadelphians, to the Christians of Smyrna, and to their bishop, Polycarp, were written at Troas. Their authenticity, in spite of some remarkable opinions put forward by a not unbiased "higher criticism", is now considered certain.

In attempting to assess the value of this *corpus Ignatianum* as a source of information on post-apostolic theology and religion, one must not overlook the fact that the seven letters were written more or less *extempore* by a prisoner condemned to death, under the eyes of his not very considerate gaolers. They are, therefore, not well-weighed theological treatises composed in conditions of tranquillity, but the spontaneous outpourings of a courageous leader, full of the love of Christ and a longing for martyrdom. All the more precious is this direct evidence, springing from the crowded

---

[31] L. Sanders, *L'hellénisme de S. Clément de Rome et le paulinisme* (Louvain 1943); W. C. van Unnik, "Is 1 *Clem* 20 purely Stoic?" in *VigChr* 4 (1950), 181–9.
[32] J. Daniélou, *La théologie du judéo-christianisme* (Paris 1958), 53–55, Eng. tr. *The Theology of Jewish Christianity* (London 1964).

life of the second century, concerning the beliefs, the piety and way of life in Christian communities at that time.

Polycarp of Smyrna, to whom one of the seven letters was addressed, was already bishop of that Asiatic see when he met Ignatius. As a bearer and transmitter of apostolic traditions he ranks high, for he had been, according to the testimony of his pupil Irenaeus, in direct contact with several of the apostles, whose eyewitness accounts of the life and teachings of the Lord he knew well. [33] As Polycarp met Pope Anacletus in Rome (*circa* 154–5 to 166–7), [34] the teachings handed down by the apostles were thus passed on to the second half of the second century by a highly qualified witness. Of the numerous pastoral letters that he wrote, [35] only one short note and a longer letter to the congregation of Philippi have been preserved, written shortly after the death of Ignatius. This letter gives us a valuable glimpse of the problems which seemed urgent to a Christian pastor of that time when he addressed the faithful of a congregation known to him.

Some of the writings attributable to the first or second post-apostolic generation are either anonymous or apocryphal, but they are nevertheless of great value as evidence concerning the religious life of the period. Chief of these is the "Doctrine of the Apostles", the *Didache*, which was probably written about the year 100 in Syria and incorporates a Jewish work on the "two ways". Its statements about circumstances within the Church oblige us to give it an early date, though some of its supplementary matter may have been written later. [36] Its editor's object was clearly to give newly-founded congregations in Syria a guide for the internal organization of their community life.

The so-called *Letter of Barnabas* — Alexandrian tradition early ascribed it to Paul's companion, though the text itself names no author — is the work of a Christian making no pretensions to learning, who after the destruction of Jerusalem and probably shortly before 130, engages in controversy with Judaism. In spite of his unfavourable estimate of the latter, which he reproaches with a fundamental misunderstanding of the Old Testament, his way of thinking is Jewish, and he is a witness to the Jewish-Christian character of post-apostolic theology. [37]

A strange, obscure work, the author of which calls himself Hermas, brings us to the end of the post-apostolic period. According to the Muratorian fragment, Hermas was a brother of Pius, bishop of Rome (*circa* 140–154). He gave his book the title of *The Shepherd* after the central figure, who

---

[33] *Euseb. HE* 5, 20, 6.
[34] Irenaeus in *Euseb. HE* 5, 24, 16.
[35] Ibid. 5, 20, 8.
[36] Thus A. Adam in *ZKG* 58 (1957), 1–47, whose opinion is to be preferred to that of Audet, *La Didachè* (Paris 1958), who considers an earlier date necessary.
[37] Cf. J. Daniélou, *op. cit.* 43–46.

appears in the second part as teacher of the Christians and preaches penance in commandments and parables. The first part is more apocalyptic in tone; in it the Church appears under various figures. A simple member of the community from a Jewish-Christian background here expresses himself about his own hard lot, interwoven with the description of which are sincere, sometimes naive, pictures of the life of the Church. The author is troubled about the lives of many Christians; without theological or speculative interests, he demands with great earnestness a moral reform of the Christian community. The *Shepherd* is a very important source for our knowledge of contemporary Christian ideas in Rome about the significance of penance in the life of the Church as a whole.

Finally there are the so-called second letter of Clement, probably the oldest extant example of a sermon delivered during a religious service (perhaps at Corinth) about the middle of the second century, and the *Epistula Apostolorum,* a work in letter-form which first gives alleged words of Christ to his disciples after his resurrection and then goes on to speak, like a kind of apocalypse, of the *parousia* of the Lord and of the resurrection of the body and the last judgment, as well as of the missionary work of the apostles, uttering at the same time a warning against false doctrines.

Besides these written documents, there also existed in post-apostolic times a mass of oral traditions which handed down the teachings of the apostles: the so-called traditions of "the Elders",[38] attested mainly by Papias and Clement of Alexandria. The former, according to Irenaeus "a pupil of John and companion of Polycarp",[39] zealously collected them from the elders or from those who had been in contact with them, as he himself relates;[40] by the "Elders" he probably means members of the earliest community at Jerusalem. Clement also stresses the fact that he had taken down from old presbyters oral traditions which went back to the time of the apostles.[41] As the presbyters of Clement cannot be identical with the Asiatic elders of Papias, they may have been descendants of Jewish Christians belonging to the original community who came to Alexandria after the destruction of Jerusalem. In content, these traditions of the elders concern the doctrine of angels, the interpretation of the first chapter of Genesis and chiliastic ideas, so that this stream of tradition also informs us about the nature of post-apostolic theology.

If we base an account of the theological principles and religious life of the post-apostolic age on this body of writings, we find that its most characteristic feature is the controversy with contemporary Judaism. This can be shown to have existed everywhere where numerous Christian

[38] Ibid. 55–64.
[39] Irenaeus, *Adv. haer.* 5, 33, 4.
[40] *Euseb. HE* 3, 39, 3–4.
[41] Clement of Alexandria, *Stromata* 1, 1, 11–12; *Euseb. HE* 6, 13, 8–9.

congregations encountered the Judaism of the Diaspora, especially therefore in Syria, Asia Minor, and Egypt, but also in Rome. The claim of the Jews to be the chosen people, the sole heirs of God's promises, was opposed from the Christian side with the thesis that after the unfaithfulness and falling away of the Jewish people the Christians were the true Israel, who had taken over the inheritance of the rejected nation.

This thesis is most strongly expressed by the author of the letter of Barnabas, but it also plays an important part in the writings of Ignatius of Antioch. God (the argument runs) did indeed once make his covenant with Israel, but the latter relapsed again and again into idolatry and thereby rejected it. The promises made to the people of the covenant were fulfilled when Jesus was recognized as the Messiah by a new people, the Christians.[42] Jewish invocation of the Old Law was in vain; the Jews in their literal-mindedness had so missed the sense of the Law's religious and ceremonial ordinances that their worship had become almost idolatrous, their attitude one of "lawlessness" ($\dot{\alpha}\nu o\mu\acute{\iota}\alpha$);[43] God had finished with them when he allowed the Temple to perish and gave mankind the "New Law of our Lord Jesus Christ".[44] The rejection of Jesus by the Jews was ultimately due to their misunderstanding of the Old Testament; they did not see that in him the promises of the Old Law were fulfilled. The christology of the post-apostolic age was largely characterized by this scriptural proof that Jesus was the Messiah, which was based upon testimony collected from the Old Testament itself.[45]

Whereas the strongly anti-Jewish attitude of Barnabas limited his view of the soteriological significance of Christ, this was more clearly seen by other post-Apostolic writers, as for example, Clement of Rome, who knew that Jesus had shed his blood for our salvation and thus atoned for the sins of the whole world;[46] even more clearly is this idea expressed by Ignatius of Antioch according to whom the flesh of Christ had suffered for our sins and won us eternal life, giving us a new relationship with the Father.[47] Anti-Jewish polemics figure largely in the *Didache,* which warns against Jewish fasting and prayers, but at the same time takes over Jewish elements for the liturgy of the Lord's supper.[48] In other writings of the time this anti-Jewish attitude is less evident, for instance in the first letter of Clement; while in the *Shepherd* of Hermas it actually gives way to one which is markedly friendly towards Judaism.

[42] Ps.-Barnabas, *Ep.* 4, 6–8; 14.
[43] Ibid. 9, 6; 16, 2.
[44] Ibid. 16, 5; 2, 6.
[45] M. Simon, *Verus Israel* (Paris 1948), 186 f.
[46] 1 *Clem* 8:1 f.
[47] Ignatius, *Smyrn.* 7, 1; *Trall.* 9, 2; *Eph.* 11, 1; *Rom.* 2, 2; 7, 2.
[48] *Didache* 8, 1 f.; 9–10.

The central place that the Lord gave to *prayer* in the religious life of his disciples remained unaffected in the Church of post-apostolic times. Christian prayer was still in many respects akin to that of the Jews; it was still addressed to the God of Abraham, Isaac, and Jacob, but every Christian knew that he was the Father of Jesus Christ. It also continued to employ Old Testaments forms, for the Old Testament had been inherited as a priceless possession by the new and true Israel. But a fresh note is audible in more than one of the prayers of this time — a note of victorious confidence, of buoyancy arising from the consciousness of being redeemed. Thus the Father is thanked with gladness for the new life which he has given to men in Jesus.[49] With joyous gratitude Polycarp thanks the Father of Jesus Christ for the gift of martyrdom; for this and for all things he praises and glorifies him now and for ever, confirming his thanks with the word *Amen* that had been taken into the Christian liturgy.[50] In the same tone of freshness is the great song of praise in the epistle of Clement, which does pray for the blessings which a Christian will always ask his God for: for peace and justice in this world, as well as for help for those in distress and wisdom for the mighty. But it is ever mindful of the one great fact, that Christians have been chosen by the Father from among all men as being those who love the Father through his son Jesus Christ, by whom they have been made holy.[51]

In their hieratic restraint these texts unmistakably show their nearness to liturgical prayers as they were formulated by the bishops who conducted the eucharistic celebration. They are therefore addressed exclusively to the Father, according to the example of the Lord in his prayers; prayer is offered to the Father in the name of his son Jesus Christ, the high priest.[52] This does not mean that private prayers were not also quite early addressed to Jesus Christ; even Pliny (*circa* 112) knew that the Christians sang hymns to their Lord,[53] the prayers of the martyrs to Christ give us in their fullness and frequency an idea how familiar direct invocation of Christ must have been in the earliest times.[54]

The sacraments do not figure so prominently in the writings of the apostolic fathers as at a later period. Their ritual forms were still in process of development, but their essential place in the Christian life as a whole is clear. This is especially true of the sacrament of initiation, *baptism*. The *Didache*[55] stresses the importance of carrying out the rite properly;

---

[49] Ibid. 9, 2–5.
[50] *Martyr. Polyc.* 14, 1–3.
[51] 1 *Clem* 59–61.
[52] Ibid. 61:3.
[53] Pliny the Younger, *Ep.* 10, 96; for examples in the N.T., cf. 1 Tim 3:16; Rev 5:9–13.
[54] K. Baus, "Das Gebet der Märtyrer" in *TThZ* 62 (1953), 19–32.
[55] *Didache*, 7, 1–4.

immersion in "living" (flowing) water is desirable,[56] but in exceptional cases it suffices to pour water thrice over the head of the person to be baptized. More important is it that every time baptism should be administered "in the name of the Father, and of the Son, and of the Holy Spirit" — the trinitarian formula is the essential formula of baptism. This is what is meant when the *Didache* elsewhere[57] speaks of "baptism in the name of the Lord". The Christian was aware that in baptism he received the seal of the tri-personal God, to whose sovereignty he thereby submitted. The Pauline representation of baptism as a burial with Christ and a rising again with him is perhaps indicated by the practice of immersion as the regular form.

The importance of baptism was underlined by the requirement of a preparatory fast, to which both the person to be baptized and the one administering the sacrament were obliged, but in which, if possible, other members of the congregation were also to take part, for baptism concerned them all — a new member was being incorporated into the community of those who were united in belief in the Lord. That baptism would give a special character to the life of a Christian, that it would be like a suit of armour to him, is emphasized by Ignatius of Antioch, for whom the healing power of the baptismal water is founded upon the sufferings of Christ.[58] The author of the epistle of Barnabas is also aware of the profound connexion between the Cross and baptism; through the latter, the redemption by Jesus Christ becomes applicable to man, for it brings forgiveness of his sins.[59] Hermas also is convinced of this; the question of the meaning and effect of baptism is one with which he is much preoccupied. According to him it is the foundation of the Christian's life; "he plunges as a dead man into the water and emerges from it a living man".[60] In baptism Christians receive the seal of the Son of God, without which there is no salvation; only this sealing makes a man a disciple of Christ. It unites all who receive it in one Spirit, in faith and love, and it admits them into the kingdom of God, into the fellowship of the Church.[61] This seal can indeed be broken, the gifts conveyed by baptism can be lost; therefore every baptized person has a moral obligation "to keep the seal intact".[62]

Statements about the *Eucharist* in the writings of the post-apostolic age

---

[56] See T. Klausner, "Pisciculi" in *Festschrift F. J. Dölger* (Münster 1939), 157–60.
[57] *Didache*, 9, 5.
[58] Ignatius, *Polyc.* 6, 2; *Eph.* 18, 2.
[59] Ps.-Barnabas, *Ep.* 11, 1, 8.
[60] Hermas, *Past. Simil.* 9, 16, 4.
[61] *Past. Simil.* 9, 17, 4; 9, 16, 3; *Vis.* 3, 3, 10; 8, 2, 2–4.
[62] *Past. Simil.* 8, 6, 3; thus also 2 *Clem* 8:6; cf. F. J. Dölger, *Sphragis* (Paderborn 1911), 70–73.

are rarer and more restrained. It was celebrated on the Lord's Day. According to the *Didache,* it is a sacrifice the purity of which can be endangered by sin; therefore Christians ought to confess their sins before its celebration. Moreover, he who lives unreconciled to his neighbour ought not to take part in the eucharistic celebration. [63] The Eucharist has been given to Christians as food and drink which are above all earthly nourishment, for it gives eternal life through Jesus. [64] Ignatius of Antioch sees the Eucharist as a bond uniting all who believe in Christ. For the individual it is an elixir of life, an antidote against death, because it nourishes life in Christ and so guarantees resurrection to eternal life. [65] The man who excludes himself from it, because he will not confess "that it is the flesh of our Saviour Jesus Christ", lives under the threat of death. [66] Just as the Eucharist joins the individual to Christ, so it unites all the faithul among themselves, since they all partake of one flesh and one chalice at one altar. [67] But it can effect this unity only when celebrated in the presence of the rightful bishop or his delegate; "if a man is not within the sanctuary, he must refrain from the bread of God." [68] Eucharistic communion not only symbolizes the unity of the Church, it also creates it.

The outstanding feature of post-apostolic piety is its christo-centricity. The will of Christ is the norm for the moral life of Christians, his commandments govern their behaviour; the Son of God himself is now the Law. [69] Christ's life has become the model which his faithful follow, the imitation of Christ the basis of Christian piety, [70] which sees in martyrdom its noblest proof. [71] Certainly the Christian knew that behind the will of Christ there was the will of the Father; but this was revealed in the example of Jesus Christ, and he who followed it came to the Father or lived in the Father.

Life in Christ and the imitation of him represented an ideal towards which all indeed were to strive, but which many Christians failed to attain. Hence the admonitions of the bishops, who were constantly calling upon their congregations to imitate God and his Son. The failure of such Christians faced the young Church with a problem that found its expression

---

[63] *Didache,* 14, 12.

[64] *Didache* 10, 3 can hardly be understood as referring to Christian truth as such, as thanks have already been given for that in 10, 2. The eucharistic character of the prayers in *Didache* 9 and 10 being by no means certain, they cannot be taken into consideration here.

[65] *Eph.* 20, 2; *Smyrn.* 18, 2.

[66] *Smyrn.* 7, 1.

[67] *Phil.* 4.

[68] *Eph.* 5, 2.

[69] 1 *Clem* 3:4; Polyc., *Phil.* 4, 1; Ignatius, *Magn.* 13, 1; 2 *Clem* 3:4 f.; Hermas, *Past. Simil.* 8, 3, 2.

[70] 1 *Clem* 16:17; 33:7, 8; Polyc., *Phil.* 10, 1; Ignatius, *Eph.* 10, 3; *Trall.* 2, 1.

[71] Ignatius, *Rom.* 4, 2; 5, 3; 6, 3.

with some asperity in the *Shepherd* of Hermas. Most of the members of the Roman congregation had indeed remained faithful to the obligation of their baptism, and some had distinguished themselves in persecution as confessors or martyrs;[72] but others had been unable to bear this trial. They had vacillated, full of fear, considering whether to deny or to confess, and only after lengthy hesitation had they decided to suffer for the Christian name. In the face of a threatening new persecution, certain Christians seemed likely to adopt a similar wavering and timorous attitude.[73]

Besides this lack of hope and courage in the hour of danger, Hermas saw other failings in the Roman church. Tepidity and slackness had become widespread, because the desire for possessions and riches had seduced many from the practice of religion, and they lived the same kind of life as the pagans. For them persecution constituted the greatest danger, since they preferred earthly possessions to loyalty towards their Lord.[74] Another evil that was rife among the Roman congregation was ambition and striving after the first places, with regrettable consequences for the peace and unity of the faithful. The elders and deacons especially were liable to such rivalry.[75]

Did there exist a possibility of atoning for such grave failings, or had the offenders finally forfeited their salvation? The Shepherd tells Hermas that it would be in conformity with the Christian ideal if baptism remained the only way of forgiving sin; some teachers had made this a law. But God grants to all those who have fallen another chance to repent, for he knows to what trials man is subject on account of his frailty and the wiles of the Devil. However, if a man falls again and again, and every time wishes to atone by repentance, he is not to entertain any deceptive hopes: his salvation is in jeopardy.[76] There was evidently an opinion that repeated repentance was possible. Between this and the rigid doctrine mentioned above, Hermas desires to show a middle way, but like an anxious preacher he stresses with great earnestness that after this second opportunity of atonement has been granted, the forgiveness thus won must not again be imperilled at any price, all the more so as the "building of the tower" will soon be finished. Hermas therefore bases the impossibility of further repentance on eschatological grounds; soon the Church would be complete, and he who did not then find himself inside the tower, who did not belong as a pure member to the Church, could not be saved.[77] Hermas does not discuss the problem of the unforgivability of certain sins; but the question of repentance was already

---

[72] Hermas, *Past. Simil.* 8, 1, 16.

[73] Ibid. *Simil.* 9, 23, 2–5.

[74] Ibid. 8, 8, 1; 9, 1; 9, 20, 1.

[75] Ibid. 3, 9, 7; 8, 7, 4; 9, 26, 2.

[76] *Past. Mandat.* 4, 3.

[77] *Past. Vis.* 3, 5, 5.

a burning one about the year 140. The *Shepherd* gives us an instructive glimpse of the discussion it raised in the Roman congregation. In the third century it was to be taken up again on a broader basis and with louder repercussions.

CHAPTER 10

The Development of the Church's Organization

IN comparison with the development of theology in the post-apostolic age, progress in completing the ecclesiastical organization in that period was far more extensive and significant. The links which bound the constitution of the post-apostolic Church to the organization of the Pauline community were still indeed apparent; but everywhere a further development from the early beginnings is observable, leading to more highly organized forms both within the individual congregation and in the Church as a whole. This fact gives the post-apostolic age of the Church a special importance.

First of all, the individual congregation is more clearly defined as regards its significance and function as part of the Church's organism. The Christians of a city were now everywhere joined together in separate congregations or local churches. The church of God, dwelling far away in Rome, greets the church of God in Corinth; Ignatius addresses his letters to clearly defined local churches, to those of Ephesus and Magnesia, to the church which, in the territory of the Romans, stands first; the congregation of Smyrna sends to the church of God in Philomelion an account of the martyrdom of its bishop, Polycarp. [78] This joining together of the followers of Christ in a city to form a single congregation differs markedly from the organization of contemporary Judaism in the Diaspora, which had several synagogues in the same place, several congregations but smaller groups. [79]

There was no Christian that did not belong to such a local congregation. He joined with all his brethren in the eucharistic celebration, at which the unity of the post-apostolic congregation is most clearly apparent. Ignatius of Antioch unwearyingly proclaims this unity, which he seeks to explain by various images and comparisons: the congregation is like a choir whose singers praise the Lord with one voice, or like a company of travellers following the directions of its Lord. For the author of the first letter of Clement the unity of the congregation is symbolized by the harmony of the

[78] 1 *Clem prooem.;* the *inscriptiones* of the letters of Ignatius and the *Martyrium Polycarpi.*
[79] Cf. for Rome J. B. Frey, "*Le judaïsme à Rome aux premiers temps de l'église*" in *Biblica* 12 (1931), 129–56.

universe or by the arrangement of the human body, in which each member has its appropriate function. Hermas sees it in the image of a tower built upon the cornerstone that is Christ.[80]

This vital, compact unity of the congregation was a possession to be constantly guarded, for it could be dangerously threatened by the tendency to disputatiousness and petty jealousy which led to divisions in the community, or by self-will in interpreting Christ's teaching. Schism and heresy were therefore regarded as the great enemies of unity in the early Church, even though they were not as sharply distinguished from one another as in later times. There is hardly a written work of the post-apostolic period which does not mention the schismatic tendencies which appeared now here, now there; it was not always a definite splitting away hardening into irreconcilability, but often ambition, jealousy, or back-biting, which created a climate of dissatisfaction against which the *Didache* and pseudo-Barnabas gave warning, but which was also present in the Roman congregation at the time of Hermas.[81] More serious was the situation at Corinth, a congregation formerly distinguished by its spirit of brother-hood; although we cannot discover all the details of the events at Corinth, the epistle from Rome attributed to jealousy the deep division which had caused once leading members of the congregation to be removed from office — jealousy, which was the root of so many evils in the religious past of Israel and also even at that early date in the young Christian Church. The Roman congregation was profoundly grieved by these happenings and condemned them severely.[82]

To the apostolic fathers, the danger of heresy was even greater. As the pastoral and Johannine epistles had had to warn against heretical falsification of Christian doctrine, so it was also Asiatic Christianity in particular that was exposed to danger from heretical groups in post-apostolic times. Ignatius of Antioch directed his attack against spokesmen of Docetism, who said that Christ had not possessed a real body and asserted that the Jewish Law was still valid. There was only one attitude for members of the Christian community to adopt towards them, and that was strict avoidance of all association with them and a closer drawing together of the faithful among themselves, not only in Antioch, but also in Smyrna, Philadelphia, and Philippi. In Rome, too, Hermas knew of attempts to introduce strange doctrines.[83] The leaders of the Church organized the campaign against heresy with exhortations and with warnings to other congregations, almost

---

[80] Ignatius, *Magn.* 7, 1–2; *Eph.* 9, 2; *Philad.* 1, 2; *Rom.* 2, 2; 1 *Clem* 19:2–3; 20:1–4, 9–11; 37:5; Hermas, *Past. Vis.* 3 and *Past. Simil.* 9.

[81] *Didache*, 4, 3; Ps.-Barnabas, *Ep.* 19, 12; Hermas, *Past. Simil.* 8, 7, 4, *Past. Vis.* 3, 9, 7–10

[82] 1 *Clem* 4:1–7; 5–6; 54:1–2.

[83] Ignatius, *Smyrn.* 4, 1; *Philad.* 6, 2; *Polyc.* 7, 1; 6, 3; Hermas, *Past. Simil.* 8, 6, 5.

in the same way as they would soon have to do, with all energy, in opposing Gnosticism.

According to what is perhaps the oldest document of the post-apostolic period, the letter of the church of Rome to that of Corinth, the leaders of the congregation were divided into two groups: one bore the double designation of elders (presbyters, πρεσβύτεροι) and overseers (episcopi, ἐπίσκοποι), the other was represented by the deacons (διάκονοι). [84] At the end of the post-apostolic age we also meet in the *Shepherd* of Hermas the two names *overseers* or *elders* for the holders of leading offices in the Church, deacons and teachers being mentioned as well. [85] The *Didache* names only overseers and deacons, Polycarp on the other hand only elders and deacons.[86] Only the letters of Ignatius distinguish clearly between the three offices of overseers, elders and deacons. Every congregation had only one overseer or bishop, to whom the college of elders (priests) and deacons was subordinate. [87]

In Antioch and in a number of congregations in Asia Minor there existed therefore in the second decade of the second century a monarchical episcopate: the government of the church was assigned to one bishop, whereas elsewhere both previously and subsequently, this development was not complete, or at least our sources do not confirm that it was. The one office, which in apostolic times bore the double designation of episcop or presbyter, was divided into two and the term overseer or bishop reserved exclusively for the holder of the highest office in the congregation. The sources do not make it possible for us to follow the phases of this development, nor do they tell us if it took place everywhere in the same way. Soon after 150 the monarchical episcopate seems to have generally prevailed throughout the area of Christian expansion.

The apostolic fathers also partly worked out a theology of ecclesiastical offices, the authority of which is ultimately derived from God. He sent Jesus Christ, who gave the apostles the commission to proclaim the Gospel; they, in accordance with this commission, appointed overseers and deacons, whose places were to be taken at their death by other approved men who would continue their work among the faithful. Thus Clement of Rome[88] regarded the authority of heads of congregations as based upon Christ's commission to the apostles, from whom all power of government in Christian communities must be derived by uninterrupted succession.

Ignatius further developed the theology of the episcopate in another direction; he was the most eloquent advocate of the complete and

---

[84] 1 *Clem* 44:2–6.
[85] Hermas, *Past. Vis.* 2, 4, 2–3; 3, 5, 1; *Past. Simil.* 9, 26, 2; 9, 27, 2.
[86] *Didache* 15, 1; Polyc., *Phil.* 5, 3; 11, 1.
[87] Ignatius, *Magn.* 2, 1; 6, 1; *Philad.* 4; 1, 2; *Smyrn.* 8, 1; 12, 2; *Trall.* 2, 2–3; *Polyc.* 1, 2.
[88] 1 Cor 42; 44: 1–3.

unconditional bond of union between bishop and congregation. The latter was one with its bishop in thought and prayer; only with him did it celebrate *agape* and Eucharist. Its members should follow him in obedience as Christ did the Father; nothing should take place in the congregation without the bishop. Even the administration of baptism and the performance of marriage ceremonies were reserved to him.[89] Presbyters and deacons had a share in his authority; the faithful were to obey the presbyters as the apostles, and in the deacons they were to honour the law of God.[90] The bishop could demand such an attitude from his people only because he represented Christ to them; he who, like the teachers of false doctrines, rejected the authority of the bishops was a rebel against the Lord, who was the actual if invisible bishop of every congregation.[91] The office-holders for their part saw their mission wholly in the light of its supernatural origin and were conscious that in the fulfilment of their task they were guided by the Spirit. Ignatius felt himself thus guided when he urged the Philadelphians to be in agreement with their bishop and presbyters; he was conscious of being the possessor of heavenly mysteries, he knew things visible and invisible. To Polycarp of Smyrna the manner of his death was supernaturally revealed; the Spirit moved Clement of Rome to address his admonition to the Corinthians.[92]

Two factors then worked together in order that the bishop and his assistants might fulfill their official duty: the apostolic, that is, God-given origin of their authority, and guidance through the divine Spirit. Thus supported, they conducted the eucharistic celebration, presided at the *agape*, proclaimed the true doctrine and were guarantors of the purity of the Gospel, guardians of the apostolic traditions.

The working of the Holy Spirit was not, however, limited to the leaders of the congregation; it could be felt everywhere among the faithful. Clement of Rome saw in the faith, the wisdom and the chastity of the Corinthians special graces from the Spirit, which were shared by the congregations of Magnesia, Ephesus and Smyrna.[93] Individual members of such congregations claimed to possess very special gifts, like Hermas or the author of the epistle of Barnabas, who speaks of a deep "insight" which he was able to transmit only in part.[94] Charismatic gifts were therefore also present in post-apostolic times, and there were also, as in the earlier period, similar tensions between those of the laity who were favoured by the Spirit and the leaders of the community. This is especially apparent in the *Didache*, which gives to the "prophets" a special rank. They appear

---

[89] Ignatius, *Eph.* 4, 1; 5, 2; *Polyc.* 5, 2; *Trall.* 7, 1–2.
[90] Idem, *Smyrn.* 8, 1–2.
[91] *Trall.* 1, 1; 2, 1; *Magn.* 3, 2.
[92] *Philad.* 7, 1–2; *Eph.* 20, 2; *Martyr. Polyc.* 5, 2.
[93] 1 *Clem* 28:1–2; 48:5; Ignat., *Magn.* 14, 1; *Eph.* 9, 1–2; *Smyrn.* inscr.
[94] Ps.-Barnabas, *Ep.* 1, 4–5; Hermas, *Past. Vis.* 5, 5–7; *Past. Simil.* 9, 331.

as teachers, they devote themselves to the service of the poor and they have to "give thanks"; they therefore have a particular role in the assemblies. But they had to prove before the congregation their claim to special gifts; for there were false prophets who did not preach the truth and were out to make money. Recognition was due to the tried and true prophet; he was above criticism, to submit him to judgment would have been to sin against the Lord.[95] One has the impression that the editor of the *Didache* is here fighting for a prophetic ideal which was sinking in general esteem, no doubt in favour of the "teacher", whose suitability had to be strictly examined.

Hermas, the author of the *Shepherd*, was a prophet of the Roman church to whom were vouchsafed many visions which he had to make known to the faithful. They concerned the single important subject of repentance, and he sought to win over to his point of view the presbyters, the official leaders of the congregation. Hermas claimed no teaching authority to which the heads of the congregation were obliged to submit; when he stepped forward in the assembly he was received with respect, for the Spirit spoke through him. That the Spirit did speak through him, it was the business of the authorities to make sure. Hermas knew too that there were false prophets who were known by their works.[96] In the case of Hermas there was clearly no rivalry between the possessor of special gifts and the office-holders; harmony seems to have been established and their respective tasks recognized. A few decades later Montanism was to bring prophecy once more into the foreground and compel the ecclesiastical authorities to take up a definite position.

The congregation of post-apostolic times did not however exist in isolation and self-sufficiency. It knew itself to be linked with all the others and united in one organism, through which flowed a supernatural principle of life: Christ the Lord. All the congregations together formed a new people, the universal Church, which was made manifest in every individual congregation. All nations were to recognize that Christians were "the people of God and the sheep of his pasture";[97] under the banner of Christ the faithful, both Jews and Gentiles, were united in one body, the Church of Christ;[98] all who had received the seal were one in the same faith, in the same love;[99] Christ had given his flesh for his new people.[100] Ignatius of Antioch was the first to call this international community of the faithful "the Catholic Church", whose invisible bishop was Christ.[101] Its catholicity

---

[95] *Didache*, 10, 7; 11, 3, 7–11; 13; 15, 1–2.
[96] Hermas, *Past. Mand.* 11, 1–14, on which see G. Bardy, *La théologie de l'église de S. Clément de Rome à S. Irénée* (Paris 1947), 140–3.
[97] 1 *Clem* 60:4.
[98] Ignat., *Smyrn.* 1, 2.
[99] Hermas, *Past. Simil.* 9, 17.
[100] Ps.-Barnabas, *Ep.* 7, 5.
[101] Ignat., *Smyrn.* 8, 2.

was such a striking characteristic that by its presence the true Church could be recognized.[102]

The Christian experienced the unity and catholicity of his Church in many ways in his daily life. Not only was the missionary welcomed like a brother when he met some of the faithful in a city; the bishop, priest, or deacon who brought a message, even the simple Christian whose business took him to foreign parts — they were all received with brotherly hospitality wherever there was a group of Christians.[103] An active correspondence between one congregation and another kept alive the consciousness of belonging to a great universal community. News was exchanged, joys and sorrows shared; long journeys were even undertaken in order that important questions of a religious nature might be discussed in common.[104]

The inner unity of the universal Church was assured by other powerful ties. Christians sought to maintain religious unity by a rule of faith which, beginning with simple forms, gradually acquired more precise and definite expression;[105] it was in essential points the same everywhere and was impressed upon all Christians at baptism. Unity of worship was established in the celebration of the Eucharist, which did indeed show local variations in form and in the text of many prayers, but which was essentially the same central act of the Christian liturgy, so that Bishop Polycarp of Smyrna in Asia Minor could celebrate it also in the church of Rome.[106] Unity in faith and worship was further preserved by the fact that the tradition of the Church was always the standard to be followed. For here no novelty of human origin could or should be admitted; loyalty to tradition was a prerequisite for the preservation of the truths of the faith and the unity of worship. With striking frequency we find the apostolic fathers, even at this early date, invoking tradition, which was looked upon as a legacy from the apostles and therefore inalterable.[107] Unity in belief, worship and apostolic tradition could ultimately be guaranteed only by him who was their Lord and protector, Christ; therefore the Church turned to him in prayer, imploring him to gather together the people of God from the ends of the earth, to bring them to unity and to preserve them in it.[108]

Even though the bishop's sphere of activity was his own congregation, he was not exempt from all responsibility for the Church as a whole. It was not only a feeling of solidarity with the faithful of other congregations

---

[102] The development of this idea is already indicated in *Martyr. Polyc.* 16, 226.

[103] *Didache* 11, 1–10; 13, 1–4; Hermas, *Past. Simil.* 8, 10, 3; 9, 27, 2.

[104] 1 *Clem* 55:1; Ignat., *Eph.* 1, 3; 2, 1; *Magn.* 2, 1; *Trall.* 1, 1.

[105] We already find in Ignatius, *Smyrn.* 1, 1–2; *Trall.* 9, forms which show a marked development compared with those of the N. T.

[106] *Euseb. HE* 5, 24, 17.

[107] Especially Papias in *Euseb. HE* 5, 20.

[108] *Didache* 9, 4; 10, 5; 1 *Clem* 59:2; Ignat. *Eph.* 4, 1–2.

that prompted bishops like Ignatius and Polycarp to address to them words of encouragement or rebuke; they acted thus from a sense of duty. There was, indeed, no bishop of the post-apostolic age who intervened in the affairs of other local churches with the same authority as in his own congregation, or could give instructions to the whole Church. Even Clement of Rome was too much of a background figure, as compared with the Roman church as such, to make it possible for us to attribute to him, on the strength of his epistle to the church of Corinth, a right to admonish, in the sense of a primacy, supported by a special authority. Rather was it the Roman congregation as such that made a claim exceeding the limits of brotherly solidarity. There are no grounds for supposing that Rome's advice had been asked for; the Roman letter seeks to re-establish peace by admonition and counsel, though sometimes its language takes on a more decisive, almost threatening tone that seems to expect obedience.[109] Noteworthy too is the respect which Clement's first epistle gained in Corinth and in the rest of the Church during the period immediately following, so that it was sometimes regarded as inspired scripture.[110] This implies the existence in the consciousness of non-Roman Christians of an esteem of the Roman church as such which comes close to according it a precedence in rank. It is especially noticeable in Ignatius' letter to the Romans. Its enthusiastic introduction is unique when we compare it with the prefaces to his other letters; the accumulation of honorific and fulsomely respectful epithets is hardly to be explained by personal temperament or by the purpose of the letter alone. In obvious allusion to the epistle to the Corinthians, the letter states that the Roman congregation acted as teacher to others.[111] Ignatius does not however mention the Bishop of Rome, and his words about the precedence of Rome in charity[112] (i.e. in charitable activities) can in no way be understood in the sense that any special personal dignity was accorded to its bishop.

In conclusion it may be added that the stream of Christians coming from elsewhere to Rome indicates a special attraction of that church which cannot be explained solely by the fact that Rome was the capital of the empire. Orthodox Christians, as well as adherents or founders of sectarian and heretical movements (we need merely mention Polycarp of Smyrna, Justin, and Hegesippus, and the Gnostics Valentinus, Cerdon, and Marcion), sought support or recognition at Rome which would count as legitimation in their own country. This fact also is evidence of the precedence allowed to the church of Rome.

[109] 1 *Clem* 57:1–2; 59:1–2.
[110] G. Bardy, *op. cit.* 112 f.
[111] Ignat., *Rom.* 3, 1.
[112] Ignat., *Rom.* inscr.

CHAPTER 11

Heterodox Jewish-Christian Currents

QUITE early there developed alongside the orthodox Jewish Christianity of the Jerusalem community and of the post-apostolic period, other Jewish groups which took over Christian elements in doctrine and worship. But, in contrast with genuine Jewish Christianity, they transformed these elements and thereby separated themselves from it as well as from post-biblical Judaism. With the latter, however, they shared the main ideas of late Jewish apocalyptic literature, and they recognized the Mosaic Law. It seems indeed not impossible that Jewish sectaries, who already had religious practices different from official Judaism,[113] borrowed Christian elements and thus emphasized their differences. Their separation from orthodox Jewry was not so much the result of changes in religious practice as of fundamentally different doctrines. These were concentrated on two main questions: Christology and the binding force of the Mosaic Law.

The latter question was, as we have seen, a cause of considerable conflict in the congregations founded by Paul and was bound sooner or later to lead to the disavowal of the "judaizers" by the Church, if they insisted on imposing observance of the Law upon Gentile Christians as necessary to salvation. Evidently it came to a separation soon after the death of James, when the judaizing group endeavoured to set up their candidate, Thebutis, against the lawfully elected successor of James, Simeon.[114] The emigration of the orthodox Jewish Christians to the region east of the Jordan and their consequent dispersion in Coelesyria weakened their inner cohesion and rendered them more open to the influence of Jewish sectaries. For the Church as a whole, however, the christological question grew more and more important and became a criterion of orthodoxy for individual Jewish Christians and Jewish-Christian congregations.

The Christology of Kerinthos[115] was, for orthodox Jewish Christians, a ground for bitterly opposing him. His character and doctrine have indeed been distorted by the addition of fantastic and legendary features, notably by Epiphanios;[116] but Irenaeus, with his connexions with Asia Minor, may well be reporting what is essentially correct when he states that Kerinthos lived towards the end of the first century in western Asia Minor, and that he asserted of Jesus that the latter was the natural son of Mary and Joseph.

---

[113] Cf. M. Black, "The Patristic Accounts of Jewish Sectarianism" in *BJRL* 41 (1959, 302.

[114] Hegesippus in *Euseb. HE* 4, 22, 4–5.

[115] For Cerinthus, see G. Bardy, *RB* 30 (1921), 344–73; W. Bauer, *RGG*, 3rd ed. I, 1963.

[116] Epiphanius, *Panar.* 28, 5.

As Jesus had distinguished himself above all other men by his justice and wisdom, Christ in the form of a dove had descended upon him after his baptism; from then on he had proclaimed the hitherto unknown Father and performed miracles. Before the end, Christ had again left him; only Jesus suffered death and rose again.[117]

This image of Christ, tinged with Adoptionism and Docetism, was bound to be unacceptable to the Christians of Asia Minor; an indication of this is to be seen in the curious note of Irenaeus that the apostle John was prompted to write his Gospel by the teachings of Kerinthos. Kerinthos also had Gnostic ideas, for according to Irenaeus, he distinguished the "highest God" from the creator of the world, who did not know the former. Eusebius[118] says moreover that Kerinthos favoured a crude form of chiliasm which may have had its origin among the Jewish sects. He does not seem to have gained a large following; the statements of Epiphanios, who speaks of a sect of Kerinthians, are open to question.

The Jewish-Christian group that in Irenaeus goes by the name of *Ebionites* was, however, a considerable movement. Early Christian heresiologists derive this name from a person called Ebion, but it is more probable that it comes from the Hebrew word *'ebjon* (poor). The adherents of this movement would, then, have seen in the name a descriptive designation which referred to their simple way of life. Perhaps the Ebionites were, in the beginning, orthodox Jewish Christians, who, so far as they personally were concerned, had remained faithful to the Law. There would then be much in favour of the assumption that they were originally successors to those members of the primitive Church who settled beyond the Jordan and in Coelesyria. Later, however, they began to propound views on christology and on the binding nature of the Mosaic Law which were heterodox and led to their breaking away from the Church. A clue to the date of their separation is perhaps to be found in Justin Martyr,[119] who distinguishes two groups of Jewish Christians: those who saw in Jesus a mere man, and those who acknowledged him as the Messiah and Son of God. The separation between heretical and orthodox Ebionites must therefore have taken place about the year 150.

Among the writings of the Ebionites, a Gospel of their own must first be mentioned. It was probably the Gospel of Matthew, revised in an Ebionite sense; Epiphanios has preserved fragments of it.[120] Ebionite ideas are also to be found in a treatise dating from the first half of the second century, containing the "Sermons of Peter", rewritten by the editor of the pseudo-Clementines. An Ebionite theological writer, known to us by name,

---

[117] Irenaeus, *Adv. haer.* 1, 26, 1; 3, 34; 3, 11, 1.
[118] *Euseb. HE* 3, 28, 4.   [119] Justin, *Dial.* 47–48.
[120] Epiphanius, *Panar.* 30, 3, 13; cf. *Hennecke-Schneemelcher*, I 3rd ed., 75–108.

is the translator of the Bible, Symmachus, whose various works on the Scriptures were extant in the time of Origen.[121]

No uniform picture can be given of the subsequent history of the Ebionite movement. Both in the attitude towards Christ and in the degree of importance attached to the Law and to sacrifices, there were different tendencies and shades of opinion. Some of the Ebionites accepted Gnostic ideas and indulged in bizarre speculations. The following characteristics are typical of the Ebionite movement in so far as it was heterodox. In their concept of the origin of the world the Ebionites took a dualistic view. God, in the beginning, set up a good and an evil principle: to the latter was given dominion over the present world; to the former, dominion over that which is to come. The good principle is Christ, the promised messianic prophet. Jesus of Nazareth was consecrated by God as Messiah and supplied on the day of his baptism in the Jordan with divine power. He was not the existing Son of God, but the naturally begotten son of a human couple, raised to the rank of Messiah because of his exemplary fulfilment of the Law of God. He was, besides, the "true prophet", who had already appeared in Adam and Moses, each time with a special mission, and who as Jesus was to bring the Jews back to the pure observance of the Law and to win the Gentiles for God.[122] This task he was to fulfill by preaching the word of God, not, therefore, by an extraordinary act of salvation, nor by dying for man's redemption. The Ebionites rejected belief in his redemptive death, as Christ had withdrawn himself from Jesus at the time of the crucifixion. The Ebionite image of Christ is thus essentially conditioned by its adoptionist character and by its denial of the soteriological significance of his life and death.

Joined to this christology was the Ebionites' demand for observance of the Law, which was, it is true, to be purged of its distortions. Such, for instance, were the false pericopes which had been later added to the Law of Moses, and above all the bloody sacrifices which represented a falsification of the divine will. This reform of the Law had been effected by Jesus in his teaching; he had shown what was genuine in the Law and in conformity with the will of God, and what contradicted it. He had rejected every form of worship by sacrifices, and therefore his death too had not the character of a sacrifice. Sacrifices were replaced by a life of poverty and community of goods; the Ebionite purified himself by daily washings, by participation in a ritual meal of bread and water, and by celebrating both Sabbath and Sunday.

Together with their esteem for the Mosaic Law and their rejection of the soteriological significance of Christ's death, the Ebionites also showed

---

[121] *Euseb. HE* 6, 17.
[122] L. Cerfaux, "Le vrai prophète des Clémentines" in *RSR* 18 (1928), 143–63.

a certain "anti-Paulinism, expressed particularly in the "Kerygmata Petrou" an Ebionite treatise of the first half of the second century which influenced the pseudo-Clementines. According to it, Paul was the great opponent of the Law, "the hostile man", who falsified the true ideas of Jesus. The Ebionites did not accept his elevation to the rank of apostle, for this dignity belonged only to those who had personal acquaintance with Jesus, whereas Paul's vocation rested upon visions and revelations that were nothing more than illusions inspired by devils. Here the Ebionites may be said to represent the heirs of those judaizers who appear in Paul's epistles as opponents of his missionary activity. The "Kerygmata Petrou" also shows an anti-Trinitarian tendency and rejects the Trinitarian interpretation of some Old Testament passages usual in Christian circles.

Recently, certain common features shared by Ebionites, Essenes and Qumran Jews have been pointed out.[123] These are especially evident in their attitude towards the Temple, its priesthood and the bloody sacrifices. Thus the Ebionite movement may have been part of a larger current of opinion, which in its extreme forms broke altogether with the official worship of the Temple. The originality of the Ebionites would then have lain in the evaluation they set upon the person of Christ.

Close to the Ebionites stood other Jewish-Christian groups which, on account of certain opinions held by them, can likewise not be regarded as belonging to orthodox Christianity. First, there was the sect of the *Elchasaites,* which, by the third century, had spread to some extent. It was founded by a man named Elchasai, who was active on the borders of Syria and Parthia during the early decades of the second century. This sect sent out missionaries and gained adherents in the East as far as the Euphrates and Tigris. It had considerable success in Palestine, and, through Alcibiades of Apamea, it even tried to get a footing in Rome at the time of Hippolytus. Its message was based upon a holy book to which a supernatural origin was ascribed. In it, two heavenly beings played a principal part, a female one, called the Holy Spirit, and a male one, the Son of God or Christ, who came into the world in repeated incarnations. The sect practised a baptism, fully clothed, which was believed to effect forgiveness of sins, as well as frequent washings, which delivered from sickness and defects.[124] The foundation of the Elchasaites' way of life was the Law. Circumcision, observance of the Sabbath, and praying towards Jerusalem were obligatory. They disapproved, however, of the Old Testament sacrifices, as well as of certain parts of the Scriptures; Paul they emphatically rejected. The prophecy of an approaching great war, that would usher in the end of the world, shows

[123] O. Cullmann, "Die neuentdeckten Qumrantexte und das Judenchristentum der Ps.-Klementinen" in *Festschrift R. Bultmann* (Berlin), 68–86.
[124] E. Peterson, *Frühkirche, Judentum und Gnosis* (Freiburg i. Br. 1959), 221–35.

apocalyptic traits; he who, when the time came, was in possession of a mysterious formula would be saved. The teaching of the holy book of Elchasai was to be kept secret since not all were worthy of it.

The question as to the original source of Elchasaitism cannot be definitely answered from the evidence at present available. Jewish elements were clearly present; and Christian influences, such as the baptismal formula and a vision of Christ, said to have been enjoyed by Elchasai, are easily recognizable. But the treatment of Christ as a mere man and a simple prophet shows the Christianity of the movement to have been undoubtedly heterodox. Gnostic elements also point in the same direction; among these may be mentioned the repeated incarnations of Christ, the concept of a "highest God" and the use made of magical formulas.

The sect of the *Mandaeans* can be included here, inasmuch as it was probably connected originally with heterodox Jewish baptist sects which had grown up in eastern Syria and Palestine. Baptism played a predominant part in their worship. It was carried out by immersing the candidate thrice in flowing water, and it could be repeated several times. Great importance was also attached to the liturgical celebration of the ascent of the souls of the dead to the realm of light. According to the Mandaean mythology, there was a great king of light or Great Mana, besides whom there existed innumerable lesser manas; opposing him was a world of black water peopled by demons. John the Baptist was highly revered by the Mandaeans, whereas Jesus was regarded as a false prophet and liar whom John unmasked. Mandaean influence on Christian baptism cannot be proved; the ritual of the baptist sects was evidently supplemented by later borrowings from Nestorian baptismal customs. Other alleged Christian elements in the Mandaean cult are of secondary importance and recede into the background when compared with the Gnostic, Iranian, and Babylonian influences (e. g. astrology). That it originally had links with early Jewish Christianity cannot be assumed.[125] The sect, which still survives with a strength of about 5000 members in the region of the Tigris and Euphrates, did not develop a literature of its own until the seventh or eighth century. It regards Judaism, Christianity, and Islam as false religions.

Finally, the influence of heterodox Jewish Christianity in some early Gnostic groups can be noted, even though the course of these influences is hard to trace. One cannot indeed speak of a Jewish Gnosis in the strict sense, for Judaism does not accept radical dualism in the shape of two original principles of good and evil, equal in rank.[126] Some Jewish schools

---

[125] M.-J. Lagrange, "La gnose mandéenne et la tradition évangélique" in *RB* 36 (1927), 321–49, 481–515, 37 (1928), 5–36; H. Lietzmann, "Ein Beitrag zur Mandäerfrage" in *SAB* 27 (1930), 596–608.

[126] Cf. esp. H. J. Schoeps, *Urgemeinde, Judenchristentum, Gnosis* (Tübingen 1956), 37 ff.

of thought did preach a relative dualism, accepting a world of angels and demons subordinate to one God; these governed the destinies of nations and individuals. [127]

Such a Gnostic tendency in heterodox Jewish Christianity can be seen in Samaritan Gnosis, which went back to Simon Magus, [128] who was of course not unfamiliar with Jewish Christianity (Acts, 8:10). Its speculations about the creation of the world by angels, the battle of these with one another and the liberation of mankind by the "virtues and powers", may have been derived from heterodox Jewish sources. Such views could have come via Simon's pupil Menander and the latter's pupils Saturninus (more correctly Satornil) and Basilides to Syria and Egypt, and there joined the Gnostic currents already existing.

The so-called "Apocryphon of John" among the Gnostic writings of Nag Hammadi, with its interpretation of Genesis and its doctrine of archons and angels and the part played by them in the Creation, clearly points to kindred speculations in later heterodox Judaism and in heretical Jewish Christianity. [129] The early Church did not have to engage in controversy to a great extent with all these heterodox Jewish-Christian schools of thought, because she did not come into close contact with all of them. Where, however, such disputes did arise, Christianity had an opportunity to clarify and affirm its beliefs.

---

[127] K. Schubert, "Problem und Wesen der jüdischen Gnosis" in *Kairos* 3 (Salzburg 1961), 2–15.

[128] Cf. L. Cerfaux, "La gnose simonienne" in *RSR* 15 (1925), 480–502, 16 (1926), 5–20, 265–85, 481–503.

[129] For details see below, chapter 15.

The Church in the Second Century

CHAPTER 12

The Position of the Church under the Emperors Marcus Aurelius and Commodus. Martyrdom of the Congregations of Lyons and Vienne

THE writers of early Christian apologetical works ascribed to the emperor Marcus Aurelius (161–80) an edict favourable to the Christians, which Apollinaris of Hierapolis and Tertullian invoked, when they wished to oppose, as unjust, the proceedings of provincial authorities against the Christians of their day.[1] They saw the explanation of this emperor's attitude in the miraculous fall of rain which, it was said, came in answer to the prayer of a Christian legion and saved the imperial army from defeat in the war against the Marcomanni.[2] It may be that the idea of a philosopher on the throne, who endeavoured, as ruler, to put the Stoic ideal into practice, favoured such an estimate of the emperor.

The reality was otherwise. The emperor's own writings show how much he despised the Christians in his heart, because (as he believed) they threw their lives away for an illusion. That he was determined not to let the State religion be jeopardized by fanatical sectaries and by the introduction of hitherto unknown cults is shown by a rescript of 176–7, which was not indeed specially directed against the Christians, but which could easily be employed against them by provincial authorities.[3] Whether this was so in individual cases cannot be proved, but the increase in the number of complaints from the Christians during the reign of Marcus Aurelius, expressed in the apologetical writings of Melito of Sardes, Apollinaris of Hierapolis, and the Athenian Athenagoras, clearly indicate a worsening of their situation. Melito drew the emperor's attention to the

---

[1] *Euseb. HE* 5, 5, 1–7; Tertull., *Apol.* 5; *Scapul.* 4.
[2] W. Zwikker, *Studien zur Markussäule* (Amsterdam 1941), 206 ff.; J. Guey, "La date de la 'Pluie miraculeuse' (172 après J.-C.) et la colonne aurélienne" in *MAH* 60 (1948), 105–27, 61 (1949), 93–118.
[3] J. Beaujeu, *La politique romaine à l'apogée de l'empire I: la politique religieuse des Antonins* (Paris 1955), 356–8.

fact that the Christians of Asia Minor were exposed day and night to plundering and robbery at the hands of people of the baser sort, treatment such as even hostile barbarian tribes would not be subjected to; their attackers invoked new decrees, which however the author could not believe the emperor had issued.[4] Athenagoras also complained in his apologia, addressed to Marcus Aurelius, that the Christians were being hunted, robbed, and persecuted, and begged him to put an end to the denunciations of which the Christians were victims.[5]

That such was the situation is confirmed by a series of individual martyrdoms in different parts of the empire which can be dated in the reign of Marcus Aurelius. In Rome the philosopher Justin was the most notable victim among a group of Christians who were put to death between 163 and 167 after a trial conducted by the city prefect himself, Junius Rusticus. Justin's pupil Tatian seems to attribute part of the responsibility for the death of these Christians to the intrigues of the pagan philosopher Crescens.[6] The martyrdoms of three bishops in the East, of which Eusebius gives a reliable account, also belong to the decade 160–70.[7] The execution of Publios, Bishop of Athens, between 161 and 170 is attested by a letter from Bishop Dionysius of Corinth to the church of Athens. Bishop Sagaris of Laodicea died a martyr's death "when Servilius Paulus was proconsul of Asia", therefore about the year 164. At the same time Thraseas, Bishop of Eumenia in Phrygia, probably also met his death; Polycarp of Ephesus informed Pope Victor that he was buried at Smyrna. There are good reasons for assigning the martyrdom of a group of Christians from Pergamum to the reign of Marcus Aurelius; Karpos, Bishop of Thyatira, and a deacon, Papylos, were there condemned to be burnt at the stake. A Christian woman, Agathonike, who was present, openly professed her faith and voluntarily threw herself into the flames.[8]

The clearest account of the background, circumstances, and course of a wave of local persecution under Marcus Aurelius is provided by a joint letter from the Christian communities of Lyons and Vienne in Gaul, in which they tell their brethren in Asia Minor what befell them in the year 177; Eusebius has included nearly the whole of it in his History of the

---

[4] *Euseb. HE 4, 26, 5–6.*
[5] Athenagoras, *Suppl.* 1, 3.
[6] The Acts of the martyrdom of Justin and his companions are in Knopf-Krüger, *Ausgewählte Märtyrerakten* (Tübingen, 3rd ed. 1929), 15–18, which contains a bibliography, esp. *Delehaye PM* 119–21; Tatian, *Or.* 19, 1.
[7] *Euseb. HE 4, 23, 2; 4, 26, 3; 5, 24, 4.*
[8] New revision of the Latin and Greek texts by H. Delehaye in *AnBoll* 58 (1940), 142–76. Cf. H. Lietzmann, *Festgabe K. Müller* (Tübingen 1922), 46–57, and A. M. Schneider in *JdI* (1934), 416 ff.

Church.[9] The Bishop of Lyons was then the aged Potheinos, who was assisted by a priest called Irenaeus; a deacon, Sanctus, belonged to the congregation of Vienne. A considerable number of the Christians in these cities came directly or indirectly from Asia Minor, such as, for instance, the Phrygian physician Alexander or Attalos of Pergamum, who possessed Roman citizenship. Besides these members of the upper class, the lower ranks of society, including slaves, were represented in the congregation of Lyons, in which, on the whole, there was an active religious life.

In the summer of 177, when representatives of all Gaul were assembled in Lyons for the festival of the imperial cult, the popular rage suddenly vented itself on the Christians, who were supposed, as elsewhere in the empire, to be guilty of atheism and immorality. After some initial vexations (the Christians were forbidden to enter Government buildings and to walk in public squares) the mob drove a group of them into the market-place, whence the Roman tribune, after examining them, had them led off to prison until the absent governor could deal with the matter personally. At the inquiry instituted by the latter on his return, a Christian who had not previously been arrested, Vettius Epagathos, volunteered to prove before the court that the accusations of crimes against religion and the State which were made against his brethren were unfounded. As he confessed, on being questioned by the governor, that he was himself a Christian, he too was arrested. Statements made by pagan slaves in the service of Christians accused their masters of heinous crimes; and thus in a few days the *élite* of both congregations found themselves in prison. During the trial, about ten Christians abjured their faith; the remainder were condemned to death, the execution of the sentence being accompanied by exquisite torments. Bishop Potheinos died in gaol after brutal ill-treatment; the others were thrown to wild beasts in the arena.

When the governor heard that Attalos, a distinguished man, was a Roman citizen, he postponed his execution in order to inquire of the emperor what line of action he should follow. He was told that apostates were to be pardoned; those who stood fast in their profession of Christianity were to be put to death. All proved steadfast, and so the executions continued. Besides the newly baptized Maturus, the deacon Sanctus, Attalos, and Alexander, the report specially singles out for praise the courage of the young girl Blandina and fifteen-year-old Pontikos. The bodies were not handed over to the families of the Christians for burial, but after six days they were burnt and the ashes scattered in the Rhône. The letter gives no exact number of the victims; only a later tradition mentions about fifty names.

[9] *Euseb. HE* 5, 1, 1–2, 8; see H. Quentin, "La liste des martyrs de Lyon" in *AnBoll* 39 (1921), 113–38.

Christians under Marcus Aurelius were not always condemned to death, but were sometimes sentenced to forced labour in the mines. This appears from a fragment of a letter quoted by Eusebius which was addressed by Dionysius of Corinth to the Bishop of Rome, Soter (167–75).[10]

If we seek the reasons for this obviously increased severity of the Roman authorities towards the Christians, fresh legal measures on the part of the emperor cannot indeed be adduced. His decision in reply to the governor's inquiry clearly shows that the legal position remained as it appears in Trajan's rescript and in the resultant practice under Hadrian. Neither are there grounds for supposing that the provincial authorities, even though the legal position remained the same, had been urged from Rome to take sterner measures. The circumstances of the persecution at Lyons and the above-mentioned complaints in the writings of the apologists show rather that it was public opinion under Marcus Aurelius which had become more unfavourable to the Christians. This hostile atmosphere now found expression more frequently and more intensively than under Hadrian, who had still been able to intervene to curb such excesses. If a provincial governor now gave in to the pressure of popular rage oftener than before, in Rome also public feeling was taken more into account and was given an outlet in the baiting of Christians.

The general discontent of the population of the empire under Marcus Aurelius was fed by various causes. The endless campaigns of that emperor laid many burdens on the people; the constant threat of hostile invasion increased the irritation of frontier populations. People were further aggravated by natural disasters such as the overflowing of the Tiber and outbreaks of the plague. Pogroms were the almost inevitable result. When it was noticed, at the ceremonies of propitiation, ordered by the emperor to avert the pestilence, that the Christians were conspicuously absent, the popular anger found its obvious outlet.

The Christian communities, for their part, had, albeit unwittingly, drawn attention to themselves more than usual about that time. The disputes with the Gnostics in particular congregations could hardly remain concealed from the pagans around them; even if the latter could not understand the background to these disputes, the Church's increased opposition to pagan culture and the Roman State nevertheless became apparent. Mention might also be made of the Montanist movement, at least in certain cases, if the growing irritability of the pagans is to be understood. The exalted desire for martyrdom that was peculiar to the Montanists, and their fanatical refusal to have anything to do with the pagan culture on which the State was based, could easily be attributed to Christianity as such, with disastrous results. Of course, the fact that

[10] *Euseb. HE* 4, 23, 10.

in the congregation of Lyons for instance one member came from Phrygia is not sufficient to prove that it contained a Montanist group.

The situation did not change under Marcus Aurelius' son Commodus (180–92), although it is known that he was personally tolerant towards individual Christians, some of whom were able to hold influential offices at his court. Later therefore, Christian writers such as Eusebius[11] attributed to the reign of Commodus a higher rate of conversions. The emperor's attitude was partly due to the influence of his wife, Marcia, who according to Dio Cassius[12] had the Christian presbyter, Hyacinth, as her teacher and was in friendly relations with the church of Rome, although she cannot necessarily be regarded as having been a baptized Christian. Thanks to her, Commodus ordered the release of the Christians who had been condemned to forced labour in the Sicilian mines.[13]

This emperor did not issue any new instructions for the conduct of the State authorities towards the adherents of the Christian faith, a fact proved by isolated trials of Christians during his reign, which can be understood only in the light of the previously existing practice. The first extant document of Christian origin in the Latin language[14] gives an account of proceedings against six Christians in the African town of Scili, who were condemned to death by the proconsul Vigellius Saturninus in July 180. It may be presumed that these Christians had been denounced to the Roman authorities, for the proconsul tried to make them renounce their faith and had them executed only after their refusal to do so. A denunciation was no doubt also the cause of the trial of the Roman senator Apollonius in 183–4, which Eusebius relates in an extract from the original acts of this martyr.[15] The prefect Perennis even canvassed opinions in the Senate on this case and clearly was very unwilling to pronounce sentence upon a man of such high rank, doing so only when the latter obstinately persisted in his profession of faith.

That the representatives of the Roman State did not always act against Christians in a spirit of brutal fanaticism is also shown by the attitude of the proconsul Arrius Antoninus, of whom Tertullian relates[16] that he once, when a large group of Christians stood before his tribunal, imprisoned

---

[11] Ibid. 5, 21, 1.

[12] Dio Cassius, 72; cf. also Irenaeus, *Adv. haer.* 4, 30, 46, and Hippolytus, *Philosophoumena* 9, 11, 12.

[13] See A. Bellucci, "I martiri cristiani 'damnati ad metalla' nella Spagna e nella Sardegna" in *Asprenas* 5 (Naples 1958), 25–46, 125–55; J. G. Davies, "Condemnation to the Mines" in *Univ. of Birmingham Hist. Journal* 6 (1958), 99–107.

[14] Text in Knopf-Krüger, *op. cit.* 28–29; see F. Corsaro, "Note sugli Acta martyrum Scillitanorum" in *Nuovo Didaskaleion* (Catania 1956), 5–51.

[15] Knopf-Krüger, *op. cit.* 30–35; see J. Zeiller in *RSR* 40 (1925), 153–57, and E. Griffe, *BLE* 53 (1952), 65–76.

[16] Tertullian, *Ad Scapul.* 5, 1.

only a few of them, releasing the others with the words: "You unhappy wretches, if you wish to die, have you not ropes and precipices enough?"

There are accounts of martyrdoms during this period at Apamea in Phrygia;[17] and Theophilus of Antioch alludes to actual persecutions in Syria when, at the end of his apologia, he remarks that the Christians "are subjected to cruel torments even to this hour".[18] This general formula implies the continuance of individual martyrdoms, of which, because of the incompleteness of our sources, we have no exact knowledge.

This survey of the persecution of Christians under the last two Antonines shows clearly that the attitude of the Roman State towards Christianity, which had been developed under Trajan, still existed; Christians were brought to judgment only when they had been denounced as such to the authorities, but profession of the Christian faith sufficed for their condemnation, proof of other crimes not being required. For these reasons, we have only sporadic evidence that trials of Christians took place; under Marcus Aurelius they were forced upon the authorities more than before by a public opinion that had grown more hostile and often expressed itself in riotous behaviour. The cause of this attitude was the increased nervousness of the pagan population. The situation is reflected in the growing apologetical literature of the second half of the century, which will be dealt with more fully later.

CHAPTER 13

Literary Polemic against Christianity

THE animosity of the pagans which we have described, with its explosions of popular anger and the action taken by the State authorities in consequence, brought the Christians more and more into the public eye, especially during the first half of the second century. Accordingly, there developed a new reaction of paganism against Christianity, this time on the intellectual plane. A will to resist arose in pagan intellectual circles. The resources of profane culture were employed in the battle against Christianity. Mocking speeches, pamphlets, and books became the means of carrying on a literary war, which began about the middle of the second century and soon reached its first climax in the satirical writings of Lucian of Samosata and in the "True Doctrine" (᾽Αληθὴς λόγος) of the philosopher Celsus.

[17] *Euseb. HE* 5, 16, 22.
[18] Theophilus, *Ad Autol.* 3, 30.

This was of great significance for the history of the Church, because it was one of the factors that provoked a reaction from the Christian side; the Christians took up the pen and adopted an attitude of defence and counter-attack. The resultant body of apologetical works became a special department of early Christian literature, giving a characteristic note to the second half of the second century.

The first beginnings of a pagan literary polemic are discernible in the report of Tacitus on Nero's persecution, mentioned earlier. Even though that author did not regard the Christians as responsible for the burning of Rome, his ironic words about their abominable superstition, their heinous crimes and their hatred of mankind reveal the extent of his contempt for them. His opinion of them could not have been without effect among his readers. A little later we meet in Suetonius a similar characterization of the Christians when he calls them adherents of a *superstitio nova ac malefica* and thus clearly and contemptuously distinguishes them from those who practised the old, true religion. [19] A like opinion was held by Epictetus, who coldly disapproves of the readiness of the "Galileans" for martyrdom, since it was (he says) based on blind fanaticism. [20] These, however, are casual remarks made by pagan writers who show no real knowledge of the new religion.

From the middle of the second century a growing unrest becomes evident among educated pagans on account of the increase of the Christian movement, which evidently could not be halted in spite of popular tumults and police measures. The representatives of pagan philosophy now had occasion to become more closely acquainted with the intellectual and religious phenomena of Christianity and to engage in controversy with it. An early example of a discussion between a member of the Church and a pagan philosopher is the encounter between the apologist Justin and the Cynic, Crescens, in Rome. According to Justin's account, [21] Crescens went about proclaiming that the Christians were "atheists and fellows of no religion"; though he did so more to please the pagan majority than because he had any sound knowledge of the facts. If he did learn anything at all of the teachings of Christ, he certainly did not, Justin thinks, grasp their scope and importance. In his disputation with Crescens, no doubt conducted in public, Justin did not feel that he had had the worst of it and was quite ready for further debate. Justin's pupil Tatian hints that Crescens sought to avenge himself on his Christian adversary by other means than those of argument. [22]

---

[19] Suetonius, *Vita Neronis* 16.
[20] Epictetus, *Diss.* 4, 6, 7.
[21] Justin, *Apol. append.* 3.
[22] Tatian, *Or.* 19, 1.

165

This example shows that the polemic of the educated adopted the reproach of the masses that the Christians were atheists. The same applies to the pagan rhetor Fronto, who enjoyed a certain consideration, not because of his intellectual importance, but on account of his position as tutor to the imperial princes Lucius Verus and Marcus Aurelius. In a speech before the Senate or in a public lecture (afterwards, no doubt, circulated in writing), Fronto took up the grave suspicions which the common folk repeated about the Christians: at their gatherings they were supposed, after having indulged in luxurious meals and partaken copiously of wine, to give themselves up to the worst excesses, including incest.[23] It is noteworthy that this member of the intellectual upper class obviously took no trouble to inquire into the justification for such evil rumours, and gave them, in his speech, an importance which could not fail in its effect on public opinion. This effect lasted until the beginning of the third century at least, when Minucius Felix wrote his Dialogue; the passage quoted by him from Fronto was obviously equally well known to pagans and Christians.

The picture of the Christians which Lucian of Samosata gives in his satire "On the Death of Peregrinos Proteus" cannot strictly speaking be regarded as a polemic against them. For this mocker, who with his sharp pen so readily exposed the weaknesses of his fellow men to the laughter of their contemporaries, was free from hatred against the Christians; he saw in them neither a danger to the State nor a threat to public order, and therefore scorned to repeat the venomous atrocity stories that were current about them. He regarded their religious convictions and their everyday behaviour as belonging to the human follies and errors which he enjoyed pillorying; but he regarded the folly of the Christians as particularly harmless. On his numerous journeys, Lucian had often heard of the adherents of this new faith, and no doubt he had occasionally been able to observe them at first hand. As, however, his alert eye was intent only on what might provide material for burlesque or be exploited for its comic possibilities, his knowledge of Christianity remained quite superficial. The writings of the Christians seem not to have interested him, and of their inner religious world he had no idea. Thus it was that he drew the following caricature of them.

The swindler Peregrinos easily succeeds in exploiting the credulity of the men of Palestine; he is soon playing a leading part in the assemblies of the Christians. He interprets their scriptures, writes some new ones himself, and in a short time he is enjoying almost divine honours. When, on account of his having murdered his own father, he is thrown into prison, this only increases the respect the Christians have for him. With

[23] Minucius Felix, *Octav.* 9, 6.

166

unwearying zeal they seek to ease his lot, visit him day and night in prison and procure him every assistance at his trial, while he unscrupulously exploits their helpfulness and unselfishness for his own enrichment. For the Christians' belief in immortality and their readiness to die Lucian had sympathy rather than cynical mockery; he felt the same about their brotherly love, their contempt for earthly possessions and their community of goods; every clever swindler could exploit this attitude and could soon became rich among them. It is only when the Christians see that Peregrinos Proteus disregards some of the commandments of their religion that they forsake him.[24]

Through this caricature of the Christian life we see a perceptible glimmer of the real situation. Lucian had heard something of the esteem in which one who professed the faith was held by his brother-Christians; he knew of their solicitude for the imprisoned, of their community spirit, and their courage in the face of death. But, even in a critic so free from hatred, we cannot fail to notice the lack of depth and the gaps in Lucian's knowledge of essential features of the Christian religion. Of Christ himself he had only the vaguest ideas; what Christ's life and teaching, death and resurrection meant to the Christians of that period was quite unknown to him. His notion that Peregrinos could be regarded by the Christians as the author of sacred books is as grotesque as his statement that they honoured the deceiver as a god. The distorted image of true Christianity which Lucian produced could hardly have appeared very attractive to the pagans who read his work. Towards a religion whose adherents were indeed harmless, but at the same time naïve fools, and who moreover were completely uncritical with regard to their own traditions of belief, one could scarcely react other than with pitying amusement. Lucian's portrait of Christianity could not fail to produce its effect in the intellectual battle with paganism.

Celsus

Celsus, who wrote in the eighth decade of the second century, raised the controversy to quite a different level in an extensive work to which he gave the equivocal title Ἀληθὴς λόγος. We no longer possess the whole work, but lengthy excerpts quoted by Origen in his refutation of Celsus, while not enabling us to make a complete reconstruction, do give us a clear idea of its basic arguments. Its author cannot be assigned exclusively to any philosophical school. His idea of God is largely coloured by a moderate Platonism; he therefore recognizes an absolutely transcendent,

---

[24] Lucian, *De morte peregrini* 11–13.

first and supreme God, immutable and without form, who should be honoured rather in the individual soul than in fixed forms of communal worship. Besides this supreme God, revealed through philosophical deduction, numerous lower gods claim the reverence of mankind, since to them have been assigned special tasks; these gods include the constellations and the tribal gods of the different nations. The demons are also inferior gods, who indeed often occupy a place in the thoughts and actions of men exceeding their actual importance. Finally, Celsus ranks earthly rulers nearly as high as the lower gods, because men owe their welfare to the order maintained by them in the world.

Celsus thus represented a philosophical creed which rejected monotheism and tolerated, in the Greek manner, popular religion and the mystery cults, provided they in some measure corresponded to the fundamental ideas of his own philosophically based religion. Every new religion must, according to Celsus, justify itself, whether as a popular belief or as a local cult. Christianity appeared to him as a new religious movement, and therefore he subjected it to examination. He had learnt as much as possible about this new religion. He had taken pains to understand its scriptures, he knew parts of the Old Testament, the Gospels, and other Christian literature as well. Evidently he had also sought personal contact with its adherents and spoken with them about questions concerning their faith. Jewish sources and Jewish-Christian polemical writings had provided further information. He summed up the results of his studies in a learned and substantial work, which does not however limit itself to displaying theoretical knowledge but also draws practical conclusions. Since his conclusions were wholly unfavourable to Christianity and were expressed moreover in a highly aggressive way, Celsus' Ἀληθὴς λόγος was a decisive event in the history of literary polemic between paganism and Christianity. The importance attached to the work and its possible effect on the public can be seen from the fact that the most significant theologian of the third century, seventy years after its appearance, thought it worth while to write a detailed refutation of it.

Celsus' philosophical principles did not allow him to accept either the Christian doctrine of Creation or the idea of Revelation. A world which was created out of nothing and will pass away again was something that did not fit into his cosmology; even the manner in which the Old Testament describes the creative activity of God seemed to him irreconcilable with the dignity of the Supreme Being. God, according to the idea of Celsus, sat enthroned at an inapproachable distance from the world and could not reveal himself without changing his nature or subjecting himself to the vicissitudes of history and coming into dangerous proximity to evil. Platonic dualism and Stoic cosmology were the basis of Celsus' attitude; to him the idea of God's becoming man appeared positively shameful: "No God and no Son of God has ever descended to earth, nor ever will." [25]

With this rejection of the doctrine of the Incarnation, Celsus coupled a characterization of the person of Jesus of Nazareth which was bound to offend every Christian deeply. According to him, Jesus was only a man who had gained respect and authority through the means employed by Egyptian sorcerers; but no one would think of giving one of these the title of "God's Son". Jesus was really nothing but a juggler, a boaster, and a liar, whose moral life was by no means blameless. The veneration which Christians had for him was comparable to the cult of Antinous, the favourite slave of Hadrian; their worship was addressed to a dead man, not to a divine being.

The opposition of Celsus to the Christian doctrine of angels was connected with the Greek idea of the impossibility of divine intervention in the course of human history. A God, who at a definite time in history sent a messenger with a mission of salvation, would be breaking the inalterable law to which all earthly things were subject.

Far more effective than his attacks on Christan doctrines was the unfavourable description Celsus gave of the Christians themselves and of their daily life. They were (he said), for the most part, men of limited intelligence, who did not understand their own doctrines and would not discuss them; they even regarded "foolishness" as a mark of distinction. Their faith was the religion of the stupid and of stupidity; [26] their deliberate exclusion of the Logos from their religious life was in itself a condemnation of Christianity in Greek eyes. Christian preaching even warned its hearers against earthly wisdom and thus frightened away those to whom Greek culture represented an ideal. That was why it found its audience in those social classes to which, in any case, culture was foreign, namely among the slaves, the lower orders of the despised manual workers and their like, among immature children and women. This was no wonder, for the founder of Christianity belonged to the lower classes, having been only a carpenter.

Celsus based his moral judgment of the Christians as deceivers and liars on their having consciously borrowed ideas from the Greek past, distorting and falsifying them in their propaganda; whereas the Greeks revered their intellectual heritage. Thus Christianity sinned against the Logos and was the irreconcilable opponent of the ἀληθὴς λόγος, the "true doctrine" of the Greeks. It offended furthermore against that other Greek ideal, that of loyalty to the Nomos, the reverent regard for tradition in

---

[25] Celsus, *Fragm.* 5, 2.
[26] Cf. for the following C. Andresen, *Logos und Nomos. Polemik des Kelsos wider das Christentum* (Berlin 1955; with Bibliography).

religion and worship, which was respected as an unwritten law by all nations. Moses had already disregarded this law when he established Jewish monotheism instead of Egyptian polytheism; but when Jesus of Nazareth began to proclaim a new faith, it was rebellion against the Nomos and an act of apostasy. This falling away from the Nomos forced Christianity into isolation and made it a miserable, hole-and-corner religion, the adherents of which Celsus compared to a group of earthworms assembled on a dunghill, vying with one another as to which of them was the greatest sinner.[27]

The revolt of the Christians against the sacred ideals of Logos and Nomos gave Celsus a pretext for branding them as a gang of lawbreakers who had to shun the light of publicity. Jesus had picked out men of evil repute to be his apostles, men who carried on the unclean businesses of publicans and sailors; he himself was nothing but a "robber chief"[28] at the head of his band of brigands. The successors of the apostles, the Christian preachers of the author's own time, were no better. Their words found an echo only among criminals, whom they incited to further crimes. It was therefore the duty of the State authorities to intervene against a religion which, in a secret and forbidden confederacy, rebelled against all traditional law and order. Sympathy for the victims of the resulting persecution would be out of place.

Here we must stop to ask the question: how far was such a powerful attack effective? It could hardly count on any appreciable success among the Christians themselves. The distorted picture of Jesus was bound to fill them with disgust, especially as it came from a man who was acquainted with the Gospels. The same is true of his characterization of the apostles and early disciples, as well as of his contempt for the martyrs, to whom Celsus denied all moral worth, although elsewhere he highly praised loyalty to religious convictions. His complete misunderstanding of the Christian concept of sin and of what gave the Christians their inner cohesion was bound to prevent his work from having any profound effect on the members of the Church. One may, indeed, justly point out that Celsus was guided in his polemic against the Christians by the motive of saving from destruction the high Greek ideals of a life according to Logos and Nomos. But in considering it necessary to employ in the process a language of contempt and mockery, which did not shrink from the vilest abuse of what he knew to be sacred to the Christians, he served his cause badly. His appeal to the Christians to come out of their isolation and to take part in the social life of the Roman State thereby lost all appearance of sincerity.

[27] Contra Celsum 4, 23.
[28] Fragm. 2, 12; 2, 44b.

The effect of Celsus's book upon contemporary paganism may well have been different. An educated pagan who, without personal knowledge of Christianity, read this work which described, with pretensions to extensive learning, a movement threatening all Greek culture held sacred, could with difficulty bring himself to take much positive interest in such a contemptible religion. The book may indeed have done much to strengthen the conviction that severe measures against such a movement were necessary. Whether Celsus succeeded in bringing about a renaissance of pagan religion in the face of the menace of Christianity may justly be doubted. Subsequent developments indicate that the latter's powers of defence were rather strengthened than weakened by this attack.

CHAPTER 14

The Early Christian Apologists of the Second Century

EVEN before the middle of the second century, some writers on the Christian side had begun a task which, because of its purpose, later earned them the name of apologists. They belonged entirely to the Greek-speaking part of the empire and form a compact group, which in the second half of the century grew in number and importance. In many respects they introduced a new phase in the development of early Christian literature; for the aim of the apologists was intentionally wider than that of their immediate predecessors, the apostolic fathers. They wanted to do more than provide the members of nascent communities with the most important truths of Revelation in a simple form. They saw clearly that the situation of Christianity in the first half of the century, especially in the Hellenic East, presented its writers with new tasks.

The apologists perceived that the faith was meeting with ever-increasing hostility in every department of public life. This development led them to address their pagan neighbours directly, in order to give them, in more or less extensive explanatory writings, a truer picture of the Christian religion. Thus an unbiased judgment of its adherents and a juster treatment of them would be made possible. In the situation then obtaining, any explanatory work on the true character of Christianity was necessarily also a defence against the suspicions and false judgments of the pagan world. Hence such a work was called ἀπολογία, "apologia" or speech for the defence. But it was not difficult to combine missionary and propagandist intentions, and these authors worked at least indirectly towards the spread of the faith among their readers.

171

The Christian apologists did not need to create the literary form for their purpose; it existed already in the speech for the defence, the *logos*, which was delivered before the judicial authorities and subsequently published. There was also the *dialogue*, the immediate occasion and circumstances of which were usually fictitious. Both forms were used in Christian apologetics. The defensive speech, in pamphlet form, was employed especially when addressing the pagans; the dialogue was more used in controversy with Judaism.[29] This controversy had entered a new phase now that the political existence of Palestinian Jewry had come to an end through the Roman victory over Bar Cochba. In the changed circumstances renewed discussion with the Diaspora Jews about the true Messiah had become possible.

The method and choice of theme varied according to the adversary addressed. In dialogues with the Jews, the main theme was already given: only Jesus of Nazareth could be the true Messiah, for in him alone were fulfilled the messianic prophecies of the Old Testament. In debate with pagan religions and Hellenistic culture there was a wider choice. First of all, the persistent rumours accusing the Christians of sexual immorality, atheism, and inadaptibilty for social life had to be refuted, for it was these rumours that kept alive the animosity of the pagan masses. More space was devoted to setting forth the truths of the Christians and the ethic on which it was based. In this connexion the Christian writers were fond of adding some more or less sharp criticism of the pagan gods and mythology for which contemporary philosophers might sometimes have provided both stimulus and example. A few of the apologists endeavoured to prove that the religious quest of the most profound pagan thinkers found its fulfilment in Christianity. Alongside such a more or less positive appreciation of the cultural achievements of paganism there was also, however, a purely negative attitude which treated all that Greek civilization had produced with cheap mockery. Repeatedly, the apologists draw the conclusion that the right to existence of such a lofty religion as Christianity could not be denied, and that, therefore, the measures taken against its adherents by the authorities were completely lacking in justice.

The series of apologetic writers begins with the Athenian Quadratus, who, according to Eusebius,[30] addressed an apologia to the emperor Hadrian. The single fragment of his work which is certainly genuine, permits no conclusions about its general character. Various attempts to see the *Apologia* of Quadratus in this or that extant apologetical work of the early Christian period must be regarded either as unsuccessful or

---

[29] Such as the lost work by Ariston of Pella: *Disputation between Jason and Papiscus concerning Christ* (circa 140); cf. *Quasten P*, I, 195 f.

[30] *Euseb. HE* 4, 3, 1; the fragment ibid. 4, 3, 2.

as hypotheses which have not met with unanimous acceptance by historians.[31]

On the other hand it has been possible to rediscover complete in a Syrian translation the long-lost work of his fellow-countryman and contemporary, Aristides, and to show that the Greek novel *Barlaam and Joasaph*, in the version of John Damascene, is a free adaptation of it. Aristides was no doubt addressing the same emperor, Hadrian, as Eusebius (who knew his *Apologia* in the original text) was aware of.[32] The author, however, did not succeed in presenting and developing his theme effectively. His main argument was that the three races, barbarians, Greeks, and Jews, did not possess the true idea of God; only the fourth race, the Christians, had the true doctrine and moral code. He was not above borrowing some of the Epicureans' religious criticism and employing Jewish arguments against polytheism. His clumsy style is no doubt partly due to his efforts to use the language of contemporary philosophy in order to bring home to his readers the fundamental truths of Christianity. These, for him, consisted in the belief that Jesus Christ as Son of God had come down from Heaven and taken flesh of a virgin, and that after his death and resurrection he had commanded the apostles to proclaim the true God to all nations and to make them observe his commandments; he who obeyed these would become a partaker in eternal life.

Aristides' tone becomes warmer when he speaks of the daily life of the Christians (c. 15), which recommends itself by its lofty purity of morals. He was deeply permeated with the belief that Christianity alone could bring salvation to mankind. This earliest surviving attempt of a Christian apologist to introduce his faith to his pagan fellow-citizens leads one to suppose that a recent convert from paganism was bold enough to undertake a task which he was not yet quite capable of fulfilling.[33]

An incomparably higher achievement was the work of Justin, a convert from a Greek family of Flavia Neapolis in Palestine, who as director of a school in Rome, died a martyr's death about the year 165.[34] An Apologia with an appendix, addressed to Antoninus Pius and his son Marcus Aurelius, together with a lengthy *Dialogue with the Jew Tryphon* have

---

[31] Cf. *Altaner* 117 f. The most interesting view so far is that of P. Andriessen, who considers that the Apologia is identical with the *Letter to Diognetus;* cf. his essays, *RThAM* 13 (1946), 5–39, 125–49, 14 (1947), 121–56, and *Vig Chr* 1 (1947), 129–36; *SE* 1 (1949), 44–54; *Bijdragen* 11 (1950), 140–50. On this question see also G. Bardy, *APhilHistOS* 9 (1949), 75–86; B. Altaner, *RAC* I, 652–4.

[32] *Euseb. HE* 4, 3, 3, The Syrian translation is addressed to "Adrianos Antoninos", i. e. Antoninus Pius; but the translator is more likely to have been mistaken than Eusebius.

[33] Cf. W. Hunger, "Die Apologie des Aristides eine Konversionsschrift" in *Scholastik* 20–24 (1949), 390–400. On its doctrinal content see P. Friedrich in *ZKTh* 43 (1919), 31–77.

[34] The account of his martyrdom is in Knopf-Krüger, *op. cit.* 15–18.

come down to us, the remnant of eight works by Justin which were known to Eusebius.[35] The *Apologia* to the two emperors was written about 150. Whether the appendix, often called the *Second Apologia*, was published with it as its original conclusion, or was a supplement added later, it is difficult to decide.[36] The *Dialogue* refers to the *Apologia* as having already appeared; more precise indications as to its date are lacking.

The career and the superior education of their author give these writings a special importance. Justin belonged to the educated upper class. As a professional philosopher he was acquainted with all the principal intellectual movements of his time, and as an unswerving seeker after truth he had tried them all in turn and found inner peace only when he recognized Christianity to be "the only certain and adequate philosophy" (*Dial.*, c. 8). He thereupon embraced it and devoted the rest of his life to proclaiming and defending it. It is understandable that, as a teacher of this philosophy in Rome before a pagan public and pupils, he made use of philosophical ideas and ways of thought that were familiar to them and were in some measure akin to the truths of Christian Revelation. He attacked polytheistic mythology with the methods placed at his disposal by the "enlightened" philosophers. To it he opposed the one true God, the "Father of the universe" (*Apol.* app. 6), who is without origin and himself the first cause of the world, and for whom there is no name that can express his nature. He is enthroned above the world, in which he cannot be directly apprehended by the senses. Justin does not argue that this one God is called "Father" because he has favoured men with a kind of divine sonship, but, rather, because he is the first cause of creation. He seeks to connect this philosophical idea of God with elements of the Christian doctrine of the Trinity as expressed in the Creed, so that the Christian belief in God is shown as including also belief in Jesus Christ his Son and in the prophetic Spirit.[37] The Logos was in the beginning with God; he was begotten by the Father and appeared in his divine fullness in Jesus Christ, as Holy Scripture had foretold. He has not indeed the same rank as the Father, but, as his Son, he shares the divine nature (*Dial.* 61). Even before his manifestation in Christ, the Logos was active; not only did the Father create the world through him, but he also appeared frequently as the "angel of the Lord", he spoke in the prophets of the Old Testament, and he was active too in such eminent men as Heraclitus, Socrates and Musonios, in whom he was at work as "germinal Logos", so that these

---

[35] *Euseb. HE* 4, 18, 1.

[36] Cf. A. Ehrhardt in *JEH* 4 (1953), 1–12. He repeats the theory of two independent apologias.

[37] W. Pannenberg, "Der philosophische Gottesbegriff in frühchristlicher Theologie" in *ZKG* 70 (1959), 1–45.

and many others who lived in accordance with the Logos working in their reason are actually to be reckoned as Christians.

If in Justin's teaching about God and the Logos Stoic influence is especially evident,[38] his ideas on the activities of angels and demons show a strong affinity with the Platonic philosophy of his time.[39] God gave the good angels charge over men and earthly affairs (*Apol.* 2:5). They are not pure spirits but possess aerial bodies, nourished by a kind of manna (*Dial.* 57). The fall of the angels was caused by their having sexual intercourse with women. Their children are the demons, who from their kingdom of the air exercise their baleful influence on mankind, until at Christ's return they will be cast into everlasting fire. They are the actual founders of the pagan cults; they also made the Jews blind to the Logos and so caused his death on the Cross. They continue by their cunning to prevent the conversion of mankind to him and to God. But in the name of Jesus Christ the redeemer, a power has been given to Christians which protects them against the demons (*Dial.* 307).

Justin's Christianity has another side, less influenced by philosophical abstractions, which appears when he writes of the daily life of the Christians, in which he took part like any other member of a congregation. Its high moral level was for him a convincing proof that the Christians were in possession of the truth. They led a life of truthfulness and chastity, they loved their enemies and went courageously to death for their beliefs, not because they had been persuaded of the importance of these virtues by philosophical considerations, but because Jesus had demanded of them a life in accordance with such ideals. It was for Justin an incontrovertible proof of the truth of Jesus' message that in him all the prophecies of the Old Testament were unequivocally fulfilled. He esteemed the Old Testament as highly as the Gospels, the "memoirs of the apostles" (*Apol.* 66 and *Dial.* 100).

With the artlessness of a simple member of the Church he speaks of baptism and the eucharistic liturgy as essential components of Christian worship. Baptism, performed "in the name of God the Father and Lord of the universe and of our redeemer Jesus Christ and of the Holy Spirit" (*Apol.* 61), frees us from sins previously committed and creates a new man

---

[38] G. Bardy, "S. Justin et la philosophie stoïcienne" in *RSR* 13 (1923), 491–510, 14 (1924), 33–45; M. Spanneut, *Le stoïcisme des Pères* (Paris 1957); R. Holte, " Logos Spermatikos. Christianity and Ancient Philosophy according to St Justin's Apologies" in *StTh* 12 (1958), 109–68; N. Pycke, "Connaissance rationelle et connaissance de grâce chez S. Justin" in *EThL* 37 (1961), 52–85.

[39] C. Andresen, "Justin und der mittlere Platonismus" in *ZNW* 44 (1952–3), 157–95; W. Schmid, "Frühe Apologetik und Platonismus (Prooimion des Dialogs mit Tryphon)" in *Festschrift O. Regenbogen* (Heidelberg 1952), 163–82.

through Christ; as the Christian is spiritually enlightened by it, baptism is also called "enlightenment".[40] The purest form of worship is the eucharistic sacrifice,[41] at which the faithful, joined in brotherly union, bring bread and wine over which the head of the congregation utters a prayer of thanksgiving. These gifts are again distributed among the faithful, but now they are no longer ordinary bread and wine but the flesh and blood of that Jesus who himself became flesh. This change is wrought by the words which Jesus spoke over the bread and wine at the Last Supper and which he told the apostles to repeat (*Apol.* 62). This food the Christians call the Eucharist; it has replaced the Old Testament sacrifices, which God rejects. It is the perfect sacrifice which Malachy foretold, and the fulfilment of the spiritual sacrifice which the Greek philosophers longed for and which they regarded as the only worthy form of divine worship. It is the only true λογική θυσία, because the Logos himself, Jesus Christ, is its centre.[42]

In other matters, too, Justin's views reflect the traditional teaching of the early Church, even when this was in contradiction to pagan sensibilities. Quite naturally he speaks of the mystery of the cross and the redemption of mankind by the bloodshed and death of the Son of God. His belief in the resurrection of the body, which would one day bring incorruptibility to the just, was unshakeable. Although, according to his own words (*Dial.* 80), not all good Christians agreed with him in this, he expected a millennium — thousand-year kingdom — in Jerusalem which would begin at the end of time, when the souls of the dead would be delivered from Hades.

We could certainly give a more complete picture of Justin's theology if his other works had been preserved. In these he stated his attitude towards the heresies of his time and dealt in more detail with questions such as the Resurrection, the universal dominion of God, and the human soul.[43] His apologetical purpose in controversy with the pagans required him to show a philosophical and rational basis for his faith, whereas the dispute with the Jews limited him very much to the question of the

---

[40] C. I. Story in *VigChr* 16 (1962), 172–8 (Justin on Baptism).

[41] See O. Casel, "Die Eucharistielehre des hl. Justinus" in *Katholik* 94 I (1914), 153–76, 243–63, 331–55, 414–36; O. Perler, "Logos und Eucharistie nach Justinus Apol. 66" in *DTh* 18 (1940), 296–316; Otilio de N. Jesús, "Doctrina eucarística de San Justín" in *RET* 4 (1944), 3–58.

[42] J. Gervais, "L'argument apologétique des prophéties messianiques selon S. Justin" in *Revue de l'Univ. d'Ottawa* 13 (1943), 129–46, 193–208.

[43] *Euseb. HE* 4, 11, 8; 4, 18, 4–5. Cf. B. Seeberg, "Die Geschichtstheologie Justins des Märtyrers" in *ZKG* 58 (1939), 1–81; H. Bacht, "Die Lehre des hl. Justinus Martyr von der prophetischen Inspiration" in *Scholastik* 26 (1951), 481–95, 27 (1952), 12–33; N. Hyldahl, "Tryphon und Tarphon" in *StTh* 10 (1957), 77–90. On the influence of Justin on Irenaeus cf. F. Loofs, *Theophilus von Antiochien adv. Marcionem* (Leipzig 1930), 339–74.

Messiah. Nevertheless, one is bound to say that he did not confine himself to a purely philosophical Christianity; his survey represents a significant advance in the development of early Christian theology when compared with the world of the apostolic fathers and the earlier apologetic of Aristides.

Justin's pupil, the Syrian Tatian, shared with him a similar way to Christian faith, for he too had found his way to the truth only after long searching (he had been initiated into the Mysteries) and by reading the holy books of the Christians (*Orat.* 29). His "Speech to the Greeks", written to justify his conversion, marks a retrograde step in comparison with Justin's *Apologia*. Whereas the latter found elements of truth everywhere in Greek philosophy and spoke with high esteem of some of its representatives, Tatian had, for the cultural achievements of Greece, only mockery and contempt. None of these, he said, was of Greek origin, but everything was borrowed from the barbarians, upon whom the Greeks looked down with such arrogance; and even then, they had misunderstood or maliciously distorted that which they had borrowed (*Orat.* 1 ff.). The theology of the Greeks was folly, their theatres were schools of vice, their philosophy full of deception, their games, music, and poetry, sinful (*Orat.* 21–28). Such a whole-sale condemnation was not exactly likely to make an educated Greek receptive to what Tatian had to say about the Christian religion.

The centre of this religion, he said, was the one God without a beginning, clearly distinct from the material world he created through the Logos. God intended man to rise again after the consummation of all things and would also be man's judge. Man, endowed with free will, could decide to be on the side of goodness and so enter into immortality, in spite of the influence of the demons, who sought to lead him astray. It was they who tried to force upon mankind belief in Fate, and for this they would finally suffer eternal damnation. Man, as God's image, could free himself from their domination if he renounced matter by strict self-mortification. This the Christians did, though they were calumniously accused of every possible vice.

The incomplete and fragmentary nature of Tatian's theology strikes us at once. What is especially noticeable is his failure to give any details about the person and the redemptive action of Christ, particularly when addressing pagan readers. Indeed, he states only a few of the fundamental points of his theology, the selection of which was governed by a predetermined schema of missionary preaching. The want of moderation in Tatian's attack on Hellenistic culture was in accordance with his character, namely his tendency to extremes, which eventually after his return to his native Syria about the year 172 was to lead him outside the Church to become the founder of the Encratites, a Christian sect which rejected marriage as sinful and renounced the use of flesh or wine in any form. [44]

Tatian's other surviving work, which he called Τὸ διὰ τεσσάρων εὐαγγέλιον, had a much more far-reaching effect than his apologetical work. It was a harmony of the Gospels which was intended to reduce the four separate gospels to a single account. This *Diatessaron,* which the fragment of Dura-Europos (dating from before 254) seems to show was written in Greek, was used as a liturgical book in the Syrian church until the fifth century, and St Ephraem wrote a commentary on it. It was early translated into Latin, and it evidently influenced the text of the Gospels outside Syria. The surviving Armenian text of Ephraem's commentary and versions of the *Diatessaron* in Arabic, Latin, and Middle Dutch enable us to make a reconstruction of its original form. [45]

Athenagoras, the "Christian philosopher of Athens", wielded a more skilful pen than any of the apologists above mentioned. About the year 177 he addressed a petition to the emperor Marcus Aurelius and his son Commodus, in which he refuted the calumnies against the Christians, claimed for Christianity equal rights with pagan philosophies, and therefore demanded its toleration by the State. The nobility of tone of the work as a whole is matched by Athenagoras' attitude towards the Greek philosophers, many of whom showed monotheistic tendencies without on that account being looked upon as atheists. The reproach of atheism made against the Christians ought therefore to be dropped, for they believed in one God, the Father, the Son and the Holy Spirit, and were convinced of the existence of a world of angels to whom was entrusted the ordering of the universe (*Suppl.* 10). The existence of this one God can be proved even by reason alone (*Suppl.* 8). Revelation shows the divinity of the Logos; the working of the Holy Spirit, who is an emanation of God, is especially perceptible in the prophets (*Suppl.* 7 and 10). The high standard of Christian morality was proved by the purity of their married life and the esteem in which virginity was held among them, a second marriage being regarded as "decent adultery" (*Suppl.* 31–35). The Christian doctrine of the resurrection of the body, so difficult for the Greeks, Athenagoras sought to prove philosophically in a special work. It is clear that in the writings of this apologist the philosophical argument had gained in quality and the theological understanding of Christianity in depth.

---

[44] R. M. Grant, "The Heresy of Tatian" in *JThS NS* 5 (1954), 62–68; G. Blond "L' 'hérésie' encratite vers la fin du IVe siècle" in *Science religieuse* (Paris 1944), 157 to 210; F. Bolgiani, "La tradizione ereseologica sull'encratismo" in *Atti Accad. Scienze Torino* 91 (1956–7), 1–77.

[45] I. Ortiz de Urbina, "Trama e carattere del Diatessaron di Taziano" in *OrChrP* 25 (1959), 326–57.

Only the *Three Books to Autolykos* survive out of the considerable body of writings left by Theophilos, a men of Hellenistic education who, after his conversion about the year 180, became head of the Christian congregation at Antioch. [46] Autolykos was his pagan friend, to whom he wished to prove, in a pleasing Greek style, that the Scriptures of the Christians (that is, the Old Testament) were superior, both in antiquity and in religious and philosophical content, to everything that the Greek intellect had produced. The line of argument and the defence against pagan calumnies follow the usual course. In Theophilos' account of the faith we meet for the first time in a Christian writer the designation τριάς (Trinity) (2:15), for the persons of which he always uses the terms Θεός (God), Λόγος (Logos), Σοφία (Sophia) (1:7; 1:10; 2:18). The evangelists were for him, like the prophets, bearers of the Spirit; their writings, with the epistles of Paul, were the "holy, divine word" (2:22; 3:13–14). The human soul was potentially immortal; immortality would be given as a reward for freely choosing to observe the commandments of God (2:27).

Except for a few fragments, the apologia of Bishop Melito of Sardes, as well as the works of the rhetor Miltiades of Asia Minor and Apollinaris, Bishop of Hierapolis, are lost. [47] With courage and dignity Melito pointed out to Marcus Aurelius the unjust plundering and persecution to which the Christians were exposed, whereas the benevolent attitude of the emperor's predecessors, except Nero and Domitian, had brought God's blessing on the Roman Empire. [48] Eusebius has preserved a list of the other works of this much respected bishop, the titles of which show the astonishing range of his interests. [49] It is highly probable that a homily on Exodus 12, rediscovered in a papyrus of the fourth century, is by Melito. This, preached no doubt at a Paschal celebration of the Quartodecimans, gives important information about early Christian teaching in Asia Minor on original sin, on the redemptive act of Christ, on baptism, and on the character of sermons at that time. A hymn in the same papyrus fits so well with the Easter liturgy of the Quartodecimans and with the ideas of Melito that it too has been claimed for the Bishop of Sardes. [50]

There are finally two other apologetical writings which belong to the closing years of the second century or the beginning of the third. The anonymous *Letter to Diognetus* attracted attention more by its elegant Greek than by its theological content; it has repeatedly tempted scholars to identify its author, but it is difficult to prove anything. A short criticism

[46] *Euseb. HE* 4, 24; Jerome, *De vir. ill.* 25; *Ep.* 121, 6, 15.
[47] See *Quasten P,* I, 228 f.
[48] *Euseb. HE* 4, 26, 5–11.
[49] Ibid. 4, 26, 2.
[50] The Easter Hymn has been edited with a commentary by O. Perler, *Ein Hymnus zur Ostervigil von Meliton?* (Fribourg 1960); see also J. Daniélou in *RSR* 48 (1960), 622–5.

of the Jewish and pagan religions is followed by the oft-quoted hymnic chapter on the Christians' daily life: "Every foreign place is their home, and their home is a foreign place to them; ... they dwell on earth, but their conversation is in heaven; they love all men and are persecuted by all; they are poor and enrich many. They are despised and are thereby glorified. They are insulted and they bless; they are mocked and show honour to those that mock them; punished with death, they rejoice as if they were awakened unto life. In brief, what the soul is to the body, the Christians are to the world" (chapters 5 and 6). The reality, it is true, did not in the year 200 everywhere correspond to the ideal. The satire of Hermias, Διασυρμὸς τῶν ἔξω φιλοσόφων, is rather an audacious pamphlet than a reasoned study. It makes fun of the contradictions in the teachings of various philosophers or schools of philosophy about God, the universe and the human soul.

A general appreciation of the achievement of the second century apologists can no longer defend, without qualification, the thesis that their endeavours to make Christianity intelligible to the Hellenistic world played a decisive part in hellenizing the Church. The genuinely Christian content of apologetical literature is too unequivocal to support such a thesis, especially when we remember its purpose. In their efforts to appeal to pagans and Jews the apologists could not give a complete exposition of Christian theology. For this reason also they had to renounce any intention of describing in detail the Christian mysteries. Compared with the apostolic fathers, however, they show a considerable development in their teaching about God, in the christology of the Logos, in the doctrine of the Trinity, and in Christian anthropology. Great progress was made in biblical studies; a start was made at establishing a canon; the doctrine of inspiration began to be developed, and the Old Testament became the foundation of a christology based on the Bible. Finally, in the works of the apologists we get valuable information on the building up of the inner life of the Church in the second century, notably for instance in the liturgical parts of Justin, in the accounts of the relations between Church and State and of the missionary activity of the young Church.

The question as to the success of the second century apologists is, of course, difficult to answer. They did not attain one of their objects, which was to place the Christian religion on the same footing as other cults and thus put an end to persecution by the State. But their works may well have increased the self-confidence of the Christians not a little; and the missionary and propagandist purpose which motivated the work of the apologists certainly played a considerable part in the expansion of Christianity before the end of the second century, especially in the East.

CHAPTER 15

The Dispute with Gnosticism

IF the literary polemic of paganism represented no great danger to the Christian community, there arose in so-called Christian Gnosticism an adversary which, from the first decades of the second century, constituted to an increasing degree a threat to her very existence. It was part of the manifestation of late classical religious syncretism which, based on oriental dualism, united Jewish religious ideas with certain elements of the Christian revelation, albeit in a distorted form. Now, as a mighty current bent on sweeping all before it, it came flooding in from the East.

Gnosticism had a great attraction for Hellenistic man; it made a real appeal to him, demanding that he make up his mind. Its impetus was derived ultimately from its claim to bring to religious-minded persons a valid interpretation of the world and of themselves — the claim made by Christianity itself. Its message was expressed in a copious literature, often of considerable stylistic beauty, and proclaimed by teachers and heads of philosophical schools with respected names. The power of Gnosticism to win recruits was supported by a liturgy which borrowed its forms from the mystery cults or from Christianity and which made skilful use of its symbolic content. The Gnostics carried on a well-planned propaganda, which employed sacred hymns as well as fascinating novels, and they strove to organize their newly-won adherents into a close-knit community. With a sure instinct, Gnosticism felt the Church to be a serious competitor, and it made a bold attempt to conquer her from within, to infiltrate into her congregations and to disrupt them by forming Gnostic cells inside them. The existence of ecclesiastically organized Christianity depended on whether the heads of the Christian congregations saw this danger and were able to sustain a defensive struggle that would tax all their energies.

Until recently, the incompleteness of our sources prevented the writing of any satisfactory account of the basic teachings of Gnosticism and of its manifestations. Only a few works of Gnostic origin were known in the original, as, for instance, the *Pistis Sophia,* which is fairly late, and the *Books of Jeû,* containing alleged revelations of Christ to his disciples. The reason for this state of affairs is that after the victory of Christianity a large part of Gnostic literature — which, in the second century, must certainly have exceeded Christian literature in quantity — was destroyed or else perished through lack of interest. To a great extent therefore the only available material was that contained in quotations and excerpts preserved in the works of Christian anti-Gnostics, especially in those of Irenaeus, Tertullian and Hippolytus, and to a lesser degree in the writings

181

of Clement of Alexandria, Origen, and the later authors, Epiphanius of Salamis and Filastrius of Brescia.

But even anti-Gnostic literature survives only in part. Thus, what was perhaps the earliest work of this kind, Justin's *Against all Heresies*, written at the time when Gnosticism was most flourishing, is now lost.[51] The anti-Gnostic literature of the Church was naturally polemical, deliberately picking out from Gnostic works that which it was most easy to attack; this selection therefore hardly permits us to form a complete picture of the whole realm of Gnostic ideas, for the Christian writers' account of it could not be other than one-sided.

A completely new situation with regard to source-material was brought about by the discovery in 1945–6 of the extensive library of a Gnostic community near the Upper Egyptian town of Nag Hammadi in the vicinity of the former Pachomian monastery of Chenoboskion. It contained in thirteen papyrus manuscripts more than forty hitherto unknown works in the Coptic language, mostly direct translations from the Greek. These translations belong to the end of the fourth or the beginning of the fifth century; the Greek originals were probably written in the second century. Many of the titles of the newly-found treatises at first led to the supposition that they were already known Christian apocrypha; but closer inspection revealed that their contents are quite new. For example, there are apocryphal gospels of Thomas and Philip, a "Gospel of the Egyptians" and a "Gospel of Truth". There are Acts of the apostles Peter and Matthias. Apocalyptic literature is particularly well represented by apocalypses of Peter, Paul, John, James (three), Dositheos, and Seth (Sem). As in many of the manuscripts the prophet Seth plays a central role, we may assume that the library of Nag Hammadi belonged to the Sethian sect, which is often mentioned by early Christian writers. There are, moreover, works of Hermes Trismegistos, doctrinal works by Gnostic leaders such as Silvanos and Eugnostes; others claim to be an "Explanation of Gnosis" or an account of the nature of the archons.[52] Up till now only a fraction of the newly discovered manuscripts is available in the original language or in translations;[53] only the publication of all the texts will make possible an account of Gnosticism that will be accurate in detail.

[51] Justin refers to this work in *Apol.* 1, 26.

[52] Cf. the general account in J. Doresse, *Les livres secrets des gnostiques d'Égypte* (Paris 1958), 165 ff. and W. C. van Unnik *Evangelium aus dem Nilsand* (Frankfurt a. M. 1960), 26 ff., Eng. tr. *Newly Discovered Gnostic Writings* (London 1960).

[53] To the texts named above in the Sources may be added: "Abhandlung über den Ursprung der Welt" in *Muséon* 72 (1959), 349–52; "Traktat über die drei Naturen" in *ThLZ* 84 (1959), 243–56.

On first acquaintance, Gnostic writings convey an overall impression of a confusing mass of ideas and questions, often expressed in strange forms. When examined, however, they reveal a basic theme which recurs in all the variations of Gnostic opinion and can be reduced to one question and the attempt to answer it. The question is: How can man find the true knowledge which will explain the riddle of the world and the evil therein, as well as the riddle of human existence? The Gnostic, Theodotos, gave a rough definition of gnosis. Knowledge (Gnosis) of the answers to the following questions gives freedom: "Who were we? What have we become? Where were we? Whither have we been cast? Whither do we hasten? From what will we become free? What is birth? What is rebirth?"[54] In the answers to these questions the same basic ideas recur: man's inmost being longs for union with the true, perfect, but unknown God. Man, however, by a peculiar destiny has been banished to this imperfect world, which is not the creation of the supreme God, but can only be the work of a lesser, imperfect being, who rules it with the help of evil powers. Man can be free of their domination only if he rightly knows himself and is aware that he is separated from the perfect God. Only this knowledge makes possible his return to the upper world of light where the true God dwells.

This basic theme of Gnosticism, giving mankind an interpretation of the universe and of being, cannot in the present state of research be ascribed to any single, clearly comprehensible and generally recognized source. Rather are its elements derived from different religious movements which are known to have existed during the syncretic period in the Near East and the eastern Mediterranean area. These elements were connected with one another in a variety of ways, so that Gnosticism continually appears under different aspects according to the regions to which it spread and the formulations of its leading representatives. The observer is not confronted with any compact system of clearly defined concepts or dogmatic teachings, but with a multicoloured stream of religious ideas and opinions, which can look different from different points along its banks. Nevertheless, certain currents are discernible which show from which tributaries the river as a whole was formed.

First of all, there already existed a certain substratum of Gnostic ideas independent of any contact with Christianity.[55] Among these was a strongly marked *dualism*, which made an absolute opposition between light and darkness, between good and evil. The home of this dualism is to be found in ancient Iran. When these Iranian ideas met the Genesis account of Creation, this was interpreted in a Gnostic sense. The Creator God of

[54] *Excerpta ex Thodoto* 78, on which see W. C. van Unnik, *op. cit.* 33.
[55] Compare J. Doresse, *op. cit.* 332.

the Old Testament became the Demiurge who did not know the light. Another source whose waters flowed into the Gnostic stream was astrological learning. Since the time of Alexander the Great, astrology had spread through the Hellenistic world from its Babylonian place of origin and had had a far-reaching effect with its doctrine of the influence of the planets on the destinies of man and the world. If such concepts were already widespread in Hellenistic times, it was in the Gnostic movement that they acquired a special force, as we can see from the speculations about the constellations, about the Pole star as the beginning of the kingdom of light, and about the spheres of the seven evil planets or archons.

The new discoveries at Chenoboskion stress the fact that Egypt was a fruitful soil for the growth of Gnostic ideas. It is true that the influence of Egyptian religion needs to be more closely studied, but the hermetic writings in the library at Nag Hammadi certainly point to an undeniable connexion between Egyptian Hermetism and Gnosis. Even though in these writings a demiurge plays no part in the creation of the world and the bizarre figures of the demons are lacking, the opposition which they proclaim between light and darkness, the encounter of a higher being with matter, the liberation of man who is tied to matter and his ascent to God once he is free — all this is part of Gnostic thought, only here the biblical and Christian elements are absent.

The relationship between Judaism and Gnosis constitutes a difficult problem.[56] It is generally admitted that the world of the Old Testament played a significant part in Gnostic literature. The latter is, besides, full of images and ideas such as were current in Jewish apocalyptic works. Biblical influence is particularly strong (even though the Gnostics disagreed with the Bible) in the Gnostic account of Creation. It seems not impossible that late Jewish sectarianism exercised a mediatory function between Iranian and Hellenistic religious currents on the one side and the Gnostic movement on the other, since it can be proved that there were Jewish heretics who were prepared to accept dualistic ideas. One feels compelled to ask if there were not here and there connecting links between Essenes and Gnostics. The Qumran community imposed, like the Gnostics, a strict commandment of absolute secrecy regarding certain parts of its doctrine; the *Book of Discipline* further teaches that God, when he created man, appointed two spirits to govern him, the spirit of truth and the spirit of wickedness, which could make a man into a son of light or a son of darkness — a fundamentally dualistic conception which is strongly

---

[56] G. Scholem, *Major Trends in Jewish Mysticism* (New York 1943); J. Maier, "Das Gefährdungsmotiv bei der Himmelreise in der Jüdischen Apokalyptik und 'Gnosis'" in *Kairos* 5 (1963), 18–40; see also the works of H. J. Schoeps.

reminiscent of similar ideas in Gnosticism. It has also been suggested that remnants of the Qumran community survived in Gnostic circles.[57]

Lastly there were the religiously-tinged philosophical currents of Hellenism, which undeniably found expression in syncretic Gnosticism. Certain themes of Gnostic theology are already foreshadowed in the Platonic doctrine of the fall of the soul and its attachment to the matter of the body. Stoicism too contributed its share to Gnostic thought. The Gnostic writings of Chenoboskion eagerly take up the allegorical interpretations of Homer and Hesiod which Hellenism had developed. Probably, however, the borrowings of Gnosticism from Hellenistic philosophy were in its terminology rather than in its ideas.

When *syncretism* was at the peak of its development, Christianity entered the Hellenistic world from its Palestinian birthplace and, in the syncretic climate of the time, it became the object of growing interest. Many men of that age could not but listen when a new redemption was promised to them through a person who was also the bringer of hitherto unknown revelations. Moreover, the new tidings of salvation came accompanied by a corresponding form of worship whose mysterious rites were alleged to ensure salvation. Such a message and such a cult offered many points of contact through which a connexion with the prevailing religious syncretism might be attempted.

Even, though the process of adopting Christian elements is no longer possible to follow in detail, nevertheless the figure of Christ had soon become a part of Gnostic thought, and many who followed syncretic tendencies were soon claiming to be Christians. About the year 160 Justin mentions men of his time who called themselves Christians, acknowledging Jesus as Lord, but who saw in the Creator of the world only an evil god; there were already several groups of such Christians, who were named after their leaders Valentinians, Marcionites, or Basilidians.[58] A little later Celsus refers to Christian communities known to him as Valentinians and Gnostics.[59] Both Justin and later Origen emphasize, however, that such groups did not represent true Christianity and did not belong to the Church. The syncretic character of such sects is even more clearly shown in Irenaeus' account of a certain Marcellina, who came to Rome in the time of Bishop Anicetus and tried with some success to make converts to her ideas. Her adherents called themselves Gnostics. Among the images of the religious leaders whom they revered was to be found, beside those of Pythagoras and Plato, that of Christ, which supposedly came from Pilate.[60]

[57] Cf. J. Doresse, *op. cit.* 326 f. and R. M. Grant, *Gnosticism and Early Christianity* (London – New York 1959).
[58] Justin, *Dial.* 35, 1–6.
[59] Origen, *Contra Celsum* 5, 61.
[60] Irenaeus, *Adv. haer.* 1, 25, 6.

The leaders of such Gnostic communities appealed in support of their teachings to apostolic tradition or to the words of Christ himself; Ptolemaeos, for instance, a pupil of Valentinus, in his *Letter to Flora*.[61] Others incorporated in their systems Christian ideas in a distorted form, as for example the Valentinians when they stressed the need for redemption, without which no man could reach the *pleroma* or "fulfilment"; the baptism of Jesus effected the remission of sins, but only redemption by Christ, who had descended into him, brought perfection. One became a partaker of this redemption by a mysterious rite and certain formulas to be recited during its performance. Thus the redeemed was to say: " I am confirmed and redeemed; I redeem my soul from this aeon and from all that derives from it, in the name of Jao, who redeemed this soul in Christ, the Living One."[62] Besides echoes of New Testament phraseology, what is here chiefly remarkable is the splitting of the person of the redeemer into an earthly Jesus and a heavenly Christ in a way quite unacceptable to the Christian Church.

Although Christian writers give no precise information on the subject, it may be presumed that the teachers and proselytizers of Gnosis found some of their adherents among the members of the Church, who often lacked the critical power to recognize at once the heterodox character of such opinions. Two factors may have contributed to the success of Gnostic propaganda. First there was the stress laid on ecclesiastical tradition, on which the doctrine of the "true Gnosis" and the salvation to be attained through it alone was supposed to be based; this tradition, because of its exalted nature, could be transmitted only in secret and was clothed in parables that could be explained only to those who were capable of understanding them.[63] Was not this what the gospel of Mark said (4:33-34): "And with many such parables he spoke to them the word, according as they were able to hear. And without parables he did not speak to them: but apart, he explained all things to his disciples"?

From this secret source came the abundance of Gnostic scriptures, which invoked now this apostle or disciple, now that, as the specially chosen messenger of revelation. The very fact that the contents of these revelations were so wrapped in mystery was bound to make them interesting to many Christians, particularly when their attention was directed to them by veiled allusions. Moreover, the success of the Gnostics in winning adherents was founded upon the thesis that they, as Christians of a higher rank, "spiritual men" (πνευματικοί), alone possessed the true interpretation of cosmic events and were thus the only ones capable of attaining to

---

[61] Ptolemy, *Ep. ad Flor.* 7, 8–9.
[62] Irenaeus, *Adv. haer.* 1, 33, 3–7.
[63] Ibid. 1, 3, 1.

186

perfect knowledge of God. He who, like the great mass of Christians, tried to work out his salvation merely by faith and good works, remained for ever on a lower level, a lesser Christian or "psychic".[64] It was unavoidable that a far-reaching conflict should arise between the prophets of such a distorted form of Christianity and the leaders of the Church, if the latter did not wish the substance of their faith to be dissolved.

The Principal Manifestations of Gnosticism

Though the different currents in Gnosticism show a certain basis of opinions held in common, they also show equally clearly how much room there was in the movement as a whole for variations and even contradictions.

The Syrian group belongs to the early phase of Gnosticism and it formed around Menander and Satornil (called Saturninus by Irenaeus) with its centre at Antioch. Menander, a Samaritan by origin, is said to have proclaimed himself as the Redeemer, who had been sent into this world by the invisible powers. The author of the *Philosophoumena* gives more details about the teachings of Satornil. The unknown supreme Father created the angels, powers and aeons of the upper world; the lower, earthly world, however, was the work of seven lower spirits, the highest of whom was identified with the God of the Jews, the Creator of Genesis. To them, man owed his wretched existence, since they had not been able to create him in the image of the Supreme Being. But the Power from above had sent him also a spark of life, which after his death would enable him to return to those higher beings whom he could claim as his kindred.[65] Satornil is said to have been the first Gnostic to mention Jesus; but he was also regarded as a pupil of Simon Magus, in whom Christian apologists saw the actual founder of Gnosis.

The Basilidian school owed its origin to the Syrian Basilides. It ushered in the golden age of Gnosticism and attained great influence, especially at Alexandria, but it also had adherents at Rome. Basilides was very active as an author and, among other works, wrote a commentary on the Gospels in twenty-four books, besides hymns and prayers. A Christian, Agrippa Castor, is said to have attempted a refutation of Basilides in a lost work, *Elenchos*. This Gnostic addressed himself to the Christians with the claim that he was the recipient of secret doctrines which the Redeemer had entrusted to the apostle Matthias in special conversations before his ascension.[66] He was familiar with Persian dualism and taught an elaborate

---

[64] Ibid 1, 6, 1–2.
[65] *Philosophoumena* 7, 28.
[66] J. Doresse, *op. cit.* 21.

doctrine of emanation; according to him innumerable angels inhabited the four heavens and their 365 firmaments. Christ was sent into the world by his unbegotten Father to save from the power of the archons those who believed in him; it was only apparently that he took a human form, and Simon of Cyrene died on the cross in his stead.

The Egyptian Valentinus was evidently Gnosticism's most gifted exponent. In the form in which he preached it, with lofty religious and poetic enthusiasm, it became the most dangerous threat to genuine Christianity. He began to teach at Alexandria about the year 135 and then propagated his opinions in Rome for nearly thirty years. There he seems to have played a leading part in the Christian community, but after a quarrel with the Roman Christians he returned to the East. His teachings were spread by means of letters, hymns, and sermons, and a *Treatise on the Three Natures* is also attributed to him. Irenaeus mentions a *Gospel of Truth* which was said to have been written by Valentinus, and among the finds at Nag Hammadi is a work of this title, the contents of which do not contradict what we know of Valentinus' doctrines. Many of these can be gleaned from writings or fragments of works by his pupils, for example Ptolemaeos, who in his *Letter to Flora* is a moderate propagandist for the Gnostic religion; or Heracleon, who had a predilection for the Gospel of John and wrote commentaries on it which Origen was later to discuss. Perhaps another work of Heracleon survives among the manuscripts at Chenoboskion.

Valentinus' Christian opponents reproached him with having borrowed his wisdom largely from Pythagoras and Plato; they rightly saw that the Gnostic's ideas were similar to those of these philosophers. He also, however, frequently follows Pauline lines of thought and employs words of Christ, interpreted in a Gnostic sense, and this gives his teaching a biblical colouring that may have made it seem familiar to many Christians. The basis of his doctrine of the universe is the common Gnostic myth of the invisible Father, from whom the "syzygies" of the emanations proceed, of which the thirty highest aeons form the pleroma. This is the upper spiritual world, wherein all earthly events have their origin, and to return to which is the longing of imperfect creation.[67] The latter is the work of the Demiurge, who created man and breathed into him the psychic or "natural" element which binds him to matter. Unknown to the Demiurge, however, man also received a pneumatic or "spiritual" element; if this has been awakened and formed by the true Gnosis which the Redeemer brought to earth, the spiritual part of man will be saved at the end of the world and can be again united with the light. In order to make possible the ascent of the lower world towards the light, Jesus became man, and

[67] H. Leisegang, *Die Gnosis* (Stuttgart, 4th ed. 1955), 297.

upon him at his baptism the Spirit descended. For the passage to the light, which led the soul through the realm of the hostile powers, the dying Gnostic was, among the Valentinians, prepared by anointings and secret formulas, in which he said to the angels of the Demiurge that he possessed the true knowledge (gnosis) about himself and whence he came, so that they could not harm him. [68]

On the fringe of these main Gnostic schools, there existed also various sectarian groups representing a highly popularized Gnosticism in which now this, now that particular doctrine often blossomed forth in the most luxuriant forms. Among such sects, anti-Gnostic literature mentions in particular the Barbelo-Gnostics, the Ophites, Naassenes, and Sethians. The first of these took their name from Barbelo, a female emanation of the Father who had the functions of the Logos. In their dualistic interpretation of the universe they employed the Old Testament, allegorically explained; the *Apocryphon Johannis* belongs to this sect, whose adherents were mainly in Egypt and Syria. [69] In the mythology of the widespread sect of the Ophites [70] a special place was given to the serpent, a religious and cosmic symbol in various pagan cults; it represented the son of Jaldaboath, the creator of the heavens and of the angels and demons, who had rebelled against the supreme Father and God. The first human couple was cast out of Paradise by Jaldabaoth, but the serpent too was banished to earth and there he sowed discontent among men and sought, with his six sons, to prevent their return to the supreme Father. But one of the highest aeons, Christ, came into the world in the man Jesus, through whom he proclaimed the truth to mankind. Since his resurrection, the elect had been initiated by Jesus into the mysteries and thus could escape the domination of the Demiurge. Not all Ophite groups regarded the serpent as evil; to some he was neutral, to others the symbol of saving knowledge. The Naassenes probably represented a large sub-group among the Ophites, who, according to Hippolytus, considered themselves to be the true Gnostics and found confirmation of their opinions in all religions. [71]

The sect of the Sethians, both by its use of the serpent-symbol and its borrowings from Greek mythology, closely resembled the Ophites and Naassenes. The author of the *Philosophoumena*, in describing their teachings, mentions a holy book of this sect called the *Paraphrase of Seth*. In its myth of creation, there are not two but three principles in the universe: light, darkness, and between the two, a pure *pneuma* resembling the per-

---

[68] Irenaeus, *Adv. haer.* 1, 21, 5.
[69] Cf. L. Cerfaux, "Barbelo-Gnostiker" in *RAC* I, 1176-80.
[70] Cf. E. Amman, "Ophites" in *DThC* XI, 1063–75; G. Kretzschmer, "Ophiten und Naassener" in *RGG,* 3rd ed. IV, 1659.
[71] *Philosophoumena* 5, 6.

fume of balsam. These three forces are reflected in many forms throughout the cosmos, especially in the symbol of the womb, which through the co-operation of light, darkness, and *pneuma* gives birth to man. The perfect Logos also had to enter into the womb of a virgin; but he was able to cleanse himself and drink the cup of living water, without which no man can find salvation. In one of the manuscripts of Nag Hammadi, entitled *Paraphrase of Sem,* we find the same doctrine of the three principles of the universe (light, darkness, and *pneuma*), so that there is hardly any doubt that it is a Coptic version of the work mentioned in the *Philosophoumena.* [72]

The myth of the triad of world principles is thus a characteristic of the Sethian sect. As other manuscripts in the library of Chenoboskion refer to the prophet Sem or Seth or claim to have been written by him, it may be presumed that the whole collection belonged to a Sethian community, and that further knowledge about the doctrines of the sect may be expected from it. Even now, a preliminary inspection of its contents shows that its ideas were often clothed in a mantle of Christianity, [73] so that the Sethians can undoubtedly be regarded as representatives of a Christian form of Gnosticism.

Marcion

Even if Marcion cannot be called a Gnostic in the full sense, he nevertheless adopted so much of Gnostic thought in his teaching that he may not unjustly be included here as representing a Christian Gnosticism of his own. The facts of his life show us a man of strong will, energy, and initiative combined with organizing ability. A well-to-do native of Asia Minor (he owned a shipping business at Sinope in Paphlagonia), he came into conflict while still quite young with the leaders of the local Christian community, probably because of differences of opinion about the interpretation of Pauline doctrines. His exclusion from the congregation in his own city was followed by his rejection on the part of leading Asiatic Christians such as Papias and Polycarp of Smyrna.

About the year 140 Marcion came to Rome, where he joined the Christian congregation, which he supported with generous financial contributions. His connexion with the Syrian Gnostic Cerdon, who also lived in Rome, no doubt made him more closely acquainted with Gnostic ideas, from which he took especially his doctrine about the Old Testament Creator. The latter was not for Marcion the true God, the Father of

[72] J. Doresse, *op. cit.* 171 ff.
[73] Ibid. 215–37, 237–56.

Jesus Christ, but only the strict and just God who in the Mosaic Law laid upon the Jewish people an unbearable yoke. In Rome too, Marcion's peculiar opinions met with no recognition, and in the autumn of 144 he left the Christian Church, albeit unwillingly.

He at once began with skill and energy to win over adherents, to whom he gave a close-knit organization. Everywhere there arose, alongside the Christian congregations, Marcionite associations, governed by bishops who in turn were assisted by presbyters. As their liturgy continued to follow closely the usage of the Catholic Church,[74] the change-over to Marcion's church was for many Christians not too difficult; and the initial success of the Marcionites, which was evidently considerable, was no doubt largely due to the influx from Christian circles. The strict organization of his establishment distinguished Marcion's community from the other Gnostic groups and gave it a special impetus which made it a serious danger to the Church. She soon recognized this threat, and the majority of ecclesiastical writers from Justin to Tertullian felt obliged to take up the pen against Marcion and his doctrines. Only when their irreconcilability with apostolic tradition was convincingly proved could their attraction for orthodox Christians be neutralized.

Marcion's teaching was based upon a clearly defined canon of scripture, from which the whole of the Old Testament was *a priori* excluded, for therein spoke the God of justice, the creator of the universe, the Demiurge, who was a stranger to goodness and love. The good God revealed himself only when he sent Christ as the Redeemer, who brought to tormented mankind the Gospel of the love of God. Paul was the only apostle who accepted this Gospel without falsifying it. It found expression in his epistles and in the Gospel of Luke, though even these writings had been corrupted by interpolations due to the apostles who adhered to the Old Testament God. Therefore everything had to be removed from them which sought to introduce into the revelation of Christ the justice and legalism of the Old Testament. Marcion wrote a commentary on these purified scriptures, the *Antitheses,* preserved only in a few fragments, which was primarily concerned with explaining his fundamental thesis, the contrast between the Old and the New Testament.

Marcion's thesis, with its dualistic approach, was a direct attack on the Christian concept of God, which did not permit of a division between a strict, merely just Creator and a God of love unknown till the coming of Christ. This doctrine alone might have caused the Christian writers to include Marcion among the Gnostic teachers. But his christology also justified them in doing so; it was less its modalistic colouring than its

---

[74] Tertullian, *Adv. Marc.* 3, 22. Even Augustine, *De Bapt. contra Donatistas* 7, 14, 31, recognizes the validity of Marcionite baptism.

Docetism which provoked their opposition. For Marcion, the idea that the Redeemer Christ sent by the good God should have chosen impure human flesh to be the bearer of the Deity was impossible; a real human birth would have subjected Christ to the dominion of the Demiurge. The Christian adversaries of Marcion, who pointed out that the latter's doctrine of the apparent birth of Christ led to the conclusion that his death on the cross was also apparent and that therefore the redemption was ineffective, were difficult to refute, even though Marcion tried to maintain the reality of the crucifixion. The fact that his pupil Apelles corrected him on this very point clearly shows the weakness of the Marcionite doctrine compared with that of the Catholic Church. In the eyes of his opponents Marcion was finally placed in the Gnostic camp by his rejection of marriage, which, in consequence of his view of the body as a part of evil matter, he forbade to all baptized persons.

Marcion's theology was indeed free from the bizarre speculations of Gnosticism about the emanations of the *pleroma,* free from astrological beliefs, from fantastic cosmogony and from the overestimation of pure gnosis as opposed to faith with its consequent gradation of Christians into "pneumatic" and "psychic". The Gnostic ideas which he adopted were enough, however, to make him suspect in the eyes of the Church and to make his teaching seem in an increasing degree a grave danger to essential features of the Christian faith. That the Church opposed him and his sect with more determination and energy than she did many other Gnostic groups was due to his disturbing success, to which the gravity of his ascetic demands and, perhaps most of all, his strong personality contributed. Like no other figure in the Gnostic world, Marcion compelled the Church to consider and to reconsider her own attitude to Scripture and criteria of faith, to overhaul her organization and to deploy her whole inner strength in face of such a menace.

The Church's Self-Defence
and the Importance of the Christian Victory

The Church's campaign against the threat to her existence caused by the manifold attractions of Gnosticism was waged in two ways, each supplementing and supporting the other. First, the leaders of individual congregations immediately took practical steps against those Gnostics who endeavoured to infiltrate into them, or who, having previously belonged to the congregation, sought from within to win over its members to their new faith. Secondly there were the theological writers of the time, who attacked the Gnostic movement on the literary plane, demonstrating the irreconcilability of its doctrine with Christian revelation and opposing its main theses with the corresponding truths of Christianity, now more precisely formulated as the result of profound study and development.

The defensive struggle at the pastoral level naturally left little evidence in the literary sources and it is therefore harder to reconstruct it in detail. The immediate object was bound to be the suppression of centres of infection within the congregations; that is, the exclusion of the bearers of Gnostic doctrine from the community and the prevention, for the future, of the formation of Gnostic cells in their midst. Only the excommunication of Marcion himself found much of an echo in early Christian literature, but it serves as an example for many similar occurrences that are not mentioned. Probably it was already his Gnostic convictions at their earliest stage, which led to his expulsion from the Christian congregation of his home town, Sinope. Bishop Polycarp of Smyrna also cast him out; in Rome likewise the leaders of the church came to recognize that the exclusion of such a wealthy and influential man was the only means of protecting the Christians from the errors which he preached.[75] Similar measures were no doubt taken in all places where the danger of the formation of Gnostic cells within Christian congregations was seen. The complaint of many Gnostics that the Catholics would have nothing to do with them and called them heretics, although they held the same doctrines, implies such defensive action on the part of the senior clergy. Other Gnostics voluntarily separated themselves from the Christian congregations when they found themselves isolated and unable to carry on their activities; such isolation was itself due to the initiative of the Church authorities or to the congregations' own efforts. Valentinus seems to have been late in breaking with the Church, but he had been repeatedly reprimanded in the congregations to which he had belonged.

The eradication of Gnostic cells was accompanied by sermons explaining the insidious nature of false doctrines, and Christians were warned by their pastors of the danger to the true faith. Irenaeus gives excerpts from the sermons of an Asiatic priest which he had himself heard;[76] they are entirely affirmative in tone and are concerned with expounding the orthodox Catholic teaching, but they unmistakably constitute a refutation of characteristic Marcionite doctrines, without any mention of Marcion by name. We are led to suppose that instruction and immunization against the Gnostic menace was the practice of most Christian leaders of the time.

That this form of defence was not merely local is shown by the example

---

[75] A. von Harnack, *Marcion* (Leipzig, 2nd ed. 1924), 24–27; for the documentary proofs, see ibid. 3*–5*, 15* f.
[76] *Adv. haer.* 4, 27–31.

of Dionysius, Bishop of Corinth about the year 170. Eusebius devotes some informative lines to his pastoral activities.[77] Dionysius carried on a lively correspondence not only with the churches in Greece itself but even with Asia Minor and far-off Pontus, seeking to build up a broad defensive front against the heresies of the age. He urged the Christians of neighbouring Athens and the island of Crete to hold fast to the true doctrine and warned them against false teachings, just as he warned the congregations of Amastris and Nicomedia in Bithynia. The heresy of his time was primarily Gnosticism; indeed, his letter to Nicomedia expressly names Marcion, to whose errors he opposed the "Canon of Truth". The special situation in which Christianity found itself placed with regard to Gnosticism made the bishops more fully aware of their duties as guardians of orthodoxy, and the increased activity of the heads of congregations which resulted made the faithful more conscious of the monarchical episcopate and of its significance for the future.

Parallel to this activity of the bishops in combating Gnosticism ran that of the theological writers, to whom the rise and growth of the Gnostic movement acted as a powerful stimulus. An extensive body of literature from the Catholic side supported the Church authorities and provided a theological basis for the counter-attack. Most of this anti-Gnostic literature has perished, especially since the fourth century, when, because of the completely changed situation, there was no need to take any interest in the products of the second. A considerable part of these writings was still extant when Eusebius wrote, and he mentions a number of authors who were active in their production, but he evidently gives only a selection. Among them were Agrippa Castor, who opposed Basilides, Rhodon from Asia Minor who wrote against Marcion and his pupil Apelles, and Modestus, whose refutation of Marcion was specially praised by Eusebius.[78] Bishops who wrote anti-Gnostic works include Melito of Sardes, Philip of Gortyna in Crete and Theophilos of Athens, all of whom were concerned with refuting Marcion; this shows how much importance was attached to the man and his work. He was also the object of attacks by Justin Martyr and several other theologians whom Eusebius does not name.[79]

Certain apocryphal writings on the Catholic side, such as the *Acta Pauli*[80] and the *Epistula Apostolorum*[81] were also of anti-Gnostic tendency and were intended as the orthodox counterpart to similar literature of

---

[77] *Euseb. HE*, 4, 23, 2–6.
[78] Ibid. 4, 25.
[79] Ibid.
[80] Cf. C. Schmidt, *Acta Pauli* (Leipzig, 2nd ed. 1905); Πράξεις Παύλου (Hamburg 1936).
[81] C. Schmidt, *Gespräche Jesu* (Leipzig, 1919); H. Duensing in *Hennecke-Schnee-melcher*, I, 126–55.

Gnostic provenance. Hegesippus, who was of oriental origin, wrote his *Memorials* (of which some fragments are extant) against the Gnostics; soon after the middle of the second century, seeking instruction in the true doctrine in view of the widespread success of Gnosticism, he came to Rome. Irenaeus, Bishop of Lyons, in his "Unmasking and Refutation of the False Gnosis", gives an analysis of Gnosticism based on his own reading of Gnostic writings, which is of outstanding merit. Another work which he planned to write against Marcion seems not to have been carried out. To his account of Gnostic systems Irenaeus added a refutation of their errors. He opposed them, using his own exact knowledge of Scripture and tradition, with the true doctrine of the Church. The author's interest in his subject and the soundness of his work make us forget any stylistic failings; his achievement was not surpassed by any of the anti-Gnostic writers who succeeded him. Of equal merit is the author of the *Philosophoumena* or *Refutatio,* which is generally ascribed (though not with absolute certainty) to the priest Hippolytus, who came from the East and was active in Rome at the beginning of the third century. [82] His work presupposes a knowledge of Irenaeus; but he brought a new point of view into the discussion, inasmuch as he sought to show that the opinions of the Gnostics were not taken from Holy Scripture but from the works of the Greek philosophers, from the mysteries, from writers on astrology and magic — in fact, from non-Christian sources. Hippolytus' account of the catholic attitude is concise and jejune compared with that of Irenaeus and gives little information about the nature of the Church's campaign against Gnosticism. In this respect his work resembles the *Syntagma,* [83] a review of the heresies that had arisen down to the author's time. The original is lost, but it can be reconstructed from the writings of later users.

More important are the works of the only Latin writer who engaged in the controversy with Gnosticism, Tertullian of Carthage, who, however, did not write until the third century. The two short treatises, *De carne Christi* and *De resurrectione carnis* prove positively from Scripture that two of the Gnostics' theses were untenable: their doctrine of Christ's "apparent" body and their rejection of the resurrection of the body. Three other writings were directed against particular Gnostics: Hermogenes, the Valentinians, and Marcion. To the last work, consisting of five books, Tertullian devoted special care; it gives a detailed account of the principal

---

[82] Ed. by P. Wendland, GCS 26 (Berlin 1916). For discussion of the authorship, see P. Nautin, *Hippolyte et Josipe* (Paris 1947); idem in *RHE* 47 (1952), 5–43; *RSR* 41 (1954), 226–57 (against Hippolytus); G. Bardy and M. Richard in *MSR* 1948, 1950–1, 1953 are in favour of Hippolytus. Further bibliography in *Altaner* 185.

[83] P. Nautin, *Hippolyte, Contre les hérésies* (Paris 1949).

Marcionite doctrines followed by a skilful refutation based on reason and the Bible. In *De praescriptione haereticorum*[84] he explains the meaning and value of apostolic tradition as opposed to the claim of the heretics, especially the Gnostics, to possess the true doctrine of Christ. The language he uses is that of the Roman law courts.

On the basis of this surviving anti-Gnostic literature we are able to give some account of the character and quality of the theological struggle against Gnosticism, at least in its main features. In general one may say that the Church's theologians thought out anew and established on a firmer foundation those points of Christian revelation which were particularly attacked and threatened by Gnostic teachings.

The claim of the heretics to be the sole possessors of the revelation imparted by Christ to his apostles meant nothing less than a depreciation of the Christian scriptures, which dated from apostolic times, and of the other, extra-biblical apostolic traditions; furthermore it implied a rejection of the Christian bishops' claim to be the only lawful witnesses to that body of tradition. If this Gnostic thesis were correct, then the whole foundation crumbled on which the inner cohesion of the Church had hitherto rested. The Christian theologians set to work to prevent the threatened collapse by bringing into the foreground the concepts of *apostolic tradition* and *succession*, and by deciding and confirming what constituted the Christian scriptures. A starting-point for the establishment of a *canon* of New Testament scriptures was already given in the books of the Old Testament, recognized as sacred; these served as a model and an encouragement to accord rank and respect to books from the period of the primitive Church. Even though we can no longer clearly discern the beginnings of this development, it is evident that two originally separate collections, the four Gospels and the Pauline epistles, gradually came closer together, although the latter were not yet accorded parity of esteem with the Gospels. According to Melito of Sardes, in the years 170–80, books of the New Testament were placed on the same level as those of the Old. No doubt the example of Marcion, who declared a clearly defined canon of New Testament writings to be necessary, hastened a development already begun in the Church. She did not however copy Marcion, but, in sharp contrast to him, accepted the Old Testament as sacred scriptures — the Christian understanding of them being made easier by developing allegorical interpretation — and then incorporated in her New Testament canon other books rejected by Marcion, notably the Acts of the Apostles and the Apocalypse. In the controversy with Gnosticism this canon became widely accepted, and in the "Muratorian

[84] The works mentioned are in *CSEL* 47 (1906) and 70 (1942); reprinted in *CChr* 1–2 (1952–3).

Fragment", a list (made by the Roman congregation or one closely attached to it) of the New Testament books held to be canononical, it is already approaching its final form before the end of the second century.[85]

In deciding which individual writings were to be included, the Church had to be able to invoke an undisputed, objective principle. This was to be found in ecclesiastical *tradition*.[86] Only those books could be recognized as canonical which went back to apostolic times and had from an early date been particularly esteemed in the traditions of the whole Christian community. The only guarantors of the genuineness of such traditions were those leaders of congregations who could trace their unbroken succession back to the apostles. The positive effect of this principle of apostolic *succession* was to assure the place of *tradition* as an essential element of the Church's faith and theology. Its negative effect was to strip the Gnostic apocrypha and doctrinal works of their authority and cut them off from the Church, for in no case could they claim to be acknowledged by the witnesses and guardians of apostolic tradition.

A second principle was employed by the Christian theologians in their war against error, that which Irenaeus calls the *Canon of Truth*,[87] given to the faithful at baptism. This seems to refer to the baptismal "symbol" or profession of faith, or at least to the summary of truths to which the catechumens had been introduced during their instruction before baptism. Whoever compared the teachings of the Gnostics with this norm or rule of faith could immediately see how they contradicted the true doctrine. The profession of faith at baptism had in fact about the middle of the second century been expanded in a christological sense[88] to affirm more emphatically the reality of the human birth and of the Passion and death of Christ. This was a blow at the Docetism of many Gnostic sects and a declaration of the historicity of our Lord's miracles in the face of "spiritualist" attempts to explain them away. The same creed proclaimed the one God and Lord and Creator of the universe and thus rejected all Gnostic speculations about the origin of the cosmos as well as Marcion's doctrine of two gods. The Christian conviction of the resurrection of the body contrasted with the Gnostics' contempt for the body as part of matter, held by them to be radically evil.

---

[85] Cf. Wikenhauser, *New Testament Introduction* (Freiburg – New York – London, 3rd ed. 1963), 20–40, and O. Cullmann, *Tradition* (Zürich 1954), 42–54.

[86] J. Ranft, *Der Ursprung des katholischen Traditionsbegriffes* (Würzburg 1931); H. von Campenhausen, *Kirchliches Amt* (Tübingen 1953), 163–94; A. Ehrhardt, *The Apostolic Succession in the First Two Centuries of the Church* (London 1953), and esp. H. E. W. Turner, *The Pattern of Truth* (London 1954), 241–58, 322–48.

[87] *Adv. haer.* 1, 9, 4; 1, 22, 1, on which see Turner, *op. cit.* 349 ff.

[88] The texts are in *Denzinger* nos. 1–12 and H. Lietzmann, *KlT* 17–18, (Berlin, 4th ed. 1935); see also Bibliography.

During the course of the conflict some individual theologians were moved to lay stress on certain truths of revelation which were endangered or distorted by Gnostic opinions. Thus Irenaeus made it his special concern, in the face of the dualistic misunderstanding of original sin, to expound the true doctrine of the Fall, and in oppostion to Gnostic self-redemption to emphasize the gratuitousness of the gift of grace.[89] The exaggeration by the Gnostics of the value of "knowledge" for redemption was later the occasion for Clement of Alexandria and Origen to consider more deeply the relationship between faith and knowledge and to acquire a Christian understanding and a true theological appreciation of Gnosis.[90]

The Christian doctrines and principles brought into prominence by the opponents of the Gnostics do not of course contain any hitherto completely unknown elements of the faith. The Church could hardly have saved her independence, threatened as it was by the innovations of Gnostic propaganda, by combating them with novelties of her own. For the Church, the rise of the Gnostic heresy was nevertheless a very efficient stimulus to reconsider the truths she possessed, to formulate some of them more clearly and to emphasize them more decidedly. Marcionitism in particular hastened the process of the development of dogma and of the Church's consciousness of her own identity, and thus it played its part in forming the character of the "Great Church" of the future. But it would be a distortion of historical reality to see in that Church merely an anti-Marcionite movement. Her inner riches exceeded the sum-total of the doctrines defended in the attack on Marcionitism; the very strength of the independence with which the young Church defeated Marcion and the other Gnostics reveals the extent of those riches.

The decisive victory in the Church's favour occurred before the end of the second century; within a few decades the poison had been ejected, and Gnosticism was thrown back upon itself. Marcion's church, because of its strict organization, lasted longer; but the other Gnostic groups lost all cohesion and lapsed into sectarianism, even though their ideas exercised a certain power of attraction upon educated members of Christian congregations in the big cities down to the middle of the third century, as the works of the Alexandrines, of Hippolytus and Tertullian testify. After that time, anti-Gnostic polemic writings appeared only sporadically, and

---

[89] Esp. Irenaeus, *Adv. haer.* 1, 3, 4; 3, 18, 2; 3, 18, 7; 3, 23, 1; see E. Scharl, *Recapitulatio Mundi. Der Rekapitulationsbegriff des Irenaeus* (Freiburg i. Br. 1941); A. Houssiau, *La christologie de S. Irénée* (Louvain 1955).

[90] O. Casel, "Glaube und Gnosis" in *JLW* 15 (1951), 164–95; T. Camelot, *Foi et gnose chez Clément d'Alexandrie* (Paris 1945); J. Moingt, "La gnose de Clément d'Alexandrie dans ses rapports avec la foi et la philosophie" in *RSR* 37 (1950), 195–251, 398–421, 537–64, 38 (1951), 82–118; W. Völker, *Der wahre Gnostiker nach Klemens von Alexandrien* (Berlin 1952).

their complete cessation in the fourth century proves that the once so powerful movement had become insignificant. The actual importance of this swift and permanent victory lies in the fact that the Church, faced by the Gnostic attack, preserved her special character as a supernatural community sharing the same faith and way of life and founded by Christ. Thus she escaped the danger of being swallowed up and of perishing in the sea of Hellenistic syncretism.

CHAPTER 16

The Rise of Montanism and the Church's Defence

THE conflict with Gnosticism was not yet over when a new movement arose in the bosom of the Church which called itself the "New Prophecy". Its opponents called it the "heresy of the Phrygians", thus indicating the geographical area which saw its birth. Only in the fourth century was the term "Montanism" invented, when it was desired to emphasize the part played by Montanus in originating it.

The name "New Prophecy" aptly describes the basic idea of this movement. It took up again that form of religious enthusiasm, so much esteemed in the primitive Church, which regarded certain individual believers as specially favoured messengers of the Spirit and as prophets who placed their gifts at the service of the community. False prophets, illusionaries and swindlers among them had indeed, here and there, brought discredit on prophecy and created mistrust of any new "bearers of the Spirit" that might arise. There had also been tension between those favoured by the Spirit and those who wielded ecclesiastical authority; but good relations had always been restored, for charismatic gifts and the authority of the clergy were not necessarily mutually exclusive. This time, however, it came to a clash between prophecy and authority, which led to the exclusion of adherents of the movement from the community of the Church.

The development of the Montanist movement had an early phase, then a period when it underwent modification by Tertullian, and finally a stage of decline after the Church had defeated it. The early phase began about 170, when the recently baptized Montanus, in the village of Ardabau on the borders of Phrygia and Mysia, proclaimed to his fellow-Christians, with ecstatic behaviour and in strange, obscure language, that he was the mouthpiece and prophet of the Holy Spirit, who was now, through him, to lead the Church to all truth. At first this message was received with some doubts; but when two women, Priscilla and Maximilla, joined

Montanus and in a similar ecstatic manner uttered their prophecies, while Montanus himself promised his adherents a higher place in the approaching heavenly Jerusalem,[91] a wave of enthusiasm swept away all hesitation. No connexion can be proved between the old Phrygian cults and the New Prophecy, though the population of the interior of Asia Minor does seem to have had a certain tendency towards religious excesses. The initial success of the three prophets was considerable, although they confined themselves to oral propaganda and at first had no writer of consequence to proclaim their message to the world. For this very reason the prophecies of Montanus and his female companions were treasured by the followers of the movement, and they were soon collected and circulated. Only a few of these *oracula* are to be found in the works of anti-Montanist writers or of Tertullian, so that we have to rely largely on the accounts of opponents to find out what the New Prophecy consisted of.

The most prominent feature of it was its *eschatological message:* the second coming of the Lord was at hand and with it the heavenly Jerusalem would be set up in the plain near the Phrygian town of Pepuza. In many parts of the empire men were not unprepared for this message, due to the grave tribulations which pestilence, war, and social distress under Marcus Aurelius had brought in their train. Hippolytus relates that a Syrian bishop had gone out at the head of his congregation to meet Christ, whom he intended to await in the desert, and that a bishop in Pontus had announced what had been revealed to him in a dream — that the last judgment would take place in a year's time. There would be no need to believe the Scriptures any more (this bishop had added) if his prophecy were not fulfilled.[92] Probably the Montanist movement would have had little effect either in depth or in extent if it had confined itself to the proclamation of its eschatological message; when the prophesying ceased, a more sober frame of mind would, as in similar cases, have returned. But the prophets drew consequences from their alleged heavenly mandate which involved far-reaching interference with the existing practice of the Church and eventually forced the ecclesiastical authorities to condemn the whole movement.

Fasting suggested itself as a means of spiritual preparation for the coming of Christ, for it had long been recognized as a form of inner sanctification, and the official fasts known as "stations" had also been instituted from eschatological motives.[93] Hitherto these fasts had been limited to two half-days in the week and recommended by the Church

---

[91] Epiphanius, *Haer.* 48, 10; Tertullian, *De exhort. cast.* 10.

[92] Hippolytus, *In Daniel.* 4, 18–19.

[93] Cf. H. Kraft, "Die altchristliche Prophetie und die Entstehung des Montanismus" in *ThZ* 11 (1955), 258 ff.

to the faithful as a voluntary exercise. Montanus went beyond the previous practice when he made continual fasting a matter of precept for all Christians, since Christ's return might be expected at any hour. When it did not take place, the fast was confined to the customary stational days but prolonged till the evening and two weeks of abstinence were added, during which only dried food was permitted. [94]

The same eschatological attitude lay behind the second demand of the Montanist prophets, that which forbade the Christian who was waiting for his Lord to make any attempt at flight from martyrdom. Evasion would have meant a renewed attachment to this world, which was after all approaching its end. Earthly possessions, too, had no value any more, so it should not have been difficult for Montanists to give up their gold, silver, and other valuables to pay for the support of their preachers and prophets.

The Montanists' demand for the *renunciation of marriage* (as far as this was possible) was bound to have the most decisive effect. In their eyes it was marriage that most strongly attached men and women to this world. Both prophetesses set a good example by ceasing to live with their husbands; they evidently represented it as a duty that others should imitate this example and forbade marriages to take place in the brief span of time before the second coming of the Lord. Tertullian later amended this rule to prohibition of second marriages. Priscilla had a further reason for requiring total continence: it made one better able to see prophetic visions and to utter prophetic messages. [95]

Montanism naturally showed most enthusiasm in its early phase. New communities in Lydia and Galatia soon added to its already numerous adherents in Phrygia. From the provinces of Asia Minor it passed to Syria (ever receptive to new ideas), where it was especially successful at Antioch; soon it appeared in Thrace also. The Gallic congregations of Lyons and Vienne heard about the Montanist movement surprisingly early, as appears from Eusebius, [96] who writes of a correspondence between those congregations and "brethren" in Asia and Phrygia in which it figures. Eleutheros, Bishop of Rome, was independently informed of the rise of the New Prophecy, but he clearly did not regard it as a serious danger, for he uttered no judgment upon it. Perhaps he was confirmed in this attitude by the Christians of Lyons, who sent their presbyter Irenaeus to Rome with a letter which likewise did not condemn the Phrygian movement. Pope Zephyrinus (199–217) also looked favourably upon it at first, for he sent its members letters of peace, which were the expression of

---

[94] Tertull., *De ieiun.* 1, 2, 10.
[95] *Euseb. HE* 5, 18, 3.
[96] Ibid. 5, 3, 4.

fellowship within the Church. Tertullian ascribes the later change in Pope Zephyrinus' attitude to Praxeas of Asia Minor, who had given him more detailed information, admittedly somewhat distorted, about the prophets and their churches.[97] The Roman bishops, then, were at first unaware of the danger which the New Prophecy represented to the existence of the ecclesiastical organization and of an ordered congregational life.

The first setback to the further spread of the movement was the death of the three original bearers of the prophecy. Maximilla died in 179. It was she who had announced: "After me no other prophet will come, but there will be the consummation of all things."[98] She had with these words enabled many followers to form a judgment upon the genuineness of her prophesying, and it could not be other than unfavourable. Perhaps the movement would have declined more rapidly — certainly the conflict with it would have taken a different form on the Church's side — if a man of the stature of Tertullian had not joined it and, on the level of literary discussion at least, given it a new importance.

We have no evidence as to when and how the African writer came into contact with the New Prophecy. From about the years 205–6 onwards his writings show not only that he knew its basic teaching and its demands on the faithful, but that he approved of them. Even in a man of the spiritual greatness of Tertullian one might have assumed there would be a period of inner struggle preceding the change from Catholic to fanatical Montanist, for his new faith involved a contrast, patent to all the world, with his previous convictions; he now scorned in unmeasured invective what he had once ardently defended and respected. What it was that appealed to him in the New Prophecy is not difficult to see when we read his Montanist writings. He found in it an attitude towards the Christian way of life which, in its pitiless severity to all that was mediocre, corresponded to his own rigoristic approach, but which could not in any way be connected with the Gnostic heresy or with the false doctrines of a man like Praxeas. What attracted him even more perhaps was that in the Montanist form of Christianity one could directly invoke the Holy Spirit in support of one's opinions; before this highest court of appeal all others had to be silent — the martyrs, the episcopal Church, the Bishop of Rome himself.

Tertullian was not, however, the man to accept the New Prophecy quite uncritically. He thought out afresh its doctrines and organization and modified it so much in detail that Tertullian's Montanism is something altogether different from that of the early days. The three great prophets of that first phase were for him no inviolable authority. He

[97] Tertull., *Adv. Praxean* 1.
[98] Epiphan., *Haer.* 48, 2, 4.

possessed indeed a collection of their prophetic utterances, but he made sparing use of them and preferred to lend weight to his views by appealing to the Paraclete directly. Especially did he deny to women in the Montanist community, as conceived by him, a rank like that accorded to Priscilla and Maximilla. They were not to hold any priestly function, nor were they to be allowed to teach or to speak at divine worship, even if they possessed the gift of prophecy; their use of it, if so endowed, was to be confined to private utterances.[99] He also disavowed the more concrete prophecies referring to the descent of the heavenly Jerusalem — Pepuza he never mentions. One gets the impression that he wished to detach the New Prophecy from its connexion with the personalities of its early phase and its local associations with Asia Minor and to give it a universal character. His grand design, of which neither Montanus nor his female assistants were capable, is clear from the new basis in salvation history which Tertullian gave the movement. Its real mission consisted, according to him, in bringing Christianity and mankind in general to adult maturity through the working of the Paraclete.[100]

Tertullian's principal Montanist writings[101] repeat the rigoristic demands of the New Prophecy with undiminished severity and in passionate language. With a sophistry that sometimes borders on the acrobatic he defends the prohibition against flight in time of persecution, and represents one marriage only as a commandment of the Paraclete that admits of no exception (secundae nuptiae adulterium).[102] In like manner he proves the obligation to fast, which the "natural men" or "psychics", whom he reviles in unmeasured terms, refused to accept. His attack on the Church's practice in the matter of penance is of ruthless severity towards sinners and the fallen. It was his attitude on this question that made him into an opponent in principle of the episcopal Church and led him finally to break away from ecclesiastical authority based upon the apostolic succession.

He soon had to give up his attempt to win over the Christian congregation in his home town of Carthage to the Montanist movement. It is remarkable that after Tertullian's time the sources are at first completely silent about Montanism; in no work or letter of Cyprian is there even a remote echo of it. Evidently the exaggerated rigorism of its African advocate had been unable to gain any large body of adherents among the simple Christian folk of that region. Tertullian's writings, however, undoubtedly found readers; their literary quality and the

[99] Tertull., De virg. vel. 9.
[100] Ibid., 1.
[101] De fuga in persecutione, De monogamia, De ieiunio adversus psychicos, De pudicitia.
[102] De monog. 15.

uniqueness of their contents would have ensured that. But there were only readers, not converts. Shortly before Augustine's death a remnant of Tertullianists rejoined the Church in Africa and brought their basilica into Catholic possession.

The defensive campaign of the ecclesiastical authorities against Montanism began, as we have said, slowly, because the latter's opposition to the Christian way of life and to the tradition of the Church became apparent only on closer examination. Emphasis on fasting and readiness for martyrdom, as well as praise for high moral standards in marriage had always been staple themes of Christian preaching; even the renewal of esteem for the prophetic gifts of the early Church gave no cause for alarm. In the message of the New Prophecy there was, moreover, no connexion to be seen with the errors the Church had hitherto been fighting against. Only when it became clear that its genuinely Christian aims were distorted by an immoderate exaggeration of their real significance, and that they represented a falsification of Christian tradition, did defensive action become necessary.

The bishops of Asia Minor must sooner or later have had to face the question, which is bound to arise in the case of every enthusiastic movement, whether the claims of the New Prophecy were not based upon an illusion. Some of them therefore tried to test the genuineness of these prophetic gifts, but they were repulsed by the Montanists. The bishops repeatedly took counsel together (the first example of such synods in the history of the Church) and came to the conclusion that it was not the Spirit of God which spoke through the new prophets. They were therefore to be excluded from the fellowship of the Church together with their adherents. Even towards the middle of the third century a synod of bishops in Iconium was concerned with Montanism; splinter groups were to be found in Spain at the end of the fourth, in Rome at the beginning of the fifth, and in the East even as late as the ninth century.

The victory of the Church over Montanism had consequences for her which brought her unique nature into greater prominence and determined her future development. By refusing to make the excessively ascetic programme of the Montanists a norm binding on all Christians, she escaped the danger of sinking to the level of an insignificant sect of enthusiasts and preserved herself for the task of bringing the message of Christ to all men and making it possible for that message to be effective in every cultural milieu. Moreover, by eliminating uncontrollable religious subjectivism as represented by the Phrygian prophets, with its claim to the sole leadership of the faithful, the Christian community was assured of objective guidance by the traditional office-holders whose calling was based on objective criteria. Finally by renouncing an eschatological hope which believed its fulfilment to be impending, it became possible for the Church to consider with an objective eye her tasks for the present and the future and to embark upon them with confidence: these were her own inner strengthening and her further missionary activity in the Hellenistic world.

CHAPTER 17

The Expansion of Christianity down to the End of the Second Century

THE question of the Church's expansion in the second century brings us back to Palestine again. The Jewish war of the first century had, for the time being, put an end to the missionary work of the Jerusalem congregation and of the Christians dwelling in the countryside. Many of the Christians who had fled to Pella, east of the Jordan, probably did not go back to Palestine; those who returned were faced with the task of rebuilding community life in and outside Jerusalem, so that by the years 73–74 a new period of Palestinian Jewish Christianity had begun. Its centre was again at Jerusalem, where the congregation was presided over by Simeon until his martyrdom about the year 107.[103] Regarding the size of the congregation our sources make only vague statements; but a remark of Eusebius is noteworthy, according to which "very many of the circumcision had come to the faith in Christ" down to the time of Simeon's death.[104] From this it is clear that the new community, like its predecessor, engaged in missionary activity; for Jews in large numbers had settled again in the city after the catastrophe of the seventies, but they now lacked a Temple as a centre for their religious life.

Hegesippus states that at this time there were also Christians outside Jerusalem, especially in Galilee, and this information is confirmed by rabbinical sources.[105] The missionary efforts of the Christians certainly encountered enormous difficulties. First of all they had to deal with heterodox Jewish Christianity, which, partly at least, continued to assert that the Law was still binding on all Christians and recognized Jesus of Nazareth as a great prophet indeed, but not as the Messiah and Son of God; moreover, it had been permeated by Gnostic ideas, as formulated by Simon Magus, Dositheos, Menander and Kerinthos.[106] Samaria especially

---

[103] *Euseb. HE* 3, 32, 1–3.
[104] Ibid., 3, 35.
[105] Ibid., 3, 20, 6; 3, 32, 6; cf. A. Schlatter, *Die Geschichte der ersten Christenheit* (Gütersloh 1927), 363.
[106] J. Daniélou, *La théologie du judéo-christianisme* (Paris 1958), 67–89, Eng. tr. *The Theology of Jewish Christianity* (London 1964).

was under the influence of Simon and Menander and offered little scope to the Christian mission. [107]

The Christians met the most determined opposition from orthodox Palestinian Jewry, based as it was upon a profound hatred of the "apostates" who had renounced the Sabbath and proclaimed as Messiah him whom the Jews had nailed to the cross. [108] According to the evidence of Justin, [109] not only was this hatred deliberately fomented in the synagogues of Palestine, but it led to powerful missionary counter-activity; from Palestine the Jews sent forth "chosen men" who were to work against the spread of the Christian faith everywhere, especially in the main centres of the Jewish Diaspora. The denunciation of Bishop Simeon also came from anti-Christian circles in Palestine. He was denounced before the proconsul Atticus as being a descendant of David and a Christian, and in the year 107 he was, according to the principle of Trajan's later rescript, crucified after steadfastly professing the faith. [110] Accessions from paganism were probably not considerable in Palestine; the only convert from paganism who is mentioned is Aquila, the translator of the Bible, who, according to the late account of Epiphanios, joined the Church at Jerusalem, but because of his superstitious tendencies was subsequently excluded from the congregation. [111]

As the Jewish war had brought to an end the original community, so did the rebellion of Bar Cochba in the years 132–5 conclude the second phase of Palestinian Christianity and with it the possibility of missionary work among the Jews of Palestine. Persecution by the leader of the rebellion caused the deaths of many Jewish Christians; [112] others again fled beyond the Jordan. As no person of Jewish race was allowed to live in the city of Aelia Capitolina, built on the site of Jerusalem, a Christian congregation could be recruited only from pagan converts. Its first bishop, Marcus, was therefore, as Eusebius states, a Greek; and all his successors down to the middle of the third century bore Greek or Roman names. [113] The Gentile-Christian congregation of Jerusalem played no remarkable role during the rest of the second century, at the end of which the bishopric of Aelia ranked below that of Caesarea. In the rest of Palestine too, the Christians were now mainly Greeks, dwelling almost exclusively in the towns. All attempts at christianizing the Jewish rural population failed

---

[107] Justin, *Dial.* 120, 6; *Apol.* 26 56.
[108] *Euseb. HE* 3, 27, 5.
[109] Justin, *Dial.* 133, 6; 137, 2; 17, 1; 108, 2.
[110] *Euseb. HE* 3, 32, 3–6.
[111] Epiph., *De mensuris* 14–15; Irenaeus, *Adv. haer.* 3, 21, 1, calls him a proselyte.
[112] Justin, *Apol.* 31.
[113] *Euseb. HE* 4, 6, 4.

down to the time of Constantine, because of determined hostility towards everything Christian.[114]

In neighbouring Syria the Christian churches dating from apostolic times maintained themselves or increased in importance. The Christians in Damascus, Sidon, and Tyre, likewise had increased in numbers during the course of the second century, while the Phoenician countryside remained largely pagan. In Antioch especially — its earliest important mission-centre — Christianity gained in consideration on account of its bishop, Ignatius, and acquired new converts from among the Greek-speaking population. The letter of Bishop Theophilos, written shortly after 180 to Autolykos,[115] is both apologetical and propagandist in tone and shows that missionary work was going on among the pagan upper class.

In the second half of the second century new territory was opened up to Christianity in the east Syrian district of Osrhoëne, when the Jewish Christian Addai began to work in Edessa and its immediate neighbourhood. His labours were continued by the future martyr Aggai and the leaders of the Edessan congregation, Hystaspes and Aggai, the latter of whom had to excommunicate Bardesanes (converted to Christianity in 179) on account of his Gnostic errors. The existence of Christians between Nisibis and the Euphrates in the second half of the second century is suggested by the Aberkios inscription.[116] At that time other congregations were established around Edessa, among which we must presume there existed a certain degree of organized union, for a synod at Edessa discussed the question of the date of Easter.[117] Tatian may have compiled his *Diatessaron* for these communities. The consecration of Bishop Palut for the see of Edessa, which took place at Antioch about the year 190, shows Antioch's interest in this promising mission-field, which was soon to be contested by various heretics. That the royal house was converted to Christianity in the second century and that Christianity was established as the State religion has often been accepted as fact; it remains, however, open to question.[118] The destruction of a Christian church at Edessa in the flood of 201 is evidence of a well developed ecclesiastical organization. Bardesanes mentions regular Sunday assemblies and fasting on particular days.[119] It is characteristic of the young Syrian church that it did not confine itself to the cities, but from the beginning concerned itself with the evangelization of the country folk. From Edessa Christianity

---

[114] Cf. *Harnack Miss* 638–43.
[115] See above, chapter 14.
[116] Cf. I. Ortiz de Urbina, *Gr* 15 (1934), 84–86.
[117] *Euseb.* HE 5, 23, 4.
[118] I. Ortiz de Urbina, *loc. cit.*, 86–91.
[119] Cf. H. H. Schaeder, "Bardesanes von Edessa" in *ZKG* 51 (1932), 21–74, esp. 72.

penetrated farther east into Mesopotamia, thanks to the labours of the missionary Addai.

Whereas southern Arabia appears to have had no Christians for a long time, northern Arabia or Transjordan shows evidence that Christianity was known there in the first and second centuries. "Arabs" were represented among the Jews and proselytes staying in Jerusalem at the first Pentecost (Acts 2:11). The faith may also have been brought to the lands east of the Jordan by Jewish Christians fleeing from Jerusalem and Palestine. The apologist Ariston, who wrote his *Dialogue between Jason and Papiskos concerning Christ* shortly before the middle of the second century, belonged to the congregation of Pella.[120] But before the third century there can have been only individual Arab conversions, most likely in cities such as Bostra, which had come into contact with Hellenistic civilization.

The beginnings of Christianity in Egypt are obscure, in spite of the discovery of numerous papyri of the first and second centuries. As the account of the founding of the Egyptian church by Peter is based on later legends,[121] the fragment of John's Gospel on papyri of the early second century may be regarded as the earliest proof of the presence of Christians on Egyptian soil.[122] We must also bear in mind that the Gnostic mission had more initial success there than orthodox Christianity, of the existence of which in Alexandria we have no clear evidence dating from before the last two decades of the second century. Pantaenus is the first mentioned preacher of the Christian faith; about the year 190 Bishop Demetrios was the head of an already considerable congregation, consciously preparing for the growth of the Church in the third century.

Besides the district of Osrhoëne, the provinces of Asia Minor were the most receptive to Christian preaching in the second century. Both inland and on the west coast, missionaries could continue to build on the foundations laid by Paul. Even by the end of the first century a number of cities in the west of Asia Minor had organized churches (Apoc 2-3) in addition to those founded by the apostle. Ignatius of Antioch maintained relations with these and with the churches of Magnesia and Tralles. The testimony of Pliny is particularly significant: he states that about the year 112 there was in Bithynia a considerable Christian rural population.[123] In the following decades the names of cities in Asia Minor in which Christianity had gained a footing continued to multiply; they are found in nearly all provinces.[124] The correspondence of Dionysius, Bishop of

---

[120] *Quasten P*, I, 195 f.
[121] *Euseb. HE* 2, 16.
[122] See above, chapter 7, note 4.
[123] Pliny the Younger, *Ep.* 10, 96.
[124] *Harnack Miss* 737 f.

Corinth, of which Eusebius tells us,[125] is addressed to a whole series of congregations, such as those of Nicomedia, Amastris, and "the communities in Pontus". It shows us a well-organized Christianity, able, in the synods of the eighties, effectively to oppose the Montanist movement.[126] Bishop Polycrates of Ephesus could point to the glorious Christian tradition of his congregation, which gave it a special place among those of the west coast.[127]

In Crete the churches of Gortyna and Knossos are now known by name, as the correspondence of Dionysius of Corinth shows,[128] whereas we have no information about the growth of the Pauline foundations in Cilicia and Cyprus during the second century. Compared with the rapid expansion of Christianity in Asia Minor, the areas of Greece and Macedonia evangelized by Paul clearly lagged behind. Corinth surpassed all other churches in the intensity of its life, which, under Dionysius, attained a high degree of ecclesiastical organization. Athens, at this time gave to the Church the apologist Aristides. We have no reliable information about attempts at christianizing the Danubian provinces in the second century; Christians among the soldiers stationed there may have won occasional converts to their faith.[129]

In the Latin West, the growth of the Christian congregation at Rome was probably greatest. The letter of Clement, Bishop of Rome, to the church of Corinth shows that despite the persecutions under Nero and Domitian the Gospel had gained many more believers before the end of the first century, though these may have been largely non-Romans.[130] The respect in which the Roman church was held appears from the powerful attraction it exercised upon the Christians of the eastern provinces; Ignatius speaks of it, as we have seen, with expressions of the deepest reverence. Marcion, Aberkios, Hegesippus and Irenaeus, Valentinus and Theodotos, Justin, Tatian, and Polycarp of Smyrna — all travelled for various reasons to the capital in the West; some to seek recognition for their peculiar doctrines, others to learn there the true Christian teaching or to work for the peace of the Church. Hermas, still writing in Greek, gives us a glimpse of ecclesiastical life in Rome with its everyday problems. With Bishop Victor towards the end of the second century the Latin element begins to predominate.[131] The educated Greek Justin set himself

---

[125] *Euseb. HE* 4, 23, 1–13.

[126] Ibid. 5, 16, 10.

[127] Ibid. 5, 24, 1–6, on which see V. Schultze, *Altchristliche Städte und Landschaften*, II/2 (Gütersloh 1926), 107 f.

[128] *Euseb. HE* 4, 23, 5 7–8.

[129] Cf. *RAC* IV, 166 f.

[130] The list of popes (cf. *Harnack Miss* 818–32) shows predominantly Greek names during this period.

[131] Jerome, *De vir. ill.* 53.

a missionary task in Rome when, in a school like those of classical Greece, he taught "the true philosophy" to interested persons among the intellectuals of the capital. From the extensive charitable activity which the Roman congregation was able to carry on in the second half of the century[132] we may conclude that its membership was considerable. There is little evidence concerning Christian advances in other parts of Italy during the second century. One might well expect there to have been missionary expeditions from the capital, but, quite possibly, the fact that the majority of the congregation consisted of non-Latins made such undertakings too difficult. At the most, we can say that in the second half of the century some bishoprics had been established south of Rome.

Whereas Sicily does not appear to have been touched by Christian missionaries before the third century, Roman North Africa proved relatively early to be a profitable field for their activity, although we do not know their names nor the route they followed. The first document that gives information about African Christians, the Acts of the martyrs of Scili,[133] already presupposes the existence there of Latin Christianity, for the six Christians who were put to death in July 180 (a later addition to the Acts shows that other Christians of the province fell victims to the persecution) evidently possessed the epistles of Paul in Latin. The place in which a large Christian community first grew up was, naturally enough, the capital, Carthage, where the catechetical and literary work of Tertullian about the year 200 was so extensive that it would have been possible only in a Christian group that was already numerically strong. The way in which the Roman, Scapula, proceeded against the Christians[134] also compels us to assume that a considerable number of Christians had existed for some time in Africa. And if Bishop Agrippinus, about 220, could summon seventy bishops to a synod,[135] we may conclude that intensive evangelization had been going on in the countryside for a considerable period. North Africa is the only large area of the Latin West at this time which can in any way be compared with the mission fields of eastern Syria and Asia Minor.

The populations of the delta and middle valley of the Rhône owed their first contact with Christianity to the commercial relations between Asia Minor and the south coast of Gaul. For the old Greek colony of Massilia this contact must have come quite early.[136] The numerical strength

---

[132] Dionysius of Corinth thanks the Roman church for its support of many congregations: *Euseb. HE* 4, 23, 10.
[133] Knopf-Krüger, *Ausgewählte Märtyrerakten* (Tübingen, 3rd ed. 1929), 28 f.
[134] Tertull., *Ad Scapul., passim.*
[135] Cyprian, *Ep.* 71, 4.
[136] E. Griffe, *La Gaule chrétienne,* I (Paris 1947), 45.

of the churches of Lyons and Vienne, which is implied in the account of forty or fifty Christians of those cities martyred under Marcus Aurelius, also presupposes a long period of development. Irenaeus of Lyons can be regarded as a missionary bishop, concerned for the Celtic population of his adopted homeland; no doubt he intended to preach the Gospel among the Gauls, although, as he himself hints, the language problem was a source of difficulties.[137] To him too we owe our knowledge of Christian congregations then existing "in the Germanies" — probably in the Rhenish provinces with their chief towns of Cologne and Mainz — and in the Spanish provinces.[138] But if Christianity had already penetrated to the frontier towns on the Rhine, it had certainly also reached Trier, situated further inside the frontier and much more frequented by traders. Its relations with the cities of the Rhône valley suggest too the way by which the faith reached the Moselle.

This survey of the expansion of Christianity in the course of the second century gives a clear impression that the missionary enthusiasm of the primitive Church was still fresh and active. Intensive work continued in the original mission fields of the apostles, with great success in the parts of Asia Minor, where Paul had preached. New areas were opened up, especially in east Syria and Mesopotamia in the Orient, in North Africa, Gaul, Germany, and Spain in the West. The bearers of the Gospel were primarily the congregations and the enthusiasm of individual Christians; there is no indication of a central direction and organization of missionary work. The names of the missionaries are for the most part unknown.

Besides the type of preaching familiar from the apostolic period, new ways of proclaiming the Gospel were being employed. First there was the written word, used by the apologetical writers of the second century, whose intentions were also missionary and propagandist. Then there were some Christians who made use of the classical system of education; as teachers in private schools, they expounded the Christian faith. Finally, the heroic behaviour of the martyrs in times of persecution became a missionary factor of the first importance, gaining for Christianity a body of new adherents which, if not numerically great, was spiritually of the highest quality.

---

[137] Irenaeus, *Adv. haer.*, *praef.* 1, 3; see E. Griffe, *op. cit.* 43.
[138] Irenaeus, *Adv. haer.* 1, 10, 2.

PART TWO

The Great Church of Early Christian Times

(c. A.D. 180–324)

Introduction

THE transition to the third century introduces the period of the early Christian Church in which it finally became the "great Church" through a combination of external expansion and inner development. In a space of some one hundred and thirty years an interior stability was attained in organization, ritual, day-to-day parish life and clarity of aim in theological studies. Upon attainment of external freedom, it was immediately possible for the Church to assume the tasks inherent in the promising new situation.

In the first place the decisive missionary advance within the Roman Empire was successfully continued through the third century. This gave both previously existing and new communities of Christians a numerical strength which provided a large degree of immunity to deliberate attack. The organization necessary to cope with this growth was supplied by the formation of larger associations of churches. These developed around certain centres: Antioch in Syria, Alexandria in Egypt, Ephesus in Asia Minor, Caesaria in Pontus, Carthage in North Africa, and Rome, which served the rest of the Latin West. Rome, under such bishops as Callistus, Stephen, and Dionysius, developed a remarkable initiative in the domain of dogmatic teaching, revealing an increasingly distinct awareness of a duty, and a corresponding claim, to leadership within the one great Church.

Everywhere within the Church new forms in liturgy and parish life were created and testify to an intense determination to lead the Christian life. Systematic organization of the catechumenate shows a clear pastoral awareness of the importance of serious introduction to the sacramental world of Christianity. The differentiation of the lower grades of the sacramental order illustrates the clergy's ability to adapt itself to growing pastoral demands. The shock resulting from the large number of Christian defections during the Decian persecution led to thorough reflection, and the regulation of the practice of penance. The rise of the order of ascetics and of the early eremitical movement demonstrated a serious striving after Christian perfection, and laid the foundations for the full growth of monasticism in the fourth century. Various ecclesiastical ordinances served to stabilize liturgical forms in the life of the parish communities; and, in addition, there were at least the beginnings of the separate rites and liturgies which were to characterize the greater groupings within the Church. Christian art developed, and testifies to the growing sureness and confidence of Christian feeling and attitude towards life.

The most enduring effect resulted from the further elaboration of Christian theology in the third century. This development received new impulses from pagan opponents and writers, and from controversies within the Church. The encounter with Middle Platonism proved especially valuable, for it contributed to the rise of the theological school of Alexandria, which had Origen as its outstanding creative figure. Through the work of scholars from Alexandria and Antioch the central position of the Bible in the work of theology was recognized, and great commentaries expounded its significance for faith and religious life. The Trinitarian question formed the centre of an important theological discussion. The monarchical attempt at a solution to this problem was rejected, but a subordinationism was advanced which held the seeds of the fourth century's great dogmatic controversy.

The Inner Consolidation of the Church in the Third Century

CHAPTER 18

The Attack of the Pagan State on the Church

The Persecutions under Septimius Severus

WITH the accession of the Syrian dynasty's founder Septimius Severus (193–211), a tranquil phase of potential development, both internally and externally, seemed to begin for Christianity. This emperor soon publicly demonstrated his goodwill towards individual Christians. His contemporary, and fellow-African, Tertullian gives definite and impressive proofs of this attitude.[1] Christians held influential positions at court, as they had under Commodus. For example, Proculus, who had once succeeded in curing the emperor of an illness, lived until the end of his life in the imperial palace; and Prince Caracalla's nurse was a Christian woman. Men and women of Roman senatorial families, whose adherence to the Christian faith was known to the emperor, were openly protected against the mob, while he vouched for their loyalty. It is possible that the emperor's tolerance was encouraged by the Syrian princesses who accompanied his wife Julia Domna to court, for they looked sympathetically on all religious trends, especially those of oriental origin. It is a further indication of the freedom of Christianity in the first years of his reign that, about the year 196, the bishops were able to meet in synods at which the date of Easter was discussed.[2] It is true that proceedings against individual Christians were not unknown, for the legal situation created by the rescript of Trajan was still unaltered. Tertullian's *Liber apologeticus* (*c.* 197) was provoked by the occurrence of such cases. It was not until the tenth year of his reign that Septimius's attitude altered drastically and created a completely new situation for Christianity.

In the year 202 an imperial edict was issued forbidding conversion to Judaism or Christianity under pain of heavy penalties.[3] In practice this

---

[1] Tertullian, *Ad Scap.* 3–4.

[2] *Euseb. HE* 5, 23–5.

[3] Spartianus, *Septim. Sever.* 16, 9: "Iudaeos fieri sub gravi poena vetuit; idem etiam de Christianis sanxit." Schwarte disputes the genuineness of the last part in "Das angebliche Christengesetz des Septimus Severus" in *Historia* 12 (1963) 185–208.

meant the abandonment of Trajan's principle *conquirendi non sunt* (they are not to be searched out), for the new ordinance could only be implemented by police supervision of the Church's activities. It was not only the individual Christian who was at the mercy of a denunciation; the Church as an organization was affected. Every activity which aimed at winning new members could be punished; therefore all missionary work would be made impossible and Christianity would slowly die out within the empire. This change in the emperor's attitude is intelligible only if we believe that he had come to recognize that Christians had not attained new religious convictions merely as isolated individuals. He must have realized that their faith bound them together in a universal organized community of belief possessing a strong cohesive power of resistance. For practical reasons of State this development may have seemed undesirable to him, so he hoped to avert it by cutting the Church's artery and making her further growth impossible. The voices of a few Christians who refused military service[4] may have strengthened Septimius in the conviction that the Christian religion was just as dangerous to the maintenance of the order of the State as was the radical opposition of the Montanists to everything connected with it. It was this anxiety which was expressed by Dio Cassius, when he made Maecenas warn Augustus to abhor and punish those who wished to introduce foreign customs into the native Roman religion. They could only give rise to conspiracies and revolutionary machinations against the monarchy, counselled Maecenas, and for the same reason no atheism or black magic should be tolerated.[5] The immediate consequences of the imperial edict showed its purpose even more clearly. In Alexandria and Carthage two places within the empire possessing large Christian communities, the persecution now affected catechumens and newly baptized persons, for they particularly transgressed the new edict. The Christian school of Alexandria, which had led many a pagan religious inquirer to the new faith, was now subjected to such supervision that its teachers were compelled to leave the town in A.D. 202. Six pupils of Origen, who was working at that time as a Christian teacher, were executed. Two of them were still catechumens, and another had only just been baptized.[6] At the beginning of the year 203, a group of catechumens were arrested, and their heroic bearing at their execution forms the theme of one of the most precious accounts of a martyrdom surviving from the third century.[7] The noble Perpetua and her

---

[4] Tertullian, *De cor. passim;* Origen, *Contra Cels.* 5, 33; 7, 26; 8, 70, 73; cf. A. Harnack, *Militia Christi* (Tübingen 1905), 55–75.

[5] Dio Cassius, *Hist. Rom.* 52, 36.

[6] *Euseb. HE* 6, 3, 1; 4, 1–3.

[7] *Passio ss. Perpetuae et Felicitatis,* ed. J. van Beek (Nijmegen 1956); an editio minor, *FlorPatr* 43 (Bonn 1938). On Chap. 7 of the*Passio,* see F. J. Dölger, *AuC* II (1930), 1–40; and on Chap. 10, ibid. III (1932), 177–91.

slave Felicitas, together with her teacher Saturus and fellow catechumens Revocatus, Saturninus and Secundulus, were never forgotten in the African Church. The account of their act of testimony to the faith, which may well have been composed by Tertullian, was read and re-read during divine service down to the days of Augustine.[8]

Proceedings against Christians as individuals were also continued. In one instance three Christians of Carthage were condemned to death at the stake; another died in prison.[9] Augustine himself was acquainted with the record of a woman martyr of Carthage, Gudentis, beheaded in 203.[10] From occasional references by Tertullian we can infer that the anti-Christian attitude of various individual Roman officials or the hostility of the pagan populace prompted renewed recourse to the rescript of Trajan. Tertullian's early work *To the Martyrs* (A.D. 197)[11] was addressed to Christians in prison awaiting trial. His later work concerning flight in time of persecution, indicates that under Septimius Severus many African Christians including clerics, escaped arrest through timely flight, or obtained their safety by bribing the police. One such persecution, which took place in Egypt in 202, is expressly attributed by Eusebius to the edict of Septimius against the catechumens. The prefects Laetus and Aquila secured the arrest of Christians from as far away as the Thebaid and had them brought to Alexandria, where they were executed, in many instances after repeated torture.[12] The most outstanding figures among these were Origen's father Leonides, the virgin Potamiaina (who was later held in high honour), her mother Marcella, and the soldier Basilides, who had been prompted by the example of Potamiaina to adopt the Christian faith.[13] One Christian writer was so impressed by the harshness of this wave of persecution that he saw in it the coming approach of Antichrist.[14] For other provinces of the empire the available sources are scanty. In Cappadocia the governor Claudius Herminianus persecuted the Christians because he could not forgive the conversion of his wife to the new faith.[15] It is possible that Alexander, later Bishop of Jerusalem, confessed the faith at this time with other Christians of Cappadocia, just as Bishop Asclepiades of Antioch stood firm under persecution.[16] No reliable information is available on the course of the persecutions in Rome. They either abruptly ceased or died away gradually in the last years of Septimius's reign.

[8] Cf. J. Moreau, *La persécution du christianisme* (Paris 1956), 82.
[9] *Passio ss. Perpetuae et Felicitatis* 11, 9.
[10] Augustine, *Sermon* 294: "in natale martyris Gudentis"; see also 284 and 394.
[11] New critical edition by A. Quacquarelli (Rome 1963).
[12] *Euseb. HE* 6, 1; 6, 2, 2.
[13] Ibid. 6, 5, 1–7.
[14] Ibid. 6, 7.
[15] Tertullian, *Ad Scap.* 3.
[16] *Euseb. HE* 6, 8, 7; 6, 11, 4-5.

Certainly Caracalla (211–17) inaugurated a period of religious toleration which was of considerable advantage to Christianity, as was recognized
by the early Christian writers themselves. It has indeed been thought that
an anti-Christian motive lay behind the so-called *Constitutio Antoniniana*
(by which Caracalla in 212 granted Roman citizenship to all free men in
the empire), because it made it easier to bring a charge of *laesa maiestas.*
But this contention is refuted both by the unrestricted praise that Augustine
accords this act[17] and by Caracalla's whole attitude to Christians whom
he knew personally. We find them once again in influential positions at
court: the freedman Prosenes was private chamberlain under Caracalla,[18]
and when, on the emperor's accession to the throne, an amnesty was granted
to deportees, Christians were not excepted from it. The proceedings of the
proconsul Scapula (211–12) against the Church in the three North African
provinces are, therefore, not to be ascribed to an order of Caracalla, but
were rather provoked by rigorist tendencies among African Christians.
Tertullian was their constant spokesman, advocating rigid principle in such
works as *On the Soldier's Crown,* a rejection of military service for
Christians.[19] Scapula may have been led to take the steps he did by the
jurist Ulpian's publication of the various existing imperial rescripts
concerning Christians, in his *De officio proconsulis.*[20] Tertullian leaves no
doubt that the methods of execution employed were particularly cruel,
though he names only one of the victims: the Christian Mavilus from
Hadrumet, who was thrown to the wild beasts.[21]

The short reign of Heliogabalus (218–22)[22] records no event by which
his attitude to Christianity can be judged, unless it be his plan to make
the cult of the sun-god of Emesa obligatory in the empire. This favourable
situation for Christianity improved still further under his successor, Severus
Alexander (222–35). The intellectual and religious atmosphere of the court
was determined by the emperor's gifted mother, Julia Mamaea. She may
be judged to have had definite leanings towards Christianity; a hagio-
grapher of the fifth century actually considered her a Christian. During a
stay in Antioch she sent for Origen requesting his presence to discuss
religious questions;[23] and Hippolytus of Rome dedicated one of his treatises
to her.[24] Her tolerance is reflected in the attitude of the young emperor,

---

[17] Augustine, *De civitate dei,* 5, 17.
[18] Cf. L. Hertling–E. Kirschbaum, *Die römischen Katakomben und ihre Martyrer*
(Vienna, 2nd ed. 1955), 213.
[19] *De cor. passim; De idol.* 17.
[20] Lactantius, *De inst. div.* 5, 11, 18.
[21] Cf. *Ad. Scap.* as a whole; and on Mavilus, ibid. c. 3.
[22] K. Gross, "Elagabal" in *RAC* IV, 998 ff.
[23] *Euseb. HE* 6, 21, 3–4.
[24] *Quasten P,* II, 197.

who accepted numerous Christians among his closer associates and entrusted the building of the library near the Pantheon to the Christian Julius Africanus.[25] His policy of religious toleration is accurately characterized by a phrase of his biographer in the *Historia Augusta*, which states that he left the Jews their privileges and allowed the Christians to exist.[26] This latter assertion is borne out by the unhampered development of Christian life in the East. Christian inscriptions of this period are found in great numbers in Asia Minor, and it was possible to erect a Christian place of worship in Dura-Europos before 234. In the West Christian burial was now organized quite freely at Rome.[27] It is characteristic that no legal proceedings against a Christian and no Christian martyrdom can with certainty be assigned to Alexander's time.

A reaction did not occur until the reign of the former guards officer Maximinus (235–8). The change of policy first affected the numerous Christians at court; but, as Eubesius emphasizes,[28] it was directed principally against the Church's leaders. To that extent it introduced a new note into the anti-Christian actions of an emperor. Had this reign lasted longer, it could have been of grave consequence for the Church. In Rome itself, it can be established that the two Christian leaders there, namely Bishop Pontianus and the priest Hippolytus, were deported to Sardinia, where both died.[29] Origen reports the danger to some Christians; it was at this time that he dedicated his *Exhortation to Martyrdom* to his friend Ambrose and the priest Protoctetus. A typical reaction of the pagan masses produced an attack on the Christians in Cappadocia following an earthquake, for which they regarded the Christians as responsible.[30]

The struggle for power by the soldier emperors who followed left them no leisure to occupy themselves with the question of the Christians. But in Philippus Arabs (244–9) a ruler came to power who showed such sympathy for the Christians that a complete reconciliation seemed possible between Christianity and the government of the Roman State. Indeed Bishop Dionysius of Alexandria tells us that about twelve years after Philippus' death many people were saying that the emperor had been in fact a Christian; Eusebius mentions the claim as merely talk.[31] On the basis of another unconfirmed rumour that the emperor once joined the crowd of

[25] Ibid. 138.
[26] Lampridius, *Alex. Sev.* 22, 4: "Iudaeis privilegia reservavit, Christianos esse passus est."
[27] Cf. also A. Alföldi in *Klio* 31 (1938), 249–53, on his decision favourable to the Christians in a land dispute.
[28] *Euseb. HE* 6, 28.
[29] G. Bovini in *RivAC* 19 (1942), 35–85.
[30] *Euseb. HE* 6, 28; Firminian of Caesarea in Cyprian, *Ep.* 75, 10.
[31] *Euseb. HE* 6, 34; 7, 10, 3.

penitents in a Christian congregation before Easter, hagiography wove the assertion that Philippus was the first Roman emperor to have accepted Christianity. But on 21 April 248 the emperor still took an active part in a celebration of the official worship on the thousandth anniversary of the foundation of Rome. And the idea that he was secretly a Christian, but publicly an adherent of the State religion, is not in accord with the attitude of the men of antiquity, to whom a sophistical distinction of that sort was alien. Nevertheless, the rumours indubitably had their root in the high degree of goodwill towards Christianity exhibited by Philippus' government. The consul in office in the year 249 was certainly a Christian.[32] And the emperor's personal inclination and that of his wife Severa are mirrored in the correspondence between the imperial pair and Origen, which Eusebius had, at least in part, available to him.[33] But not even so much sympathy could protect the Christians of Alexandria from an outburst of popular rage in the year 249. A refusal to revile their religion[34] cost many of them their lives.

A retrospective survey of the relations between the Roman State and Christianity in the first half of the third century makes it clear that the phases of really peaceful co-existence, and sometimes of positive toleration, predominate over the waves of harsh persecution. Only twice can the features of a systematic policy against Christianity be observed: first when Septimius Severus made adherence to Christianity an indictable offence; and secondly when Maximinus Thrax took action against the leaders of the Christian communities. For the rest, the haphazard, unsystematic proceedings against individual Christians reveal the vacillating religious policy of the holders of power in the State and of their subordinate authorities in the provinces. The unsettled course adopted by these officials was partly a result of the political decline of the empire under the soldier emperors. At the beginning of the second half of the century the possibility of a definitive reconciliation between State and Church which had emerged under Philippus Arabs, was brusquely reduced to a utopian dream. The emperor Decius came to power and determined to re-establish the old brilliant reputation of the Roman State by restoring its ancient religion.

The Persecution under Decius

The first measures of the new emperor might appear as a typical or common reaction against the rule of a predecessor. Christians were arrested as early as December 249, and in January 250 the head of the Roman community,

---

[32] J. Moreau, op. cit. 92.
[33] Euseb. HE 6, 36, 3.
[34] Ibid. 6, 41, 1–9.

Bishop Fabian, was put to death.[35] A general edict in 250, however, soon proved that Decius was pursuing aims concerning the Christians which far exceeded those of his predecessors. The text of his edict has not been preserved, but its contents can be largely reconstructed from contemporary sources. All the inhabitants of the empire were summoned to take part in a general sacrifice to the gods, a *supplicatio*. This appeared to be a summons to the people for the purpose of invoking the protection of the gods. They were to entreat for the well-being of the empire by an impressive and unanimous demonstration. But it was significant that, at the same time, exact supervision of the edict's implementation was ordered throughout the empire. Commissions were set up to see that the sacrifice was performed, and to issue everyone with a certificate, or *libellus*.[36] Before a certain date the *libelli* were to be exhibited to the authorities; and anyone refusing to sacrifice was thrown into prison, where attempts were often made to break his resistance by torture. Although the decree did not explicitly condemn the Christians, their leading representatives and writers rightly considered it to be the most serious attack that their Church had yet sustained. It is impossible to state with precision what motive exercised greater influence upon the emperor: the opportunity to determine the exact number of adherents to Christianity, or the expectation of a mass return to the old State religion. The undoubted initial success of the measures favours the latter motive. The bitter laments of the bishops Dionysius of Alexandria and Cyprian of Carthage leave no doubt that the number of those who in one way or another met the demand of the edict especially in Egypt and North Africa, far exceeded the number of those who refused it. What Origen had recently remarked was verified to a terrifying extent: the heroic days of his youth were past. That former spirit had yielded to the laxity and barrenness of the present.[37] Some of the Christians of Alexandria appeared before the commission trembling with fear, and performed the sacrificial rite as required; others denied that they had ever been Christians, and still others fled. Many offered sacrifice when on the point of arrest; others endured a few days in prison refusing to sacrifice until they were due to appear in court; and some submitted only after torture.[38] In North Africa many Christians thought they could avoid a decision by not actually offering sacrifice. They secured for themselves from a member of the verification commission, through bribery or other means, a certificate of having done so. These were the so-called *libellatici*, whose fault was not considered as grave as that of the *thurificati* who offered incense or of the *sacrificati* who offered

[35] Cyprian, *Ep.* 37, 2; 6, 3–9, 1. Cf. *Duchesne LP*, I 4.
[36] Forty-three such *libelli* have been found so far on Egyptian papyri.
[37] Origen, *In Ierem. hom.* 4, 3.
[38] *Euseb. HE* 6, 41, 10–13.

a full sacrifice before the image of the gods.[39] In Rome, some Christians resorted to the device of having their *libelli* taken and attested by intermediaries.[40] The large number of the *lapsi* in North Africa is proved by Cyprian's statement that, when the danger slackened, they flocked to those who had confessed the faith, in order to obtain "letters of peace" from them and facilitate their readmission into the Christian community.[41] The Bishop of Carthage felt it particularly disturbing that two of his own fellow-bishops in North Africa were among those who fell away. One of them had even persuaded the majority of his flock to offer sacrifice, and the other subsequently wished to remain in office without making atonement. He had also to number two Spanish bishops among the *libellatici*.[42] In the East, the martyr Pionius saw his own bishop zealously arranging the precise accomplishment of the ritual of sacrifice.[43]

In contrast to these, however, there was in every province of the empire an *élite* ready to answer for their belief with their lives. Here, too, Cyprian's letters provide the most informative account of the situation in North Africa. He had sought out a place of refuge in the neighbourhood of Carthage, but was able to keep in touch with his flock by correspondence and convey words of encouragement and consolation to the Christians who were already under arrest. Those in prison, including many women and children, showed an intense and genuine longing for martyrdom that was not always fulfilled, for many were released even before the end of the persecution. Cyprian deplored the pride and moral lapses by which some of these latter detracted from the worth of their true confession of faith, but he was able to enroll others among his clergy, so exemplary was their behaviour. Cyprian does not give exact figures regarding those who offered the sacrifices, and names only a few of the *confessores*.[44] Naturally, the number of those put to death, the *martyres coronati* or *consummati*, was smaller by comparison. Cyprian mentions two by name, but presupposes a larger number. The confessor Lucianus once mentions sixteen by name, most of whom were left to die of hunger in prison.[45] In Rome, too, Christians were released from gaol after resolutely confessing their faith, among them a certain Celerinus whose brave bearing so impressed the emperor Decius that he gave him his freedom; Cyprian later ordained him lector.[46] The case of the two Spanish bishops mentioned above reveals that the commission

[39] Cyprian, *De laps. passim*, and *Ep.* 55, 2.
[40] Ibid. *Ep.* 30, 3.
[41] *Ep.* 20, 2.
[42] *Ep.* 65, 1; 59, 10; 67, 6.
[43] *Mart. Pionii* 15, 2; 16, 1; 18, 12.
[44] Cyprian, *Ep.* 6, 10, 13, 38, 40.
[45] *Ep.* 10 and 22.
[46] *Ep.* 37 and 39.

was effective in Spain, but we have no certain information about Gaul. For Egypt, Bishop Dionysius of Alexandria mentions the kind of death suffered by fourteen martyrs: ten of them died at the stake and four by the sword. But he knew of numerous other martyrs in the towns and villages of that country, just as he knew that many Christians died of hunger and cold while fleeing from persecution. Finally, he mentions also a group of five Christian soldiers who voluntarily confessed their faith when they encouraged a waverer to stand fast; because of their outspoken courage the court left them unmolested.[47] In neighbouring Palestine Bishop Alexander of Jerusalem died a martyr's death at that time, as did Bishop Babylas, the leader of the Antioch community.[48] The aged Origen's longing for martyrdom was at least partly satisfied in Caesaria where he was subjected to cruel torture. The fundamentally trustworthy account of the five Christians of Smyrna who were imprisoned, and of whom Pionius was burnt to death, is the only echo of the effects of the Decian persecution in Asia proconsularis.[49] Gregory of Nyssa provides late and vague reports about events in Pontus: he tells us that numerous Christians were arrested under Decius, while their bishop, Gregory Thaumaturgus, fled with many others.[50] A host of further accounts of early Christian martyrs places the death of their heroes in Decius's reign. As sources they are worthless, for the cult of these alleged martyrs cannot in any way be substantiated and perhaps their martyrdom was attributed to Decius's persecution only because he had acquired the reputation in later times of being one of the cruellest persecutors of the Christians.[51]

The rapid cessation of the Decian persecution is in a sense surprising. One would have expected that the considerable initial success attained by such shock tactics would have been exploited and deepened by further systematic measures. The impression gained is that the administrative apparatus was overtaxed by so extensive an undertaking. The departure of the emperor for the Danubian provinces, occasioned by a new invasion of the Goths, halted it completely; and his death on the battle-field prevented its rapid resumption. From the point of view of Roman government, no tangible and lasting success was gained by this calculated and systematic attack on the Catholic Church. The great mass of those who had fallen away soon clamoured to be received into the Church again, while many *libellatici* atoned for their fault by a new confession of faith shortly after their lapse. The number of former Christians won over to the State religion does not

---

[47] *Euseb. HE* 6, 41, 14–23; 6, 42, 1–4.
[48] Ibid. 6, 39, 2–5.
[49] Text in Knopf–Krüger, *Ausgewählte Märtyrerakten* (Tübingen, 3rd ed. 1929), 45–57; on this cf. *Delehaye PM*, 28–37.
[50] Gregory of Nyssa, *Panegyr. in Greg. Thaumat.* in PG 46, 944–53, esp. 945 D.
[51] *Delehaye PM*, 239 ff.

seem to have been particularly high. The Christian community, for its part, recognized that much within it was decayed and ready to crumble. Conscious leaders of communities, like Cyprian, were spurred by this condition to serious reflection, which after long controversies about the question of penance, was to lead to a regeneration of the Church.

Valerian and Gallienus

The ensuing seven years of tranquillity for the Church (250–7) were disturbed only by a short wave of persecution in Rome. The emperor Trebonius Gallus had Cornelius, the head of the Christian community in Rome, arrested and exiled to Centum Cellae (Città Vecchia), where he died in 253.[52] The latter's successor, Lucius (253–4),[53] was likewise banished, but the death of the emperor soon permitted his return to Rome. Dionysius, Bishop of Alexandria, reports arrests in Egypt also occurring at that time.[54] Gallus's repressive action was probably aimed at indulging popular sentiment, which blamed the Christians for the plague then devastating the empire. The first years of the reign of his successor, Valerian (253–60) produced for the Church a situation which Dionysius of Alexandria celebrates in enthusiastic tones. No predecessor of Valerian had been so well-disposed towards the Christians. Indeed so friendly was Valerian's attitude that his household was, so to speak, one of God's communities.[55] But the fourth year of the emperor's reign brought a surprising change, introducing a short but extremely harsh and violent persecution. Like that of Decius, this policy could have proved a severe threat to the Church, because it too was based on a well-considered plan. Dionysius blames the emperor's minister and later usurper, Macrianus, for this reaction. Macrianus certainly may have suggested the idea of remedying the precarious financial state of the empire by confiscating the property of wealthy Christians. Valerian was probably also impelled by the threatening situation of the empire in general. He sought to counter a possible threat from within by a radical move against the Christians. The plan is clear even in the edict of 257: the blow was to strike the clergy; bishops, priests, and deacons were to be obliged to offer sacrifice to the gods and any of them celebrating divine worship or holding assemblies in the cemeteries were to be punished with death.[56] In North Africa and Egypt,

---

[52] *Duchesne LP*, I, 150 ff.; Cyprian, *Ep.* 60 and 61.

[53] Cyprian, *Ep.* 61, 1.

[54] *Euseb. HE* 7, 1.

[55] Ibid. 7, 10, 3.

[56] Cf. A. Alföldi, "Der Rechtsstreit zwischen der römischen Kirche und dem Verein der popinarii" in *Klio* 31 (1938), 323–48.

the leaders of the churches, Cyprian and Dionysius, were at once arrested; and, in addition, many Christians of the African provinces were condemned to forced labour in the mines. The edict of 258 took a further decisive step: clerics who refused the sacrifice were to be immediately put to death. But this time the leading laity in the Christian communities were also included. Senators and members of the order of knights were to lose their rank and possessions, as were their wives; the latter could be punished with banishment and their husbands with execution, if they refused to offer sacrifice to the gods. Imperial officials in Rome and the provinces, the *caesariani*, were also threatened with forced labour and the confiscation of their possessions for similar offence.[57] The aim of this policy was clear: the clergy and prominent members of the Christian communities, who enjoyed wealth and position, were to be eliminated; and the Christians, thus deprived of leaders and influence, were to be condemned to insignificance. The victims were numerous, especially among the clergy. North Africa lost its outstanding bishop in Cyprian, who met his death with unforgettable dignity. His flock showed their love and respect once again when he was beheaded, soaking cloths in his blood and interring his remains with reverent joy.[58] Rome had its most distinguished martyr in Pope Sixtus II, who was joined in death by his deacons.[59] There is an authentic account of the death of the Spanish bishop, Fructuosus of Tarragona, and two of his deacons.[60] The head of the Egyptian church, Dionysius of Alexandria, was condemned only to an exile which he survived.[61] The victims were also numerous among the lower clergy: in May 259, the deacon James and the lector Marianus[62] died in Lambaesis, North Africa; there were clerics also in the group with Lucius and Montanus.[63] The deacon Laurence, later transfigured by legend, achieved the greatest posthumous fame among the Roman victims of this persecution.[64] The report of the historian Socrates that Novatian also died for his Christian convictions in the reign of Valerian was formerly treated with some reserve. It has recently received considerable support from the discovery of an epitaph which a certain deacon Gaudentius dedicated "to the blessed martyr Novatian".[65] The proportion of laity

---

[57] Cyprian, *Ep.* 80.

[58] *Acta Cypr.* in *CSEL* 3, 3, CX–CXIV; Knopf-Krüger, *op. cit.* 62–64 (with bibliography).

[59] Cyprian, *Ep.* 80, I.

[60] Text in Knopf-Krüger, *op. cit.* 83–85; on this cf. P. Franchi de Cavalieri in *SteT* 65 (1935), 183–99, and J. Serra-Vilaró, *Fructuós, Auguri i Eulogi, martirs sants de Tarragona* (Tarragona 1936).

[61] *Euseb. HE* 7, 11, 4–6.

[62] *Martyr. ss. Mariani et Iacobi*, Knopf-Krüger, *op. cit.* 67–74.   [63] Ibid. 74–82.

[64] H. Delehaye in *AnBoll* 51 (1938), 34–98.

[65] *Socrates HE* 4, 28; cf. C. Mohlberg in *ELit* 51 (1937), 242–9; and A. Ferrua in *CivCatt* 4 (1944), 232–9.

among the victims of the persecution was not inconsiderable: it was probably quite large in Egypt[66] and highest in North Africa.

The persecution ceased with the tragic end of the emperor who was taken prisoner by the Persians in 259 and soon died. The general impression left by the attitude of the Christians on this occasion is far more favourable than in their previous tribulation. Only in one African record of martyrdom is there a mention of lapsed Christians. The shock of the Decian persecution had produced its salutary effect; the Christians met this trial with far more calm determination than they had displayed eight years previously, and withstood it extremely well. The political situation both at home and abroad would have prevented Valerian's son and successor, Gallienus (260–8), from continuing the fight against the Christians. But he was not content, with a merely tacit cessation of the persecution and issued an edict of his own in the Christians' favour. This is referred to in a further rescript of 262 to Dionysius of Alexandria. In this the emperor says that he had restored their places of worship to the Christians some time previously, and that nobody was to molest them in these places.[67] This recognition of ecclesiastical property by the highest civil authority represented a far-reaching act of toleration, and had a favourable effect on the future of the Church. Although Christianity was not yet officially recognized thereby as a *religio licita,* nevertheless there began with Gallienus' edict a period of peace which lasted more than forty years, and which could not but further its development both within and without. It was with good cause that Eusebius celebrated this time as a period of glory and freedom for Christianity. It was possible to build churches without hindrance, and preach to the barbarians and Greeks, while Christians occupied high offices of State, and enjoyed warm sympathy everywhere.[68]

[66] Cyprian, *Ep.* 76 and 80, and *Euseb. HE* 7, 11, 18–26.
[67] *Euseb. HE* 7, 13.
[68] Ibid. 8, 1, 1–6.

CHAPTER 19

Further Development of Christian Literature in the East in the Third Century

The Beginnings of the Theological School of Alexandria

THE inner consolidation of Christianity in the third century is particularly evident and impressive in the domain of early patristic literature. More and more frequently, members of the ruling classes joined the new faith and felt impelled to serve it by word and writing in ways which corresponded with their level of culture. This created an essential condition for the development of a learned theology. The earliest attempts of this kind are found of course as early as the second century, when educated converts such as Justin and his pupil Tatian presented themselves publicly in Rome as teachers of the "new philosophy", and gave a well-grounded introduction to the understanding of the Christian faith to a relatively small circle of pupils.[1]

The "schools" of these teachers were not, however, institutions of the Roman Christian community itself, but private undertakings by learned Christians. Out of a sense of missionary obligation, and in the manner of philosophical teachers of the time, these men expounded their religious beliefs to a circle of those who might be interested, and substantiated them by constant comparison with other religious trends. In a similar manner Gnostics like Apelles, Synerus, and Ptolemy, appeared in Rome as private teachers; and men like Theodotus from Byzantium and perhaps Praxeas, too, tried within the framework of such private schools to win support for their particular Monarchian views. While no objection was raised against the teaching activities of orthodox laymen like Justin, the authorities of the Roman community took exception to the activities of Gnostic or Monarchian teachers, and finally excluded them from the community of the Church. These problems induced the Roman bishops of the third century to seek to bring private Christian schools under their control and to transform them into a purely ecclesiastical institution which would administer the instruction of the catechumens. No theological school within the proper sense of the word developed either in Rome or elsewhere in the Latin West, because certain conditions of an intellectual kind were just not present. Neither were the personalities to whom they might have been of use. But both prerequisites were existent in great quantity in the East.

---

[1] Tatian's pupil Rhodon must also be reckoned among these; he attracted some attention by his controversy with the Marcionite Apelles, cf. *Euseb. HE* 5, 13, 5–7.

In the Greek East the Egyptian capital, Alexandria, with its scientific tradition and the interest generally shown by its educated upper classes in religious and philosophical questions, was to prove the most favourable soil for the development of a Christian theology on a learned intellectual basis. By establishing the two great libraries of the Sarapeion and the Museion, the first Ptolemies had laid the foundation of that lively interest in the most varied branches of learning which had developed in Alexander's city during the Hellenistic period. This cultural development, especially in the areas of Hellenistic literature and neo-Platonic philosophy, helped to create a general atmosphere which was to prove particularly fruitful when it encountered Christianity. Educated Alexandrians who had adopted the Christian religion were inevitably moved to confront it with the intense cultural life around them; and those of them who felt impelled publicly to account for their faith became the first Christian teachers in the Egyptian capital. The available sources of information about the beginnings of Christian teaching in Alexandria are not very rich; only Eusebius speaks of them in any detail, and his treatment is relatively late and rather un-critical. Nevertheless, the intensive research of recent years has produced some reliable results. According to these sources it is impossible to speak of a "school of catechists in Alexandria" as early as the end of the second century.

The first Christian teacher whose name is known is Pantainus, of Sicilian origin, who was giving lessons about the year 180, expounding and defend-ing his Christian view of the world; but he was teaching without ecclesias-tical appointment, just as Justin or Tatian had earlier done in Rome. Any interested person, pagan or Christian, could frequent this private school, and the syllabus was entirely a matter for the teacher's judgment. Clement of Alexandria must be considered to have been the second teacher of this kind, but he cannot be regarded as the successor of Pantainus at the head of any school. He publicly taught the "true gnosis" independently of, and perhaps even simultaneously with Pantainus. The first phase of Origen's teaching activity still had this private character. At the request of some friends who were interested in the Christian religion, he gave up his position in a grammar school and devoted himself as an independent teacher to instruction in the Christian religion, which was clearly open to Christians and pagans alike. It was only later,[2] perhaps about 215, that he undertook the instruction of catechumens at the request of Bishop

---

[2] There are contradictions in Eusebius's account. It seems extremely unlikely that a young man of seventeen would be placed in charge of a school for catechumens; cf. M. Hornschuh, in ZKG 71 (1960), 203–7.

Demetrius,[3] and so became the ecclesiastically-appointed head of a catechetical school. He soon further expanded this role assigning the actual teaching of the catechumens to his friend Heraclas, certainly with the consent of the bishop. He provided a circle of educated persons and advanced students with a systematic exposition of the philosophic knowledge of the age, crowned by instruction in the Christian religion.[4] In this respect, Origen had taken a decisive step; the work which Clement before him had undertaken as a private teacher was now placed directly at the service of the church of Alexandria, which thereby received a school of its own in which instruction in the Christian religion was given in no way inferior in quality to the contemporary pagan course of education. This institution alone has a claim to the title of a theological school. It is true that its real importance was due to the intellectual quality of the man who was its leader and soul until the year 230. And it is not surprising that Origen's bold step was received with some reserve: he soon had to defend himself against the accusation of attributing too much importance to profane philosophy,[5] but the success and enthusiastic support of his students made him keep to the path he had taken. When the rift between Origen and Bishop Demetrius led to his quitting the country, the Alexandrian school of theologians quickly reverted to a simple school for catechumens, giving to those seeking baptism their first introduction to the Christian religion. Origen took the nature and spirit of his foundation with him to Caesarea and Palestine. Here he tried until his death to realize his ideal of a Christian institute for advanced teaching, this time with the full approval of the Palestinian episcopate.

After Origen's death, it is only possible to speak of an Alexandrian theological school in a wider sense; we can only denote a theology bearing the characteristic marks which the two first great Alexandrians, Clement and Origen, gave it: namely, the drawing of philosophy into the service of theology, a predilection for the allegorical method of scriptural exegesis, and a strong tendency to penetrate by speculation on an idealistic basis the supernatural content of the truths of revelation.

Clement of Alexandria

While none of the writings of the first Alexandrian teacher, has come down to us,[6] three longer works and a small treatise survive from the pen of

[3] *Euseb. HE* 6, 14, 11.

[4] Ibid. 6, 18, 3–4. Origen expounds his educational ideal in a letter to his pupil Gregory of Neo-Caesarea: *Ep. ad Greg.* 1.

[5] *Euseb. HE* 6, 19, 13–14.

[6] H.-I. Marrou considers he may well be the author of the *Letter to Diognetus*; cf. Marrou's ed., *SourcesChr* 33 (1951), 266 ff.

Clement. Though they are merely the remnants of a more extensive production, they permit us to form an impression of his characteristics as a writer, his theological interests, and the aim of his teaching. Clement was the son of a pagan family of Athens, became a Christian in adult life and, after extensive travels, reached Alexandria towards the end of the second century. There he was active as a Christian teacher until the persecution under Septimius Severus forced him to emigrate to Asia Minor about the year 202, and he died still in this area, about 215.

Clement's secular learning is shown by the very title of the first of the three main works mentioned above. On the model of Aristotle, Epicurus, and Chrysippus, he too wrote a *Protrepticus*, a discourse of admonition and propaganda, which presupposes educated pagan readers who are to be won over to his "philosophy". His aim is, therefore, in fact the same as that of previous apologists, but his work is far superior to their writings in form and tone. Naturally, in a Christian apologia, polemic against pagan polytheism could not be lacking, but it is conducted by Clement in a calm and thoughtful manner. He concedes that many of the pagan philosophers, Plato above all, were on the way to a knowledge of the true God; but full knowledge, and with it eternal salvation and the satisfaction of all human aspiration, was only brought by the Logos, Jesus Christ, who summons all men, Hellenes and barbarians, to follow him. A level of discourse on the Christian faith was here attained that had not been known before, and one which could appeal to a cultivated pagan. Many a discerning reader must have had the impression that inquiry into this religion and discussion with its enthusiastic spokesman might be worthwhile.

Anyone who allows himself to be won over as a follower of the Logos must entrust himself absolutely to the latter's educative power. Clement's second main work, the *Paidagogus,* is therefore intended as a guide in this respect, and at the same time as an aid to training in Christian things. The fundamental attitude required is first developed: the Logos-Paidagogos has provided by his life and commands in Holy Scripture the standards by which the life of a Christian should be directed; the Christian who acts in accordance with them fulfills to a higher degree the "duties" to which, for example, an adherent of the Stoic philosophy knows he is obliged, since the demands of the Logos are in the fullest sense "in conformity with reason". Clement illustrates the application of this basic principle with many examples from daily life, and displays a gift of discernment and a balanced and fundamentally affirmative attitude to cultural values. Both Christian ascesis and Christian love of one's neighbour must prove themselves in the actual circumstances of civilization. The magnificent hymn to the Paidagogus Christ, which ends this work,[7] effectively

[7] *Paidag.* 3, 12, 101.

emphasizes the position occupied by the person of Christ in Clement's personal piety.

Their formal treatment and intellectual structure show that the *Protrepticus* and the *Paidagogus* are essentially related works. The second further suggests [8] that Clement intended to complete a literary trilogy with another work, the *Didascalos*, which was to follow the others and offer a systematic exposition of the chief doctrines of Christianity. But the third surviving work, the *Stromata*, cannot be considered as the conclusion of this trilogy, for its themes are quite different from those announced, and in style and form it in no way corresponds to the first and second studies. The title itself indicates its literary category: a number and variety of questions are treated in an informal manner, as in the *Deipnosophistae* of Athenaeus, or the *Attic Nights* of Aulus Gellius, and are intended in the first place to appeal to pagans interested in religious and philosophical matters. There is good reason to think that these questions relate to the themes which Clement treated in his oral teaching, and that consequently their very form reveals the marks of their origin. [9] One purpose certainly pervades the whole work: to prove by reasoned confrontation with contemporary Gnosticism that the Christian religion is the only true gnosis, and to represent the faithful Christian as the true Gnostic.

At baptism every Christian receives the Holy Spirit and thereby the capacity to rise from simple belief to an ever more perfect knowledge; but only those rise to attain it in fact who perpetually strive to do so, and who struggle for ever greater perfection in their manner of life. Only by an increasing effort of self-education and by penetrating more and more deeply into the gospel, and that solely within the Church, which is the "only virgin Mother", [10] does a man become a true Gnostic and so surpass the cultural ideal of the "wise man" of pagan philosophy. That pagan ideal certainly represents a value which must be acknowledged, but it is only a preliminary stage. The model of the Christian Gnostic is the figure of Christ, whom he must come to resemble, and by following whom he becomes an image of God. [11] Linked with this is a perpetual growth in the love of God, which makes possible for the Gnostic a life of unceasing prayer, makes him see God and imparts to him a resemblance to God. This ascent from step to step, does not, however, remove the true Gnostic from the company of his brethren to whom such an ascent has not been granted; rather does he serve them, ever ready to help, and summons them

[8] Ibid. 1, 1, 3.
[9] Cf. A. Knauber in *TThZ* 60 (1951), 249 ff.
[10] *Paidag.* 1, 6, 42.
[11] *Strom.* 7, 13, 2.

to follow his path by the example of the purity of his life. Such practical questions of actual living stand in the centre of Clement's thought and teaching. Speculative theological problems occupy only the fringe of his interests. He takes over the idea of the Logos from St John, but does not penetrate more deeply into it. The Logos is united with the Father and the Holy Spirit in the divine Trias; the world was created by him, and he revealed God with increasing clarity, first in the Jewish Law, then in Greek philosophy, and finally in becoming man. By his blood mankind was redeemed, and men still drink his blood in order to share in his immortality.[12] The Redeemer Christ recedes, for Clement, behind the Logos as teacher and lawgiver. He did not further speculative theology properly so-called, but he is the first comprehensive theorist of Christian striving after perfection, and posterity allowed him to be forgotten far too readily.

Origen

Fortune did not favour the life-work of Origen, the greatest of the Alexandrian teachers and the most important theologian of Eastern Christianity. The greater part of his writings has perished because the violent quarrels which broke out concerning his orthodoxy led to his condemnation by the Synod of Constantinople in 553. As a consequence, his theological reputation suffered for a long time, and the reading of his works was proscribed. Few of these works remain in his Greek mother-tongue, and the greater part of his biblical homilies has survived only in Latin translations, notably those by Jerome and Rufinus. Friends and admirers in the third and fourth centuries preserved a little of his canon and this helps to throw light on the aim and purpose of his life's work, the most useful of this evidence being preserved in the sixth book of Eusebius' *Ecclesiastical History*. Though this sketch is transfigured by retrospect vision, Eusebius had at his disposal a collection of Origen's letters, and obtained many details from men who had known him personally in Caesarea.

The first decisive influence on Origen was that of the Christian atmosphere of his parents' home.[13] There he inherited and never lost the high courage to confess his faith, and the constant readiness to be active in the ecclesiastical community. An excellent education in secular studies made it possible for him, after the martyr's death of his father, Leonides, to support the family by teaching in a grammar school. Quite soon, while

---

[12] *Paidag.* 2, 19, 4.
[13] Eusebius's precise details are to be preferred in this to Porphyry's vague allusions to a pagan period in Origen's life. It is certainly correct that Origen was familiar with Greek culture.

instructing interested pagans in the Christian faith on his own initiative, he felt the need of a deeper philosophical training; and this he found in the lectures of the neo-Platonist Ammonius Saccas, whose influence on him was strong and lasting. Journeys in his early manhood took him to Caesarea in Palestine, where he became a friend of the bishop, Theoctistus, and of Alexander, the head of the Jerusalem community, to Arabia at the invitation of the imperial governor; and also to the West, where he travelled to Rome. These journeys gave him a vivid idea of the life of the Church as a whole, and strengthened his inclination to work everywhere through his lectures for a deeper understanding of Scripture and belief.

His appointment as teacher of the catechumens and his duties as head of the theological school in Alexandria brought his rich intellectual and spiritual powers to full development, and initiated the creative period of his life. This was not fundamentally disturbed when, in the years 230–1, conflict with Bishop Demetrius forced him to transfer his activities to Caesarea in Palestine. The ostensible cause of his estrangement from the local bishop was his ordination to the priesthood without the former's knowledge. It was conferred on him by Palestinian bishops, although Origen, being a eunuch (he had castrated himself in a youthful excess of asceticism), was not, according to the views of the time, a suitable candidate. The deeper reason, however, was the bishop's inability to have a man of such high reputation and intellectual quality by his side. The understanding which was shown to Origen in his second sphere of activity, namely in Palestine, was munificently repaid by him; for, in addition to his actual teaching, he served the life of the Church directly, both by his tireless preaching and by public theological discussions about problems of the day, which repeatedly took him as far as Arabia. He had occasion to crown his fidelity to faith and Church by manfully confessing the faith during the Decian persecution, when he was imprisoned and subjected to cruel torture. About the year 253 or 254 he died in Tyre as a result of this treatment, when nearly seventy years of age.

The kernel of Origen's theological achievement was his work on the Bible, his efforts for its better understanding and the use made of it to create a right attitude in belief and true piety. The bulk of his literary production derived from this concern. It took the form of critical and philological work on the text of Scripture, scientific commentaries on individual books, and finally in his abundant discourses on the Bible, which were recorded by stenographers and later published. These are works of edification; not merely intellectually stimulating, they delve into the ultimate depths of Christian life. The impressive undertaking of the Hexapla [14] served to establish a trustworthy text of the Bible. It presented

---

[14] See *Quasten P*, II, 44 ff., and G. Mercati, *Psalterii Hexapli reliquiae* I (Rome 1958).

in six parallel columns the original Hebrew in Hebrew characters, a Greek transcription, the translations by Aquila and Symmachus, the Septuagint and the Theodotion translation. What was probably the only copy of this work was placed in the library of Caesarea, where it could still be consulted in the time of Jerome and even later. A particularly hard fate overtook the great scriptural commentaries; many of which perished completely, or did so with the exception of a few fragments, such as the commentaries on Genesis, the Psalms, Proverbs, Isaias, Ezechiel, the Minor Prophets, Luke, and most of the Epistles of St Paul. Larger portions of the commentaries on the Canticle of Canticles, the Gospels of St Matthew and St John were preserved, partly in Greek and partly in Latin translations. The works which most frequently survived were homilies, particularly esteemed for their pastoral use of the Old Testament. About six hundred of them have come down to us, but only twenty-one in the original Greek.

It was with an attitude of deepest reverence that Origen undertook this service of Holy Scripture; for in it he encountered the living word of God which it embodies. Consequently, the understanding of Holy Scripture is for him "the art of arts" and "the science of sciences". [15] And just as all events take place in mysteries, so Scripture also is full of mysteries which unveil themselves only to one who implores this revelation in insistent prayer. [16] From this consideration sprang Origen's spontaneous appeals to "his Lord Jesus" to show him the way to a right interpretation of a difficult passage of Scripture. [17] He knew that this is only found when the deeper spiritual and divine sense is recognized, that which is hidden behind the letter is the treasure hidden in a field. That is why the allegorical interpretation of Scripture was not for Origen merely a traditional and easily applied method, taken over from the exposition of secular texts. It was often a compelling necessity for him, absolutely essential if what is sometimes offensive in the purely literal sense of Scripture is to be transcended. Origen was fully aware that allegory has its limits. [18] Nevertheless, in the hand of the master and despite all errors in detail, this method remains the path that leads him to the very heart of Scripture, affording ultimate religious insight and knowledge.

The daily reading of Scripture, to which Origen exhorts us, [19] became for him the well-spring of his personal religious life; and it also made him a teacher of the Christian ideal of striving after perfection, whose subsequent influence was immeasurable: first on Eastern monasticism, and then in the Latin West, by way of St Ambrose. The ultimate goal of the ascent to

[15] *In Ioannem comm.* 13, 46.
[16] *In Exod. hom.* 1, 4; *Ep. ad Greg.* 4.
[17] *In Levit. hom.* 1, 1; 5, 5; *In Matth. comm.* 10, 5.
[18] *In Num. hom.* 9, 1.
[19] *In Gen. hom.* 10, 3.

perfection is the resemblance to God, to which man was called when God created him in his own image and likeness. The surest way to this goal is the imitation of Christ; and to be so centred on Christ is the characteristic attitude of Origen's piety, just as later the principle "Christus" was the basic concept of his pupil, Ambrose of Milan.[20] A man who imitates Christ chooses life and chooses light.[21] A presupposition for the success of this imitation is correct self-knowledge, which brings awareness of one's own sinfulness; and this, in turn, imposes a stubborn fight against the perils which threaten from world and from one's own passions. Only a person who has reached *apatheia* is capable of further mystical ascent, but this cannot be attained without a serious ascetic effort, in which fasting and vigils have their place just as much as the reading of Scripture and the exercise of humility.[22] Those who, following Christ's example, freely choose a celibate life and virginity will more easily reach the goal.[23] The ascent to mystical union with the Logos takes place by degrees, a progress which Origen sees prefigured in the journey of the people of Israel through the desert to the promised land.[24] The profound yearning for Christ is fulfilled in a union with him which is accomplished in the form of a mystical marriage;[25] Christ becomes the bridegroom of the soul, which in a mystical embrace receives the *vulnus amoris*.[26] Origen here is not only the first representative of a profound devotion to Jesus, but also the founder of an already richly developed Christocentric and bridal mysticism, from which the medieval Christocentric spirituality of William of St Thierry and Bernard of Clairvaux derived, and from which it drew considerable substance. In this way the personality of the great Alexandrian had its deepest ultimate influence precisely where it is most authentically evident: in its calm, limpid, and yet ardent love for Christ.

While in Alexandria, Origen wrote a systematic exposition of the chief doctrines of Christianity. He gave this first dogmatic handbook in the history of Christian theology the title Περὶ ἀρχῶν (Concerning Principles), and dealt in four books with the central questions concerning God, the creation of the world, the fall of man, redemption through Jesus Christ, sin, freedom of the will, and Holy Scripture as a source of belief. The Greek original has perished, as has also the literal Latin translation made by Jerome. This surviving version by Rufinus, has smoothed down or eliminated entirely many things to which

---

[20] Cf. K. Baus, in *RQ* 49 (1954), 26–29.
[21] *In Levit. hom.* 9, 10.
[22] *In Ierem. hom.* 8, 4; *In Exod. hom.* 13, 5.
[23] *In Num. hom.* 24, 2; *In Cant. comm.* 2, 155.
[24] *In Num. hom.* 27.
[25] *In Cant. comm.* 1.
[26] Ibid. 2, 8.

objection might be raised. There is, consequently, some uncertainty about the precise view which Origen held on certain questions.[27]

In his introduction, Origen speaks with great clarity about the principles of method which guided him in his work; Scripture and tradition are the two primary sources for his exposition of Christian doctrine. He knows that they cannot be approached with a philosopher's inquiry, but only with the attitude of a believer. The Old and New Testaments, the books of Law, the Prophets and the Epistles of St Paul: all contain the words of Christ and are a rule of life for the Christian, because they are inspired.[28] The authority of the Church guarantees that no spurious writings intrude; only what is accepted in all the communities as indubitably Holy Scripture is free from the suspicion of being apocryphal.[29] Only that truth can be received in faith which does not contradict ecclesiastical and apostolic tradition, and this is found in the teaching of the Church which per *successionis ordinem* was handed down from the apostles.[30] Consequently, the Church is not only intended to be the guardian of Holy Scripture, but is also its authentic interpreter, for she alone has received from Christ the light which enlightens those who dwell in darkness.[31] She is the true Ark in which alone men can find salvation: the house which is marked with the blood of Christ and outside which there is no redemption.[32] She is like a fortified city, and anyone who remains outside her walls is captured and killed by the enemy.[33] Men enter Jesus' house by thinking like the Church and living according to her spirit.[34]

As the rule of faith contains only the necessary fundamental doctrines preached by the apostles, without giving further reasons for them or showing in any detail their inner connexions, a wide field of activity remains open to theology. According to Origen, this is where the task lies for those who are called to it by the Holy Spirit through the special gifts of wisdom and knowledge. Theirs is the vocation of penetrating deeper into the truths of revelation and of framing by an appropriate method a theological system from Scripture and tradition.[35] The execution of his own project makes it plain that Origen was not a born systematizer; he had not the power to carry through his conception on a strictly logical plan. But of much greater

---

[27] Cf. M. Harl, "Recherches sur le Περὶ ἀρχῶν d'Origène en vue d'une nouvelle édition" in *Studia Patristica* 3 (Berlin 1961), 57–67.
[28] Origen, *De princ. praef.* 1; *In Matth. comm.* 46.
[29] *De princ. praef.* 8; *In Matth. comm.* 61.
[30] *De princ. praef.* 2.
[31] *In Gen. hom.* 1, 5.
[32] Ibid. 2, 3; *In Jesu Nave hom.* 3, 5.
[33] *In Ierem. hom.* 5, 16.
[34] *Disput. cum Heracl.* 15.
[35] *De princ. praef.* 3 and 10.

weight than this imperfection of form, are the particular theological views which gave rise to the later controversies about their author's orthodoxy. In his doctrine of the Trinity, Origen still thinks in Subordinationist terms: only the Father is ὁ Θεός or αὐτόθεος: the Logos, of course, likewise possesses the divine nature, but in regard to the Father he can only be called δεύτερος Θεός.[36] Yet Origen clearly expresses the eternity of the Logos and characterizes him as ὁμοούσιος;[37] and so an advance is made here as compared with early Subordinationism. Origen, one might say, is on the path that led to Nicaea. In Christology, too, he devises modes of expression which point to the future: the union of the two natures in Christ is so close in his doctrine that the communication of idioms follows from it;[38] as far as can now be traced the term God-man, Θεάνθρωπος, first occurs with Origen, and probably he prepared the way for the term Θεοτόκος.[39] Origen also followed paths of his own in the doctrine of Creation; before the present world, a world of perfect spirits existed to which the souls of men then belonged; these were, therefore, pre-existent. Only a fall from God brought upon them banishment into matter which God then created. The measure of their pre-mundane guilt actually determines the measure of grace which God grants each human being on earth.[40]

All creation strives back towards its origin in God, and so is subjected to a process of purification which can extend over many aeons and in which all souls, even the evil spirits of the demons and Satan himself, are cleansed with increasing effect until they are worthy of resurrection and reunion with God. Then God is once more all-in-all, and the restoration of all things (ἀποκατάστασις τῶν πάντων) is attained.[41] The eternity of hell was practically abandoned as a result of this conception. That a new Fall would be possible after this process and consequently a new creation of the world and a further series of purifications necessary, was presented by Origen merely as an arguable possibility and not as certain Christian teaching. Critics have reproached Origen with further errors in his theology, which might be described as spiritualism and esotericism. By this is meant his tendency to undervalue the material creation and to except the spirit from the need for redemption, and also his tendency to reserve the innermost kernel and meaning of the truths of revelation for the circle of the perfect, the *pneumatikoi*, or the spiritual ones. Both accusations have a certain justification but have often been very much exaggerated. Origen recognized perfectly the proper value of what pertains to the senses and the body, and

[36] *De princ.* 1, 2, 13; *Contra Cels.* 5, 39.
[37] *In ep. ad Hebr. fragm.*
[38] *De princ.* 2, 6, 3.
[39] *In Ezech. hom.* 3, 3; *In Luc. hom.* 6, 7.
[40] *De princ.* 2, 8 ff.; *Contra Cels.* 1, 32–3.
[41] *De princ.* 1, 6, 1 and 3; 3, 6, 6; *Contra Cels.* 8, 72.

in fact, saw its importance precisely in its function as an image of a spiritual world that lies behind it. Consequently, he did not call for its annihilation, but for its spiritualization and transfiguration. He was likewise convinced that every baptized person is called on principle to perfection, but that there are many stages on the way to it, and that every stage can assimilate only an appropriate part of the truth of revelation. He believed in consequence that the full grasp of Christian truth is only possible at the final stage.

Like every theological achievement, that of Origen must be judged according to the possibilities and conditions which the age provided. He approached theological problems with the equipment and questions of a third-century man trained in philosophy; and most of the defects of his theology can be seen to derive from the limits and conditioning circumstances of this philosophy. But, viewed as a whole, his theological work, and especially his systematic treatise Concerning Principles, represents a creative personal achievement and consequently an enormous advance in Christian theology. For a judgment of the whole, the fact is important that the work was inspired by the purest ecclesiastical spirit. For all the independence and freedom of his theological questioning and inquiry, Origen wanted only to serve the Church, and was always ready to submit to her judgment. "If I", he once addressed the Church, "I, who bear the name of priest, and have to preach the word of God, offend against the doctrine of the Church, and the rule of the gospel and were to become a scandal to the Church, then, may the whole Church with unanimous decision cut off me, her right hand, and cast me out."[42] Such an attitude should have prevented posterity from proscribing Origen's work as a whole merely because of particular errors and mistakes, in the way that happened later.

Dionysius of Alexandria; Methodius; Lucian of Antioch and his School

Subsequent teachers in the school of Alexandria, which after Origen's departure, as has been said, assumed once more the character of a school for catechumens, are overshadowed by their great predecessors. The title of "great" was given to Dionysius, later bishop of the Egyptian capital (247–8 to 264–5), more on account of his personal bravery in the Decian persecution and his zealous activity in ecclesiastical affairs than because of any theological achievement. The orthodoxy of his teaching on the Trinity was doubted in Rome, and he attempted to demonstrate it in an apologia composed in four books against Dionysius, Bishop of Rome. He opposed the chiliastic ideas of Bishop Nepos of Arsinoë in his work On the Promises, in which he rejected John the apostle's authorship of the Apocalypse.[43]

[42] In Ios. hom. 7, 6.
[43] Euseb. HE 7, 24 ff.

Dionysius is the first Bishop of Alexandria for whom we have evidence of the custom of announcing the date of the day of the Resurrection each year to Egyptian Christendom in the so-called "Easter letters". With the exception of two letters, his extensive correspondence has been lost. The written works of Theognostus and Pierius, Dionysius's successors at the head of the school for catechumens, drew on Origen's achievement. The *Hypotyposes* of Theognostus was a dogmatic work, while Pierius occupied himself more with exegesis and homiletics. [44] Whether Peter, who was Bishop of Alexandria from about 300, also worked in the catechetical school is uncertain: the fragments of his treatises indicate particularly pastoral interest, as do those on penitential regulations and on the Pasch, though some opposed the alleged errors of Origen.

Other Eastern writers are also found within the range of Origen's influence, and their inferior performances make the greatness of the master stand out in sharper relief. We owe a panegyric on Origen to his pupil Gregory Thaumaturgus († c. 270), a miracle-working bishop in central Asia Minor who was soon transfigured by legend and became a highly honoured figure in the Byzantine church. Gregory's panegyric gives an instructive glimpse at the teaching method of the revered master. The laity, too, took an interest in theology and exegetical questions. This is proved by Julius Africanus of Palestine († *post* 240), a friend of Origen, who in a letter to the latter raised doubts about the authenticity of the story of Susanna, and in another inquired into the genealogies of Jesus in Matthew and Luke. [45] The learned priest Pamphilus of Caesarea in Palestine sought to serve Origen's aims by continuing the tradition of the master in his teaching and learned inquiries. His interests lay particularly in the text of Scripture, as well as in collecting Origen's writings and in taking care of the library founded by Origen in Caesarea. The Diocletian persecution brought him martyrdom after long imprisonment (310), during which he wrote an Ἀπολογία ὑπὲρ Ὠριγένους, or *Defence of Origen*, in six books, of which only the first survives in the Latin translation by Rufinus. [46] The writer Methodius is included in the opposition that formed against Origen. According to Jerome and Socrates, [47] he was Bishop of Olympus in Lycia, but more probably he lived as an ascetic and as a private Christian teacher. In his discussion of Origen he rejected the latter's doctrine of the pre-existence of souls and the theory of a cycle of several creations of the world, but could not free himself from Origen's allegorical interpretation of Scripture. For his literary works he

---

[44] Fragments in R. Routh, *Reliquiae sacrae* 3 (Oxford 1846), 405–35; cf. L. B. Radford, *Three Teachers of Alexandria, Theognostus, Pierius and Peter* (Cambridge 1908).

[45] W. Reichardt, *Die Briefe des S. Julius Africanus* (Leipzig 1909); E. Blakeney, "Jul. Africanus" in *Theology* 29 (1934), 164–9.

[46] *Euseb. HE* 6, 32, 3; *PG* 17, 521–616.

[47] Jerome, *De vir. ill.* 83; *Socrates HE* 6, 13.

preferred the dialogue form, and he displays a good knowledge of Plato.[48] His *Symposium* was in fact an important work, especially in its influence on the history of spirituality. It praises the Christian ideal of virginity and ends with a famous hymn to Christ the bridegroom and his bride the Church.

The beginnings of the second theological school in the East are no less obscure than those of the Alexandrian school. It sprang up in the Syrian capital of Antioch, an important centre of the Hellenic world where conditions were similar to those in Alexandria. Tradition unanimously names the Antiochan priest Lucian as founder of the school, which may have been preceded by undertakings on a smaller scale and more private in character. In the time of Bishop Paul of Samosata, a priest named Malchion enjoyed a considerable reputation in Antioch for wide learning, but was a teacher in a secular Greek school. He demonstrated his superior theological training in the controversy with Paul of Samosata at the Synod of Antioch (268) which led to the latter's condemnation.[49] Another priest of Antioch whose biblical interests and knowledge of Hebrew were praised, was Dorotheus, a contemporary of Lucian, but he is not expressly said to have been a Christian teacher.[50] It is only with Lucian that the records in the sources become more precise. The fact that Lucian was one of the clergy of Antioch permits the assumption that his activity as a Christian teacher was authorized by his bishop. His theological learning, which is praised by Eusebius,[51] did not find expression in extensive publications. His real interest was in biblical work and more particularly in a new recension of the Septuagint, for which he consulted the Hebrew original. It enjoyed high repute and was widely used in the dioceses of Syria and Asia Minor. Lucian's exegetical method must be gathered from the biblical works of his pupils; it takes principally into account the literal sense and only employs typological interpretation where the text itself demands it. Similarly, it is only from the works of his pupils that it is possible to form an idea of Lucian's other theological characteristics. He always starts from biblical data, not from theological presuppositions, and attains, among other things, a strict Subordinationism in the doctrine of the Logos. This was represented soon after by Arius and some of his fellow-pupils, the so-called Syllucianists, and they expressly referred to their teacher for it. The characteristics of the Antioch school became fully clear only in the great age of the Fathers, in connexion with the Trinitarian and Christological controversies.

[48] Cf. M. Margheritis, "L'influenza di Platone sul pensiero e sull'arte di s. Metodio d'Olimpo" in *Studi Ubaldi* (Milan 1937), 401–12. On the dialogue technique, cf. G. Luzzati, ibid. 117–24.
[49] *Euseb. HE* 7, 29, 2.
[50] Ibid. 7, 32, 3–4.
[51] Ibid. 9, 6, 3.

CHAPTER 20

The Development of Christian Literature in the West in the Third Century

The Rise of Early Christian Latin and the Beginning of a Christian Literature in Latin. Minucius Felix

THE essentially different course taken by the development of Christian literature in the West in the third century, particularly in Rome, was determined by the linguistic tradition of the Roman Christian community, which at first was composed for the most part of Greek-speaking members and consequently used Greek for preaching and the liturgy. Only with the disappearance of the Greek majority did the necessity arise for translating the Holy Scriptures of the new faith into Latin, of preaching in Latin, and finally of using Latin as a liturgical language too. The first traces of the existence of a Latin Bible extend back, as far as Rome is concerned, into the latter half of the second century, for the Latin translation of the *First Letter of Clement* must have been made at that time.

In Africa, at the turn of the century, Tertullian also quoted from a Latin Bible which he had at hand. The unknown translators thereby initiated the development of early Christian Latin, and with this achievement created the conditions for the rise of an independent Christian literature in the Latin tongue. Old Christian Latin was firmly based in one respect on the colloquial language of the common people, to whom the missionaries at first addressed themselves. On the other hand, it borrowed certain words from the Greek, for many Latin words were impossible to employ because of their previous use in pagan worship. And, finally, for many central concepts of Christian revelation and preaching, existing Latin terms had to be given a new content. In this way there arose, by a lengthy and extremely important process, a sector of early Christian Latin within the wider field of later Latin. It is clearly distinct from the language of secular literature, possessing its own unmistakable style. No single person, therefore, created early Christian Latin: not even Tertullian, the first writer to attest its existence through his writings. Naturally, it took a certain time for this Christian Latin to acquire such flexibility and clarity that it could be used for more important literary works. It is characteristic that the theological discussions in Rome at the end of the second and in the third centuries were still conducted to a large extent in Greek. Justin wrote his *Apologia* in Greek; Marcion and the early disputants in the Trinitarian controversies were from Asia Minor; and even Hippolytus, the first theologian of rank to live and write in Rome, was of Eastern origin, and published his works in the Greek language.

A further characteristic of Latin Christian theology in the third century was that it was not developed in theological schools as was its Eastern counterpart. There was no lack of institutions for the instruction of catechumens at key points of christianization such as Rome and Carthage; but schools where important theological teachers of Origen's kind provided an introduction to the Christian religion for cultivated pagans were unknown in the West. Tertullian, it is true, exercised a strong influence, and Novatian was certainly a theologian of importance; but neither of them was head of a school in its proper sense.

The *Octavius Dialogue* of Minucius Felix presents a defence of Christianity written in a distinguished and polished style by a lawyer trained in philosophy who was particularly influenced by Stoic thought. Caecilius, the pagan speaker in this dialogue, views pagan polytheism with marked scepticism, but, because Rome owed its greatness to it, would give it preference over the Christian religion, whose invisible God seemed to him a figment of the imagination, whose adherents were without culture and gave themselves up to shameless orgies. The Christian Octavius proves by purely philosophical arguments, without any appeal to Holy Scripture, that a sceptical standpoint on religious questions is untenable, and he rejects as calumnies the accusations made against the Christians. The dialogue does not go deeper into the content of the Christian faith. Its diction is still free from the typical features of early Christian Latin, and its style still strongly recalls the artistically cultivated prose of the later Antonines. One may for these reasons be inclined to date this elegant apologia before Tertullian's *Apologeticum* in the much-disputed and still open question of priority.

Hippolytus

Hippolytus can be regarded as a link between East and West. His person and work even today present many unsolved problems for research. It can be said with certainty that he was not a Roman by birth but a man from the East, thinking Greek and writing Greek, whose home was possibly Egypt and very likely Alexandria: a true Roman would scarcely have expressed as low an opinion of Rome's historical past as Hippolytus does.[1] He came to Rome probably as early as Pope Zephyrinus's time and belonged as a priest to the Christian community there, in which his culture and intellectual activity assured him considerable prestige. His influence is evident in all the theological and disciplinary controversies which stirred Roman Christianity in the opening decades of the third century. His high conception of the functions of a priest, among which he emphatically

[1] See in particular J.-M. Hanssens, *La liturgie d'Hippolyte* (Rome 1959), 290 f.

reckoned the preservation of apostolic traditions, did not permit him to shrink from bold criticism of the Roman bishops when he thought those traditions threatened by their attitude and measures. The position he assumed in the controversy over Modalism must be mentioned later. His rigoristic attitude on the question of penance made him an irreconcilable opponent of Bishop Callistus (217–22), and the leader of a numerically small but intellectually important opposition group. Nevertheless, the conjecture that he had himself consecrated bishop at that time, and so became the first anti-pope in the history of the Church, finds no adequate support in the sources. And there is just as little reliable evidence that it was the writer Hippolytus whom the emperor Maximinus Thrax banished to Sardinia with Pope Pontian, that it was he who was there reconciled to the latter and died in exile.[2] But it is possible that Hippolytus lived on through the period of the Novatian schism, belonged to this movement for a while and after being received once more into the Christian community survived until later than 253.[3] Both Eusebius and Jerome give a list of his writings;[4] and their titles reveal him as a writer having such notable breadth of interest as to suggest comparison with Origen, though certainly he never achieved the latter's originality and depth. If the statue of a teacher which was discovered in 1551 actually represents Hippolytus — an incomplete catalogue of his works and an Easter calendar are carved on the side of the teacher's chair — it is tangible evidence of his reputation.

Hippolytus most clearly shares with Origen an inclination to the study of Scripture, which he expounds in the same allegorical way, though a more sober use of this method is unmistakable in his case. It is true that only a small remnant of his biblical writings has survived, but among them is a significant commentary on Daniel in the Greek original, and an exposition of the Canticle of Canticles, complete but in translation. In the Susanna of the Book of Daniel he considers that the Church, the virgin bride of Christ, is prefigured, persecuted by Jews and pagans. Likewise the bride and bridegroom of the Canticle of Canticles are understood as Christ and his Church, and sometimes the bride is considered to be the soul that loves God, an interpretation that was taken up particularly by St Ambrose in his exposition of Psalm 118, and so transmitted to the Middle Ages.

---

[2] There are sound reasons for supposing that confusion later occurred with another Hippolytus, who was also a priest and who was honoured as a martyr: cf. Hanssens, op. cit. 317–40. It would then be the latter Hippolytus who was referred to in the Depositio martyrum of 354.

[3] The supposition is based chiefly on a letter written to Rome in 253 by Dionysius of Alexandria, which presupposed that Hippolytus was still alive; cf. Euseb. HE 6, 46, 5, and Hanssens, op. cit. 299 f.

[4] Euseb. HE 6, 12, and Jerome, De vir. ill. 61.

Anxiety for the preservation of apostolic traditions was the second motive determining Hippolytus's work as a writer. They seemed to him threatened in doctrine and in the performance of divine worship. Consequently, he wrote a *Church Order* designed to ensure the maintenance of traditional forms in the most important rules and formulas for conferring Orders, the various functions of ecclesiastical offices, the conferring of baptism, and the celebration of the eucharist. This *Traditio Apostolica* no longer survives in its original language, but it forms the kernel of a series of further Church Orders such as the *Apostolic Order*, the *Testament of our Lord Jesus Christ*, the *Canons of Hippolytus* and the eight books of the *Apostolic Constitutions*. Its principle impact was felt in the East, especially in Egypt, as the many translations into Coptic, Ethiopic, and Arabic show, while the Latin version (*c.* 500) is incomplete. For Hippolytus, his *Church Order* probably represented an ideal form which was not designed for the needs of a particular community, but intended to provide a norm by which the Church leaders could test the conformity of their liturgical prescriptions with apostolic tradition.[5] It drew its material chiefly from Eastern sources, and consequently cannot be regarded as a Ritual which Hippolytus based on the liturgical forms customary in Rome at the beginning of the third century.

The anti-heretical dogmatic writings of Hippolytus served to safeguard apostolic tradition in doctrine. An early work was his *Syntagma* against thirty-two heresies, treating of the erroneous doctrines which had appeared in the course of history down to his own day. Unfortunately only its concluding part, which refutes the teaching of Noëtus, is extant. Another anti-heretical work is attributed to Hippolytus: *The Refutation of All Heresies*, also called the *Philosophoumena*, which indicated in its first part the errors of pagan philosophers and the aberrations of pagan religions (Book 1–4), and then proceeded to oppose the Gnostic systems in particular (Books 5–9). The argument in this work owes a great deal to Irenaeus. The Tenth Book provides a recapitulation of the whole work, and adds a brief account of the content of Christian belief. The chief purpose of the author is to demonstrate his thesis that the root of all heresies is that they did not follow Christ, Holy Scripture, and tradition, but reverted instead to pagan doctrines.[6] The historical transmission of this work is extremely confused. The First Book was ascribed to Origen, but the manuscript containing Books 4–10 was not discovered until 1842 and names no author. Only the fact that the writer refers to other works of Hippolytus as his own writings[7] — his *Chronicle* and his study *On the Universe* — makes the

---

[5] See *Trad. apost.*, ed. E. Hauler, *Didascaliae Apostolorum Fragmenta Veronensia* (Leipzig 1900), 56, 1–13; 78, 30—5; 80, 30–5.
[6] *Refut., praef.*   [7] Ibid. 10, 30 and 32.

attribution to Hippolytus at all possible. The *Philosophoumena* have very much the character of a compilation, and give the impression of being a first draft which did not receive further revision. The polemic is caustic and oversteps all bounds when a personal opponent is attacked, so that an Hippolytus different from the author of his other works seems to be speaking here.[8] The concept of the Church, which the *Philosophoumena* express, is particularly striking. In the commentary on Daniel and the exposition of the Canticle of Canticles the Church appears as the spotless bride of Christ, permitting no place for a person who has incurred grievous moral guilt, but here in the controversy with Callistus the Church is addressed as the bearer and safeguard of truth, whose purity and authenticity have to be watched over by bishops in legitimate apostolic succession. The author turns passionately against those who forget their task and who, though appointed members of the hierarchy, open too wide to sinners the gate of the Church of the saints.

Novatian

Novatian may be considered as the first Roman theologian of importance, but his culture and gifts had to overcome manifold contradictions within the Roman community. Although he had received only the baptism of the sick, and so, according to the conception of the time, displayed a lack of courage to confess the Faith, Pope Fabian had nevertheless ordained him priest;[9] and about the year 250 he played a decisive role in the Pope's *collegium*. When the papal see was vacant, he continued the correspondence of the Roman Church with other communities abroad, and in two or three letters to Cyprian[10] expounded the Roman position concerning the treatment of those who had lapsed during persecution, a position identical with Cyprian's prudent practice. About 250 Novatian wrote his chief theological treatise on the Trinity. Here he made use of the work of earlier theologians, especially Hippolytus and Tertullian, and carefully formulated the state of the question in clear language of much formal distinction. The theology of Marcion is rejected in his treatise, as well as the Modalist conception of the Monarchians; Novatian propounds a very definite Subordinationism, which however much it emphasizes Christ's Godhead subordinates him to

---

[8] This caused P. Nautin to ascribe the *Philosophoumena*, the *Chronicle*, and the work *On the Universe* to another author, whom he called Josipos. Even if his arguments are not convincing on this, he clearly perceived and rightly emphasized the striking difference of style and particular range of themes in the *Philosophoumena* as compared with the other writings of Hippolytus.

[9] See *Euseb. HE* 6, 43, 6–22; cf. also ibid. for the one-sided characterization of Novatian by Cornelius.

[10] In Cyprian's *Letters*, nos. 30, 36, and perhaps 31.

the Father almost more strictly than in earlier theology. He expresses himself very briefly on the relation of the Holy Spirit to the Son and the Father, but here too emphasizes the subordination of the Spirit to the Son. He lays great stress on the role of the Holy Spirit within the Church, which is preserved by his gifts inviolate in holiness and truth. This work of Novatian brought the theology of the Trinity in the West before Constantine's time provisionally to an end, until Augustine later revived discussion on the subject.

Novatian's other writings are pastoral in character and belong to the later phase of his life when, after leaving the Roman community, he led his own rigoristic, strictly organized society, as its bishop. His separation from the Roman community was due in the first place to personal motives especially aroused when Cornelius was preferred to him in the election of bishop in 251. The rift became irreparable when Novatian tried to justify his own secession by a concept according to which there could be no place for a mortal sinner in the Church of the saints, however ready he might be to atone by penance. While African circles, contrary to Novatian's expectation, ultimately refused him a following, he found numerous adherents in the East, who regarded themselves as the Church of the "pure" (καθαροί).[11] Dionysius of Alexandria had difficulty in preventing a greater defection than occurred,[12] and in the West a synod of sixty bishops under the leadership of Pope Cornelius clarified the situation by excommunicating Novatian and his followers. The first of Novatian's three pastoral letters to his communities deals with the question of the obligation of Jewish food laws, which he rejected; the second adopts a negative position on visits to the pagan theatre and circus; the third, *De bono pudicitiae*, presents a lofty exposition of the early Christian ideal of chastity in which marital fidelity and high esteem of virginity are forcefully proclaimed. Regarding Novatian's end, we have only the report of Socrates that he died as a martyr in the persecution by Valerian. An epitaph found in a catacomb in Rome in 1932, which reads: "Novatiano beatissimo martyri Gaudentius diaconus fecit", appears to confirm this report.[13]

Tertullian

The contribution made by the young African Church to early Christian literature in the third century was of greater weight and consequence. All evidence seems to indicate that Christianity found its way from Rome to these provinces beyond the sea, and that the first missionaries still used

---

[11] *Euseb. HE* 6, 43, 1.
[12] He tried to persuade Novatian to return; see his letter in *Euseb. HE* 6, 45.
[13] *Socrates HE* 4, 28; see Chapter 18, above.

Greek in their preaching. Towns provided the earliest points of contact for Christian teaching, especially and above all Carthage, which had flourished again under Roman rule and where the upper classes were quite familiar with Greek. [14] But the transition to Latin for preaching and liturgy took place earlier in Africa than in Rome. The *Acts of the Martyrs of Scili*, the first dated Latin document of Christian origin (A.D. 180), probably already presupposes a translation of the Pauline epistles into Latin; a few years later Tertullian used a Latin translation of the Bible, which was not to his taste; and, about the middle of the third century, Cyprian quoted it so habitually that it must have been generally known by that time. [15]

The Christian literature which begins with Tertullian vividly reflects the special features of the world of African Christianity in the third century. This area was exposed to most grievous tribulations in the persecutions of the time and had to pay a very heavy toll in blood for its steadfastness in the faith, which was rewarded by a proportionately rapid growth of the Church. The African church was characterized to an almost equal extent by the internal controversies which it suffered with the Gnostic sects and Montanism, by the struggles for its unity which it waged against the schismatical movement of Novatian and Felicissimus and, after the middle of the third century, by the quarrel concerning baptism conferred by heretics. All this left its mark on the early Christian literature of North Africa, and gives it its lively and sometimes pugnacious quality. At the same time the first differences which were to divide the Greek and Latin literature more and more sharply from each other are already apparent within it. The latter was not as much concerned as was the East, in grasping the metaphysical content of revelation and demonstrating its superiority over Hellenistic religious trends. Its prime interest lay, rather, in directly practical questions of actual living in pagan surroundings, such as logically follow from the Christian doctrine of redemption; and it was concerned, furthermore, with the translation of belief into action, which demands a fight against sin, and with the positive practice of virtue as a contribution of the individual Christian to ensuring salvation.

In Tertullian we meet the first and at the same time the most productive and distinctive writer of pre-Constantinian literature in North Africa. Born about 160 in Carthage, he was the son of a pagan captain, received a solid general education in the humanities, and pursued special studies in law and

---

[14] See J. Mesnage, *Le christianisme en Afrique*, I (Paris 1915); C. Cecchelli, *Africa christiana, Africa Romana* (Rome 1936); G. Bardy, *La question des langues dans l'église ancienne* (Paris 1948), 52–72.

[15] See G. D. Aalders, *Tertullianus' citaten uit de Evangeliën* (Amsterdam 1932); B. Botte in *DBS* 5 (1952), 334–7; H. J. Vogels, *Handbuch der neutestamentlichen Textkritik* (Bonn, 2nd ed. 1955).

Greek. He entered the Church as an adult, as a result of the impression made on him by Christians' fidelity to their beliefs under persecution, and immediately placed his wealth of gifts at her service. The sources do not make it clear whether he became a priest or remained a layman. The period of his activity as a writer covers approximately a quarter of a century (c. 195–220), and comprises two parts of roughly equal length but of quite contrasting nature. Until c. 207 he was a convinced and declared member of the Catholic Church, but then he joined the Montanist movement and rejected wholesale what he had previously revered. This change accounts for a double feature in Tertullian's nature which is apparent to every reader of his works. He is a man who gives himself utterly and uncompromisingly to whatever he professes at any given moment: anyone who thinks differently than he is not only an opponent of his views but is morally suspect. His temperament, which inclined him to extremes, led him almost inevitably out of the Church when he encountered in Montanism a form of Christian belief in which the utmost rigorism was the law. For the defence of his conviction of the moment, he had at his command a mastery of contemporary Latin such as no other writer of those years possessed. In expounding his own position, he employed an impressive eloquence supported by comprehensive learning in every field, which he drew upon with brilliant effect. He had also the gift of that brief incisive turn of phrase which holds the reader's interest. His acute intellect relentlessly uncovered the weakness of an opponent's argument, and helds up to ridicule those who differed from him. There can be no doubt that Tertullian's work was read, but its power of conviction is open to suspicion. It seems that even Montanism was not in the end sufficient for his excessive and immoderate nature; and Augustine credibly reports that before his death he became the founder of a sect named, after himself, the Tertullianists.[16]

In a series of writings Tertullian tried to place before the pagans a true picture of the Christian religion. After a first attempt in *Ad nationes,* he found in the *Apologeticum* a form that suited his ideas. The work is directly addressed to the *praesides* of the Roman provinces, but indirectly to paganism as a whole. Tertullian takes in each case ideas familiar to the pagans as the starting point of his argument, and contrasts them with Christian doctrine and Christian life. He effectively makes it clear that the most grievous injustice is done to the Christians by condemning them without knowing the truth about them. Tertullian therefore asks not for acquittal but for justice based on impartial investigation of the truth. In this way his apologetics advances in content beyond that of the Greeks of

---

[16] *De haeres.* 86. G. Säflund, *De pallio und die stilistische Entwicklung Tertullians* (Lund 1955), would like to consider Tertullian's *De pallio* as his last work, and as giving the defence of that step; but Säflund's arguments are not convincing.

the second century, and at the same time achieves an artistic form superior to any coming before.

Tertullian also defended the claim of the Church to truth and her possession of truth against the heresies of the age and especially against Gnostic trends. This he accomplished in a treatise on principles which makes brilliant use of his legal knowledge: the *De praescriptione haereticorum* demonstrates that Christianity, as opposed to heresy, can substantiate a clear legal claim to the possession of truth. Long before heresies appeared, Christian teachers were preaching that message which they had received from the apostles and which had been entrusted to the latter by Christ. Consequently, Holy Scripture is in the possession of the Church alone; only she can determine its true sense and so establish the content of belief. A series of monographs was also directed by Tertullian against individual Gnostics or their particular tenets; such a work was that against Marcion, mentioned above, which refutes his dualism and defends the harmony between Old and New Testaments. He seeks to safeguard the Christian doctrine of Creation, the resurrection of the body and the status of martyrdom against volatilization by the Gnostics; and against Praxeas he expounds the Church's conception of the Trinity with a clarity hitherto unknown. He deals with practical questions of Christian daily life in his short works on the meaning and effects of baptism, prayer, theatrical shows, patience, and the spirit and practice of penance. A rigoristic strain is often perceptible even here, and it becomes predominant in the works of the Montanist period. In this latter phase he made demands in utter contradiction of his earlier views, as for instance when he opposes second marriages in his *De monogamia*, military service and all trades in any way connected with idolatry in the *De corona* and *De idolatria*, and proclaims the most rigorous practice of fasting in *De ieiunio*. His fight against the Church took particularly harsh forms; he disputed her right to remit sins, which he reserved in the *De pudicitia* to the Montanist prophets alone.

Viewed as a whole, Tertullian's interests as a writer were not of a speculative kind, and he gives no systematic exposition of Christian doctrine. His importance in the history of dogma rests on the value of his writings as evidence of the stage of development which various particular doctrines had reached in his time; but it must also be borne in mind that his adherence to Montanism essentially modified his views. He was speaking as a Montanist essentially about the nature of the Church when he rejected an official priesthood and affirmed: *ubi tres, ecclesia est, licet laici.*[17] A pre-eminent position with the power of binding and loosing belonged only to Peter, and was not therefore conferred on later bishops.[18] The

[17] *De exhort. cast.* 7; cf. *De fuga* 14; *De pud.* 21, 17.
[18] *De pud.* 21, 9–11.

conception of original sin as a *vitium originis* was familiar to him, in the sense that through Adam's sin evil concupiscence has poisoned human nature, but he does not infer the necessity of infant baptism from this.[19] Tertullian thinks in very concrete terms about the Eucharist; those who take part in the *orationes sacrificiorum* receive the body of the Lord which is just as truly the real body of Christ as was the body on the cross; and the soul is nourished on the body and blood of Christ.[20] In Christology and the theology of the Trinity, he employs a terminology which influenced subsequent developments in the Latin West: according to him, Jesus Christ is true God and true man, both natures are united in one person but not confused.[21] The expression "Trinitas" as well as the term "persona", is found for the first time in Latin literature in Tertullian:[22] in this Trinity, Father, Son, and Holy Spirit are "unius substantiae et unius status et unius potestatis".[23] The Logos existed already before the creation of the world, but only became Son at the creation, and consequently as such is not eternal.[24] The more precise relation of Father and Son is viewed in a Subordinationist manner: the Father alone has the fullness of the Godhead; the Son has only a derivative part.[25] The Holy Spirit too is thought of as a person: he is the real teacher in the Church, who first of all led the apostles into all truth, but who is also operative as the representative of God and Christ in every Christian community,[26] especially through Holy Scripture which is his work and in which his voice is audible.[27]

Cyprian

A notable influence on posterity was also exercised by Bishop Cyprian of Carthage as a writer of the African Church. The authenticity of his personality and the example of his pastoral care stamped characteristic features on the Christianity of his native land.[28] The interest taken in his writings was likewise due to the deep impression produced by these qualities. In theology he owed much to Tertullian, whom he called his master and

---

[19] *De an.* 41; *De bapt.* 18.

[20] *De or.* 19; *De cor.* 3; *De pud.* 9, 16; *Adv. Marc.* 3, 19; *De res. carn.* 8.

[21] *Adv. Prax* 27; *De carne Christi* 5.

[22] *Adv. Prax.* 3.

[23] Ibid. 12.

[24] Ibid. 7; *Adv. Hermog.* 3.

[25] *Adv. Prax.* 9, 13; B. Piault, "Tertullien a-t-il été subordinatien?" in *RSPhTh* (1936), 181–204.

[26] *De bapt.* 6, 12; *De praescr.* 22, 8–10; 13, 5.

[27] *Adv. Hermog.* 22, 1; *De idol.* 4, 5.

[28] For Cyprian's influence on Augustine, see J. B. Bord in *RHE* 18 (1922), 445–68; also B. de Margerie in *Sciences Ecclésiastiques* 15 (1963), 199–211.

whose works he constantly read.[29] His treatises and letters deal mostly with the solution of questions of the day, as they arose through persecution and the threat to ecclesiastical unity from sectarian divisions. A personal note is struck in the little work *Ad Donatum,* in which the religious certainty attained in baptism after long search finds attractive expression. Cyprian as a pastor turned with a word of consolation to the Christians of North Africa in time of plague, and summoned them to be ready to make sacrifices in order to perform works of mercy. This he did in his *De mortalitate* and *De opere et eleemosynis.* He extols the Christian ideal of virginity and utters warnings against the destructive consequences of dissension in the *De habitu virginum* and *De zelo et livore* and here too he takes up the ideas of Tertullian in his writings on the Our Father and on patience. His treatise *On the Unity of the Church* shows greater independence both in content and in the personal position it reveals; and it has greater value as evidence of the concept of the Church held in the mid-third century. The representative and guarantor of ecclesiastical unity is the bishop, who is united with his fellow bishops through the common basis of the episcopate in the apostolic office.[30] Among the holders of the latter, Peter had objectively and legitimately a special position which rested on the power of binding and loosing imparted to him alone.[31] As this was committed by Christ to only *one* apostle, the unity that Christ willed for the Church was established for ever.[32] Cyprian does not yet infer from this an effective jurisdiction of Peter over his fellow apostles, nor a transmission of his personal prerogatives to his successor as Bishop of Rome. Rather does there belong to the Roman church a position of honour, founded on the fact of Peter's work and death in Rome.[33] Cyprian unambiguously rejects a Roman right of direction, for instance in the question of the validity of baptism for heretics. The individual bishop is responsible to God alone for the guidance of his community even in such matters.[34] Cyprian sets a very high value on membership in the Church of Christ: nobody has a claim to the name of Christian who has not his own name in this Church; only in her is his salvation assured, according to the pregnant formula: "salus extra ecclesiam non est."[35] Children, too, should share in the membership of the Church as early as possible, and so infant baptism is a practice which Cyprian takes for granted.[36] Fidelity to the Church in persecution merits the highest

---

[29] See Jerome, *De vir. ill.* 53.

[30] *Ep.* 54, 1; 68, 5.

[31] *De eccl. unit.* 4.

[32] Ibid. 7.

[33] *Ep.* 71, 3.

[34] *Sent. episc. init.,* CSEL 3, 1, 435 f.

[35] *Ep.* 73, 21; 55, 24.

[36] *Ep.* 64, 2 and 5.

recognition; those who in martyrdom have sealed their testimony to Christ and his Church with the sacrifice of their lives obtain immediately the vision of God.[37] In this belief, Bishop Cyprian himself accepted a martyr's death in a manner which kept his name in undying remembrance in the African Church.

CHAPTER 21

The First Christological and Trinitarian Controversies

THE apologists of the second century in their discussions of pagan poly-theism emphasized above all strict monotheism which they did not consider imperilled by their conception of Logos-Christology. In the Church's defensive action against Gnosticism, the emphatic stress on the unity of the divine nature was similarly prominent, and so theology in the second century did not concern itself in great detail with the problem of the relation between Father, Son, and Holy Spirit. It was obscurely felt that, in the one indivisible God, certain distinctions were present which were manifested particularly in the Creation and the Redemption. The apologist Theophilus had even employed the term "Trias" for this reality,[1] but a deeper conceptual penetration of this truth of revelation and a correspond-ing linguistic formulation of it had not been attained. Theological reflection was now, at the end of the second century, to concern itself precisely with the question of the Trinity. The Logos-Christology presented by the apologists, and further developed by the second-century writers, was defective to the extent that it subordinated the Son to the Father. According to this concept, the Logos, existing from all eternity within God (λόγος ἐνδιάθετος), came forth from the Father only as Creator and ruler of the world (λόγος προφορικός), only then was begotten and only then became the personality distinguishing him from the Father; and, therefore, he was not eternal in the same sense as the Father.[2] But this Subordinationism at first less disturbed people's awareness of the faith, because they saw in it no direct threat to the divinity of Christ. Emphasis on the difference between the Father and the Son must, however, have given cause for hesitation when the unity of God was brought into greater prominence. In fact this Christological Subordinationism led at the end of the second century and the beginning of the third to a vigorous reaction by Christian

---

[37] *De eccles. unit.* 14; *Ep.* 55, 20.
[1] *Ad Autol.* 2, 15.
[2] Already in Justin, *Apol.* app. 6; Theophil., *Ad Autol.* 2, 10–22; further in Hippol., *Refut.* 10, 33, 1; Orig., *De princ.* 1, 3, 5; *In Joh.* 2, 21.

circles who were anxious at all costs to safeguard the divine unity. The movement owed its origin to men of the Greek East; but the controversies about their theories took place chiefly in the West and especially in Rome. We owe the very name Monarchianism, by which we try to characterize this theology, to a Latin theologian: the African Tertullian renders by the formula "monarchiam tenemus" the slogan[3] by which its adherents tried to express their holding fast to the one God and to a single divine principle.

Emphasis on the unity of God, however, necessitated a decision on the Christological problem, and in this process the Logos-Christology was contested in two ways. Some regarded Christ as merely a man, but one born of the virgin Mary and of the Holy Spirit, and in whom God's power (δύναμις) was operative in quite a special way. This so-called Dynamist Monarchianism safeguarded the one divine principle but virtually abandoned the divinity of Christ. Another solution of the problem was proposed by those who declared that the one God revealed himself in different ways or *modi*, now as Father, now as Son. This theory so effaced the distinction between Father and Son that it was said that the Father had also suffered on the Cross; and the supporters of this attempted solution are therefore called Modalist or Patripassian Monarchians. Dynamist Monarchianism, which is also not inappropriately called Adoptionism, betrays a rationalist attitude which found the idea of God's becoming man difficult to accept. Consequently, it seems to have gained a wider hearing in intellectual circles, but small support among the common people. The sources name as its first exponent an educated leather-merchant called Theodotus of Byzantium, who came to Rome about 190 and there sought support for his theological ideas. He and his followers tried to prove from Scripture, by means of philological textual criticism, their fundamental thesis that Jesus, until his baptism in the Jordan, led the life of a simple but very upright man on whom the Spirit of Christ then descended.[4] Their interest in logic and geometry, their esteem for Aristotle and their relations with the doctor Galen and his philosophical interests gave offence to the faithful.[5] Theodotus's expulsion from the ecclesiastical community by the Roman Bishop Victor (186–98) did not mean the end of the Adoptionist movement; and a series of disciples — including Asclepiodotos, Theodotus the younger, and later Artemon — transmitted the ideas of its founder. The first two attempted to organize the Adoptionists in a church of their own, and won over even the Roman confessor Natalis as its leader, though he shortly left their movement.[6] Theodotus the younger added a new element to

---

[3] *Adv. Prax.* 3.
[4] Hippol., *Refut.* 7, 35.
[5] *Euseb. HE* 5, 28, 13–14.
[6] Ibid. 5, 28, 1–3 and 9.

previous theories by designating Melchizedech as the highest power, standing higher than Christ, as the actual mediator between God and man.[7]
About the mid-third century a double argument inspired the Adoptionists'
doctrine: on the one hand, they attacked the orthodox view as ditheistic;[8]
and on the other, they also claimed that as true guardians of apostolic tradition
they would teach regarding Christ only what had always been believed at
all times.[9] An exponent of a particularly crude Adoptionism in the East,
in the second half of the third century, was Paul of Samosata, a bishop of
Antioch in Syria, whose teaching and life preoccupied several synods.[10]
It is true that he employed in his theology the Trinitarian formulas of his
age, but he divested them of their orthodox meaning by teaching that "the
Son" designated only the man Jesus, in whom the wisdom of God had
taken up abode; that, furthermore, "the Spirit" is nothing other than the
grace which God gave the apostles. And by "wisdom of God", or Logos,
Paul did not understand a person distinct from the Father, but an im-
personal power. Although at a first synod in the year 264 he skilfully
evaded being pinned down to definite views, the learned priest Malchion
demonstrated his errors to him at a second assembly of bishops, which
removed him from office and expelled him from the Church's community.
At the same time, the synod rejected the statement that the Logos is of the
same nature as the Father (ὁμοούσιος), because Paul of Samosata meant
by this term to deny the Logos a personal subsistence of his own. The
Catholic community of Antioch, under the new bishop Domnus, was
obliged even to call in the help of the civil authorities against Paul
following his deposition, to make him vacate the episcopal residence.
Yet, even after his condemnation, Paul had a considerable following
in the so-called Paulicians, who were condemned by the nineteenth canon
of the General Council of Nicaea. After his death the leadership of the
group passed to a certain Lucian who later joined the orthodox community.
It is unlikely that the latter is the same man as the martyr, Lucian of Antioch
(† 312), the founder of the school of Antioch, though this Lucian also held a
Subordinationist Logos-Christology.

Modalist Monarchianism

The Modalist attempt at a solution of the Logos-Christological problem
spread relatively widely because it obviously appealed more strongly to
simple religious minds, for whom the biblical statements about the unity
of God and the full divinity of Christ were deep convictions. Any

[7] Hippol., *Refut.* 7, 36.
[8] Novat., *De Trin.* 30.
[9] In *Euseb. HE* 5, 28, 3 f.
[10] Ibid. 7, 27–30.

conception which separated the Son or the Word too sharply from the Father seemed suspect here, because it could lead to the existence of two Gods being deduced from it. Once again, the first representative of Modalist teaching whose name is now known was a Greek, by name Noëtus, who according to Hippolytus came from Smyrna in Asia Minor. He vigorously emphasized the dogma of the one God, the Father, asserted also that Christ is identical with the Father, and affirmed the inference that the Father became man and suffered on the Cross.[11] Following two discussions with the priests of Smyrna, Noëtus was expelled from the Church, yet nevertheless found supporters for his ideas. His disciples appealed to passages in the Old and New Testaments (such as Exod 3:6; Isa 44:6; 45:14–15; Jn 10:30; 14:8 ff.; Rom 9:5), which they construed in the sense of implying an identity of Father and Son. They countered the difficulty which the Prologue of St John's Gospel presented in this respect by allegorical interpretation.[12] Epigonus, a pupil of Noëtus, brought the doctrine to Rome, where it was taken up by Cleomenes. Praxeas, whose character and origin remains obscure, also perhaps came from the East to Rome, where he was still pursuing Modalist lines of thought in the time of Pope Victor. According to Tertullian's polemic against Praxeas, written about 213, the latter taught the complete identity of Father and Son, and denied that the Logos had any subsistence peculiar to himself,[13] so that in reality it was the Father who suffered, died, and rose from the dead. Praexas seems to have modified his view to the extent that he distinguished the man Jesus from the God Christ, who was identical with the Father, so that the Father is said to have suffered together with the Son.[14] Despite their different starting-points, the Dynamist and Modalist conceptions resemble each other here in a striking way.

Another member of the Patripassianists, as the adherents of this doctrine were later called by Cyprian,[15] was Sabellius, who is said to have come to Rome from Libya when Zephyrinus was bishop (199–217). It was probably he who gave Modalist doctrine a more systematic character, when he attributed to the one Godhead three modes of operation, so that the Father was its actual essence which, nevertheless, expressed itself also as Son and Spirit: as Father, God was the creator and law-giver; as Son, he was operative in the redemption; as Spirit, he conferred grace and sanctification.[16] It is impossible to obtain a completely clear and incontestable picture of Modalist ideas, since only their opponents — Hippolytus, Tertullian, and Epiphanius — report them. In Rome, the centre of Modalist propaganda, there was at first

---

[11] Hippol., *Contra Noetum*, 1.
[12] Ibid. 15.
[13] Tertull., *Adv. Prax.* 5 and 7.
[14] Ibid. 27.
[15] Cyprian, *Ep.* 73, 4.
[16] Epiph., *De haeres.* 62, 1.

no clash with the authorities of the community there. But there was a reaction by the leading theologian, the learned Hippolytus, who sharply attacked the Roman bishops Zephyrinus (199–217) and Callistus (217–22), because of their favouring, as he alleged, and even recognizing this false doctrine. He accused the former, an "ignorant and uneducated man", of maintaining two conflicting theses simultaneously: firstly, "I know only one God, Christ Jesus and no other, who was born and suffered"; and, secondly, "It was not the Father who died, but the Son." [17] But what is apparent from these two formulas is rather the concern of the Roman bishop to emphasize the divinity of Christ on the one hand, and to insist on the distinction between Father and Son on the other hand, though he lacked an unobjectionable terminology for his purpose. Hippolytus's criticism that Zephyrinus entertained Modalist views was probably provoked by the mistrust that the latter felt for Hippolytus's manner of expression, which sounded to him suspiciously ditheistic. That Hippolytus's judgment was far too harsh is plain from his verdict that Callistus had let himself be misled by Sabellius, though it was Callistus himself who expelled the latter from the Church. It is clear that Callistus was also trying to pursue a middle course between the downright Modalism of Sabellius and, in his judgment, the ditheistic tendency of the learned Hippolytus. In opposition to the latter, he laid all emphasis on the unity of God, when he said that Father and Son are not separate beings; in opposition to Sabellius, he held fast to the distinction between the Father and the Logos, who existed before all time and who became man. He was conscious, therefore, of the dubiousness of Modalist doctrine, but he likewise regarded the doctrine of two or three distinct divine "persons" as an even greater danger to the content of faith concerning the one God. Yet neither did he, in his search for the right balance between the two tendencies, have yet the appropriate terminology at his disposal.

Nevertheless, the struggle of Hippolytus and Tertullian against Modalism bore fruit, as can be seen from the advance in Trinitarian theology in the work of Novatian about the mid-third century. The latter turned Tertullian's thought and preparatory work to account, and clearly moved away from Modalism in saying that the Son begotten of the Father, that is the Word, is not a mere sound but has subsistence proper to him, and thus is a "second person"; that the Son was not begotten in view only of Creation, but existed before all time, since it is in the nature of the Father as such ever to have a Son. [18] Novatian seeks with even greater emphasis to reject ditheistic lines of thought by stressing that the Son is God only in being the Son, who received his Godhead from the Father, and only as Son is distinct from the

---

[17] Hippol., *Refut.* 9, 11.
[18] Novat., *De Trin.* 31.

Father, so that there is no division of the divine nature. But Novatian does not express himself so plainly regarding the "person" of the Spirit, whom he regards as a divine power operative in the prophets, the apostles, and the Church.[19] According to him, the Son is subject to the Father, is less than the Father, and is obedient to the Father.[20] Novatian's manner of expression is, therefore, strongly Subordinationist; and his progress beyond Tertullian and earlier theology consists in his recognizing that the personal distinction between Father and Son does not have its ground in the economy of salvation, that the Son was begotten before all time, and that he subsisted, that is as a person, before the creation of the world.[21] This much was achieved, even if Novatian did not yet clearly grasp the doctrine of an eternal generation of the Son.

The discussion about Monarchianism extended beyond the West to other territories where Christianity had penetrated. In Arabia in the time of the emperor Gordianus (238–44), according to a rather obscure report by Eusebius,[22] a Bishop Beryllus of Bostra held the view that Christ had not existed in a way proper to himself before his incarnation, and that he possessed no divinity of his own but only that of the Father dwelling within him. This teaching suggests an Adoptionist Christology; and Beryllus's doctrine encountered contradiction from his fellow bishops, who devoted various synods to it and finally summoned Origen to debate the issue. The latter succeeded in refuting Beryllus and winning him back to the true faith.

Attention was further aroused by the controversy in which Bishop Dionysius of Alexandria engaged about the year 260 with Patripassianists of the Libyan Pentapolis. In several letters,[23] of which one was addressed to bishops Ammonius and Euphranor, Dionysius attacked the Modalist theories with an incisive yet reckless manner of expression; and he gave such imprecise formulation to the distinction between Father and Son, whom he termed a creature ($\pi o i \eta \mu \alpha$), that the unity of essence of both seemd blurred.[24] A denunciation of this doctrine in Rome caused the bishop there, also called Dionysius (259–68), to make a pronouncement which in several respects is important. He requested the Alexandrian bishop to make his views more precise, and at the same time adressed a letter to the community of Alexandria expounding the Roman conception of the Trinity. Without identifying Bishop Dionysius, but with an unmistakably sharp reference to the school of theologians from which he sprang, he said he had heard that there were catechists and teachers of theology in Alexandria who split up

[19] Ibid. 29.
[20] Ibid. 18, 26, 27 and 31.
[21] Ibid. 31 and 16.
[22] *Euseb. HE* 6, 33, 1–4.
[23] Ibid. 7, 26, 1.
[24] According to Athanas., *De sent. Dionys.* 14–18.

the most venerable kerygma of the Church, the monarchy or the unity of God, into three separate hypostases and three divinities, and taught a doctrine diametrically opposed to that of Sabellius. Whereas the latter maintained that the Son was the Father, and vice versa, these men in a certain way preached three Gods. In contrast with this view, the unity of God should be held just as firmly as the divine Trinity; yet, on the other hand, to speak of Christ as a creature, or to assert that there had been a time when he did not exist, was just as blasphemous as it was to call "his divine and inexpressible generation" a creation (ποίησις).[25] Dionysius of Alexandria thereupon replied with a detailed apologia,[26] in which he admitted that certain of his formulas were liable to misinterpretation, but pointed out also that justice had not been done to his view as a whole. He likewise rejected a separation of Father, Son, and Spirit, but maintained firmly that they are three "hypostases", for otherwise the Trinity would be dissolved. He stressed equally definitely the eternity of the Son. He said he had avoided the expression ὁμοούσιος (of the same nature) as not biblical, though rightly understood, it was nevertheless acceptable.[27] His résumé of his position, that the unity of God must be maintained but the three persons must also be acknowledged, clearly satisfied Rome, since the discussion was not pursued further. These issues, it is true, involved the problem of correct terminology, of which the differing senses of "hypostasis" afford a typical example, since it could be easily identified in Rome with Tertullian's "substantia". But behind these linguistic problems were the different aspects through which the theology of the Trinity was approached from East and West. In the West, the "dogma" of God's unity was sacrosanct, and it was difficult for people to recognize and acknowledge as "persons" the distinctions in the Trinity, of which they were convinced. The East was more sensitive to the mystery in the Trinity, as a consequence of its familiarity with the world of neo-Platonic thought concerning the hierarchy of being. This difference in mode of theological thought, together with the imperfection of the terminology worked out so far, found clear expression in the following century and gave rise then to a comprehensive discussion of the dogma of the Trinity.

[25] Partly according to Athanas., *De decr. Nic. syn.* 26.
[26] Both Euseb., *Praep. evang.* 7, 19, and Athanas. *De sent. Dionys.*, quote parts of this apologia.
[27] Athanas., *De sent. Dionys.* 14–18, tries to represent Dionysius as being orthodox in every respect. Basil, *Ep.* 9, 2 (esp. *sent.* 4), realized with greater penetration that his opposition to Sabellian Modalism made him incline dangerously near to the opposite extreme.

CHAPTER 22

Manichaeism

A few decades after the great Gnostic movement of the second century had passed its peak, there was born the founder of a new religion, which came on the stage with a definite claim to be the most universal of all religions, and promised true redemption to all nations. It took its name from its founder, the Persian Mani or Manes, who is called in the Greek and Latin sources Μανιχαῖος or Manichaeus. Until the beginning of the present century, our knowledge of Manichaeism was mainly dependent on information from non-Manichaean sources, since a large part of the abundant Manichaean literature was destroyed as a consequence of the struggle waged against it by civil authorities and ecclesiastical circles, both in the Latin West and in the Byzantine East, and later also in lands under Islamic rule. Since the beginning of the present century, however, a number of discoveries have brought to light authentic Manichaean sources which permit a much more exact and comprehensive idea of this religion to be formed. The first in order of time among these are the texts which were discovered about 1900 in the caves of Turfan in the Chinese province of Turkestan and which contain fragments from Mani's *Book of Giants*, liturgical documents, confession formularies, a type of catechism, and dogmatic texts. But far more important was the 1930 finding of a Manichaean library in Medinet Madi in Upper Egypt, which contained letters and sermons of Mani, the so-called Cephalaea-fragments of a textbook of Manichaeism and an important large volume of psalms. These texts had been translated from Syriac into Coptic about the year 400 and they give an insight into the religious world of a Manichaean group which had created a powerful centre of propaganda in Upper Egypt about one generation after Mani's death. On the basis of these newly-discovered sources, the life and teaching of the Persian religious founder can now be represented more or less as follows.

Mani was born on 14 April A.D. 216, probably in the Parthian capital Seleucia-Ctesiphon, and belonged to a family related on both his father's and his mother's side to the Persian princely house of the Arsacides.[1] Mani's father belonged to a religious sect, perhaps the Mandaeans, in which strict abstinence from meat and wine was combined with purification ceremonies of many kinds. Mani was at first brought up in this sect, too, but repeated visions revealed to him very early that he was destined to be the missionary and herald of a new universal religion, the content of which was made known to him through further revelations. Mani quickly undertook a

---

[1] G. Widengren, *Mani und der Manichäismus* (Stuttgart 1961), 30 f.

missionary journey to India, where, he preached with particular success in the province of Baluchistan. After his return home to Persia, he won the favour of his king, Shapur I (241–73), who permitted him freely to preach his religious message throughout the Sassanid kingdom. Mani now developed a comprehensive missionary activity, was himself engaged as a missionary in the West, as far as Nisibis, and sent out on a systematic plan other messengers of his faith, who, even during his lifetime, gained entry for his teaching into Egypt and the eastern provinces of Iran. Under King Bahram I, however, a radical change occurred affecting Mani's favour at court. It is probable that the priests of the Zoroastrian religion accused him of subversive plans and heresy; and, after a short imprisonment, Mani died in captivity in 277. His followers described his manner of death as crucifixion, but by the term was meant only his martyr's death for his beliefs. Upon Mani's death there ensued a powerful wave of persecution against his adherents, some of whom fled to the West, while others emigrated to India and China, where they secured great influence which persisted as late as the fourteenth century.[2]

Mani set down the content of his missionary teaching in a series of writings which soon attained canonical force. The most important of these are: *The Great Gospel from Alpha to Tau,* which was provided with an album of pictures; the *Treasure of Life,* from which Augustine frequently quoted; the *Book of the Mysteries,* in twenty-four chapters; and finally his letters discovered in Upper Egypt.[3] According to these works, a radical dualism in the doctrine concerning God characterizes Manichaeism: there are two highest beings or principles of equal rank, the one of light and the other of darkness. Both are unbegotten and eternal; both possess equal power but stand in irreconcilable opposition to one another, each in a realm of his own: the region of light or the good, which lies in the North, and the region of evil, which lies in the South.[4] Each realm has a king: the realm of light is ruled by the Father of greatness; the realm of evil by the Prince of darkness who commands numerous demons. Between the two primary principles and their realms a conflict breaks out: the realm of matter seeks to swallow up the light; and, to defend the latter, the Father of greatness creates the first man, who with his five sons goes out to battle, but is conquered by evil. The first man becomes aware of his fate, and begs the Father of greatness for help. The latter emits from himself, after a series of intermediary emanations, the Living Spirit, who frees the first human being from evil matter and so redeems him.[5]

[2] Ibid. 47; 127–9; 132–5.
[3] For a description of this Manichaean literature, cf. ibid. 79–96.
[4] See No. 5 in A. Adam, *Texte zum Manichäismus* (Berlin 1954).
[5] Adam, *op. cit.* No. 7.

This mythical occurrence is a symbol and image of the way of redemption for man, who is a mixture of light and darkness. As soon as a man becomes aware of this fact, that is to say knows himself, his redemption begins. And thereafter the Father of light helps him to free himself more and more from the darkness in him. For this purpose he sends the heralds of true religion to earth, who give men correct knowledge about themselves. These messengers are Buddha, Zoroaster, Jesus, and Mani. They are representatives of the Manichaean redeemer, the emissary of light, and each of them brings to a part of mankind the true religion or gnosis, whose spread, however, is impeded from the opposite side. Before Mani, the heralds of religion had been assigned only certain parts of the world to which they were to bring true gnosis: Buddha worked in India, Zoroaster restricted himself to Persia, and Jesus to Judaea, or at least to the West. Neither did these three establish their message in writing; and consequently the religions they founded, especially the Christian religion, quickly fell to pieces or were falsified. Against such a background, Mani's mission stands out more sharply in its uniqueness: he is the last envoy of light, the apostle of the ultimate generation, the "seal of the prophet";[6] his message is the last summons to salvation; the world can now only be converted or for ever perish. Mani preached the highest, the perfect, gnosis; to reject it, is definitively to refuse salvation. The movement founded by Mani is, therefore, also the most universal religion ever known, comprising all earlier religions in itself, and at the same time leading beyond them. It will conquer the East and the West, and will be heard preached in all languages.[7]

From this Manichaean doctrinal system Manichaean ethics necessarily follow, the fundamental characteristic being the demand for abstinence from everything which links men to matter. In man light and darkness mingle; anyone who forgets this condition, or who does not repent, adheres more to matter, persists in ἀγνωσία, determined not to recognize his situation, and so rejects gnosis and thereby salvation. Consequently, the perfect Manichee renounces this world, seeks to possess nothing in it and subdues all his appetites; he binds himself by the triple seal of the mouth, the hands, and the womb; that is to say, he refrains from impure words and pleasures, and rejects menial work, for by these things the world of light, fragments of which are present in all visible, tangible things, is violated; he exercises absolute sexual continence and rejects marriage. In practice these lofty demands of Manichean ethics could not be fulfilled, a condition which led to the division of Manichaean believers into the elect, or *electi*, and the hearers, or *audientes*;[8] and there were special commandments for each

---

[6] Ibid. No 1b.
[7] Adam, *op. cit.* Nos. 3 and 17.
[8] Ibid. No. 16.

according to their capacities. The hearers or catechumens served the elect, gave them food and clothing, and so hoped to be born sometime in the body of an elect and then to attain salvation.

In addition to being divided into such categories as these, the followers of the Manichaean religion were united in a well-organized church,[9] and this factor ensured them considerable impact in their missionary work. At the summit of the Manichaean church was a supreme head, the head of the apostles or the king of the religion, who had his residence in Babylon. The first head was naturally Mani himself, from whom every successor derived his authority. Subject to this supreme head was a hierarchy with numerous members comprising, in a series of grades, twelve apostles, seventy-two bishops or teachers of truth, and three hundred and sixty priests to whom all other members of the elect, both men and women, were attached as deacons. The great mass of hearers represented the last and lowest grade. The elect, particularly in China, were assembled in monastic communities, which were supported by the alms of the hearers. The ascetic exercises of Manichaeism included an elaborate practice of fasting. By fasting they prepared for a sort of confession,[10] in which they acknowledged transgressions of the commandments of abstinence. In their temples the Manichaean faithful gathered for a pure divine service of the word, which consisted of readings from Manichaean writings and the singing of their own hymns,[11] often possessed of high qualities of form. Other rites were rejected, since in them the body, which is bound to matter, is active, and only true gnosis brings salvation.

Of special importance is the marked dependence of Manichaean doctrine on Christian ideas. The high rank that is attributed to the person of Jesus is particularly striking. It is true that Mani lists the heralds of true gnosis, who had preceded Mani himself, as Buddha, Zoroaster, and Jesus and likewise his brethren; but the chief role is ascribed to Jesus. At the beginning of his letters, Mani emphatically calls himself "apostle of Jesus Christ".[12] This Jesus, as a heavenly "aeon", had appeared on earth with the semblance of a body, in order to teach mankind its real origin and true way of redemption. According to Arius, the Manichees called Christ "a part of the Father having the same nature as he";[13] and this use of the *homoousios* idea made the Arians their determined opponents. Thus, Jesus has become the guide of souls, whom the Manichees praised in many of their hymns. These sound in places so like purely Christian prayers, that the ear of a simple Christian could scarcely detect the Manichaean undertone when,

[9] See Widengren, *op. cit.* 97–100.
[10] Adam, *op. cit.* No. 48.
[11] For examples of such hymns, ibid. Nos. 24–30.
[12] Adam, *op. cit.* Nos. 10 and 12.
[13] Letter of Arius to Bishop Alexander in Epiphanius, *Panar.* 69, 7–8.

for instance, he heard: "Come to me, living Christ! Come to me, O light of the day! O merciful one, O comforter, I cry to you so that you may turn to me in the hour of tribulation. Your sweet yoke I have taken upon me in purity. Honour and victory be to our Lord, the comforter and to his holy elect and to the soul of the blessed Mary."[14] Finally, this Jesus has sent the Paraclete promised by him, in order to free his teaching from falsification. The Paraclete came down upon Mani, and revealed hidden mysteries to him; and Mani became one with him, so that Mani could now come forward and teach as the promised Paraclete:[15] from Mani and through him there speaks the Spirit sent by Jesus. Neither does Mani pass over and ignore the Holy Scripture of Christianity.[16] It is true that he adopts a critical attitude to the Old Testament, because, in striking similarity to Marcion, he did not recognize the God of the Old Testament as the God of light; nevertheless, angels of light laid down some isolated truths even in the Bible of the Jews. But more important for Mani are the Gospels and Paul's letters: these also he considers as interspersed with Jewish errors, but they contain a rich store from Jesus' message regarding the profound structure of the world, the meaning of human destiny, the battle between light and darkness, and the liberation of the soul from the fetters of matter. Mani recognized these truths in the New Testament writings, singled them out and absorbed them into his preaching. Manichaeism showed particular interest also in New Testament apocrypha, such as the Gospel of Thomas and the legend of Abgar, and made use likewise of a version of the *Shepherd* of Hermas. This considerable adaptation of Christian elements in Manichean preaching was intended by Mani to facilitate contact with Christians in the West, and to win them over to his movement, just as he made similar use of the ideas of Zoroastrianism or Buddhism for his missionary work in the East. By taking over these various elements, Manichaean doctrine was intended to show that it was the fulfilment of all the religious aspirations of mankind.

The syncretic character of the new religion certainly ensured those initial successes which were everywhere apparent. The doctrines which Mani's zealous missionaries had to proclaim did not sound alien and did not come from a distant and unknown world. The fundamental ideal of a safe way to liberation from the evil in the world and of redemption through true gnosis was familiar to men of the third and fourth centuries. The Manichaean religion quickly spread in Mesopotamia, pressed on from there to Syria and Arabia, and soon found a particularly firm base in Egypt which was developed into a propaganda centre for the Mediterranean countries.

[14] Psalm 247 ed. by C. R. Allberry, *A Manichaean Psalmbook*, part II (Stuttgart 1938), 55 f.
[15] Adam, *op. cit.* No. 1b.
[16] See Widengren, *op. cit.* 125–7.

It clearly had marked success in Rome and North Africa, for the extremely severe edict which the emperor Diocletian issued in 297 to the proconsul of Africa, against this "pernicious innovation",[17] was based on the official complaints of the Roman authorities of that area. Death at the stake was ordered for leaders of the movement; their followers were to be beheaded, and Roman citizens of rank among them were to be punished by forced labour in the mines. Such measures, however, could not prevent the spread of Manichaeism. It can be shown to have existed in Rome under Pope Miltiades (311–14); from there it probably found its way to Gaul and Spain, also appearing in the Balkans.

The emperor Constantine was likewise disturbed by the doctrines of the movement, and had special reports drawn up on the subject.[18] Synods of the fourth century had to deal with Manichaeism repeatedly. A law of the emperor Valentinian I in the year 372 ordered the confiscation of houses in which the Manichees held their assemblies.[19] Theodosius II intensified the sanctions against them, and Justinian I reintroduced the death penalty for the profession of Manichaeism.[20] In North Africa Manichaeism exercised a peculiar fascination, to which the young Augustine succumbed for ten years, as did both with him and after him many members of the African upper classes. Augustine's fight against his earlier coreligionists introduces us to a number of Manichaean bishops, and reveals their extensive ecclesiastical organization which is confirmed by archaeological finds in North Africa. After the Vandal invasion, persecution affected them just as harshly as it did the Catholics; the formulas of abjuration for former Manichees on reception into the Church testify to their continued existence in the West extending into the sixth century. The Byzantine church in the East had to fight against them much longer, and the neo-Manichaean movements of the Middle Ages, especially in the Balkans, once again strikingly manifest the vitality of Mani's foundation.

Since Mani did not allow his followers to belong to another religion, the position of the Church in relation to Manichaeism was different from her defensive struggle against the Gnosticism of the second century. The penetration by individual Manichees into Christian communities, and the destruction of these from within, was less to be feared than direct apostasy or the conversion to the Manichaean religion, for which its missionaries openly strove. Its claim to sole possession of true and unfalsified Christianity, forced the Church authorities to take up a definite attitude and

[17] Adam, *op. cit.* No. 56. On the question of authenticity, see W. Seston in *Mélanges A. Ernout* (Paris 1940), 345–54.

[18] See Ammianus Marcell. 15, 13, 1–2.

[19] Adam, *op. cit.* No. 57.

[20] See E. H. Kaden, "Die Edikte gegen die Manichäer von Diokletian bis Justinian" in *Festschrift H. Lewald* (Basle 1953), 55–68.

to put the faithful on their guard. Moreover, the Church could not but experience the Manichaean movement as a dangerous rival in her own missionary endeavour among the pagan population; thus a Christian defence was initiated relatively early. In a letter to his community[21] about the year 300 a bishop of Alexandria, perhaps Theonas, issued a warning against Manichaean doctrines of marriage and against their elect. Like Cyril of Jerusalem, Afrahat and Ephraem in the East, and like Leo the Great later in the West, other unnamed bishops must have combated the movement by their preaching. The Church enjoined particular vigilance when a Manichee wished to become a Catholic; and an attempt was made to ensure the genuineness of such a conversion by precisely-worded formulas of abjuration. Just as Augustine himself signed such a formulary,[22] so also it was imposed on others. He himself decreed that trust should be placed in the Manichee Victorinus only when he had given the names of all the Manichees known to him;[23] and Cyril of Jerusalem showed similar circumspection.[24] Very detailed formulas of abjuration, which had often to be signed even on the mere suspicion of Manichaeism, were in use both in the Latin West and in the Greek East.[25]

Hand in hand with these pastoral efforts to immunize the faithful against this heresy, there developed the theological defence carried on by writers. This was waged not only as occasion arose in theological studies, but also in special monographs, of which some have been lost.[26] The success which the Manichaean mission very early enjoyed in Egypt especially roused Egyptian authors to counter-measures. Even if Alexander of Lycopolis and his anti-Manichaean polemical treatise cannot be considered as Christian,[27] the work of Bishop Serapion of Thmuis represents an achievement against the Manichees which won special approval from Jerome,[28] and deserved it. In many of his writings, Didymus of Alexandria attacked this work, and wrote in addition a short treatise Κατὰ Μανιχαίων.[29] The four books of the Arabian bishop, Titus of Bostra,[30] against the Manichees have been

---

[21] Pap. Rylands 469, which is Adam, op. cit. No. 35; Cyril of Jerusalem, Catech. 6, 32, 34 and 36; Afrahat in Adam, op. cit.

[22] See Adam, op. cit. No. 61.

[23] Ep. 236. The so-called commonitorium Augustini also warns against allowing former Manichees too readily to be baptized, CSEL 25, 979 f.

[24] Catech. 6, 36.

[25] Adam, op. cit. Nos. 62–4.

[26] See editions listed in Bibliography, p. 491, 2. Indirect Sources.

[27] See O. Bardenhewer, Gesch. der altkirchlichen Literatur, III (Freiburg i. Br., 2nd ed. 1923), 102 f.

[28] De vir. ill. 99; on this, see Quasten P, III, 82 f.

[29] PG 39, 1085–110.

[30] PG 18, 1069–264; Syriac text ed. P. de Lagarde (Berlin 1859; reprinted Hanover 1924).

preserved, as have the *Acta Archelae* of a certain Hegemonios who came presumably from Syria. Written in the form of a debate, these severely attacked Mani, the founder of the religion, and are a rich source for the early history of Manichaeism.[31] The anti-Manichaean works of Eusebius of Emesa, George of Laodicea, and Diodorus of Tarsus do not survive. In the Latin West, anti-Manichaean writers were less numerous; but, on the other hand, the West produced in Augustine the theologian who overcame the threat to the Church through years of reflection and argument, and in so doing made profitable use of Manichaean modes of thought, transposing suggestions derived from them into Christian terms.[32] From the evidence of his dialogue with Manichaeism, it is quite clear that the followers of the latter in Africa did not constitute a mass movement but were mainly recruited from intellectual circles. The Church's defensive struggle derived much benefit from the persecution of Manichaeism by the State. With Diocletian this persecution was still partly motivated by anti-Persian feeling; but, when the empire had itself become Christian, it represented a defence against heresy by means of the civil authority. So the Manichaean religion won its greatest successes in the Asiatic East; while, in the Mediterranean area proper, from the fourth century onwards, despite its obstinate persistence in individual cases, it never again became a danger to the Church as a whole in the way earlier Gnosticism had been.

CHAPTER 23

Further Development of the Liturgy

THE growth of theological literature within the Church of the third century was accompanied by an equally important development in the liturgical domain. Here, too, new creative impulses are perceptible, from which the forms of divine worship grew, and which answered the needs of the communities of the great Church as they increased in strength.

Easter and the Easter Controversy

In the first place the feast of Easter was given an elaboration which made it in the minds of the faithful the central and pre-eminent celebration and memorial of Christian redemption. Two factors are especially responsible

[31] Ed. C. H. Beeson (Leipzig 1906); cf. *Quasten P*, III, 357 f.
[32] See especially Adam in *ZKG* 69 (1958), 6–23.

for this development: first of all the unfolding of the previous Easter festival itself, by increasing the duration of preparation and celebration; and, secondly, the bringing of the administration of the sacrament of Christian initiation into the Easter liturgy. The beginnings of this double movement extend back probably into the second century, since they are already apparent in an advanced stage early in the third. The sources which show this development most clearly, such as the Syrian *Didascalia*, some writings of Tertullian and the *Apostolic Tradition* of Hippolytus, belong in all instances to the third century. The homilies on the Psalms by Asterius the Sophist were in fact written in the early fourth century, but often reflect a state of liturgical development which can be ascribed to the late third century.

Despite differences of emphasis in detail, considerable similarity of view concerning the root idea of the celebration of the Easter festival can be assumed in both the East and West. It commemorated the fundamental truths and facts of Christian redemption, which were conferred upon mankind by the death and triumphant resurrection of the Lord.[1] In second-century Asia Minor and a few neighbouring regions, a Christian Passover was kept which naturally placed the thought of the Lord's passion in the foreground, but also included the idea that this passion leads to the resurrection. In accordance with Jewish custom, 14 Nisan was kept as the date for this Passover, by the Quartodecimans of Asia Minor and perhaps generally at first; it was prepared for by a strict fast and included a homily on Exodus 12 (as did the Jewish Passover). It was not exclusively a day of mourning nevertheless, and had a joyous conclusion with the agape and celebration of the Eucharist early on 15 Nisan. The Sunday Passover, the celebration of Easter on the Sunday following 14 Nisan, such as was known for instance in Syria, Egypt, Pontus, and the Latin West, likewise in no way excluded the thought of the Lord's passion from the fundamental idea of the feast. This thought was in fact incorporated into it by explicit commemoration, linked in this case also with a strict fast, because the recollection of the passion was the necessary condition for significant celebration of the triumphal resurrection of the Lord. The Easter vigil brought this Easter fast to an end, and constituted the bridge to Easter joy in the redemption perfected by the resurrection.

The so-called Easter controversy at the end of the second century is therefore misconstrued, if its basis is thought to have been a dispute over Easter festivals with fundamentally different content between the Quarto-decimans[2] and the supporters of the Sunday pasch. It was rather a dispute

[1] Of fundamental importance: O. Casel, "Art und Sinn der ältesten christlichen Oster-feier" in *JLW* 14 (1938), 1–78.
[2] So, for example, B. Lohse, *Das Passafest der Quartadecimaner* (Gütersloh 1953), who does not go into the views of O. Casel.

about the date of the same Easter festival, and about the nature and duration of the same Easter fast. It led initially to no agreement, for both groups thought they could appeal to apostolic tradition in support of their own view.[3] It is no longer possible to determine when and by whom this Sunday Passover was introduced in Rome, but it must have become established there early in the second century, for Irenaeus plainly assumes the festival to have existed in the time of the Roman Bishop Xystus.[4] And the practice referred to by him is unlikely to have been a special creation in Rome itself, for such a supposition finds no support in the sources. Furthermore, the common elements shared by the Sunday celebration of the Easter festivities and the Passover feast of the Quartodecimans are very clear: the introductory strict fast; the reading of Exodus 12 with a homily appended; and, incorporated into a vigil celebration, a concluding eucharistic supper. These are best understood if we take the Sunday Easter celebration as a further development of the original Quartodeciman custom, but one which made the Sunday after 14 Nisan the culmination of the festival. This was done in order to emphasize more strongly the contrast with Judaism, and at the same time to bring more vividly into consciousness faith in the resurrection of the Lord as the crown of his work of redemption.

The remaining differences in the manner of keeping the feast, whether according to the Sunday Easter rite or the Quartodeciman practice, were certainly felt and also disputed, as Irenaeus reports with reference to Bishop Polycarp of Smyrna and Anicetus of Rome;[5] but they did not at first burden the relations of the communities to one another in such a way as to endanger peace within the Church. That the differences in practice easily caused controversy is proved by the debate between Melito of Sardes and Bishop Claudius Apollinaris of Hierapolis about the year 170 in Asia Minor: a debate in which Clement of Alexandria also intervened. The latter based his argument on the Johannine chronology so as to criticize, in a work of his own, the custom of the Quartodecimans, and emphasized that Jesus, the true Paschal lamb, died and was buried on one day, the day of preparation of the Passover. In his reply, Melito justified the Quartodeciman practice by the dating of the Synoptics, according to which Jesus

---

[3] *Euseb. HE* 5, 23, 1; 5, 24, 6.

[4] Ibid. 5, 24, 14, and on this see B. Lohse, *op. cit.* 117. The interpretation of the passage in Irenaeus suggested by M. Richard seems untenable. Irenaeus definitely restricts the subject of the dicussion to the date of the already existing feastday, and the duration and nature of the fast usual before it; there was no question at issue whether the festival should be celebrated or not. According to M. Richard, a specifically Roman dispute about the date of Easter is to be postulated, within the Roman community under Soter's predecessors, in which the actual introduction of the Easter feast was controverted.

[5] *Euseb. HE* 5, 24, 16.

had celebrated the Passover before his death; and he asserted that this was what should still be maintained.[6]

A few years before the turn of the century, the dispute over the date of the Easter celebration assumed graver forms. The immediate occasion is most probably found in Rome, where the priest Blastus sought to introduce the Quartodeciman custom, and managed to secure support among the Christian immigrants from Asia Minor.[7] About 195 the Roman Bishop Victor wished to establish a uniform regulation for the Church as a whole, and caused synods to be held everywhere for this purpose. Later Eusebius still possessed the results of the deliberations of some of these synods, which took place in Palestine, Pontus, and Osrhoëne; and he also knew the corresponding resolutions of a Roman synod, as well as the decisions of the churches of Gaul and of some individual bishops.[8] The majority expressed itself in favour of the Sunday practice; but determined contradiction came from the stronghold of the Quartodecimans, the province of Asia, for whose communities Bishop Polycrates of Ephesus made himself the spokesman. In accordance with a Roman request, he had likewise summoned the bishops of the province to a synod. This assembly came to the conclusion that the traditional practice was to be retained, as in Asia it was founded upon apostolic tradition.[9] The decision of the majority of all the synods moved Pope Victor to more severe action against the churches of Asia Minor, which he "attempted", as Eusebius emphasizes,[10] to exclude from the ecclesiastical community. But his action did not meet with general approval; and Irenaeus of Lyons resolutely advocated a course of tolerant treatment towards the followers of the divergent practice, which was evidently adopted.[11] The bishops of Palestine, too, strove for a uniform manner of celebrating Easter in accordance with the majority decision. The Quartodeciman minority remained faithful to their previous practice throughout the whole of the third century, and the Novatians in Asia Minor followed them in this.[12] The first canon of the Synod of Arles in 314 imposed the Sunday Easter, and the Council of Nicaea expelled the Quartodecimans from the ecclesiastical

---

[6] Fragments of Apollinaris from the *Chronicon paschale: PG* 5, 1297. The title of Clement's work, Κανὼν ἐκκλησιαστικὸς ἢ πρὸς Ἰουδαΐζοντας seems to indicate that in other places the Quartadeciman practice was felt to be a Jewish custom; cf. A. v. Harnack, *Dogmengeschichte*, I (Tübingen, 5th ed. 1931), 314.

[7] On Blastos, see, as well as *Eusebius HE* 5, 15, Ps.-Tertullian, *Adv. haer.* 8.

[8] *Euseb. HE* 5, 23, 3–4.

[9] Ibid. 5, 24, 1–8.

[10] Ibid 5, 24, 9.

[11] Ibid. 5, 24, 15–17. It seems impossible to limit Victor's action to the group of Quartodecimans at Rome; Eusebius' account is too plain. Victor would scarcely have summoned the synods outside Rome for such a limited purpose.

[12] *Socrates HE* 5, 21.

community.[13] Thereafter, their numbers continually declined, though even into the fifth century the great Church had to deal with them on occasion.[14]

According to the most important sources for the third century, the pattern of the Easter celebration itself was also largely uniform in East and West. It was introduced by a strictly obligatory fast, which was viewed as an integral part of the Easter festival. The length of the fast was different from place to place, and could last for one, two, or even more days, as Irenaeus already attests.[15] It was kept most strictly in the East, where from the Monday of the appropriate week onwards, only bread, salt and water were taken, and on Friday and Saturday all food was dispensed with.[16] Fasting on these last two days was also demanded by the *Traditio apostolica,* but could be restricted to the Saturday in special cases.[17] Tertullian emphasizes that this fast gave special character to the days on which the Church was deprived of the Bridegroom.[18] Consequently, it was felt to be inseparably linked with the festival which had the whole occurrence of redemption as its content, the passage of the Lord and his community from death to life and from sorrow to joy.

The heart of the Easter celebration was the nocturnal vigil, for which all the Christians of a community assembled, so that it was not a family rite like the Jewish Passover, but essentially a social rite for all members of a congregation. Participation in it was a strict duty, so that Tertullian was afraid that the pagan husband of a Christian wife might have hesitation in allowing her to go to such a nocturnal festival.[19] The community assembled first of all for a service of prayer and readings, which occupied the first hours of the night; psalms, readings from the prophets and the Gospel are specially mentioned.[20] According to the *Didascalia,* the vigil belonged essentially to Easter day and consequently had a joyful conclusion;[21] and this aspect came increasingly to the fore with the further elaboration of the vigil celebration, such as must have occurred at the beginning of the third century. The solemn baptism must particularly be mentioned here, since about this time it was incorporated as a new element into the framework of the Easter liturgy. Tertullian had already regarded Easter, on account of

[13] For Arles: *Acta et symbola conciliorum, quae saec. IV habita sunt* (Leyden 1954), 23; For Nicaea: Eusebius, *Vita Constantini* 3, 18.

[14] B. Lohse, *op. cit.* 128 ff.

[15] In *Euseb. HE* 5, 24, 12.

[16] *Didasc. apost.* 5, 18: see ed. by Funk, *Didascalia et Constitutiones apostolorum* I (Paderborn 1905), 288.

[17] *Trad. apost.* 29: see ed. by Botte in *SourcesChr* 11 (1946), 64.

[18] Tertullian, *De ieiun.* 12–13

[19] *Ad uxor.* 2, 4.

[20] *Didasc. apost.* 5, 19 (290 Funk); according to Asterius Soph. (*Hom.* 8 and 9, and 28) psalms 5 and 15 in particular were used.

[21] *Didasc. apost.* 5, 20 (300 Funk).

its festive character, as being a particularly suitable date for baptism, without actually indicating the vigil in particular. But if Easter were really, as he says, the "dies baptismo solemnior", the liturgical location of the administration of baptism on this day could scarcely be sought outside the vigil celebration. [22] Although Hippolytus's *Church Order* does not formally name Easter day as a date for baptism, its statements concerning the immediate preparations for baptism make sense only if they refer to the last days of what was later to become Holy Week. The observation that people "must keep watch all night and have readings and instructions given to them (that is, to those to be baptized)" clearly points to the baptismal rite as part of the Easter vigil. [23] Asterius in the early fourth century speaks so much as a matter of course of the baptismal liturgy as an integral part of the festival of Easter night that the introduction of this liturgical custom must be ascribed to the third century according to him also. [24] In one of his homilies there is a hymn of praise to Easter night, which may rightly be described as a prefiguration of corresponding parts of the later Latin *Exsultet*. It gives authentic expression to the high place which the liturgy of the Easter vigil already occupied in the religious devotion of the early Christian Church: [25] "O night, brighter than day! O night, more radiant than the sun! O night, whiter than snow! O night, more dazzling than lightning! O night, more shining than torches! O night, more precious than Paradise! O night, freed from darkness! O night, filled with light! O night, which banishes sleep! O night, which teaches us to watch with the angels! O night, terror of the demons! O night, longing of the year! O night, which brings the Bridegroom to the Church! O night, mother of the newly baptized!" The crown and conclusion of the vigil was formed by the eucharistic celebration of Easter Sunday, which in all probability was very early distinguished in the East by the *Trishagion*. [26]

The third century also produced the first outline of a paschal season which then became the nucleus and the first ritual cycle, of the developing ecclesiastical year. For fifty days after Easter the faithful commemorated

---

[22] *De bapt.* 19: "diem baptismo solemniorem Pascha praestat." Hippolytus, too, *In Dan. comm.* 16, gives Easter as a date for baptisms.

[23] *Trad. apost.* 20 (48 ff. Botte).

[24] Asterius, *Hom* 11, which also makes the ritual use of light in the liturgy of baptism quite probable.

[25] Ibid. *Hom.* 11, 4, and on this see H. J. Auf der Maur, "Der Osterlobpreis Asterios' des Sophisten" in *LJ* 12 (1962), 72–85.

[26] Once again Asterius provides the earliest certain evidence in *Hom.* 16, 15; he says that on this night the newly baptized would sing for the first time the ὕμνος τῶν πιστῶν. As Gregory of Nyssa also views the Trishagion in connexion with the solemn baptism, it was probably first used in the Easter liturgy. Gregory exhorts a catechumen to receive baptism so that he can sing it with the faithful (*De bapt.* PG 46, 461).

with joyful hearts the resurrection of the Lord and their own salvation which this bestowed; the joyful character of this pentecost was emphasized by refraining from fasting and from kneeling at prayer.[27] The development of a definite octave of Easter is perhaps to be assigned to the end of the third century or the beginning of the fourth, since Asterius takes it for granted as a well-established custom. Several of his extant homilies were pronounced on various days of Easter week to the newly-baptized, and consequently represent the earliest known example of mystagogic catechetics. He also accepts the Sunday after Easter as the conclusion of the octave.[28]

The final day of Pentecost at first had no festive character. A single reference indicates that in Spain, about the year 300, no uniform practice was followed regarding the final date of Eastertide: one group of Christians kept the fortieth day after Easter, while others kept the fiftieth. The Synod of Elvira disapproved of the former of these customs, and expressly declared that the fiftieth day after Easter was to be celebrated as the feast which ended the Easter cycle.[29] Since the feast of the Epiphany cannot be shown with certainty to have existed in the universal Church before the fourth century, its possible pre-Constantinian roots in Egypt must be discussed later.

The basis for the development of a third-century Christian calendar of feasts can be observed in the commemoration of the martyrs, which was already customary in the Church at that time. This practice sprang from the general honour paid to the dead which was also shown by the Christians to their own departed. On their private initiative, Christians often had the eucharistic oblation made for their dead at the grave-site on the anniversary of death, and customarily remembered them in their prayers. Tertullian repeatedly attests this custom at the beginning of the third century.[30] That such commemoration was emphatically held in honour of the Christian martyrs can easily be understood from the deep veneration which was very early shown them by the faithful. In the East a commemoration for the martyrs, as can be seen from the account of the martyrdom of St Polycarp of Smyrna, which in its concluding report speaks of the celebration on his "birthday", that is, the anniversary of his death.[31] In the West, such a development is perceptible from the sources only much later: The commemoration of a martyr, officially celebrated by the Church, is found in Rome in the first half of the third century: the *Depositio martyrum*, the

---

[27] Cf. Tertullian, *De cor.* 3; *De ieiun.* 14: "...quinquaginta exinde dies in omni exsultatione decurrimus." The custom of standing up to pray during Pentecost was sanctioned by the Council of Nicaea, canon 20.

[28] Asterius, in the headings to *Homilies* 8, 11, 30, 31; cf. *Homily* 21 as a whole.

[29] Synod. Illib., can. 43.

[30] Tertullian, *De cor.* 3; *De exhort. cast.* 11; *De monog.* 10.

[31] *Martyr. polyc.* 18; but see on this H. v. Campenhausen, *Bearbeitungen und Interpolationen des Polykarpmartyriums* (Heidelberg 1957), 3.

Roman calendar, names the Roman Bishop Callistus († 222) as the earliest example of a martyr honoured in this way, perhaps because it was only then that the Roman community acquired its own cemeteries, and so obtained by this legal right the possibility of organizing a commemorative ceremony.[32]

For North Africa, Cyprian testifies to a cult of the martyrs, regulated by the Church, in which the *confessores* were also included. He ordered that the days of their deaths also should be carefully noted, so that the eucharistic sacrifice might be offered[33] on those days, too, as well as on those of the martyrs. The giving of special prominence to the grave of a martyr by the architectural elaboration of his tomb probably occurred in places even in the third century, but only the *Memoria apostolorum* on the Appian Way outside Rome can be said with certainty to be a construction in that period, of a kind which was later generally called *martyrion*.[34] There are reasons for thinking that the pre-Constantinian memorial under the *Confessio* in St Peter's which must be identified with the *Tropaion* on the Vatican Hill mentioned by the Roman presbyter Gaius, should also be mentioned here.[35] At all events, the organization of a cult of the martyrs as a whole becomes in the third century a matter for ecclesiastical authority, that is, of the bishop of the community, whose influence on the development of liturgical worship is here particularly evident.

Catechumenate and Baptism

With the introduction of the catechumenate under ecclesiastical direction, as an institutional preparation for the reception of baptism, the growing Church at the end of the second century and beginning of the third accomplished one of its most important achievements and one very rich in consequences. Several causes were decisive in the Church's gradual construction of a carefully planned and organized course of instruction, containing provision for moral and religious training of those seeking baptism. The first impulse must have come from the considerable missionary success of the Church which developed towards the end of the second century. Such progress must have suggested the idea of an intensive probation of the pagan neophytes, if the previous level in the Christian communities was to be maintained. The urgent need for better instruction in the faith and deeper knowledge of it, was also increased by the

---

[32] *Depos. mart.*, 14 Oct., ed. H. Lietzmann, *Die drei ältesten Martyrologien* (Bonn, 2nd ed. 1911) 4; cf. A. Stuiber, "Heidnische und christliche Gedächtniskalender" in *JbAC* 3 (1960), especially 30 ff.

[33] Cyprian, *Ep.* 12, 2; 39, 3. On the whole question, see *Delehaye OC* 24–49.

[34] See, in particular, F. W. Deichmann in *JdI* 72 (1957), 44–110 and, in general, A. Grabar, *Martyrium* (Paris 1946).

[35] See above, pages 115 ff.

threatening growth of propaganda from heretical groups, especially from the powerful Gnostic movement which penetrated even into the communities of the great Church. Finally, a systematic introduction on firm principles into the world of the Christian sacraments of initiation was found desirable, in view of the rival mystery cults, whose influence on pagan religious inquirers is not to be minimized.

In the development of the ecclesiastical institution of the catechumenate, certain earlier forms must be taken into account, which at first lay principally in the domain of private initiative. In particular, the first instruction in the faith must generally have been given on a private basis, but it was placed at a later stage under ecclesiastical supervision or made to depend on ecclesiastical authorization. Often an individual Christian was the first teacher of a pagan who had become acquainted with the new faith, and whose subsequent community membership was in question. Later it was the educated convert who came forward on his own initiative as a private teacher of the Christian religion, as the activity of Justin and of the earlier Alexandrian teachers shows; and who could then be taken into service by the Church.[36] These forms of private preparation of candidates for baptism were gradually incorporated by the Church, until by the beginning of the third century the organized institution was in existence, as it is found in the *Church Order* of Hippolytus. Concurrently, the development in North Africa was just reaching completion, as Tertullian testifies. These sources indicate the following general picture of the catechumenate in its standard form.

The admission of catechumens to instruction was controlled by the Church, who submitted the candidate for baptism to a strict examination, especially of his moral qualities. For this reason she first of all required that the candidate should name a Christian acquaintance as guarantor, who could vouch for the seriousness of his intention in conversion.[37] One may generally consider this guarantor to have been an apostolically active Christian, to whom the candidate for baptism owed his acquaintance with the Christian religion, and who now introduced him to the leader of the Christian community. There was as yet no special name for these witnesses in the catechumenate; they were not identical with a godfather in the later sense, since they undertook to guarantee only the worthiness of the candidate, and assumed no responsibility for his future manner of life. The acceptance into the catechumenate depended, moreover, on an examination of the candidate by the teacher of the catechumens, who might be a cleric or layman,[38] and whose inquiry extended to the motives of the candidate's

---

[36] See above, pages 229 ff., and Justin, *Apol.* 61, 1.

[37] *Trad. apost.* 16 (44 Botte).

[38] Ibid. 16 and 19. According to Origen, *Contra Cels.* 3, 51, it was still the Christians as a whole who had the duty of examining the candidates for baptism.

request, his marital status, profession, and social position.[39] In the case of the slave of a Christian master, the latter's agreement and testimonial were required; and if this was unfavourable, the candidate was rejected. A number of professions were forbidden to the Christian of the third century, and therefore a candidate for the catechumenate might have to abandon his previous trade. Those occupations in particular were incompatible with his future status as a Christian which stood in a direct or highly potential connexion with pagan worship, such as those of a sacrificial priest, temple guard, actor,[40] astrologer, or magician, to which the Synod of Elvira added that of a charioteer in the circus[41]. Service in the army or in the civil administration gave rise also to hesitation. Tertullian could not believe that soldiers or officials could avoid every situation in which participation in pagan sacrifice and worship would be required of them, or in which they would come into contact with the service of the temples, or have to employ violence or weapons against others.[42] Anyone who joined the army after being accepted into the catechumenate was, according to Hippolytus's *Church Order*, immediately to be excluded from further instruction. The Christian attitude to sexual offences in the candidate for baptism was quite uncompromising: every prostitute was to be rejected and, if need be, the marital situation was to be regularized before admission to instruction. It is clear that, in the investigation of all these questions, decisive weight was attributed to the testimony of the guarantor. The precision of all these regulations shows the mentality of a Church conscious of her responsibility, who took her moral ideal seriously and courageously laid down clear conditions for those who wanted to become her members.

A favourable outcome of this initial inquiry opened the way to the catechumenate, into which the candidate was then received by a special rite, the marking with the sign of the cross; and thus became a *Christianus* or *catechumenus*.[43] A detailed set of rules regulated the life and activity of the catechumens.[44] They were placed under the *doctor audientium* for three years, though this period could be shortened in particularly zealous individual cases.[45] Their time was now occupied with special instruction, introducing them to the world of Christian belief, and with practical training in Christian spiritual life. The teaching was based on Holy

---

[39] For what follows, cf. *Trad. apost.* 16 as a whole (43–46 Botte).

[40] Cyprian, *Ep.* 2 also includes a man who instructs actors; the original connexion with the worship of the gods was still vividly felt.

[41] Canon 62.   [42] *De idol.* 17.

[43] Cf. F. J. Dölger, *Sphragis* (Paderborn 1911), 177; Tertullian, *De idol.* 1 and *De cor.* 2. In North Africa the catechumens were also known as *audientes* or *auditores*, as opposed to the *fideles*, the baptized: Cyprian, *Ep.* 29.

[44] In Hippolytus, *Trad. apost.* 17–20 (46–49 Botte); B. Capelle has attempted a reconstruction of the Latin translation in *RThAM* 5 (1933), 136–9.

[45] *Trad. apost.* 17; the Synod of Elvira (canon 42) lays down two years.

Scripture, with which attendance at the service of the Word and the homily also made them more familiar. Every lesson ended with a prayer and imposition of hands by the catechist.[46] The three-year period of the catechumenate was concluded by yet another examination of the candidate for baptism extending over his moral and religious performance during that time. The examination took place a few weeks before Easter, the principal date for baptism, and was conducted probably by the bishop. Once again a guarantor was required to appear for the candidate;[47] and the latter's performance was measured by "good works", among which visiting the sick and respect for the widows were expressly included.[48] An eminent form of excellence in a catechumen was arrest for Christ's sake; and if thereby death was suffered without baptism, the catechumen was nevertheless saved, because he had been "baptized in his own blood".[49]

A satisfactory outcome of the second inquiry led to the second and final stage of the catechumenate, which served directly to prepare the candidates, now called *electi*, for the reception of baptism soon to ensue. This stage was characterized by a greater use of liturgical prayers of purification or exorcisms, intended to heal and liberate more completely from Satanic power.[50] The bishop as leader of the community came even more prominently into the foreground. As the day of baptism approached, he tested once more by an exorcism the purity of the candidates and excluded the energumens. He prayed with them on the Saturday before baptism, laid his hands on them, and blessed their senses with the sign of the cross.[51] Perhaps the beginning of this second stage of the catechumenate was also the special time for the first renunciation of Satan, of which Tertullian speaks.[52] He also mentions that the weeks of final preparation included more intense practices of penance and frequent prayer and fasting,[53] which emphasized the importance of the event which was to come. A baptismal fast was imposed on the candidates on the Friday and Saturday preceding the Sunday when baptism was to be conferred.[54] In addition to this preparation of a liturgical kind, Hippolytus also mentions as a special task of the *electi* that "they are to hear the Gospel".[55] This comment probably means that they were now strictly obliged, and no longer merely authorized, to be present at the service of the Word at the celebration of the Eucharist, and there to hear readings from the Gospels and the homily.[56]

---

[46] *Trad. apost.* 18 and 19.   [47] Cf. E. Dick in *ZKTh* 63 (1939), 25–27.
[48] *Trad. apost.* 20, 1.
[49] Ibid. 19, 2; Tertullian, *De bapt.* 12 and 14; Cyprian, *Ep.* 57, 4; 73, 21 and 23.
[50] Cf. A. Stenzel, *Die Taufe, eine genetische Erklärung der Taufliturgie* (Innsbruck 1958), 62 and 72.
[51] *Trad. apost.* 20, 3, 5 (48 f. Botte).
[52] *De cor.* 3.   [53] *De bapt.* 20.   [54] *Trad. apost.* 20, 5.   [55] Ibid. 20, 2.
[56] Cf. A. Stenzel. *op. cit.* 64 ff.

The act of baptism was enclosed in the impressive framework of a night-long vigil, which time was occupied with readings and final liturgical instructions. It was chiefly during the Easter vigil that the greatest number of candidates were baptized; otherwise it was during a Saturday to Sunday night that the ceremony took place, if a special reason required a different date for baptism. The break of day, signalized by the crowing of a cock, brought the beginning of the baptismal action proper.[57] The candidates had set aside their clothes and all ornaments, and advanced to a font with a flow of clear water. The bishop had first of all consecrated the oils to be used at the baptism: the oil of thanksgiving and the oil of exorcism, which were each held ready by a deacon on the left and right of the priest. The sequence of candidates was prescribed as follows: children were baptized first,[58] with their parents or perhaps a member of their family giving the answers to the priest's questions for them; the men came next and then the women. The priest required each candidate individually to say the words of baptismal renunciation, turning to the West as he did so: "I renounce you, Satan and all your pomp and all your works"[59] Then followed the anointing with the oil of exorcism, together with the formula: "Every evil spirit go forth from you." Thereupon the candidate went to the priest by the font, and a deacon accompanied him into the water. The officiating bishop or priest laid his hands on him, and asked in sequence three questions regarding his belief:[60] "Do you believe in God the Father almighty? Do you believe in Jesus Christ, the Son of God who was born by the Holy Spirit of the virgin Mary, who was crucified under Pontius Pilate, died, and was buried, who rose alive from the dead on the third day, ascended into heaven, sitteth at the right hand of the Father, who will come again to judge the living and the dead? Do you believe in the Holy Spirit, Holy Church, and the resurrection of the flesh?" To each question the candidate answered "I believe"; and as he did so the officiant poured water over his head.[61] A priest then anointed him with the oil of thanksgiving: "I anoint you with the oil in the name of Jesus Christ"; the baptized person now put his clothes on again, and after the end of the baptisms all went from the baptistery into the church. There a new rite was carried out with each of the baptized individually, the *consignatio*,[62] performed by the bishop. The latter placed

---

[57] *Trad. apost.* 21, 1 (49 Botte).

[58] Infant baptism prevailed everywhere from the end of the second century, though hesitation was expressed on occasion, cf. K. Aland, *Die Säuglingstaufe im Neuen Testament und in der alten Kirche* (Munich 1961).

[59] *Trad. apost.* 21, 6 (50 Botte).

[60] Ibid. 21, 8–12.

[61] For North Africa, cf. Tertullian, *De cor.* 3; *Adv. Prax.* 26. For the accompanying anointing, *De bapt.* 7, 1.

[62] *Trad. apost.* 22 (52 f. Botte).

his hand on the baptized person, and said a prayer as he did so, imploring the grace of God for the newly-baptized that he might serve God according to his will. Then he anointed the head of each with oil, made the sign of the cross on their brows, and gave each a kiss with the words: "The Lord be with you"; whereupon the confirmed person answered: "And with thy spirit." Then the newly-baptized joined the congregation of the faithful and celebrated the Eucharist with them for the first time.

The foregoing account of the catechumenate and the baptismal liturgy are derived from the *Church Order*, or *Liturgy*, of Hippolytus, a document which is by far the most advanced ritually and, one might say, rubricistically, in the period. Since this is now considered to have been an ideal liturgical plan, originating in the East and suitable for adoption by any community, it can no longer be viewed with complete confidence as the typical baptismal liturgy of the Roman church. [63] The only informative material on the subject apart from this source and in any way comparable to it, concerns the North African church. Tertullian's occasional, but nevertheless valuable observations about the baptismal liturgy and practice of his country show points both of agreement and difference with those described above. The agreement is found mostly in factual details: chiefly in the existence of the catechumenate, the form of administration of baptism, and the way baptismal symbolism was employed. The differences consist less in the absence of particular features than in a different kind of assessment of the significance of preparation for, and administration of this sacrament. There seems to be no second stage in Tertullian's version of the catechumenate; the days of immediate preparation before the date of baptism are not described in detail; the special work *De baptismo* gives not a single text of the prayers used in the administration of baptism: all of these elements being necessarily related to a stage of organization of the ritual which had not yet been reached in North Africa. On the other hand, in the catechumenate of North Africa, the moral and ascetical training of the candidates had clearly greater weight than their introduction to a knowledge of the faith; the demand made on their moral quality was very high. The rejection of failures or dubious candidates was inexorable. The "juridical" evaluation of the act of baptism was especially marked; the latter appears as the "sacramentum militiae" or "sacramentum fidei", as the "pactio fidei" and "sponsio salutis"; a binding pact is concluded with the Church, which enrols the baptized in the "militia Christi." [64]

Broadly speaking, at the beginning of the third century the early Christian

---

[63] Cf. J. M. Hanssens, *La liturgie d'Hippolyte* (Rome 1959).
[64] Cf. Tertullian, *De cor.* 11; *De spect.* 24; *Ad mart.* 3; *De bapt.* 6; *De pud.* 9. On the whole question cf. F. J. Dölger, "Sacramentum militiae" in *AuC*, II (1930), 268–80. Fundamentally the *pactio* is also present for Hippolytus in the baptismal renunciation.

Church as a whole had laid down the essential pattern regulating baptism which remained in force for the two centuries that followed. That pattern was still capable of completion, and underwent considerable modifications when peace came, but these only emphasized the quality of the foundations.

The Celebration of the Eucharist

In order to be able to survey more clearly and better estimate the development reached in the eucharistic liturgy by the end of the third century, it is well to start with the description given by Justin Martyr about the year 150. He first sketches the course of the ritual linked to baptism, then speaks of the common ceremony to which all came "on the day named after the sun". [65] From this double description, it can be seen that the service of readings which opened the liturgy had kept its place on Sundays: "The memoirs of the apostles or the writings of the prophets are read aloud"; the reading is followed by the homily of the man presiding; and then come the prayers in common "for ourselves, for the newly-baptized and for all others wherever they may be". The reference to prayer for the newly-baptized permits the supposition that it was possible to insert prayers at this point for some special purpose, their formulation being left to the leader. The service of prayers and readings was terminated by the kiss of peace. [66] The second part of the ceremony stands out in clear contrast: it began with the bringing in of the sacrificial gifts though it is not said who brought the bread and the chalice with wine and water to the president. The essential element of this part is the prayer of the man presiding, which is called εὐχαριστία, and in which he sends up praise and honour to the Father of all things through the name of the Son and the Holy Spirit, and gives thanks that the faithful had been given those gifts. The whole congregation taking part confirmed and ratified the εὐχαριστία of the president with the Hebrew word "Amen". The consecrated eucharistic gifts were then given by the deacons to all present, to be consumed, and portions were also taken to those who were absent. Justin emphasizes that only the baptized could receive this food, which was itself called Eucharist. [67]

Two features stand out in an especially clear manner in this eucharistic liturgy: first of all, there was its social character, drawing all the participating faithful into the actual liturgical action; they ratify expressly the thanksgiving uttered by the leader, and also share as a whole in the eucharistic meal. Moreover, the eucharistic great prayer is primarily one of thanksgiving. Justin insists on this idea in other contexts too, as other writers of the second

[65] *Apol.* 65 and 67.
[66] Only mentioned in c. 65.
[67] Ibid. c. 66.

and third centuries do after him, [68] so that the word "eucharistia" could now become a technical term for the Christian celebration of Mass. [69] The absence of explicit mention in Justin's *Apology* of the idea of sacrifice in the eucharistic liturgy may be due to the fact that he does not quote a complete text of the prayer. The concept was by no means unknown to him, [70] and εὐχαριστία could certainly include for him the idea of sacrifice. [71] Irenaeus speaks more clearly on this point, emphasizing especially that the gifts of bread and wine, which by God's word have become Christ's flesh and blood, represent the pure sacrifice of the New Covenant. [72]

The elaboration which the eucharistic liturgy underwent between the period of the Apologists and the first half of the third century is again most clearly revealed by Hippolytus's *Church Order*, which also records a double description of the celebration of Mass, explaining firstly how it is carried out in connexion with the consecration of a bishop, and secondly how the Christian community celebrates Mass with its newly-baptized members. [73] The chief value of this source lies in the formulary of the eucharistic great prayer, of which a text is provided in full. The first of these two Mass liturgies starts with the introduction of the sacrificial offering carried by the deacons; the bishop, with the presbyters, stretches out his hands over the offering as he begins the great prayer of thanksgiving; the latter is introduced by a prayer of versicle and response between him and the whole congregation, just as it is found to the present day in the liturgy of the Roman Mass. The thanksgiving of the great prayer is addressed to the Father "through his beloved Son Jesus Christ", whom he has sent as saviour and redeemer. Christ is the Father's Word through which he created all things; he took flesh in the womb of the Virgin and was born of the Holy Spirit and of her; he took suffering freely upon himself to break the power of death and of Satan, and made known his resurrection. The congregation is following his example and command at the Last Supper (here the words of Christ are quoted), when it is mindful of his death and resurrection, offers to the Father the bread and the chalice, and gives thanks to him for considering them worthy to stand in his service. The bishop also prays that the Father may send down his Holy Spirit on the sacrificial offering of Holy Church, so that they may strengthen their faith in truth, "so that we may praise and glorify thee through thy Son Jesus Christ, through whom is glory and honour to thee,

---

[68] Justin, *Dial.* 41, I; Irenaeus, *Adv. haer.* 4, 17, 5; Origen, *Contra Cels.* 8, 57.
[69] Cf. T. Schermann in *Philologus* 69 (1910), 375–410.
[70] *Dial.* 41, 2; 117, 2 and 3.
[71] Cf. T. Schermann, *loc. cit.* 385 ff. On the sacrificial character of the Eucharist before Justin's time, see J. A. Jungmann, *The Mass of the Roman Rite*, I, 25 ff. (New York 1951).
[72] *Adv. haer.* 4, 18,1; 3, 18, 1 and 19, 3.
[73] *Trad. apost.* 4 and 23 (30–33 and 53–56 Botte).

the Father and the Son with the Holy Spirit, in thy Holy Church, now and for ever." The Amen of the whole congregation here, too, ratifies the bishop's prayer.[74]

Just as Hippolytus's liturgy of the Mass was intended as a guide, which the leader of a community could keep to a greater or less extent, so too the eucharistic great prayer, in particular, was not intended as an obligatory text for all churches and all purposes, but as a model formulary, the structure and fundamental ideas of which could be retained, but which might be varied and developed in detail.[75] The bishop could therefore still on occasion freely create and shape the text, so that various types of eucharistic prayers of thanksgiving were possible for the celebration of Mass in the third century; and they can still be traced in the formularies which have been preserved in more recent liturgies. It is not possible to decide whether the *Trishagion* was already present in some of them. Hippolytus does not mention it; and the way in which Tertullian, and before him Clement of Rome, speak of the liturgy does not require the assumption that the *Trishagion* was always used in the Mass at that time.[76] But the "form of Mass" presented by Hippolytus can be regarded as a basic outline of the eucharistic liturgy as it was generally celebrated in the Church in those days: it is a liturgy still quite clear in structure and without much detailed elaboration. But when Pope Anicetus could invite Bishop Polycarp of Smyrna, during the latter's visit to Rome about the year 154, to celebrate the liturgy in the Roman community, and when in the Syrian *Didascalia,* about a hundred years later, it is said that an episcopal guest should be given the honour of "offering the sacrifice",[77] such evidence presupposes in different geographical regions a regulation of the ritual of the Mass which was uniform at least in its main features.

Occasional observations by other writers confirm and complete this picture of the eucharistic liturgy drawn by Hippolytus. Tertullian's writings in particular show on many points the identity or similarity of the African Mass liturgy with it.[78] In Tertullian's record also bread and wine were the gifts which the faithful provided for the sacrifice.[79] The eucharistic great prayer was addressed to the Father "per Christum Jesum";[80] but Tertullian

---

[74] Ibid. 4 (33 Botte).
[75] Hippolytus says quite plainly, *Trad. apost.* 10 (41 Botte), that the texts he provides were not to be learnt by heart by the bishop: "Each must pray according to his capacities."
[76] Cf. W. C. van Unnik, "1 Clement and the 'Sanctus'" in *VigChr* 5 (1951), 204–48.
[77] *Euseb. HE* 5, 24; *Didasc. apost.* 2, 58, 3 (168 Funk).
[78] See on this E. Dekkers, *Tertullianus en de geschiedenis der liturgie* (Brussels-Amsterdam 1947), 49–67.
[79] *De monog.* 10; *De exhort. cast.* 11; and even clearer Cyprian, *De op. et eleem.* 15.
[80] *Adv. Marc.* 4, 9.

does not expressly quote from it, though many echoes can be detected in his style and thought. He explicitly stresses that Christ, with the words "Hoc est corpus meum", makes the bread his body;[81] but he does not clarify the position of the Our Father and the place of the kiss of peace in the Mass liturgy. His remarks about the communion ritual are more informative:[82] the Eucharist was received under both kinds, as in Hippolytus's rite;[83] but while the latter cites the formulas with which the species were distributed by the bishop or priests to the faithful, that is "panis caelestis in Christo Jesu", "In Deo patri omnipotenti", and "Et Domino Jesu Christo et spiritu sancto et sancta ecclesia", with a confirmatory "Amen" from the communicant, Tertullian mentions only the Amen, which certainly presupposes that there was some preceding formula.[84] He demanded reverent care in handling the consecrated bread and wine; the faithful could take the former home, in order to receive the Eucharist privately when they were prevented from attending divine worship.[85] Tertullian also implies the existence of a formula for dismissing the congregation when he speaks of the people being sent away at the end of the eucharistic ceremony.[86] He does not name Sunday as the day preferred for celebrating the Eucharist, but he does mention Wednesday and Friday as days of the Stations, together with Mass.[87] That Mass was also celebrated at the funeral and on the anniversary of the death of one of the faithful has already been made clear. Since the second century, the time for Mass had been in the early morning before sunrise, as Tertullian clearly testifies.[88] Therefore, it was not linked, or was no longer linked, with the agape, which persisted as an independent meal.

The first beginnings of the so-called "discipline of the secret" can also be traced in the third century. This is a modern term for the early Christian custom of keeping secret from the uninitiated the most important actions and texts of liturgical worship, especially baptism, the Eucharist, the Our Father, and the creed, or of referring to them in the presence of unauthorized persons in veiled terms only. In particular, the nature and form of liturgical initiation were to be kept secret, and "discovered" solely through the initiation itself. As this attitude took shape slowly, its beginnings cannot be discerned with complete clarity. It is scarcely possible to refer to Tertullian for elucidation since his occasional relevant remarks are obscure, and he moreover speaks ironically of the passion for secrets in the pagan mystery

---

[81] Ibid. 4, 40.
[82] Cf. E. Dekkers, *op. cit.* 59 ff.
[83] Tertullian, *De resurrect. carn.* 8; *Trad. apost.* 23 (54 Botte).
[84] *De Spect.* 25.
[85] *De cor.* 3; *De orat.* 19; *Ad uxor.* 2, 5.
[86] *De an.* 9, 4, and cf. F. J. Dölger in *AuC*, V (1940), 108–17.
[87] *De orat.* 19.
[88] *De cor.* 3; *De orat.* 19; *De fuga* 14; cf. also *Didasc. apost.* 2, 60, 2 (172 Funk).

cults, in a manner which would hardly have been possible if the North African Christians had observed a similar custom in his time.[89] But the attitude is apparent in Hippolytus's *Church Order*, according to which an unbeliever was not to be instructed about baptism and the Eucharist before he had been baptized or admitted to communion.[90] The use of the language of the mysteries was also probably in conformity with a growing discipline of the secret.[91] Similary, in Origen, formulas are found which may be interpreted as echoes of this thinking when he refrains from disclosing details to his hearers concerning the Eucharist, or when he tells the future candidate for baptism that he would later "be initiated into the exalted mysteries already known to those for whom such knowledge is appropriate".[92] Since most of this evidence comes from the East, the place of origin of the discipline of the secret is perhaps thus indicated. It attained its real force only in the fourth and early fifth centuries; consequently, its deeper motives and relation to the pagan mysteries will be discussed in greater detail later.

The Beginnings of Christian Art

A Christianity which had increased in numbers and self-awareness was provided for the first time in the third century with the possibility of engaging in artistic activity inspired by a Christian spirit, for only the longer periods of peace coming at that time afforded the special conditions required. Christian art was, however, initially opposed by a trend of considerable strength within the Church itself that stood in irreconcilable opposition to artistic activity as such.[93] The Old Testament prohibition of images (in Exod 20:4) was influential in this respect. Origen, for example, refers to it in saying that the Christians abominated temples, altars and images.[94] The pure spirituality of the Christian God was also felt by Minucius Felix to be an obstacle that obstructed worshipping Him in a special building.[95] The close connexion between the art of antiquity and pagan worship was in the forefront of Tertullian's mind when he radically rejected Christian activity in this domain. The devil alone, he says, had sent sculptors and painters

---

[89] The references usually given are to *Apol.* 7, 6; *Ad ux.* 2, 5; *Adv. Val.* 1. On this see E. Dekkers, *op. cit.* 80–82.

[90] *Trad. apost.* 23 (56 Botte), with variants. This is so although Hippolytus himself speaks in detail of baptism and the Eucharist.

[91] Cf. *Protr.* 12, 118–20; *Paed.* 1, 5, 26.

[92] Origen, *In Lev. hom.* 9, 10; *In Iesu Nave hom.* 4, 1: " si ... initiatus fueris venerandis illis magnificisque sacramentis, quae norunt illi, quos nosse fas est."

[93] Cf. H. Koch, *Die altchristliche Bilderfrage nach den literarischen Quellen* (Göttingen 1917); W. Elliger, *Die Stellung der alten Christen zu den Bildern* (Leipzig 1930).

[94] *Contra Cels.* 7, 64.

[95] *Octavius* 32.

into the world.[96] Even at the beginning of the fourth century the synod of Elvira decreed for the territories of the Spanish bishops that: "Images are forbidden in Church; what is honoured and worshipped must not be represented on the walls."[97] This hostile tendency to art and images could not, however, prevail over the positive trend which succeeded in making an important advance in the third century. Tertullian knew Christians who possessed drinking vessels bearing the image of the Good Shepherd.[98] Clement of Alexandria, for all his reserve regarding a representation of God, nevertheless suggested to the Christians of his day some symbols which their signet rings might bear, as the dove, fish, ship, anchor, and fisherman.[99] Giving due regard to such a favourable attitude towards art in the private domain, it was nevertheless the needs of liturgical worship in the stronger communities of the Church as a whole which finally obtained for art an official recognition by ecclesiastical authority. Another contributory factor was the inclination of the Christians, surrounded by a widespread pagan cult of the dead, to express in artistic form on the tombs of their dead whatever their faith proclaimed to them concerning death and resurrection.

First of all, the desire must have developed among the Christians for a place of worship of their own where the worthy celebration of the eucharistic liturgy would be possible, when the size of the congregations made this increasingly difficult in private houses. The written evidence for the existence of specifically Christian places of worship appears at the beginning of the third century.[100] About 205 a flood in Edessa in the East of Syria destroyed, among other things, "the temple of the Christians".[101] Hippolytus reports in his commentary on Daniel that the enemies of the Christians forced their way "into the house of God", just when the faithful had gathered there for prayer.[102] About the same time, Tertullian spoke of the "house of our dove", in a context which most probably indicates that the Christian place of worship in Carthage was referred to.[103] For the second half of the third century, evidence is available of Christian "churches" in Palestine[104] and Sicily.[105] About the end of the third century and the beginning of the fourth, the Christian churches had become very numerous.

[96] De idol. 3.
[97] Synod. Illib., can. 36.
[98] De pud. 7, 10.
[99] Paed. 3, 59, 2, and cf. L. Eizenhöfer in JbAC 3 (1960), 51–69.
[100] Cf. J. R. Laurin, "Le lieu du culte chrétien d'après les documents littéraires primitifs" in AnGr 70 (1954), 39–57, and W. Rordorf in ZNW 55 (1964), 110–28.
[101] Chronicum Edessenum in CSCO 4, 3.
[102] In Dan. comm. 1, 20.
[103] Adv. Val. 3, and cf. F. J. Dölger in AuC, II (1930), 41–56. See also Tertullian, De fuga 3; De idol. 7.
[104] Euseb. HE 7, 15, 1–5.
[105] Porphyry, Fragment 76.

Eusebius indicates that the earlier places where the Christians had worshipped, prior to Diocletian, were everywhere replaced by more spacious buildings[106]. Christian places of worship were destroyed in Bithynia, Galatia and Pontus, Thracia, Africa, Spain, and Gaul, as a result of the Diocletian decree of persecution[107]. In contrast to these abundant and plain statements of the written sources, archaeological findings have not until now been rich. It has of course been thought, that the remains of older Roman houses found during excavations under some of the most ancient titular churches of Rome, such as San Clemente, St Pudenziana, St Martino ai Monti and others, are the remnants of the pre-Constantinian *domus ecclesiae* in each case;[108] but definite proof of the liturgical character of these earlier buildings has not been discovered.[109] An undoubted example of a pre-Constantinian Christian church has, however, been brought to light by excavations in Dura-Europos, a Roman frontier garrison on the west bank of the Euphrates, built about 232. The Christian character of this private house, adapted for use in divine worship, is clearly demonstrated by the frescoes of a room which was perhaps used as a baptistery: they depict the Good Shepherd among tombs, the healing of the man born lame, and Christ walking on the water.[110]

New possibilities of Christian artistic activity presented themselves when the Church in the first half of the third century came into possession of her own burial-grounds,[111] which were at first called cemeteries. In Rome from the ninth century onwards these were called the catacombs; this appellation deriving from the name of the field *in* or *ad catacumbas,* at the cemetery of St Sebastian on the Appian Way. The *cemeterium Callisti* must be considered the earliest purely Christian underground burial-place; it stood on land which Bishop Zephyrinus (199–217) donated to the Roman Church from his private estate, and the administration of which he entrusted to the deacon Callistus. The wall and ceiling surfaces in the grave-chambers of the catacombs were furnished with pictures. The painters were naturally dependent in form on contemporary secular art, but their choice of themes was mostly determined by Holy Scripture or other Christian sources. Among the earliest subjects were, for instance, Daniel between two lions in the den, Noah in the Ark, Jonah swallowed by the fish and cast out again, or the

---

[106] *HE* 8, 1, 5.

[107] See J. R. Laurin, " Le lieu du culte chrétien, d'après les documents littéraires primitifs" in *Studi sulla chiesa antica* (Rome 1954), 55 f.

[108] Cf. J. P. Kirsch in the Italian edition of *Fliche-Martin*, III, 537 ff.

[109] Cf. A. M. Schneider, "Die ältesten Denkmäler der römischen Kirche" in *Festschrift der Akad. der Wiss. Göttingen*, II (Göttingen 1951), 195–7.

[110] See illustrations 42–51 in Hopkins-Baur, *Christian Church at Dura-Europos* (New Haven 1934).

[111] Cf. F. de Visscher, "Le régime juridique des plus anciens cimetières chrétiens à Rome" in *AnBoll* 69 (1951), 39–54.

New Testament scene of the resurrection of Lazarus.[112] They must all be understood as references to the biblical accounts of the saving of a man from deadly peril, and consequently aim at proclaiming the Christian hope of entering into an eternal life, safe from all peril and threat from the powers of evil. Proceeding from the same current of ideas is the figure of the Good Shepherd, which is found in the early catacomb paintings and in epitaphs.[113] In this instance Christ is seen as the saviour who, as shepherd, brings life and, as teacher, brings true knowledge of God. Christ appears also as a teacher in the early Christian carvings on sarcophagi.[114] The image of Christ in pre-Constantinian times was enriched by a representation in mosaics in a mausoleum under St Peter's in Rome. These show the Christ-Helios journeying from Hades to the Father.[115] And so the third century had already in various ways laid the foundations of the flourishing art of the Christian empire in the following century.

CHAPTER 24

Spiritual Life and Morality in the Communities of the Third Century

IF THE sources are studied for the essential concepts and convictions which characterized the piety of the third century, two ideas and realities stand out, namely baptism and martyrdom. All writers of the period, who discuss in any detail Christian perfection and its actual realization, speak so insistently of baptism as the well-spring, and of readiness for martyrdom as the touchstone of the genuineness of a Christian way of life, that devotion to baptism and to martyrdom must be generally considered to be the fundamental twofold attitude to religious life in the early Christian Church.

Baptismal Spirituality

The first attempts of any magnitude to develop a theory of Christian perfection were undertaken by the early teachers of Alexandria. Clement of Alexandria tried to trace such a theory in the portrait of the Christian Gnostic which he sketched in the *Paedagogus* and the *Stromata*. There is no mistaking, in his account, the fundamental importance, theoretical and

[112] Cf. J. Kollwitz, *Das Christusbild des 3. Jahrhunderts* (Münster 1953), 7.
[113] Ibid. 11, with illustrations 2–4.
[114] F. Gerke, *Christus in der spätantiken Plastik* (Berlin 1940), 7–14.
[115] O. Perler, *Die Mosaiken der Juliergruft im Vatikan* (Fribourg 1953).

practical, which baptism held for perfection.[1] Using the terminology of the pagan mystery-cults, but in no way abandoning his conviction of the reality of the Christian sacrament of baptism, he describes its profoundly transforming effects: it brings complete forgiveness of sins, and liberates from the dark power of the demons.[2] In its positive aspect, it is a rebirth to new life in the kingdom of the Father, and so grants immortality; and, by the infusion of the Holy Spirit into the soul, gives also true knowledge of God, or *gnosis*.[3] Essentially, this gnosis is imparted to every baptized person, not merely to *pneumatikoi*, or spiritually endowed persons; and by it the grace-given root of all perfection is in principle implanted; this must grow throughout life.[4] For, even if the gnosis received in baptism cannot increase in its essential nature, it can nevertheless grow in extent within the baptized person; and above all it must stand the test in the struggle with evil.[5] In baptism there is a real, not merely a symbolic, repetition for the Christian of what baptism in the Jordan once effected for Christ. Consequently, the life which springs from baptismal grace is an imitation of Christ, with whom the believer is indissolubly united at his baptism.[6]

What is expressed by Clement quite plainly, but with some reserve and a certain formulary concision, is developed by Origen in rich abundance. This is particularly evident in his homilies, in an ardent metaphorical style with insistent kerygmatic appeal. It was in this way that Origen became the most zealous preacher of a deep-felt baptismal spirituality for the early Christian Church generally. He lays the foundation first of all in a theology of baptism, which bases all exhortations to live in accordance with baptismal grace on the supernatural sacramental event which occurs at baptism. He prefers to explain that event by reference to those principal Old Testament prefigurations of baptism which were to play such an important part in the mystagogical preaching of the fourth century.[7] He regards the whole path of the person seeking baptism from his first wish for instruction in the Christian faith through his acceptance into the catechumenate and his introduction to the law of God, to the day when in the midst of the priests he is initiated into the mysteries of baptism as prefigured in the exodus of Israel from Egypt, the passage of the Red Sea, the stages of the wandering in the desert and the crossing of the Jordan,

---

[1] W. Völker, *Der wahre Gnostiker nach Clemens Alexandrinus* (Berlin 1952), 147–53.

[2] *Paed.* 1, 26, 2; 1, 30, 1; *Strom.* 4, 26, 5; *Exc. ex Theod.* 77, 3.

[3] *Paed.* 2, 118, 5; 1, 28, 1; *Protr.* 117, 4.

[4] *Paed.* 1, 25, 1; *Strom.* 7, 14, 1; 4, 160, 3.

[5] *Paed.* 1, 26, 3; *Protr.* 116, 4.

[6] *Paed.* 1, 25, 3; *Strom.* 7, 14, 1.

[7] Cf. J. Daniélou, "Traversée de la mer rouge et baptême aux premiers siècles" in *RSR* 33 (1946), 402–30, and F. J. Dölger, "Der Durchzug durch den Jordan als Sinn-bild der christlichen Taufe" in *AuC*, II (1930), 70–79.

after which the Promised Land is opened to him. Jesus instead of Moses is his guide on his further paths.[8] Just as Israel was then freed from the power of Pharaoh, so the baptized person is liberated from the dominion of Satan; and just as Israel journeyed through the wilderness, guided by the column of cloud and fire, so also the believer, who with Christ passed through Christ's death and burial, will rise on the third day through baptism in water and the Holy Spirit; and God will henceforth lead him on the way of salvation: "You become healthy, sound, and cleansed from the stains of sin; you come out a new man, ready to sing the new song."[9] By this act the Christian is summoned to follow Christ, the new guide who has been given him in baptism. Before, he was an *imitator diaboli;* now in baptism he has found a new example to follow: the Logos with whom and in whom he sets out on the paths of his spiritual life which is to lead him to the Father.[10] Baptism is, therefore, the beginning of this new life, since its life-giving power has its source in the death of Christ on the cross, and the life of baptismal grace derives ultimately from the crucifixion.[11]

Origen bases his doctrine of the spiritual life as a baptismal one on these truths of the faith concerning the nature of baptism. That element which received its foundation by what happened sacramentally in baptism, must further develop; the new life then received must prosper in the spiritual life of the soul, but can do so only if it is renewed daily.[12] The Logos must be able to act in the soul of the baptized person like a vine, whose grapes reach their full sweetness gradually.[13] The Logos already exercises this purifying power in a soul which is preparing for baptism; the whole ascetical struggle of the catechumen to train himself in the life of Christian virtue receives its effectiveness from the anticipatory radiance of the grace of baptism.[14] But the spiritual life receives its accomplishment and stamp after baptism, and from the sacrament. The *apotaxis* of Satan pronounced in baptism must be constantly repeated if the grace of baptism is to be preserved. Its corresponding *syntage,* or covenant with Christ, imposes an obligation of absolute fidelity to the baptismal vow, which some keep without faltering, but which others break and so bear with them the shame of Egypt.[15] The task set every Christian in his religious life can be expressed,

---

[8] *In Iesu Nave hom.* 4, 1; cf. also *hom.* 5, 1; *In Num. hom.* 26, 4; *In Ioann. comm.* 6, 42, 220.

[9] Cf. the whole fifth *Hom. in Exod.*, especially 1, 2, and 5.

[10] *In Num. hom.* 12, 4; *In Exod. hom.* 10, 4; *In Gen. hom.* 2, 5.

[11] *In Gen. hom.* 13, 4; *In Exod. hom.* 11, 2.

[12] *In Rom. comm.* 5, 8.

[13] *In Cant. comm.* 2.

[14] *In Ioann. comm.* 32, 7; *In Iesu Nave hom.* 4, 1; *In Lev. hom.* 6, 2.

[15] *In Exod. hom.* 8, 4; *In Iesu Nave hom.* 26, 2; 4, 2.

according to Origen, in the concise phrase τηρεῖν τὸ βάπτισμα, that is to preserve baptismal grace.[16] But the obligation of fidelity to the baptismal vow does not derive simply from the renunciation of Satan's world. By baptism Christ becomes the bridegroom and spouse of the soul, and marital fidelity must be preserved; a return to the impure spirits of the pagan period of life would break this fidelity and sully the white robe of baptism.[17] Fidelity to baptismal vows and to the divine espousals can be kept solely by a perpetual fight against the powers of the evil one. In this combat the baptized persons follow once more the example of their master, who was likewise tempted after his baptism in the Jordan; and so the daily practice of a baptismal spirituality is an actual imitation of Christ.[18] Viewed positively, the fidelity to baptism ensured by perpetual combat leads to the abundant development of all virtues. Two attitudes, which early Christianity held in particularly high esteem grow from a baptismal piety truly lived. These are genuine love of one's neighbour and readiness for martyrdom. Brotherly love is a transmission of the Father's love for us, which we receive in baptism: we imitate him when we give our love to our neighbour.[19] And, further, the Spirit conferred by baptism bestows the courage to suffer:[20] baptismal renunciation includes a willingness for martyrdom.[21]

In their doctrine of baptismal spirituality as the development of the grace of baptism and the imitation of Christ's example, the Alexandrian teachers were not framing the demands of an esoteric teaching on perfection addressed merely to an *élite*. Indeed, because in this context Origen was speaking to all Christians, he was therefore aware of the failure of many in the face of this lofty religious ideal;[22] and that is precisely what led him to preach repeatedly on a right understanding of the mystery of Christian baptism, and to call for its realization in daily life. Other pastors and writers of the third century speak in a similar way to the Alexandrians, if not with equal force. For Cyprian, Christian life is the continuance of the *renuntiatio saeculi*, which, once expressed in baptism, must now be made effective by following our Lord when God tests the Christians through persecution.[23] Cyprian's biographer Pontius reveals the same notion of Christian life as the carrying out of the obligations of baptism by not beginning his description of the bishop's life until the latter's

---

[16] *In Ier. hom.* 2, 3.

[17] *In Exod. hom.* 8, 5; 1, 5; 11, 7.

[18] *In Exod. hom.* 2, 3; 1, 5.

[19] *In Cant. comm.* 2; *In Ioann. comm.* 20, 17.

[20] *Contra Cels.* 6, 44.

[21] *Protr.* 11, 107.

[22] *In Rom. comm.* 5, 8; *In Num. hom.* 5, 1.

[23] *Ep.* 13, 5, 3.

baptism: "The deeds of a man of God should be counted only from the moment when he was born to God." He expressly emphasizes that Cyprian always preached during persecution that Christians must prove themselves worthy of their birth, and that a man born again of God could not belie his origin.[24] It was in accord with this judgment on the importance of baptism for the daily religious life of the Christian that such care was taken by the leaders of the Christian communities to provide a preparation for baptism in the catechumenate, and to organize a solemn celebration of it. The whole impact of initiation into the mysteries of the Christian faith was to work itself out in a religious life which never forgot the radiance of that hour nor the gravity of the solemn baptismal vow. When Christian art, in the previously-mentioned baptistery of the house church of Dura-Europos, represented the Good Shepherd among his sheep,[25] (signifying in this case Christ among the newly baptized Christians), it sought to inculcate forcefully in the faithful the importance and meaning of the baptismal sacrament.

Devotion to Martyrdom

Whereas the preaching of baptismal spirituality was to increase in extent and depth in the spiritual doctrines of the fourth century, devotion to martyrdom as the second fundamental attitude in the striving for Christian perfection reached its height in the third. Closely linked with the idea of the imitation of Christ, esteem for martyrdom as the summit and crown of all perfection became the most widespread, and ascetically fruitful, watchword in the world of early Christian spirituality. At the end of the second century, when the Church increasingly made it a theme of preaching to her own members, there was already a rich tradition on which to build. With Ignatius of Antioch the connexion between martyrdom and imitation of Christ was already clearly grasped and forcefully expressed: a man is a true disciple of Christ only if he dies for Christ's sake; anyone who does not accept death willingly with eyes fixed "on his Passion" has not the life of Christ within him.[26] The recorder of the martyrdom of Bishop Polycarp of Smyrna expressly drew a parallel between Christ and the martyr; he saw the justification for the honour which was beginning to be paid to martyrs in the fact that they are the authentic disciples and imitators of the Lord. Similarly, the communities of Lyons and Vienne said proudly that their martyrs of the year 177 were emulators and imitators of Christ. They expressed the idea in biblical terms, saying of Vettius Epagathus that

---

[24] Pontius, *Vita Cypr.* 2: "hominis dei facta non debent aliunde numerari, nisi ex quo deo natus est"; ibid. 9 "quos renatos per deum constat, degeneres esse non congruit."
[25] See above p. 287.
[26] Ignatius, *Ad Rom.* 4, 2; *Ad Magn.* 5, 2; cf. *Ad Rom.* 6, 3.

"he was a true disciple of Christ, because he followed the Lamb wherever he went", even to the death of martyrdom.[27] Origen declared the same view,[28] and the pastor Cyprian took advantage of the persecutions to remind his flock that they had at such times to imitate Christ as a teacher of patience and suffering, and that in the daily celebration of the Eucharist they drank the Blood of Christ in order to be able one day to give their blood for him.[29] Anyone who suffers for confessing the name of Christ becomes thereby a "sharer and companion of his Passion", as Roman priests stressed in a letter to Cyprian.[30] The concept of following Christ and of imitating him occurs with especial frequence in the accounts of the martyrs and in the pronouncements of Christian writers concerning martyrdom.[31]

Devotion to martyrdom received a particular force of attraction from the idea that a martyr's violent death led in a unique way to union with Christ. It was a widespread conviction in the third century that this union with Christ is already manifest when a Christian confesses his fidelity to his Lord under torture. At that moment it is Christ who strengthens him, and so fills him with his presence that, in a kind of exaltation, he scarcely feels the pain of torture and execution.[32] Thus, the Christian captive Felicity replied to the jailer who derided her for groaning at the birth of her child: "Now it is I who suffer what I suffer; but there (that is, at her martyrdom), it will be another in me who will suffer for me, because I too will be suffering for him."[33] Cyprian comforted and strengthened Christians facing martyrdom with the assurance that the Lord "himself contends in us, goes to battle with us, and in our hard struggle himself gives the crown and receives it."[34] It was this idea which culminated in the custom of honouring the martyrs with the title of *Christophorus:* union with Christ attains perfection by suffering martyrdom.[35] The martyrs were convinced that nothing united them with Christ as directly as a violent death while bearing witness to him. From this belief sprang the aspiration, found as early as Ignatius of Antioch, precisely for this kind of death, which is described by Cyprian as "the baptism which, after our departure from

---

[27] *Mart. Polyc.* 17, 3; 19, 1; *Euseb. HE* 5, 2, 2; 5, 1, 10.

[28] *In Ioan. comm.* 2, 34.

[29] Cyprian, *Ep.* 58, 1, 3.

[30] *Ep.* 31, 3: "collega passionis cum Christo."

[31] Cf. *Passio Perpet. et Felicit.* 18, 9; Clement of Alex. *Strom.* 4, 3, 14; Tertullian, *Scorp.* 9; *De resurrect. carn.* 8; Cyprian, *Ep.* 76, 7, 1; Pseudo-Cyprian, *De laude mart.* 6; 26; 29.

[32] Cf. *Mart. Polycarp.* 2, 2 and the Christians of Lyons, *Eusebius HE* 5, 1, 23, 42.

[33] *Passio Perpet. et Felic.* 15, 3; Cf. *Ep. ad Diogn.* 7, 9.

[34] Cyprian, *Ep.* 10, 4; 37, 2; 76, 7. Further references in H. v. Campenhausen, *Die Idee des Martyriums in der alten Kirche* (Göttingen 1936), 90, note 1.

[35] F. J. Dölger in *AuC,* IV (1934), 73–80.

the world, unites us directly to God",[36] and which consequently, as a baptism in blood, completely replaces the other baptism, and in fact surpasses it in efficacy, because there is no danger of later relapse. Ultimately, the value set on martyrdom as absolute perfection was based on the double conviction that martyrdom represents the highest form of imitation of Christ and unites us in a unique way with him. Clement of Alexandria equates martyrdom with τελείωσις, since anyone who dies for his faith "has accomplished the work of perfect love".[37]

There is no plainer way of proving love of God and of Christ than by suffering violent death under persecution. Consequently, the *exhortatio ad martyrium* was a regular part of early Christian preaching and literature; not a dull cliché, but a very real factor in the actual realities of the third century itself. Origen and Cyprian are its purest and most convincing exponents. Origen's work on the meaning and dignity of martyrdom is the expression of a genuine readiness and desire for martyrdom, exhorting his own father in prison not to be dissuaded by the thought of the fate of his family from bearing witness unto death, and pointing with pride to friends and pupils who had travelled the road to the end.[38] Origen regarded the times of persecution as the truly great age of the Church because of the martyrs, whereas he had to recognize with sorrow that long periods of peace quickly led to slackening of enthusiastic faith.[39] Cyprian's letters to his flock during persecution present the same picture. In his own behaviour the Bishop of Carthage displayed the balanced and wise prudence that the Church demanded, which did not foolishly and fanatically seek martyrdom,[40] yet did not fail in the hour of trial. When, during the Decian persecution, an alarmingly large number of lapsed Christians created no small problem for the Church authorities, Cyprian had also to observe that readiness for martyrdom was found only in an *élite*.

Devotion to martyrdom is also clearly seen in the efforts of Christian circles to find substitutes for actual death by martyrdom, when for various reasons this was not in fact attainable. In very early times there were those who considered a serious striving for moral purity as an attitude which, though certainly not equal in value to real martyrdom, nevertheless revealed in a way a martyr's mentality which put God first.[41] Origen was convinced that in a community there are Christians "who have taken up their cross and follow Christ and are ready to shed their blood for him",

---

[36] *Ad Fortun. praefat.* 4.
[37] *Strom.* 4, 4, 14.
[38] *Euseb. HE* 6, 2, 3–6; 6, 3, 4.
[39] *In Ier. hom.* 4, 3.
[40] Like the Montanists, cf. Tertullian's *De fuga in persecutione.*
[41] Already in Clement of Alexandria, *Strom.* 4, 7, 43.

and so are martyrs before God.[42] Cyprian clearly expressed the difference between actual martyrdom and martyrdom of desire, and worked out a spirituality centred on martyrdom.[43] What was of essential importance here was the evolution of martyrdom into a criterion for Christian perfection, even if in detail only a greater or lesser resemblance to martyrdom was retained. Dionysius of Alexandria judged the self-sacrifice of some Christians who died in the time of the plague in the service of the sick almost on the same level as a martyr's death.[44] But a new development took place when certain ascetic modes of live, such as the state of virginity and retirement from the world, became considered as real substitutes for actual death by martyrdom, and were praised as a new way of following Christ.

The Asceticism of the Third Century

Christians of both sexes who renounced marriage, who dissociated themselves more than others from secular life, yet remained with their families and put themselves at the service of the Christian community, are not found for the first time in the third century. The biblical basis for such a mode of life and the example of a celibate life given by Christ and St Paul produced at a very early date their effect, for the letter of the Roman Bishop Clement presupposes the existence of celibates, and the *Didache* refers to a type of wandering ascetic which was commonly active in the missionary field.[45] Ignatius of Antioch and Hermas of Rome knew of groups of virgins in their communities who enjoyed high esteem.[46] The apologists, in their descriptions of the life of the Christian communities, did not fail to point out to the pagans that a notably high number of men and women leading celibate lives testified to the high moral quality of the followers of Christianity; and the pagans themselves were impressed by this feature of Christian spiritual life.[47] Occasional references in second-century texts are followed in the third century by a series of writings which expressly concern Christian asceticism, and provide a detailed account of its ideals and of the dangers which beset it. Its adherents had become so numerous in the meantime that they represented an important factor in Christian daily life in the churches of both East and West. They were not yet committed

---

[42] *In Num. hom.* 10, 2.

[43] *Ad Fortun.* 13; *De zelo et liv.* 16.

[44] *Euseb. HE* 7, 22, 7.

[45] 1 *Clem.* 38:2, which terms this life ἐγκράτεια; *Did.* 11 and 12.

[46] Ignatius, *Ad Smyrn.* 13, 1; *Ad Polyc.* 5, 2; Hermas, *Pastor Sim.* 9, 2; 10, 3; *vis.* 1, 2, 4.

[47] Justin, *Apol.* 15; 29; Athenagoras, *Suppl.* 33; Min. Felix, *Oct.* 31, 5. For the judgment of the pagan Galen regarding the Christians, cf. R. Walzer, *Galen on Jews and Christians* (Oxford 1949).

to a definite mode of life with a fixed rule; and so they mostly remained with their families and still disposed of their own private property. Only the pseudo-Clementine letters *Ad virgines* indicate a tendency in that period for closer groupings, just as they also refer to missionary and charitable activity by the ascetics.[48] Moreover, there was still no set rite by which the Church herself received them into their state of life; they simply bound themselves by a very serious promise to a life of continence.[49] That promise, however, was known to the community authorities, who punished its transgression very strictly, namely by excommunication. On the other hand, the promise did not bind for ever; the ascetic for special reasons could forego his mode of life and contract matrimony.

Within the community and among its rulers, the ascetics enjoyed unique esteem. For Clement of Alexandria, they were the "elect of the elect", while Cyprian saw in them "the more splendid part of Christ's flock, the flower of Mother Church".[50] A new element with increased prestige was ascetic virginity, since this was connected with the idea of the soul's espousal to Christ. Tertullian was already acquainted with the title "bride of Christ", used to honour virgin ascetics, both men and women;[51] and the term later became part of the customary official language of the Church. Origen's exposition of the Song of Songs,[52] in terms of the individual's conception of it as a description of the relationship between the particular soul and its heavenly bridegroom, Christ, inaugurated the triumphant progress of this idea through the centuries which followed. At first this notion was at the service of the ideal of virginity; Methodius of Olympus meant by his lyrical praise of virginity that it is not to be separated from espousal to Christ. The records of the martyrdom of virgins consecrated to God, such as Agnes, Pelagia, and Caecilia, are pervaded by this idea.[53] A theological basis was sought for the worth of the ascetics. Their mode of life was declared to be the worthiest substitute for death by martyrdom; like the latter, it called for total self-sacrifice,[54] and consequently, according to Cyprian's warning, the spirit of the martyrs must be living in the ascetics also. Methodius directly compares virginity with martyrdom, while others list the ascetics immediately after the martyrs: the latter bearing fruit a hundredfold, the former sixtyfold. The *corona virginitatis* is accorded to

---

[48] Cyprian, *De hab. virg.* 7–12, 18–19; Pseudo-Clement, *Ad virg.* 1, 8, 4; 1, 2; Origen, *In Iudic. hom.* 9, 1; *In Ier. hom.* 20; *Contra Cels.* 5, 49.

[49] Cyprian, *De hab. virg.* 4 and *Ep.* 62, 3. Canon 13 of the Synod of Elvira speaks of a *pactum virginitatis.*

[50] Clement of Alexandria, *Quis div. salv.* 36; Cyprian, *De hab. virg.* 3.

[51] *De orat.* 22; *De resurr. carn.* 61; *De exhort. cast.* 13.

[52] Both in the commentary as well as in the homilies on the Song of Songs.

[53] Cf. the texts collected by J. Schmid in *RAC* II, 560 ff.

[54] Methodius, *Symp.* 5, 4; 11.

the *virgines utriusque sexus,* just as the *corona martyrum* is to the martyrs, for their life is a true following of Christ.[55] Such a lofty ideal is liable to particular perils. Tertullian warned the ascetics especially against pride, to which the high esteem in which they were held in the community might tempt them; the pseudo-Clementine letters show a similar awareness of the threat of vanity and empty show. Cyprian saw clearly the practical dangers which life in the world involved for the ascetics, and consequently demanded of them a high degree of all the virtues. Methodius tried to strengthen them positively by directing their minds to meditation and the wealth that lies therein; virginity should be a means of individual sanctification.[56]

Ascetical excess and a disproportion between the individual's moral strength and such lofty idealism explain a grave aberration in Christian asceticism, especially in the third century. Christian ascetics lived together as "sister and brother" in a sort of spiritual matrimony, and so imperilled the virginity they had vowed to keep. Not only did they expose themselves to the insinuations and derision of the people around them, but they also failed grievously themselves. The sources leave no doubt about the existence and considerable extent of the aberration.[57] The system of agapetae extended through the East, in Syria and Egypt as well as in North Africa,[58] and forced the ecclesiastical authorities to decisive action. In Cyprian's time a deacon who was guilty in this matter was excommunicated. Cyprian's clearsightedness and freedom from illusion made him intervene even where there were as yet no serious lapses.[59] The *De singularitate clericorum,* an anonymous treatise of the third century, could not conceal the fact that the evil had penetrated certain clerical circles, which sometimes employed biblical texts to justify their attitude. Already in the third century some synods imposed heavy sanctions on the guilty, but the custom persisted obstinately in East and West, surviving in Spain down to the sixth century.[60]

The asceticism of the third century not only continued in its previous form, but also provided the source of two new developments which were

---

[55] Cyprian, *De hab. virg.* 21; Methodius, *Symp.* 7, 3; Pseudo-Clement, *Ep. ad virg.* 1, 5, 5; 1, 7, 1–2.
[56] Tertullian, *De virg. vel. passim;* Cyprian, *De hab. virg. passim;* Methodius, *Symp.* 4, 5; 7, 2; Pseudo-Clement, *Ep. ad virg.* 1, 3, 2; 1, 4, 2.
[57] Especially the *Ep. 2 ad virgines* of the Pseudo-Clement, Cyprian, *De hab. virg.* and *De singularitate clericorum.*
[58] Dionysius of Alexandria (*Euseb. HE* 7, 30, 12) calls them γυναῖκες συνείσακτοι, which was later rendered in Latin as *virgines subintroductae.*
[59] Cyprian, *Ep.* 4 and 13.
[60] So the Synods of Antioch (*c.* 267–8), Elvira (canon 27), Ancyra (canon 19), Nicaea (canon 3). Jerome, *Ep.* 117, and John Chrysostom still had to take up a definite position on the matter. Later Synods: Carthage (348) canon 3; Hippo (393) canon 20; Carthage (397) canon 17; Arles (443) canon 3; Agde (510) canon 10; Toledo (531) canon 3.

rich in consequences. From this practice sprang the early monasticism of the East, which, in its first eremitical phase, was merely a transference of the life and activity of the ascetics from the Christian community into solitude, such as Athanasius's account of the eremitical period of St Antony's life records for the end of the third century. The baptismal spirituality and devotion to martyrdom of the second and third centuries, in conjunction with ascetical virginity, continued to exert influence as fundamental ideas of monasticism, and so proved their intense vitality. The vows taken by the monk were compared in value with a second baptism, and his life with a spiritual martyrdom which made him, like the actual martyr, an *athleta Christi*, while his continence ranked him in the company of those who are the brides of Christ.[61] The ideal of virginity additionally prepared the way for the concept of priestly celibacy.[62]

Within the Church as a whole the manner of life of the ascetics was an highly esteemed ideal, but nevertheless one which was always freely accepted, and only by a minority. As soon as individual Christians or groups attempted to make it a norm binding on all Christians, it inevitably led to conflicts between them and the ecclesiastical authorities. The Encratites, followers of the Syrian Tatian, represented such an ascetic ideal carried to extremes; they characteristically named themselves not after their teacher but after the ascetical principle of their life.[63] The Encratites of Mesopatamia admitted no one to baptism who did not observe absolute sexual continence, and thus forced married people who did not want to renounce matrimony into a perpetual catechumenate existence.[64] It is true that the other heretical views held by Tatian were decisive in his expulsion from the great Church about 172, but his ascetical rigorism certainly contributed to that judgment. Encratite tendencies are perceptible in many apocryphal acts of apostles, as well as in the lives of individual Christians. As long as *encrateia* was not imposed by these on every Christian as necessary for salvation, the Church could tolerate them or excuse individual cases, such as Origen's self-castration, as ascetical enthusiasm carried too far. The intense attachment of the third-century Church to the ascetical ideal can certainly be taken as a general proof of her high moral quality.

[61] Cf. E. E. Malone, *The Monk and the Martyr* (Diss. Washington 1950); J. Schmid, "Brautschaft (heilige)" in *RAC* II, 561.
[62] Cf. Origen, *In Lev. hom.* 1, 6, which demands continence of the priest, for he serves the altar.
[63] Οἱ ἐγκρατεῖς according to Irenaeus, *Adv. haer.* 1, 28, 1; and cf. Origen, *Contra Cels.* 5, 65.
[64] See A. Vööbus, *Celibacy a Requirement for Admission to Baptism in the Early Syrian Church* (Stockholm 1951).

Prayer not only maintained, as a matter of course, its position in the third century as an indispensable element in Christian worship of God, but to an increasing extent became the subject of theological reflection and practical concern for its right performance both liturgical and private. Alexandrian theologians worked devotedly at a theological interpretation of Christian prayer and endeavoured to incorporate it into their conception of Christian perfection as a whole. The Latins, Tertullian and Cyprian in particular, display in their expositions of the Our Father the greater interest of the Latin mind in questions of the actual practice of the life of prayer and in its importance for the detail of Christian daily life. For Clement of Alexandria the Christian's duty to pray is self-evident, for the soul must thank God without ceasing for all his gifts; and in the striving for perfection, prayer of petition is likewise indispensable, and it must be used to implore true gnosis and the forgiveness of sins. [65] After the example of his master, brethren and enemies are included in this prayer of the Christian, and he is mindful, too, of the conversion of the whole world to the true God. Prayer accompanies him in all he does, binds him most closely to God, makes him "walk in God". [66] Clement's best answer to the pagan reproach of ἀσέβεια (impiety) addressed to the Christians, is to point out that for them, prayer is the most holy and precious sacrifice with which to honour God. [67] With a certain hesitation he hazards the definition that prayer is "intercourse with God". [68] So the Christian consecrates his everyday life to God when he conscientiously keeps the hours of prayer and in this way bears witness to the Lord throughout his life. [69] The highest form of prayer for the true Gnostic is interior mental prayer, which Clement clearly distinguishes from vocal prayer. He does not, of course, reject the latter, but unquestionably assigns the highest rank to interior prayer: it needs no words; it is unceasing; it makes the whole life a holy day; and gives θεωρία, the vision of divine things. [70] In this distinction between vocal and mental prayer the later division of the spiritual life into active and contemplative is already indicated in a purely Christian sense. Clement is its first important pioneer.

Where Clement provided an outline sketch of prayer, Origen gives a whole monograph, which deepens and carries farther what Clement had begun. In order to gain a full view of Origen's teaching on prayer one

[65] *Strom.* 6, 113, 2; 6, 102, 1; 5, 16, 7.
[66] Ibid. 7, 62, 2 ff.; 7, 41, 4, 6; 7, 40, 3; 7, 44, 5; 7, 35, 5.
[67] Ibid. 7, 31, 7.
[68] Ibid. 7, 39, 6: ὁμιλία πρὸς τὸν θεὸν ἡ εὐχή, ὡς εἰπεῖν τολμηρότερον.
[69] Ibid. 2, 145, 6.
[70] Ibid. 7, 49, 6 ff.; 6, 102, 1; 7, 35, 6; 7, 49, 4.

must draw upon his theoretical exposition and upon the lively observations and the spontaneous prayers found in his homilies and biblical commentaries. Like Clement, Origen is profoundly aware that the life of the Christian must be a perpetual prayer, in which daily prayers have their indispensable place.[71] To be blessed, such prayer requires a certain disposition in the soul. Origen very definitely includes in this a continual defence against sin, lasting freedom from emotional disturbance, and finally interior recollection and concentration, which excludes all from without and within that cannot be consecrated to God.[72] Under such conditions, a Christian's prayer develops in an ascent by stages. The first stage being prayer of petition, which should request the great and heavenly things: the gift of gnosis and growth in virtue.[73] At the stage of the προσευχή, the praise of God is linked with prayer of petition.[74] The summit of Christian prayer is reached in interior, wordless prayer which unites the soul to God in a unique way.[75] This mirrors Origen's basic conception of a spiritual ascent by stages, ending in the loving knowledge of God in which the soul is "divinized".[76] A more concrete view of Origen's practice of prayer is given by the many actual texts of prayers which occur frequently in his homilies.[77] Somewhat surprisingly, they are often addressed to Christ, though in his treatise on prayer, Origen always maintains that prayer is to be addressed to the Father; theoretical conviction was overborne by the spontaneous devotion to Christ which is also apparent in many other ways in the homilies. Not only does Origen repeatedly exhort his hearers to pray to Jesus, but in his addresses, he himself continually turns to him in supplications of his own composition which reveal a rich and heartfelt devotion to Jesus. It is an eminently important fact in the history of spirituality, and consequently in the history of the Church, that the theory and practice of prayer represented by the Alexandrian Origen exercised an extensive influence. His teaching on prayer decisively affected the spirituality of the Eastern Church, particularly in its monastic form, and the practice of devotion to Jesus formulated in his prayers influenced, by way of Ambrose, Western mystical devotion to Jesus down to St Bernard's day.[78]

The commentaries on the Our Father by the two Latins, Tertullian and

[71] Origen, *De or.* 1, 12, 2.
[72] Ibid. 8, 1; 9, 1, 3; *Contra Cels.* 8, 17; 7, 44.
[73] The kinds of prayer are dealt with in connexion with 1 Tim. 2:1 in *De or.* 14, 2. On the prayer of petition, see also *De or.* 1, 17; 2, 2; 13, 4; *Contra Cels.* 7, 44.
[74] *De or.* 14, 2; 13, 5.
[75] *In Num. hom.* 10, 3; *Contra Cels.* 7, 44; *De or.* 9, 2; 10, 2.
[76] Cf. K. Rahner in *RAM* 13 (1932), 113–45.
[77] Cf. K. Baus in *RQ* 49 (1954), 46–55.
[78] Cf. F. Bertrand, *Mystique de Jésus chez Origène* (Paris 1951), 153 ff.

Cyprian, introduce us to a view and atmosphere of Christian prayer that is both independent of, and very different from that of the Greeks. Both of them, of course, are like the Alexandrians, profoundly convinced of the obligation of prayer. Both they and the Greeks are inspired through the example given by Christ, who prayed himself and taught how to pray;[79] they know the same times for prayer and the biblical grounds for them, and have similar ideas about the mental conditions necessary for proper prayer.[80] But the two Latins are very far removed from the lofty idealistic strain of the Greeks. Deeper speculation about the nature and dignity of interior prayer and its significance for growth in the spiritual life is alien to them, and there is certainly no hint in their writing of a theory about the various stages of prayer. Their urgent concern is with the actual concrete form of prayer and its place in the daily life of the Christian community. For them the form of prayer to be preferred is the Our Father, the new form of prayer taught by Christ, and known to the Christians alone, because they alone have God as their Father.[81] Both understand the petition for daily bread in a predominantly eucharistic sense, which Cyprian expresses with warmth and emphasis.[82] For both, humility is the right attitude in which to pray; all passions and faults must be laid aside if the prayer is to find acceptance with God.[83] A trait of the Latin organizing spirit is evident in Tertullian's detailed treatment of questions concerning the external order of prayer, such as the times for prayer — morning prayers, evening prayers, grace, prayer at the third, sixth, and ninth hours — and the physical posture of those at prayer: they are to pray with hands raised and extended, in imitation of their suffering Lord on the cross.[84] Tertullian propounds an actual theological feature in what he says about the unlimited efficacy of Christian prayer,[85] and in his exposition of the second petition of the Our Father, which like Origen he understands in a directly eschatological sense: "Yes, very soon, Lord, may thy kingdom come; that is the longing of Christians, the confounding of the pagans, the joy of the angels."[86] Perhaps Cyprian's undeniable dependence on Tertullian has sometimes caused the original contribution of the African bishop in his exposition of the Our Father to be too easily overlooked. The much greater religious warmth and persuasiveness with

---

[79] Tertullian, *De or.* 1; Cyprian, *De dom. or.* 1, 3.

[80] Tertullian, *De or.* 11–15; Cyprian, *De dom. or.* 4–6, 34. For the Greeks, cf. Clement, *Strom.* 2, 145, 1; 7, 40, 3; Origen, *De or.* 31, 2.

[81] Tertullian, *De or.* 2; Cyprian, *De dom. or.* 9–11.

[82] Tertullian, *De or.* 6; Cyprian, *De dom. or.* 18.

[83] Tertullian, *De or.* 11–14, 17; Cyprian, *De dom. or.* 4, 6.

[84] Tertullian, *De or.* 18–25; more briefly, Cyprian, *De dom. or.* 35–36.

[85] *De or.* 29.

[86] *De or.* 5.

which he speaks of prayer are to be appreciated, and he deserves further recognition for his emphatic identification of the Kingdom of God with Christ: "For whose coming we daily long, and whose early arrival we desire and long for." [87] Of paramount importance however, is the ecclesiological emphasis which he would like to see in the prayers of Christians: "When we pray, we do not pray for one but for the whole people, for we are all one"; the Christian people at prayer is joined together in the unity of the Father and the Son and the Holy Spirit; anyone who breaks this unity sins grievously, and lacks an essential condition for genuine prayer. [88]

Besides the Our Father, Tertullian and of course, Cyprian too, freely recognize improvised prayers. [89] Early Christianity had also at its disposal a collection of set prayer texts in the Old Testament Psalter. Its liturgical and private use presupposed, of course, its christianization, which must have taken place in the second century, as the singing of the psalms in divine worship and at the agape was an established custom by the beginning of the third century. [90] This christianization took place by way of a typological interpretation of the psalms, which either viewed the speaker in the psalms as Christ himself addressing the Father, or heard in them the voice of the Church recognizing in the *Dominus psalmorum* her glorified Lord and speaking directly to him. A particularly striking example of the first kind is Psalm 3, verse 6: "ego dormivi et soporatus sum et exsurrexi", which was already regarded by Justin as spoken by the Risen Christ on Easter morning. This interpretation is also found in Irenaeus and was taken over by Hippolytus and Cyprian. [91] Origen, too, has examples of praying the psalms to Christ [92] and thus illustrates the strength of the trend, for despite theoretical hesitation he cannot refrain from it. The christianization of the Psalter, which made it the prayer and hymn book absolutely preferred by the early Church, was furthered and facilitated by the importance and extent of prayer to Christ in early Christian popular devotion. This is strikingly evident in those prayers which rose spontaneously to the lips of martyrs when they were summoned to bear last testimony to their Lord. Most of these are words of gratitude to Christ for giving them the grace of bearing witness to him, or protestations that they accept death for his name's sake, or cries of supplication for Christ's strength and support in that hour of trial. A comparison of the number of prayers

[87] *De dom. or.* 13.
[88] *De dom. or.* 8, 24, 30.
[89] Cyprian, *De dom. or.* 3; Tertullian, *De or.* 9.
[90] Tertullian, *Apol.* 39, 18; Hippolytus, *Trad. apost.* (Ethiopic) in *Hennecke-Schneemelcher* 581; Πράξεις Παύλου (Hamburg 1936), 50 ff.
[91] Justin, *Dial.* 97, 1; Irenaeus, *Adv. haer.* 4, 33, 13; Hippolytus, *Comm. on Psalms,* Frag. 37 (*GCS* 1, 2, 153); Cyprian, *Test.* 2, 24.
[92] Cf. for example, *In Ioann. comm.* 19, 3; *In Psalm.* 29, 3.

addressed to Christ by the martyrs with those addressed to the Father reveals their overwhelmingly Christocentric character.[93] In the domain of popular piety there are the strikingly numerous prayers to Christ in the apocryphal acts of apostles,[94] and many of the above-mentioned prayers to Christ in Origen's homilies must have been an echo from private popular piety.

Finally, prayer addressed to Christ was expressed by turning to the East when praying. The first signs of this custom appear at the beginning of the second century, and it established itself widely in East and West in the third century. The grounds adduced for the custom are theologically notable: people prayed facing the East because the return of the Lord was awaited from that direction and because Paradise, the desire of all Christians, lies there.[95] This manner of praying to Christ therefore had an eschatological significance. For some Christian circles in the Greek and Syrian East, it was also a way of expressing the theological contrast to Judaism, whose followers prayed facing the Temple in Jerusalem. Another custom had been associated with it since the second century, that of praying before a crucifix, wooden or painted, so arranged that those praying stood facing the East. Here too the early Christian texts plainly indicate an eschatological motive for this custom: as a sign of the Lord's triumph, the cross will precede him, on his second coming, from the East.[96] This emphasis on the crucifix in the Christian's position at prayer was probably based on the extensive use of the sign of the cross in both private devotion and the liturgy, many testimonies to which are found in the writers of the third century.[97] Tertullian's statement can stand for many: "Whenever we go out or depart, at the beginning or end of anything, when we dress or put on our shoes, before the bath or before sitting down to table, when putting on the lights, when we lie down to rest or sit down on a chair, in every action of daily life, we sign our foreheads with the sign of the cross."[98] The texts of prayers and the position adopted for prayer therefore show private prayer in the early Christian Church as a whole that was centred to a large extent on Christ and on the cross.

[93] The proportion is about 6:1; cf. a selection of these prayers by K. Baus in *TThZ* 62 (1953), 23–8.
[94] A survey is found in E. v. d. Goltz, *Das Gebet in der ältesten Christenheit* (Leipzig 1901), 343–56.
[95] Cf. particularly, F. J. Dölger, *Sol salutis*, 136–70, 198–242. In the first concluding hymn of Methodius' *Symp.*, the virgins go in solemn procession eastwards to meet the heavenly bridegroom, Christ.
[96] This has been established by E. Peterson, "Das Kreuz und das Gebet nach Osten" in *Frühkirche, Judentum und Gnosis* (Freiburg i. Br. 1959).
[97] Cf. F. J. Dölger, "Beiträge zur Geschichte des Kreuzzeichens" in *JbAC* 1 (1958), 5–19; 2 (1959), 15–22; 3 (1960), 11–16; 4 (1961), 5–17.
[98] *De cor.* 3, 4.

The ascetical enthusiasm of the third century also led to a considerable practice of fasting both in connexion with liturgical worship and in the private devotion of Christians. The weekly fasts on Wednesdays and Fridays that had descended from apostolic times[99] became more firmly established and received a further development in the *statio* of the North African church. In Tertullian's time the *statio* was still quite definitely an ascetical exercise freely undertaken; it lasted until the ninth hour (3 p.m.), and was linked with a special divine service.[100] This latter, however, must be understood to have been the celebration of the eucharist, which would take place at the usual time before sunrise. The high esteem of Station fasting among Christians of North Africa can be judged from the refusal of many of the faithful to take part in the celebration of the Eucharist on Station days, because they thought the reception of Communion would break the fast.[101] In the East, the observation of the weekly fasts was, according to the evidence of the Syrian *Didascalia*, early imposed as an obligation.[102] In Carthage, Station fasting was sometimes extended to Saturday; the Roman church must also have known this custom, and it is encountered in Spain at the end of the third century.[103] The Church had to defend the voluntary character of Station fasting against the rigorism of Montanists and Encratites who represented it as an obligation strictly binding on all Christians. At this period, too, the motive for the choice of the two fast days in the week changed; while earlier it emphasized the independence of the Christian custom from the Jewish one (the Jews kept Monday and Thursday as fast days), now it was the connexion of the two days with the events of our Lord's Passion that was indicated: the betrayal by Judas on a Wednesday and death on the cross on a Friday. Thus fasting on these days was understood to be a fast of mourning and grief.[104]

The high value placed on fasting by the Church authorities is particularly evident from the various ways in which they incorporated it into the liturgy. As preparation for the feast of Easter, a Passover fast had been early introduced, but its duration differed from local church to local church and could extend over one, two, or even six days.[105] The baptismal fast of which there is evidence as early as the *Didache*, and in Justin, and which at first only lasted one or two days,[106] was now extended further; in the

---

[99] *Did.* 8, 1; Hermas, *Past. Sim.* 5, 1, 2.

[100] Tertullian, *De ieiun.* 2, 10, 12–14.

[101] Tertullian, *De or.* 19; *De cor.* 3.

[102] *Didasc.* 5, 14, 15.

[103] Tertullian, *De ieiun.* 14; Hippolytus, *In Dan. comm.* 4, 20, 3; Synod. Illib., canon 26, and cf. J. Schümmer, *Die altchristliche Fastenpraxis* (Münster 1933), 152–9.

[104] Tertullian, *De ieiun.* 10; *Didasc.* 5, 14, 15.

[105] Tertullian, *De ieiun.* 2; Irenaeus, in *Euseb. HE* 5, 24; *Trad. apost.* 29 (64 Botte); *Didasc.* 5, 18; Dionysius of Alexandria, *Ep. ad Basil.* 1.

[106] *Did.* 7, 4; Justin, *Apol.* 61, 2; *Trad. apost.* 20 (48 Botte).

first period of preparation for baptism it consisted of restriction to bread, water, and salt, but in the days immediately preceding baptism it involved total abstention from food and drink.[107] The baptismal fast was envisaged in close relation to prayer, which fasting effectively supports; it was also considered a means of atoning for former sins and of preparing for the reception of the Spirit.[108] Finally, fasting became an extremely important factor in the penitential discipline of the early Christian Church generally, which imposed on the sinner for the duration of his penance restrictions on food and drink and sometimes days of strict fasting as well. Here, too, the significance of the fast was seen to be in the support it gave to the atoning prayer with which the sinner turned to God; but the Church always stressed in addition the salutary character of such penitential fasts in themselves.[109]

Fasting as a means to gaining mastery over concupiscence and unregulated sense pleasure and consequently as a way to higher perfection, found special favour in early Christian ascetic circles. It brought with it the danger of over-emphasis, and this sometimes found expression in heroic record-breaking performances such as are reported repeatedly from the monastic groups which superseded the ascetics.[110] As opposed to such aberrations, Christian authors very early emphasized that what was decisive was the spirit, a genuine penitential attitude and self-denial, which alone give bodily fasting its value.[111] Others stressed corporal works of mercy to the neighbour as a motive for fasting, for by its means a brother in need could be given more help.[112] The most valuable views here also are those that envisaged fasting in close conjunction with prayer; which can be given greater efficacy by this ascetical attitude.[113] Similarly efficacious was the widespread conception of fasting as an important preparation for every kind of reception of the Spirit, so that fasting became an indispensable requirement for men of the Spirit, prophets, teachers, and bishops.[114] This explains the inner link between prophecy and fasting which is encountered in Montanism; fasting there became an absolutely necessary condition for the gift of prophecy, and Tertullian in his work De ieiunio bitterly attacked from his own standpoint the great Church which should not approve such overrating of an ascetical practice.[115]

[107] Cf. J. Schümmer, op. cit. 166–8.

[108] Tertullian, De bapt. 20; De ieiun. 8, 12; Clement of Alex. Exc. ex Theod. 83, 84.

[109] Tertullian, De paen. 9–11; Ad ux. 2, 8; Didasc. 2, 16, 2; 2, 41, 6; Cyprian, De laps. 35.

[110] Euseb. De mart. Pal. 3; Palladius, Hist. Laus. 1–2, 11, 18, 22, 36, 38, 43, 45, 48, 52.

[111] Hermas, Past. Sim. 5, 1, 4; 5, 36; Justin, Dial. 15; Origen, In Lev. hom. 10, 2.

[112] Aristides, Apol. 15.

[113] Tertullian, Apol. 40, 13; De fuga 1.

[114] Cf. Acts, 13:2 and also Hermas, Past. Vis. 2, 2, 1; 3, 1, 2; 3, 10, 6 ff.; Tertullian, De ieiun. 13; Fragm. Murat. 9–16.

[115] Cf. particularly R. Arbesmann, "Fasting and Prophecy in Pagan and Christian Antiquity" in Tr 7 (1949–51), 52–71.

The ideals of Christian perfection just described, represented, as has already been emphasized, maximum demands, the achievement of which was only possible to an *élite* and consequently to a minority among the Christians. There arises, therefore, the question how the great majority of the community members in town and country lived their daily religious lives in pagan surroundings and within a secular civilization determined by pagan principles. Unfortunately the sources, even for the third century, still do not provide very much information on this, and do not make it possible to draw a complete picture of Christian life valid for all the territories where Christianity had spread at that time. Most informative are the sources for North Africa, where the leading writers Tertullian and Cyprian, because of their marked concern with the practical questions of daily religious life reveal much that is interesting. In addition to these men, the Alexandrian teachers Clement and Origen must be mentioned, for they frequently speak of similar features in the Christian daily life of the Egyptian communities.

Any attempt to estimate objectively the achievements of Christianity in this domain must indicate very plainly the difficulties that the implementation of Christian moral ideals inevitably met with day after day. First of all, there were the afflictions to which Christian minorities are liable in any period of Christian missionary activity when forced to form and establish themselves in the midst of a pagan environment encompassing every section of private and public life. A large number of professions and trades directly served the polytheism of later antiquity and the Christians had to exclude themselves from these if they were not to imperil their own religious convictions.[116] The whole pagan atmosphere further presented a perpetual temptation to relapse into former habits of life, and this demanded of all Christians a renunciation that had to be continually and precisely renewed in daily life. The sexual licentiousness which characterized moral life in later antiquity particularly necessitated a very high degree of self-discipline. This itself created a test case where the Christian moral ideal had to prove its real quality.

The sources show that precisely in the third century, the Christian communities were exposed to searching trials which they did not entirely withstand. In the longer periods of peace which that age provided, the poison of the surrounding pagan atmosphere could exercise its slow but enduring effect. This became terrifyingly evident when a powerful wave of persecution such as those of Decius and Diocletian broke upon the Christian communities as exceptional tribulations. The large number of

---

[116] See page 277 above, in the description of the catechumenate.

those who lapsed in the years 249–50 revealed a considerable slackening of Christian self-discipline, a condition which could oppose no decisive resistance to the tempting amenities of a pagan civilization. The picture which Cyprian had to draw speaks for itself.[117] Eusebius too, in his description of the general situation of Christianity before the outbreak of the Diocletian persecution was forced to indicate many suspicious features. Among these were especially the slackening of moral discipline and not a few lamentable quarrels of Church leaders among themselves. The Christians "like so many pagans . . . piled sin upon sin", and Eusebius was moved to explain the persecution as a divine judgment.[118] What we have to say about the question of penance will presently show that grave transgressions by Christians, especially those of a sexual kind, again and again moved the Church authorities to serious admonition and strict measures regarding atonement. But despite these undeniable dark shadows in the picture of general Christian life in the third century, it is indisputable that Christianity succeeded at that time in raising the moral level of the various churches and communities high above that of the pagan world around them.

Marriage and the Family

This is particularly striking in the matter of marriage and the family. It is true that Tertullian's description of the beauty of Christian marriage is an ideal picture which transfigures reality, but it proves that this ideal was recognized and that earnest efforts were made to realize it. Ignatius of Antioch had already recommended that the contracting of matrimony be sanctioned by the bishop. In Tertullian's time, too, Christians celebrated their marriage in the presence of the *ecclesia,* and had it sealed with a blessing, although this cannot have signified an actual liturgical rite or an indispensable participation of the bishop at the marriage in that period. The inner harmony of such a marriage derived from the common religious convictions of the two partners, and it drew its strength in good days and bad from a common sharing in the eucharistic repast.[119] As such conditions could not be present in marriages between Christians and pagans, these were disapproved of by the Church. Furthermore the Christian party was exposed all too easily to contact with pagan worship and the accomplishment of many religious duties and customs of the faith was made difficult by such an arrangement. When Cyprian lists the abuses in the North African church which called down the judgment of the Decian persecution, he assigns a special place to the marriages between Christians and unbelievers, through

---

[117] See above, page 224.
[118] *Euseb. HE* 8, 1, 7–9.
[119] Ignatius, *Ad Polyc.* 5; Tertullian, *Ad ux.* 2, 8.

which "the members of Christ were abandoned to the pagans". Consequently, such marriages were expressly forbidden by the Church, and parents who gave their consent to the marriage of their daughter to a heretic, a Jew, or a pagan priest, incurred heavy ecclesiastical punishment.[120] The indissolubility of Christian marriage which had since St Paul found its deepest ground in its symbolical representation of the union of Christ and the Church (Eph 5:32; 1 Cor 7:10ff.), is emphasized by most writers of the third century.[121] The Church was also concerned with maintaining the sanctity of matrimony by preserving conjugal fidelity and reverence for children. Adultery was strictly punished by ecclesiastical penitiential discipline, any kind of abortion was proscribed as murder, and the exposing of children after birth was condemned. It was here that the demands of Christian ethics came into sharpest conflict with pagan lasciviousness or the Roman legal view, which regarded only the born child as a human being.[122]

Within Christian marriage of this kind, the position of the wife was that of a partner with equal rights, and Christianity thereby showed in principle a far higher regard for her than most of the pagan religions held at that time. Second marriages were not looked upon with favour; they were not of course forbidden as they were among the Montanists, but in accordance with the trend of the age towards asceticism, they were viewed as signs of diminished moral effort and even stigmatized by the apologist Athenagoras as "a respectable adultery". This opinion is not merely an isolated one, it corresponded to the Church's view which, on account of it, forbade clerics to take part in the celebrations of such marriages and treated a second marriage as an impediment to the assumption of or continuance in the clerical state. A third or fourth marriage was very definitely held to be a serious failure regarding the demands of Christian discipline and excluded one, as Origen said, from the circle of the perfect.[123]

Early Christian Works of Mercy

A criterion of the value of Christian ethical principles in daily life is provided by the way in which the commandment of Christian love for one's neighbour is fulfilled. Practical exercise of active charity towards a needy

[120] Tertullian, *Ad ux.* 2, 4–6; Cyprian, *De laps.* 6; Synod. Illib., canons 15–17; Synod. Arel. canon 11.
[121] Clement of Alexandria, *Strom.* 2, 23; Origen, *In Matth. hom.* 14, 16; Tertullian, *Adv. Marc.* 4, 34; *De pat.* 12; *De monog.* 9.
[122] Synod. Illib., canons 14, 47, 64, 70, 78. Athenagoras, *Suppl.* 35; Tertullian, *Apol.* 9, 8; Min. Felix, *Oct.* 30, 2; Hippolytus, *Refut.* 9, 12, 25, and cf. F. J. Dölger in *AuC*, IV (1934), 23–55.
[123] Athenagoras, *Suppl.* 33; cf. Hermas, *Pastor. Mand.* 4; Theophilus, *Autol.* 3, 15; Clement of Alexandria, *Strom.* 2, 23; 3, 11; Origen, *In Luc. hom.* 17, 10; *In Ier. hom.* 20; *In Matth. comm.* 14, 22; Synod. Ancyr., can. 19; Neocaes., can. 3 and 17.

brother in the faith or towards a pagan afflicted with illness or misfortune was, in very striking contrast to the corresponding pagan attitude, an undeniable title of glory in the early Christian Church. One of the earliest forms of charitable activity was the "agape", meals in the Christian community which were intended to strengthen community spirit among their members of different social rank, but which at the same time provided the possibility of extending effective material help, in a tactful way, to the poor and needy within the community. They were held either in the private dwelling of a well-to-do member of the congregation or in premises belonging to the church with the bishop presiding — he could also be represented by a priest or a deacon — and inaugurating the meal with a prayer said over the gifts that had been brought. The bishop discussed with those in charge questions concerning the life of the community, and made sure that the absent sick and widows also received their share of the gifts. Sometimes the widows were invited separately by a fellow-Christian or foodstuffs were taken to them in their houses. The abuses that occurred here and there in connexion with the agape do not lessen the value of these meetings which, according to Clement of Alexandria, represented an original form of Christian sociability in marked contrast to pagan custom, and were intended to prevent social conflicts arising within the churches.[124]

Tertullian in his *Apologeticum* gives an instructive glimpse of the beginning of the third century. There was a sort of common fund for the voluntary contributions of members and from it the poor were fed, old people in need looked after, orphans and destitute children cared for, brethren in prison helped, and those condemned to forced labour in the mines given support.[125] A special kind of early Christian charitable work was hospitality, taking in and looking after, with warm generosity, brethren in the faith who were travelling through. This custom was already praised in apostolic and subapostolic times and was no less esteemed and recommended in the third century. Origen made hospitality the theme of two of his homilies. Cyprian left money with one of his priests to be spent on strangers in need during his absence. The Syrian *Didascalia* insistently urges care for strangers on the bishop, and the Synods of Elvira and Arles stress it too. In the fourth century there grew from this charitable obligation a comprehensive organization which established hostels and hospices.[126] The impression made

---

[124] Clement of Alexandria, *Paed.* 2, 1, 4 ff.; Tertullian, *Apol.* 39, and cf. E. Dekkers, *Tertullianus en de geschiedenis der liturgie* (Brussels-Amsterdam 1947), 67–71; Hippolytus, *Trad. apost.* 26–7 (57–62 Botte); *Didasc.* 2, 28, 1–3.

[125] *Apol.* 39.

[126] Cf. G. Stählin in *ThW* V, 1–36 (φιλοξενία). According to *Euseb. HE* 4, 26, 2, Melito of Sardes wrote Περὶ φιλοξενίας. Origen, *In Gen. hom.* 4 and 5; Cyprian, *Ep.* 7; *Didasc.* 2, 58, 6; Synod. illib., can. 25; Synod. Arel., can. 9. See also Justin, *Apol.* 67, 6; Tertullian, *Ad ux.* 2, 4.

on pagan circles by this kind of practical charity is confirmed, despite himself, by Emperor Julian when he wrote that Christianity had been most lastingly furthered "by philanthropy to strangers and care for the burial to the dead".[127] The last-mentioned feature, concern for the worthy burial of poor brethren in the faith, was felt to be a duty of love, and was specially praised as something that characterized Christianity as opposed to paganism. Whenever possible, the dead were buried among their deceased brethren in the faith, and love was shown them beyond the grave by having the eucharistic sacrifice offered for them and by being mindful of them at prayer.[128]

Pre-Constantinian Christianity had, of course, no slave problem in any sense that would have made it work for the abolition of slavery, but early Christian charity could not fail to be interested in the lot of the slaves. It contributed decisively to the improvement of their condition by recognizing slaves who became Christians as equal brothers and sisters with the rest of the faithful and by according them complete equality of rights[129]. Ecclesiastical offices, including that of bishop, were open to a slave. It did not detract at all from the reputation of the *Shepherd* that its author Hermas had been born a slave.[130] Slaves among the martyrs, both men and women, were held in unqualified esteem; Blandina, for instance, in Lyons and Felicity in Carthage. Degrading treatment of slaves by Christian masters was severely censured and, if need be, punished with ecclesiastical penalties. On the other hand, slaves who patently misunderstood "Christian freedom" and tried to have their freedom purchased from the common fund of the community were reminded of the deeper sense of Christian service which made it possible for them to bear their position for the honour of God.[131]

Christian brotherly love had really to prove itself in the times of extraordinary catastrophes which were not lacking in the third century. Dionysius of Alexandria sang a paean to the Christian readiness for sacrifice which distinguished the laity as well as the clergy in Alexandria during an epidemic about the year 250. Without fear of infection, they had cared for their sick brethren and given their lives thereby, while the pagans had avoided their sick relatives and abandoned their dead without burial. When plague was raging in Carthage, Cyprian summoned his flock by word and example to organized relief action which did not deny care and attention to the pagans. And once again the attitude of the Christians contrasted

---

[127] *Sozom. HE* 5, 15.
[128] Aristides, *Apol.* 15; Tertullian, *Apol.* 39; Lactantius, *Div. instit.* 6, 12; Cyprian, *Ep.* 67, 6. Tertullian, *De monog.* 10; *De cor,* 3; *De exhort. cast.* 11; Cyprian, *Ep.* 1 and 12.
[129] Tatian, *Or.* 11; Aristides, *Apol.* 15; Irenaeus, *Adv. haer.* 4, 21, 3; Tertullian, *De cor.* 13; Euseb. *De mart. Pal.* 11, 1.
[130] See the references in E. J. Jonkers in *Mnemosyne* 10 (1942), 286–302.
[131] Synod. Illib., can. 5. — Ignatius, *Ad Polyc.* 4, 3.

honourably with that of their pagan fellow-citizens during an epidemic in Maximinus Daia's time, when they cared for the hungry and the sick without distinction of creed.[132]

Practical Christian charity also extended to any communities which were in special need in any of the territories to which Christianity had spread. They were helped with an impressive, matter-of-fact spontaneity which reveals a sense of community among the faithful of the whole Church, and which was shown by no other religious group of the time. The sources give the strong impression that the conduct of the Roman church was felt to be exemplary in this regard. Apparently the church of Rome was immediately ready to give active assistance whenever news was received of special need in any community no matter how remote. What Dionysius of Corinth praised in this respect in 170 is also valid for the third century: "From the beginning it was your custom to do good to all the brethren in many ways and to send assistance to many communities in towns everywhere. In this way you have lightened the poverty of the needy, supported the brethren in the mines and so, like Romans, held fast to a custom handed down from of old by your fathers. Your blessed bishop Soter not only maintained this custom but carried it further."[133] For Dionysius of Alexandria reports about a hundred years later that Rome regularly sent relief to the churches in Arabia and Syria, and in Cappadocia it was not forgotten in the days of Basil that the Roman church under Bishop Dionysius (259–69) sent funds there so that Christian prisoners might be ransomed from pagan rulers. A remark by Eusebius implies that Rome gave similar help during the Diocletian persecution also.[134] A similar sense of responsibility for other churches distinguished Cyprian of Carthage; he had a collection made among his flock for the communities in Numidia and its considerable yield was employed in caring for their prisoners.[135]

The practical accomplishment of the tasks imposed by the duties of brotherly love required, in the bigger communities of the third century, a certain administrative organization and personnel. Women were increasingly employed in order to supplement the efforts of deacons who were the appointed helpers of the bishops in charitable welfare work; they were in any case indispensable in the care of their own sex. Widows were the ones first considered for such work; they were regarded as a special order within the community and held in high regard on account of Timothy 5:3–16. Only approved women were received — a judgement on this was a task of the bishop — without consecration and without prescribed vows. They were

---

[132] *Euseb. HE* 7, 22, 7–10 and 9, 8, 1; Cyprian, *De mortal. passim;* Pontius, *Vita Cypr.* 9.

[133] *Euseb. HE* 4, 23, 10; cf. Ignatius, *Ad Rom. proem.:* ἡ προκαθημένη τῆς ἀγάπης.

[134] *Euseb. HE* 7, 5, 2; 4, 23, 9; Basil, *Ep.* 70.

[135] Cyprian, *Ep.* 76–79, especially *Ep.* 62.

particularly employed in private pastoral work in the home and in missionary work among women. They devoted themselves to educating orphans, worked as nurses, and sometimes undertook the care of those in prison.[136] From the second century onwards, unmarried women were also admitted for such purposes, and later for them as well as for the widows engaged in charitable works the title of deaconess was used. When the order of widows and virgins, through its adoption of an ascetical manner of life, detached itself more and more from this kind of task, the function of the deaconess became, especially in Syrian territory, a definite office in the community; she was now especially concerned in looking after women catechumens and candidates for baptism, in domestic pastoral work with Christian women in pagan families, and in caring for sick women. In the fourth century, as a consequence of the entry of the pagan masses into the Church, the office of deaconess increased even more in importance and attained its definitive form and full development.

As the office of deaconess cannot be shown to have existed in the Latin West before the fourth century, the widows who were already known to Hermas in Rome as a special order, probably retained the same functions.[137] The deliberate creation of an institution so adapted to the talents and disposition of women is to that extent a praiseworthy original achievement of the early Christian Church. The benefits it brought caused later centuries to maintain it in principle even if in ever-different forms.

Christian charitable activity inevitably confronted the Church with a series of social problems, such as those of property and wealth, labour and poverty, which obliged her to adopt definite positions. The most detailed treatment of these is found in Clement of Alexandria, though his views cannot be taken as those of the Church as a whole. He maintains in principle the New Testament detachment from property and wealth, though his estimate of these is not so pessimistic as that of some other Christians. Wealth in itself does not exclude from the kingdom of heaven, just as poverty alone cannot guarantee access to it, but Clement is also profoundly convinced of the serious danger which wealth brings to any Christian. Whether wealth and property prove a curse to a Christian depends on whether or not he is the slave of these possessions and makes them the business of his life. Those who possess inner freedom in regard to them and bear their loss calmly, belong to the poor in spirit whom the Lord declared to be blessed. A right use is made of them when they are put to the use of the brethren.[138] Hence the high

---

[136] Clement of Alexandria, *Paed.* 3, 97; Origen, *De or.* 28, 4; *In Luc. hom.* 17, 10; *In Is. hom.* 6, 3; *Euseb. HE* 6, 43, 11; *Didasc.* 3, 1, 2; 3, 21. Tertullian, *De virg. vel.* 9; *Ad. ux.* 1, 7; *De exhort. cast.* 13.

[137] The name "deaconess" occurs for the first time at the Council of Nicaea, canon 19. — *Didasc.* 3 12, 1–4; Hermas, *Past. Vis.* 1, 4, 3.

[138] Clement of Alexandria, *Quis div. salv. passim; Paed.* 3, 35; *Strom.* 2, 22, 4; 4, 31, 1.

praise of almsgiving that is found in most writers of the age culminates, as far as pre-Constantinian times are concerned, in Cyprian's special treatise on this subject. Already in the so-called *Second Letter of Clement,* almsgiving had been ranked higher than fasting and prayer and with Cyprian it attains the rank of a means of grace by which the Christian can atone for daily faults committed after baptism. [139] Without doubt the bishop's exhortations to benevolence were willingly followed by many Christians, as is proved by the forms of Christian charitable action which we have just described. Some in ascetical enthusiasm gave all they had or distributed their gifts without discretion, so that Origen for example utters the warning that the situation of anyone in need should be carefully investigated and appropriate help given. [140]

For all her welfare work, however, the Church in no way failed to proclaim the high personal worth of labour and she opposed the view of antiquity which regarded manual labour as an evil and a bitter necessity, as a sign of lack of freedom and of slavery. She followed the Jewish and New Testament pattern in this and emphasized that even simple work was estimable and was preferable to the idle luxury of many pagans. Church ordinances simply regarded work as a duty and proclaimed that a Christian who was capable of working should not receive any relief from the community. [141] It is only with Augustine that deeper reflection on the moral and religious meaning of labour began and led to the formation of a Christian ethic of work. The contribution which the Church of the third century made to the practical solution of the problem of labour was so comprehensive that it attracted the attention of the pagans. Tertullian reports how many of them, in light of this, said with ironic disdain, "Look how they love one another!" [142] What was meant as derision, was in the last analysis high praise.

The Attitude of Early Christianity to Secular Civilization and Culture

It was in accord with the fundamentally ascetical attitude of early Christianity that it regarded with marked reserve the amenities of late-antiquity civilization. Though Tertullian's rigorism may have gone too far in its radical rejection of most of civilization's benefits as the inventions of pagan demons, even level-headed men condemned pagan luxury. Clement of Alexandria, for example, repudiated everything that served an exaggerated

---

[139] Clement, *Ad Cor.* 2, 16; Cyprian, *De op. et eleem.* 1.
[140] Cf. Hermas, *Pastor. Mand.* 4–6; Origen, *In Matth. comm.* 61.
[141] *Did.* 12, 2–5; Aristides, *Apol.* 15; Tertullian, *De idol.* 5, 12; *Apol.* 41; Clement of Alexandria, *Paed.* 3, 11; *Didasc.* 2, 4, 3.
[142] *Apol.* 39.

cultivation of beauty and the body and which degenerated into pleasure-seeking luxury, though he by no means opposed reasonable care for health and a moderate use of jewellery.[143] The great threats to the Christian ideal of morality represented by pagan entertainments, gladiatorial contests, theatrical shows, and dances, were deliberately shunned if for no other reason than their connexion with idolatry, even though this was often no longer very perceptible. But the discussions which Tertullian and Novatian had to engage in on the subject show that many Christians found it difficult to free themselves from their deep-rooted liking for these things.[144]

The estimate of pagan literature and learning by Christian writers of the third century is very mixed. The Greeks with some reservations show themselves far readier than the Latins (excepting Lactantius) to attribute importance to them. Clement of Alexandria could not concur in the opinion of those who regarded philosophy as an invention of the devil. He even accorded to Greek philosophy a providential significance as a preparation for Christianity, while admitting that some of its representatives, in their preoccupation with words and style, had let themselves be misled into losing sight of the relevant content. Philosophical thought, even in Christianity, can still help to prepare the way for faith. In literature, Clement sets a positive value on tragedy because it teaches men to raise their eyes heavenwards.[145] Origen, too, felt and expressed open-minded sympathy with many achievements of secular learning. In his controversy with Celsus he defended himself against the latter's accusation that he was illogical in adducing the testimony of pagan philosophers in favour of the immortality of the soul; he also contested the assertion that the dialectical method was rejected by Christians. Origen recognized the importance of secular studies for Christian instruction, but compared unfavourably the sophistry and rhetoric of many teachers with the simplicity and conscientiousness of the evangelists.[146] The attitude of Hippolytus was much more reserved. He explained the rise of heresies by their dependence on Greek philosophies, though he still gave Greek literature preference over the wisdom of Egypt, or of Babylon and the Chaldees.[147]

On the Latin side, Minucius Felix arrived at a radical repudiation of pagan poetry and literature, the mythological content of which rendered it unsuitable, he considered, for use in Christian education of young people. He was just as unwilling to overlook philosophical scepticism in the question

---

[143] Tertullian, *De cor. passim; De cultu fem. passim;* Clement of Alexandria, *Paed.* 2, 8 and 11–12; 3, 2 and 10–11; Min. Felix, *Oct.* 12, 38; Cyprian, *De laps.* 6.

[144] *De spect. passim,* especially 1; Novatian, *De spect.* 2–3.

[145] Clement of Alexandria, *Strom.* 6, 17, 156; 6, 8, 66; 6, 17, 153; 1, 5, 28; 6, 16, 151; 5, 14, 122; *Protr.* 4, 59.

[146] Origen, *Contra Cels.* 3, 81; 6, 7; 6, 14; 3, 39.

[147] Hippolytus, *Refut. I proem.;* 10, 5; 10, 34.

of knowledge of God, though he passes a favourable judgment on the endeavours of other thinkers to arrive at a true conception of God.[148] Tertullian's attitude was of a particularly complex nature and was, of course, expressed with varying intensity and differently based according to his theme and the moment of writing. In his early apologetic works, the possibility of attributing some value to philosophical endeavour is at least indirectly conceded when Tertullian himself quotes the critical works of pagan philosophers on religion for the purposes of his own argument.[149] In his polemical works of controversy against heresies his judgment on the value of philosophy is more sceptical; he makes philosophy at least partly responsible for erroneous doctrine and its theses are only utilizable when they agree with Christian truth.[150] His practical, ascetical writings then reveal intense pessimism in his judgment of all pagan literature, which can make scarcely any contribution to the formation of Christian moral life. Consequently, the profession of teacher in pagan schools is intolerable for a Christian; Tertullian could not conceive of anyone teaching something of which he was not genuinely convinced.[151] Here something of the contradictions in Tertullian's soul become apparant. He himself possessed a comprehensive knowledge of pagan literature and learning which he often placed in a very distinguished manner at the service of his work as a Christian writer. Yet he contested in an increasingly radical manner, and as it were despite himself, the idea that these studies possessed any worth whatsoever for the culture of a Christian. Cyprian, as a man of deeds, only expressed himself sporadically on these questions; according to him, the truths of Christian faith have no need of rhetoric; pagan tragedy only taught immoral behaviour, pagan ethics failed to provide motives for virtue and dealt with empty words, "but we are philosophers not in words but in deeds".[152] Even more incisive in form is the uncompromising rejection of pagan literature found in the apocryphal writings of the third century that are attributed to Cyprian. It is only shortly before the turning-point under Constantine that in Lactantius there is found a Christian writing in Latin whose regard for the greatness of the past of Rome made possible a more favourable estimate of its literary achievements. As a former teacher of rhetoric, he also saw some value in this branch of knowledge, and he found more in philosophy, which teaches how to distinguish truth and falsity, even though pagan philosophy had often failed. Cicero remained for him *eloquentiae unicum exemplar,* and he esteemed Virgil as the *poeta summus*

---

[148] Min. Felix, *Oct.* 23, 1; 23, 8; 38, 5; 20, 1–2; 14, 2; 31, 1.
[149] *Ad nat.* 1, 10; 2, 4–7; 2, 16; *Apol.* 14, 19, 24, 46–47.
[150] *De praesc.* 7; 43; *De resurr. carn.* 3; *De an.* 2.
[151] *De spect.* 30; *De pat.* 1; *De paen.* 1; *De cor.* 10.
[152] *Ad Don.* 2; 8–9; *De bono pat.* 2–3.

of Latin literature, but in regard to the theatre he expressed certain reservations.[153]

The counterpart to the predominantly unfavourable estimate of pagan literature and philosophy made by the majority of third-century Christian writers was their proud awareness that in the the Old Testament, the Gospels, Epistles and other documents of apostolic tradition, they possessed an intellectual patrimony far superior to the wisdom of the Greeks. The works of the apologists and exegetes and the achievements of the writers of Alexandria and North Africa who professed the Christian faith, represented in the eyes of their fellow-believers an intellectual life which provided a perfectly adequate substitute for what they had given up. If Christianity in the third century was not yet able to develop any systematic and specifically Christian ideal of culture, it nevertheless laid foundations upon which a later age could build.

The Early Christian Church and the Pagan State

Of particular interest is the relation which developed in the third century between the pagan State and the Church. The Christian society became clearly aware of her growing inner strength and felt herself to be the "great Church". This increase in strength within and without was not hidden from the pagan State either, and it now reckoned with her as a power that required the adoption of a new attitude. This consciousness existed on both sides and is most strikingly revealed by Cyprian's proud remark that the emperor Decius heard the news of the rebellion of a rival usurper much more calmly than the announcement of the election of a new Bishop of Rome.[154] Both sides considered the relationship afresh and the outcome was of far-reaching importance for the period that followed. Among the Christians there was really only one voice at the beginning of the century that expressed a radical rejection of the Roman State; Hippolytus saw the power of Satan behind the Roman *imperium,* he envisioned it as represented by the first beast in the Apocalypse (13:1 f.) and the fourth beast in Daniel (chapter 7); in diabolical imitation the Roman empire copied the faithful Christian people which the Lord had gathered together from all nations and tongues.[155] Such a judgment expresses the overwhelming pressure that sometimes weighed upon a Christendom fixed within a structure of power that worshipped its emperor as a god. The position of the Alexandrian teachers was quite different. Clement was fundamentally loyal to the pagan

---

[153] *Div. instit.* 1, 1, 9; 3, 13, 17 ff.; *Epit.* 25, 7 ff.; on Cicero and Virgil: *De opif.* 20, 5; *Div. instit.* 1, 19, 3.
[154] *Ep.* 55, 9.
[155] *In Dan. comm.* 4, 9; *De antichr.* 25.

State when he affirmed the obligation of taxes and military service and recognized Roman law; if that State persecuted the Church, the hand of Providence was to be worshipped.[156] The only limit to this recognition was set by the cult of the emperor and the idolatry encouraged by the State. Origen is the first to attempt to cope theoretically with the relation between the Church and the pagan State. On the basis of Romans 1:13 ff., he derives the power of the *Imperium Romanum* from God, who has conferred judicial authority on it in particular. To the intrusive and insistent question of how a State authority that came from God could combat the faith and religion of the Christians, he answered that all the gifts of God can be abused and that those who held the power of the State would have to render an account before the judgment-seat of God.[157] God's providence permitted persecutions but always gave back peace again.[158] In principle the Christian showed loyalty to this State and followed all its laws as long as they did not stand in contradiction to the clear demands of his faith, as, for instance, the required recognition of the cult of the emperor did.[159] Origen, however, thought that a special providential mission had been assigned to the Roman empire; its unity which comprised the civilized world of that time and the *pax Romana* effective within it, had according to God's will smoothed the way for the Christian mission and so the empire acted, ultimately, in the service of the faith.[160] Tertullian, too, for all his bold defence of the freedom of the Christian conscience in the face of the Roman State, was profoundly convinced that it was under the authority of God. As the God of the Christians is therefore also the God of the emperor, they pray for the emperor's well-being and in fact for the continuance of the Roman Government.[161] Tertullian's positive affirmation of the Roman State, in principle, is not altered by the frequent reservations he has to express regarding political activity by Christians. These latter spring from his conception of a considerable permeation of public life by Satanic influences which make Christians strangers in this world despite their loyalty as citizens.[162]

It is not surprising that with so much recognition in principle of the authority of the Roman State, contacts in practice between it and the Church became frequent in the third century. Origen could lecture to the womenfolk

---

[156] *Paed.* 2, 14, 1; 3, 91, 3; 2, 117, 2; 3, 91, 2; *Strom.* 1, 171 and 4, 79, 1.

[157] *In Rom. comm.* 9, 26.

[158] *Contra Cels.* 8, 70.   [159] *In Rom. comm.* 9, 29.

[160] *Contra Cels.* 2, 30.

[161] *Apol.* 30; 32; 39. Dionysius of Alexandria also stresses prayer by the Christians for the emperor: *Euseb. HE* 7, 1. The prayer *pro salute imperatorum* is an inheritance from very early Christian times, cf. L. Biehl, *Das liturgische Gebet für Kaiser und Reich* (Paderborn 1937).

[162] *De idol.* 17; *De cor.* 13.

of the Syrian rulers in Antioch; his correspondence with Emperor Philippus Arabs is a significant sign of tolerance. At the beginning of the reign of Valerian many Christians worked in the Roman imperial palace.[163] Emperor Gallienus ordered by rescript that the Christians should be restored their consecrated places and he forbade further molestation.[164] The Christian community of Antioch could even dare to appeal directly to Caesar Aurelian for an edict in a lawsuit between itself and the deposed Paul of Samosata.[165]

All this shows that in the third century the relation between State and Church cannot in many spheres be regarded as one of hostility nor, from the point of view of the Church, even as a matter of indifference. A process is perceptible which may be described as one of gradual mutual approach even though the Church unmistakably expressed the limits of her recognition of Roman power. Only twice, under Decius and Diocletian, was this development harshly interrupted. This occurred because both still believed in the possibility of a violent solution. How completely their opinions failed to recognize the signs of the times was shown by the enormously rapid change after Constantine's victory. A view of the exhaustive way the foundations of a reconciliation between Church and State were laid even in the third century shows that the events following the failure of the Diocletian persecution were not as revolutionary a turning-point as they have often been interpreted to be.

CHAPTER 25

The Holiness of the Christian and his Church

THE faithful of early Christian times had to conduct their religious life on the foundation of a baptismal spirituality and "preserve the seal of baptism". This implied a lofty awareness of the obligation of all the baptized to holiness in a holy Church. Despite their vivid knowledge of this duty, and despite all efforts to conform to it, the ideal was never carried out by all members of the various communities, and the writings of the apostolic and sub-apostolic age in particular reveal with perfect clarity that at no period in the young Church was there complete absence of sin. Paul himself had to excommunicate an incestuous person from the church at Corinth (1 Cor 5:1–13), and on frequent other occasions had to reprimand individual members of a community for sinful behaviour

---

[163] *Euseb. HE* 6, 21, 3–4; 6, 36, 3; 7, 10, 3.
[164] Ibid. 7, 13.
[165] Ibid. 7, 30, 18–19.

(Eph 4:17–31; 1 Cor 6). The author of the Apocalypse deplored grave faults in the communities of Asia Minor (Apoc 1–3). Clement of Rome had to exhort the Corinthian community not only to avoid as possible dangers but to give up as deplorable realities a whole series of grave failings such as sedition, covetousness, licentiousness, fraud, and envy.[1] Similar or identical sins are implied in the community of Philippi by the letter of Polycarp of Smyrna, and the so-called *Second Letter of Clement*.[2] About the middle of the second century the *Shepherd* of Hermas drew a grave picture of the failure of many Christians of the Roman community, in which there were adulterers, swindlers, drunkards, covetous people, and the like.[3] Then the third century sources make it plain that with the growth in size of the individual congregations, the number of those increased within them who did not succeed in avoiding sin even in its most serious forms. The ideal of a holy Church all of whose members persevered in the grace of baptism until death, remained a high aim which was never achieved.

This undeniable situation created a serious problem for the individual Christian, the single community, and the Church as a whole. Had the Christian who lost baptismal grace forfeited salvation for ever, had he definitely left the Church, or was there still a way for him to "recover the (lost) seal of baptism"?[4] Were some sins perhaps of such gravity that no penance, however strict, could atone for them? Were they unforgivable, and did they make return to the Church's society for ever impossible?

The discussions about the possibility of a penance which atones for sins committed and gives back participation in the life of the ecclesiastical community, accompany the Church, it might be said, from her very first hour, and in the third century they reached an almost dramatic culmination. The struggle for the holiness of Christians and the sanctity of their Church assumed concentrated form in the question of penance and, in the controversies about penance, became a factor of the first importance in the Church's own life. This is reflected, too, in ecclesiastical history research. Until now it has not been possible to reach generally accepted conclusions, since both the complicated condition of the sources and the close involvement of the problem of penance with the concept of the Church made objective decision difficult. To understand the questions regarding penance in the third century, it is necessary to have an acquaintance with previous developments; a brief sketch of these must, therefore, be given first.

---

[1] Clement, *Ad Cor.* 1, 3, 13, 30, 35.
[2] Polycarp, *Ad Phil.* 2–3, 5–6, 11; Ps-Clement, *Ep.* 2, 4.
[3] *Pastor Sim.* 6, 5.
[4] Ibid. 8, 6, 3.

Jesus' preaching indubitably demanded an absolutely radical renunciation of evil (Lk 9: 62; 14: 25), and also judged the situation of someone who has relapsed as graver than that of someone who has not yet been converted (Mt 13:3 ff.). On the other hand, he knew the sinfulness of his closest followers and did not exclude even the disciples who were unfaithful to him from reconciliation and from responsibility for important tasks in the *basileia* of God. God's readiness to forgive a sinner many times, is the basis for the precept that they must be equally ready to go on forgiving their brethren (Mt 18:22; 6:12; 7:11). With the conferring of the power of binding and loosing on the apostles as bearers of authority, the Church was appointed to pass judgment on the faithful who sinned, that is to say, to expel them from the community or to free them from the bond again, and forgive them their sins (Mt 18:15 ff.; Jn 20: 21 ff.). That authority was given without restriction; no sin was excepted as unforgivable, and so no sinner was excluded permanently from the Church unless he hardened himself impenitently in the "sin against the Holy Spirit" (Mt 12:31 ff.). St Paul acted in accordance with this when he "delivered to Satan" the incestuous sinner of Corinth, excluded him from the sacramental company of the faithful, "excommunicated" him (1 Cor 5:3 ff.). In accord with such individual measures, Paul expects that members of the community who have sinned grievously by lewdness and debauchery will be converted (2 Cor. 12:21). In other New Testament writings, too, the view prevails that every sinner can obtain forgiveness again if he does penance (Jas 1:21; 5:19 ff.; 2 Pet 3:9; 1 Jn 2:1 ff.). Only if he refuses penance and atonement does his fault become for him "the sin unto death" (1 Jn 5:16). The prayer of the sinner, and that of the community praying for him, open the way to forgiveness (1 Jn 5:14 ff.; Jas 5:14 ff.); the community of the faithful occupies itself with the sinner who is doing penance, and who makes his confession before it (1 Jn 1:9).[5] The Apocalypse admonishes bishops not to tolerate idolatry and licentiousness in their communities, but also recognizes that God himself can still bring the worst sinner to penance (Apoc 2:2; 2:14 ff.; 2:20–3).

This New Testament conviction of the possibility of penance and reconciliation of the sinner with God and with the community of the faithful, also persisted in the sub-apostolic period. Its writers suffer intensely when they see that the ideal of a society of brethren sanctified by baptism is thoroughly disgraced by some,[6] but they all issue an urgent summons to penance, which will restore salvation to each.[7] By such penance they meant genuine conversion, that is, renunciation of sin and a

---

[5] See *Did.* 14, too.
[6] Cf. Ps-Clement, *Ep.* 2, 14, 1.
[7] Ibid. 8, 1–3; Ignatius, *Ad Philad.* 3, 2; 8, 1; *Ad Symrn.* 9, 1; 1 *Clem* 7: 4, 5.

return to obedience to God's commandments.[8] This is expressed in prayer of repentance, fasting, and alms-giving,[9] and an integral part of it consists in confession of sinfulness before God and the community of the brethren.[10] In the sub-apostolic period, too, penance was always something that concerned the community. The authorities attended to ecclesiastical discipline and excommunicated the obstinate sinner, that is, they excluded him from participation in religious life and broke off all association with him "until he did penance". During the sinner's "time of excommunication", the community tried to help him by its impetrative prayers.[11] The judgment as to when the sinner had, through penance, sufficiently atoned for his fault, was clearly a matter for the Church authorities. Their favourable judgment brought him pardon and re-incorporation into the religious life of the ecclesiastical community, which was convinced that he had thereby obtained pardon also from God.[12]

Penance in the *Shepherd* of Hermas

Gaps occur even in the rather occasional remarks regarding penance which we can find in the writings of the Apostolic Fathers. They give no details about the duration of penitential excommunication, nor about its enforcement and control, nor about the procedures of release and reception. Yet they clearly reveal the fundamental affirmation of the possibility of doing penance for all sins without exception. In this context it is difficult to understand the attitude of some with respect to Hermas, the author of the *Shepherd*. They have assigned the author of this mid-second century work as the first Christian who attempted to break a previously strict practice of denying any possibility of penance to a Christian who had placed himself outside the Christian community by grave sins committed after baptism. Hermas is said to have proclaimed a single opportunity of penance after baptism, and this has been construed as a display of Christendom's deviation from the original ideal of a Church of the saints. It is further said that the disastrous consequences of Hermas' proceeding are not mitigated even by an attitude regarding these possibilities of penance as an exceptional measure. This is considered to be similar to the jubilee of the Old Testament, which by its very nature had time limits set to it. Such an interpretation of the purpose of the Hermas document[13]

[8] Ibid, 56, 1; Ps-Clement, *Ep.* 2, 8, 4.
[9] 1 *Clement* 48, Justin, *Dial.* 90, 141; Ps-Barnabas, *Ep.* 19, 10; Ps-Clement, *Ep.* 2, 16, 14.
[10] *Did.* 14, 1; 4, 17; Ps-Barnabas, *Ep.* 19, 12.
[11] Ibid, 19, 4; Ignatius, *Ad Smyrn.* 4, 1; 7, 1; Polycarp, *Ad Phil.* 6, 11; 11, 2; Ps-Clement, *Ep.* 2, 17, 3; *Did.* 15, 3.
[12] Ignatius, *Ad Phil.* 3, 2; 1 *Clem* 57: 2.
[13] The latest representative of this view was R. Joly in *RHR* 147 (1955), 35–49, but

is certainly favoured to some extent by its literary genre. Hermas chose the form of an apocalypse in order to preach his conception of penance in visions and parables; consequently his basic purpose only reveals itself on closer examination and even this leaves an obscure and contradictory residue.

Hermas receives the new revelation about penance in his second vision; his former ideas regarding the question can therefore be gleaned from his statements that are prior to this event. In the first vision he states without reservation that his children are written again in the books of life "when they do penance from the bottom of their hearts"; yet these had lapsed from the faith and had denounced their parents as well.[14] Only those who refused penance, or undertook it merely in appearance, could not reckon on forgiveness.[15] The revelation imparted to Hermas receives a new element with the announcement that the previous possibility of penance has a time limit set to it; it lasts until a certain day with a single possibility of penance for sins committed after bapism. The end of the world, heralded by an imminent persecution[16] is approaching and no further chance is available for subsequent sins. The modification in the time available for penance is, therefore, given eschatological grounds. In support of the thesis that Hermas here proclaims, for the first time in the history of the Church, a fundamentally new possibility of penance after baptism, reference has been made in the first place to his conversation with the Shepherd to whom Hermas submits his doubts. Here: "some teachers" are said to hold the view that only the penance afforded at baptism and with baptism brings remission (ἄφεσις) of sins and that no further possibility of penance exists. The "Shepherd" confirms the correctness of this view; he says that anyone who has received forgiveness of sins by baptism ought really (ἔδει) not sin any more; the mercy of God, however, grants to those who have fallen again through human weakness a single, last penance.[17] Whether these teachers should be regarded as the spokesmen of a minority inclining to rigorism, or as the representatives of a catechetical practice which unswervingly proclaimed the ideals of a baptismal spirituality and the preservation of baptismal grace,[18] may remain an open question. It remains established in any case that a majority, including Hermas himself, were aware of a possibility of penance subsequent to baptism. As compared to the repeatedly proclaimed demand

with the notable qualification that Hermas is said to be here opposing a rigorist trend in the Roman community.

[14] Hermas, *Past. Vis.* 1, 3, 2; 2, 2, 2–4.

[15] *Past. Vis.* 1, 4, 2; *Sim.* 8, 6, 4; 8, 7, 2; 9, 26, 3.

[16] *Past. Vis.* 2, 2, 5; 2, 3, 4; 3, 5, 5; 3, 8, 8 f.; *Sim.* 9, 9, 4.

[17] *Past. Mand.* 4, 3, 1–7.

[18] Cf. K. Rahner in *ZKTh* 77 (1955), 398 f.

for the realization of the baptismal ideal in daily life it was less emphatically stressed and, according to the "Shepherd's" words, was only to be preached with great discretion, out of regard for the newly baptized.[19] Hermas is obviously disturbed and anxious over the possibility that penance after baptism might contain some element of uncertainty; it might, for example, be prevented by some unforeseen circumstance. In the mind of the faithful its efficacy must have probably seemed less certain when compared with the radical effect of baptism. The Shepherd's answer gives Hermas confidence again, and makes him hope that his children, and all who are willing to make use of the proffered second chance of penance will obtain forgiveness even though a time limit is set.[20] While Hermas unquestionably states that there is only one possibility of post-baptismal penance, the reason given is not that there is simply no more time left for penance after the proclamation of his revelation. Rather it is explained as being something that is unrepeatable in principle, probably on the idea that just as there is only one baptism which confers forgiveness, so there is only one penance which blots out post-baptismal sins.[21] Furthermore, Hermas is convinced that the penance of someone who has relapsed a second time could not have been an irrevocable rejection of evil; it could not therefore have been genuine penance; and God could not have thereby granted forgiveness. The principle of the singleness of *paenitentia secunda* is clearly formulated for the first time by Hermas and remained in force for a long time.

Among penitential practices for the sinner, Hermas reckons confession of sins, prayer, fasting, almsgiving, and the humility with which he takes all these exercises upon himself.[22] When the atonement is complete, that is to say, when it corresponds to the measure of guilt, its double effect supervenes: it brings forgiveness of sins, and healing, while restoring life to the soul, the seal of baptism that had been lost.[23] Hermas makes it clear by his image of the tower, which is symbol of the Church, that penance is not only a matter between God and the sinner, but involves the Church. The sinners stand outside this tower, some near and others farther from it.[24] Anyone not in the tower is excluded from the community

---

[19] Hermas, *Pastor Mand.* 4, 3, 3.

[20] *Past. Vis.* 2, 2, 2–3, 4; *Mand.* 4, 3, 7.

[21] *Past. Mand.* 4, 1, 8; 4, 3, 6; on this see K. Rahner, *op. cit.* 405.

[22] *Past. Vis.* 1, 1, 3; 3, 1, 5; 3, 9, 4–6; 3, 10, 6; *Sim.* 5, 1, 3; 9, 23, 4; *Mand.* 8, 10.

[23] *Past. Vis.* 2, 4; 1, 9; 8, 6, 3.

[24] Ibid. 3, 2, 7 and 9; 3, 7, 1–3; 3, 5, 5. It is not possible to conclude, as Grotz does in *Die Entwicklung des Bußstufenwesens in der vornicänischen Kirche* (Freiburg i. Br. 1955), that there are two groups of sinners, one excommunicate, the other not, though the latter are subjected to ecclesiastical penance; what is decisive is that they are all outside the tower. The different distances at which they stand from the tower is an index of their guilt or of their "excommunication-penance."

of the Church; anyone who is no longer taken into the tower is lost. As, however, it is the Church which excludes, which, in the sense of that time, excommunicates the adulterer or the man who has relapsed into idolatry,[25] all who stand outside the tower are persons who have been so excommunicated by her. Reception again into the tower presupposes an examination on whether the excommunication penance can be regarded as sufficient or "completed". Such an examination was, of course, the prerogative of the Church authorities[26] who either kept the sinner back at a "lesser place"[27] or, granting him complete reconciliation, let him back into the tower again, received him once more into the community of salvation of the Church. It is to be noted that Hermas' intention was not to completely describe the ecclesiastical penance of his time, but rather simply to preach penance.

Tertullian's Two Views of Penance

The increased membership of the communities, especially in the phase of intense growth that characterized the latter half of the second century, involved more frequent cases of failure in Christian life and so heightened the importance of the question of penance. Even if convinced in principle that a second penance was not to be refused to such sinners, it was possible in the practice of penitential discipline to choose stricter or milder forms according to whether emphasis was placed on the Christian ideal of holiness or on the Christian motive of mercy. Both tendencies could be represented in the same community and both are perceptible here and there in the sources, too. When Dionysius of Corinth, about 170, requires that all "who repent of some fall, error or even a heresy", are to be received again, he not only expresses the generally recognized view, but also clearly opposes a tendency of another kind.[28] A rigoristic trend emerged in Phrygian Montanism. At first this appeared to be a protest against the excessively lax view and manner of life of many Christians, but later revealed itself as an extremist movement whose first prophet Montanus upheld the thesis: "Potest ecclesia donare delicta, sed non faciam, ne et alii delinquant." "The Church can forgive sins, but I shall not, lest others fall away."[29] This amounted to demanding that for the sake of discipline in its communities, the Church should refuse sinners the possibility of penance, the granting of which she was in principle admitted to possess. The initial success of Montanism shows that this demand met

---

[25] Hermas, *Past. Mand.* 4, 1, 8–9.

[26] Cf. *Past. Vis.* 3, 9, 7–10.

[27] On this, see K. Rahner, *loc. cit.* 410–24.

[28] *Euseb. HE* 4, 23, 6.

[29] Recorded as an "oracle" of Montanus by Tertullian, *De pud.* 21, 7.

with a certain amount of sympathy, because it was apparently trying to achieve an uncompromisingly high ideal of holiness. The question of penance became a prime problem at one stroke when Tertullian by his adherence to Montanism made this demand his own. He proclaimed it with all the subtlety of his intellect and the pitiless rigour of his will. However, as a member of the Catholic community of Carthage, he had previously expounded the traditional view of the question of penance in his own work. The twofold position he adopted offers an exceptional opportunity of investigating the problem more closely through comparison.

When Tertullian wrote his monograph *On Penance* in the first years of the third century, the existence of the possibility of a single penance for the baptized was something of which he had no doubt whatever.[30] God knows the perils to which the Christian is exposed, even after baptism, and which are due to the malice of the devil. For those who fall victims, God has "established the second penance in order to open the door to those who knock, but only once, because it is already the second time, but not again any more, because the next time is already too late."[31] As opposed to this, Tertullian quite unmistakably expresses his real ideal and in doing so reminds us by the very words he uses of the same attitude in Hermas. He speaks of the possibility of this penance only against his will because it might easily mislead some into far too careless an attitude towards sin.[32] Tertullian also clearly reveals that the loss of baptismal grace was felt to be a very grave failure in the Catholic community, so that some almost lost the heart to make a new beginning and in a sort of despair were no longer willing to undertake the second penance. It is to them that his admonition was addressed: "It certainly ought to be hard for us to sin a second time but to do penance a second time ought not to daunt us."[33] It is of special importance for judging Tertullian's later attitude to observe that in his Catholic days he maintained the universality of penance and excepted no sin as unforgivable. Moreover, only grave sins are in question as matter for penance — penance is of course intended to restore the lost grace of baptism[34] — and he names a few incidentally, not in the sense of an exhaustive catalogue or list, such as "to succumb to carnal lust or the allurements of the world, to deny the faith for fear of the secular power, to stray from the right path as the result of false teachings".[35] In another passage he mentions lust *(stuprum)*, eating of idol-offerings, and heresy *(perversa docere)*.[36]

---

[30] The chapters 7–12 in *De paen.* deal with them together.
[31] *De paen.* 7, 10.   [32] Ibid. 7, 2.   [33] Ibid. 7, 12.   [34] Ibid. 7, 11.   [35] Ibid. 7, 9.
[36] Ibid. 8, 1. Other sins of course are matter for penance in Tertullian's view and he mentions them on occasion as grave transgressions in other works. See K. Rahner, *Festschr. K. Adam* (1952), 141–4.

A radical change in Tertullian's view about penance is revealed in *De pudicitia,* a later open polemic in which he now denies the Church any right to forgive grave sins and reserves this to the spirituals of the Montanist movement which he had joined in the meantime. In the very introduction a Catholic bishop is sharply attacked for publishing a definite edict saying "I also forgive the sins of adultery and fornication for those who have done penance."[37] It was tempting to see in this bishop the then leader of the Roman community, because the expression *pontifex maximus* and *episcopus episcoporum,* by which Tertullian refers to him, at first sight seemed to point to Rome. But the alleged identification of the bishop under attack with Callistus or Zephyrinus of Rome cannot be maintained because Tertullian himself excludes it by saying later that this bishop presumptuously asserted that the power granted to Peter of binding and loosing had passed to every church, "which is related to Peter". That can only mean that Tertullian's opponent was a (North African) bishop who saw the power of binding and loosing present in every church that was in communion with Peter.[38] This interpretation gains considerably in weight from a remark of Cyprian's that some African bishops had earlier refused penance to adulterers;[39] Tertullian's African opponent was defending the view opposed to theirs.[40]

By praising himself for his unashamed renunciation of his earlier error, namely the Catholic teaching,[41] Tertullian himself says with all desirable clarity that the attitude expressed in *De pudicitia* regarding penance represents something new. This obliged him, it is true, to reinterpret his earlier scriptural proofs of the universality of ecclesiastical penance by a display of what can only be called exegetical acrobatics. What is fundamentally new is his division of sins into remissible and irremissible, among which those of idolatry, adultery, and murder play a special part. It is not really admissible to speak of a triad of capital sins in Tertullian, for he mentions other unforgivable sins as well as the three above named,[42] even though he tried to adduce special reasons for these three from the decalogue and the apostolic decree in Acts.[43] To prove the irremissibility

---

[37] *De pud.* 1, 6.
[38] *De pud.* 21, 9. The attempts of K. Stockius, "Ecclesia Petri propinqua" in *AkathKR* 117 (1937), 24–126, and of W. Koehler, *Omnis ecclesia Petri propinqua* (Heidelberg 1938), to show that Tertullian meant the Roman Church here, must be considered to have failed; cf. C. B. Daly, *Studia patristica,* III (Berlin 1961), 176–82.
[39] *Ep.* 55, 21.
[40] In view of Tertullian's liking for employing literary fictions in his controversies, it is not impossible that the *episcopus episcoporum* is not intended to designate some particular bishop but to represent all the bishops of North Africa who took up the attitude which Tertullian was attacking; cf. A. Ehrhard, *Kirche der Märtyrer,* 366 ff.
[41] *De pud.* 1, 10–13.
[42] *De pud.* 9, 9; 19, 25; *Adv. Marc.* 4, 9.   [43] *De pud.* 5 and 12.

of certain sins by the Church, Tertullian appeals to the fact that they would not be forgiven by God either,[44] but he has to contradict himself by saying, in another passage, that forgiveness of these sins must be left to God.[45] It is not that the three capital sins were treated as unforgivable in the Church's penitential discipline before Tertullian's Montanist period, for in that case he could not have passed them over in silence in his work *De paenitentia*. The triad is rather to be considered a construction of Tertullian which he thought to use effectively in his polemical writings against the Catholic Church.

In his monograph on penance and in some parts of the Montanist polemic, Tertullian becomes the first Christian writer to provide enough detail about the penitential procedure for a clear picture of its operation to be obtained. The first stage was an external action that Tertullian liked to call by the Greek term *exhomologesis,* confession.[46] The sinner had openly to admit *(publicatio sui)* that he was in a condition that forced him to perform the official penance. How this public confession was actually carried out in fact is not really clear. When penance for notorious faults was involved, the summons to do penance probably came from the church authorities themselves, who in particularly serious cases could on their own initiative inflict exclusion from the ecclesiastical community, that is, excommunication. The question is more difficult in regard to secret grievous sins, for which the same duty of penance certainly existed as for those publicly known.[47] Various considerations suggest that, in this case, the sinner himself spoke to the leader of the community. For, in the first place, he himself might be in doubt whether his sin necessitated his doing penance at all. Then, too, the gravity of the works of penance which was required, and particularly their duration, depended on the gravity of the sins committed; their allocation presupposes adequate confession by the sinner to the church authority. This explains Tertullian's emphatic admonition to undertake penance whatever the very understandable obstacles in the soul; for after all it was better for the sinner to be publicly absolved than to remain hidden in damnation.[48]

Performance of public penance began with exclusion from participation in the eucharistic service and the prayer of the community; the penitent now no longer possessed *communicatio ecclesiastica.*[49] This act, which belonged to the head of the community, was not identical with the present canonical procedure of excommunication. It consisted rather of installation in the status of penitent, who thereby stood "outside the church" *(extra*

---

[44] Ibid. 17, 8.   [45] Ibid. 19, 6.   [46] *De paen.* 9, 1, 5 etc.
[47] Ibid. 10, 8.
[48] Ibid. 10–12, especially 10, 8: "an melius est damnatum latere quam palam absolvi?"
[49] *Apolog.* 39; *De pud.* 18, 2.

ecclesiam stare).[50] The sinner could prepare for the beginning of public penance by private works of penance. Tertullian is the first to speak of these in some detail;[51] in addition to continual prayer in a contrite frame of mind, he mentions fasting intended to increase the efficacy of that prayer, the wearing of sackcloth and ashes as an expression of a penitential spirit, and restrictions in care for the body. The sinner performed public penance in two stages. First he stood at the entrance to the church *(pro foribus ecclesiae* or *in vestibulo),* probably in penitential clothes; clerics and laity passed by him and on his knees he asked for the help of their prayers and for readmittance into their society.[52] The second stage restored entry to the inside of the church itself, where the penitent again had to implore the impetratory prayer of the congregation and the restoration of his former membership.[53] Such penance extended over a considerable space of time, which varied according to the gravity of the fault, and probably according to the contrite attitude of the penitent; lifelong penance does not seem to have been imposed in Tertullian's time.[54]

To the first act of excommunication at the beginning of the penance there corresponded the act of reconciliation at the end through which the bishop granted pardon *(venia)* and "restoration" *(restitutio).* The outward form in which this took place cannot be clearly gathered from Tertullian, but most probably it corresponded to the rite customary in Cyprian's time: imposition of hands in conjunction with a prayer.[55] Although Tertullian does not go into detail about the act of reconciliation performed by the bishop until the *De pudicitia,* this certainly existed already in his pre-Montanist days. A second penance intended to restore the grace of baptism[56] loses its meaning if there is not at the end of it a recognizable concluding action which incorporates the penitent into the community again, granting him what he has requested so imploringly. That this act was definitely performed by the bishop of the community is demonstrated in the fact of Tertullian's polemic against the bishop of the Catholic Church who claimed to pardon sins of adultery. But the community, too, was drawn into the process of reconciliation by its impetratory prayer for the penitent, which can certainly be understood in a deeper sense of collaboration. The absolution and reception again of a sinner into the sacramental community can be felt as a special concern of the Christ-society, without any claim being made thereby to share the

---

[50] *De pud.* 1, 21.
[51] *De paen.* 9–10.
[52] *De pud.* 1, 21; 9, 4 and 6; 4, 5; 7, 10; *De paen.* 10, 5–6.
[53] *De pud.* 13, 7; 18, 13.
[54] *De paen.* 7, 11; 12, 7.
[55] Cyprian, *De laps.* 16; *Ep.* 15, 1; 16, 2; 18, 1; 20, 3 etc.
[56] *De paen.* 7, 11; and on this, see K. Rahner, *Festschrift K. Adam* (1952), 149 ff.

sacramental authority of the bishop.[57] The reconciliation pronounced and accomplished by the bishop gave back to the former sinner *pax* with his Church,[58] and conferred and guaranteed at the same time, reconciliation with God, just as baptism as first penance blotted out sins and gave the grace of being a child of God.[59] This reconciliation was guaranteed on the one hand by the power of the impetratory prayer of the Church, which is at the same time the prayer of Christ, and therefore infallible, and on the other hand, it was vouched for by the authority of the Church to forgive sins as God's representative. In respect to this last assurance, appeal was made on the Catholic side to Matthew 18:18.[60] Immoderate and lacking in objectivity as the Montanist Tertullian's controversy about penance and penitential discipline was in regard to the Catholic Church, it nevertheless had positive effects. It caused the Catholics to rethink the biblical and theological foundations of the customary practice of penance and very likely prompted a more precise formulation of these in their preaching. Tertullian was not able to win a large or lasting following in Carthage and North Africa.

More serious consequences for ecclesiastical unity seemed at first to portend from a controversy about the practice of penance that broke out almost at the same time in Rome. In this dispute the learned priest Hippolytus sharply opposed the Roman bishop Callistus (217–22) and it is clear that it had no intrinsic connexion with the African disputes. Hippolytus here appears as the representative of a rigorist trend such as had perhaps already existed in the Rome of Hermas' time. He accused Callistus of general laxity in administering ecclesiastical discipline and alleged a few examples. Callistus allowed a bishop to remain in office even if he were guilty of grave offences; all clerical appointments were open to men who had married twice or even three times; clerics who married were not guilty of sin; and finally Callistus declared that marriages between free women and men of lower rank, not excluding slaves, were valid, although these were forbidden by Roman law. Hippolytus summed up his indictment in the reproach that even as the member of a sect he would be free from charge for his sins, provided he joined the "school of Callistus".[61] It is evident that the actual question of penance was not at issue here. Callistus issued no regulation introducing innovations in penitential practice or even any conceding for the first time in contrast to earlier custom the possibility of penance for adulterers. It certainly was

[57] K. Rahner, ibid. 152–4.
[58] *De pud.* 1, 21; 12, 11 *(pax)*; 3, 5; 15, 5 *(communicatio)*.
[59] *De paen.* 7, 14; 10, 8; *De pud.* 2, 15; 3, 1–3 etc.
[60] *De paen.* 10, 6 ff.; *De pud.* 5, 14. — *De pud.* 1, 6; 21, 9.
[61] Hippolytus, *Refut.* 9, 12 (the whole chapter).

neither a matter of remissible and irremissible sins nor one of the Church's authority to forgive sins, as it was with Tertullian. Callistus plainly held to the general customary doctrine and practice of penance which based the view that there are good and bad in the Church on the parable of the tares among the wheat. Hippolytus himself admitted that Callistus had the majority of the Catholics of Rome on his side. And even Hippolytus himself cannot be described as an adherent of the opinion that some sinners cannot be forgiven; perhaps he was only demanding stricter and perhaps even lifelong penance for some offences. In fact, if the author of the *Philosophoumena* is identical with the Hippolytus of the *Apostolic Tradition,* he conceded in principle that a bishop had authority to absolve from every sin. [62] And the practice of reconciling a heretic after he had performed public penance, was already in existence even under Callistus' predecessor Zephyrinus (199–217). This is proved by the account handed down by Eusebius regarding the confessor of the faith, Natalis, who after rigorous penance was received once more into the community of the Church by the Roman bishop. [63] Hippolytus' followers were only a minority which formed a "school" of their own in Rome, but with apparently no adherents outside the city and which disintegrated when Hippolytus died, if it had not done so already.

Penitential Discipline in North Africa in Cyprian's Time

Renewed discussion of the question of penance in North Africa and subsequently in Rome was occasioned by the course taken by the Decian persecution which was so deplorable for the Church as a whole. By the end of it, the large numbers of lapsed forced the Church's leaders to review the previous penitential practice, at least in certain respects. This phase of early Christian controversies about penance is of the greatest consequences for the history of the Church, because it substantially threatened ecclesiastical unity and led in actual fact to divisions which culminated in the extensive anti-Church of the Novatians.

Bishop Cyprian of Carthage saw himself faced with a new situation when news came to him where he was hiding from the pagan authorities, not only of the large numbers who had lapsed during the persecution, but also about a serious breach of the penitential discipline which had previously been under his own firm control. Some priests were receiving into the Church again those who had fallen, without requiring any work of penance from them at all. Many of the lapsed produced "letters of peace" *(libelli pacis),* which had been issued to them by martyrs before their death,

[62] See the prayer of consecration of the bishop in *Trad. apost.* 3.
[63] *Euseb. HE* 5, 28, 8–12.

or by confessors of the faith, and in which prompt or immediate granting of their readmission to the community of the Church was recommended. Cyprian at once forbade his priests under pain of deprivation of office, to receive the lapsed again; he informed the confessors that he could only regard their letters of peace as a recommendation to the Church authorities; they did not represent an ecclesiastical decision having force of law. When more news arrived about growing unrest in his flock, he gave his clergy instructions to grant ecclesiastical *pax* at once to lapsed persons who were on their death-bed, if they could produce letters of peace from martyrs, but to other dying persons only if they had previously given proofs of genuine willingness to do penance; he would make further regulations for the rest of the lapsed after his return to Carthage. [64] Some of the lapsed immediately accepted these measures of Cyprian and declared themselves willing to do penance, although they were in possession of letters of peace. Others, however, revolted and wrote to Cyprian that they had already been given back their peace with the Church by a martyr. Cyprian ironically described these proceedings by saying that the lapsed behaved as though they were the Church [65] and it was his place to graciously request from them their admission into the Church. A cleric called Felicissimus soon put himself at the head of this group. In Cyprian's absence and without his knowledge he had been appointed deacon of the Carthaginian community by the priest Novatus. He was joined by a few other clerics who were already opposed to Cyprian on other grounds. They won over a considerable part of the community, regarded themselves as the rightful Catholic community of Carthage, and developed an intense propaganda against Cyprian. [66]

This was the situation that Cyprian met when he returned to Carthage at Easter in 251. He soon published his work *On the Lapsed*, which gives an instructive description of the general situation of the North African Church before and after the Decian persecution. In this work Cyprian once again expounded his standpoint in the matter of penance; he opposed strongly the lax practice of his opponents and demanded serious and comprehensive penance from the lapsed as a condition for their reception [67]. The opposition group now provided themselves with their own episcopal leader in the person of the priest Fortunatus and also endeavoured, through a delegation to Rome, to obtain recognition from Pope Cornelius. The latter, however, repulsed them and informed Cyprian of his attitude [68].

---

[64] Cyprian, *Ep.* 1; 15; 16; 18 and 19.
[65] *Ep.* 33 and 35, especially 33, 1.
[66] Ibid., 41, 1 ff.; 42 and 43, 1–7; 52, 3.
[67] *De laps.* 15 and 16.
[68] *Ep.* 59, 1, 9, 16.

Cyprian's energy soon succeeded in ensuring that the ecclesiastical authorities would alone handle the penitential discipline for the lapsed. At a synod summoned by him and attended by numerous African bishops in the year 251, serious penance was unanimously required from all the lapsed, but with special treatment prescribed for the *libellatici* and the *sacrificati;* the former could quickly obtain the *pax* after a careful examination of each individual case; the *sacrificati,* however, who had been guilty of downright denial of their faith by a complete performance of the pagan sacrifice, were only to be received again when in danger of death. But anyone who thus far had not shown himself ready to undertake penance should be excluded from peace with the Church even when in danger of death, because clearly no will to do penance was present at all. Cyprian justified the milder treatment of the *libellatici* by the much lesser gravity of their offence. [69]

When a new persecution threatened under Emperor Gallus and seemed likely to surpass the Decian persecution in intensity, a second synod in Carthage in 252 again dealt with penitenial discipline for the lapsed. It was decided, in view of the grave situation, to concede to all the lapsed admission to the peace of the Church if they had begun their works of penance from the very day they lapsed. This decision was justified by the considerations: that peacetime practice could not be maintained now, that all now needed strengthening by the Church, and that it was impossible to debar from the Blood of Christ those who were expected and required to shed their blood for Christ. It was indicated that only those were capable of accepting martyrdom whom the Church had armed for that struggle, and that the Holy Spirit could only speak through those who had received the Spirit of the Father through peace with the Church. [70] As the persecution of Gallus, however, did not assume the proportions that had been feared, the argument about penance for the *lapsi* was settled by the victory of Cyprian's views, which the North African bishops made their own. The opposition group round Felicissimus and Fortunatus likewise lost its importance, so that soon after the Second Synod of Carthage, peace was to all intents and purposes restored in Cyprian's community.

This sketch of the course of the North African dispute about penance shows clearly that discussion extended to two definite questions: first whether the restoration of peace with the Church was possible without performance of works of penance, and secondly, if a decision about it belonged to the Church's leaders or whether a testimonial from martyrs or confessors of the faith possessed binding force over ecclesiastical authority. Cyprian's opponents advocated a relaxation or even abolition

---

[69] Cf. the account of this to Bishop Antonianus, *Ep.* 55, 6; 55, 13–16; 55, 23.
[70] Ibid. 57.

of the previous stricter practice and, as opposed to this, Cyprian defended the maintenance of a full performance of penance and its control by church authority. His attitude in no respect reveals any break with an earlier severer practice of a kind which rejected the possibility of atonement by public canonical penance for the sin of apostasy; in other words the remissibility or the irremissibility of this sin was not the subject of this controversy at all. The possibility of admission to penance, or of definitive reception into the church community again, was in fact presupposed by both parties. After initial hesitation, Cyprian allowed himself to be won over to a milder handling of penitential practice on one point only: he was persuaded to grant reconciliation to the dying even though they had not yet carried out the customary penance, the only qualifying condition being the possession of a letter of peace from a martyr or a confessor of the faith.[71]

As regards the outer form of the institution or liturgy of penance, the following can be gathered from Cyprian's writings. The first act was the *paenitentiam agere* or *satisfacere* of the sinner, his works of penance, that is, prayer, fasting, wearing penitential clothes, almsgiving, and other such works of self-denial.[72] But these acts were not placed at the private discretion of the penitent; they were carried out with the knowledge of the Church who supported them with her prayer and determined their duration.[73] The second stage was the *exhomologesis*, the part of the penance which took place in the presence of the community. It consisted in the request of the penitent to the bishop, clergy, and congregation, that they should receive him back into the community of the Church and grant him reconciliation.[74] Whether this happened only once or more often, cannot be determined with certainty. It nevertheless presupposed a non-public admission of guilt to the head of the community (the bishop), which Cyprian terms *confessio*.[75] Cyprian's *exhomologesis* is misunderstood when it is regarded as special form of penance. The "real ecclesiastical penance" was different from excommunication penance or "full penance" and is said to have developed from the *exhomologesis*.[76] The third and final act was reconciliation proper and took place through imposition of hands by the bishop. It is first mentioned for the Latin church by Cyprian but it was a long-established rite and one that was, of course, in use even earlier in the East.[77] The bishop accomplished the act of reconciliation

---

[71] *Ep.* 8, 3; 30, 8; 18, 1; 29, 2; 20, 3. — *Ep.* 55, 6; 57, 1; 64, 1.
[72] *De laps.* 24, 30, 35.   [73] Ibid. 32; *Ep.* 4, 4.
[74] *Ep.* 15, 1; 16, 1; 19, 2; 20, 3.
[75] *De laps.* 28, 29; *Ep.* 55, 17, 19.
[76] J. Grotz, for example, in *Die Entwicklung des Bußstufenwesens in der vornicänischen Kirche* (Freiburg i. Br. 1955); against this view, S. Hübner in *ZKTh* 84 (1962), 171–95.
[77] Cyprian, *Ep.* 16, 2; Origen, *In Lev. hom.* 2, 4; *Didasc.* 2, 18, 7; 43, 1.

by reason of the power of binding and loosing committed to him.[78] The community took part in the judgment which decided whether reconciliation was to be granted, but no details are given about this collaboration. Reconciliation, when accomplished, restored to the penitent *communicatio* with the Church, he again received the *pax ecclesiae*.[79] He was thereby permitted to take part once more in the eucharistic service and to receive the Eucharist.[80] Furthermore Cyprian was convinced that the *pax* accorded by the Church was also ultimately significant for salvation, for by it the former penitent was again incorporated into the community of the Church in which alone it is possible to work out one's salvation.[81]

The Roman Controversy on Penance and the Schism of Novatian

While Cyprian had to oppose a tendency to laxity in the imposition of penance on the part of his own clergy in North Africa, Rome was faced about the middle of the century, by a rigorist movement which derived particularly effective and dangerous impetus from the personality of the man who led it and gave to it theological foundation. In striking similarity to Tertullian, the Roman priest Novatian also originally upheld the traditional teaching on penance but soon proclaimed an extremely rigoristic view though for reasons different than those which motivated the African. In particular he rejected any reception of the lapsed into the Church's community as incompatible with her holiness. The Roman attitude on the reconciliation of the lapsed was expressed even before Novatian's time in a letter which some priests of that church had addressed to Cyprian; they had demanded even more definitely than the African bishop that sick persons among the lapsed who repented of their fault and desired reconciliation should be "helped".[82] This view was at first held by Novatian, too. As secretary of the Roman college of priests while the see was vacant in the years 250–1, he had had to deal with correspondence to churches abroad, and his elegant pen was able to express it eloquently and attractively. When (he wrote to Cyprian) humanly speaking, the death of one of the lapsed seemed imminent, he should with appropriate prudence be "helped", provided he had already performed works of penance publicly, had repeatedly expressed abhorrence for his defection and had demonstrated his sorrow by his tears.[83] There was agreement between Rome and Carthage on another point, too. Just as Cyprian was to undertake a definite settlement of the question of penance upon his return to Carthage, so too a final decision would be

---

[78] Cyprian, *Ep.* 57, 1.   [79] Ibid. 64, 1.   [80] Ibid. 4, 4; 16, 2; 18, 1; 55, 29.
[81] Ibid. 73, 21; 74, 7; *De eccl. unit.* 6.
[82] Cyprian, *Ep.* 8, 3.   [83] Ibid. 30, 8.

given in Rome when the community again had a bishop. In connexion with this, a principle of Roman practice in questions of law and faith which was to play an outstanding part in the dispute about heretical baptism and later on, was here formulated for the first time: *nihil innovandum*, they would hold fast to tradition.[84] This letter of Novatian's also contains an interesting detail in that the Roman confessors of the faith unlike their friends in Carthage, refused to issue letters of peace to the lapsed, and were resolute opponents of any relaxation of previous practice in ecclesiastical discipline; they consequently disapproved the vehement demand of the African *lapsi* for immediate reconciliation. To grant it to them too quickly would be to act like a doctor who only closes a wound without giving it time to heal and so only makes the illness worse.[85] When Novatian also observes that the apostasy had assumed such proportions in the whole Church that a final settlement ought only to be made by common consultation of bishops, priests, deacons, and the laity who had stood firm, he seemed to have a Roman synod in mind.[86] A further letter to Cyprian, the style of which likewise identifies Novatian as the author, sharply criticized the lapsed in Carthage who were not willing to wait for Cyprian's return and who despite their serious offence, demanded the *pax* with the Church and even asserted it had already been granted them by heaven. It was high time the letter states that they did true penance, proved the genuineness of their contrition, and brought down God's mercy on themselves by humble submission.[87] Neither of Novatian's two letters justifies the view that in the Roman church until then, no forgiveness had been granted for the sin of denial of the faith; on the contrary, reception of the lapsed into the Church is also presupposed by Novatian when he says at one point that prayer should be made that the penance of the lapsed might obtain forgiveness for them and at another point, that a humble attitude on the part of the fallen would facilitate their request for readmission.[88] Two observations still spring to the mind of one who reads the masterly formulation provided in these two letters of Novatian. Whilst merciful love is always perceptible in Cyprian's whole outlook on the fallen, it is quite lacking in Novatian; he is cold, almost harsh towards them and appeals with an undertone of pride to the glorious Roman tradition.[89] It is also difficult to avoid the impression that his suggestion that a settlement of the whole question of penance for the lapsed could only be undertaken after the election of a new Roman bishop, was not given without a certain reservation. Was he perhaps to be the man to whom this task would fall?

---

[84] Ibid.   [85] Ibid. 30, 2 and 3.   [86] Ibid. 30, 5.   [87] Ibid. 36, 1–3.
[88] Ibid. 30, 6; 36, 3.   [89] *Ep.* 30, 2.

The change in Novatian's attitude on penance occurred when the election of a successor to Pope Fabian, possible with the end of the Decian persecution, elevated not him but Cornelius as Bishop of Rome. The picture that Cornelius draws of his opponent in a letter to Fabius of Antioch [90] is certainly distorted by personal resentment, but it is confirmed in many factual details by the correspondence of Cyprian, who was level-headed and not easily given to exaggeration, and by other sources. Novatian had himself set up as a rival bishop in Rome with the assistance of the priest Novatus from Carthage [91] and tried to win more supporters with the slogan that the readmission of the lapsed into communion with the Church was to be refused on principle. A Roman synod of sixty bishops and numerous other clerics excommunicated Novatian and confirmed by synodal decree the previous Roman practice of admitting apostates to penance. [92] Novatian, however, immediately set about building an opposition church everywhere in East and West. He moved energetically and with undeniable skill in propaganda, taking the organization of the universal Church as a model. [93] In Rome and Italy the success of his endeavours was certainly small, for the prompt action of Cornelius in calling the Roman synod clarified the situation. According to Cornelius' ironical account, Novatian adjured and implored his followers to remain faithful to him, even when he was administering the Eucharist to them, but their numbers continued to shrink. [94] His propaganda took no root in North Africa either, because Cyprian had the situation well in hand there and probably also because the conversion of the leader of the lax party, Novatus, to the opposite camp did not particularly recommend the Novatian movement. Nevertheless, Novatian's letters designed to win over African bishops actually had a certain effect, as the case of Bishop Antonianus shows. He had resisted Novatian from the start, but when he received a letter from him, became hesitant nevertheless and turned to Cyprian for enlightenment. Cyprian's answer is available in a long letter that develops his whole conception of the doctrine of penance. [95] Cyprian also gave Pope Cornelius his support in the struggle against Novatianism by a brisk exchange of letters with Rome and succeeded in inducing some of Novatian's followers to rejoin the legitimate bishop of Rome. [96]

In other regions the successes of Novatian propaganda were more considerable. In Gaul, Bishop Marcian of Arles joined the movement and pitilessly refused reconciliation to the lapsed, even on their death-bed, so

---

[90] *Euseb. HE* 6, 43, 5 ff.   [91] Cyprian, *Ep.* 52, 2.   [92] *Euseb. HE* 6, 43, 2.
[93] According to Cyprian, *Ep.* 73, 2, he imitated this.
[94] *Euseb. HE* 6, 43, 18, 19.
[95] *Ep.* 55, which has already been quoted several times.
[96] *Ep.* 44–54.

that many of them died in despair. Cyprian took up the case and requested Pope Stephen (254–7) in a special letter, to excommunicate Marcian and to give the church in Southern Gaul a new leader.[97] Signs of Novatian infiltration into Spain also exist but were not really perceptible until later. Bishop Pacian of Barcelona († before 329), still remembered a document shown to him by a Novatian, Simpronianus, containing the assertions, "After baptism there is no penance any more; the Church cannot forgive any mortal sin and she destroys herself when she admits sinners."[98] That might very well be a sequel to the Novatian doctrine of penance. This likelihood is increased by the many decrees of the Synod of Elvira, which by their rigorist tendency show a sympathy of this kind existing very early in Spain.

What influence Novatian and his doctrine had on many distant communities in the East is notable; it found supporters particularly in Syria and Palestine, in the Asia Minor provinces of Bithynia, Phrygia, Cappadocia, Pontus, Cicilia, and even in Armenia and Mesopotamia. Novatian took part personally in propaganda in the East by writing letters to leading bishops. There is for instance a letter to Dionysius of Alexandria, in which he seeks to justify his step in founding a church of his own. Dionysius' reply to Novatian has been preserved. The Bishop of Alexandria adjures him insistently to desist from his project, to urge his followers to return to Catholic unity and so at least to save his own soul.[99] A particular danger of the inroad of Novatian influence existed in Fabius of Antioch who had a tendency to rigorist views and consequently "was rather inclined to schism" as Eusebius put it. Dionysius of Alexandria, however, succeeded in keeping him to the traditional conception by expounding the doctrine of penance in detail and by providing examples from real life which showed the longing of the lapsed for reconciliation.[100] Eusebius transmits a few valuable indications about the extent of Dionysius' correspondence for he still had access to it.[101] From one of these letters it appeared that Novatian's schism threatened so strongly to consolidate itself in the East that the leading bishops in Cicilia, Cappadocia, and Palestine wanted to discuss the whole question in a synod at Antioch and had invited Dionysius to it.[102] The latter contributed substantially, by his vigorous work of making the issues clear through letter-writing, to halting the Novatian movement. But he was certainly mistaken about the measure of his success when he later reported to Pope Stephen that peace was restored to the Church in the East, that "the innovation of Novatus" (= Novatian) had been "rejected", and that there was everywhere great

---

[97] *Ep.* 68, 1–3.
[98] Pacianus, *Ep. ad Sympronianum* 3, 1.
[99] In *Euseb. HE* 6, 45.   [100] Ibid. 6, 44, 1–6.   [101] Ibid. 6, 44–6.   [102] Ibid. 6, 43, 3.

joy over the restoration of unity.[103] Novatianism still persisted for a long time in the East, even if only in small sectarian communities which went further than the rigorism of their first founder and pretentiously called themselves Cathars, the church of the pure.[104]

Doctrine and Practice of Penance in the East in the Third Century

A sketch of the doctrine and practice of penance current in the eastern regions to which Christianity had spread, may well begin with a reference to Irenaeus of Lyons, who came from Asia Minor. He, too, was one of those who still represented the strict ideal of holiness inherited from the beginnings of the Church, and who would have refused readmission into the Church to those who had incurred the guilt of serious offences.[105] Irenaeus himself was particularly imbued with the thought that the likeness to God given to man by redemption, obliges him to a perfectly holy and sinless life.[106] Because Christians had been given such high graces, they must be subjected to a much stricter judgment than the men of the Old Testament, and consequently, after their baptism, ought to be on their guard against any sin, because the death of Christ is not efficacious for them a second time.[107] On the question whether there is any salvation at all for a sinner after baptism, Irenaeus makes no pronouncement, but on another occasion he expresses perfectly clearly the possibility of such penance; he believes that God gives his peace and friendship to those "who do penance and are converted"; only those who persist in apostasy impenitently are eternally lost.[108] Particularly important is a remark in the so-called "rule of faith" of Irenaeus (*Adv. haer.* 1, 10, 1), that summary of ancient belief inherited from the apostles,[109] where it is said that God will "graciously grant life to those who persevere in his love — some from the beginning, some since penance — will grant them incorruptibility and surround them with eternal glory". It follows from this, that the conviction that men could regain the love of God by penance even after baptism, has always belonged to the belief of the Church.[110] To designate this penance, Irenaeus commonly uses the expression *exhomologesis;*[111] he is in fact

---

[103] Ibid. 7, 5.

[104] Ibid. 6, 43, 1; *Concil. Nicaen.* can. 8. Some Novatian inscriptions in Asia Minor, *DACL* XII, 1759. Also cf. *Cod. Theodos.* 16, 5, 2; *Socrates HE* 5, 21, 22.

[105] Cf. B. Poschmann, *Poenitentia secunda* (Bonn 1940), 212.

[106] *Adv. haer.* 3, 18, 1; 3, 9, 1; *Epid.* 42.

[107] *Adv. haer.* 4, 27, 1–4.

[108] Ibid. 4, 40, 1; 5, 26, 2.

[109] Ibid. 1, 10, 1.

[110] Cf. K. Rahner in *ZKTh* 70 (1948), 452–5.

[111] *Adv. haer.* 1, 13, 5, 7; 3, 4, 3.

silent about a reconciliation of the penitents but this follows indirectly from his belief in the efficacity of penance. That penance after baptism is a concern of the Church, is clear from his observation that priests had the duty of watching over the moral life of Christians and, when necessary, of expelling a sinner from the Church.[112]

The position of the Alexandrian teachers on penance and penitential discipline is characterized by the fact that it is lacking in the polemic note of the controversies of the Latin West; their statements were not formulated in the heat of argument against hostile views. Clement's conception of penance is, in the first place, marked by his idea of purification, which was influenced by Plato; in accordance with it, he represents liberation from sin as a rather long process, but one that is not possible without penance.[113] What is also striking, is his considerable agreement with Hermas' doctrine on the subject. Like him, he stresses that the ideal of Christian life is to avoid all offences after the great forgiveness of sins in baptism;[114] God knows human weakness and grants the possibility of a second, but single, penance; this cannot be repeated because renewed penances would show that no serious penitential attitude of mind was present.[115] Clement views the effect of penance in a similar way to Hermas; it confers indeed, like baptism, forgiveness of sins, but not solely as a gift of divine pardon, and only after previous painful purification consisting of prayer, fasting, and works of brotherly love.[116] To penance there belongs, too, a confession of guilt, but details about the course of this exhomologesis are not given.[117] No fault is considered irremissible, as what he has to say about the woman taken in adultery, the good thief, and heretics, shows.[118] Like Irenaeus, Clement does not speak of a reconciliation, but that for him, too, penance ended with readmission into the Church, follows from his story of the young man who had fallen into error and whom the apostle John "brought into the Church" again after long prayer and fasting.[119] Clement is the first writer who recommends for the penitent a sort of spiritual guide, whose help by prayer and admonitions would be of great profit to him.[120] Such spiritual directors are, in addition to the Church authorities, the perfect Christians, the

---

[112] Ibid. 4, 26, 2, 3; 4, 27, 4.

[113] *Quis div. salv.* 40, 3–6; 42, 14, 15; *Strom.* 7, 10, 56.

[114] *Strom.* 56, 1.

[115] Ibid. 2, 13, 56 ff.; 2, 13, 59.

[116] Ibid. 2, 12, 55, 6; 2, 70, 3; *Quis div. salv.* 40, 1; 42, 14, 15; *Strom.* 2, 15, 71.

[117] *Strom.* 2, 59, 3.

[118] Ibid. 2, 23, 147; *Quis salv.* 38, 4–39, 2; 42, 7; *Strom.* 7, 16, 102.

[119] *Quis div. salv.* 40, 1. A temporary exclusion from the Church is indicated by *Strom.* 7, 16, 102, 4; see on this A. Méhat in *VigChr* 8 (1954), 232.

[120] *Quis div. salv.* 31, 1; 41, 1–6; *Strom.* 7, 12, 79.

Gnostics, and the poor of the community. The efficacy of their help by prayer and mortification is founded on their personal perfection.[121] In this way, Clement introduces the *pneumatic* (Spirit-endowed) spiritual guide into the penitential practice of the Eastern Church, in which he was to play an outstanding role after the rise of monasticism.

Like Clement, Origen was less interested in the concrete details of penitential practice than in its theoretical basis, which, however, he does not expound systematically, either. His high esteem for baptism and the effects of its grace made him painfully aware of the gross contradiction to the ideal patent in the daily life of many Christians. Sin after baptism in all classes, in all the grades of the hierarchy, as well as in all its forms, was for him an undeniable fact. Lighter sins, of course, do not lead to the loss of the grace of baptism and consequently do not exclude from the sacramental community life of the Church. But the sinner's grave offences bring death to his soul and place him in a condition worse than that before his baptism; such a sin can no longer be wiped out by grace, as in baptism, there is only forgiveness through an appropriate penance of atonement.[122] The model of this penance was given in the punishment imposed by Paul on the incestuous Corinthian which was designed "for his salvation on the day of judgment".[123] Origen, therefore, taught the possibility of forgiveness of sins after baptism by penance even in fact for those grave faults which he counts among the deadly sins, such as idolatry, adultery, unchastity, murder, or other serious offences.[124] He only excepts from forgiveness the sin of impenitence, which by its nature is an unreadiness to do penance;[125] penance for grave sins cannot be repeated.[126]

Origen makes many remarks which indicate that the Church authorities were involved in the accomplishment of penance; he compares them with doctors to whom one must show the wounds so that they might apply the correct remedy.[127] An important part is played for him by admonitory reprimand, *correptio*. Its severest form is excommunication, and Origen sternly blames those in authority in the Church who through cowardice omit to impose it where necessary.[128] Even though he also demands that penance should not be so hard as to discourage the sinner, its duration is nevertheless greater than that of preparation for baptism. A novelty in

---

[121] *Eclog. proph.* 15, 2.

[122] *In Joann. comm.* 2, 11; 15, 15; *Exhort mart.* 30; *In Exod. hom.* 6, 9; *In Lev. hom.* 11, 2.

[123] *In Lev. hom.* 14, 4.

[124] *In Ioann. comm.* 19, 4; *De or.* 28, 9, 10.

[125] *In Ioann. comm.* 19, 13.

[126] *In Lev. hom.* 15, 2.

[127] *In Ioann. hom.* 37, 1, 1.

[128] *In Lev. hom.* 3, 2; *In Iesu Nave hom.* 7, 6.

Origen is the remark that reconciled Christians could no longer be admitted to office in the Church.[129] The sinner has to open himself by confession to the bishop as the physician of souls, and the bishop will also determine whether the character of the sin makes public penance necessary at all.[130] In his discussion of the spiritual director, Origen goes further along the road indicated by Clement; the guide must not be a priest, and he can be of particular help to the sinner in the blotting out of lesser offences, if he takes part in the penitential performance of works and prayer voluntarily undertaken.[131] Sharp disapproval is shown to some priests who claimed to be able to forgive sins as grievous as idolatry, adultery, and unchastity "by their prayer".[132] In Origen's perspective, that can only mean that these clerics ascribed efficacy for forgiveness, even for such serious offences, presumptuously to their personal care for the sinner by way of *correptio,* instead of requiring of him the acceptance of public canonical penance. In no way can the remark be interpreted in the sense that Origen taught certain capital sins to be ecclesiastically irremissible.

Even more definitely than Clement, Origen maintains the thesis that the priest's power of remission is bound up with his personal perfection. He attributes the power of forgiveness even to ordinary Christians who have attained a high degree of personal perfection.[133] That, however, does not mean that someone not a priest could accomplish ecclesiastical reconciliation, for Origen reserves this, as well as excommunication, to the bishops. But it remains true that the Alexandrian theologians attributed quite special value to the collaboration of a perfect Christian in the performance of penance. With Origen, this view is connected with the importance that he ascribes to the "saints" in the life of the Church; just as the sin of one of her members always affects the whole Church, so, too, she is involved as a whole in reparation. The reincorporation into the Church that follows on reconciliation has a salutary effect, because the salvation of the individual and his membership of the Church are inseparably bound up with one another.[134] Consequently, the act of reincorporation must in fact also effect forgiveness of sins, even if, for Origen, this effect is not as predominant among his interests as desire to emphasize the task of the spiritual physician of the soul in the process of freeing the penitent from sin.

---

[129] *In Ioann. comm.* 28, 7; *Contra Cels.* 3, 51.

[130] *In Lev. hom.* 2, 4; *In Matth. comm.* 13, 30; *In ps. 37 hom.* 2, 6.

[131] *In Lev. hom.* 5; *In Matth. comm.* 4, 16, 8. These texts cannot be used to prove the existence of private penance in the present-day sense in Origen: cf. K. Rahner in *RSR* 37 (1950), 452–6.

[132] *De or.* 28, 10.   [133] *De or.* 28, 8; *In Matth. comm.* 12, 11–14.

[134] *In ps. 36 hom.* 2, 4; cf. *In Ezech. hom.* 10, 1.

Particularly informative on the penitential liturgy in the East is the Syrian *Didascalia*, the composition of which can be assigned to the first decades of the third century. This is especially true since alleged anti-Novatian features cannot definitely be established in it or in any case can be regarded as later additions.[135] It emphasizes most persistently the duty incumbent on the bishop of care for sinners; to him also belongs the occasionally indispensable exclusion of an obstinate offender from the ecclesiastical community, which should be carried out without respect for persons, without favouritism. The bishop's authority in the whole matter of penance is founded on the power of binding and loosing committed to him.[136] The measures he takes in regard to the sinner have always a double aim; they should strengthen the community of the faithful in what is good, while giving the sinner hope of forgiveness. The bishop should act on the model of the Good Shepherd, who is forgiving sins and imparting peace through him.[137] No fault, however grave, is excluded from the bishop's power to forgive.[138] According to the *Didascalia*, the process of penance takes more or less the following course: when the bishop has heard of a sinner in his flock, he takes him to task, reproaches him sharply with his faults and then excludes him from taking part in the common life of the Church; members of the community, too, castigate his sinful behaviour.[139] After a certain time, however, they intercede with the bishop for him, especially through the deacons; the bishop assures himself of the genuine quality of the sinner's repentance and, with renewed admonitions and advice, imposes on him a penance, in which fasting occupies a special place, proportionate to his guilt.[140] With the acceptance of this penance imposed by the bishop, the "liturgical" phase of the sinner's penitential course begins and this lasts until the act of reconciliation proper. The *Didascalia* warns the bishop when a sinner is denounced by members of his flock, not only to check conscientiously the foundation of the accusation but also to consider the motives of such denunciations.[141] During the official period of penance the sinner is admitted to the readings and the sermon; consequently the excommunication is already in a sense mitigated.[142] Full reconciliation is only granted with the imposition of hands by the bishop which takes place to the accompaniment of prayer by the congregation; it makes the sinner a member of the Church again

---

[135] Cf. P. Galtier, "La date de la Didascalie des apôtres" in *Aux origines du sacrement de pénitence* (Rome 1951), 189–221.

[136] *Didasc.* 2, 20, 3–4; 2, 8, 4; 2, 10; 2, 11, 1–2; 2, 18, 2.

[137] Ibid. 2, 15, 8; 2, 20, 9.

[138] Ibid. 2, 22–23, 1; 2, 24, 3.

[139] Ibid. 2, 16, 1–2.

[140] Ibid.

[141] Ibid. 2, 37, 4–5.   [142] Ibid. 2, 39, 6; 2, 41, 1.

and restores to him the Holy Spirit, lost by sin. A special reference is here made to the parallel giving of the Spirit by baptism.[143] The ecclesiastical nature of penance is made clearer in the *Didascalia* than anywhere else, for it is linked with the episcopal head of the community. Consequently the sacramental character of the forgiveness of sin, conferred by him, is apparent too.

A special feature of the doctrine of the *Didascalia* on penance must also be particularly noticed; it is nowhere said that the post-baptismal penance, described at such length and with such care, was unique and unrepeatable. That is striking in a work that so often emphasizes the remissibility of sins committed after baptism. The *Didascalia* seems rather to presuppose that penance can be repeated after a reconciliation has already taken place, because it does not concede this in one particular case, that of an informer who lapses. Yet it could have simply appealed here to the principle that penance is only possible once; in fact, however, it adduces the reasons for this case at length and in detail, giving different grounds.[144] The supposition that the *Didascalia* recognized the possibility of repeated penance and reconciliation after baptism, is strengthened by a further observation, that between the practice of canonical penance in the *Didascalia* and the practice of excommunication from the synagogue there are so many striking parallels,[145] that some features in the *Didascalia* account are only intelligible as a slightly developed continuation of the synagogue custom. But in this, every excommunication could be lifted repeatedly. If we add that the *Apostolic Constitutions,* which also originated in Syrian territory, likewise do not recognize ecclesiastical penance as occurring only once,[146] the conclusion becomes inescapable that the single unrepeatable canonical penance was not everywhere current in the East, and that this cannot simply be held to have been the original practice. In the West, as has been shown above, it appears for the first time with Hermas, and pastoral reasons are given for it. If he was the very first to introduce it, perhaps as a concession to a rigorist trend, this would permit the whole attitude of the Church to penance before his time to be characterized as a period of greater mildness, and the assumption of a contrary development from an original strictness to a growing laxity, would be shown to be erroneous.

With a single exception other accounts from the East regarding the question of penance give no new information at variance with the picture that has been drawn.[147] Origen's pupil, Gregory Thaumaturgus, mentions

---

[143] Ibid. 2, 41, 1.   [144] Ibid. 2, 43, 1–4.

[145] Cf. K. Rahner in *ZKTh* 72 (1950), 278 ff.

[146] *Const. Apost.* 2, 40, 1.

[147] On the view of Bishop Dionysius of Alexandria, see above, p. 337.

the division of penitents into various classes as an arrangement established long since, but the terminology he uses was, it seems, not yet fixed.[148] Some consider the classes of the "hearers" and "fallen" as definitely attested, others think that those of the "weepers" and "bystanders" are, too.[149] The synods of the fourth century gradually gathered penitential regulations into canons and so formed the transition to the juridically formulated canonical penance of succeeding generations.

Disputes Concerning Penance after the Persecution of Diocletian

The Diocletian persecution again made the question of the treatment of apostates a topical one. For this time, too, in various regions the Church had to deplore *lapsi*, even though, as will presently be shown, the whole outcome on this occasion was far from being as deplorable for her as it had been during and after the wave of attack under Decius. As regards Rome, the fact of disputes about the question of penance under Pope Eusebius (310) is established, but the circumstances remain obscure. An inscription dedicated by Pope Damasus (366–84) to his predecessor Eusebius, says that the latter had required the fallen to do penance, but had met with contradiction over this from a certain Heraclius, who "forbade" penance to the *lapsi*.[150] The text does not permit us to attribute with certainty to Heraclius one of the two possible extreme positions, the rigorist view, which refused penance to the apostates or the laxist view, which demanded their reception without penance, though the first is more likely. According to Damasus, the discussion of these matters led to serious unrest and to a split in the community; the dispute brought about the intervention of the emperor, Maxentius, who banished the leaders of the two parties, Bishop Eusebius and Heraclius. On the other hand, a connexion between the disputes about penance under Eusebius' predecessor, Marcellinus (296–304), and the Diocletian persecution, can no longer be maintained. Marcellinus,[151] too, Damasus reports in another epigram,[152] required the performance of penance from the fallen and had met with strong opposition over this. As Marcellinus did not live to see the beginning of the Diocletian persecution, the offences of these *lapsi* cannot be determined more precisely.

---

[148] In his so-called *Epistula canonica*, PG, 10, 1019–48, and J. B. Pitra, *Iuris ecclesiastici Graecorum historia et monumenta*, I (Rome 1864), 562–75.

[149] B. Poschmann, *HDG* IV/3, 39. — J. Grotz, *op. cit.* 400–8.

[150] Ferrua, *Epigrammatica Damasiana* (Rome 1942), 129: ..."Heraclius vetuit lapsos peccata dolere, Eusebius miseros docuit sua crimina flere."

[151] Damasus actually names Marcellus, but he is probably to be identified with Marcellinus. Cf. R. H. Röttges in *ZKTh* 78 (1956), 385–420.

[152] Ferrua, *op. cit.* 181.

The controversy connected with the Diocletian persecution in North Africa cannot, strictly speaking, be considered as a dispute about penance. Many Christians had submitted to Diocletian's demand that they should hand over their holy books, and were regarded as *traditores*. The consecrations of bishops who were *traditores* were held by a rigorist section to be invalid. When in 311 the newly-elected bishop of Carthage, Caecilian, was consecrated by an alleged *traditor,* Bishop Felix of Aptungi, the violent Donatist conflict burst out. An account of this belongs, however, to the history of the fourth century.

The problem of the *lapsi* occupied the Alexandrian church, too, when the Diocletian persecution abated, and its bishop, Petrus, laid down in an *epistula canonica* the principles on which penitential practices were there to be determined. These canons which are still extant, show no real development in penitential practice since Origen, but they reveal a warm sympathy for the fate of the fallen.[153] Bishop Petrus, however, is also named as one of the leaders of the two parties which opposed one another over the question of penance in an early phase of the so-called Meletian schism[154] in Egypt. The leader of the other group was Meletius himself who, according to the admittedly late account of Epiphanius, firmly opposed, with numerous confessors, the readmission of the lapsed.[155] The question of penance was, however, not the starting-point of this division in the Egyptian church; it was provoked rather by Meletius, bishop of Lycopolis, in the Thebaid, who encroached upon the bishop of Alexandria's rights of consecration. Meletius, however, used the question of penance to win supporters in the struggle against the bishop of the Egyptian capital and to give the churches dependent on himself a distinctive and effective slogan. After a few years the question of penance ceased to be topical in the Meletian disorders and Meletius' supporters soon joined the Arians and made common cause with them against Athanasius.

After the revolutionary change under Constantine, the controversies about the problem of penance ceased. It is the lasting merit of the Church of the third century, in the often intense struggles for a right understanding of Christian penance in the face of the rigorism that kept flaring up again and again, to have defended the spirit of compassionate understanding for the sinner which the founder of the Church had preached, and yet to have prevented the incursion of lax tendencies into Christian penitential discipline.

---

[153] The Canons are given in J. B. Pitra, *op. cit.* 551–61; cf. J. Grotz, *op. cit.* 409–13.
[154] Cf. K. Baus in *LThK* VII, under Meletius of Lycopolis.
[155] Epiphanius, *Haer.* 68.

CHAPTER 26

The Development of the Church's Constitution in the Third Century

THE third century led in many ways to a further development of the Church's constitution. In addition to the three grades of the ministry in the second century, new lower clerical grades develop, the episcopal office is increasingly consolidated and gains in prestige, the organization of the various individual communities becomes more complex, and in the East, in particular, ecclesiastical provinces take form; the system of synods receives new and intense impetus, and finally, the pre-eminent position of the Roman church and its bishop grows unmistakably stronger by recognition and by contradiction. The sum of these developments in the Church's constitution confirms that here, too, Christianity had grown from its origins into the "great Church" of early Christian times.

The Clergy

The existing orders of bishop, presbyter, and deacon remained unchanged in intrinsic significance, of course, but in many ways were more sharply differentiated, and to some extent, too, underwent an extension in the scope of their functions. The conditions for admission to a particular ministry were further developed, and for the office of bishop a deeper theological grounding was attempted. This strongly emphasizes the ever-growing importance of the bishops for the life of the Church as a whole in the third century. The various problems within the Church, such as the defence against Gnosticism and Montanism, the greater demands made on the authorities by the various waves of persecution, the elucidation of the question of penance, and the struggle against threats of schism, display a monarchical episcopate functioning fully in the third century and in unquestionable possession of the plenary powers that its ministry conferred. The bishop was now the undisputed leader of the ecclesiastical community in all the expressions of its life; he proclaims the faith to it by preaching, and is ever vigilant for the purity of the faith, the correct performance of the liturgy, especially in baptism and the celebration of the Eucharist; he is the guardian of Church discipline and responsible for the observance of the Christian ideal of life by his flock. He guides its works of charity from day to day, and organizes its relief measures in times of need and crisis. He represents his community in its relation with other local churches or at the synodal assemblies of church leaders of a province, which were now becoming important, or at even larger regional assemblies. In this way the bishop became an important link between the individual community and the Church as a whole, and an effective furtherer of Church unity.

It is understandable that theological reflection, too, turned more and more to an office in the Church, the holder of which occupied so central a position in Church life and in the minds of the faithful. A deeper grasp was sought of its nature and basis, with a consequent emphasis on the duties that such an office imposes. Origen, more than any other writer of the third century, concerned himself with the ecclesiastical ministry. He met many of its representatives during his lifetime and in his maturity was himself ordained priest. Not for a moment did he doubt the right and justification of the ministry. The bishop's authority is founded on our Lord's words conferring the power of the keys on Peter; consequently, it is God who calls a man to such an office, and the choice should always be left to God when it is a question of appointing a new bishop in a community.[1] The holder of this office has the task of leading men to the kingdom of God, consequently, he should be a model of every virtue.[2] He has to preach the word of God, therefore he must read and meditate the Holy Scriptures, not preaching his own ideas, but what the Holy Spirit has taught him.[3] He has to accomplish liturgical worship and he should only raise in prayer hands that are undefiled.[4] Origen evidently holds the view that the efficacy of priestly authority is bound up with the personal holiness of the man who bears it.[5] Hence his unmistakably sharp judgment on the clergy of his time, when he compared the reality with the ideal held out to them. The Church which ought to be the temple of God and the house of prayer, had become a den of thieves; bishops, priests, and deacons were full of avarice, ambitious of power, ignorant and even irreligious; ambitious men intrigued for these offices which had become a traffic and which were transmitted from unworthy occupants to unworthy successors.[6] In the choice of a new bishop, therefore, the community should be present and take care that the man chosen is outstanding by reason of his learning, holiness, and virtue.[7]

In the West, it was Cyprian who, a few years after Origen, was the first Latin writer to try to determine the nature and function of the office of bishop in the Church. There can be only one bishop in the local church, who is its judge, and takes the place of Christ.[8] The bishop is in

---

[1] *In Matt. comm.* 12, 14; *In Lev. hom.* 6, 6; *In Num. hom.* 22, 4; *In Jesu Nave hom.* 32, 2.
[2] *In Matth. comm.* 14.
[3] *In Ezech. hom.* 2, 2.
[4] *In Rom. comm.* 9, 42.
[5] *In Matth. comm.* 12, 14; *De or.* 28, 8.
[6] *In Matth. comm.* 16, 21–2; 15, 26; *In Ezech. hom.* 10, 1; *In Num. hom* 22, 4.
[7] *In Lev. hom.* 6, 3.   [8] *Ep.* 59, 5.

the Church, and the Church in the bishop; anyone who is not with the bishop, is not in the Church, either.[9] The Church, by the will of her founder, is an episcopal Church; "it is built up on the bishops and is ruled by them as overseers."[10] At his election, God in some way expresses his consent, and consequently, the bishop is responsible to God alone.[11] But the responsibility is not limited to his own community; it extends to the whole Church. Origen, too, emphasized that a bishop is called to the service of the whole Church.[12] With Cyprian, this responsibility is expressed in the serious concern of the bishop for maintenance of ecclesiastical unity.[13] He links the idea of succession with the office of bishop by saying that it is founded on our Lord's words to Peter (Mt 16:18), and from there proceed the ordination of bishops and the organization of the Church through the changes and succeeding course of time.[14] According to Cyprian, Bishop Stephen of Rome, too, claims to have the see of Peter *per successionem*.[15]

On account of the importance of the office of bishop, the appointment of a man to the position had to be ensured by a sound method of choice. Like Origen, Cyprian, too, expects the community to collaborate in it. This was required because the congregation would be acquainted with a candidate who was a member of it, and be able to form a judgment of his manner of life.[16] The bishops of the province were to play a decisive part in the choice, too, and its validity depended on their consent, which included a judgment about the legitimacy of the way in which the election had been carried out.[17] The right of consecrating the chosen candidate also belonged to these bishops; the Canons of Hippolytus had already recognized this.[18] When it is stated, with a certain emphasis, that the bishop to be consecrated must have been chosen by the whole people, that must be understood in a way that does not exclude the collaboration of neighbouring bishops.[19] Cyprian regards the method of election observed in North Africa as a divine tradition and apostolic custom, and one that was widespread.[20]

---

[9] *Ep.* 66, 8.

[10] *Ep.* 33, 1: "... (ut) ecclesia super episcopos constituatur et omnis actus ecclesiae per eosdem praepositos gubernetur."

[11] *Ep.* 59, 5; 55, 21; 69, 17; 72, 3.

[12] *In Cant. comm.* 3: "qui vocatur ad episcopatum, non ad principatum vocatur, sed ad servitium totius ecclesiae."   [13] *Ep.* 73, 26.

[14] *Ep.* 33, 1: "inde per temporum et successionum vices episcoporum ordinatio et ecclesiae ratio decurrit."   [15] *Ep.* 75, 17.

[16] *Ep.* 67, 5; 59, 5 *(populi suffragium)*; 55, 8.

[17] *Ep.* 67, 5 *(episcoporum iudicium)*; 59, 5 *(coepiscoporum consensus)*.

[18] Ibid. 67, 5 and *Trad. apost.* 2 (26, Botte).

[19] Cf. K. Müller in *ZNW* 28 (1929), 276–8.

[20] *Ep.* 67, 5: "traditio divina et apostolica observatio."

The Syrian *Didascalia* indicates in a very special way the pre-eminent position of the bishop in his community and pays homage to his dignity by the most laudatory expressions; he takes God's place in the community, he is the image of God and the mediator between him and the faithful.[21] In his office as preacher, he is "the mouth of God", encouraging righteousness, urging on to good works, enthusiastically extolling God's benefits, but speaking, too, of the future wrath at God's judgment.[22] The *Didascalia* speaks more insistently than any other pre-Constantinian work of the qualities required by the episcopate and the shortcomings that would exclude one from it. The first requirement is close familiarity with Holy Scripture, of which the bishop must be the interpreter. A wider intellectual formation is desirable, but is not an indispensable condition.[23] As all his conduct is to be a model to his flock, he must fulfill the highest demands on moral qualities and character.[24] Guarantees of this are more likely to be provided by a certain maturity in age and so the bishop chosen should be fifty years old if possible, and in the case of a younger candidate, his real suitability should be determined by conscientious investigation.[25] Access to episcopal office was barred to a man who had been married more than once; the manner of life of the wife and children had to be in harmony with the high dignity of the head of the family.[26] The presbyters or priests occupy, generally speaking, in the *Didascalia*, the position that the *Letters* of St Ignatius of Antioch had already assigned to them; they are the advisers and associates of the bishops, and collaborate particularly in judicial proceedings against a Christian, but have no claim to share by right the gifts of the community.[27] The third century, however, also saw signs of increasing importance in the office of priest, at least in some of the regions to which Christianity had spread. This was connected with growing numbers of Christians in country districts for whom no bishop, but only a presbyter, could be appointed as leader of the community. This was certainly the case in Egypt after the middle of the century as Dionysius of Alexandria testifies.[28] It can scarcely be doubted that a village presbyter, appointed to such small communities, had also the right of celebrating the Eucharist. An extension of priestly faculties was also granted in times of need, such as persecutions, when the bishop, through arrest or flight, could no longer

---

[21] *Didasc.* 2, 18, 2; 2, 11; 2, 25, 7.
[22] Ibid. 2, 28, 9; 2, 17, 6.   [23] Ibid. 2, 1, 2; 2, 5, 3.   [24] Ibid. 2, 6, 5.
[25] Ibid. 2, 1, 1–3.
[26] Ibid. 2, 2, 1–4. There was, therefore, no obligation to celibacy yet in the third century; Canon 6 of the Synod of Elvira then imposed it on clerics from deacons upward.
[27] Ibid. 2, 34, 3; 2, 46, 6; 2, 48, 4.
[28] In *Euseb. HE* 7, 24, 6–9; cf. also ibid. 6, 44, 2–5.

personally care for his flock. A letter of Cyprian is instructive here, which empowered presbyters and deacons in times of special peril through sickness, to hear the confessions of the lapsed and to reconcile them.[29] Finally, the growth of priestly functions was due to the growth in this century of large Christian communities, often with several thousand members in the more important towns of the Roman Empire such as Rome, Carthage, Alexandria, and Antioch. The frequent mention of priests at the administration of baptism in the rite described by Hippolytus, is just as noticeable in this respect as the emphasis on the part they played in the ordination of new priests, on whom they laid hands with the bishop.[30] In Rome, the setting up of the *tituli* as actual pastoral districts[31] gave a more independent position to the priests to whom they were entrusted than was possible in smaller communities. The care of Christians in the countryside around Alexandria by travelling priests (περιοδευταί)[32] at the beginning of the fourth century, already points clearly to the incipient development that led to the "parish", which likewise was to give the presbyter a new and wider sphere of activities, and so bring increased importance to his office.

In the daily life of an average Christian community, the presbyters, however, were still less prominent than the deacons. As the chief official assistants of their bishops, especially for the care of the poor, and in the administration of funds, they came into more frequent contact with individual members of the congregation and so, as the *Didascalia* says, were the bishop's "ear and mouth, heart and soul".[33] As the deacon had to keep the bishop informed about all that happened in the community, discussions of its affairs gave him, by the nature of things, much influence. The *Didascalia* considers that the well-being of the community depended on harmonious collaboration between bishop and deacon.[34]

The growing needs of the communities in the third century finally led to the development of further grades in the series of clerical ministries which, however, all remained below the rank of deacon. They are listed in the catalogue of the Roman clergy which Bishop Cornelius drew up in a letter to Fabius of Antioch.[35] According to this, there were seven subdeacons, forty-two acolytes, and fifty-two exorcists, lectors, and doorkeepers, in the Church's service. The holders of these offices mostly

---

[29] *Ep.* 18, 1.
[30] *Trad. apost.* 8; 21 (37, 49–51 Botte).
[31] See below, page 380.
[32] *Euseb. HE* 8, 13, 7; *Epist. episc. Aegypt.* in *PG* 10, 1566.
[33] *Didasc.* 2, 44, 4.
[34] Ibid. and 3, 13, 7.
[35] *Euseb. HE* 6. 43, 11; they are also all mentioned, with the exception of the *ostiarius*, by Cyprian.

figured in a liturgical role, others had special tasks in connexion with corporate works of mercy, such as care for those mentally ill and for epileptics. The exorcists had charge of this latter task, whilst the subdeacons are to be regarded as direct assistants of the deacons, with the acolytes, in turn, as helpers of the subdeacons. The most frequently mentioned office among the minor orders is that of the lector,[36] whose duty was to read aloud at divine service; this presupposed a certain education in the man entrusted with it, and gave special prestige. The doorkeeper looked after the entrances to the place of divine worship, and kept out unauthorized persons.

Appointment to these offices, as to those of priest and deacon, belonged exclusively to the bishop who, of course, could consult his flock about suitable candidates. The bishop handed the lector the book of readings when he was inducted into his office, but as the *Traditio apostolica* emphasizes, he received no ordination. The subdeacon was not ordained by imposition of hands, either.[37]

The beginnings of the so-called "irregularities", or canonical impediments are already clearly perceptible in the third century. As has already been said, anyone who had once been obliged to perform public canonical penance was incapable of receiving holy orders; similarly, baptism received in sickness *(baptismus clinicorum)*, which was considered to show a lack of courage to confess the faith, excluded from ecclesiastical office; finally, voluntary self-mutilation was regarded an an impediment to orders, though in Origen's time this was not yet generally recognized.

As the bishop and deacons were completely occupied with their duties, in the larger communities, it was the obligation of the faithful to see to their upkeep; this was a charge on the general gifts of the faithful for the whole needs of the Church.[38] The other clerics were dependent on private means, or on their income from a profession in civil life. Cyprian even had to complain of the excessive acquisitiveness of some bishops, and the Synod of Elvira was obliged to lay down quite definite regulations about the clergy's commercial transactions.[39]

Little information is available about the training of the clergy for its religious and ecclesiastical tasks at this period; it was not yet subject to fixed rules laid down by the Church authorities. Consequently, the cleric obtained his theological knowledge first of all in the lessons of the catechumenate and further by private study, sometimes, perhaps, with a learned Christian teacher, who after the fashion of the philosophers of

---

[36] Tertullian *De Praescr.* 41 mentions it; the East at first only had the grade of lector, reader (ἀναγνώστης).
[37] *Trad. apost.* 12 and 14 (43 Botte).   [38] *Didasc.* 2, 25,4 and 14.
[39] Cyprian, *De laps.* 6; Synod. Illib. can. 19.

antiquity, now also gave lessons in the "philosophy" of Christianity. Knowledge of liturgical functions was provided by direct participation in the prayer and worship of his church. The growing variety of ecclesiastical orders provided the possibility of being tested in a lower grade, and of gradually acquiring deeper religious knowledge and increasing familiarity with the tasks of a higher office. [40]

The Bishop and his Church

The growth of the Christian communities in the third century and the development of their organization which this involved, has already been pointed out several times. The elaboration of divine worship in the liturgy of baptism and the celebration of the Eucharist, and the creation of more grades in the ministry, are among the most significant phenomena of this kind. In this connexion, we have still to speak specifically about the position of the individual church under its bishop as the holder of ecclesiastical property. This, particularly in the large town communities of the third century, was becoming of considerable importance. The gifts of the faithful which were expended on the manifold activities of the local church, were collected in a common fund which probably became a permanent institution quite early. [41] In Tertullian's time, these gifts had assumed the character of a voluntary monthly personal contribution, the proceeds of which were placed in the community chest *(arca)*. [42] In this way, the local churches everywhere acquired property and funds, the control and administration of which ultimately belonged to their bishops. As well as contributions in money and things in daily use (foodstuffs and clothes), there soon came gifts of houses and land, so that even before Constantine's time, the property of the church communities consisted of money and real estate. [43] The existence of this church property was not unknown to the civil authorities; Tertullian and Origen, of course, discussed quite openly the problems connected with it. Since this property was not touched by the State, except in the abnormal circumstances of various particular persecutions, this presupposes the recognition of the individual communities as the legal owners in civil law. [44] The decrees of

[40] On this, see *Harnack Miss* 860–6.
[41] Ignatius of Antioch was already familiar with it: *Ad Polyc.* 4, 3; and so was Justin, for *Apol.* 67, 12 implies its existence.
[42] *Apol.* 39; the common chest of Alexandria was called γλωσσόκομον, cf. Origen, *In Matth. comm.* 11,9.
[43] Cf. Tertullian, *Ad Scap.* 3; Origen, *In Lev. hom.* 11, 1; Cyprian, *De op. et eleem.*, *passim.* On the property of the Roman church in houses and cemeteries, cf. *Liber pontif.* 26; *Euseb. HE* 4, 23, 10; for Antioch, ibid. 7, 30, 7.
[44] Cf. G. Krüger, *Die Rechtsstellung der vorkonstantinischen Kirche* (Stuttgart 1935, reprinted Amsterdam 1961), 191–226.

the State authorities after the end of the Diocletian persecution, which provided for the return of the confiscated property to the various Christian communities as its legal owners, similarly indicate that the capacity of the churches to own property was recognized by the State in the third century.[45] This development, too, shows clearly that the Church of the third century had grown into a condition and circumstances which plainly distinguish it from the preceding period, and justify the designation "great church" of early Christian times.

Another development in the sphere of organization was also important for many episcopal churches. They grew not only in numbers, but also in geographical extent. When, in Egypt,[46] there were churches in the country which were served either by a resident priest or by a cleric from the bishop's centre, it followed that as the communities came into existence, they did not automatically receive a bishop as their head, but remained subject to the bishop of the nearest larger community. In that way a development began in the third century which led in the direction of a bishop's centre, it followed that as the communities came into existence, A reshaping of organization was taking place which led to two new forms: a bigger episcopal diocese comprising several Christian communities in town and country, but with only one bishop at their head, and a Christian community which received a pastor of its own for its immediate religious needs; he however, whether priest, or, as in a few places, chorepiscopus,[47] was always subject to the bishop.

Forms of Organization Larger than the Local Community

The coming into existence of the "great church" is made very tangibly clear by the association of the various individual communities under their bishops into a higher structure, the church province. The rise of this was determined particularly by two factors. One of these followed from the method of the early Christian mission which first tried to gain a footing in populous towns, which would mean the provincial capitals in the Roman Empire, and attempted to found its first communities there. Normally, the evangelization of further larger centres in the province would begin from the bishop's community in the provincial capital, and the new churches that had come about in that way naturally maintained close relations with the mother-church. Consequently, all the daughter communities founded by a central episcopal church were bound together

---

[45] Ibid. 231–42.
[46] Cf. *Euseb. HE* 7, 24, 6. On the division of the Roman community into districts for pastoral purposes, see *Harnack, Miss* 854–60.
[47] *Euseb. HE* 7, 30, 10; Syn. Ancr., can. 13.

by mutual ties. In this association a certain leading role naturally fell to the bishop of the mother-church, and from the fourth century, this was expressed by the title "metropolitan". But more decisive than the link created by such missions, was the formation of ecclesiastical provinces by the establishment of synods which, from the end of the second century, brought together the bishops of specific regions to discuss important Church affairs. The question of the date of Easter, and the Montanist movement, are mentioned as motives for such meetings which, of course, were not limited to the bishops of particular political provinces, but extended beyond these. In this way, a synod on the occasion of the Easter controversy brought together the bishops of Caesarea in Palestine, Aelia, Ptolemais, and Tyre, whose sees, in fact, lay in two provinces, namely, Syria and Palestine. These bishops also kept in touch with the bishop of Alexandria and came to an agreement with him about the date of Easter.[48] In the same way, bishops from various civil provinces such as Cappadocia, Galatia, Cicilia, and others, took part in the middle of the third century in the Synod of Iconium in Asia Minor.[49] In any case, such synods were a regular custom in the East at the beginning of the third century, while in North Africa they were still unknown, as appears from a remark of Tertullian which also shows that such synodal assemblies were felt to be an important and impressive outward manifestation of Christianity.[50] It is clear from the list of those who took part in the Council of Nicaea that, at least in the East, the association of the local churches into church provinces was later adapted to the frontiers of the political provinces, for the list follows the order of the latter.[51] The same Council took for granted the existence of the ecclesiastical provinces by assigning to all the bishops of a province the right to install a bishop in his diocese and reserving the right of confirming this to the metropolitan of the province.[52]

In the Latin West, the tendency for wider associations of this kind only appeared later, and then assumed different forms. What happened was not really the formation of several ecclesiastical provinces in the proper sense, as in the East, but directly a supra-provincial association of all the episcopal sees in North Africa on the one hand and of central and southern Italy on the other. The leadership of these forms of organization fell to the bishops of Rome and Carthage, particular weight attaching to the fact that the communities of these great cities had been the starting-points in the christianization of the territories of which they were now the

[48] *Euseb. HE* 5, 23, 25.
[49] Cf. Cyprian, *Ep.* 75, 7.
[50] Tertullian, *De ieiun.* 13.
[51] Cf. E. Schwarz in *AAM NF* 13 (1937), 14 ff.
[52] Conc. Nic., can. 4.

ecclesiastical leaders. When the Bishop of Carthage summoned synods in the third century, his invitation was addressed to the bishops of all the civil provinces in North Africa, and was so accepted.[53] Similarly, the synods held by the Roman bishops of the third century brought together all the bishops there were in Italy at that time. Consequently, Rome and Carthage were ecclesiastical administrative centres of a rank far superior to that of a mere ecclesiastical metropolis. Two such higher centres also became increasingly prominent in the third century East, Antioch and Alexandria. In Antioch, synods met which were attended by the bishops of all Syria and of eastern Asia Minor, like the one planned in 251 against Novatianism,[54] or those of the years 264–8, which were particularly concerned with the case of Paul of Samosata.[55] The missionary interests of the Antioch bishops extended further than the territory of a church province, too, as their concern about Cicilia or Osrhoëne shows.[56] The same applies to the episcopal see of the Egyptian capital, whose occupant controlled the affairs of the episcopate of the Lybian Pentapolis, although this belonged administratively to Crete. Here, too, the third century development was confirmed by the Council of Nicaea:[57] all the bishoprics of Egypt, Libya, and the Pentapolis were made subject to the bishop of Alexandria, and at the same time, express reference was also made to the similar pre-eminence of Rome. Antioch had similar rights, obviously in the sphere of the political diocese of Oriens. In this way, the occupants of these two eastern episcopal sees were recognized as a sort of higher metropolitans, and so the foundation was laid for the development of later patriarchates. There is only a hint in Canon 6 of the Council of Nicaea that similar tendencies were showing themselves in other places. It is only Canon 2 of the Council of Constantinople (381), that makes it clear that the bishops of Ephesus, Heracleia, and Caesarea were also trying to obtain such supra-metropolitan rights for the political dioceses of Asia, Thrace, and Pontus — without, in the long run, succeeding.

The Pre-eminent Position of Rome and its Bishop

The preceeding account has repeatedly had occasion to indicate the special influence which the Roman community exercised on questions and events that exceeded the sphere of interest of an average episcopal community.

[53] Cf. for example, the introduction to the *Sententiae episcoporum*. They come from the provinces of Africa (proconsularis), Numidia, Mauretania; cf. the list of the synods from 251–6 with the numbers of those taking part and the names of the provinces represented in *DHGE* 1, 747–50.

[54] *Euseb. HE* 6, 46, 3.   [55] Ibid. 7, 5, 1–2.

[56] Ibid. 6, 12, 2; see below, chapter 27, p. 372.

[57] Conc. Nic., can. 6.

Similarly, too, there was perceptible the echo of a claim to a pre-eminent position, of a kind that revealed special recognition and regard for the Roman community within the Church as a whole. In that way a development was powerfully pursuing its course, the bases of which were clearly visible in the sub-apostolic period.[58] The features already indicated must now be brought together into a unified view with other facts and statements of ecclesiastical writers that have not yet been mentioned.

In the description of the Church's fight to defend herself against Gnosticism, the importance which Irenaeus of Lyons attributed to apostolic tradition for the recognition of true doctrine has already been mentioned.[59] Now it must be particularly stressed that he ascribed very high value to the Roman church for the ascertaining of apostolic tradition. This latter can, indeed, be established, he maintains, in every church whose bishops can be derived in a genuine series of succession from the apostles.[60] But it is sufficient to prove this succession in the "greatest and oldest church known to all", that of Rome; for "it was founded and built by the two glorious apostles Peter and Paul" and its list of bishops proves that in it, "the apostolic tradition and preaching of the faith" has come down to our time.[61] Here, therefore, a special pre-eminence of Rome is linked with the fact that its church rests on the most distinguished apostolic foundations and has always remained true to the doctrine of the apostles. Consequently, anyone seeking the truth, will find it in Rome; all the Gnostic founders of sects can be refuted by the traditional truth found in Rome. The relevance of the Roman church to the discovery of truth, which is already expressed very strikingly in all this, would certainly gain even more weight if the statement of Irenaeus which has been discussed for centuries[62] without yet receiving an absolutely satisfactory interpretation, could also be quite certainly taken as referring to the Roman church and to it alone.[63] This reference, however, is neither imperatively demanded by the context, nor is it free from serious philological difficulties. Irenaeus' line of thought is, plainly, as follows: The apostolic

---

[58] See above, chapter 10, p. 152.

[59] See above, chapter 15, p. 197.

[60] *Adv. haer.* 3, 3, 1.

[61] Ibid. 3, 3, 2.

[62] Cf. the survey of the various attempts at interpretation in L. Spikowski, *La doctrine de l'église dans s. Irénée* (Strasbourg 1926), 146–55.

[63] *Adv. haer.* 3, 3, 3: "ad hanc enim ecclesiam propter potiorem (al. potentiorem) principalitatem necesse est omnem convenire ecclesiam, hoc est eos qui sunt undique fideles, in qua semper ab his qui sunt undique conservata est ea quae est ab apostolis traditio (For with such a church, on account of the greater authority of its origin, every church must agree, that is to say, all the faithful everywhere, in which (church) the tradition which is from the apostles has always been preserved by these who are everywhere)."

tradition is found with certainty in the communities which rest on a directly apostolic foundation; there are several of these and each of them has a stronger power, grounded in its (apostolic) origin, for the ascertaining of truth, than any other Christian community whatever. But Rome stands out even from this series of apostolic foundations, because, as is everywhere recognized, Peter and Paul were its founders. Then Irenaeus summarizes; with such a church of apostolic foundation every individual church must agree, because precisely such a church has always preserved the apostolic tradition. One of these churches is the Roman church; which is even in a particularly favourable position for establishing the apostolic tradition, but not exclusively so.[64]

The Jewish Christian Hegesippus, living about the same time as Irenaeus, showed an interest for the succession of Roman bishops, deriving from similar motives. In his fight against the Gnostic heresy, he sought to ascertain the tradition of belief in the more important Christian communities of his time. Where he found a tradition transmitted from bishop to bishop (διαδοχή), that for him was a proof of the authenticity of its doctrine. His journey to the various churches led him to Rome, where he convinced himself of the existence of such a *diadoche* right down to the last bishop, Eleutherius.[65] Here, too, a specific importance is attributed to the Roman church for a knowledge of apostolic tradition purely preserved. Tertullian, likewise, names Rome, and Smyrna in addition as examples of a church which could trace back to an apostle the list of its bishops in succession.[66]

Consciousness of a pre-eminent position of the Roman church in determining apostolic tradition, was also the basis of the attitude of the

---

[64] The difficulty of interpretation is partly due to the loss of the original text. Of special importance appear to be the attempts of P. Nautin in *RHR* 151 (1947), 37–78, and B. Botte in *Irénikon* 30 (1957), 156–63. P. Nautin succeeds in proving that the grammatical structure of the sentence makes it impossible to construe *hanc ecclesiam* as referring exclusively to the Roman church. On the other hand, it does not seem possible that, as he maintains, it refers to the *ecclesia universalis;* for in that case *omnis ecclesia* would also have to refer to each Gnostic community to which a certain *principalitas* belonged, yet Irenaeus never calls a Gnostic sect *ecclesia.* If, however, *hanc ecclesiam* is regarded as a church of directly apostolic foundation, it is easy to see that it has a *potior principalitas* in regard to any other Christian community at all which derives its origin only indirectly from the apostles. The suggestion of B. Botte (*op. cit., ad fin.*), is worth considering: that *conservare* might be understood in the sense of τηρεῖν and those referred to by *ab his qui sunt undique* as the Gnostics from whom the apostolic tradition is being "guarded". Even if the famous text of Irenaeus must be abandoned as one of the proofs of early Christian awareness of the primacy, this does not affect the development of this awareness elsewhere, where it is manifest in various ways.

[65] Cf. *Euseb. HE* 4, 22, 3.

[66] *De praescr.* 32.

Roman Bishop Victor (189–98) in the dispute about the keeping of Easter.[67] He appealed to apostolic tradition to justify the Roman practice of keeping Easter on the Sunday after 14 Nisan. He then demanded quite definitely that the churches of Asia Minor should also follow this custom, threatening in the event of a refusal the most serious of measures, that is, exclusion from the ecclesiastical community, because he regarded the Asia Minor practice as heterodox.[68] A claim by Rome to leadership is here apparent which goes far beyond the pre-eminence attributed to it as the guardian of apostolic tradition. It is only explained by the Roman bishop's awareness of his ability to intervene authoritatively in the affairs of even distant churches. Victor did not state the source of this awareness in his own case. In any event, his instruction[69] that synods were to be held about the matter was followed even by the bishops of Asia Minor, although they held different views from Rome. The majority of the synods decided on the Roman custom. Opposition to the Roman demand was raised by Bishop Polycrates of Ephesus and his fellow bishops, because they also believed themselves bound to an apostolic tradition. When Polycrates in his answer to Pope Victor, emphatically recalled the great figures of the Asiatic church of the past, this suggests that Victor had supported the Roman claim on the foundation of its church by Peter and Paul; but that Victor also felt himself to be the guardian of orthodoxy, is proved by his excommunicating the Monarchian Theodotus. A few decades later, Sabellius was excommunicated for heresy by the Roman Bishop Callistus.[70]

An unmistakable expression of the bishop of Rome's awareness that he occupied a special position within the Church as a whole, is encountered in various measures of a disciplinary nature taken by Pope Stephen (254–7). Two Spanish bishops, Basilides of Emerita and Martialis of Asturica, had got sacrifice certificates in the Decian persecution and on account of this and other transgressions, had been deposed.[71] Basilides went to Rome and obtained, by false representation of the case, as Cyprian emphasizes,[72] his own rehabilitation and that of his colleague. Two things are notable about this incident. A Spanish bishop had recourse to Rome because he was convinced that it was the place to which he could appeal against the decision of a Spanish synod, and that there, a disciplinary case of this sort could be dealt with and decided with legal authority. Even more significant is the case that has already been mentioned, that of Bishop

[67] See above, chapter 23, p. 271, with the references in the notes.
[68] *Euseb. HE* 5, 24, 9,   [69] Ibid. 5, 24, 8.
[70] Ibid. 5, 28, 6 and Hippolytus, *Refut.* 9, 12. Both matters can of course be regarded as internal affairs of the Roman community.
[71] See the whole *Ep.* 76 of Cyprian.
[72] *Ep.* 67, 5.

Marcion of Arles, a convinced follower of Novatian, who allowed the lapsed in his community to die without reconciliation, despite their readiness to repent. This time, it was Cyprian of Carthage who turned to Pope Stephen in a very significant letter[73] that demanded from him decisive action against Marcion, that is to say, his deposition and the appointment of a new head of the community, whose name was to be sent to the African episcopate so that they might know with whom they were to maintain fellowship.[74] The whole tenor of the letter implies the view that the Arles case concerned the pope alone, and could only definitively be decided by him, and that Rome could determine authoritatively who was to be granted ecclesiastical fellowship and who was not. The same conviction was current in Gaul, because Cyprian's letter was sent as a result of steps taken by Faustinus,[75] the bishop of Lyons.

This public recognition of the pre-eminent position of the Roman bishop by Cyprian, at least as regards Spain and Gaul, is rather surprising when it is compared with his theoretical standpoint and attitude to Rome in the dispute about baptism by heretics. It is true that in Cyprian's writings there are statements about the Roman church which at first sight seem to amount to recognition of a special authority of Rome. In one of his letters to Pope Cornelius he denounces the conduct of that section of his clergy that was opposed to him, in sending representatives to Rome in order to win over its bishop to their side. They brought letters "to the chair of Peter and to the chief church, from which the unity of the bishops took its rise".[76] The Roman see is elsewhere called by him "the place of Peter".[77] In his work *On the Unity of the Church,* Cyprian speaks about the foundation of the Church, which he considers is expressed in our Lord's words at Matthew 16:18. By designating Peter as the rock, Christ proclaimed that he "is building the Church on one man, that the origin of unity derives from one".[78] The other apostles were, to be sure, equal to Peter in dignity and power, but the beginning of unity is identified with Peter. Apparently favourable to the primacy, too, is the version of the fourth chapter of this work that is found in some manuscripts, where we read: "Is anyone who leaves the see of Peter, on which the Church is founded, still convinced that he is within the Church?" and: "Certainly the others were what Peter was, but *Petro primatus datur* and so one

---

[73] *Ep.* 68.   [74] *Ep.* 68, 3–5.

[75] *Ep.* 68, 1.

[76] *Ep.* 59, 14: "ad Petri cathedram atque ad ecclesiam principalem, unde unitas sacerdotalis exorta est." This text remains just as important even if we see it as expressing the view of Cyprian's opponents; cf. J. Ludwig, *Der hl. Märtyrerbischof Cyprian von Carthago* (Munich 1951), 44.

[77] *Ep.* 55, 8.

[78] *De eccles. unit.* 4.

Church and one *cathedra* is manifest."[79] It can be considered probable that these sentences, which bear the unmistakable stamp of Cyprian's style, were to be read in the "first edition" of his work and were only suppressed when it was revised at the time of the dispute about heretical baptism; there is no need to assume any later interpolation from some Roman partisan.[80] But closer analysis of Cyprian's linguistic usage obliges us to abandon these texts as conclusive proofs that the idea of the Roman primacy existed in the mind of the North African bishop. Cyprian is here still simply expressing a chronological pre-eminence of Peter over the other apostles in the conferring of the power of binding and loosing, for they, of course, according to his own words, possessed the same plenary power as he. Consequently, all the bishops possess, even now, one and the same equal episcopal office. In the *cathedra Petri*, Cyprian sees the well-spring of ecclesiastical unity, which has its beginning in Peter. Cyprian does not, however, voice the consequence that this well-spring even now, in his own day, has this function of bringing about unity, in the *cathedra* of the Bishop of Rome. He does not seem to draw it in his own mind, either, for he maintains most emphatically the thesis that bishops are responsible to God alone for the administration of their bishoprics.[81] What Cyprian thought in an actual concrete situation about the right of a Roman bishop to issue binding ordinances with decisive authority for the Church as a whole is shown by the test case of the dispute about heretical baptism which may appropriately be described at this point.

The Controversy about Heretical Baptism

The Christian communities first encountered the problem of heretical baptism when heretical (or schismatical) groups of some size formed, and when members of these wanted to enter the Catholic Church. When it was a case of persons who had been pagans, and who had received baptism in the heretical community, the question arose whether the baptism that had been conferred on them was to be considered valid. The same reply was not given in all the Christian communities. In North Africa, Tertullian's treatise on baptism contains a first standpoint rejecting validity.[82] A synod

---

[79] Ibid. "qui cathedram Petri, super quem fundata ecclesia, deserit, in ecclesia se esse confidit? — hoc erant utique ceteri, quod fuit Petrus, sed primatus Petro datur et una ecclesia et cathedra una monstratur." On the problem, see M. Bénevot, *St Cyprian's De Unitate c. 4 in the Light of the Manuscripts* (Rome 1937); and compare the two versions side by side in J. Ludwig, *op. cit.* 33.

[80] Cf. in particular D. van den Eynde in *RHE* 29 (1933), 5-24, with the older literature there given; further references in *Altaner* 197 f.

[81] *Ep.* 59, 14; see A. Demoustier in *RSR* 52 (1964), 337–69.

[82] Tertullian, *De bapt.* 15; cf. *De praescr.* 12; *De pud.* 19.

about 220, under Bishop Agrippinus of Carthage, maintained a similar view.[83] In the East (especially in Asia Minor), there was a widespread practice of baptizing again on reception into the Church, persons baptized in heresy. Firmilian of Caesarea himself took part in a synod in Iconium (not earlier than 230), at which bishops from Galatia, Cicilia, and other neighbouring provinces, decided they would continue to rebaptize Montanists at their reception.[84] The Alexandrian theologians were also critical of the baptism of heretics, even if they did not make a clear pronouncement about its validity.[85] It is true that the Alexandrian church under Bishop Dionysius took up the same position as Rome, where persons baptized in an heretical sect were received into the Roman community merely by imposition of hands. The different estimation of heretical baptism and the resulting difference of treatment of those who had received it, could plainly have existed side by side for decades in the Church without one side having felt the practice of the other to be intolerable. But shortly after the middle of the third century a serious clash occurred over the matter, when the various views found unyielding defenders in Cyprian of Carthage and Stephen of Rome. An African bishop, Magnus, had submitted the inquiry to Cyprian whether "those who came from Novatian" had to be baptized again in the Catholic Church. Cyprian's comprehensive answer is clear; baptism is entrusted to the Catholic Church alone and her baptism alone is valid; anyone who has not got the Holy Spirit cannot confer that Spirit.[86] Cyprian submitted a similar inquiry from eighteen Numidian bishops to a synod in 255 and it came to the same conclusion.[87] But according to Cyprian "a few colleagues" were still in doubt whether the African practice were the correct one; in a letter that Cyprian wrote after the synod, a tone of irritation with them is unmistakable. There is also a certain sting in it against Rome; for Cyprian attacks the thesis that in such questions appeal should not simply be made to tradition, but that rational reflection should be allowed to have its say; Peter, whom the Lord chose first, did not make any arrogant claims on that account, and did not presumptously occupy the first place *(primatus)*.[88] A synod considered the question again early in 256 and Cyprian wrote at its request to Pope Stephen, enclosing the resolutions of the previous year's synod as well as his previous correspondence on the subject. The whole file clearly showed that Cyprian regarded the Roman custom, and the view of the validity of heretical

[83] Cyprian, *Ep.* 73, 3; 71, 4.
[84] Firmilian in Cyprian, *Ep.* 75, 7; a synod with the same result took place about this time in Synada, cf. *Euseb. HE* 7, 7, 5.
[85] Clement of Alexandria, *Strom.* 1, 19; Origen, *In Ioann. comm.* 6, 25.
[86] *Ep.* 69, 1 and 2 and *passim*.
[87] Cf. *Ep.* 70.   [88] *Ep.* 71, 3.

baptism on which it rested, as a grave dogmatic error, but, with remarkable lack of logic, he wrote that he did not want to impose his view on anyone, as each bishop was free to administer his own flock. He added with heavy irony that there were, of course, people who, in their stubbornness, were not to be dissuaded once a decision had been made. [89]

Pope Stephen's answer to this letter has not survived, but a clear echo of it is found in Cyprian's correspondence. One of his letters describes it as "uninformed and written without due reflection", and Stephen's standpoint is termed an error. [90] Cyprian was particularly up in arms over the principle with which the Roman bishop justified his standpoint. "No innovation, but stand by tradition", because in intention it stamped Cyprian as an innovator. [91] Furthermore, he considered that Stephen's letter had also contained some "haughty matters, beside the point". [92] The letter of Firmilian of Caesarea, preserved among Cyprian's correspondence, throws welcome light on the meaning of these remarks. Cyprian was informed that Pope Stephen's initiative in the matter of heretical baptism was not limited to North Africa. A letter had been sent from Rome to the churches of Asia Minor too, demanding that they should abandon their practice of rebaptism, and threatening excommunication. [93] Cyprian's deacon, Rogatianus, conveyed to Firmilian a report from his bishop about the previous course of the discussion in North Africa. The detailed answer of the Cappadocian bishop shows how deeply concerned they were in Asia Minor over Stephen's action; all the blame for the split was placed on him, and Firmilian compared him with Judas. [94] It is also said that Stephen, in his folly, "glories in his position as a bishop and claims to hold succession of Peter, on whom the foundations of the Church rest". [95] This makes it clear that Stephen was appealing to Matthew 16:18 and claiming for himself, as Peter's successor, Peter's position in the Church. Previous Roman bishops' awareness of a pre-eminence belonging to them in the Church as a whole, which had already been present earlier was, as a matter of fact, now for the first time given a formal basis in that biblical text which in future was to be increasingly regarded as the decisive attestation of the Roman primacy. The two leading bishops of North

---

[89] *Ep.* 72, especially c. 3.   [90] *Ep.* 74, 1.

[91] *Ep.* 74, 1–2. On the formula "nihil innovetur, nisi quod traditum est", cf. F. L. Dölger in *AuC* I (1929), 79 ff. It is a principle with which Rome had already defended its liturgical tradition, when Novatian wrote in the matter of the *lapsi*, "nihil innovandum putavimus" (Cyprian *Ep.* 30, 8).

[92] *Ep.* 74, 1: "superba quaedam et ad rem non pertinentia."

[93] *Euseb. HE* 7, 5, 4–5.

[94] *Ep.* 75, 2.

[95] *Ep.* 75, 17: "de episcopatus sui loco gloriatur et se successionem Petri tenere contendit, super quem fundamenta ecclesiae collocata sunt."

Africa and Asia Minor did not bow to Stephen's claim. Cyprian had his position confirmed again at a third synod in September 256, in which eighty-seven bishops took part from the three provinces of Africa proconsularis, Mauritania, and Numidia, — not actually comprising the majority of the approximately two hundred bishops who there were at that time.[96] The episcopal delegation sent to Rome with the resolutions of the synod was not even received by Stephen, and he went so far as to give instructions that it was not to be received in the church community there either.[97] That meant a breach with the church of North Africa led by Cyprian. It was the most important demonstration of Rome's position of pre-eminence yet undertaken by one of its bishops, and Stephen undertook it, even at the cost of a rupture, in the consciousness of occupying and of having to fulfill the office and function of Peter in the Church as a whole. It is not surprising that this claim met with resistance. Just as in the history of the Church, Rome's task of leadership only became more clearly manifest in situations which demanded its active exercise, such situations becoming gradually more frequent with the Church's growth; so also from an historical point of view the idea of the Primacy had to develop and became clearer through a process of some length. Cyprian of Carthage, in his striving for an understanding of Matthew 16:18, is an example of a transitional stage in the process of clarification. It seems much more worthy of note that in the face of such contradiction the idea of the primacy prevailed and held its ground.

The question of heretical baptism did not, however, lead to a division of long duration in the early Christian Church. The two leaders of the opposed views in the West, died shortly after one another, Pope Stephen in 257 and Bishop Cyprian as a martyr on 14 September 258. Their followers were not so personally involved in the dispute and at first let it rest, one side tolerating the practice followed by the other. In the East, the zealous Bishop Dionysius of Alexandria endeavoured to mediate between the two camps; six letters on the matter went to Rome. A brief reference in one of these letters, written "imploringly", to Pope Stephen, praises the unity of all Eastern bishops in repulsing Novatianism.[98] His implication is clear: ought it not to be possible to avoid a schism in the discussion about heretical baptism, too? Dionysius appealed in the same sense[99] to Stephen's successor, Sixtus (257–8). Under Sixtus' successor, Dionysius (260–8), the conflict between Rome and the bishops of Asia Minor seems to have been settled. In the West, after a first approach at the Synod of Arles,[100] a final clarification was achieved by the dogmatic work of Augustine, in the sense of the Roman view and practice.

---

[96] See *Sent. episcop. 87 de haer. baptiz. proem.*   [97] *Ep.* 75, 25.
[98] *Euseb. HE* 7, 5, 1–2.   [99] Ibid. 7, 5, 3; 7, 9, 1 and 6.   [100] Can. 8 (314).

The Alexandrian Bishop Dionysius, who was so zealously concerned with peace in the Church, experienced personally, however, that the Roman bishop demanded an account of anyone who put forward false or misleading views in matters of faith, when, in about 260, in controversy with the Patripassians, he used insufficiently precise formulas regarding the distinction between Father and Son.[101] The Bishop of Rome not only required of him a precise exposition of his views but directly addressed himself to Dionysius' flock and warned them of teachers who threatened to falsify the previous teaching of the Church about the Trinity. Here too, the intervention of Rome, even against a bishop of such undeniable merit as Dionysius of Alexandria, demonstrates that its bishop knew he was responsible for safeguarding right belief in the whole Church.

The pre-eminence of the Roman position also received spontaneous recognition. The lyrical homage of the Christian Aberkios of Phrygia to the Church of Rome dates from the early third century. He is sent to Rome by a holy shepherdess in order to see a realm, a queen in golden robe and golden shoes and a people possessing a shining seal.[102] Here poetic expression is given to the power of attraction radiating from this Christian community in the West even as far as the eastern provinces of the empire. Origen, too, saw Rome, and not a word from him or any other "pilgrim to Rome" of the time, indicates that it was the fame or the prestige of the imperial capital, as such, that drew them to it. What Origen says can certainly be considered as representative of many: "I wanted to see the ancient church of the Romans."[103] The visits, delegations and letters which came to Rome, and which have been so often mentioned above, frequently had only one purpose, that of obtaining from this Church and this bishop a recognition and confirmation of their aims or views. They testify thereby to the existence of a widespread conviction that both possessed a unique position.

This is also manifest in a final, very significant fact; the language of Christian symbols seized on the theme in order to express a reality in its own way or to make it accessible in a new form. The very expressive and widespread symbol of the ship of the Church[104] was developed into the picture of the Church as Peter's ship. It is encountered in the texts of the early third century, in the letter of the pseudo-Clement to the apostle

---

[101] See above, chapter 21, pp. 259 f., with references to sources.

[102] No doubt is possible regarding the Christian character of the inscription since the investigation of F. J. Dölger in *Ichthys* II (Münster 1922), 454–507; see also the text in *RAC* I, 13.

[103] *Euseb. HE* 6, 14, 10.

[104] Cf. especially H. Rahner, "Antenna crucis III" in *ZKTh* 66 (1942), 196–227, 67 (1943), 1–21, republished in H. Rahner, *Symbole der Kirche* (Salzburg 1964), 473–503; J. Daniélou, "Le navire de l'église" in *Les symboles chrétiens primitifs* (Paris 1961), 65–76.

James, which introduces the Clementine *Recognitions* and is probably of Roman origin.[105] Here Peter admonishes the hesitant Clement, to whom he entrusts his see, not to fail in service to the faithful who are in danger on their voyage through this life. The owner of this ship is God, its helmsman-pilot Christ, the bishop stands in the bows, the passengers are the brotherhood of believers; the bishop has the hardest task, he must vigilantly listen to the words of the helmsman (Christ) and repeat his orders clearly. Consequently, all the brethren must obey the bishop, who "presides in truth", for the *cathedra Christi* is entrusted to him.[106] With astonishing sureness here, conviction about the position of the Roman bishop has been transposed into the language of symbolism; he is the second pilot of the ship of the Church, over which he has full official authority. The προκαθημένη τῆς ἀγάπης (presiding by love) of the *Letter to the Romans* of Ignatius of Antioch has become the προκαθεζώμενος ἀληθείας (having the presidency of truth) and he has to preach the truth of him whose chair he occupies. Novatian, too, emphasized, not without self-satisfaction, in the letter which he wrote to Cyprian when the see was vacant in 250–1, that the Roman church held the wheel of the ship of the Church in firm hands. The greatest hour of the symbol of the *navicula Petri* was only to come in the post-Constantinian and early medieval period, when it was given an ecclesiastico-political interpretation, but its symbolism is theologically richer in the Clementine *Recognitions*.

Devotion to the Church in the Third Century

The previous chapters have attempted to portray all the important expression of the life of the Church as a whole in early Christian times. The reality revealed by this picture is manifold and full of contrasts, like everything which is living. A final feature has to be added to the picture. This Church is not only an object of knowledge, is not only given its theological basis and affirmed with understanding, its very reality is taken up into the affections of the faithful, felt as a gift of grace. Just as there was a spirituality of baptism and martyrdom, there was a spirituality centred on the Church.

This was given most profound expression by the application of one of the fundamental words of humanity to the Church, which was loved as the "mother" of the faithful. This name was prepared for by the personification of "faith" as a maternal figure in Polycarp of Smyrna[107] and by Hermas, to whom the Church appeared as a revered woman.[108] The

---

[105] On this cf. H. Rahner in ZKTh 69 (1947), 6.   [106] Ps-Clement, *Recogn.* 14–17.
[107] Phil. 3, 2 alluding to Gal. 4:26. Cf. also *Acta ss. Iustini et sociorum* 4, 8.
[108] *Pastor Vis.* 2, 1, 3; 2, 4, 1; 3, 9, 1.

Christians of Lyons were the first to apply the name "mother" to the Church, like an expression that had long been familiar to them; the martyrs of the year 177 were the children born of her who went home in peace to God without saddening their mother.[109] According to Irenaeus, the heretics have no share in the spirit of truth; they are not at the breast of Mother Church who, at the same time, is the Bride of Christ.[110] The catechists, in preparing for baptism, clearly liked to represent the Church to the catechumens as a mother who bears her children in baptism and then feeds and guards them. Tertullian speaks with deep feeling, especially in his pastoral writings, of *domina mater ecclesia* who, with motherly care, looks after those who are imprisoned,[111] and whose children, after baptism, recite the Our Father as their first prayer in common with their brethren, "in their mother's house",[112] whilst the heretics have no mother.[113] The same note of deep feeling is found in the terminology of the Alexandrians; for Clement, the Church is the Virgin Mother who calls her children to herself and feeds them on sacred milk.[114] Origen sees her both as *sponsa Christi* and as mother of the nations; bitter sorrow is caused her by impenitence and attachment to evil.[115] The term *mater ecclesia* has become a real expression of filial love and piety in the writings of Cyprian, who sings the joy this mother feels about her virginal children and brave confessors; but he also knows the tears which she sheds for the lapsed.[116] More than any other writer of the third century, he evokes the picture of this mother when the unity of the Church is threatened by schism. His urgently repeated appeals to the faithful to preserve their unity at all costs culminate in one of his most celebrated sayings: "That man cannot have God as his Father who has not the Church as his Mother."[117] In a mystical vision, Methodius of Olympus sees the Church like a richly jewelled queen with her place at the right hand of the bridegroom.[118] For her sake, the Logos left the Father and was united to her when she was born from the wound in his side. The newly-baptized are conceived in the embrace between Logos and Church; born again, from her, to an eternal life and accompanied by her maternal care throughout life, to perfection.[119]

[109] *Euseb. HE* 5, 1, 45; 5, 2, 6.   [110] *Adv. haer.* 3, 38, 1; *Fragm.* 30.   [111] *Ad mart.* 1.
[112] *De bapt.* 20; on this see F. J. Dölger in *AuC*, II (1930), 142–55.
[113] *De praescr.* 42, 10.   [114] *Paed.* 1, 6, 42; 3, 12, 99.
[115] *In Cant. hom.* 1, 7; *In Iudic. hom.* 5, 6; other texts in J. C. Plumpe, *Mater ecclesia. An Inquiry into the Concept of the Church as Mother in Early Christianity* (Washington 1943), 70–80.
[116] *De hab. virg.* 3; *Ep.* 10, 4; *De laps.* 8.
[117] *De eccles. unit.* 6: "habere non potest deum patrem qui ecclesiam non habet matrem."
[118] *Symp.* 2, 7, 50; see A. Demoustier in *RSR* 52 (1964), 554–88.
[119] Ibid. 3, 8, 70–2; cf. also, as well as Plumpe, *op. cit.* 113–22, H. Rahner in *ZKTh* 64 (1940), 71–74.

As well as this picture of the Church as Mother, which appealed most directly to the feelings of the faithful, early Christian preaching made use of other images, too, in order to make clear to the hearers the reality of the Church and impress it on their hearts. So, according to Hippolytus, the Church is "God's spiritual garden with Christ as its ground", with an inexhaustible stream of water, from which the four rivers of Paradise flow, the four Gospels which announce the Lord to the world.[120] Origen compares the Church with Paradise in which the newly-baptized fulfill the works of the Spirit.[121] The Johannine parable of the vine and the branches (Jn 15:1–7), must have proved particularly rich as a catechetical theme; it is applied to the Church by the Fathers repeatedly with far-ranging symbolism.[122] All these metaphors were of a kind to give the Church distinctive emotional associations in the mind of her members and to make the Church dear to them in a sense of very real affection.

A widespread devotion to the Church of this kind in the third century is like the spirituality of baptism and martyrdom spoken of above, an important factor in the history of the Church, and must not be passed over unnoticed. Even if the depth and extent of its influence is often difficult to measure and determine, there is no doubt of its presence; it gave the consciousness of the Church in the third century a characteristic stamp, and may be regarded as one of the sources from which the early Christian Church as a whole drew some of its vitality.

CHAPTER 27

The Extent of Christianity prior to the Diocletian Persecution

RUNNING parallel to the rich development of life within the Church, in literature and liturgy, organization and the practice of spirituality, was a growth in numbers which gave Christianity at this period, even when viewed from outside, the character of a "great Church". The inner strengthening of the Church in this century created the conditions for her decisive missionary success in the world of Hellenic civilization right up to the beginning of the Diocletian persecution. This eminently important process in the history of the Church was influenced not only by

---

[120] Hippolytus, *In Dan. comm.* 1, 17; similarly Cyprian, *Ep.* 73, 10.
[121] Cf. J. Daniélou: "Sentire ecclesiam" in *Festschrift H. Rahner*, (Freiburg i. Br. 1961), 96.
[122] Ibid, 100–2. Also "Un Testimonium sur la vigne dans Barnabé 12:1" in *RSR* 50 (1962), 384–99.

such conditions, but also by the conjunction of further favourable factors of varying importance in their actual impact.

In the first place, the two long periods of peace in the third century must be mentioned. They offered the Church, to an extent unknown before, missionary possibilities of making herself known, and they were only disturbed by a few waves of relatively brief persecution. These chances were used variously in the different geographical territories of the Empire and on its frontiers. Moreover, the drive of Christianity towards expansion was furthered by developments in the paganism of antiquity itself. The crisis of the ancient world in the third century consisted not only of the threatening decay of the Roman Empire, but was also, and equally, of a crisis in the existing religious and cultural forces.[1] Under the emperor of the Syrian dynasty, the Roman State religion abandoned what had been its traditional foundations. New cults from the East gained increasingly larger followings even in the Latin world, until finally emperor Caracalla gave entry to their divinities into the Roman temples;[2] the Baal of Emesa, the Sun-God of Palmyra, Egyptian Sarapis and Persian Mithras burst the framework of the ancient Roman religion, and robbed it of its exclusiveness. In its place appeared a wide-ranging syncretism which, to be sure, aimed at offering something for every religious inquirer, but was itself poor in religious substance and consequently represented, in fact, a weakening of earlier religious forces. Christianity could advance into this increasing vacuum, and with its claim to offer, in the midst of this religious confusion, both absolute truth and what was "new" and full of promise for the future, found a ready hearing among the pagan population. The Christian preaching of the age not only presented this claim with firm assurance of victory, but increasingly found for it a distinguished form in speech and writing which won the respect of the cultivated pagans. At the beginning of the third century the Alexandrian teachers Clement and Origen dared to attempt to win to Christianity not only cultivated people but culture itself.[3] On the foundation of Christian revelation, they set up a new ideal of culture to which, they were convinced, the future belonged; and they were liberal enough to incorporate in this ideal those elements of pagan education and culture which did not contradict the fundamental truths of the gospel. In East and West, Origen gained an outstanding reputation and became an attractive force with far-reaching influence. Towards the end of the century there grew up in Antioch the second intellectual centre of

---

[1] Cf. F. Altheim, *Der Niedergang der alten Welt*, II (Frankfurt a. M. 1952), 197–233.

[2] K. Bihlmeyer, *Die syrischen Kaiser zu Rom und das Christentum* (Rottenburg 1916), 9–28.

[3] K. Prümm, *Christentum als Neuheitserlebnis* (Freiburg i. Br. 1939), 382–8.

Christianity in the East; it influenced the Syrian hinterland as much as Alexandria did Egypt. In the West, also, Christianity produced writers of quality and reputation who are a striking testimony to the higher standards of Christian literary production. This rich increase in credit and prestige brought Christianity an ever-growing number of adherents from the pagan upper class. Under the Syrian emperors, under Philippus Arabs and Gallienus, there were Christians in influential positions at the imperial court, and an increasing number of bishops sprang from the educated classes. Certainly the majority of the pagan population still met the appeal of the new religion with refusal and, especially in leading circles, so did the "conservatives" who instinctively defended existing intellectual and cultural property. But at the beginning of the fourth century, a minority of such strength and quality professed the new religion, that its resistance could not be broken by the last onslaught under Diocletian.

The East

At the beginning of the third century commenced that rise of the Christian world of Alexandria which made the Church there the intellectual centre of eastern Christianity. Origen's activity as a teacher brought many Gnostics and pagans under its spell; his later friend and patron Ambrose is the best-known example of a learned convert made by him and he was followed by many others. Naturally the Alexandrian community also formed the missionary centre from which sprang attempts to christianize the inhabitants of the Egyptian countryside and neighbouring peoples. The expansion of Christianity into the countryside is increasingly attested by the numerous finds of papyri in Egyptian territory containing biblical fragments, especially St Paul's Epistles, the Synoptic Gospels, the Gospel of St John and the Acts of the Apostles, of which more than twenty can be assigned with some certainty to the third century.[4] The Decian persecution revealed the existence of many Christians in towns and villages even outside Alexandria, and the mention of various bishops[5] shows the growth of hierarchically organized churches which may be presumed to have existed in most provincial centres. Dionysius, the leading bishop of Egypt about the middle of the century, visited several Christian communities in Fayûm which clearly had a considerable number of members.[6] When during the persecution of Decius, he himself had to go into exile, he and his companions used the opportunity to act as

---

[4] H. Idris Bell, *Cults and Creeds in Greco-Roman Egypt* (Liverpool 1954), 84 ff.
[5] *Euseb. HE* 6, 42, 1, 3; 6, 46, 2.
[6] Ibid. 7, 24, 6.

missionaries to the pagans of their place of exile.[7] A papyrus written about the year 300 speaks of two Christian churches in Oxyrhynchus, one in the north, the other in the south of the town.[8] Naturally the Greek-speaking missionaries first addressed themselves to the Greek element in the Egyptian population, but by the middle of the century, there is also evidence that members of the Coptic-speaking part of the nation were being converted to Christianity.[9] The beginnings of Egyptian monasticism stretch as far back as the third century and its early eremitical phase had its first famous representative in St Anthony, who was a Copt.[10] By the beginning of the fourth century certainly, a considerable minority of the population of Egypt was Christian.[11]

The Christian world of Northern Arabia, which became more prominent in the third century, followed the lines of the Alexandrian centre, though whether these relations had their foundations in missionary work from Alexandria, must remain an open question. Origen was held in high regard by the Christians of the province of Arabia;[12] its governor wrote a letter to Bishop Demetrius of Alexandria asking him to send Origen to him so that he might learn about Christianity. Origen answered the request, and care for the Church's doctrine frequently led him to the capital of the Arabian province of Bostra, where about 240, he took part in two synods.[13] This was plainly done at the instance of Bishop Beryllus, the leader of the Arab Christians, who was also active as a writer.[14] The recently discovered script of a religious discussion of Origen with Bishop Hieraclides, in the presence of several bishops, regarding the question of the Trinity, probably took place in a church in Arabia.[15] The later occupants of the episcopal sees of Arabia whose existence is attested here, took part in the Council of Nicaea. It is impossible to determine to what race the Christians in Arabia at this period belonged.

The motherland of Christianity, Palestine, lagged behind the more rapid development of Egypt in the third century. The country people still to a large extent shut themselves off from Christian belief and the faithful were mainly to be found among the Greek population of the cities. About twenty names of towns or villages with Christian groups or communities

---

[7] Ibid. 7, 11, 13–14.

[8] H. I. Bell, *op. cit.* 87.

[9] G. Bardy, *Mémorial Lagrange* (Paris 1940), 209 ff.

[10] K. Heussi, *Der Ursprung des Mönchtums* (Tübingen) 101 ff.

[11] According to Eusebius, *Praep. evang.* 3, 5, the majority of people in Egypt in his day had already abandoned the pagan cults.

[12] G. Kretzschmer, "Origenes und die Araber" in *ZThK* 50 (1953), 250–79.

[13] *Euseb. HE* 6, 33, 3; 6, 37.

[14] Ibid. 6, 20, 2.

[15] J. Scherer in his edition, *Sources Chr.* 67 (1960), 19–21; on Bishop Alexander see P. Nautin, *Lettres et écrivains* (Paris 1961), 105–37.

are known from pre-Constantinian times and sixteen of their bishops took part in the Council of Nicaea. In his report about the Palestinian victims of the Diocletian persecution, Eusebius quotes almost exclusively Greek names for the martyrs, whose relatively small numbers are an index of the extent to which Christianity had spread. The Christians of Jerusalem did not achieve the importance which one would have expected from its ancient Christian tradition, though pilgrimages of Christians from other parts of the Empire[16] which sprang up in the third century, contributed to a revival and increase of its prestige. Among its bishops, Alexander was prominent; he showed his interest in theological learning by establishing a library,[17] probably inspired by the example of Alexandria; he held the teachers Pantaenus and Clement in high esteem, and was on terms of friendship with Origen.[18] The leadership of Palestine in ecclesiastical affairs had been taken over at an early date by the bishops of the provincial capital, Caesarea, and they represented this church province at the synods of Antioch. The Christian community of Caesarea also became the theological and intellectual centre when Origen, after leaving Alexandria in 230, finally settled here, and with strong support from Bishop Theoctistus, was able to pursue his work. The renown of the Alexandrian, and his manifold activity as a teacher so contributed to the successful development of Christianity in this Palestinian town, that about the year 300, even the pagan part of its population was not ill-disposed.[19]

An essentially similar situation was to be found in Phoenicia which already belonged to the greater Syrian area. Here, too, conversions to Christianity at first were confined chiefly to the coastal towns where there were more Greeks, while the mission had scarcely any success in the countryside. In the interior, the great pagan centres of worship of the Sun-god in Emesa, Heliopolis, and Palmyra, occupied a dominant position which made entry for Christian teaching difficult. Syrian national susceptibilities played their part here, causing Christianity, represented by Greeks, to be judged unfavourably. In the towns of Damascus and Paneas there were Christians, because in these towns Hellenism was stronger. In the third century, as a consequence, the coastal towns of Tyre, Sidon, Berytus, Byblos, and Tripoli remained the centres from which Christianity spread, and of these Tyre took the lead about 250. In this town, Origen died and was buried and Tyre also had the most martyrs in the persecution of the fourth century.[20]

[16] Euseb. *Demonstr. evang.* 6, 18, 23.
[17] *Euseb. HE* 6, 20.
[18] *Euseb. HE* 6, 14, 8.
[19] *Harnack Miss*, 647.
[20] *Euseb. HE* 8, 7, 1; 8, 13, 3; De mart. Palaes. 5, 1; 7, 1.

In Coelesyria proper, the rise of the Christian church of Antioch, already so marked in the second century, continued. Within its walls the synods met, from the middle of the third century onwards, attended by bishops from a wide area and naturally presided over by the Antiochan bishop. When the Bishop of Antioch, Paul of Samosata, himself stood before such a synod accused of Christological heresies,[21] it became clear that this episcopal see already possessed considerable political importance even at that time. And it is very clear that the see of Antioch, as well as that of Rome, was no longer a matter of indifference to the civil government, from the fact that the case of Bishop Paul was even brought before the emperor Aurelian, his decision being sought, and given, regarding the ownership of the bishop's residence in the Syrian capital.[22] Towards the end of the third century, Antioch also became a centre of theological learning for the East, though at a certain distance behind Alexandria. Christian teachers of repute in Antioch at that time were the priests Malchion and Dorotheus[23] but above all Lucian, later a martyr (in 311),[24] who laid the foundations of the Antioch theological school. The Christian church in Antioch also became a missionary centre which not only worked at christianizing the immediate surroundings, but was also engaged in spreading Christian faith in more distant regions, such as the centre of Asia Minor, Armenia, Mesopotamia, and Persia. In the Syrian hinterland, the missionary efforts of Antioch encountered those of Edessa. Success here was considerable in the third century, for twenty bishops from Coelesyria came to the Council of Nicaea, most of them probably from larger towns, but there were also two chorepiscopi who spoke on behalf of the Christian mission in the country.[25] A certain index of the intensity of this, is given by Eusebius' remark that the prisons in Syria after the outbreak of the Diocletian persecution in 303, "were everywhere filled with bishops, priests, deacons, lectors, and exorcists".[26]

In Osrhoëne, Christianity made such strides in the capital, Edessa, in the third century, that it could be considered a Christian town at the beginning of the fourth[27] and the centre of the Syrian Christian world. The beginnings of a Christian school in Edessa probably also extend into the third century.[28] The mission to the countryside started from Edessa, and by 260 it counted several communities with bishops.[29] At the same

---

[21] G. Bardy, *Paul de Samosate* (Louvain, 2nd ed. 1929); on the charge, cf. H. de Riedmatten, *Les actes du procès de Paul de Samosate* (Fribourg 1952).
[22] See above, p. 318.
[23] *Euseb. HE* 7, 29, 2; 7, 32, 2–4.
[24] G. Bardy, *Recherches sur s. Lucien d'Antioch et son école* (Paris 1936).
[25] *Harnack Miss* 671.　　[26] *Euseb. HE* 8, 6.　　[27] Cf. *Euseb. HE* 2, 1, 7.
[28] E.-R. Hayes, *L'école d'Edesse* (Paris 1930).
[29] *Euseb. HE* 7, 30, 10.

time, Christianity advanced in adjacent Mesopotamia, to the East. On its borders, the garrison town of Dura-Europos on the Euphrates had a Christian community at the beginning of the third century. The rooms set aside for worship in a private house rebuilt for this purpose have actually been discovered. A fragment of the Greek *Diatessaron* of Tatian, also discovered in Dura-Europos, shows how widely this was known.[30] The existence of other churches in Mesopotamia is attested by a reference by Bishop Dionysius of Alexandria.[31] In the third century, too, there also arose the bishopric of Nisibis, which was later an intellectual centre of Syrian Christianity, and that of Seleucia-Ctesiphon on the Euphrates, the future ecclesiastical metropolis of the region.[32].

Nearby Persia was opened in the third century as a new missionary territory for the Christian religion. Individual missionaries were able to penetrate into the Persian highlands from the Adiabene district. Political causes then led to the settlement of larger groups of Syrian Christians in the Persian empire; about the middle of the century (252), the incursions of the Sassanid rulers into Roman territory began, as a consequence of which numerous Syrian Christians were deported into the interior of Persia where they were given the opportunity for forming settlements of their own. In the organization of their church life and the practice of divine worship, Shapur I left them complete freedom, and so there sprang up, in addition to the purely Persian Christian communities, those which had exclusively Syrian members. As one of the Persian invasions had reached Antioch, there were Greek Christians among the prisoners too, and these had a place of worship of their own in Rev-Ardashir, later the seat of the Persian archbishops.[33] When the revolutionary change in policy regarding the Church, which occurred in the Roman Empire under Constantine, became known to the Christians of Persia, their sympathies were, understandably, on the side of the now Christian empire; this led to a change in the attitude of the Sassanids to Christianity and prepared the way for the harsh persecution which under King Shapur II in the fourth century was to cost the young Persian Church a heavy toll of vicitims.

In view of the strength of that Christianity, it would be quite within the realm of possibility for east Syrian or Persian missionaries to have

---

[30] O. Eissfeldt, "Dura-Europos" in *RAC* IV, 362–70 with bibliography.

[31] *Euseb. HE* 7, 5, 2. No certain dates can be ascertained from the *Chronicle of Arbela*, for the indications for earlier times are unreliable; cf. I. Ortiz de Urbina in *OrChrP* 2 (1937), 5–32. The *Chronicle of Arbela*, however, receives a much more favourable criticism from G. Messina in *Orientalia* 6 (1937), 237 ff.

[32] *Harnack Miss* 691.

[33] A. Allgeier, "Untersuchungen zur ältesten Kirchengeschichte von Persien" in *Katholik* 98 II (1918), 224–41, 289–300.

penetrated into western India at this time. The St Thomas Christians of south-west India, of course, regard the apostle Thomas as their first missionary,[34] but the apocryphal *Acts of Thomas,* on which they have to base that belief, is not a very sound source. When Origen mentions India on one occasion, he still regards it as a pagan country.[35] Arnobius the elder, however, clearly assumes the existence of individual Christians about the year 300[36] and the well-organized Christian communities attested by Cosmas Indicopleustes about 525 in Malabar, in the region of present-day Bombay, and in Ceylon,[37] oblige us to assume a fairly long missionary development with its beginnings in the fourth or fifth century. That again suggests the possibility of evangelization by Persian Christians who had fled east from Persia under persecution and this conjecture is supported by the later dependence of the Indian Christians on Seleucia-Ctesiphon.[38]

The region of Asia Minor maintained throughout the third century the lead in christianization which it had gained by the end of the second over other parts of the East. The province of Cicilia, the geographical link between west Syria and Asia Minor preserved, however, a marked orientation towards Antioch. The Pauline origin of the church of the city of Tarsus gave it special rank and caused it to become the metropolitan see of the province. Dionysius of Alexandria is probably referring to the metropolitan dignity of the Bishop of Tarsus when he gives Hellenus of Tarsus precedence over the other bishops of Cicilia.[39] Examples of churches with bishops were those of Epiphania and Neronias, whose leaders were represented at the Synod of Ancyra in 314, and seven more were named as taking part in Nicaea, among them was a chorepiscopus, evidence that Christians in the countryside were already also joined into communities.[40] Of the provinces of Asia Minor, Cappadocia and Pontus are prominent, both on account of the prestige of their metropolitans and their strong missionary interest. Firmilian of Caesarea was the recognized leader of the Cappadocian episcopate at their annual meetings and an enthusiastic admirer of Origen, whom he invited to his diocese.[41] He corresponded with Cyprian of Carthage on the question of heretical baptism and so is already a pointer to the later theological standing of Caesarea.[42] A considerable number of martyrs also contributed

---

[34] Cf. L. W. Brown, *The Indian Christians of St Thomas* (Cambridge 1956), 43–64.

[35] Origen, *In Iesu Nave hom.* 15, 5.

[36] Arnobius, *Adv. nat.* 2; 12, and on this, G. E. McCracken, "Arnobius of Sicca" in *ACW* 7 (1949), 311 ff.

[37] Cosmas Indicopl., *Topogr. christ.* 3, 178.

[38] Cf. R. Garbe, *Indien und das Christentum* (Tübingen 1914), 153–5.

[39] *Euseb. HE* 7, 5, 1.

[40] *Harnack Miss* 730 ff.   [41] *Euseb. HE* 6, 27.   [42] Cyprian *Ep.* 75.

to its renown. At the end of the period of persecution the Christians were already in a majority in Cappadocia.

The Pontic regions, lying to the North of Cappadocia, were also a fertile mission field in the third century. Here, of course, there were certainly considerable Christian communities quite early, such as Amastris, Synope, Pompeiopolis, soon joined by the important Amaseia which was the metropolis as early as 240.[43] The missionary, however, who succeeded in winning even the majority of the country population to Christianity, was Gregory Thaumaturgus. He received his theological formation with Origen and, after his return home, was consecrated bishop of his native town, Neo-Caesarea, by the Bishop of Amaseia.[44] In his activity a well-thought-out missionary plan can be detected. After the Decian persecution he travelled systematically through the country districts, acquired precise knowledge of the strength of paganism and the religious customs of the people, and framed his missionary method accordingly. He succeeded in shaking the confidence felt by the people in the pagan priesthood and drew them to Christianity by an impressive liturgy. He seized on the liking of the population for festivals and celebrations in the course of the years, by giving these a Christian content and making festivities in honour of the martyrs the culminating points of the year. By his work, paganism was considerably overcome,[45] though the task of deepening Christian belief remained for the later bishops of Pontus, as can be seen from the discussions of a Synod of Neo-Caesarea between 314 and 325 which dealt in detail with the discipline of the churches of Pontus.[46] By that time, however, Pontus could be considered a country which, to a large extent, had accepted the Christian faith.

The evangelization of Armenia was essentially influenced by the neighbouring regions of Pontus and Cappadocia in the west and Osrhoëne in the south-east, and this had consequences of various kinds for the Armenian Church. The first missionaries probably came from the South, from the Edessa area, preached in the province of Sophene in Lesser Armenia, and used Syriac as the language of the liturgy. It was probably here in the south-east that Meruzanes was a bishop; Dionysius of Alexandria addressed a letter to him about penance.[47] The decisive impulse

---

[43] *Euseb. HE* 4, 23, 26. The bishops of Pontus had also taken part in the discussions about the date of Easter, ibid. 5, 23, 3.

[44] *Quasten P*, II, 123 ff.

[45] These details can be gathered from the account that Gregory of Nyssa gives of the life of Gregory Thaumaturgus; it is not entirely free from legendary elements in other respects: *PG* 46, 893–958.

[46] The Canons of the Synod in F. Lauchert, *Die Kanones der altkirchlichen Concilien* (Freiburg i. Br. 1896), 35 ff., and in E. J. Jonkers, *Acta et symbola conciliorum quae saeculo quarto habita sunt* (Leyden 1944), 35–8.   [47] *Euseb. HE* 6, 46, 2.

for the complete conversion of the country came, however, from Cappadocia. The Armenian, Gregory, had fled there when, in his country, struggles were taking place between the Persian Sassanids, the rulers of Palmyra, and finally, Rome. Gregory became acquainted with Christianity in Caesarea and was baptized there (c A.D. 285–90). After his return he became the great missionary of his nation, which, on this account, honoured him with the title of "The Illuminator". In his work of conversion he had the full support of his king, Trdat II, who with the upper classes of the country, embraced the Christian faith. The acceptance of Christianity by the Armenians assumed a political complexion when this was presented as a national alternative to the Persian religion previously imposed upon them. After overcoming the resistance of the pagan priests, Christianity became the State religion and the Church was richly endowed with the former temple treasure. The religious centre was Ashtishtat where the chief pagan shrine had stood and Bagravan was another important see.[48] The influence of Cappadocia remained because Gregory and his immediate successors recognized Caesarea as a kind of higher metropolitan see. In his missionary methods Gregory the Illuminator seems to have imitated Gregory Thaumaturgus of Pontus, for he, too, zealously encouraged veneration of the martyrs and replaced pagan centres and seasons of worship by Christian churches at those places and by festivals in memory of Christian saints.[49] The report of the forty martyrs of Sebaste[50] shows that Christianity, by 300, had already a strong hold in the country districts of Armenia, too. Some of the village communities had a bishop at their head, others only priests and deacons. The last great persecution fell in Armenia on a country that was, in its majority, Christian, so that the fight of Maximinus Daia against the Christians was felt as an attack upon the whole nation.[51] It was only in post-Constantinian times that evangelization of Georgia began on any considerable scale, but Christianity may well have become known there in individual cases through the busy trade that existed with the west of Asia Minor.[52]

Although there is scarcely any question in the sources of any marked clash between paganism and Christianity in the western provinces of Asia Minor in the third century, nevertheless at this period, particularly in the towns, the Christian religion had achieved the position of an important minority. This much is clear from the situation that the Roman authorities discovered everywhere when they tried to put into effect Diocletian's

[48] F. Tournebize in *DHGE* IV, 294 ff.

[49] *Harnack Miss* 760.

[50] Text in R. Knopf - G. Krüger, *Ausgewählte Märtyrerakten* (Tübingen, 3rd ed. 1929), 116–19, and bibliography.

[51] *Euseb. HE* 9, 8, 2.

[52] K. Lübeck, *Georgien und die katholische Kirche* (Aachen 1918), 6.

religious edicts and the ordinances of Maximinus Daia or Licinius. In Nicomedia itself, where the persecution began, there were many Christians in high State positions, and even at court. This corresponded to their numerical strength in the administrative centre; there were similar strong communities in the Bithynian towns of Nicaea, Chalcedon, Prusa and others, as the presence of their bishops at the Council of Nicaea shows: and further expansion in the country is indicated by the existence of two chorepiscopi.[53] A similar picture emerges for the provinces of Galatia, Phrygia and Pisidia; for their bishops met in synods in Iconium and Synnada at the time of the dispute about heretical baptism. Ancyra, the metropolis of Galatia, had quite a considerable synod in 314; its proceedings are extant.[54] Laodicea, the metropolitan see of Phrygia possessed a celebrated martyr in Bishop Sagaris and the number of bishops of this province at Nicaea was considerable (eight). In Phrygia the wealth of Christian inscriptions from pre-Constantinian times is very striking, and neighbouring Pisidia is also distinguished by them; there, the best known sees were Iconium and Laodicea and nine others whose holders figure on the list at Nicaea. Least information is available in the sources for the provinces in the south of Asia Minor, Lycia, Pamphilia, and Isauria, although once again the presence of twenty-five bishops from these areas at Nicaea proves the intensive missionary work of the previous century. The same is true of the west coast of Asia Minor where as well as the famous names of Ephesus, Smyrna, Pergamon, Sardes, Thyatira, and Miletus, a large number of other towns having churches ruled by bishops must be listed.

The impression of a far-advanced christianization of Asia Minor given by this survey of individual regions and provinces, is confirmed by a quantity of reports and indications referring to the whole of this territory. It is clear that, with the exception of the short Decian persecution, almost unrestricted freedom was available here throughout the third century for the preaching of the Christian faith. This is shown by the numerous epitaphs, even from smaller places in Asia Minor, upon which the Christian faith of the dead could be openly expressed.[55] Similarly, the building of Christian places of worship seems to have encountered no difficulties; a little town like Amaseia in Pontus had several churches in the time of Licinius[56] and would scarcely be unique in this respect. In many provinces, for instance in Phrygia and the neighbouring regions, a high degree of

---

[53] *Harnack Miss* 762–85, also for what follows.
[54] Cf. F. Lauchert, *op. cit.* 29–34; E. J. Jonkers, *op. cit.* 28–35.
[55] Collected in the *Monumenta Asiae Minoris antiqua* IV and VI published by the American Society for Archaeological Research (London-Manchester 1928–56). Cf. also, H. Grégoire, *Recueil des inscriptions chrétiennes de l'Asie Mineure* (Paris 1922).
[56] Eusebius *Vita Const.* 2, 1–2.

christianization had already been reached by the middle of the century, for Dionysius of Alexandria terms the communities of these areas "the most populous churches".[57] Lucian of Antioch no doubt had such conditions in Asia Minor in his mind, when, in a discourse in Nicomedia, he said that "whole towns" had accepted the truth of the gospel.[58] In the Diocletian persecution a town of the province of Phrygia was burnt down because the whole of it was Christian.[59] Finally, Maximinus Daia when considering Asia Minor, justified his measures against the Christians on the grounds that "almost all" would be converted to that religion.[60] The high percentage of bishops from Asia Minor present at Nicaea (and yet a number of absences must be reckoned with), shows too, that Christianity had here already given itself a thoroughly systematic organization, such as was required for the pastoral care of such a numerous following in the churches of both town and country.

The sources contain only sparse material, until the fourth century, on the progress of Christianity on the Greek islands. Certainly it was only by chance that no bishop from Crete took part in the Council of Nicaea, as of course the existence of churches with bishops in Cnossos and Gortyna, as early as 170, is proved by the correspondence of Dionysius of Corinth.[61] On the other hand, the Christian communities of the islands of Corcyra, Cos, Lemnos, and Rhodes, had sent representatives. Christianity can also presumably be taken to have existed before 300 on the island of Patmos with its rich traditions. Cyprus was represented at Nicaea by the bishops of Salamis, Paphos, and Trimithus;[62] here the proximity of Antioch had plainly been favourable to more rapid development. Finally Christianity before the Council of Nicaea had also found entry into the Greek settlements on the northern coasts of the Black Sea and in the Crimean peninsula, for the two bishops, Theophilus of Gothia and Cadmus of Bosphorus, who are known to have taken part in the Council, came from that area. Christianity had also been spread even among the Goths north of the Black Sea by Cappadocian prisoners of war who had been taken there in 258, after an attack on Asia Minor.[63]

The Greek mainland could not, about the year 300 rival either the intensity or extent of evangelization as it existed on the west coast of Asia Minor or in Bithynia, although stronger missionary activity might have been expected from towns of Pauline tradition. Something of the kind is perceptible in Corinth,[64] which concerned itself with the christianization of the Peloponnesus. The latter possessed, in the third century,

---

[57] In *Euseb. HE* 7, 7, 5.   [58] *In Rufin. HE* 9, 6.   [59] *Euseb. HE* 8, 11, 1.
[60] Ibid. 9, 9 a, 1.
[61] Ibid. 4, 23, 5, 7–8.   [62] *Harnack Miss* 786, 677.   [63] Ibid. 797.
[64] Cf. the letter of Dionysius of Corinth to the church of Lacedaemon: *Euseb. HE* 4, 22, 2.

several Christian communities, for "the bishops of Achaea" championed Origen in 231. Corinth, as the ecclesiastical metropolis, also possessed pre-eminence over Athens which preserved even into the fourth century the character of a pagan city and a centre of secular learning. It is not really clear why Origen twice stayed in Athens. He praised the order and peace of its church which, he said, contrasted with the noisy assemblies of the Athenian people.[65] Further north, the island of Euboea and the towns of Thebes, Larissa, and, of course, Thessalonica, had episcopal churches whose leaders were present at Nicaea in 325.[66]

The West

It was only gradually that the romanized Balkans with their Danubian provinces and the adjacent Noricum became receptive to the message of the gospel.[67] Reports about missionary activity by disciples of the apostles in these areas are legendary, but are supposed with no reliable evidence. Traces of Christianity can be found for Noricum, at the very earliest, in the second half of the third century; influence from Aquileia must be presumed for this. About the year A.D. 304 Florian became a martyr at Lauriacum (Lorch). It is only reports of the martyrdom of Christians in the Diocletian persecution that show that Christian faith had penetrated various Balkan areas by the beginning of the fourth century. For the provinces of Moesia and Pannonia the number of martyrs is in fact relatively high; among them were the bishops of Siscia, Sirmium, and Pettau; in Durostorum (Moesia) the soldier Dacius was executed, and a remarkable report of his trial and death is extant.[68] The list of those present at Nicaea mentions, as well as those named above, the episcopal sees of Dacus, in the province of Dardania, Marcianopolis in Moesia and Serdica in Dacia. In addition, there are about twelve other places where Christian churches may be presumed to have existed but, with one exception, they are only towns. It was in these that the Christian faith first won large numbers of adherents, and the evangelization of the country people remained a task for the fourth and fifth centuries.

In Italy the third century signified a period of strong external and inner growth for the Christian community of the capital, Rome; the number of its members was increasing considerably, its internal organization was developing and becoming firmer and its prestige within Christianity as a whole was continually increasing. When Pope Callistus declared at the beginning of the third century that marriages between slaves and Roman

---

[65] Euseb. HE 6, 23, 4; 6, 32, 2.   [66] Harnack Miss 788–92.
[67] Cf. A. Lippold - E. Kirsten in RAC IV, 166–9.
[68] Text in Knopf - Krüger, op. cit. 91–5.

matrons would be regarded as valid by the Church, it can be inferred that Christianity had also penetrated the upper classes. About the middle of the century, the total number of all Christians in Rome had increased so considerably that their pastoral needs could no longer be attended to from one church centre; a division into seven pastoral districts proved necessary, and was probably implemented under Pope Fabian.[69] Eusebius provides very precise and significant figures regarding the strength of the clergy of the city of Rome under Pope Cornelius (251–3). The total of 154 clerics included 46 priests, 7 deacons, 7 hypodeacons, 42 acolytes, and also 52 exorcists, lectors, and doorkeepers. The numbers of widows and poor people cared for by the community at that time was more than 1,500.[70] Even if the percentage of those dependent on ecclesiastical charity is put rather high, a total number of Christians of some 10,000 must probably be inferred from all this.

In the second half of the century the administrative development was continued by the introduction and arrangement of what were later known as the titular churches; various districts of Rome now received a *domus ecclesiae:* a fairly large private house obtained by the community. As well as rooms for the clergy of the district these also provided rooms for divine worship and other pastoral purposes. The titular churches formed, with the cemeteries, the properties which were given back to the Church after the Diocletian persecution.[71] It is also clear that the proportion of Christians in the total population of Rome at the beginning of the fourth century was very considerable from the attitude of Emperor Maxentius, who, though a pagan himself, deliberately refrained from any persecution, because he did not wish to turn the strong group of Christians into political opponents at home.[72] Finally, the often-quoted remark of Cyprian[73] that Emperor Decius had said that he was less concerned over the news of the revolt of a rival emperor than by the election of a new bishop in Rome, indicates the great prestige of the Roman bishop, but also, indirectly, implies the importance of the Roman Christian community in the middle of the third century.

Doubtless many a missionary campaign was undertaken by this strong and eminent church to win to Christianity the immediate and also more

---

[69] Hippolytus, *Refut.* 9, 12; on this K. von Preysing in *ZKTh* 38 (1914), 422 ff; *Duschesne LP*, I, 148.

[70] *Euseb. HE* 6, 43, 11.

[71] Cf. F. Lanzoni, "I titoli presbiterali di Roma antica" in *RivAC* 2 (1925), 195–257; R. Vielliard, *Recherches sur les origines de la Rome chrétienne* (Maçon 1941) 27 ff.; E. Josi in *ECatt* XII, 152–8.

[72] H. v. Schoenebeck, *Beiträge zur Religionspolitik des Maxentius und Constantin* (Leipzig 1939), 4–27.

[73] *Ep.* 55, 9.

distant surroundings of the capital. Unfortunately the details are lacking that would permit a more detailed account of the course of evangelization of central and southern Italy. Its success is shown by the controversy connected with Novatian's step in trying, after his separation from the great Church, to set up an ecclesiastical organization of his own for his followers. He had himself consecrated by three bishops as their leader and these three had been fetched from Italy, that is to say, in this case, from the country.[74] Pope Cornelius gave new leaders to the churches of these bishops and then summoned a synod to Rome in which sixty Italian bishops took part, with numerous presbyters and deacons. Cornelius, in his report to Bishop Fabius of Antioch, provided a register containing the names of the bishops and their sees which included the name and see of the bishops who were prevented from taking part in the Roman synod, but who had written to disapprove of Novatian's proceedings.[75] Unfortunately, this double list of bishops, which might have given information about the distribution of Christian churches in central and southern Italy, has not been preserved. If, however, as well as the sixty participants in the Roman synod and the bishops who were prevented from attending, the episcopal supporters of Novatian are also counted, the number of Christian communities in Italy about the year 250 must easily have amounted to a hundred. The signatures of those taking part in the Synods in Rome in 313 and Arles in 314 mention eight of these sees by name. About fifty other place-names can be inferred from reports of martyrdoms and archaeological finds as being probable locations of Christian communities even before Constantine's time.[76] The country population of central and southern Italy, of course, had not been effectively reached by the Christian mission at the beginning of the Peace of the Church. A surprisingly low level of christianization is also displayed by the provinces of upper and northern Italy; these obviously at that time were not envisaged in Rome's missionary interests. Particularly the Tyrrhenian side of Northern Italy seems to have remained completely devoid of Christian influence before the fourth century. One of the oldest churches in Aemilia must have been Ravenna, whose list of bishops goes back to the third century.[77] Close to it in age Rimini, Cesena, and probably Bologna, too, may have been pre-Constantinian churches.[78] The martyrdom of Antoninus indicates that there was a Christian community in Piacenza at that time.[79]

In Venetia, Aquileia was an important early Christian centre which certainly had a bishop as its head in the second half of the third century.

[74] *Euseb. HE* 6, 43, 8.   [75] Ibid. 6, 43, 2, 10, 21.
[76] *Harnack Miss* 811–16.
[77] M. Mazzotti in *ECatt* X, 558–73, and bibliography.
[78] *Delehaye OC* 328 ff.   [79] Ibid. 329.

Its fourth bishop, Theodore, and his deacon, Agathon, took part in the Synod of Arles in 314 and he was also the builder of the first Christian basilica in his city.[80] From here, Christianity could easily penetrate to Verona and Brescia, both of which received their first bishops in the third century. The presence of Christians in Padua before Constantine's time may be considered probable.[81] Perhaps even older than that of Aquileia is the Christian community of Milan, capital of the province of Transpadana. Its bishop, Merocles, who took part in the two Synods of Rome, 313, and Arles, 314, appears sixth among the bishops of Milan, so the see must have dated from the first half of the third century. The local martyrs, Felix, Nabor, and Victor, were the glory of Christian Milan in the fourth century.[82] It is doubtful whether Christians can be presumed to have existed in nearby Bergamo before Constantine. The sources give no indication about Christians in the country districts of any of these provinces before this time and the country people, in fact, were only won over to Christian belief in the fourth and fifth centuries, by apostolic bishops of the towns.

The large islands of the Tyrrhenian Sea, Sardinia and Sicily, however, lay within the sphere of Rome's interest. There is reason to suppose that Christianity came to Sardinia through Roman Christians who had been condemned to forced labour in the mines there.[83] The first bishop of the island whose name is known, is Quintatius of Calaris (Cagliari) who, with his priest, Ammonius, took part in the Synod of Arles. In the interior of the island, paganism certainly persisted for a long time. During the Decian persecution, the Roman clergy were in correspondence with Christians of Sicily.[84] Syracuse on the east coast, with its rich traditions, is a Christian centre whose catacombs date back to the third century[85] and whose bishop, Chrestus, was invited by Constantine to the Synod of Arles.[86]

The third century represents for the Church of North Africa the decisive period of its pre-Constantinian growth, when Christianity was embraced by practically a majority in the towns. Tertullian's writings in many respects reflect the vitality and vigour with which evangelization was carried on at the beginning of the century. The report of the martyrdom of Perpetua and Felicity gives a striking impression of the eager life of the

---

[80] *ECatt* I, 1722 and bibliography; J. Fink, *Der Ursprung der ältesten Bauten auf dem Domplatz von Aquileja* (Cologne 1954) and on this, L. Voelkl in *RQ* 50 (1955), 102–14.
[81] *Harnack Miss* 871.
[82] *Delehaye OC* 335–7. [83] Hippolytus, *Refut.* 9, 12.
[84] Cyprian *Ep.* 30, 5.
[85] G. Agnello, "La Sicilia cristiana" in *Atti de I° congresso nazionale di archelogia cristiana* (Rome 1952); by the same author, *Actes du Ve congrès international d'archéologie chrétienne* (Vatican City 1957), 291–301; further bibliography, ibid. 156–8.
[86] Euseb. *HE* 10, 5, 21.

church of Carthage, whose members belonged to every social class.[87] The persecution under Scapula, in 211, involved Christians of the provinces of Byzacena and Mauretania.[88] Particularly significant for the expansion of Christian communities throughout North Africa are the growing numbers of bishops who took part in the synods, which were particularly frequent there. Bishop Agrippinus (218–22) already had seventy bishops around him at a synod in Carthage, including some from Numidia,[89] and at a synod in Lambaesis about 240, their number had already risen to ninety.[90] Finally, the transactions of the synod of 256 not only record the attitude adopted to heretical baptism by the eighty-seven bishops who took part but also give the names of their sees.[91] According to this, Africa pro-consularis had the greatest proportion of bishoprics; they were also numerous in Numidia though much rarer in Mauretania and Tripolitania. The correspondence and other writings of Cyprian are a mine of information regarding the size and variety of the community of Carthage, the capital, with its numerous and strongly organized clergy, and regarding the differing quality of the members of the church,[92] a terrifyingly large part of whom gave way in the Decian persecution, while others bravely bore noble testimony to their belief. At the summit of this great community Cyprian himself ruled as a conscientious pastor and also as the sovereign head of African Christendom. By his character and personality, he put in the shade every provincial governor in the North Africa of his time and publicly and eminently illustrated the validity of the faith he represented.

The Christian religion was able, by the end of the period of persecution, to conquer for itself the majority of North African towns through its great prestige and through the impetus gained by its relatively rapid expansion.[93] Shortly before, the most distinguished representatives of pagan literature, the Africans Arnobius and Lactantius, had accepted the Christian faith. In the Diocletian persecution apostasy and fidelity seemed to have more or less balanced; it became clear that such a proportion of the population of the urban settlements had decided for Christianity that it was no longer to be defeated. The Donatist controversy gives the impression of there being two denominations of one Christian people, for whom paganism had come to be a long-past episode of history. Nevertheless, the African Church still had a great missionary task before it,

---

[87] Text edited by C. I. M. Beek (Bonn 1938, *FlorPatr* 43).

[88] Tertullian, *Ad scap.* 3–4.

[89] Cyprian *Ep.* 71, 4.   [90] Ibid. 59, 10.

[91] *Sent. episc.* 87 and cf. the cartographical expression of the information in F. van der Meer - C. Mohrmann, *Bildatlas der frühchristlichen Welt* (Gütersloh 1959), Map 4, p. 10.

[92] Cf. D. D. Sullivan, *The Life of the North Africans as revealed in the Works of St Cyprian* (Diss. Washington 1933).

[93] *Euseb. HE* 10, 5, 16–18.

that of winning, as well as the romanized population, the Punic element of the nation and then the Berber tribes in south and west on the fringes of the North African mountains, so intensively to Christianity, that in times of persecution and tribulation they could preserve it independently. It will have to be shown later that neglect of this double task was one of the reasons why Christianity could not survive the Islamic invasion to any notable extent.

Information about the progress of Christian expansion in the Spanish provinces in the third century is not exactly abundant. There is an important letter of Cyprian's which indicates that in his time there were organized churches with bishops in various places in Spain, though he only names four of them, Leon, Astorga, Merida, and Saragossa.[94] Cyprian also knew that these Spanish bishops met in synods but no missionary is named as preaching the faith there and no church from which he was sent. A certain link of Spanish Christianity with Rome can, perhaps, be inferred from the fact that one of these bishops appealed to the Bishop of Rome against the verdict of a synod. The reports of Christian martyrdoms indicate the existence of Christian groups, apart from those in the towns already mentioned, in Tarragona, Cordova, Calahorra, Alcala, Sagunto, and Astigi.[95] Particularly informative for our purpose are the transactions of a synod which took place immediately before the beginning of the period of peace, in the town of Elvira (Granada) in the South of Spain;[96] we have already frequently quoted them. Twenty-three churches of the province of Baetica (Andalusia) were represented by their bishops or other clerics; the representatives of fourteen other churches came from the province of Tarragona, eight of them from the frontier region of Baetica and two from the province of Lusitania. From the home towns of those who took part in the synod, it seems clear that the south-east of Spain had been most affected by evangelization, which had been stronger there than towards the Atlantic coast, the west or the north-west of the country.[97] The tenor of the decisions of the Synod of Elvira provides a welcome measure of the effectiveness of previous missionary work in the Spanish provinces. This must be described as alarmingly slight, even if it is taken into account that the resolutions of such congresses generally do not stress the good features of religious life. Freedom from pagan customs and superstition was far from attainment, relations between Christian masters and their slaves showed little Christian spirit, attendance at church left much to be desired, all ranks of the clergy failed morally, and sexual

---

[94] Cyprian *Ep.* 67.   [95] *Delehaye OC* 362–71.
[96] Text in Lauchert, *op. cit.* 13–26 and in Jonkers, *op. cit.* 5–23. On the list of those taking part, cf. *Hefele–Leclercq*, I, 214 ff.
[97] See Map 4 in F. van der Meer - C. Mohrmann, *op. cit.* 10.

transgressions were widespread. The impression given in this case is not that a new worldly trend had begun in previously excellent communities, but that there had been a serious lack of the intensive missionary endeavour necessary to inculcate into persons, who had, perhaps, been converted all too rapidly, a Christianity which permeated all sections of life. This is confirmed, in particular, by the fact that the attempt was made to remedy the faults that existed by stern, punitive measures.[98] The mission in Spain before Constantine's time, was not yet able to give the Church any bishop or writer of rank, and a broad field still lay open for missionary consolidation.

In Gaul, Christianity won most of its new adherents in the third century in the south-east, along the Rhone. As well as Lyons, other bishoprics existed as early as 200 but their names are not known. Arles is first mentioned in a reference by Cyprian,[99] and it soon became important. Its bishop, Marcion, took part in the Roman Synod of 313; and in 314 the town was appointed by Constantine himself as the place where the bishops' conference should meet to discuss the Donatist problem. At this, the Provincia Narbonensis was represented by five other bishops, whilst from Aquitania another three bishops were present, but from the province of Lyons, only two.[100] In short, christianization was progressively less westwards; missionary work only started there on a larger scale in the fourth century. In the province of Belgica, Trier (Trèves) became a bishopric in the second half of the century;[101] its third bishop, Agricius, was also at Arles in 314. The fact that there were Christians at the court of Constantius Chlorus in Trier,[102] is more an indication of the emperor's tolerance than of the size of the Christian community. The growth of the latter became more rapid only during Constantine's reign as sole emperor, when the previous place of worship had to be replaced by a bigger church. For the whole of the rest of the province of Belgica, there is no information about Christian missionary activity, so that before Constantine, there cannot have been any successful work here.

It is true that Irenaeus already speaks of churches even in the province of Germania;[103] if he was thinking of organized communities under bishops, only the Roman centres such as Cologne and Mainz could be meant. Only in Cologne, however, is an episcopal church definitely known to have existed before Constantine's time; its leader, Maternus, was invited

---

[98] On this see J. Grotz, *Die Entwicklung des Bußstufenwesens in der vornicänischen Kirche* (Freiburg i. Br. 1955), 414–27.

[99] *Ep.* 68, 1.

[100] Cf. Map 4 in F. van der Meer - C. Mohrmann, *op. cit.* 10.

[101] M. Schuler in *Trierer Zeitschrift* 6 (1931), 80–103.

[102] Euseb. *Vita Const.* 1, 16.

[103] *Adv. haer.* 1, 10, 2.

to the Synods of Rome and Arles. Farther down the Rhine, excavations in Xanten, which was then Colonia Traiana, have revealed a martyr's shrine and consequently proved the existence of Christians before Constantine's time, at least in this settlement on the lower Rhine.[104] Christians can also be presumed, with some reason, to have existed in Germania inferior, in Tongern, for the town was the seat of a bishopric in the first half of the fourth century, under Bishop Servatius. In South Germany, Christians are found only in Augsburg, where the martyrdom of St Afra is recorded.[105]

The first certain evidence of the presence of Christians in the British Isles is the account of the martyrdom of St Alban of Verulam,[106] but this cannot be supposed to have occurred during the Diocletian persecution because Constantius Chlorus did not permit the edict against the Christians to be put into effect in the territories he governed. The same applies to to the deaths for the faith of the martyrs Julius and Aron in Legionum urbs (Caerleon), farther west.[107] However, Britian was represented by the bishops of London, York, and, probably, Colchester at the Synod of Arles, so that, after all, communities of some size must have developed before the peace of Constantine began. But the real work of conversion, with marked success, only started here, too, in the following century.

The attempt has been made to estimate in figures the results of Christian missionary work at the beginning of the fourth century, and it has been thought that, out of a total population in the Roman Empire at that time of about 50 millions, there must be assumed to have been at least 7 million Christians, that is to say, nearly fifteen per cent.[108] As, however, the proportion of Christians was not uniform everywhere in the Empire, these figures have only a limited value. More important is the knowledge that christianization in many areas, such as Asia Minor, and the regions of Edessa and Armenia, had affected half the population, while in other provinces of the Empire, such as Egypt, along the Syrian coast, in Africa proconsularis, and in the capital Rome and its immediate surroundings, such a large minority held the new faith that the decisive missionary advance of the Christian religion had in fact been made successfully in various parts of the Empire. The fact was also important that in other areas, such as Phoenicia, Greece, the Balkan provinces, southern Gaul and southern Spain, as well as in northern Italy, so many missionary bases

---

[104] Cf. W. Neuss in *RQ* 42 (1934), 177–82 and W. Bader in *AHVNrh* 144–5 (1946–7), 5–31; W. Neuss, *Geschichte des Erzbistums Köln* I (Köln 1964), 31–108.
[105] *Delehaye* OC 259; *Bauerreiss*, 23 ff.; for the Regensburg martyrs see J. A. Fischer in *Jahrbuch für Altbayerische Kirchengeschichte* (1963), 28.
[106] *Bede HE* I, 17 ff, following older sources; cf. W. Levison, "St Alban and St Alban's" in *Antiquity* 15 (1941), 337–59.
[107] Gildas, *De exid. et conquestu Brit.* 10.
[108] *Harnack Miss* 946–55; L. Hertling in *ZKTh* 62 (1934), 243–53.

had been won, that further development would proceed there with comparable success. It was only in a few frontier districts in the East, on the north and west coasts of the Black Sea, in the Alps, in the Germanic provinces, along the Atlantic coast of Europe, and in the British Isles, that the Christian mission was still in its infancy. Anyone who surveyed this situation as a whole, at the beginning of the fourth century, and assessed it, could without great difficulty be certain that the advance of the movement of Christian belief was no longer to be stopped by the methods of a State persecution. The young Emperor Constantine drew the conclusion from such a realization.

The question might be raised: what intensity and depth actually had Christian missionary work in the course of the third century? Two phases may be distinguished in it; the long period of peace in the first half on the century had, of course, brought the Church notable outward gains, but the direct effect of the wave of persecution under Decian showed that it was not consolidated by corresponding religious growth in depth. The enormously large number of apostasies in Egypt, Asia, North Africa, and Rome made it unmistakably clear that admission to the Church had been granted far too optimistically and readily, when a more rigorous catechumenate would have been justified. Some lessons were obviously drawn from this during the second period of peace after the collapse of the Decian persecution. The last persecution, under Diocletian, showed a far more favourable balance sheet; and so more attention was given to deepening the effects of missionary work.

When it is remembered that the missionary activity of the pre-Constantinian Church was chiefly concerned with people who belonged to a relatively high civilization, with rich forms of religion and a multifarious variety of cults, it must be admitted that the results as a whole were outstanding. Comparison with the relatively slight success of Christian missions with culturally advanced nations of modern times, such as Japan, or the upper classes in India, turns out entirely to the advantage of the early Christian Church. The missionary task imposed by the founder of the Christian religion had been taken up enthusiastically by its adherents and, despite tribulations, sometimes of the most grievous kind, it was prosecuted with ever renewed energy. In the third century, the thought of missionary obligation fully prevailed in the doctrine of ecclesiastical writers. Hippolytus expressly points out that the gospel in the first place must be preached to the whole world.[109] Origen expresses similar thoughts, and he was convinced that the unified Roman Empire was the providential condition for the rapid diffusion of the gospel.[110] He knew the figure of the regular missionary, wandering not only from town to town but

---

[109] *In Dan. comm.* 4, 17.   [110] *Contra Cels.* 8, 72; 2, 30.

from village to village and from place to place, to win new believers in the Lord, receiving hospitality from well-to-do Christian men and women but taking with him on his missionary journeys only as much as he actually needed to live.[111] Individual Christians often felt obliged to missionary work in their sphere of life, soldier and merchant, slave and Christian at court, women and confessors in prison. The Christian writer, too, was conscious of his missionary task.[112] All contributed their share, so that a numerically large and internally strongly consolidated early Christian Church could undergo the supreme test of the Diocletian persecution.

[111] Ibid. 3, 9.
[112] Clement of Alex., *Stromata*, 1, 1.

SECTION TWO

The Last Attack of Paganism and the Final Victory of the Church

CHAPTER 28

The Intellectual Struggle against Christianity at the End of the Third Century

WHEN Emperor Gallienus (260–8), at the beginning of his reign, put an end to the persecution ordered by his father Valerian and adopted a series of measures favourable to the Christians, some of these, like Bishop Dionysius of Alexandria, indulged in extravagant hopes, that a new era was dawning for Christianity.[1] Gallienus' rescript was, in fact, followed by a period of peace lasting about forty years during which the Christians did not suffer any centrally organized persecution. They were able in relative freedom to pursue and consolidate the internal and external development of their society into the "great Church" of early Christian times. Eusebius paid tribute to the years before the outbreak of the Diocletian persecution as a time of the most extensive toleration of Christianity and of the public expressions of its life, and emphasized three freedoms particularly which the Christian religion was at that time permitted to enjoy: freedom of belief, which allowed the Christians of all social classes to profess their faith publicly; freedom of worship, which allowed unrestricted access to Christian church services and made it possible everywhere to build great churches; and freedom of preaching to all, unhampered by anyone. As well as this, there was the markedly benevolent attitude of the civil authorities, who treated the leaders of the Christian communities with particular respect.[2]

Seeing that such a phase of tolerance was followed by the Diocletian persecution, which brought the most violent wave of oppression Christianity had yet experienced, the question must be put whether many Christians did not overlook certain signs of the times and underestimate happenings which pointed to a development less favourable to Christianity and which make the turn of events under Diocletian intelligible.

In the first place, the situation of the Christians, even under the emperors since Gallienus, was in no way guaranteed by law. It was

[1] Cf. *Euseb. HE* 7, 23.
[2] Ibid. 8, 1, 1–6.

self-deception when some Christians thought that the tolerant attitude of individual emperors, and a consequently tolerant attitude of some high officials, had also brought about a definitive change in the mentality of the whole non-Christian population of the empire and already ensured final agreement with the pagan civil power. It was still possible for the hostile sentiment of an official to strike an individual Christian with extreme severity, for no law defended the Christian against such measures. The account of the martyrdom of the distinguished Marinus of Caesarea in Palestine, which Eusebius gives from his own certain knowledge, shows that even "when the Church was everywhere at peace" a Christian could still be brought before the court on mere denunciation and suffer execution, simply on account of his loyalty to his faith.[3] How quickly the change of mind of an emperor could lead to a completely altered situation can be seen, too, from the fact, guaranteed by Eusebius and Lactantius, that even Emperor Aurelian (270–5) allowed himself to be won over against the Christians "by certain advisers" and was preparing an edict of persecution, the application of which was prevented only by his sudden death.[4] This perpetual legal uncertainty shows that the period of toleration introduced by Gallienus was very far from a transformation of the situation as a whole such as was realized under Constantine.

It was inevitable that particularly serious consequences would in the long run flow from a new wave of intellectual intolerance towards Christianity which emerged among the educated, from Aurelian's reign onwards, and which found its exponent in the neo-Platonist Porphyry. In Phoenicia, where he was born near Tyre, about 223, Porphyry had already come into contact with Christianity, though it cannot be proved that he once believed and later abandoned it, as early assertion would have it.[5] According to his own statement, he met Origen in his youth,[6] and was able to see for himself the rapid growth in adherents to the Christian religion in the period of peace after 260. He owed his first philosophical and theological formation to Longinus in Athens; in 263, when he was thirty, he came to Rome, where he became the pupil, friend, and intellectual heir of Plotinus whose discourses he published in the *Enneads*. Plotinus himself, of course, did not engage in direct controversy with Christianity but in the second *Ennead* there are, nevertheless, some references which would seem to exclude a favourable estimate of it. When he reproached there his opponents, "the Gnostics", with despising the created world and with maintaining that, for them, there was a new

[3] Ibid. 7, 15, 1–5.
[4] Ibid. 7, 30, 20–21; Lactantius, *De port. pers.* 6.
[5] Socrates *HE*, 3, 23, 37; cf. also Augustine, *De civ. dei*, 10, 28.
[6] *Euseb. HE* 6, 19, 5.

earth to which they would come after death, and when he pillories their custom of "calling the worst of men their brothers,"[7] it is impossible to avoid the impression that it was the Christians of whom he was speaking.

With Porphyry, a negative attitude to Christianity is perceptible, even in his early writings. In his *Philosophy of the Oracles,* he has a Christian woman described, in a saying of Apollo, as unteachable and impossible to convert; she is said to grieve for a dead God who, however, was condemned to death by just judges; and the Jews are placed on a higher religious level than the Christians.[8] The fifteen books *Against the Christians,* on which Porphry worked from about the year 268, are indubitably the most important contribution to the ambitious attempt of neo-Platonism to renew Greek wisdom and religious sentiment, and to hold the educated classes especially to them, in face of the increasingly successful advance of Christianity. The task that he had in this way set himself demanded for its successful accomplishment far more than Celsus' project a hundred years before. Christianity had developed since that time literary productions that commanded the respect even of an educated pagan. A comprehensive discussion of the Bible was now particularly necessary, for through Origen's work, the Scriptures had achieved wide-ranging influence. To his plan for a comprehensive refutation of Christianity, Porphyry brought, as can be seen from the fragments which survive, genuine knowledge of the Christian Scriptures, a trained critical and philological mind, and a considerable gift of exposition. In quite a different way to the Ἀληθὴς λόγος of Celsus, Porphyry's work immediately called forth Christian defences against his design. Probably even in his lifetime the reply of Methodius of Olympus was published; Jerome mentions it with respect;[9] then Eusebius of Caesarea brought out a voluminous refutation in twenty-five books;[10] both, however, in the opinion of Jerome and Philostorgius, were excelled by the performance of Apollinaris of Laodicea in thirty books.[11] The same fate has overtaken attacker and defenders, for all these works have completely perished. Constantine ordered, even before the Council of Nicaea, the destruction of the "godless writings" of Porphyry, "the enemy of true piety", the first example of the proscription of a written work hostile to Christianity by the civil power; Emperor Theodosius II in 448 again ordered the burning of all Porphyry's writings.[12] Clearly, however, a pagan had made a selection from Porphyry at the beginning of the fourth century,

[7] *Enneads* II, 9, 5, 9, 14, 18.
[8] Augustine, *De civ. dei* 19, 23.
[9] *De vir ill.* 83; *Ep.* 48, 13; 70, 3.
[10] Quasten P, III, 333.
[11] Jerome, *De vir. ill.* 104; *Philostorgius HE* 8, 14.
[12] *Socrates HE* 1, 9, 30; *Cod. Theod.* 16, 6, 66.

summarizing his chief objections to Christianity. Macarios Magnes, perhaps Bishop of Magnesia, argued against this even as late as 400 in his *Apocriticus* and so preserved a relatively large number of excerpts from Porphyry. [13]

Even though Porphyry did not subject the figure of Christ to such a harsh judgment as the evangelists, the apostles, and Christians in general, he nevertheless finds in it many features which in his estimation are incompatible with a truly religious and heroic personality. In the first place, Christ does not show himself to possess the divine power which he claims for himself; he refuses out of fear, to throw himself from the pinnacle of the Temple; he is not master of the demons; he fails lamentably before the high priests and Pilate; and his whole Passion is unworthy of a divine being. In comparison with him, the wonderworker Apollonius of Tyana of the first century, is a far more impressive figure. [14] After his resurrection, Christ should have appeared, not to simple unknown women, but to Pilate, to Herod, in fact to the Roman Senate; he should have given his ascension a much more grandiose setting; this would have spared his followers their harsh persecutions, for in face of such demonstrations of divine power, all doubt of his mission would have been silenced. [15] The evangelists are severely rejected for their presentation of Jesus' deeds and words, which they themselves invented and did not experience. [16] Their accounts are full of contradictions, inexactitudes, and absurdities and merit no belief. [17] Porphyry felt the profoundest antipathy for the leading figures of the early Church, Peter and Paul; Peter, he considered was in no way fitted to the high office to which he was called — Porphyry does not in the slightest contest this call —, and his choice was one of Christ's worst mistakes. [18] Paul seems to him a repulsive character; double-tongued, mendacious, perpetually contradicting himself and perpetually correcting himself, he preaches in his eschatology a doctrine of the end of the world, the Last Judgment, and the resurrection of the dead, which provoked the harshest contradiction of the neo-Platonist. [19] The opposition of Peter and Paul in the question of the obligation of the Mosaic Law for Jewish and pagan Christians did not escape Porphyry; but the behaviour of both showed them up he asserts, as pitiable figures. [20]

The central doctrines of the Christian faith and the essential features of Christian worship are also decisively rejected. Christ's doctrine demands

[13] For the proof of these literary links, cf. especially A. Harnack, *TU* 37/4 (Leipzig 1911). Quotations will here be given from the *Fragments* of Porphyry in Harnack's edition, *AAB* 1916, I.

[14] *Fragm.* 48, 49, 62, 63.

[15] *Fragm.* 64, 65.   [16] *Fragm.* 15.   [17] *Fragm.* 9–17.

[18] *Fragm.* 23–26.   [19] *Fragm.* 27–34.   [20] *Fragm.* 21, 22.

irrational faith, too large a demand for thinkers and philosophically trained persons.[21] Christian monotheism really only thinly disguised polytheism, for the angels also appear as divine beings.[22] The doctrine of the Incarnation fills every Greek with abhorrence, and so does the Christian Eucharist, which Porphyry regards as a rite such as is not found even among the most savage tribes; for him the words of Christ at John 6:54, "Except you eat the flesh of the Son of Man . . ." are bestial, and these words alone place St John's Gospel far below the work of the Synoptics.[23] Christian baptism, which is supposed by one washing to expunge all faults, even the worst, of adults, can only be considered an immoral institution inciting to new vices and wickedness.[24] Christian esteem for the poor and sick meets with absolute incomprehension and for the ideal of Christian virginity Porphyry has nothing but mockery.[25] The characteristic note and tone of Porphyry's controversy with Christianity, is bitter sarcasm; here is no open mind, striving for objective understanding of an alien religious movement; Porphyry is very definitely taking sides in a struggle between the civilization of antiquity and Christianity, which had entered its decisive phase. The aim of the Christians he describes as a "barbarous venture"[26] and he clearly approves punitive measures by the civil authorities when he says, "what penalties could be too severe to impose on men who abandon the laws of their country?"[27] And here, the fate of the empire is far from being as much in the forefront of Porphyry's mind, as all that the intellectual and religious tradition of Hellenism meant to him. He was irritated and embittered that Christianity had undertaken a threatening and surprisingly successful attack on it.

Among the Christians, Porphyry's work was certainly felt to be important, or it would not have provoked the rapid and effective reaction represented by the writings that have been mentioned above. By a central item of his attack, Porphyry even exercised very considerable indirect influence on a definite sector of early Christian literature. His assertion that the gospels are unworthy of belief on account of their numerous patent contradictions, led Christian writers to give this problem special attention and to suggest solutions in the literature of *Quaestiones et responsiones*, beginning with the *Quaestiones evangelicae* of Eusebius of Caesarea and leading, by way of the *De consensu evangelistarum* of Augustine, down to Hesychius of Jerusalem's collection of sixty-one such questions.[28] It is strange that Porphyry, whose hostility to Christianity

---

[21] *Fragm.* 54.   [22] *Fragm.* 75, 76.   [23] *Fragm.* 69.   [24] *Fragm.* 88.
[25] *Fragm.* 87, 58, 33.
[26] *Fragm.* 39.   [27] *Fragm.* 1.
[28] Cf. G. Bardy, "La littérature patristique des quaestiones et responsiones sur l'écriture sainte" in RB 41 (1932), 210–36, 341–69, 515–37; 42 (1933), 211–29; H. Dörries, *Erotapokriseis* in *RAC* 6 (1964), 347–70.

was universally known,[29] was intensively studied by Latin theologians of later antiquity. Augustine especially could not conceal a certain sympathy for him, a consequence of the positive influence neo-Platonism had had on his own religious course; and he liked to think that Plato and Porphyry "would probably both have become Christians" if they had met and had been able to combine their views about the destiny of the soul.[30]

Porphyry's book against Christians had serious consequences in pagan upper-class circles. To many, a religion could not but appear unacceptable which so sinned against the Logos, against clarity and against truth as, according to his account, the doctrine and practice of the Christians did. Above all, his work made the opposition between neo-Platonism and Christianity unbridgeable. The claim of the latter to exclusive possession of truth, was felt to be a denial of all that the World Logos had until then made known to mankind.[31] If a strong civil power desired once again to take violent measures against the followers of the Christian faith, it would encounter considerable sympathy among the educated, and a favourable climate prepared by Porphyry.

The possibility of literary polemic against Christians being linked with the will to actual persecution by the State was realized in the person of Sossianus Hierocles who as a high civil servant (he was successively Praeses of the provinces of Arabia Libanensis and Bithynia, then Prefect of Egypt[32]) took up his pen and attacked Christianity in two works which he entitled Λόγοι φιλαληθεῖς, with obvious reference to the work of Celsus.[33] He played an essential part in preparing the Diocletian persecution;[34] although it cannot be determined whether or not the appearance of his two treatises preceded its outbreak. It is true that Hierocles ostensibly presented himself as a benevolent adviser, for, as Lactantius emphasizes,[35] he spoke "to the Christians", not against them. That this attitude was not honest, is clear not only from the shameless treatment to which he permitted Christian virgins to be subjected as Prefect of Egypt,[36] but also by the content of his polemical writings as reported by Lactantius. Hierocles took his material largely from Porphyry's work, that is evident from the most important arguments that he deploys against the Christian religion: the Holy Scriptures of the Christians are composed of lies and

---

[29] Firmicus Mat., De err. prof. rel. 13, 4 calls him "hostis dei, veritatis inimicus, sceleratarum artium magister"; Augustine, De civ. dei 9, 12: "Christianorum (sermo 242, 7: fidei christianae) acerrimus inimicus."

[30] Serm. 241, 6, 7.

[31] Cf. H. Dörries, "Porphyrios" in RGG, 3rd ed. V, 463 ff.

[32] On the difficulties of this career, cf. J. Moreau: Sources Chr 39 II, 292–4.

[33] Lactantius, Div. inst. 5, 3, 23.

[34] Lactantius, De mort. pers. 16, 4 calls him "auctor et consiliarius ad faciendam persecutionem."   [35] Div. inst. 5, 2, 12.   [36] Eusebius, De mart. Palaes. 5, 3.

contradiction; the apostles generally and Peter and Paul in particular, were uneducated, ignorant men, who spread lies everywhere; Christ was the head of a robber band of nine hundred men and his alleged miracles were far surpassed by those of Apollonius of Tyana; finally, non-Christians, too, believed in a highest God, the creator and sustainer of the world.[37] Hierocles' only contribution here from his own resources is his description of Christ as the leader of a robber band and the great prominence given to Apollonius of Tyana, that wandering philosopher with the aureole of legend of the first century, whose life had been written by Philostratus at the request of the emperor's mother Julia Domna about the year 220.[38] Perhaps in this biography Philostratus himself was trying to present his age with a religious figure who could compare favourably with Christ.[39] That, in any case, was the sense in which the miraculous power of Apollonius was exploited by Porphyry, so that Eusebius of Caesarea in his reply to Hierocles made the comparison between Apollonius and Christ the central point of the refutation. Eusebius denied any originality or independence to Hierocles' work, because he thought he had based himself on Celsus.[40] Clearly, therefore, Eusebius had not yet in his possession a copy of Porphyry's work which was Hierocles' real source, and to which Eusebius himself later composed a reply.

Lactantius knew of another philosopher, teaching in his time in Bithynia, who at the beginning of the Diocletian persecution, published a work called *Three Books against the Christian Religion and Name,* but it is no longer possible to establish who he was. According to Lactantius' brief indication of its contents, the opportunist author, in an unctuous style, wanted to lead back to the cult of the gods those who had strayed, and prevent them from being exploited, in their simplicity, by unscrupulous men. Consequently, he praised the emperors who had taken the necessary measures to suppress a godless superstition, only worthy of old women; he had no knowledge of the nature of the Christian religion.[41] Though Lactantius seems to attribute no great importance to the work of this unknown philosopher, and does not appear to regard him as any special danger to Christianity, nevertheless he was a link in the chain of general animosity against Christianity, especially among the educated, which characterized the atmosphere of the pagan side on the eve of the persecution.

As a last source of anti-Christian polemic and propaganda, the pagan priesthood must be mentioned; it observed with understandable disquiet

---

[37] Lactantius, *Div. inst.* 5, 2, 13–15, 3–23.
[38] Cf. G. Gross, "Apollonius von Tyana" in *RAC* I, 529–33 with bibliography.
[39] Cf. P. de Labriolle, *La réaction païenne* (Paris 1934), 311 ff.
[40] *In Hieroclem* 1. [41] *Div. inst.* 5, 2.

the powerful rise of the Christian movement, and inevitably felt itself threatened in its prestige and privileges. Its influence on the renewed friction is clear in the report of Lactantius, which is confirmed by Eusebius, that Diocletian, who still shrank from violent persecution, sent an augur to question the oracle of Apollo of Miletus; only the utterance of this oracle, which was unfavourable to the Christian religion brought about, he alleges, the decision.[42] The guiding hand of the pagan priesthood is also easy to perceive in an event that perhaps occurred even earlier. Once when Diocletian wanted to proceed with the taking of the auguries, the priests explained to him that they remained without effect because the presence of "profane men" nullified them. That was a reference to the Christians at court, and Lactantius affirms that Diocletian thereupon prescribed a sacrifice to the gods for all at court and in the army; those who refused were to be flogged, or expelled from the army, as the case might be.[43] It can be inferred that this method of the priesthood was not limited to isolated cases but was employed on a wide scale, from the reference in Arnobius the Elder with which he opens his work *Ad Nationes*: the atrocities already attributed earlier to the Christians would be revived and would be exploited by augurs, soothsayers, oracle-mongers and people of that kind, who saw their clientèle evaporating.[44]

The features described indicate that, about 270, a wave of anti-Christian polemic and propaganda set in which tried in the first place to win over the educated classes, but later also influenced wider circles. This must be counted as an essential factor in any understanding of why, at the beginning of the fourth century, there could still have been such a violent, yet for paganism fundamentally hopeless, trial of strength between the power of the Roman State and the Christian religion.

CHAPTER 29

Outbreak and Course of the Diocletian Persecution down to Galerius'
Edict of Toleration, 311

THE growing hostility to Christianity that has just been described cannot itself explain Diocletian's relatively sudden transition from liberally exercised toleration to the harshest of persecutions. The emperor practised toleration for years, quite deliberately, for he could not have been unaware of the Christian religion's growing successes and its ceaselessly increasing

---

[42] Lactantius, *De mort. pers.* 11, 7–8; Eusebius, *Vita Const.* 2, 50, 51.
[43] *De mort. pers.* 10. [44] Arnobius, *Adv. nat.* 1, 24.

power of attraction. From the imperial palace in Nicomedia he could see an obviously representative Christian place of worship.[1] The Christian faith of high civil servants who every day were at their work around him, could no more be unknown to him than that of numerous court officials[2] or the reported, and very likely, inclination of his wife Prisca and his daughter Valeria towards the Christian religion.[3] That tolerance of the emperor led historians of his own and of modern times largely to absolve him from responsibility for the outbreak of the persecution. Lactantius sees in the *Caesar* Galerius the driving force which practically wrung from the vacillating Diocletian the order to proceed against the Christians.[4] In this he certainly contradicts himself, for in another passage as we have seen, he names Hierocles as the "originator and adviser" in preparing the persecution.[5] In fact, a number of causes and influences were operative which profoundly influenced Diocletian's decision to use measures of State compulsion, but he made the decision with full freedom and personal responsibility. The central motive for his action can most probably be found in a conviction that Christianity stood in the way of the work of reconstruction which he had so successfully undertaken in the most various spheres of life of the Roman Empire. After securing the frontiers, strengthening the civil government and eliminating financial difficulties at home, he now turned to the burning religious problem, the solution of which he envisaged solely in terms of a restoration of the old Roman religion. He referred to this as early as 295, in his edict concerning marriage; and two years later, in his decree against the Manichees, he described them as worthless men "who set up new and scandalous sects against the older religions".[6] His collaborators and advisers, such as Galerius and Hierocles, propounded to him a solution which they thought correct, and perhaps confirmed him in the line in which he, too, saw the solution. The renewed mood of hostility to Christianity in the educated upper classes and to some degree in the common people, too, seemed to him to recommend this course. But he undertook it on his own responsibility.

---

[1] Lactantius, *De mort. pers.* 12, 2.

[2] Adauctus and Dorotheus, the first a high official in the finances, the other in the administration of crown-lands: *Euseb. HE* 8, 2; 7, 22, 3; Christians employed at court: Lactantius, *De mort. pers.* 10, 4.

[3] *De mort. pers.* 15, 1.

[4] Ibid. 11; Eusebius varies in his judgment on the question of responsibility, cf. R. Laqueur, *Eusebius als Historiker seiner Zeit* (Berlin 1929), 77–80.

[5] *De mort. pers.* 16, 4; *Div. inst.* 5, 2, 12: "qui auctor in primis faciendae persecutionis fuit".

[6] *Coll. mos. rom. leg.* 6, 4, 1; 15, 3 and on this cf. J. Vogt, *Constantin der Große und sein Jahrhundert* (Munich, 2nd ed. 1960), 123.

It is understandable that Diocletian began the fight against Christianity by a purge of the army, for the reliability of the army was the highest principle of Roman State power. But it was also suggested by some very recent disturbing events. In 295 in Numidia the Christian Maximilian had vehemently refused to be recruited, and in Mauretania three years later the Christian centurion Marcellus refused to continue in military service when on the anniversary of the assumption of the titles of *Jovius* and *Herculius* by the two emperors, he would not break the vow which bound him to Christ.[7] Further incidents were caused by two veterans, Tipasius and Julius, in 298 and 302 when, on the occasion of a special gift, they refused the coins on which the emperors were represented as sons of the gods. Fabius, an official in the civil administration and *vexillifer* of the governor of Mauretania, refused to carry "pictures of dead men", that is to say, the standard with the device of the divinized emperors.[8] In all these cases the conflict had a religious foundation; the Christians in question were not opposed to military service as such; they were refusing to take part in an act of pagan worship, which is what the various forms of honour paid to the emperors signified for them, after the rulers had proclaimed themselves sons of Jupiter and Hercules. A decree issued by Diocletian as early as 300 aimed at removing such unreliable elements from the army; it laid down that all soldiers had to sacrifice to the gods or leave the army.[9] The failure of the augury already mentioned, and the oracle given when the Milesian Apollo was consulted, then led him, after a consultation with the Senate, to publish the general edict of February 303. This ordered in the name of the four emperors, the destruction of all Christian places of worship, the surrender and burning of all their sacred books, and it forbade all their assemblies for divine worship. Extremely serious, too, was the degradation of the Christians which was laid down by the edict; if they were in the imperial administration, they were enslaved; notabilities among them lost the privileges of their rank, and their offices, and all Christians in the empire were declared incapable of performing legally valid acts.[10] In Nicomedia a beginning was made by demolishing the church opposite the palace; a Christian who, in spontaneous indignation, tore down the edict that had been nailed up, was immediately executed.[11] Two outbreaks of fire in the imperial palace whose authors could not be discovered, even by the harshest interrogation, made the situation worse; the Christians in the court administration were subjected

---

[7] The *Acta* of both are in Knopf–Krüger, *Ausgewählte Martyrerakten* (Tübingen, 3rd ed. 1929) 86–9.

[8] Cf. W. Seston, *Mélanges Goguel* (Paris 1950) 242 ff.

[9] *Euseb. HE* 8, 4, 2–3.

[10] Lactantius, *De mort. pers.* 13; *Euseb. HE* 8, 2, 4; *De mart. Palaest. proem.* 1.

[11] Lactantius, *De mort. pers.* 12 and 13; *Euseb. HE* 8, 5.

to severe tortures, then burnt or drowned; in particular, distinguished Christians were compelled to offer sacrifice, among them Diocletian's own wife and daughter.[12] And now the real impact of the persecution was aimed against the clergy; in the town where Diocletian resided, Bishop Anthimus was executed, and elsewhere, too, many clerics suffered imprisonment or death,[13] presumably because they did not comply with a provision of the edict requiring them to hand over the sacred books. That was certainly the reason for the decapitation of Bishop Felix of Thibica in North Africa,[14] and for the execution of a number of laity from Numidia.[15] It is true that there were those among the clergy who failed in this, too, especially in North Africa and Rome, and they later were stigmatized as *traditores*.[16] The sources do not provide a survey of the outcome of the first edict in all parts of the empire. Being a decree of the supreme emperor, the edict was of course addressed to the three other members of the tetrarchy and they were expected to put it into effect. This did happen in all parts of the empire, but with differences of intensity. In the west, Emperor Maximian showed himself particularly compliant, whilst his *Caesar* Constantius carried out the decree very negligently in Gaul and Britain, for though he destroyed buildings he did not imprison or put to death.[17]

Diocletian was soon driven further on the course he had begun. In Syria and in the Melitene region disturbances broke out which were attributed to the persecution.[18] These occasioned a second edict which robbed the Christian communities of their pastors, and so struck the ecclesiastical organization at a vital spot; the prisons everywhere filled with "bishops, priests, deacons, lectors, and exorcists", so that no room was left for common criminals.[19] A third edict contained more detailed instructions for proceedings against the clergy; anyone who carried out the pagan sacrifices went free; anyone who refused was tortured and put to death.[20] The fourth and last edict, early in 304, completed the imperial legal measures against Christians by imposing sacrifice to the gods on all of them without exception.[21] In the previous autumn, Diocletian had celebrated in Rome

---

[12] De mort. pers. 14 and 15, 1; *Euseb. HE* 8, 6, 6 and on this P. Collinet in *RHE* 45 (1950), 136–40.

[13] *Euseb. HE* 8, 6, 6; Lactantius, *De mort. pers.* 15, 2–4.

[14] Account of the martyrdom in Knopf - Krüger, *op. cit.* 90 ff.

[15] Augustine, *Breviculus collat.* 3, 25–7.

[16] See below, chapter 30, p. 418.

[17] Lactantius, *De mort. pers.* 15, 6–7; *Euseb. HE* 8, 13, 13 absolves Constantine's father even from this measure.

[18] *Euseb. HE* 8, 6, 8.

[19] Ibid. 8, 6, 9.

[20] Ibid. 8, 6, 10.

[21] Euseb. *De mart. Palaest.* 3, 1.

the twentieth anniversary of his rule, the *vicennalia*, and had given great prominence in this to faith in the Roman religion which had been revived by him. The Romans in fact were less interested in the display of serious piety, than in the games and gifts that the *vicennalia* celebrations brought with them. On his return journey from Rome to Nicomedia the emperor, who was disappointed with the inhabitants of the ancient imperial capital, contracted a serious illness which weighed heavily on his mind and gave rise to profound anxiety in the imperial palace.[22] Whether the fourth edict was the result of his depression, or of the disappointing outcome of previous measures, can scarcely be determined. Recourse was now had to the method of Emperor Decius, and the persecution was extended to a part of the population that numbered six to seven millions, bringing down unspeakable suffering on them by the most brutal methods of oppression; at the same time admitting by that very fact that success could now only be looked for from such desperate expedients. The intensity of the persecution did not alter when on the common abdication of the two *Augusti*, Diocletian and Maximian, there began on the first of May 305, the second tetrarchy which placed Constantius Chlorus in the West and Galerius in the eastern part of the empire in the highest rank and conferred the title of *Caesar* on Severus and Maximinus Daia, thus passing over young Constantine, son of Constantius, contrary to what the army had anticipated. Since Constantius as *Augustus* held firm to his previous tolerance, and as his *Caesar*, Severus, adopted this attitude too, it was only during the two-year rule of Maximian and in the territory under his jurisdiction that the edicts of persecution were systematically carried out. The later changes in the head of the government in the West did not cut short the toleration practised there; both Constantine, who succeeded his father in 306, as well as Maxentius who, in the same year, ousted Severus from power, were averse to any persecution of the Christians though from different motives. The eastern part of the Empire, in contrast, was forced to bear the full burden from the first edict of the year 303 until Galerius' decree of toleration in 311; an exception was Pannonia where, after 308, Licinius ruled as *Augustus*, and out of tactical considerations, desisted from molesting his Christian subjects.

The two chief witnesses on the Diocletian persecution, Eusebius and Lactantius, are unfortunately completely silent about the course and scope of Maximian's proceedings in the West. Consequently, definite details about the names of martyrs and their home provinces are often difficult to ascertain with certainty, though here and there the history of the cult of the martyrs provides some evidence for the existence of individual martyrs in this period. Even if the large number of alleged Roman martyrs

---

[22] Lactantius, *De mort. pers.* 17.

mentioned in some not very trustworthy accounts, without indication of the time of their martyrdom, cannot be ascribed *in globo* to the Diocletian persecution, some of them certainly fell victims to it; the history of their cult shows them to have been historical persons. So there is a certain probability that St Agnes, who has been very much transfigured by legend, was martyred at this time[23] and so were Sebastian, Felix and Adauctus, Peter and Marcellinus;[24] perhaps the most important epigram of Pope Damasus refers to the latter.[25] When Eusebius says of Pope Marcellinus (296–304), "persecution carried him off", this phrase certainly strongly suggests death by persecution,[26] yet the lack of his name in the oldest list of martyrs and bishops raises difficulties. There is a fragmentary but authentic account of the interrogation and execution of the Sicilian martyr Euplius of Catania.[27] The report of Bishop Eucherius of Lyons († about 450) regarding the martyrdom of an entirely Christian legion under its commander Mauritius in Agaunum (Switzerland) about 286, is legendary; in the first place, no persecution of Christians can be shown to have taken place in the early part of the reign of Maximian and Diocletian; secondly, there scarcely existed at that time in Roman army a self-contained Christian legion like the Theban; and, finally, all other sources are completely silent about such a spectacular occurrence.[28] The number of victims was not small in the North African provinces, and Spain, too, had a series of martyrs[29] among whom greatest honour fell to deacon Vincentius of Saragossa; for some names, however, an absolutely certain ascription to the years 303 to 305 is not possible.[30]

In the Balkans, and in the eastern provinces, the persecution raged for eight years, though with occasional local interruptions. There, Galerius and after 305 his *Caesar*, Maximinus Daia, supplied the impetus; they

---

[23] *ActaSS Ian.* II 350 ff.; E. Schäfer, "Agnes" in *RAC* I, 184.

[24] J. Moreau, *La persécution du christianisme dans l'empire romain* (Paris 1956), 120 ff.

[25] In Ihm, *Damasi epigr.* 29; Delehaye OC 280 ff.

[26] *Euseb. HE* 7, 32, 1; cf. J. Zeiller in *Fliche–Martin*, 466 n. 6.

[27] Critical text in P. Franchi de' Cavalieri, *Note agiografiche* VII (Rome 1928), 1–46; on this F. Corsaro, "Studi sui documenti agiografici intorno al martirio di S. Euplo" in *Orpheus* 4 (London 1957), 33–62; published separately (Catania 1957).

[28] Cf. D. van Berchem, *Le martyre de la légion thébaine* (Basle 1956); G. Curti, "La passio Acaunensium martyrum di Eucherio di Leone" in *Convivium Dominicum* (Catania 1959), 297–327; L. Dupraz, *Les passions de s. Maurice d'Agaune* (Fribourg 1961); H. Büttner, "Zur Diskussion über das Martyrium der Thebäischen Legion" in *ZSKG* 55 (1961), 265–74. It is not impossible that the cult of a Maurice (of Apamea perhaps) was transferred from the East by Bishop Theodore of Agaunum.

[29] J. Zeiller in *Fliche–Martin* II, 467 lists the best-known names. On Vincent cf. M. Simonetti, "Una redazione poco conosciuta della passione di s. Vincenzo" in *RivAC* 32 (1956), 219–41.

[30] Most of them are attested for the first time in Hymns 3–5 of Prudentius, *Peristephanon*.

were also responsible for the cruel ingenuity of the methods of persecution. For Palestine and Phoenicia, some of Eusebius' reports are eye-witness accounts and he also collected reliable information about the martyrdoms in Egypt. There are credible accounts of some of the Illyrian martyrs, for instance Bishop Irenaeus of Sirmium and the three women of Salonica, Agape, Chione, and Irene.[31] In the Asia Minor provinces of Cappadocia and Pontus, the persecuted Christians were faced with particularly inventive torturers who ironically described putting out the right eye or maiming the left leg with red-hot iron as humane treatment and who tried to outdo one another in discovering new brutalities.[32] When it was found that all the inhabitants of a little town in Phrygia were Christians, they burnt it down with everybody in it.[33] Eusebius includes the report of the martyr-bishop Phileas of Thmuis about the exquisite tortures inflicted in Egypt which exploited all the technical possibilities of those days;[34] the doubts that arise when reading this letter, as to whether such inhumanities were even possible, can unfortunately be removed by recalling similar events in the very recent past.

Eusebius gives us no actual information about the number of victims, except in Palestine. From his special account of this area, it seems that the number was less than a hundred. Elsewhere, however, the figure was considerably higher, certainly in Egypt, for example, where Eusebius, who clearly was closely acquainted with events there, states that ten, twenty, or sometimes even sixty or a hundred Christians were executed on a single day.[35] Applied to the eastern provinces, with their relative density of Christian population, this reckoning gives a total of several thousand dead. In addition there were the numerous confessors of the faith who were tortured at this time and dispatched to forced work in the mines.[36] Eusebius mentions by name only the most distinguished victims, especially among the clergy; for example, he notes in addition to those already listed: the priest Lucian of Antioch, the founder of the school of theology there; the bishops of Tyre, Sidon, and Emesa in Phoenicia; among the prominent Palestinian martyrs are Bishop Sylvanus of Gaza and the priest Pamphilus, "the great ornament of the church of Caesarea"; at the head of the Egyptian martyrs he placed Bishop Peter of Alexandria, besides whom he also mentions by name six other bishops and three priests of the Alexandrian community.[37] It is striking that Eusebius is silent about

---

[31] Texts in Knopf - Krüger, *op. cit.* 103–5, 95–100; on the latter cf. *Delehaye PM* 141–3.
[32] *Euseb. HE* 8, 12, 8–10.
[33] Ibid. 8, 11, 1.
[34] Ibid. 8, 10, 4–10; on the martyrdom of Phileas, see F. Halkin in *RHE* 38 (1963), 136–9; *AnBoll* 81 (1963), 5–27.
[35] Ibid. 8, 9, 3.
[36] Ibid. 8, 12, 10.   [37] Ibid. 8, 13, 1–7.

those who failed in the persecution; both among clergy and laity there were those who did, as is shown by the re-emergence in Egypt of the problem of how to treat the *lapsi*.

Although the manner of proceeding against the Christians, particularly as Maximinus Daia practised it, was strongly disapproved of by many pagans[38], it was only in 308 that there was a momentary lull[39] which may have been connected with Maximinus Daia's annoyance at Licinius' elevation to the position of *Augustus*. Some of the Christians condemned to forced labour in the mines were set free, or they were granted some relief. Among the Christians, people were already beginning to breathe again when Maximinus Daia introduced a new wave of oppression with a decree ordering the rebuilding of the ruined pagan temples and announced new detailed ordinances for the conduct of sacrifices to the gods.[40] The real turning-point came with the serious illness of the *Augustus* Galerius, which seemed to the Christians only intelligible as an intervention of divine providence. A beginning had already been made with plans for his *vicennalia* when the emperor fell ill in 310 and in the vicissitudes of his dangerously worsening condition he took to reflecting on the scope of the whole action against the Christians. The outcome was the edict of the year 311 ordering the cessation of the persecution throughout the empire. The text of the decree, which is reproduced by Lactantius and, in a Greek translation, by Eusebius in his *Ecclesiastical History*,[41] still reveals the emotion that Galerius must have experienced when he realized that his policy of violence against the Christians, determined upon by him from the start and energetically put into effect, had been an error and a failure. The edict bears the names of the four rulers, but the tone is that of Galerius, in whose mind a new understanding was only with difficulty taking shape. It begins with the affirmation that the emperors had in their earlier measures only the good of the State in view and had been striving for a restoration of the old laws and Roman manner of life and had wanted to win the Christians, too, back to these. For the Christians had fallen away from the religion of their ancestors and in revolutionary upheaval had made their own laws for themselves. However, the edicts of persecution had not been able to bend the majority of Christians, many of them had had to lose their life and others had become confused. The outcome was religious anarchy in which neither the old gods received appropriate worship nor the God of the Christians himself received honour. In order to put an end to this state of affairs, the

---

[38] According to Eusebius, *De part. Palaest.* 9, 3, many called it oppressive and excessive, disgusting and stupid.

[39] Eusebius, *De mart. Palaest.* 9, 1.   [40] Ibid. 9, 2.

[41] Lactantius, *De mort. pers.* 34; *Euseb. HE* 8, 17, 3–10.

emperors grant pardon and permit "Christians to exist again and to hold their religious assemblies once more, providing that they do nothing disturbing to public order". [42] Another document addressed to governors is promised, which will provide more detailed instructions for the accomplishment of the edict. The Christians are charged to pray to their God for the welfare of the emperor, the State and themselves.

Galerius' edict was a document of the greatest importance; by it the highest representative of the power of the Roman State rescinded a religious policy which had been in force for more than two hundred years. From now on, the Christians were relieved of the oppressive legal uncertainty of the past; for the first time an imperial edict expressly recognized them; their belief was no longer *superstitio* and *religio illicita*, but by an imperial juridical pronouncement of toleration, put on the same footing as other cults. That was more, and must have meant more, to the Christians than all their freedom, however welcome, in the so-called periods of peace which were devoid of any legal basis.

The two rulers in the West had no difficulties in proclaiming the edict in their dominions; it only gave legal foundation to a state of affairs that had already existed for some time. In the East, Maximinus did not in fact have the text of the edict published, but he gave his prefect of the guard, Sabinus, instructions to announce to subordinate authorities that no Christian was any longer to be molested or punished for the practice of his religion. [43] They drew the immediate conclusion from this, at once liberated all Christians who were in custody and recalled those who had been condemned *ad metalla*. A monstrous psychological weight was lifted from the Christians of the eastern provinces and this intensified religious activity; the places of worship that still existed filled again, people flocked to divine worship; in the streets cheerful groups of exiles were seen returning home. Even those who had given way in the persecution, sought reconciliation with the Church and asked their brethren who had stood firm, for the help of their prayers and for readmission into their company. Even the pagans shared the Christians' joy and congratulated them on the unexpected turn of events. [44] This toleration, legally guaranteed, rightly appeared to open to the Christians the gate to a brighter future.

[42] *De mort. pers.* 34, 4: "ut denuo sint christiani et conventicula sua componant ita ut ne quid contra disciplinam agant."
[43] Sabinus' circular letter in *Euseb. HE* 9, 3–6.
[44] Ibid. 9, 1, 7–11.

CHAPTER 30

The Definitive Turning-Point under Constantine the Great

Reverse under Maximinus Daia

In Galerius' mind the edict of toleration in 311 was intended to introduce a new state of affairs in religious matters. In his experience the God of the Christians had proved to be a real power which was to be recognized, together with its followers, and incorporated among the numerous religious beliefs of the empire so that the religious peace so attained might prove a blessing to the State and the tetrarchy ruling it. In this way the edict corresponds to the views of a pious polytheist and adherent of the Diocletian conception of the State such as Galerius was, and does not need to be made intelligible by other influences brought to bear on him. The view that the *Caesar* Licinius was the first to advocate the idea of toleration and was the intellectual originator of the change in the East because he wanted to ensure by it the favour of the Christians for his plans of conquest in the Orient,[1] finds no support in the sources. Others have wanted to discover in Constantine the driving force which made Galerius, in his sickness, change his religious policy.[2] But such an early and striking proof of sentiments favourable to Christianity in Constantine would certainly have found an echo in Eusebius and Lactantius; yet they are completely silent about it.

Galerius died a few days after the publication of the edict and Licinius guaranteed that toleration would be observed in his dominions, but the joy of the Christians over the freedom they had acquired was short-lived in the eastern provinces and in Egypt. Maximinus Daia who had scarcely concealed his inner resistance to the policy of toleration, even in the way he announced this, returned after a few months step by step to his earlier methods of oppressing the Christians. He began by forbidding the Christians to assemble in their cemeteries[3] and tried to expel them from the larger towns. Recourse was had to other crude means, such as inspired petitions by pagans to the emperor requesting him to forbid Christians to stay in their towns. A leading role was played in this by the treasurer of the city of Antioch, Theotecnus, who also spread alleged oracles calling for the banishment of Christians from the Syrian capital and its surroundings.[4] This device set a precedent, and petitions to the emperor

---

[1] So H. Grégoire in *Revue univ. Brux.* 36 (1930–1), 259–61.
[2] For example, H. Lietzmann, *Geschichte der alten Kirche* 3, 57, referring to E. Schwarz, *Kaiser Konstantin und die christliche Kirche* (Leipzig, 2nd ed. 1936), 58.
[3] *Euseb. HE* 9, 2.   [4] Ibid. 9, 2–3.

from all kinds of towns multiplied. Maximinus answered such addresses with rescripts of his own which were published throughout the province and most graciously conceded the requests.[5] The towns felt most highly honoured by the imperial answers and had the petitions and rescripts recorded on tablets or pillars as a lasting memorial.[6] One of the plaques with its inscription has been found in the little town of Arycanda in Lycia and bears an incomplete Latin text of the imperial rescript and the petition, in Greek, "of the people of the Lycians and the Pamphilians".[7] The imperial propaganda against the Christians did not shrink from even meaner methods. In Damascus an imperial official forced women of bad repute, by threats of torture, to declare that formerly, as Christians, they had taken part in the debaucheries in which the Christians indulged in their places of worship. The text of this declaration was conveyed to the emperor and on his orders published in town and country.[8] Another method of denigration consisted in fabricating documents attributed to Pilate which were "full of blasphemies of every kind against Christ"; they, too, at the wish of the ruler, were posted up in public and the teachers in schools had to use them instead of textbooks and make the children learn them by heart.[9] With this harsh anti-Christian propaganda Maximinus combined energetic reorganization of the pagan cults; all the towns received priests and high-priests chosen from officials particularly attached to the State.[10] All these measures of the emperor quickly recreated an atmosphere in which the officials thought themselves justified in taking active steps against the Christians. The punishment of banishment from the towns was once more imposed, even if it was not fully implemented; leading Christians were once more arrested, imprisoned and condemned to death; death by wild beasts and by beheading were once again used as methods of execution. Eusebius assigns to this phase of the persecution the martyrdom of bishops Sylvanus of Emesa and Petrus of Alexandria mentioned above, as well as the priest Lucian of Antioch.[11] The situation which had become very serious again for the Christians was relieved, however, in a surprising way by a communication from the emperor at the end of 312, to his prefect Sabinus, of which Eusebius provides a translation.[12] The same aim, it is true, is maintained in principle, that "of recalling the population of our provinces ... to the service of the gods"; the earlier measures of Diocletian and Maximian are

---

[5] Ibid. 9, 4; 9, 7, 3–14, copy of the rescript to the city of Tyre.

[6] Ibid. 9, 7, 1–2.

[7] Dittenberger, *Orientis Graeci inscriptiones selectae* n. 569; *CIL,* III, n. 12132 and 13625b.

[8] *Euseb. HE* 9, 5, 2.   [9] Ibid. 9, 5, 1.

[10] Ibid. 9, 4, 2.   [11] Ibid. 9, 4, 3; 9, 6, 1–4.

[12] Ibid. 9, 9a, 1–9.

represented as just. Maximinus stresses that he had already given instructions earlier not to use violence in this matter and asserts that nobody had been banished or mishandled in the eastern territories since then. This is contradicted by the fact that, in the same document, he had to insist that the Christians might not be subjected to contumely and ill-treatment but were rather to be brought back to recognize the worship of the gods by kindness and instruction. Maximinus tries to justify his rescripts in answer to the petitions of the towns by saying that such requests deserved a gracious answer and that this was pleasing to the gods as well. The letter ends with the instruction to the prefect to bring the imperial order to the attention of all provinces. It is understandable that after so much bitter experience, the Christians mistrusted even this limited toleration; consequently they did not yet hold the assemblies they had formerly been accustomed to and certainly did not dare to build new churches or otherwise draw attention to themselves.[13] They could not at first comprehend the reasons behind Maximinus' new line of policy. It was determined by far-reaching events in the western parts of the Empire which had made Constantine master of Italy and Africa after his victory over Maxentius in October 312. The victor had immediately intervened with Maximinus in favour of the Christians[14] and the new political situation made it advisable for him to veer into a more tolerant course. The young *Augustus* of the West thus became active in religious policy in a way that extended far beyond his own dominions. We have now to consider his attitude to Christianity.

Constantine's "Conversion" to Christianity

The question of Constantine's turning to Christianity, the fact, its course and its date, was and is hotly disputed among historians and this is partly due to the nature of the sources capable of providing an answer. Constantine's own historiographer, Bishop Eusebius of Caesarea, a friend of the emperor from 325 onwards, was profoundly convinced of his hero's providential mission and he views all the events of his life, which changed the complexion of the age, in the light of this. His *Ecclesiastical History* reflects in its successive editions not only how his knowledge in particular matters increased but also how many of his views changed in the direction of a heightened glorification of the emperor. Certainly the *Life* of the emperor attributed to Eusebius is dominated by this tendency; the consequent suspicion has given rise to a series of conjectures, ranging from the hypothesis of several revisions by the author and even to the suggestion

[13] Ibid. 9, 9a, 11.
[14] Lactantius, *De mort. pers.* 37, 1; and on this, A. Piganiol in *Historia* 1 (1950), 86–90.

that it is a pseudonymous work, written only about 430.[15] The reaction against this judgment on the *Vita Constantini* led to a firm defence of its authenticity[16] which recently received considerable support from a papyrus discovery; this document from about the year 324 contains a fragment of an edict of Constantine to the peoples of the East, quoted in the *Vita* and which had been regarded by one of the harshest critics of the latter as a plain forgery.[17]

The second contemporary author, Lactantius, likewise sided with Constantine and his appointment as tutor to the emperor's eldest son, Crispus, shows the degree of trust that he enjoyed with the emperor. But for that reason he, too, is suspected of regarding Constantine in all too glowing and therefore distorting a light. Of pagan criticism of the emperor only a little has been preserved through his nephew Julian and the historian Zosimus. On the other hand the discourses of panegyrists are particularly valuable for the light they throw on the religious change in the emperor during his transitional phase. The possibility of closer understanding of the world of his religion is also provided by the numerous letters and ordinances of the emperor which have been studied more recently to considerable profit. The religious symbolism of the coinage, too, provides an insight into the changing views of the emperor. Two characteristics stand out even in early tradition regarding Constantine; the passionate partisanship he aroused for and against himself, and a tendency to the formation of legends.[18] They show that the life achievements of this ruler influenced the lot of his contemporaries and posterity as deeply as only those of the great figures of history can do.

There is little in the sources about the childhood and youth of Constantine or of his religious development at that period. Constantius and Helena, his parents, were certainly pagans at the time of his birth in 285. His attachment to his mother was deep and lasting. The former innkeeper[19] was not Constantius' legal wife, for higher officers were not allowed to marry native women of the province. A few years after Constantine's birth, his father left her in order to contract a socially appropriate marriage with Theodora, the step-daughter of Maximian. The

---

[15] Cf. most recent survey in K. Aland, "Die religiöse Haltung Kaiser Konstantins" in *Kirchengeschichtliche Entwürfe* (Gütersloh 1960), 205–15.

[16] Especially by J. Vogt in *Historia* 2 (1953), 463–71; P. Franchi de' Cavalieri, *Constantiniana* (Rome 1953), 51–65; F. Vittinghoff, "Eusebius als Verfasser der Vita Constantini" in *RhMus* 96 (1953), 330–73.

[17] See A. H. M. Jones in *JEH* 5 (1954), 196–200 and K. Aland in *FF* 28 (1954), 213–17.

[18] On Constantine's posthumous history, see E. Ewig in *HJ* 75 (1956), 1–46; W. Kaegi in *Schweiz. Zeitschr. für Geschichte* 8 (1958), 289–326; H. Wolfram in *MIÖG* 68 (1960), 226–43.

[19] Ambrose, *De obit. Theodos.* 42, states she was a *stabularia*.

son presumably remained at first with his mother Helena and probably received his first religious impressions from her as a consequence. She was gifted above the average. Through her son she later made her way to Christianity;[20] and when he became sole ruler, Constantine was able to give her the position of first lady in the empire and she filled it to perfection.[21] It is questionable whether any marked influences of a religious kind came to Constantine from his father; it would be possible to recall Constantius' striking independence in relation to the official religious policy of the Diocletian tetrarchy. He never appeared particularly in the role of a client of Hercules; he rather felt leanings towards Mars, who was specially honoured in his dominions.[22] His aloofness in regard to the policy of edicts of severe persecution has already been mentioned. It permits the inference that he deliberately rejected all compulsion in religious matters. Eusebius characterized Constantius as an adherent of monotheism[23] and so probably viewed the emperor as a representative of the religious trend in the third century which gave increasing predominance to the one divine Being, the *summus deus* which transcended all other deities. Positive relations of Constantius' family to Christian circles are perhaps indicated by the name Anastasia given to one of his daughters, for at that time it was only found among Christians or Jews;[24] another of his daughters, Constantia, later showed herself a convinced Christian. At any rate the general atmosphere of Constantine's father's house was rather well-disposed towards Christians and that is how Constantine found it when in 305 he went to his father in the West after his flight from Nicomedia. Other strong influences must also, however, be reckoned with those which he received in his impressionable years as a youth at the court of Diocletian, where he lived through the outbreak and severity of the persecution of the Christians and perhaps even then felt its questionableness. When in 306 Constantine was elevated by his father's troops to the position of *Augustus,* he maintained his father's religious policy, one of far-reaching toleration towards his Christian subjects and of conscious independence of the rulers in the East. Whether, as Lactantius seems to suppose, he issued a general edict of toleration when he took over power,[25] must remain an open question, but it is not impossible that, in isolated cases, he expressly assured Christian communities of their freedom of worship.

[20] Eusebius, *Vita Const.* 3, 47.
[21] Ibid. 3, 42–5.
[22] Cf. the examination of coins minted by him in H. von Schoenebeck, *Beiträge zur Religionspolitik des Maxentius und Constantin* (Leipzig 1939), 31 ff.
[23] *Vita Const.* 1, 17.
[24] Cf. H. Lietzmann, "Der Glaube Konstantins des Großen" in *SAB* 29 (1937), 268.
[25] *De mort. pers.* 24, 9; cf. J. Moreau in his commentary on this work, 343 ff.

It was of fundamental importance that Constantine at this time was notably alive to the religious question. He linked his personal religious sentiment quite definitely to a mission entrusted to him by the divinity for the whole empire. That became apparent in the year 310 when the fall of Maximian placed him in a situation that called for a fresh decision. The devices on coins show that Constantine at that time freed himself from the theology of the tetrarchy by choosing as his special patron-god, instead of Hercules, the *sol invictus;* [26] this expressed a new political conception. The sun-god was worshipped in all parts of the empire in different forms, in Gaul as Apollo, by the troops as Mithras; he was the god of the whole empire, as Aurelian had already regarded him. The emperor who placed himself under his protection and experienced his assistance was thereby called to determine the destinies of the whole empire. These ideas are indicated in the panegyric pronounced in 310 in Trier in the emperor's presence. [27] In this, Constantine's claim to rule was no longer based on his belonging to the tetrarchan system, but was justified by his descent from an imperial line; the patron of this dynasty and of its present member was said to be Apollo who had revealed himself in a unique way to Constantine. On a visit to a shrine of Apollo in Gaul, he was declared to have seen the god with Victoria and they had given him a laurel wreath with the figures XXX and so had promised Constantine victory and long life. [28] This was an announcement of the emperor's claim to universal dominion and his patron god was the *sol invictus* in the form of the Gallic Apollo.

Constantine took the first step towards the realization of his idea in the autumn of 312 when, against the advice of his entourage, he took the field against the usurper Maxentius, then master of Italy and Africa, and whose troops outnumbered his. Previously he had obtained Licinius' agreement to this undertaking and promised him the hand of his sister Constantia in return. It would be a mistake to interpret the background to this conflict as though Maxentius were an oppressor of the Christians and Constantine their champion. In fact Maxentius had tried to win over the Christians by going beyond what was laid down in the Galerian edict of 311 and restoring to the Christian community in Rome at the beginning of 312 its confiscated property. [29] Nor did Constantine's propaganda make out Maxentius to be a persecutor of Christians, but described him as a tyrant, plundering and oppressing his subjects and from whose

---

[26] H. von Schoenebeck, *op. cit.* 24–6 and A. Piganiol, *L'empereur Constantin* (Paris 1932), 22-7.

[27] *Paneg.* 7 in E. Galletier, *Panegyrici latini*, 2 vols. (Paris 1949–52).

[28] Ibid. 7, 21; cf. H. Kraft, "Kaiser Konstantin und das Bischofsamt" in *Saeculum* 8 (1957), 10 ff.

[29] H. v. Schoenebeck, *op. cit.* 4–23.

yoke Rome ought to be set free. In a rapid onset Constantine overran Maxentius' defences which extended in echelon as far as the Alps, brought the whole of Northern Italy under his sway and approached the city of Rome which his opponent intended to defend as his last stronghold. The decision turned in Constantine's favour at the battle of the Milvian Bridge to the north of the city on October 28, 312. Maxentius lost throne and life, and the way was open for Constantine into the Western capital consecrated by tradition. He was in possession of the whole of Western Europe and had victoriously concluded the first stage of his journey to universal rule.[30]

This campaign was followed by Constantine's decisive turning to the God of the Christians, to which contemporary Christian writers, pagan panegyrists, and Constantine's behaviour directly after the victory all testify.

The first report of it is given by Lactantius[31] who says that Constantine had been exhorted in a dream to put God's heavenly sign on his soldiers' shields and so give battle. The emperor followed this instruction, he says, and made them put an abbreviation for "Christus" on their shields by bending the upper end of the letter X placed sideways. This statement of Lactantius is in itself quite clear. It describes the sign drawn on the shields as an X stood on its side, that is, $+$, which, by having its top arm bent over was changed to a ⊥, that is to say a *crux monogrammatica*, a sign which at that time was not unknown to the Christians as well as their real Christ monogram ☓.[32] Lactantius does not claim that what he relates was a miraculous occurrence. A dream of the emperor, which in view of the situation shortly before the battle was quite an understandable one, was the cause of the instruction, which was easy to carry out and the significance of which could be easily understood by all: emperor and army were not taking the field as usual, under a pagan magical sign, but under the protection of the God of the Christians. The victorious outcome showed that the Christian God had brought about this decision and that he now must be recognized as a divine patron. That was the picture of the remarkable event that was current in the emperor's entourage when Lactantius in 318 published his book *On the Manner of Death of the Persecutors*. Lactantius did not permit himself any interpretation of the psychological foundation of this event and it is most certainly impossible

---

[30] Cf. for the course of the campaign, E. Stein, *Geschichte des spätrömischen Reiches*, 1 (Vienna 1928), 139 ff. and J. Vogt, *Constantin der Große und sein Jahrhundert* (Munich, 2nd ed. 1960), 155–60.

[31] *De mort. pers.* 44: "Commonitus est in quiete Constantinus ut caeleste signum dei notaret in scutis atque ita proelium committeret. Facit ut iussus est et transversa littera X summo capite circumflexo Christum notat."

[32] Cf. C. Cecchelli, *Il triunfo della Croce* (Rome 1954), 65–79 and 151–70.

for the modern historian to reconstruct this; the fact can only be accepted. There are no grounds for emending Lactantius' text,[33] for it is clear in itself and there is certainly no ground at all to look for a literary model of his report and to claim to find this in the pagan panegyrist who reported Constantine's visit to the shrine of Apollo in Gaul in 310;[34] neither in form nor in content can this narrative be claimed as a basis for Lactantius' story.

The same event is clearly at the bottom of the account given by Eusebius about twenty-five years later in his biography of the emperor,[35] but how much more extensive it is now, in comparison with Lactantius' brief report! According to Eusebius, Constantine wanted to wage the campaign against Maxentius under his father's protector-god and prayed to him to reveal himself and grant his aid. Straightaway the emperor and the army saw in the late afternoon "in the sky above the sun the radiant victory sign of the cross", and near this the words: "By this, conquer: τούτῳ νίκα ". The following night, Christ appeared to him with the cross and told him to have it copied ánd to carry it as protection in war. The emperor had a standard made according to his specifications; a long shaft with a cross-bar ending in a circle which bore in the middle the monogram of Christ, ✗, such as Constantine later had attached to his helmet, too. A rectangular banner hung down from the cross-bar and above this on the shaft were fixed the images of the emperor and his sons. Eusebius appeals to the fact that he had seen this banner himself[36] and this could not have happened before 325 when his closer relations with the emperor began. At that time, however, the banner had already become the imperial standard, which was later called the *labarum*.[37]It is noteworthy that Eusebius does not give this report of the vision of the cross in the last edition of his *Ecclesiastical History* (about 324). The conclusion that strongly suggests itself, that he knew nothing about it, and that as a consequence it was added to the *Vita Constantini* by another hand later on, is, however, excluded because Eusebius clearly refers to the vision of the cross in his speech on the anniversary of the emperor's accession in 335 and also says in the *Ecclesiastical History* that at the beginning of his campaign against Maxentius, Constantine had prayed and appealed to Christ for help.[38] Consequently in the *Vita* he gives the version of what had happened as this took shape in Constantine's mind after a certain

[33] As J. Moreau does in his edition, 1, 127.
[34] So H. Grégoire and his school.
[35] *Vita Constant.* 1, 27–32.
[36] Ibid. 1, 30.
[37] First found in Prudentius, *Contra Symm.* 1, 486, probably derived from *laurus*, laurel; cf. H. Grégoire in *Byz(B)* 12 (1937), 227–81.
[38] Euseb. *Tric.* 6; *HE* 9, 9, 2.

lapse of time from the event itself and in the transfiguring light of the memory of his victorious course. The accessory details dressing it out in legendary fashion must not, however, distract the view from the essential kernel common to both reports. Constantine was convinced that the sign of the cross had been revealed to him at the beginning of his campaign against Maxentius; he had changed it into the monogram of Christ and with his help had triumphed over his opponent who trusted to the power of the pagan gods. His veneration for Christ as his protector-god was due to this event and it occasioned his turning to Christianity.

The question arises whether and in what form this turning found expression in Constantine's still pagan entourage. In the autumn of 313 in Trier, the pagan panegyrist celebrated Constantine's victory over Maxentius and in accordance with tradition, had to speak of the god who had given victory. It is striking that the speaker does not name him, but says that Constantine in agreement with the god present to him and with whom he was linked by a profound secret, had taken the field, despite the fears of his officers, because this god had promised victory.[39] A god who is near, who conveys direct instructions to his protégé,[40] who secretly encourages him and assures him of victory, are all forms of expression which were intelligible to Christians as well as to educated people of neo-Platonic views; they indicate the way in which Constantine conveyed his experience to those around him. Even more important, the same speaker, in his description of the solemn entry of Constantine into Rome, does not mention the traditional procession of the victor to the Capitol and the usual sacrifice there to Jupiter: evidently the emperor omitted it and so again proclaimed that he owed his victory to another god.[41] This is also in agreement with another break with the usual pagan practice of taking the omens by examining entrails; Maxentius had done this before the battle, but Constantine, the panegyrist points out, trusted to his god's instructions.[42] The panegyrist conveys a strong impression that after his victory over Maxentius, Constantine moved away from the customary pagan worship.

The triumphal arch in Rome, dedicated to the emperor after his victory by the Roman Senate and completed in 315, was naturally decorated with carvings which corresponded to the ideas of the pagan senate; the latter regarded the *sol invictus* as the emperor's protector-god and consequently had Constantine represented as entering the city in triumph with the

---

[39] *Paneg.* 9, 2, 4–5; 9, 3, 3.

[40] Ibid. 9, 4, 4: *divina praecepta.*

[41] Ibid. 9, 19, 3, and cf. especially J. Straub in *Historia* 4 (1955), 297–313; in a contrary sense, F. Altheim in *ZRGG* 9 (1957), 221–31.

[42] Ibid. 9, 2, 4; 9, 4, 4, and on this H. Dörries, *Das Selbstzeugnis Kaiser Konstantins* (Göttingen 1954), 248 ff.

attitude and gesture of the sun-god.[43] The inscription on the triumphal arch is more reserved and does not mention his god's name but ascribes the victory to an "inspiration of the divinity" and the emperor's greatness of soul.[44] Here this divinity is still the neo-Platonic "highest being", but could also be understood by Christians in their sense.

Another monument is of greater importance; it too was intended to commemorate the victory and Constantine's view of it. This is the statue of the emperor in the Forum, bearing in the right hand, on Constantine's personal directions, "the sign of suffering that brought salvation". The inscription is due to Constantine's own initiative and explains the sign in his hand. "By this salutary sign, the true proof of power, I saved and freed your city from the yoke of the tyrant and gave back to the Senate and Roman people, as well as freedom, their ancient dignity and their ancient glory."[45] In view of this emphatic indication of the inscription, there can be no question of its being the usual *vexillum* in the emperor's hand which the Christians had then interpreted in the form of a cross;[46] it is the *signum caeleste dei* of Lactantius, the Christian cross, probably in the form of the monogram. Consequently this statue is not only a novelty by its form, being the first example of an emperor's statue with a standard,[47] but it expresses in a particularly clear manner both Constantine's conviction that he had been led by this standard, and his will publicly to proclaim this.

Finally the process of turning towards Christianity, even in a very qualified way, is indicated in the coins Constantine had struck. Christian symbols gradually appear beside the images of the old divinities especially the *sol invictus,* which can be traced on coins down to the year 322. From Ticinum a silver medallion struck on the occasion of the *decennalia* of 315 shows the helmeted head of Constantine bearing a clear Christ monogram ☧ on the crest of the helmet.[48] Coinages from the Siscia mint have, after 317–18, the same sign on the emperor's helmet, and from 320 on, coins appear with the Christ monogram in the field next to the *vexillum.*[49]

---

[43] Cf. H. P. L'Orange-A. v. Gerkan, *Der spätantike Bildschmuck des Konstantinbogens* (Berlin 1939).

[44] In Dessau, *Inscriptiones latinae selectae* n. 694: "instinctu divinitatis — mentis magnitudine."   [45] *Euseb. HE* 9, 9, 10–11; cf. *Vita Const.* 1, 40 and *Tric.* 9, 8.

[46] So H. Grégoire in *Antiquité classique* 1 (1932), 141–3.

[47] Cf. A. Alföldi in *Pisciculi* 11; P. Franchi de' Cavalieri, *Constantiniana* (Rome 1953), 98–100. Recently the possibility is seriously entertained that the gigantic head of Constantine in the Palazzo dei Conservatori belongs to this statue; cf. H. Kaehler: *JdI* 67 (1952), 1–30 and C. Cecchelli, *op. cit.* 13–40.

[48] Illustrations in *Pisciculi* plates 1 and 2, and see also A. Alföldi, ibid. 4 ff. and *Studies in Honour of A. C. Johnson* (Princeton 1951), 303–11; better illustrations in H. Kraft, *Kaiser Constantins religiöse Entwicklung* (Tübingen 1955), 35–58.

[49] Cf. H: v. Schoenebeck, *op. cit.* 35–58.

Even though the introduction of the significant Christ symbol among the devices on coins was slow, it was not possible without the emperor's approval. Even if it is regarded as nothing more than a proof of the neutral attitude of an emperor who was now taking Christianity into account as well as paganism, nevertheless the use of the Christ monogram on the helmet can scarcely be interpreted otherwise than as a personal proclamation of Constantine himself.

Of considerable significance, too, for the emperor's attitude to Christianity were some measures directly connected with the victory of October 312. That very same year a letter must have gone from Constantine to Maximinus calling for an end to persecution of Christians in the eastern regions. It has already been shown how this wish was carried out.[50] Are we to suppose that the emperor was only impelled to this rapid step because he was anxious to inform Maximinus that he regarded himself as the highest *Augustus*? Similarly in the same year 312, he commanded in a letter to prefect Anullinus in North Africa that confiscated Church property should be restored.[51] Another letter was addressed directly to the Catholic Bishop of Carthage, Caecilian, who received quite a large sum for the clergy "of the lawful and most holy Catholic religion".[52] Both measures go far beyond the intention of the edict of Galerius and the second already shows the emperor taking special interest in the liturgical concerns of the Catholic Church. This may have been awakened in him by the Spanish bishop, Ossius of Cordova, who appears already in this letter as Constantine's adviser on Church affairs. The Church's worship forms the centre of a third very important document[53] which freed the clergy of the Carthaginian church from obligation to public service so that they might devote themselves unhindered to the performance of the liturgy. Constantine gave as a reason for this measure, appealing as he did so to the lessons of experience, that neglect of the worship of God had brought the State into grave danger, whereas its careful observance would bring happiness and prosperity. In adopting this position it is quite clear that, in the emperor, opinions drawn from the Roman conception of religion were struggling with new religious ideas; Constantine has become aware of the importance of Christian worship even if no understanding of its real content is perceptible. He feels obliged not merely to ensure freedom for this worship, for that was done by the edict of Galerius, but to ensure its exact and worthy accomplishment, because he sees in it a condition for the success of the work he has begun.

---

[50] See above, pages 406–7.   [51] *Euseb. HE* 10, 5, 15–7.
[52] Ibid. 10, 6, 1–5.
[53] Ibid. 10, 7, 1–2, and on this Dörries, *op. cit.* 18 ff.; H. Kraft, *op. cit.* 164 ff.

The features of Constantine's proceedings in regard to Christianity in the year 312–13, which have been discussed, vary, it is true, in evidential force. Taken as a whole they nevertheless impose the conclusion that during this period Constantine had accomplished his personal turning to Christianity. By themselves and quite apart from the further measures belonging to the emperor's religious policy until the beginning of his period of rule as sole emperor, they exclude the date 324 as the beginning of this change. Constantine's "conversion" must, it is true, only be understood in the sense of a "turning" founded on a recognition which perhaps had already been maturing in him for some time, that the God of the Christians alone had a claim to the worship due to the highest Being. The features mentioned do not themselves permit us to judge how far Constantine had advanced towards an understanding of the Christian message of redemption, or to what extent he had made principles of Christian ethics the guiding standard of his personal activity.

From the Convention of Milan, 313, to the Beginning of Sole Rule, 324

In February 313 Constantine and Licinius met in Milan to discuss the new political situation created by the former's victory. The marriage between Licinius and Constantia was also then celebrated. In regard to religious matters, discussions led to a settlement which, however, did not find expression in the form of an Edict of Milan, as was formerly thought.[54] But it is clear that this agreement was not merely concerned with putting into effect the measure of toleration laid down by the edict of Galerius;[55] it rather involved in principle a substantial extension of this as a comparison of the Galerian text with the content of two decrees of Licinius published after his victory over Maximinus Daia will show. One of them is dated from Nicomedia and Lactantius gives the Latin text;[56] the other is in Eusebius[57] and was probably intended for Palestine. The Latin document, which diverges slightly from the Greek in Eusebius, opens with a direct allusion to the negotiations between Constantine and Licinius in Milan. It is stressed in the first place that the emperor intends to settle the religious question by toleration: everyone, including Christians, had full freedom to follow the religion he preferred; that would be a guarantee for continued favour from the *summa divinitas*. Then, however, come a series of special ordinances for the Christian Church, which, by their content, intensity of insistence and tone of

---

[54] Cf. J.-R. Palanque, "A propos du prétendu édit de Milan" in *Byz(B)* 10 (1935), 607–16, and H. Nesselhauf, "Das Toleranzgesetz des Licinius" in *HJ* 74 (1955), 44–61.
[55] So J. Moreau in *Annales Univ. Sarav.* 2 (1953), 100–05.
[56] *De mort. pers.* 48, 2–12.   [57] *HE* 10, 5, 1–14.

respectful goodwill, far exceeded Galerius' grudging grant of toleration. All places in which the Christians had been accustomed to assemble, that is, churches and cemeteries, were returned to them without charge, whether they were in public or private possession.[58] Moreover this property was to be conveyed directly to the various Christian communities, whose corporate legal existence was thereby recognized.[59] Finally a conviction is expressed which would have been quite impossible with Galerius; that through this treatment of the Christian religion, the divine favour, that the emperors had experienced in such great matters, would continue for ever in its beneficial effect on public welfare.[60] There is little likelihood of mistake if the allusion to divine favour is understood as referring to the successes of Constantine's campaign. The special decrees about Church property correspond to the measures that Constantine had already adopted for Africa, and reveal the part he played in the making of the Milan agreement. The latter can be considered as the religious policy which he was chiefly striving to carry out. The benefits it accorded could not, however, be enjoyed by the Christians of the eastern provinces and Egypt, until the conflict between Licinius and Maximinus, which still persisted, had been brought to an end. The latter sought a quick military decision when, early in 313, he moved to the Balkans at a moment when he knew that Constantine was occupied by his war with the Franks of the Rhine. Lactantius represents the battle between the two rulers as a religious war; he describes Maximinus making a vow to Jupiter before the battle that in case of victory he would destroy the Christian name; an angel reveals to Licinius a prayer to the *summus deus* which would bring him victory if it were recited before the battle by the whole army.[61] The prayer is neutral in content; perhaps the only Christian element being the angel who reveals it. Maximinus was decisively defeated at Adrianople and harried by Licinius in a rapid pursuit which struck deeply into Asia Minor. He still tried to win the sympathies of his Christian subjects by an edict of unrestricted toleration,[62] and prepared for a new battle. His death in Tarsus in the autumn of 313 abruptly ended the struggle and brought all the eastern territories under Licinius' authority and the Milan agreement. The conqueror showed little magnanimity to the family and closest supporters of Maximinus; they were mercilessly exterminated, among them Diocletian's wife and daughter who had sought Maximinus' protection.

The conquest of the oriental territories brought Licinius an enormous increase of power and Constantine had to postpone for the moment his ultimate aim of establishing a universal Roman rule. The two *Augusti*

---

[58] Lactantius, *De mort. pers.* 48, 7.
[59] Ibid. 48, 8–9.
[60] Ibid. 48, 11.   [61] Ibid. 45–7.   [62] *Euseb. HE* 9, 10, 7–11.

occupied themselves first with consolidating and strengthening what had been won. In the religious question, Licinius maintained the principles of the Milan agreement; Constantine, with his mental alertness, already saw the approach of a problem and a task which were to attract him more and more as time went on: that of bringing the Christian Church closer to the State, of discovering a form of mutual relation for them which would correspond to his view of their respective missions. These views changed and became clearer in a process that took some time. He moved to a solution through the experience afforded him by his gradually deepening penetration into the specific nature of the Christian world and the questions belonging to it. He encountered them for the first time on a large scale through developments within the Church in North Africa which, shortly before his victory, had led to a profound split among adherents of Christianity there. The beginnings of the Donatist movement must be here recalled because they explain the personal attitude of the emperor to the Christian religion; a connected account and evaluation of it will only be possible later.

The superficial occasion of the Donatist schism was the question of church discipline regarding what judgment was to be passed on the action of Christians who had handed over the Holy Scriptures to the pagan authorities in the Diocletian persecution. One group among those who had remained faithful regarded it as grave betrayal of the faith and called the guilty *traditores;* among the latter were laymen, clerics, and even bishops. The question became theologically important when it was linked to the particular opinion traditional in North African theology, according to which the validity of a sacrament depended on the state of grace of its minister; consequently the sacraments conferred by a *traditor,* an apostate ultimately, could not be regarded as valid. The controversy became extremely acute when it was involved in the personal difficulties provoked by the quarrel about the succession to Bishop Mensurius of Carthage. In 312 when Caecilian, who had previously been deacon of Carthage, was called to the see, one group in the church which felt slighted because of the sharp treatment of one of its most influential members, whom Caecilian had criticized for his over-enthusiastic cult of the martyrs, pointed out that one of those who had consecrated him bishop, Felix of Aptungi, had been a *traditor.* The case was taken up by the first Bishop of Numidia, Secundus of Tigisis, and brought before a synod of seventy Numidian bishops, which declared Caecilian deposed. In this action of the Numidian episcopate, a certain rivalry with Carthage no doubt also played its part. First, Majorinus became rival bishop to Caecilian and then, after 313, Donatus, the real intellectual head of the opposition, from whom the rapidly developing schismatical church, the *pars Donati,* took its name.

When Constantine in 312 sought information about the situation in his newly acquired territories, he found himself faced by this complicated situation, very difficult for an outsider to grasp in its ultimate connexions, and even more difficult to comprehend on account of the hostility of both groups, embittered by personal rancour. He probably received his first report from the point of view of Caecilian's supporters, perhaps from Bishop Ossius, who very early showed himself to be well-informed about the African clergy. Of course, Constantine at that time could not understand the dogmatic background to the dispute, but he immediately recognized its adverse effects on the unity of the Christian society and strove as occasion offered to restore that unity. In the first place he saw that by the dissension the correct accomplishment of Christian worship was no longer assured, and this, as has already been indicated, was of particular concern to him. Consequently he was ready to make the help of State officials available to bring back into line the disturbers of the peace, for that is how the Donatists chiefly appeared to him. [63] Thereupon the Donatists addressed themselves directly to the emperor, handed in a memorandum through proconsul Anullinus, explaining their attitude to Caecilian and asking for the dispute to be settled by Gallic judges. [64] Constantine accepted this suggestion and turned to the Bishop of Rome, Miltiades, informing him what he had decided in the matter: Caecilian was to come to Rome with ten bishops of his choice and so was his opponent; there an ecclesiastical court consisting of Miltiades and three bishops of Gaul, those of Arles, Autun, and Cologne, was to hear the case and give judgment. The emperor stressed that the inquiry into Caecilian must determine whether he answered to ecclesiastical requirements "which are to be held in high respect". Finally, he affirmed that he had the greatest reverence for the Catholic Church and did not wish any division to be found in it anywhere. [65]

It is clear from this document that the emperor realized he was in a position which in many respects was completely novel to him. A Christian denomination had invoked the help of the civil power and requested the appointment of impartial judges. The emperor tended to think in legal terms and could not refuse such a request but was it possible for him to hand over such a purely ecclesiastical question to a civil court? Constantine decided on episcopal judges, leaving the matter, therefore, in ecclesiastical hands and hoping that in that way peace would be restored. [66] There can

---

[63] Letter to Bishop Caecilian, ibid. 10, 6, 1–5; in H. v. Soden, *Urkunden zur Entstehungsgeschichte des Donatismus* (Berlin, 2nd ed. 1950), no. 8.

[64] See Soden, *op. cit.* nos. 10 and 11.

[65] Soden, *op. cit.* n. 12; cf. H. Kraft, *op. cit.* 166–9.

[66] On the legal aspect of the matter, see H. U. Instinsky, *Bischofsstuhl und Kaiserthron* (Munich 1955), 59–82.

be no question, therefore, of any presumptuous intervention of imperial authority in the internal affairs of the Church, but the intense interest of the emperor in the restoration of peace within the Church is unmistakable. Miltiades invited, and this can scarcely have been contrary to the emperor's intentions, a further fifteen Italian bishops to the proceedings, clearly as members of a larger *consilium,* such as was customary for decisions of far-reaching importance.[67] The unanimous verdict of the court pronounced Donatus guilty and confirmed Caecilian as legitimate Bishop of Carthage. The Donatists, however, contested the judgment on the ground of defects of procedure, and the emperor found himself obliged to have the matter dealt with once more. The proceedings were conducted this time in Arles in the summer of 314 on a much bigger scale and with the assistance of numerous bishops, the imperial postal service being put at their disposal for the journey.

In the emperor's letter of invitation a double advance in his understanding of Christianity may be observed. He now sees the Church as a society which, in fraternal harmony, accomplishes by its rites the true worship of God.[68] Anyone who does not respect the unity of this society endangers his salvation; so the Church is felt to be a means to salvation. The emperor knows that he is on the side of this society when he claims for himself and for Aelafius, who was known to be a Christian, the designation of *cultor dei,* which here may be taken as a substitute for *christianus.*[69] He does not yet feel himself to be a complete member of the Church, but he fears for her reputation and her universal mission when he points out that the quarrels of Christians among themselves hold back from her the followers of the pagan religion. When Constantine says that, furthermore, he himself could be brought to account by the *summa divinitas* if he were to ignore the divisions in the Church and that he would only be tranquil again when the fraternal harmony was restored, his growing personal attachment to the Church is manifest. A more personal relation to the bishops was forming, too, for in his letter to those taking part in the Synod of Arles, he addressed them for the first time with what was after that to be his habitual mode, as *carissimi fratres;*[70] and he asks with feeling for their prayers "that our Redeemer may always have mercy on me".[71]

---

[67] Instinsky argues this convincingly, *Bischofsstuhl und Kaiserthron* (Munich 1955), 77 ff.

[68] Soden, *op. cit.* n. 15; H. Kraft, *op. cit.* 170 ff.

[69] H. Kraft, *op. cit.* 54 ff., and Soden, *op. cit.* no. 14.

[70] Soden, *op. cit.* no 18, and on this H. Kraft, *op. cit.* 184–191 and *Saeculum* 8 (1957), 40 ff.

[71] Ibid. conclusion: "meique mementote, ut mei salvator noster semper misereatur." The central part of this letter cannot be made use of, for it is suspected of being an interpolation, cf. H. Kraft, *op. cit.* 186–9.

After the unsuccessful outcome of the Synod of Arles, Constantine decided after all to end the Donatist schism by his own means. His attempt at pacification met with no success when he first of all refused to allow the Donatist delegation to Arles to return to Africa. He was also frustrated in his effort to install another bishop in Carthage instead of Caecilian. In a threatening tone the emperor announced to both parties that he was going to come to Africa himself and proclaimed his aim of leading all men to the true religion and the worthy worship of Almighty God.[72] In this letter to the *vicarius* Celsus, the Christian ruler's consciousness of his mission is expressed with perfect clarity: it is the emperor's task (*munus principis*) to remove all error, to be solicitous for the preaching of the true religion, to maintain concord and ensure divine worship; and the *vera religio* to which the emperor knows he is bound, is Christianity alone. Constantine did, after all, desist from a journey to Africa, but in a letter at the end of the year 316, plainly took the side of Caecilian and his supporters.[73] When disturbances occurred, from 317 onwards, he sent in troops, had Donatist bishops exiled, and their churches seized, but this only created martyrs and the sense of martyrdom until he resigned the struggle.[74] Constantine had to learn early, by experience, that divisions in Christendom are only embittered by the attempt to remove them by means of the civil power; even though his attempt sprang from the conviction that he had to take that way to save the unity of the Christian Church, as an obligation of his function as ruler. At the same time, however, dangerous possibilities are already visible which arose for the Church from the sense of mission of a Christian ruler who thought himself justified by a religious call to intervene directly in the Church's own essential concerns.

This gradual and growing attachment of the emperor for Christianity was accompanied by certain laws which revealed the influence of Christian ideas or restricted the influence of pagan religious activity.

The general line of Constantine's legislation shows increasing regard for the dignity of the human person;[75] this is seen in an ordinance of the year 315 forbidding the branding on the face of those condemned to forced labour or to the amphitheatre,[76] for the human face may not be disfigured as it is formed to the likeness of heavenly beauty. The biblical and Christian character of this explanation is unmistakable. A similarly humanitarian tendency combines with respectful recognition of those in

---

[72] Soden, *op. cit.* no. 23; To the *vicarius* Celsus, final sentence.
[73] Soden, *op. cit.* no. 25.
[74] Cf. W. H. C. Frend, *The Donatist Church* (Oxford 1952), 159–62.
[75] Cf. J. J. Van de Casteele, "Indices d'une mentalité chrétienne dans la législation civile de Constantin" in *Bulletin Assoc. G. Budé* 14 (1955), 68–74.
[76] Cod. Theod. IX 40, 2.

charge of the Christian communities, in an ordinance addressed to Bishop Ossius which declares that Christians could free their slaves in the presence of the bishop with full legal validity, and clerics likewise, in certain cases, without written documents and without witnesses.[77] As the liberation had to take place "in the bosom of the Church" it is treated as an action of religious significance. Similar regard for the episcopal office is expressed in the important decision allowing Christian bishops to set up a court of arbitration, even for civil cases, if the parties to a dispute make application to the judge to have their case transferred to one. And what *lex christiana* then decides has the force of law.[78] The law freeing those who were unmarried and without children from certain obligations may rightly be regarded as framed with the ascetics of the Christian Church in view.[79] Of decisive importance was Constantine's Sunday law, March-July 321, ordering cessation from work in the courts and from manual labour on this "venerable day".[80] The religious quality of the day makes it appropriate to distinguish it by particularly pious works such as the liberation of slaves, which could be attested on a Sunday by an official document. There is no question of seeing in the *dies solis* here a day dedicated to the sun; the introduction of a civil holiday on the first day of the week was plainly intended honourably to distinguish the Lord's day of the Christian Church, an essential feature of its liturgy. A special favour granted to the Catholic Church is represented by the edict which allowed anyone the right to bequeath in his will whatever he liked to the Catholic community.[81] There was no such provision for Jewish or schismatic communities.

Certain legal provisions were necessary to protect the right to free profession of religion laid down in the Convention of Milan, in its detailed application to Christianity. Christian converts from Judaism who were molested by their former co-religionists receive the special protection of the law.[82] Only the Catholic faith is considered here to be *cultus dei;* neither Judaism nor paganism can claim to possess it.[83] An actual incident formed the basis of a law of May 323 imposing the penalty of flogging or heavy fine on those who compelled members of the Christian community, whether clerics or laity, to take part in the pagan lustral sacrifice.[84] It is significant that Constantine here no longer designated the pagan religion as such by a neutral term, but characterized it pejoratively as *superstitio.* When in Lucania the clerical privilege of

---

[77] Ibid. IV 8, 1.   [78] Ibid. I 27, 1.   [79] Ibid. VIII 16, 1.
[80] Cod. Theod. II 8, 1a and II 8, 1.
[81] Ibid. XVI 2, 4.   [82] Ibid. XVI 8, 1.
[83] Cf. H. Dörries, *op. cit.* 170.
[84] Cod. Theod. XVI 2, 5.

immunity was not respected by pagans, Constantine reemphasized this;[85] the expressions he uses, again entail plain value judgments on the old and the new religions and make his own position quite evident: the clergy, he says, devote their pious activity to the worship of God, whilst the impious hostility of the pagans aims at impeding them in this function.

Finally a restriction of the extent to which pagan religion could be practised was introduced by the double decree on divination in 319 and 320,[86] which forbade under strict penalties the practice of this custom in private. This cannot have concerned the abolition of an abuse, for divination in public remained permissible. But it was precisely in private life that divination made possible for pagans an effective propaganda for their religion and one that escaped all control. Through restriction to public divination a check was ensured and the possibility of secret propaganda eliminated.[87]

These laws from the time when Constantine was sole ruler confirm the picture already drawn. The emperor was under the influence of Christian ideas, his concern for the accomplishment of Christian worship sprang from an inner personal interest and in this or that case a preference for the Christian religion is perceptible. Of particular importance is the unmistakable tendency of the emperor to call on the moral and religious values of the Christian religion and the authority of the Christian church leaders, for the benefit of the State. As a consequence, various features of the public life of the age already receive a Christian stamp. His attitude to paganism is in principle tolerant, but in the law against augury the first limitation of its freedom of action is seen.

The struggle for sole rule in the Roman Empire, which had been impending for some time between Licinius and Constantine, was to take the latter an important step further on the road to public and personal recognition of the Christian religion. A first military clash in Pannonia and Thrace in the autumn of 316[88] gave no decision, but the gains of territory in the Balkans that it brought to Constantine and the recognition of his two eldest sons as *Caesares* notably strengthened his position for the now inevitable final confrontation. The struggle, though ultimately concerned with the claims to the political leadership of the empire, nevertheless assumed the character of a religious war that was finally to decide the victory or the defeat of Christianity. Licinius had maintained the provisions of the Convention of Milan in his dominions since 313,[89]

---

[85] Ibid. XVI 2, 2.

[86] Ibid. IX 16, 1; XVI 10, 1.

[87] Cf. on this H. Karpp, "Konstantins Gesetze gegen die private Haruspizin" in *ZNW* 41 (1942), 145–51.

[88] On this dating see C. Habicht, "Zur Geschichte des Kaisers Konstantin" in *Hermes* 86 (1958), 360–78. [89] *Euseb. HE* 10, 2.

although by doing so he had not, like Constantine, intended to bring the Christian Church nearer to the State or even commit various public tasks to it. The marked favour shown to Christianity by the *Augustus* of the West, led Licinius gradually to diverge from the line of religious policy laid down in Milan, and after about 320 to exert pressure increasingly on the Christians in the East. Freedoms previously enjoyed were not expressly revoked, it is true, but petty bureaucratic restrictions were put on them; on freedom of worship, for example, by forbidding Christian church services inside towns or in enclosed places or by requiring separate services for men and women. Freedom of preaching was restricted by forbidding the clergy to give instruction in the Christian faith to women, and charitable activity in favour of those in prison was hampered.[90] More serious still was the abolition of freedom of belief when Christians were dismissed from the army or administration.[91] Finally came measures aimed at the Church's organization; synodal assemblies of bishops were forbidden.[92] It is not surprising that the sympathies and hopes of Christians in Asia Minor and the Near East turned to the *Augustus* in the West. The resentment of high officials was vented in violent measures. In Pontus some places of worship were closed and others demolished; some bishops were arrested, others banished; some were condemned to death and executed,[93] although no general persecution was ordered. When after massive preparations, war broke out in the summer of 324, Constantine deliberately gave it a Christian stamp by giving the army the now fully developed *labarum* as a standard in battle, whilst Licinius questioned the pagan oracles and implored the help of the gods by sacrifices.[94] Constantine's victories in battle at Adrianople and on the Bosphorus in July and at Chrysopolis in Asia Minor in September 324, forced Licinius to capitulate and accept negotiations with Constantine. The latter spared Licinius' life at the request of his wife Constantia and assigned Thessalonica as his place of detention, but later had him executed, ostensibly for treasonable plotting.

Constantine's complete victory and the position of sole ruler which it gave him, almost inevitably introduced a new phase of religious policy, for he was not now hampered by need to take into consideration the differing views of a fellow-ruler or rival. The Christians, especially in the East, looked forward with intense expectation to what was to come. Eusebius speaks in the final section of his *Ecclesiastical History* of the days of rejoicing with which the emperor's victory was celebrated. He, too, saw clearly what possibilities a unified Roman Empire directed by

---

[90] Ibid. 10, 8, 11; *Vita Const.* 1, 53 and 54.
[91] *Euseb. HE* 10, 8, 10; *Vita Const.* 1, 54.
[92] *Vita Const.* 1, 51.   [93] *HE* 10, 8, 13–17.   [94] *Vita Const.* 2, 4.

an emperor well-disposed towards Christianity could open for the Christian faith; "people rejoiced about present benefits and looked forward to future ones".[95] The first proclamations of the victorious emperor were of such a kind as to confirm these hopes. A comprehensive decree concerning the inhabitants of the eastern provinces at once cancelled the wrong done to the Christians in the time of persecution, and provided generous compensation.[96] More important still are those sections of the document in which Constantine explained the significance of recent events as the great battle for recognition of the Christian God who revealed his might in the success of Constantine's army. He stated that God had chosen him as his instrument in order "to lead (the nations) to the service of the holiest law and to spread the most blessed faith" and that not only are thanks due to the most high God for that, but: "I owe him my whole soul, every breath and every stirring of my mind, wholly and completely."[97] The earlier consciousness of a mission has now been replaced by a bold knowledge of his election which in future was to mark all the emperor's acts. The decree ends with the exhortation to serve "the divine law", that is to say, Christianity, with all reverence.[98] Constantine's personal profession of Christianity is expressed even more plainly in a second communication to the eastern provinces in which the pride of the victor is mingled with thanksgiving for divine election.[99] Here Constantine turns in prayer to God: "Under your guidance I have begun and completed these salutary deeds. I had your sign carried before us and so led the army to glorious victories; and if any necessity of the State should require it, I shall follow the same dispositions of your power and do battle against your enemies. For that I have consecrated my soul to you; ... I love your name and honour your power which you made known by many signs and so strengthened my faith. I long to set to work and build up again for you the holiest of houses."[100] The final words vividly express the intense drive of the emperor standing in the full possession of his powers; he had a clearly defined aim, the restoration of the Christian Church. The same document also shows the calibre of the victorious emperor as a statesman; he will not persecute adherents of paganism or force them to become Christians; freedom of conscientious decision is guaranteed: "Each must hold what his heart bids him."[101] Only the future could show whether Constantine would stand by this, and the programme it represented.

[95] *HE* 10, 9, 6–8; *Vita Const.* 2, 19.
[96] *Vita Const.* 2, 30–41.
[97] Ibid. 2, 28–9.   [98] Ibid. 2, 42.
[99] Ibid. 2, 48–60.   [100] Ibid. 2, 55.   [101] Ibid. 2, 56.

CHAPTER 31

The Causes of the Victory of the Christian Religion.

The Scope and Import of the Turning-Point under Constantine

THE turning-point in the history of the Church which was reached when the first Christian emperor became sole ruler, raises two questions of great importance for a right understanding of the whole situation of the Church at the beginning of the fourth century.

1. The first question regarding the causes of the final success of Christianity in its conflict both with the rival religious currents of late Antiquity and with the power of the Roman State as well has often been formulated and has received very divergent replies. A very superficial one attempts to explain the victory of Christianity by the process of decay in which the civilization of later Antiquity was involved at precisely that time; this is alleged to have given syncretist Christianity a fundamentally easy triumph over a world in dissolution.[1] This view is blind to what properly characterizes Christianity as a religion, and only postpones the problem, for at once a new question arises, why in that case did Christianity survive in the general disintegration, and not one of the other religious movements of the age? It is just as difficult to understand the final Christian success if this is viewed as the victory of a proletarian revolution in a class-war over the upper-class which until then had dominated the Roman Empire.[2] It is true that Celsus had already reproached Christianity for having a particular attraction for the lowest and uneducated social classes of the empire's population,[3] but all Christian preaching of pre-Constantinian times shows plainly that it was deliberately addressed to all classes and all races in identical fashion. In fact, this universality of the Church can rightly be regarded as one of the factors that were particularly effective in bringing about the final success of the Christian religion. But the question remains, what were the reasons for the attraction exercised by Christianity on all social classes and on all nations.

Another answer to the question regards the support given to Christianity by Constantine as the real reason for its success. Such a view of

---

[1] The first exponent of the "decadence theory" was E. Gibbon, who passionately advocated it in the *History of the Decline and Fall of the Roman Empire;* it was put forward in a modified form by F. Altheim, *Literatur und Gesellschaft im ausgehenden Altertum* (Halle 1948), 16.

[2] So, for example, A. J. Toynbee, *A Study of History,* 1, 57 ff.; and likewise Marxist histories.

[3] *Contra Cels.* 3, 59.

things, however, confuses cause and effect; Constantine acted from insight into the actual victory already achieved by Christianity when he first tolerated and then favoured it. His immediate predecessors, the persecuting emperors, realized that their persecutions had failed, even Diocletian himself, perhaps, and certainly Gallienus and Maximinus Daia, and so did Maxentius, though he was not himself a persecutor; they only drew the logical conclusions from this realization, against their will and too late. Sooner or later some emperor after Constantine would have had to seek an understanding with the victorious Church. Constantine's decisive act and what logically followed, his religious policy favourable to the Christians, certainly made the Church's task very much easier, but they do not explain the Church's victory.

The answers which seek an explanation in an element within the Church itself are closer to the facts of the case. Attention has rightly been directed, for example, to the above average level of morals and character reached by most followers of Christianity, which was proof against the heaviest trials. The fact of actual or at least always extremely possible persecution subjected candidates for baptism to an inexorable selection which provided the various Christian communities with a considerable percentage of members whose quality is scarcely paralleled in the history of the Church. The teaching in the catechumenate made it clear to them that adherence to Christianity demanded a radical break with their previous manner of life; anyone who made this break did so from a deep conviction of faith which was the source of his strength in the hour of trial. The failure of many Christians in the Decian and Diocletian persecutions does not contradict this; the frank admission of such losses by Dionysius of Alexandria and Cyprian of Carthage and their efforts to heal the wounds caused in the Church by too indiscriminate a reception of candidates for baptism in the period of peace, attest the serious determination of the Church as a whole to maintain the high level in her communities. The pagan world was also impressed by the attitude of the Christians towards their persecutors, for whom they entertained no feelings of revenge or desires for reprisals. The comprehensive charitable work of the early Christian Church as a whole also represented a strong attraction. Here, too, the question remains open what the ultimate root of this attitude and these high moral qualities was.

There is a good deal of truth in the view which attributes the success of Christianity to the values which it had to offer to a late Hellenistic world which in religious matters was in a state of unrest and inquiry. It is correct that Christianity could often advance into a spiritual vacuum which it filled with the message, proclaimed with a joyful certainty, of the new and unique way to salvation founded on a divine revelation. But this Christian message of salvation must have been characterized by an ultimate, definite quality of its own which enabled it to gain the advantage over Gnosticism, neo-Platonism, or the pagan mystery-cults, for these, too, claimed to come forward with the means of bringing the fulfilment of its longings to the human soul seeking salvation.

Augustine in the seventh book of the *Confessions* points the way to a real answer to the question of the ultimate cause of the Christian victory. He says that in the writings of the Platonists he found many assertions that he met with again later in Christian doctrine; but neo-Platonism could not in the long run hold him, because it was unaware of the sentence in the Gospel of St John: "The Word was made flesh and dwelt amongst us."[4] It was the message of the incarnate God and the conception of *humilitas* that has its ultimate roots in the Incarnation which, according to Augustine's own words, made him a Christian. This locates the decisive reason which led to the victory of Christianity, the source from which all the other factors previously mentioned received their force in the person of Jesus Christ and the message proclaimed by him; this by its unique character and absolute novelty left all other religious trends of the age far behind it. It is not difficult to perceive in the third century historical sources the unique fascination, and the power appealing to all the capacities of the human heart that is exerted by the person of Christ. Belief in his mission bound the first disciples to him, faith in his redemptive death on the cross, hope in the resurrection promised by him, are the ultimate reason for the enthusiasm of the original community, the success of Paul's missionary preaching, and the joyful readiness of the Christian martyrs to die as witnesses. The origin of this belief, its intensity and its inexhaustible vitality cannot be explained by historical means, but its existence and radiating force are plainly perceptible in its effects. By faith in the God-man, Jesus' followers joined in a society of brotherly love which, in a way never known before, abolished all social and racial barriers between men. The impression that the vitality and strength of Christianity had their roots in Jesus Christ was what in the final resort led Constantine to recognize the God of the Christians. It was similarly that absolutely new thing in his message which won the men and women of later Antiquity in increasing proportions for him. Its central content was the proclamation of the Incarnation of the only-begotten Son of God and his redemptive death of atonement on the cross; and the very contradiction aroused in pagans by the doctrine of a crucified God, shows plainly how absolutely new this message was felt to be. The way in which mankind was to share through baptism and Eucharist in the salvation won by Christ's death on the cross was also moral. It was a new demand that the genuineness of a man's belief in this redeemer had to be proved by

[4] *Conf.* 7, 9, 14.

a life imitating his, extending even to the sacrifice of life itself, and finally it was a new message that Jesus brought of another world in which human beings after their resurrection will be united with their Lord in an eternal life. Irenaeus expressed accurately the feelings of pre-Constantinian Christendom: "He brought all that is new by bringing himself."[5] It was this whole experience of novelty and originality, conveyed to the men of late Antiquity by the message and person of Christ, that we must consider as the deepest historically perceptible reason leading to Christianity's triumph over the resistances which opposed it in the first three hundred years of its existence. The Christian believer sees in this event the disposition of divine Providence which accompanied the young Church throughout all the heights and depths of the first decisive part of its journey.

2. The second question regarding the scope and import of the "Constantinian turning-point" has often been raised, and at the present time forms the central topic of a vigorous discussion[6] which unfortunately lends the theme something of a catchword character. There is general agreement that the complete change in the relation between Christian Church and Roman State wrought by Constantine was an event of first importance in the history of the world. In the estimate of its scope and consequences for Christianity in particular, however, opinions differ considerably according to the philosophical standpoint or the conception of the Church held by those who are attempting to judge. Some see its significance in the fact that the Roman emperor succeeded, by his alliance with the Church, in making that Church serviceable to the State, and so founded the system of Caesaropapism which held the Church in degrading dependence on the State, and which was the never really seriously contested practice of the Byzantine world. The Church is said to have been at fault through her silence in the face of such enslavement and to have herself contributed to narrowing her effective possibilities in regard to her divine mission. Others see in Constantine's favour and the privileges accorded to the Christian religion the first step on the road of a fateful deviation that has persisted down to the present day; the Church authorities are alleged not to have withstood temptation to power and to have bolstered their position with secular privileges, to have striven for dominion over secular spheres of civilization alien to the Church's mission; and so as a power-seeking Church to have destroyed both the credibility of her claim to a religious mission and the impact of her missionary endeavours. Both judgments agree in viewing the attitude of the Church

---

[5] *Adv. haer.* 4, 34, 1.
[6] On this discussion, see H. Rahner, "Konstantinische Wende?" in *StdZt* 167 (1960–1), 419–28, and the bibliography he gives.

at the "Constantinian turning-point" as a decline from the ideal of the gospel, in which opposition to the world, separation of secular and ecclesiastical authority, and the renunciation of the use of earthly power in the fulfilment of her missionary task are considered, on this view, to be essential. An estimate of the "Constantinian turning-point" based on criteria drawn from sources contemporary with that development might, however, lead to the following conclusions.

The closer relation brought about between the Christian religion and the Roman State had not, as a matter of fact, the radically revolutionary character that is sometimes attributed to it. As we have already seen, pre-Constantinian Christendom had already sought a tolerable relation even towards the pagan State because, as St Paul had taught (Rom 13:1–7), behind every secular power the will of God was discerned. [7] The numerous contacts in the course of the third century between followers of the Christian religion and representatives of the Roman State clearly reveal a development that would lead to mutual recognition and the collaboration of the two societies. The toleration of all religions laid down by Constantine and Licinius in the Convention of Milan in 313 could not, in the conception of that period, be of long duration. Religion and the State in late Antiquity were not known except as related to one another in principle. It would have been revolutionary if the Roman emperor and State had made absolute neutrality in regard to all religious cults a lasting principle of its policy and had been uninterested in any relations at all between the State and religion. The idea of a State necessarily neutral in religious matters in the context of a pluralist society, is an anachronism for the beginning of the fourth century. Consequently it was a perfectly normal way of thinking for Christians of the time to expect that under an emperor whose sincere conversion to their faith was not to be doubted, Christianity would gradually take the place of pagan worship. And that, in addition, their affections fixed on that emperor with unreflecting enthusiasm, is psychologically perfectly understandable. The Christians of the eastern territories of the empire, especially, had years of most severe mental and nervous strain behind them; one wave of persecution after another had broken over them from the very beginning of the century; the hope for peace that sprang up when persecution slackened was suddenly and bitterly disappointed again and again as violent oppression flamed up once more. Then with Constantine an emperor who was of their faith became sole ruler and gave every guarantee for the beginning of a lasting peace. Inevitably that released an overwhelming flood of enthusiasm which Eusebius voiced when he opened the Tenth Book of his *Ecclesiastical History* with the cry of exultation from Psalm 97: "Sing ye to the

[7] See above pp. 316–18 for the statements of Christian writers of the time on this question.

Lord a new canticle, for He hath done wondrous things"[8]. Second thoughts about a deviation or aberration in development were all the more absent because the biblical sayings about civil authority being willed by God were applied precisely to the new situation and the anointed king of the Old Testament was seen as the model for Constantine who, just like the former, bore responsibility for a correct worship of God by the nations subject to him.[9] It is asking too much of bishops of that time who attributed such a theocratic value to the Christian emperor to expect them to have seen immediately the dangers that objectively were involved in the new relation developing between Church and State and to look for prophetic warnings from any of them. Insight into the presence of such dangers could only be gained by experience and only then did a decision of the Church on the problem of the relation between Christian State and Christian Church fall due.

The positive as well as negative possibilities that presented themselves for the Christian Church at the beginning of Constantine's period of sole rule may be summarized as follows. The freedom granted to the Church released strong forces that could be devoted to the unhampered building-up of life within the Church. Freedom of worship and of preaching within the Church was guaranteed by law. New conditions were created for the worthy performance of the liturgy through the possibility for reconstruction and the erection of new Christian places of worship which were generously accorded by the State. The religious care for the faithful in the various forms of catechetical instruction, preaching and sacramental life was no longer subject to any restriction. New and attractive tasks appeared for ecclesiastical writers in unhampered work in pastoral and theological literature. The missionary function of the Church was likewise no longer impeded by any restrictions and was able to develop in a particularly fruitful way, for freedom of conscience was guaranteed in the profession of a religious faith.

It was now also possible for the Church to undertake the enormous task of christianizing secular culture and public life and to develop and give a Christian stamp to an intellectual life of her own. The Church did not feel this task to be in any way a problematic one, for ideas of the independence of secular culture and civilization were alien to her. Here the Church faced perhaps her most radical task of adaptation. Previously she had lived consciously at a distance from the cultural world around her and had withdrawn from the completely pagan public life into her own specific moral and religious domain which was easier to preserve in

---

[8] *HE* 10, 1, 3.
[9] Cf. S. L. Greenslade, *Church and State from Constantine to Theodosius* (London 1954), 11 ff.

complete isolation. Freedom now led her out of this separate existence but as a consequence, exposed her at the same time to risk; in the attempt to penetrate secular civilization with Christian ideas, she became more vulnerable to alien elements which could adulterate her belief and her morality. This imposed heavy responsibility on Christian leaders.

A danger for the high moral and religious standard of the Christian communities was created by the favour shown by Constantine to the Christian religion: people could now seek admission to the Church because adherence to Christianity offered social and professional advantages. The principle of selection that had been effective in times of persecution ceased to exist and the institution of the catechumenate became more important than ever.

Objectively the most difficult task to which the Church was set was the discovery of the right mental attitude to the new relation of Church and State. The double danger present was not, as we have already indicated, consciously realized from the start. Eusebius was still quite unconcerned and full of praise for Constantine when reporting that now, "the bishops received imperial documents and honours and subsidies".[10] It must have been a temptation for many bishops especially in the East, after being oppressed for so long, to sun themselves in the imperial favour and so lose their freedom. More dangerous was the tendency, deriving from the emperor's view, not to consider the Church as a partner *sui generis,* but to make her serviceable to the interests of the State and so to stifle her independence and necessary freedom in the realm of internal Church affairs. It has, of course, been said that Pope Miltiades recognized this tendency of the emperor even in the early phase of the Donatist dispute when Constantine refused to regard the verdict passed by the Roman bishop's court on the Donatist leaders as final and ordered the matter to be dealt with again,[11] but the sources say nothing definite about this. Only the bitter experiences under Emperor Constantius could give the episcopate some idea of how exceedingly difficult it could be to achieve a healthy, fruitful equilibrium in the mutual relations between a State under Christian leadership and the Catholic Church.

[10] *HE* 10, 2.
[11] For example, B. Lohse, "Kaiser und Papst im Donatistenstreit" in *Ecclesia und Res Publica, Festschrift für K. D. Schmidt* (Göttingen 1961), 85–88.

BIBLIOGRAPHY

BIBLIOGRAPHY TO THE GENERAL INTRODUCTION

I. The Subject Matter, Methods, Ancillary Sciences, and Divisions of Church History, and its Relevance for Today

SUBJECT MATTER

J. A. Möhler, *Einleitung in die Kirchengeschichte: Ges. Schriften und Aufsätze,* ed. by J. J. I. Döllinger, II (Regensburg 1840), 261–90; A. Ehrhard, "Die historische Theologie und ihre Methode" in *Festschrift S. Merkle* (Düsseldorf 1922), 117–36; E. Müller, "Die Kirchengeschichte. Die Darstellung der Lebensäußerungen der Kirche in ihrer zeitlichen Entwicklung im Aufbau der Theologie" in *3. Lektorenkonferenz der deutschen Franziskaner 1925* (Münster 1926), 95–108; P. Guilday, *An Introduction to Church History* (St Louis 1925); K. Adam, "Das Problem des Geschichtlichen im Leben der Kirche" in *ThQ* 128 (1948), 257–300; P. Simon, *Das Menschliche in der Kirche Christi* (Freiburg i. Br. 1948); H. Jedin, "Zur Aufgabe des Kirchengeschichtsschreibers" in *TThZ* 61 (1952), 65–78; J. Lortz, "Nochmals zur Aufgabe des Kirchengeschichtsschreibers" ibid. 317–27; H. Jedin, "Kirchengeschichte als Heilsgeschichte?" in *Saeculum* 5 (1954), 119–28; O. Köhler, "Der Gegenstand der Kirchengeschichte" in *HJ* 77 (1958), 254–69; G. Gieraths, *Kirche in der Geschichte* (Essen 1959); J. Wodka, *Das Mysterium der Kirche in kirchengeschichtlicher Sicht: Mysterium Kirche,* ed. by F. Holböck and T. Sartory (Salzburg 1962), 347–477 (Large bibliography). Protestant Works: E. Seeberg, *Über Bewegungsgesetze der Welt- und Kirchengeschichte* (Berlin 1924); W. Köhler, *Historie und Metahistorie in der Kirchengeschichte* (Tübingen 1930); H. Karpp, "Kirchengeschichte als Theologische Disziplin" in *Festschrift R. Bultmann* (Stuttgart 1949), 149–67; E. Benz, "Weltgeschichte, Kirchengeschichte und Missionsgeschichte" in *HZ* 173 (1952), 1–32; J. Chambon, *Was ist Kirchengeschichte?* (Göttingen 1957); D. Forbes, *The Liberal Anglican Idea of History* (Cambridge 1952); P. Meinhold, "Weltgeschichte – Kirchengeschichte – Heilsgeschichte" in *Saeculum* 9 (1958), 261–81 (good bibliography); E. Benz, *Kirchengeschichte in ökumenischer Sicht* (Leiden–Cologne 1961); M. Schmidt in *RGG,* 3rd ed. III, 1421–33.

THE THEOLOGY OF HISTORY at the present time: J. Wach, "Die Geschichtsphilosophie des 19. Jh. und die Theologie der Geschichte" in *HZ* 142 (1930), 1–15; J. Bernhard, *Der Sinn der Geschichte* (Freiburg i. Br. 1931); H. Rahner, "Grundzüge katholischer Geschichtstheologie" in *StdZ* 140 (1947), 408–27; K. Thieme, *Gott und die Geschichte* (Freiburg i. Br. 1948); H. Urs v. Balthasar, *Theology of History* (New York 1963); J. Endres, "Die Grenzen des Geschichtlichen" in *DTh* 30 (1952), 73–110; J. Daniélou, *The Lord of History* (Chicago 1958); J. Maritain, *On the Philosophy of History* (New York 1957); A. Dempf, *Weltordnung und Heilsgeschehen* (Einsiedeln 1958); J. Möller, "Die Frage nach der Transzendenz der Geschichte" in *Festgabe J. Lortz* II (Baden-Baden 1958), 567–84; O. Köhler, "Der neue Äon" in *Saeculum* 12 (1961), 181–204 (discussion on recent literature). — Protestant Works: N. Berdyaev, *The Meaning of History* (New York 1936); P. Tillich, *The Interpretation of History* (New York 1936); E. Rust, *The Christian Understanding of History* (London 1947); H. Butterfield, *Christianity and History* (London 1949);

K. Löwith, *Meaning in History* (Chicago 1949); R. Niebuhr, *Faith and History: A Comparison of Christian and Modern Views of History* (New York 1951); E. Harbison, "The Meaning of History and the Writing of History" in *CH* 21 (1952), 97–107; C. Fabro, "La storiografia nel pensiero cristiano" in *Grande antologia filosofica* 5 (Milan 1954), 311–503 (with Italian translation of patristic and medieval texts); W. Kamlah, *Christentum und Geschichtlichkeit* (Stuttgart, 2nd ed. 1951); H. Berkhof, *Der Sinn der Geschichte: Christus* (Göttingen 1962); S Mead, "Church History Explained" in *CH* 32 (1963), 17–31.

ECCLESIOLOGY, as far as it concerns the historical element: H. de Lubac, *The Splendor of the Church* (New York 1956); J. Beumer, "Ein neuer, mehrschichtiger Kirchenbegriff" in *TThZ* 56 (1956), 93–102; S. Sáki, *Des tendences nouvelles de l'ecclésiologie* (Rome 1957); K. Rahner, *The Dynamic Element in the Church* (London–New York 1964); K. Rahner and J. Ratzinger, *The Episcopate and the Primacy* (Freiburg–London–New York 1962); J. Auer, "Das Leibmodell und der Kirchenbegriff der katholischen Kirche" in *MThZ* 12 (1961), 14–38; "Sentire Ecclesiam" in *Festschrift H. Rahner* ed. J. Daniélou and H. Vorgrimler (Freiburg i. Br. 1961).

METHODS

J. G. Droysen, *Historik*, ed. by R. Hübner (Darmstadt, 3rd ed. 1958); C. de Smedt, *Principes de la critique historique* (Liège 1883); E. Bernheim, *Lehrbuch der historischen Methode* (Leipzig, 6th ed. 1914, new impression 1960); H. Feder, *Lehrbuch der historischen Methode* (Regensburg, 3rd ed. 1924); L. E. Halkin, *Critique historique* (Liège, 4th ed. 1959); W. Bauer, *Einführung in das Studium der Geschichte* (Tübingen, 2nd ed. 1928; new imp. Frankfurt a. M. 1961); L. Gottschalk, *Understanding History* (New York 1950); G. Garraghan, *A Guide to Historical Method* (New York, 3rd ed. 1951). The following develop their methods from the writing of history: M. Ritter, *Die Entwicklung der Geschichtswissenschaft* (Munich–Berlin 1919); F. Wagner, *Geschichtswissenschaft* (Freiburg i. Br. 1951). K. Erslev, *Historische Technik* (Munich–Berlin 1928); H. Nabholz, *Einführung in das Studium der mittelalterlichen und der neueren Geschichte* (Zürich 1948); H. Quirin, *Einführung in das Studium der mittelalterlichen Geschichte* (Brunswick, 2nd ed. 1961); L. Halphen, *Initiation aux études d'histoire du moyen âge* (Paris, 3rd ed. 1952); G. Wolf, *Einführung in das Studium der neueren Geschichte* (Berlin 1910). The views of the French school of social history are represented by the collection *L'histoire et ses méthodes*, ed. by C. Samaran (Paris 1962).

ANCILLARY SCIENCES

An excellent summary is found in A. von Brandt, *Werkzeug des Historikers. Eine Einführung in die Historischen Hilfswissenschaften* (Stuttgart, 2nd ed. 1960).

1. Chronology

H. Grotefend, *Zeitrechnung des deutschen Mittelalters und der Neuzeit*, I (Hanover 1891), II (Hanover–Leipzig 1898), the most comprehensive and detailed work, with a general account of the history of the calendar in vol. I; adequate for the student in most cases is: H. Grotefend, *Taschenbuch der Zeitrechnung des deutschen Mittelalters und der Neuzeit* (Hanover, 10th, ed. 1960). For chronology in Classical times, see W. Kubitschek, *Grundriß der antiken Zeitrechnung* (Munich 1928); for practical use, H. Lietzmann, *Zeitrechnung der Römischen Kaiserzeit, des Mittelalters und der Neuzeit* (3rd ed. revised by K. Aland, Berlin 1956). For the dating of documents, see the appropriate sections of H. Bresslau and H. W. Klewitz's *Handbuch der Urkundenlehre*, II, 2 (2nd ed. 1931, new imp. 1958) and

A. Giry, *Manuel de diplomatique*, II (Paris 1894, new imp. 1925). Comprehensive tables in C. de Mas Latrie, *Trésor de chronologie, d'histoire et de géographie* (Paris 1889); J. Finegan, *Handbook of Biblical Chronology* (Princeton 1964). For the astronomical basis: W. F. Wislicenus, *Astronomische Chronologie* (Leipzig 1895); F. K. Ginzel, *Handbuch der mathematischen und technischen Chronologie*, 3 vols. (Leipzig 1906–13). The founder of the critical method in chronology was D. Petavius with his *De doctrina temporum* (Paris 1627, with many later editions). An instructive example of the problems of medieval chronology is offered by W. E. van Wijk, *Le nombre d'Or. Étude de chronologie technique. Suivie du texte de la 'Massa Compote' d'Alexandre de Villedieu. Avec traduction et commentaire* (The Hague 1936).

2. Palaeography

A brief but excellent introduction to Latin palaeography with bibliography is B. Bischoff, *Paläographie*, 2nd revised ed. by W. Stammler (Berlin 1957) in *Deutsche Philologie im Aufriß*, 379–452. The principal Textbooks are E. M. Thompson, *An Introduction to Greek and Latin Paleography* (Oxford, 2nd ed. 1912); G. Battelli, *Lezioni di paleografia* (Vatican City, 3rd ed. 1940); H. Foerster, *Abriß der lateinischen Paläographie* (Berne 1949); M. Prou, *Manuel de paléographie latine et française*, ed. by A. de Boüard (Paris, 4th ed. 1924); G. Cencetti, *Lineamenti di storia della scrittura latina* (Bologna 1954), which takes into account recent research on the history of writing. Summary accounts of the latest researches in different countries are to be found in the principal periodical, *Scriptorium* (Antwerp 1946 seqq.).

HANDWRITING. The latest general account of the history of handwriting is J. Fevrier, *Histoire de l'écriture* (Paris, 2nd ed. 1959). For particular periods see *Nomenclature des écritures livresques du IXᵉ au XVIᵉ siècle* (Paris 1954), which contains B. Bischoff, "La nomenclature des écritures livresques du IXᵉ au XIIIᵉ siècle" (7–14); G. J. Lieftinck, "Pour une nomenclature de l'écriture livresque de la période dite Gothique" (15–34); G. Battelli, "Nomenclature des écritures humanistiques" (35–43). See also: J. Mallon, R. Marichal und C. Perrat, *L'écriture latine de la capitale à la minuscule* (Paris 1939); B. Bischoff, *Die südostdeutschen Schreibschulen und Bibliotheken in der Karolingerzeit*, I (Wiesbaden, 2nd revised ed. 1960); W. Meyer, *Die Buchstabenverbindung der sogenannten gotischen Schrift* in *AGG*, Phil. Hist. Klasse I, 6 (1897); A. Hessel, "Die Entstehung der Renaissanceschriften" in *AUF* 13 (1935), 1–14; H. Hirsch, "Gotik und Renaissance in der Entwicklung unserer Schrift" in *Almanach der Akademie der Wissenschaften zu Wien* (1932). H. Fichtenau, *Mensch und Schrift im Mittelalter* (Vienna 1946); compare however the critical discussion by A. J. Walter, "Die Schrift als Kulturobjekt" in *MIÖG* 57 (1949), 375–82; for a general survey of this subject, D. McMurtrie *The Book* (New York – London, 3rd revised ed. 1943). On the history of writing in the Middle Ages the classic work of W. Wattenbach, *Das Schriftwesen im Mittelalter* (Leipzig, 3rd ed. 1896, new imp. Graz 1958) remains unsurpassed; L. Santifaller, *Beiträge zur Geschichte der Beschreibstoffe im MA mit besonderer Berücksichtigung der päpstlichen Kanzlei*, I, in *MIÖG* Suppl. vol. 16 (1953). Palimpsests: F. Mone, *De libris palimpsestis latinis* (Karlsruhe 1855); E. Chatelain, *Les palimpsestes latins* (Paris 1903); for recent research the bibliography in the works of A. Dold is important: *Colligere Fragmenta* in *Festschrift A. Dold* (Beuron 1952) IX–XX. On penmen and penmanship: J. Destrez, *La pecia dans les MSS. universitaires du XIIIᵉ siècle* (Paris 1935); S. Haynal, *L'enseignement de l'écriture aux universités médiévales* (Budapest 1954); H. Hajdu, *Lesen und Schreiben im Spätmittelalter* (Pécs – Funfkirchen 1931).

ON WATERMARKS: G. Piccard, "Wasserzeichenforschung als historische Hilfswissenschaft" in *AZ* 52 (1956), 62–115; C. M. Briquet, *Les filigranes,* 4 vols. (Paris, 2nd ed. 1923); V. A. Mosin and M. Traljié, *Filigranes des XIIIe et XIVe siècles* (Zagreb 1957); T. Weiss ed., *Handbuch der Wasserzeichenkunde* (Leipzig 1963).

ABBREVIATIONS AND CRYPTOGRAPHY: The most practical textbook is A. Capelli, *Dizionario di abbrevature latine ed italiane* (Milan, 5th ed. 1954). J. Walther, *Lexikon diplomaticum* (Ulm, 2nd ed. 1756) is still useful. For the history of abbreviations: L. Traube, *Nomina Sacra* (Munich 1907); by the same, *Lehre und Geschichte der Abkürzungen, Vorlesungen und Abhandlungen,* I (Munich 1909); B. Mentz, *Die Tironischen Noten* (Berlin 1942); W. M. Lindsay, *Notae Latinae* (Cambridge 1915); D. Bains, *A Supplement to Notae Latinae* (Cambridge 1936); B. Bischoff, *Übersicht über die nichtdiplomatischen Geheimschriften des MAs* (Munich 1954) also in *MIÖG* 62 (1954), 1–27; A. Meister, *Die Anfänge der diplomatischen Geheimschrift* (Paderborn 1902); by the same, *Die Geheimschrift im Dienste der päpstlichen Kurie* (Paderborn 1906).

MUSIC: For the development of musical notation, see *Paléographie musicale: Les principaux MSS. de Chant Gregorien publ. en facsimile* (Solesmes 1889 seqq.), esp. vols. 2–3 (1891–2), with examples from the ninth to seventeenth centuries; J. Wolf, *Handbuch der Notationskunde,* I (Leipzig 1913), with a good historical survey; C. Parrish, *Notation of Medieval Music* (New York 1957); W. Apel, *Gregorian Chant* (Bloomington 1957); G. K. Fellerer, *History of Catholic Church Music* (New York 1960).

ILLUSTRATED WORKS: *Monumenta Palaeographica. Denkmäler der Schreibkunst des MAs,* ed. by A. Chroust, 3 series, I (Munich 1899–1906), II (Munich 1909–17), III (Munich 1918–39), arranged regionally, with more than 500 plates. Most suitable for the student are the following: F. Steffens, *Lateinische Paläographie* (Trier, 2nd ed. 1929), with 125 plates and full explanations; W. Arndt and M. Tangl, *Schrifttafeln zur Erlernung der lateinischen Paläographie,* parts 1 and 2 (4th ed. by M. Tangl, Munich 1904–6), 3rd part ed. by M. Tangl (Munich, 2nd ed. 1907); J. Kirchner, *Scriptura latina libraria* (Munich 1955); F. Ehrle and P. Liebaert, *Specimina codicum latinorum Vaticanorum* (Bonn 1912).

Illustrated works covering a limited field: E. A. Lowe, *Codices Latini Antiquiores* (Oxford 1933 seqq.), intended to include in ten parts all MSS. of the period before 800; a parallel work for documents before 800 is A. Bruckner and R. Marichal, *Chartae latinae antiquiores* (Olten – Lausanne 1954 seqq.); A. Bruckner, *Scriptoria medii aevi Helvetica,* 8 parts published to date (Geneva 1936 seqq.); E. Petzet and O. Glauning, *Deutsche Schrifttafeln des 9. bis 16. Jh.,* 5 parts (Munich 1910–30); R. Thommen, *Schriftproben aus Basler Handschriften des 14. bis 16. Jh.* (Basle, 2nd ed. 1908); G. Mentz, *Handschriften der Reformationszeit* (Bonn 1912); J. Kirchner, *Germanistische Handschriftenpraxis* (Munich 1950).

GREEK PALAEOGRAPHY: For this science founded by the Maurist Br. Mountfaucon with his *Palaeographia graeca* (Paris 1708), consult: V. Gardthausen, *Griechische Paläographie,* 2 vols. (Leipzig, 2nd ed. 1911–13); W. Schubarth, *Griechische Paläographie* (Munich 1925); H. Hunger, *Studien zur griechischen Paläographie* (Vienna 1954).

3. Libraries

GENERAL WORKS: *Handbuch der Bibliothekswissenschaft,* founded by F. Milkau, 2nd revised and corrected ed. by G. Leyh (Wiesbaden 1957 seqq.); *Répertoire des Bibliothèques de France,* I: *Bibliothèques de Paris* (Paris 1950); II: *Bibliothèques des Départements* (Paris 1950); III: *Centres et Services de Documentation* (Paris 1951); K. Schottenloher, *Bücher bewegten die Welt. Eine Kulturgeschichte des Buches,* 2 vols. (Stuttgart 1951–2). Periodical: *Zentralblatt für Bibliothekswesen* (Leipzig 1884 seqq.) *[ZblB].*

PARTICULAR FIELDS of study: T. Birt, *Das antike Buchwesen in seinem Verhältnis zur Literatur* (Berlin 1882, new imp. Aalen 1959); T. Gottlieb, *Über mittelalterliche Bibliotheken* (Leipzig 1890, new imp. Graz 1955); K. Löffler, *Deutsche Klosterbibliotheken* (Bonn–Leipzig, 2nd ed. 1922); F. Ehrle, *Historia bibliothecae Romanorum Pontificum tum Bonifatianae tum Avenionensis* (Rome 1890); A. Pelzer, *Addenda et emendanda ad Francisci Ehrle Historia*, I (Vatican City 1947); E. Muntz and P. Fabre, *La bibliothèque du Vatican au XVe siècle d'après des documents inédits* (Paris 1887). An important work for the study of medieval libraries is *Mittelalterliche Bibliothekskataloge Deutschlands und der Schweiz* ed. by the Bavarian Academy of Sciences (1918 seqq.); P. O. Kristeller, *Latin MS. Books before 1600. A list of the Printed Catalogues and Unpublished Inventories of Extant Collections* (New York, 2nd ed. 1960): this first appeared in *Tr* 6 (1948), 227–317, 9 (1953), 393–418; R. Hale, *Guide to Photocopied Historical Material in the United States and Canada* (Ithaca 1961); P. Haner ed., *A Guide to Archives and Manuscripts in the United States* (New Haven 1961).

4. Study of Documents

BIBLIOGRAPHIES AND PERIODICALS: H. Oesterley, *Wegweiser durch die Literatur der Urkundensammlungen*, 2 vols. (Berlin 1885–6); L. Santifaller, *Neuere Editionen mittelalterlicher Königs- und Papsturkunden* (Vienna 1958), with details of editions of medieval papal documents. The oldest and most important periodical is the *Bibliothèque de l'École des Chartes* (Paris 1839 seqq.) *[BECh]*; also *Archiv für Urkundenforschung* 1–18 (Leipzig 1907–44) *[AUF]*, which is specially devoted to the study of documents. A continuation, with a wider scope, is: *Archiv für Diplomatik, Schriftgeschichte, Siegel- und Wappenkunde* (Cologne–Graz 1955 seqq.) *[ADipl]*.

TEXTBOOKS AND MANUALS: H. Bresslau, *Handbuch der Urkundenlehre für Deutschland und Italien*, I (Berlin, 2nd ed. 1912), II/1 (Berlin, 2nd ed. 1915), II/2, 2nd ed. by H. W. Klewitz (Berlin 1931, new imp. Berlin 1958), index by H. Schulze (Berlin 1960); A. de Boüard, *Manuel de diplomatique française et pontificale*, I: *Diplomatique générale* (Paris 1929); II: *L'acte privé* (Paris 1948); L. Paetow, *A Guide to the Study of Medieval History* (New York 1931) revised ed.
Textbooks for particular fields of study: O. Redlich, *Allgemeine Einleitung zur Urkundenlehre*; W. Erben, *Die Kaiser- und Königsurkunden des Mittelalters* (Munich 1907) [Part I of Below–Meinecke, *Handbuch der mittelalterlichen und neueren Geschichte*]; O. Redlich, *Die Privaturkunden des Mittelalters* (Munich 1911) [Part III of Below–Meinecke, *Handbuch*]; R. Thommen, *Grundbegriffe, Kaiser- und Königsurkunden* (Leipzig–Berlin 1913) [A. Meister, *Grundriß der Geschichtswissenschaft*, I]; L. Schmitz-Kallenberg, *Papsturkunden* (Leipzig, 2nd ed. 1913) [Meister, *Grundriß*, Part II]; H. Steinacker, *Die Lehre von den nichtköniglichen Privaturkunden* (Leipzig 1906) [Meister, *Grundriß*, Part III]; R. Heuberger, *Allgemeine Urkundenlehre für Deutschland und Italien* (Leipzig 1921). For Byzantine diplomatics, see F. Dölger, *Byzantinische Diplomatik* (Munich 1956).

ILLUSTRATED WORKS. H. von Sybel and T. Sickel, *Kaiserurkunden in Abbildungen*, 11 parts (Munich 1889–91); A. Brackmann, *Papsturkunden* (Leipzig–Berlin 1914) [G. Seeliger, *Urkunden und Siegel in Nachbildungen für den akademischen Unterricht*, 2].

HISTORY OF DIPLOMATICS. The Benedictine J. Mabillon laid the foundation of the scientific criticism of documents in his work *De re diplomatica libri VI* (Paris 1681), *vide infra*, Enlightenment. Modern methods of research have been developed mainly by German and Austrian scholars: T. Sickel, *Die Urkunden der Karolinger*, 2 vols. (Vienna 1867); J. Ficker, *Beiträge zur Urkundenlehre*, 2 vols. (Innsbruck 1877–8); the various works of P. Kehr (*vide infra*) are excellent.

REGESTA. Collections of *Regesta* of papal documents: P. Jaffé, *Regesta pontificum Romanorum ab condita ecclesia ad annum post Christum natum 1198* (Berlin 1851), 2nd ed. by S. Loewenfeld, F. Kaltenbrunner, P. Ewald, 2 vols. (Leipzig 1885–8, new imp. Graz 1958); A. Potthast, *Regesta Pontificum Romanorum inde ab anno 1198 ad annum 1304,* 2 vols. (Berlin 1874–5, new imp. Graz 1957). For the new ed. under the direction of P. Kehr commissioned by the Göttinger Gesellschaft der Wissenschaften, cf. the work of L. Santifaller (p. 439). *Regesta* of papal documents are to be found in the various series published by the Bibliothèque des écoles françaises d'Athènes et de Rome (see the bibliographies to vols. II–IV).

SIGILLOGRAPHY: W. Ewald, *Siegelkunde* (Munich 1914); P. Sella, *I sigilli dell'Archivio Vaticano,* 2 vols. (Rome 1937–46); V. Laurent, *Documents de sigillographie byzantine* (Paris 1954); R. Gandilhon, *Sigillographie des universités de France* (Paris 1952).

5. Archives

MANUALS: A. Brennecke, *Archivstudien,* ed. by W. Leesch (Leipzig 1953); H. O. Meissner, *Archiv- und Aktenlehre der Neuzeit* (Leipzig, 2nd ed. 1952); A. Mazzoleni, *Lezioni di archivistica* (Naples 1954).

PERIODICALS: *Archivum. Revue internationale des archives* (Paris 1951 seqq.); *Archivalische Zeitschrift* (Stuttgart–Munich 1877 seqq.) *[AZ].*

GUIDES TO ARCHIVES: D. H. Thomas and L. M. Case, *Guide to the Diplomatic Archives of Western Europe* (Philadelphia 1959); K. A. Fink, *Das Vatikanische Archiv. Einführung in die Bestände und ihre Erforschung* (Rome, 2nd ed. 1951). A good example of a general catalogue of an important set of archives is: L. Bittner, *Gesamtinventar des Wiener Haus-, Hof- und Staatsarchivs,* 5 vols. (Vienna 1936–40).

6. Heraldry

GENERAL: J. Siebacher, *Grosses und allgemeines Wappenbuch,* Nuremberg, 1st ed. 1594, 8 new impressions (unaltered) since 1854. The best general accounts are D. L. Galbreath, *Handbüchlein der Heraldik* (Lausanne, 2nd ed., 1948) O. Hupp, *Wappenkunst und Wappenkunde* (Berlin 1928); H. Hussman, *Deutsche Wappenkunst* (Leipzig 1940); L. Fejerpataky, *Magyar Czimeres Emlekek,* 3 vols. (Budapest 1901–2); C. Fox-Davies, *A Complete Guide to Heraldry* (London–New York 1951); J. Burke, *Britain's Genealogical and Heraldic History of Landed Gentry* (London 1939); A. Wagner, *Heralds and Heraldry in the Middle Ages* (Oxford 1956); S. Konarski, *Armorial de la noblesse polonaise titrée* (Paris 1958).

ECCLESIASTICAL HERALDRY: Baron du Rouve de Paulins, *L'héraldique ecclésiastique* (Paris 1911); B. B. Heim, *Wappenbrauch und Wappenrecht in der Kirche* (Olten 1947). For papal and cardinalitial arms see A. Ciaconius-Oldoin, *Vitae et res gestae summorum Pontificum et S. R. E. cardinalium,* 4 vols. (Rome 1677); D. L. Galbreath, *A Treatise on Ecclesiastical Heraldry,* I: *Papal Heraldry* (Cambridge 1930); C. Erdmann, "Das Wappen und die Fahne der Römischen Kirche" in *QFIAB* 22 (1930–1), 227–55; by the same, "Kaiserliche und päpstliche Fahnen im hohen Mittelalter", ibid. 25 (1933–4), 1–48; O. Kirchberger, *Die Wappen der religiösen Orden* (Vienna 1895); M. Gorino, *Titoli nobiliari e ordini equestri pontifici* (Turin 1933); E. Zimmermann, *Bayrische Klosterheraldik* (Munich 1931); A. Walz, "Das Wappen des Predigerordens" in *RQ* 47 (1939), 111–47. There is no general account of the origin of the arms of the German bishoprics, but there are some good ones for individual sees, e.g. P. Bretschneider, "Das Breslauer Bistumswappen" in *Zeitschrift des Vereins für Gesch. Schlesiens* 50 (1916), 225–56. For France: J. de Meurgey *Armorial de l'Église de France* (Macon 1938).

7. Geography and Cartography

GENERAL: G. Franz, "Historische Kartographie, Forschung und Bibliographie" (Bremen – Horn 1955) in *Veröffentlichungen der Akademie für Raumforschung und Landesplanung*, Report No. XXIX; H. Hassinger, *Geographische Grundlagen der Geschichte* (Freiburg i. Br., 2nd ed. 1953); L. Mirot, *Manuel de geographie historique de la France* (Paris 1930); M. Schmidt, "Probleme, Aufgaben u. Möglichkeiten kirchengeschichtlicher Kartographie" in *Misc. Hist. Eccl.* (Louvain 1961) 158–66; J. Prinz, "Eine Konfessionskarte Deutschlands", ibid. 147–57.

ATLASES. General historical atlases: G. Droysen, *Allgemeiner historischer Handatlas* (Biele-feld – Leipzig 1886); K. von Spruner and T. Menke, *Handatlas für die Geschichte des Mittelalters u. der neueren Zeit* (Gotha 1880); *Grosser historischer Weltatlas* ed. by the Bayrischer Schulbuchverlag (Munich 1954 seqq.); F. W. Putzger, *Historischer Schulatlas* (Bielefeld – Leipzig, 65th ed. 1960); G. Niessen, *Geschichtlicher Handatlas der deutschen Länder am Rhein* (Bonn 1950). J. Horrabin, *An Atlas of European History from the 2nd to the 20th Century* (London 1935); F. van der Meer, *Atlas de la civilisation occidentale* (Paris 1952). For ecclesiastical history: O. Werner, *Orbis terrarum catholicus* (Freiburg i. Br. 1890); E. McClure, *Historical Church Atlas* (London 1897); K. Heussi and H. Mulert, *Atlas zur Kirchengeschichte* (Tübingen, 3rd ed. 1937); L. Grammatica, *Testo e Atlante di Geografia ecclesiastica* (Bergamo 1928); K. Pieper, *Atlas orbis christiani antiqui* (Düssel-dorf 1931); C. Streit, *Atlas Hierarchicus* (Paderborn, 2nd ed. 1929); A. Freitag and J. M. Lory, *Atlas du monde chrétien* (Brussels 1959); F. van der Meer and C. Mohrmann, *An Atlas of the Early Christian World* (London 1958); E. Gaustad, *Historical Atlas of Religion in America* (New York 1962).

Missionary History: C. Streit, *Katholischer Missionsatlas* (Steyl 1906); J. Thauren, *Atlas der katholischen Missionsgeschichte* (Mödling bei Wien 1932); J Neuhäusler, *Atlas der katholischen Missionen* (Munich 1932); *Atlas Missionum a Sacra Congregatione de Propaganda Fide dependentium*, ed. by H. Emmerich (Vatican City 1958); A. Freitag, *Die Wege des Heils, Bildatlas zur Geschichte der Weltmissionen* (Salzburg 1960).

TOPOGRAPHY: J. G. T. Graesse, *Orbis latinus*, 3rd ed. revised by F. Benedict (Berlin 1922); E. Förstemann, *Die deutschen Ortsnamen* (Nordhausen 1863); H. Oesterley, *Historisch-geographisches Wörterbuch des deutschen Mittelalters* (Gotha 1881–3); U. Chevalier, *Répertoire des sources historiques du moyen âge*, II: *Topo-bibliographie* (Montbéliard 1894–1903); L. H. Cottineau, *Répertoire topo-bibliographique des abbayes et prieurés*, 2 vols. (Macon 1935–9); *Germania Sacra*, ed. by the Kaiser-Wilhelm-Institut für Deutsche Geschichte (Berlin 1929 seqq.). A basic work for the later Middle Ages (bishoprics and abbeys) is H. Hoberg, *Taxae de communibus servitiis* (Vatican City 1949). For ecclesiastical geography of the Byzantine Church see H. G. Beck, *Kirche und theologische Literatur im byzantinischen Reich* (Munich 1959) 148–229; R. Janin, *La géographie ecclésiastique de l'empire byzantin* III/1: *Églises et monastères de Constantinople* (Paris 1953).

8. Statistics

For general statistics of population: E. Kirsten, E. W. Buchholz, W. Köllmann, *Raum und Bevölkerung in der Weltgeschichte*, 2 vols. (Würzburg, 2nd ed. 1956). Numbers of popu-lation, including clerics and monks in individual bishoprics and monasteries, are till the later Middle Ages based mainly on estimates. Only from the late Middle Ages onwards do church registers, tithe lists, records of visitations and other documents provide more reliable figures; cf. H. Jedin, "Das Konzil von Trient und die Anfänge der Kirchen-matrikeln" in *ZSavRGkan* 32 (1943), 419–494; H. Börsting, *Geschichte der Matrikeln von der Frühkirche bis zur Gegenwart* (Freiburg i. Br. 1959). Concerning the cardinals, the papal court and the curial authorities, the annual *Notizie per l'anno* ... have given exact statistics since 1716, from 1850–70 under the title *Annuario Pontificio*. In the *Gerarchia Cattolica*, appearing since 1872 (which in 1912 became the official *Annuario Pontificio*), holders of bishoprics are listed alphabetically. Valuable and by no means fully exploited material for the statistics of bishoprics and orders is contained in the lists of personnel and property dating mostly from the 18th century. The Congregation for the Propagation of the Faith first issued missionary statistics in 1843: *Notizia statistica delle Missioni cattoliche in tutto il mondo*, reprinted in O. Mejer, *Die Propaganda*, I (Göttingen 1852), 473–562.

The first bureau of ecclesiastical statistics following scientific methods, the *Zentralstelle für kirchliche Statistik*, was set up by the German bishops' conference at Cologne in 1915. It took over the *Kirchliche Handbuch für das katholische Deutschland*, edited since 1908 by H. A. Krose, SJ. Only in quite recent times have other countries followed this example, such as France, Holland, and Spain among others. The Federal Republic of Western Germany has now two research institutes, at Königstein and Essen, which are members of the International Federation of Catholic Research Institutes (FERES), whose headquarters are at Fribourg, Switzerland. The *Official Catholic Directory* published annually in the United States contains ecclesiastical statistics on America, Great Britain, and Commonwealth Nations, as well as the Philippine Islands and Mexico.

DIVISIONS

E. Göller, *Die Periodisierung der Kirchengeschichte und die epochale Stellung des Mittelalters* (Freiburg i. Br. 1919); K. Heussi, *Altertum, Mittelalter und Neuzeit in der Kirchengeschichte* (Tübingen 1921); O. E. Strasser, "Les périodes et les époques de l'histoire de l'église" in *RHPhR* 30 (1950), 290–304; O. Halecki, *The Limits and Divisions of European History* (New York 1950); id., *The Millennium of Europe* (Notre Dame 1963).
A general guide to the division of history: J. H. J. van der Pot, *De Periodisering der der Geschiedenis. Een overzicht der Theorien* (The Hague 1951); M. Tetz, "Über Formengeschichte in der Kirchengeschichte" in *ThZ* 17 (1961), 413–31.

RELEVANCE FOR TODAY

A. Knöpfler, *Wert und Bedeutung des Studiums der Kirchengeschichte* (Munich 1893); cf. also: H. Schrörs in *HJ* 15 (1894), 133–45; A. M. Koeniger, *Voraussetzungen und Voraussetzungslosigkeit in Geschichte und Kirchengeschichte* (Munich 1910); Y. Congar, *Vraie et fausse réforme dans l'église* (Paris 1950); M. Richards, "Is Church History Really Necessary?" in *The Clergy Review* (1964); H. F. May, "The Recovery of American Religious History" in *The American Historical Review*, 70 (1964), 79–92. For further bibliography see above under Subject Matter, Ecclesiology.

II. The Writing and Study of Church History

There is still no satisfactory account of ecclesiastical historiography and its development into a science. F. C. Baur's brilliant *Die Epochen der Kirchengeschichtsschreibung* (Tübingen 1852, new imp. Darmstadt 1962) was Hegelian in its inspiration; it confined itself, like W. Nigg's *Die Kirchengeschichtsschreibung* (Munich 1934) to the main types — in recent times Protestant — without inquiring into the reciprocal effects of research, narrative and instruction. The same applies to the concise survey by P. Brezzi, *La storiografia ecclesiastica* (Naples 1959).

Antiquity

The sources given in G. Loeschke's *Zwei kirchengeschichtliche Entwürfe* (Tübingen 1913), excellent as far as they go, have now been superseded. Brief but excellent information about the Church historians of antiquity, with full bibliography, is to be found in B. Altaner, *Patrology* (London – New York, 2nd imp. 1960) 263–93. For the Latin Fathers' consciousness of the Church see P. T. Camelot, "Mysterium Ecclesiae" in *Festschrift H. Rahner* (Freiburg i. Br. 1961), 134–51.

Eusebius and his Continuators. The first ed. of Eusebius' Church History in the Greek text is that of R. Étienne (Paris 1544), with Socrates, Sozomen, and Theodoret; critical ed. by E. Schwartz and T. Mommsen, 3 vols. (Berlin 1903–9), Greek and Latin text; Greek and English text by H. J. Lawlor and J. E. L. Ulten (London, second edition 1952–3). R. Laqueur, *Eusebius als Historiker seiner Zeit* (Berlin 1929); cf. *Altaner* 265 ff. for further bibliography. For Socrates and Sozomen see *PG* 67, 29–1630; Sozomen alone, ed. by J. Bidez and G. C. Hausen (Berlin 1960) [GCS 50]; Theodoret, ed. by L. Parmentier and F. Scheidweiler (Berlin, 2nd ed. 1954); F. Scheidweiler, "Die Bedeutung der Vita Mitrophanis et Alexandri für die Quellenkritik bei den griechischen Kirchenhistorikern" in *ByZ* 50 (1957), 74–98. *Historia Tripartita* ed. by W. Jacob and R. Hanslik (Vienna 1952) [*CSEL* 71]; for bibliography see *Altaner* 275. The *World Chronicle* of Eusebius and Jerome ed. by R. Halm, 2 vols. (Berlin 1913–26) [*GCS* 24, 34], new ed. in 1 vol. (Berlin 1956). *Lesser World Chronicles* ed. by T. Mommsen in *MGAuctant* IX (Berlin 1892). For a brief survey of the Byzantine historians not here mentioned see H. G. Beck in *LThK* VI, 212 and General Bibliography to vols. I and II.

Of the extensive literature on Augustine's view of history (*Altaner* 504–5), only A. Wachtel, *Beiträge zur Geschichtstheologie des Aurelius Augustinus* (Bonn 1960) need be mentioned, especially for its full bibliographies; Paulus Orosius, *Historiae adversus paganos*, ed. with English translation by J. W. Raymond (New York 1936); bibliography, *Altaner* 280–1.

For schemata of sacred and profane history see van der Pot, *Periodisering der Geschiedenis*, 36–64, 76–84; J. Daniélou, "La typologie millénariste de la semaine dans le christianisme primitif" in *VigChr* 2 (1946), 1–16; P. E. Hübinger, "Spätantike und frühes Mittelalter" in *DVfLG* 26 (1952), 1–48; A. D. van den Brincken, "Weltaeren" in *AKG* 39 (1957), 133–49; B. Sticker, "Weltzeitalter und astronomische Perioden" in *Saeculum* 4 (1953) 241–49.

Middle Ages

In addition to the still unfinished new edition of W. Wattenbach's standard work, *Deutschlands Geschichtsquellen im Mittelalter* (1st ed. 1858) by W. Levison and H. Löwe (Weimar 1952–7) for the early and Carolingian period and by R. Holtzmann for the 11th–13th centuries (Tübingen 1948) (referred to as Wattenbach–Levison and Wattenbach–Holtzmann respectively), consult also K. Jacob, *Quellenkunde der deutschen Geschichte im Mittelalter*, 5th ed. revised by H. Hohenleutner, I and II (Berlin 1959–61), III by F. Weden (Berlin 1952) [Sammlung Göschen 279, 280, 284]; R. I. Poole, *Chronicles and Annals* (Oxford 1926); T. F. Tout, *The Study of Medieval Chronicles* (Manchester 1934); H. Grundmann, "Geschichtsschreibung im MA" in *Deutsche Philologie im Aufriß*, ed. by W. Stammler, III (Berlin 1957), 1273–336; M. Manitius, *Geschichte der lateinischen Literatur des MA*, 3 vols. (Munich 1911, 1923, 1931, new imp. of I, 1959) (to the end of the 12th cent.); G. Misch, *Geschichte der Autobiographie*, II and III, in 4 parts (Frankfurt 1955–62), with detailed analyses; for interpretations of history, see *Geschichtsdenken und*

Geschichtsbild, ed. by W. Lammers (Darmstadt 1961), which contains sixteen essays by leading authors, already published elsewhere. Finally there is O. Brunner's study, *Abendländisches Geschichtsdenken* (434–59) with extensive bibliographies.

For the medieval beginnings of ecclesiastical history in the strict sense, an important work is H. Zimmermann, *Studien zur Kirchengeschichtsschreibung im MA* (Vienna 1960) [*SAW,* Phil.-Hist. Kl. 235, 4]; necessary for deeper study of the subject are the numerous modern works on medieval ecclesiology: J. Beumer, "Zur Ekklesiologie der Frühscholastik" in *Scholastik* 26 (1951), 365–89; by the same, "Das Kirchenbild in den Schriftkommentaren Bedas der Ehrwürdigen", ibid. 28 (1953), 40–56; by the same, "Ekklesiologische Probleme der Frühscholastik", ibid. 27 (1952), 183–209; H. Riedlinger, *Die Makellosigkeit der Kirche in den lat. Hoheliedkommentaren des MA* (Münster 1958); for the history of Joachimism and the Franciscan spirituals, see E. Benz, *Ecclesia Spiritualis* (Stuttgart 1934). For the late medieval idea of the Church, see F. Merzbacher, "Wandlungen des Kirchenbegriffs im Spätmittelalter" in *ZSavRGkan* 39 (1953), 274–361; H. Jedin, "Zur Entwicklung des Kirchenbegriffs im 16. Jh." in *Relazioni del X° Congresso internazionale di Scienze Storiche IV* (Florence 1955), 59–73; L. Buisson, *Potestas und Caritas. Die päpstliche Gewalt im Spätmittelalter* (Cologne 1958).

Special Subjects: H. Löwe, *Von Theoderich zu Karl dem Großen* (Darmstadt 1958); A. D. van den Brincken, *Studien zur lateinischen Weltchronik bis in das Zeitalter Ottos von Freising* (Düsseldorf 1957); J. Spörl, *Grundformen hochmittelalterlicher Geschichtsanschauungen* (Munich 1935). For the medieval Vita, see H. Vogt, *Die literarische Personenschilderung des frühen MA* (Leipzig 1934); O. Köhler, *Das Bild des geistlichen Fürsten in den Viten des 10., 11. und 12. Jh.* (Berlin 1934). P. van den Baar, *Die kirchliche Lehre von der Translatio Imperii bis zur Mitte des 13. Jh.;* W. Goez, *Translatio Imperii. Ein Beitrag zur Geschichte des Geschichtsdenkens und der politischen Theorie im MA und der frühen Neuzeit* (Tübingen 1958); H. Beumann, "Der Schriftsteller und seine Kritiker im frühen MA" in *StudGen* 12 (1959), 497–511.

Humanism, the Reformation, and the Beginnings of Church History as a Science

The influence of humanism on attitudes towards the Church and Church history still needs closer study. The leading accounts of modern historiography may still be mentioned: E. Fueter, *Geschichte der neueren Historiographie* (Munich–Berlin 1911); H. von Srbik, *Geist und Geschichte vom deutschen Humanismus bis zur Gegenwart,* 2 vols. (Munich–Salzburg 1950); F. Meinecke, *Die Entstehung des Historismus,* 2 vols. (Munich, 3rd ed. 1959); W. Dilthey, *Weltanschauung und Analyse des Menschen seit Renaissance und Reformation* (Leipzig, 2nd ed. 1921). See also L. Spitz, *The Religious Renaissance of the German Humanists* (Cambridge 1963). For this subject, further reference may be made to the following surveys of sources: G. Wolf, *Quellenkunde der deutschen Reformationsgeschichte,* 2 vols. (Gotha 1915–22); F. Schnabel, *Deutschlands geschichtliche Quellen und Darstellungen in der Neuzeit, I: Das Zeitalter der Reformation* (Leipzig 1931); an excellent general survey of the literature, embracing the whole of Europe, is E. Hassinger, *Das Werden des neuzeitlichen Europa* (Brunswick 1959), 401–86. For the rise of a new view of history, see A. Klempf, *Die Säkularisierung der universalhistorischen Auffassung* (Göttingen 1960); cf. O. Köhler in *Saeculum* 12 (1961), 191; W. Kaegi, *Chronica Mundi. Grundformen der Geschichtsschreibung seit dem MA* (Einsiedeln 1954). For an excellent survey of the Renaissance in its historical context: W. Ferguson, *The Renaissance in Historical Thought* (Cambridge 1948).

The only general account of the historiography of this period is E. Menke-Glückert, *Die Geschichtsschreibung der Reformation und Gegenreformation* (Leipzig 1912), which is inadequate for developments on the Catholic side. For the attitude of the Reformers towards Church history, see W. Köhler, *Luther und die Kirchengeschichte*, I (Erlangen 1900); H. W. Müller-Krumweide, *Glauben und Geschichte in der Theologie Luthers* (Göttingen 1953); H. Berger, *Calvins Geschichtsauffassung* (Zürich 1955); K. Räber, *Studien zur Geschichtsbibel Sebastian Francks* (Basle 1952). For the separation of sacred from profane history in Melanchthon, see P. Meinhold, *Ph. Melanchthon* (Berlin 1960), 90 ff. The effect of the controversial point of view on the development of Church history into a science is studied by P. Polman, *L'élément historique dans la controverse religieuse du XVIᵉ siècle* (Gembloux 1932). For the publication of sources and the rise of criticism, see H. Quentin, *J.-D. Mansi et les grandes collections conciliaires* (Paris 1900); also *LThK* VI, 534 ff.; P. Peeters, *L'Oeuvre des Bollandistes* (Brussels, 2nd ed. 1961); E. Martène, *Histoire de la Congrégation de St Maur*, ed. by G. Charvin, 9 vols. (Liguge 1928–43); E. de Broglie, *Bernard de Montfaucon et les Bernardins*, 2 vols. (Paris 1891); H. Leclercq, *J. Mabillon*, 2 vols. (Paris 1953–7), on this M. D. Knowles in *JEH* 10 (1959), 153–73; J. De Ghellinck, "L'édition de St Augustin par les Mauristes" in *NRTh* 57 (1930), 746–74. Studies of particular subjects: A. Herte, *Das katholische Lutherbild im Bann der Lutherkommentare des Cochlaeus*, 3 vols. (Münster 1943); B. A. Vermaseren, *De cath. Nederlandsche Geschiedsschrijving in de 16ᵉ en 17ᵉ eeuw* (Maastricht 1941); H. Borak, "Theologia historiae in doctrina S. Laurentii a Brindisi" in *Laurentiana* 1 (Rome 1960), 31–97.

The Enlightenment and Teaching of Church History

K. Völker, *Die Kirchengeschichtsschreibung der Aufklärung* (Tübingen 1921); E. C. Scherer, *Geschichte und Kirchengeschichte an den deutschen Universitäten* (Freiburg i. Br. 1927), a fundamental introduction to the subject; J. Engel, "Die deutschen Universitäten und die Geschichtswissenschaft" in *HZ* 189 (1959), 223–378; K. Zinke, *Zustände und Strömungen in der katholischen Kirchengeschichtsschreibung des Aufklärungszeitalters im deutschen Sprachgebiet* (Bernau 1933). A. Walz, *Studi storiografici* (Rome 1940), 40–72, on the introducing of Church history as a subject of instruction at the Roman universities in the 18th and 19th centuries; A. Pérez Goyena, "Los orígenes del estudio de la historia eclesíastica en España" in *RF* 79 (1927). Histories of the faculties of Church history have been written by S. Merkle for Würzburg, E. Säger for Freiburg, E. Hegel for Trier, H. Jedin for Bonn, and A. P. Brück for Mainz.

The 19th and 20th Centuries and the Development of Church History as a Science

On the main currents in the science of history-writing during the 19th and 20th centuries: F. Wagner, *Geschichtswissenschaft* (Freiburg i. Br. 1951), 169–377 (full bibliography); important for Church history is E. Troeltsch, *Der Historismus und seine Probleme* (Tübingen 1922); id., *Der Historismus und seine Überwindung* (Berlin 1924); E. Laslowski, "Probleme des Historismus" in *HJ* 62–9 (1949), 593–606; H. Butterfield, *Man on his Past* (Cambridge 1955), important here because it deals in some detail with Döllinger's pupil, Lord Acton. For the progress of historical research in the 19th century in which Church history also shared, the great works on published sources must be consulted (e.g. H. Bresslau, *Geschichte der MG* [Hanover 1921], and H. Grundmann, *Geschichte in Wissenschaft und Unterricht*, 2 [1951], 538–47), as well as the publications of the historical institutes (e.g. W. Friedensburg, *Das Königliche Preußische hist. Inst. in Rom* 1888–1901 [Berlin 1903]; H. Kramer, *Das Österreichische hist. Inst. in Rom* 1881–1901 [Rome 1932]; for other historical institutes in Rome, see K. A. Fink, *Das Vatikanische Archiv* [Rome, 2nd ed. 1951], 152–80), and their annual reports in their respective periodicals; and not least the correspondence and autobiographies of famous historical scholars: *Die Geschichtswissenschaft in Selbstdarstellungen,* ed. by S. Steinberg (Leipzig 1925); *Die Religionswissenschaft in Selbstdarstellungen,* ed. by E. Stange (Leipzig 1927), containing among others H. Grisar, H. Schrörs and J. Schmidlin; P. M. Baumgarten, *Römische und andere Erinnerungen* (Düsseldorf 1927); T. von Sickel, *Römische Erinnerungen,* ed. by L. Santifaller (Vienna 1947). The account in this section is an attempt to trace the reciprocal effects of research, historical writing and instruction in the field of Church history, as I have done in *Das Konzil von Trient. Ein Überblick über die Erforschung seiner Geschichte* (Rome 1948), 167–213.

MÖHLER AND DÖLLINGER: J. A. Möhler, *Die Einheit der Kirche* (1825), ed. by J. R. Geiselmann (Cologne 1957); *Gesammelte Schriften und Aufsätze,* ed. by J. J. I. Döllinger, 2 vols. (Regensburg 1939–40); S. Lösch, *J. A. Möhler, Gesammelte Aktenstücke und Briefe,* I (Munich 1928); K. Bihlmeyer, "J. A. Möhler als Kirchenhistoriker" in *ThQ* 100 (1919), 134–98; H. Tüchle, *Die eine Kirche. Zum Gedenken J. A. Möhlers* (Paderborn 1939); J. R. Geiselmann, *Lebendiger Glaube aus geheiligter Überlieferung* (Mainz 1942); id., *L'ecclésiologie au XIXᵉ siècle* (Paris 1960), 141–95; B. D. Dufourcq, "Schisme et Primauté chez J. A. M." in *RSR* 34 (1960), 197–231. The biography of Döllinger by his pupil, the Old Catholic J. Friedrich, 3 vols. (Munich 1899–1901) can be superseded only when the edition of his letters begun by V. Conzemius is completed; cf. V. Conzemius in *ZBLG* 22 (1959), 154–60; S. Lösch, *Döllinger und Frankreich* (Munich 1955). Discourse on the past and present of Catholic theology (1863) in *Kleinere Schriften,* ed. by F. H. Reusch (Stuttgart 1890), 161–96.

GENERAL BIBLIOGRAPHY TO VOLUMES I AND II

Containing the sources, historical accounts, periodicals, and other ancillary works of most importance for the study of the history of the ancient Church. The abbreviations are based on those employed in the *Lexikon für Theologie und Kirche* I (Freiburg i. Br., 2nd ed. 1957), 16–48.

I. LITERARY SOURCES

Ancient Christian Authors

The works of the ancient Christian authors are certainly of primary importance. They exist for the most part in the form of collections of writings, an account of the origin of which has been given in the Introduction. For many of these authors the editions in J.-P. Migne's two great series of patristic texts have not yet been superseded: *Patrologiae cursus completus. Series graeca,* 161 vols. (Paris 1857–66) and *Series latina,* 221 vols., of which the four last contain indexes (Paris 1844–64, several vols. reprinted 1878–90). The indexes to the *Series graeca* were compiled by F. Cavallera (Paris 1912) and T. Hopfner, 2 vols. (Paris 1928–45). A Supplement to the *Series latina* in several vols. has been begun by A. Hamman (Paris 1958 seqq.); so far (1964) vols. I, II, and III, fasc. 1 and 2 have appeared.

Critical editions of the Latin and Greek authors are still being produced by the Academies of Science of Vienna and Berlin respectively in: *Corpus scriptorum ecclesiasticorum latinorum* (Vienna 1860 seqq.) and *Die griechischen christlichen Schriftsteller der ersten Jahrhunderte* (Leipzig 1897 seqq.). A parallel undertaking is: *Texte und Untersuchungen zur Geschichte der altchristlichen Literatur,* in several series (Leipzig–Berlin 1882 seqq.). The Benedictine abbey of St Peter at Steenbrugge (Belgium) is planning a new edition of the writings of all the Latin, Greek, and Eastern Fathers: *Corpus christianorum seu nova patrum collectio,* of which the Latin series has already been begun (Turnhout–Paris 1953 seqq.). A very valuable aid to study is the following work, prepared for this series by E. Dekkers and A. Gaar: *Clavis patrum latinorum* (Steenbrugge, 2nd ed. 1961). This gives a critical survey of all existing editions of the Latin Fathers. Some late Latin ecclesiastical writers have been edited in: *Monumenta Germaniae Historica, Auctores antiquissimi* (Hanover–Berlin 1826 seqq.). For the early Byzantine period of Church history a work to be consulted is: *Corpus scriptorum historiae Byzantinae* (Bonn 1828 seqq.).

Greek and Latin texts of the Fathers (with French translation) are published in the collection edited by C. Mondésert known as: *Sources chrétiennes* (Paris 1941 seqq.); 102 vols. have so far appeared.

For the study of Greek and Latin Christian authors, M. Vatasso's *Initia patrum (latinorum),* 2 vols. (Rome 1906–8) and C. Baur's *Initia patrum graecorum,* 2 vols. (Rome 1955) are important aids. All printed works of the Fathers are listed according to their opening words.

The following are collections of Eastern Christian writers: *Patrologia Syriaca,* ed. by R. Grafin, 3 vols. (Paris 1894–1926); *Patrologia Orientalis,* ed. by R. Grafin and F. Nau (Paris 1903 seqq.); *Corpus scriptorum christianorum Orientalium* (Paris 1903 seqq.), begun by J. B. Chabot and now edited by R. Draguet, Louvain.

The smaller collections of individual writings of the Fathers listed below are intended for students' use: *Corpus scriptorum latinorum Paravianum* (Turin): *Florilegium patristicum*, ed. by J. Zellinger and B. Geyer (Bonn 1904 seqq.); *Kleine Texte*, ed. by H. Lietzmann (Berlin 1902 seqq.); *Sammlung ausgewählter Kirchen- und dogmengeschichtlicher Quellenschriften*, ed. by G. Krüger (Tübingen 1891 seqq.); *Scriptores christiani primaevi* (The Hague 1946 seqq.); *Stromata patristica et mediaevalia*, ed. by C. Mohrmann and J. Quasten (Utrecht 1950 seqq.).

For students also the so-called *enchiridia* are to be recommended. They contain a selection of characteristic patristic texts: C. Kirch and L. Ueding, *Enchiridion fontium historiae ecclesiasticae antiquae* (Freiburg i. Br., 8th ed. 1960); M.-J. Rouët de Journel, *Enchiridion patristicum* (Freiburg i. Br., 21st ed. 1959); M.-J. Rouët de Journel and J. Dutilleul, *Enchiridion asceticum* (Freiburg i.Br., 5th ed. 1958); C. Silva-Tarouca, *Fontes historiae ecclesiasticae medii aevi*, I, *saec. V–IX* (Rome 1930; selections); H. M. Gwatkin, *Selections from Early Christian Writers Illustrative of Church History to the Time of Constantine* (London 1937).

The principal series of translations of the Fathers are: *Bibliothek der Kirchenväter*, ed. by O. Bardenhewer *et alii*, 1st series, 63 vols., 2nd series, 20 vols. (Kempten–Munich 1911–39); *Sources chrétiennes*, the French translation mentioned above; *Ancient Christian Writers*, ed. by J. Quasten (Westminster, Md.-London 1946 seqq.); *The Fathers of the Church*, ed. by R. Deferrari (New York 1947 seqq.); *Ante-Nicene Christian Library* (Edinburgh Collection) 1866–72, 24 vols., and 1 supplement. vol by A. Menzies, 1897; *Ante-Nicene Fathers* (Buffalo Collection) 1884–6, supplemented by 28 vols. republished (Grand Rapids 1956); *A Select Library of Nicene and Post-Nicene Fathers*, 28 vols. (Buffalo and New York 1886–90).

The actual Church historians among the ancient writers are of special importance: Eusebius, *Historia Ecclesiastica* (down to 324) ed. by E. Schwartz in *GCS* 9, 1–3 (Berlin 1908–9); Philostorgius, *Historia Ecclesiastica* (down to 425) ed. by J. Bidez in *GCS* 21 (Berlin 1913); Socrates, *Historia Ecclesiastica* (305–439), ed by R. Hussey, 3 vols. (Oxford 1853); Sozomen, *Historia Ecclesiastica* (324–425), ed. by J. Bidez and G. C. Hansen in *GCS* 50 (Berlin 1960); Theodoret, *Historia Ecclesiastica* ed. by L. Parmentier, 2nd ed. by F. Scheidweiler in *GCS* 44 (19) (Berlin 1954); Gelasius, *Historia Ecclesiastica*, ed. by G. Loeschke and M. Heinemann in *GCS* 28 (Berlin 1918); Zacharias Rhetor, *Historia Ecclesiastica* (circa 450–540), preserved in a Syrian translation, ed. by E. W. Brooks in *CSCO* 83–4 (Paris 1919–21); Evagrius Scholasticus, *Historia Ecclesiastica* (431–594), ed. by J. Bidez and L. Parmentier (London 1898, republished Amsterdam 1964); Rufinus of Aquileia's translation of the *Historia Ecclesiastica* of Eusebius, with two supplementary books of his own, ed. by T. Mommsen in *GCS* 9, 1–3 (Berlin 1908–9); Sulpicius Severus, the *World Chronicle* or *Historia Sacra* (down to 400), ed. by C. Halm in *CSEL* 1 (Vienna 1866); Paulus Orosius, *Historia adversus paganos*, an outline of world history to the year 474, ed. by C. Zangmeister in *CSEL* 5 (Vienna 1882); *The World Chronicles* of Tiro Prosper of Aquitaine, Cassiodorus and Isidore of Seville, edited by T. Mommsen in *MGAuctant* 9 and 11 (Berlin 1892 and 1894).

ACTS OF THE MARTYRS AND THE VITAE OF THE EARLY SAINTS

The Acts of the martyrs and the Vitae of the early saints are valuable source-material for the first centuries of the history of the Church. They have been catalogued in three works ed. by the Bollandists: *Bibliotheca hagiographica latina*, 2 vols. (Brussels 1898–1901, reprinted in 1949), a supplementary vol. appeared in 1911; *Bibliotheca hagiographica graeca*, 3 vols. (Brussels, 3rd ed. 1957); *Bibliotheca hagiographica orientalis* (Brussels 1910). *Acta Sanctorum*, begun by J. Bolland at Antwerp in 1643, serves editors and commentators working on these sources. The vols. are arranged according to the saints' days of the Roman Calendar, beginning with January. The most recent vol., no. 65, contains the ninth and tenth days of November. Two important supplementary vols. are: *Martyrologium Hieronymianum*, ed. by H. Quentin and H. Delehaye (Brussels 1931) and *Martyrologium Romanum*, revised by H. Delehaye (Brussels 1940). A selection of the most important *Acta* is found in: T. Ruinart, *Acta martyrum sincera* (Paris 1689. Regensburg, 5th ed. 1859). The selection by R. Knopf and G. Krüger, *Ausgewählte Märtyrerakten* (Tübingen, 3rd ed. 1929), is intended for the use of students. A fundamental work for Byzantine hagiography is that of A. Ehrhard and J. M. Hoeck, *Überlieferung und Bestand der hagiographischen und homiletischen Literatur der griechischen Kirche*, of which vols. I–III have so far appeared (Leipzig 1937–52) (*TU* 50–2). The leading periodical for the whole field of hagiography is: *Analecta Bollandiana* (Brussels 1882 seqq.), with bibliography.

LITURGIES, CREEDS, ACTS OF COUNCILS, PAPAL DECREES

Source-works on ancient liturgies, creeds, acts of councils and papal decrees, important for our knowledge of the inner life of the Church, have been accorded separate treatment.

a) LITURGIES: Among collections of liturgical texts the following should be mentioned: J. A. Assemani, *Codex liturgicus ecclesiae universalis*, 13 vols. (Rome 1749–66, new imp. Paris 1922 seqq.); H. A. Daniel, *Codex liturgicus ecclesiae universalis*, 4 vols. (Leipzig 1847–53); N. Nilles, *Kalendarium manuale utriusque ecclesiae orientalis et occidentalis*, 2 vols. (Innsbruck 1896–7). The following contain only Oriental texts: J. Goar, *Euchologion, sive Rituale Graecorum* (Paris 1647, Venice 1730, latest imp. Graz 1959); E. Renaudot, *Liturgiarum orientalium collectio*, 2 vols. (Paris 1716, Frankfurt 1847); H. Denzinger, *Ritus Orientalium*, 2 vols. (Würzburg 1863–4); F. E. Brightman, *Liturgies Eastern and Western*, I: *Eastern Liturgies* (Oxford 1896). There is new material in: H. Leclercq, *Monumenta ecclesiae liturgica* (Paris, I, 1902–13, V, 1904); W. Bulst, *Hymni latini antiquissimi* (Heidelberg 1956) contains early Latin hymns.

The recent collection *Opuscula et textus, series liturgica* (Münster 1933) publishes select liturgical texts, as does also: *Liturgiegeschichtliche Quellen* (Münster 1918 seqq.).

Recent critical editions, especially of Latin texts, are named at the appropriate places in the present work; for them the following manuals on liturgy may be consulted: L. Eisenhofer, *Handbuch der katholischen Liturgik* (Freiburg i. Br., 2 vols. 1932–3); M. Righetti, *Manuale di storia liturgica*, I–IV (Milan, 2nd ed. 1950–5); A.-G. Martimort (ed.), *Introduction à la liturgie* (Paris 1961).

Fundamental works for the study of ancient liturgies are: L. Duchesne, *Origines du culte chrétien* (Paris, 5th ed. 1920), Eng. tr. *Christian Worship. Its Origin and Evolution. A Study of the Latin Liturgy up to the Time of Charlemagne* (New York, 2nd ed. 1954); J. M. Hanssens, *Institutiones liturgicae de rebus orientalibus*, 3 vols. (Rome 1930–2); A. Baumstark, *Liturgie comparée* (Chevetogne, 3rd ed. 1953).

b) THE CREEDS of the 'ancient Church have been collected by A. Hahn, *Bibliothek der Symbole und Glaubensregeln* (Hildesheim 1962). There is a selection in H. Lietzmann, *Ausgewählte Symbole der alten Kirche*, *KlT* 17–18 (Berlin, 3rd ed. 1931). Other collections are: H. Denzinger, *Enchiridion symbolorum* (Freiburg i. Br., 31st ed. 1960), Eng. tr. *The Sources of Catholic Dogma* (St. Louis 1957); F. Cavallera, *Thesaurus doctrinae catholicae ex documentis magisterii ecclesiastici* (Paris, 2nd ed. 1937). For the early Byzantine period: J. N. Karmiris, Τὰ δογματικὰ καὶ συμβολικὰ μνημεῖα τῆς 'Ορθοδόξου Καθολικῆς

'Εκκλησίας (Athens, 2 vols. 1952–3, 2nd ed. 1960). See also: H. Lietzmann. "Symbolstudien" in *ZNW* 21 (1922), 22 (1923), 24 (1925), 26 (1927), now contained in H. Lietzmann, *Kleine Schriften, III* (Berlin 1962), 189–281; F. Kattenbusch, *Das apostolische Symbol,* 2 vols. (Leipzig 1894–1900, new impression Darmstadt 1964); J. de Ghellinck, *Patristique et Moyen Age, I: Les recherches depuis cinq siècles sur les origines du symbole des apôtres* (Brussels, 2nd ed. 1949); F. J. Badcock, *History of the Creeds* (London, 2nd ed. 1938); J. N. D. Kelly, *Early Christian Creeds* (London, 2nd ed. 1960).

c) The Acts of the Early Christian Councils are to be found in the great collections of J. Hardouin, *Acta conciliorum et epistolae decretales ac constitutiones summorum pontificum* (Paris, 12 vols., 1714 seq.), and J. D. Mansi, *Sacrorum conciliorum nova et amplissima collectio* (Florence – Venice 1759–98, new imp. and continuation, Lyons – Paris 1899–1927, new imp. Graz 1960–1). The Acts of the councils of Ephesus and Chalcedon have been published in critical editions by E. Schwartz, *Acta conciliorum oecumenicorum* (Berlin 1914 seqq.). Smaller editions of texts are: F. Lauchert, *Die Kanones der wichtigsten altkirchlichen Konzilien* (Freiburg i. Br. 1896, new imp. Frankfurt 1961); E. J. Jonkers, *Acta et symbola conciliorum quae saeculo quarto habita sunt* (Leiden 1954). The decrees and canons of the early Christian Councils may now be conveniently found in *Conciliorum oecumenicorum decreta,* ed. J. Alberigo *et alii* (Freiburg i. Br. 1962).

A basic work for the history of the ancient councils is: C. J. von Hefele, *Conciliengeschichte* I–III (Freiburg i. Br., 2nd ed. 1873–7), and the French translation (with supplementary matter by H. Leclercq, *Histoire des Conciles d'après les documents originaux,* I–III (Paris 1907–10). On the council of Chalcedon: *Das Konzil von Chaldekon,* ed. by A. Grillmeier and H. Bacht, 3 vols. (Würzburg 1951–4).

d) The Principal Papal Decrees of the early period have been published in P. Coustant, *Pontificum Romanorum a s. Clemente usque ad s. Leonem epistulae genuinae* (Paris 1721, Göttingen 1796), and A. Thiel, *Epistulae Romanorum pontificum genuinae a s. Hilaro usque ad Pelagium II,* vol. I (Braunsberg 1867). A collection of the earliest *Vitae* of the popes is contained in: *Liber Pontificalis,* ed. by L. Duchesne, 2 vols. (Paris 1907–15); new ed. by C. Vogel in 3 vols. (ibid. 1955–7) The history of the early popes is related in E. Caspar, *Geschichte des Papsttums von den Anfängen bis zur Höhe der Weltherrschaft,* 2 vols. (Tübingen 1930–3); J. Haller, *Das Papsttum. Idee und Wirklichkeit, I: Die Grundlagen* (Urach – Stuttgart, 2nd ed. 1950); F. X. Seppelt, *Geschichte der Päpste, I: Der Aufstieg des Papsttums* (Munich, 2nd ed. 1954).

EARLY CHRISTIAN PAPYRI

Early Christian papyri form a body of source-material that is constantly increasing in importance. Collections of papyri are being published, either in separate series or in special periodicals. The following may be mentioned: *Berliner griechische Urkunden* (Berlin 1895 seqq.); *The Oxyrhynchos Papyri* (London 1898 seqq.); *Papiri greci e latini della Società Italiana* (Florence 1912 seqq.); *Select Papyri,* 3 vols. in the Loeb Classical Library, ed. by A. S. Hunt, C. C. Edgar, and D. L. Page (London 1932–41).

Christian Texts only: C. Wessely, *Les plus anciens monuments du christianisme écrits sur papyrus, POR* 4, 2; 18, 3 (Paris 1907, 1924); G. Ghedini, *Lettere Christiane dai papiri del III° e IV° secolo* (Milan 1923). Other letters: *Aegyptus* 34 (1954), 266–82. Liturgical texts: C. del Grande, *Liturgiae, preces hymni Christianorum e papyris collecti* (Naples, 2nd ed. 1934); *Aegyptus* 36 (1956), 247–53, 37 (1957), 23–31.

Periodicals and ancillary studies: *Archiv für Papyrusforschung,* ed. by U. Wilcken

(Leipzig 1901 seqq.); *Aegyptus, Rivista Italiana di Egittologia e Papirologia* (Milan 1920 seqq.), with valuable bibliography and specializing in Christian texts. W. Schubert, *Einführung in die Papyruskunde* (Berlin 1918); K. Preisendanz, *Papyrusfunde und Papyrusforschung* (Leipzig 1933); A. Calderini, *Manuale di papirologia antica greca e romana* (Milan 1938, with bibliography, 176–92); F. Preisigke and E. Kiessling, *Wörterbuch der griechischen Papyrusurkunden* (Berlin 1925 seqq.); E. Mayser, *Grammatik der griechischen Papyri aus der Ptolemäerzeit* (Berlin 1923–38); W. Schubert, *Papyri Graecae Berolinenses* (Bonn 1911), (= *Tabulae in usum scholarum*, ed. J. Lietzmann, No. 2).

PHILOLOGICAL AIDS

For work on the written sources of early Church history, a knowledge of certain branches of Classical studies, especially of philology, is indispensable. A. Gercke and E. Norden, *Einleitung in die klassische Altertumswissenschaft* give an introduction to this subject (3 vols., Leipzig, 3rd ed. 1921 seqq.). More comprehensive are the relevant volumes of the *Handbuch der Altertumswissenschaft* latest revised editions, now ed. by H. Bengtson (Munich 1955 seqq.).

A work of reference to be constantly consulted is: *Paulys Realencyclopädie der klassischen Altertumswissenschaft* in the revised version of G. Wissowa, W. Kroll and K. Mittelhaus (Stuttgart 1893 seqq.).

The most important Latin dictionaries are: C. du Cange, *Glossarium ad scriptores mediae et infimae latinitatis,* first published in 3 vols. (Paris 1678), many times reprinted and enlarged, most recently by L. Favre, 10 vols. (Niort 1883–7); *Thesaurus linguae latinae* (Leipzig 1900 seqq.); A. Souter, *A Glossary of Later Latin to* A.D. *600* (Oxford 1949); A. Blaise, *Dictionnaire latin-français des auteurs chrétiens* (Strasbourg 1954). See also C. Mohrmann, *Études sur le latin des chrétiens,* I (Rome 1961), II (Rome 1961); H. Nunn, *An Introduction to Ecclesiastical Latin* (New York 1928); M. O'Brien, *Titles of Address in Christian Latin Epistolography* (Washington 1930).

The most important Greek dictionaries are: H. Stephanus, *Thesaurus graecae linguae,* latest ed. in 8 vols. (Paris 1831–55); H. G. Liddell and R. Scott, *Greek-English Lexikon,* ed. by H. S. Jones and R. McKenzie (Oxford 1940); W. F. Arndt and F. W. Gingrich, *A Greek-English Lexicon of the New Testament and other Early Christian Literature* (Chicago, 4th ed. 1957); *Theologisches Wörterbuch zum Neuen Testament,* ed. by G. Kittel and G. Friedrich (Stuttgart 1933 seqq.), Eng. tr. *Theological Dictionary of the New Test.,* vol. I (Grand Rapids 1964); G. W. H. Lampe, *A Greek Patristic Lexicon* (Oxford 1961 seqq.); E. A. Sophocles, *Greek Lexicon of the Roman and Byzantine Periods* (A.D. *146 to 1100)* (New York, 3rd ed. 1888). See also S. B. Psaltes, *Grammatik der byzantinischen Chroniken* (Göttingen 1913); F. Blass and H. Debrunner, *Grammatik des neutestamentlichen Griechisch* (Göttingen, 11th ed. 1961).

PALAEOGRAPHY: V. Gardthausen, *Griechische Paläographie,* 2 vols. (Leipzig, 2nd ed. 1911–13); B. A. van Groningen, *Short Manual of Greek Palaeography* (Leiden 1940); R. Devreesse, *Introduction à l'étude des manuscripts grecs* (Paris 1954); H. Hunger, *Studien zur griechischen Paläographie* (Vienna 1954); F. Steffens, *Lateinische Paläographie* (Trier, 2nd ed. 1907–9); B. Bretholz, *Lateinische Paläographie* (Leipzig–Berlin, 3rd ed. 1926); G. Battelli, *Lezioni di paleografia* (Vatican City, 3rd ed. 1949); B. Bischoff, *Paläographie* (Berlin, 2nd ed. 1957). To these may be added the vols. of facsimiles ed. by H. Lietzmann: *Specimina codicum graecorum Vaticanorum* (Berlin, 2nd ed. 1929) and *Specimina codicum latinorum Vaticanorum* (Berlin, 2nd ed. 1927), as well as the periodical *Scriptorium* (Antwerp 1948 seqq.).

Patrology

The above-mentioned sources are all systematically treated in the histories of early Christian literature and in the manuals and textbooks of patrology, as follows: A. von Harnack, *Geschichte der altchristlichen Literatur*, 3 vols. (Leipzig 1893–1904); new impression of the 4th ed. with supplementary matter by K. Aland (Leipzig 1958); O. Bardenhewer, *Geschichte der altchristlichen Literatur*, 5 vols. (Freiburg i. Br., I–III, 1913–23; IV, 1924; V, 1932; repr. Darmstadt 1962). On Syriac writers: O. de Urbina, *Patrologia Syriaca*, I (Rome 1958); M. Moricca, *Storia della letteratura latina cristiana*, 3 vols. (Turin 1924–34); A. Puech, *Histoire de la littérature grecque chrétienne*, 3 vols. (Paris 1928–9); F. Cayré, *Patrologie et histoire de la théologie, I: Précis de patrologie* (Paris, 3rd ed. 1958), Eng. tr. *A Manual of Patrology and the History of Theology* (Paris 1936), several new editions have appeared; P. de Labriolle, Eng. tr. *History and Literature of Christianity from Tertullian to Boethius* (London–New York, 2nd ed. 1947); F. Cross, *The Early Christian Fathers* (London 1960); J. Quasten, *Patrology*, 3 vols. so far (Utrecht 1950–60); B. Altaner, *Patrology* (Freiburg–London–New York, 2nd imp. 1960) from the fifth German edition 1958.

Certain sections of patristic studies are dealt with in the following works: M. Manitius, *Geschichte der lateinischen Literatur des Mittelalters*, I (Munich 1911, new imp. Graz 1959); F. J. E. Raby, *A History of Christian Latin Poetry* (Oxford, 3rd ed. 1953); H. G. Beck, *Kirche und theologische Literatur im byzantinischen Reich* (Munich 1959, *HAW*); P. Nautin, *Lettres et écrivains chrétiens des IIᵉ et IIIᵉ siècles* (Paris 1961); A. Siegmund, *Die Überlieferung der griechisch-christlichen Literatur in der lateinischen Kirche* (Munich 1939).

The works of the Eastern Christian writers are treated of in: A. Baumstark, *Geschichte der syrischen Literatur* (Bonn 1922), with additions by A. Baumstark and A. Rücker in the *Handbuch der Orientalistik*, III (Leiden 1954), 169–204; J. Chabot, *La littérature syriaque* (Paris 1935); F. N. Fink, "Geschichte der armenischen Literatur" in *Geschichte der christlichen Literatur des Orients* (Leipzig 1907); K. Kiparian, *Geschichte der armenischen Literatur*, I (Venice 1944); H. Thorossian, *Histoire de la littérature arménienne* (Paris 1951); G. Peradze, *Die altchristliche Literatur in georgischer Überlieferung*, OrChr 3–8 (Wiesbaden 1930–3); J. Karst, *Littérature géorgienne chrétienne* (Paris 1934); M. Tarchnišvili and J. Assfalg, *Geschichte der kirchlichen georgischen Literatur* (Rome 1955); O'Leary, "Littérature copte" in *DACL* 9 (1930), 1599–635; S. Morenz, "Die koptische Literatur" in *Handbuch der Orientalistik*, I (Leiden 1952), 207–19; W. Till, "Coptic and its Value" in *BJRL* 40 (1957), 229–58, with bibliography; G. Graf, *Geschichte der christlichen arabischen Literatur*, 5 vols. (Rome 1944–53).

The chief bibliographical aid for the whole field is now the *Bibliographia Patristica*, ed. by W. Schneemelcher (Berlin 1956 seqq.). The *Bulletin d'ancienne littérature chrétienne latine*, since 1921 associated with the *Revue Bénédictine* (Maredsous), is concerned only with Christian Latin literature.

II. MONUMENTAL SOURCES

EARLY CHRISTIAN EPIGRAPHY

Early Christian life, in so far as it has left "monuments" of itself (taking the term in its widest sense), is the subject of Christian archaeology. One of this science's most important branches is early Christian epigraphy, which is the study of Latin and Greek Christian inscriptions. These have mostly been collected according to localities; and among such collections, that of the city of Rome is of particular significance: J. B. de Rossi, *Inscriptiones christianae urbis Romae*, 2 vols. (Rome 1864—80), enlarged by J. Gatti with a Supplement to vol. I (Rome 1915). The continuation of this work has been undertaken by A. Silvagni, *Inscriptiones christianae urbis Romae, Nova Series*, 3 vols. (Rome 1934–56). See also H. Zilliacus, *Sylloge inscriptionum christianarum veterum Musei Vaticani*, I–II (Helsinki 1963); I. Kajanto, *Onomastic Studies in the Early Christian Inscriptions of Rome and Carthage* (Helsinki 1963).

Next come the collections for separate countries: E. le Blant, *Inscriptions chrétiennes de la Gaule*, 3 vols. (Paris 1856–92, new imp. Paris 1923); A. Hübner, *Inscriptiones Britanniae christianae* (Berlin–London 1876); E. Egli, *Die christlichen Inschriften der Schweiz* (Zürich 1895); S. Gsell, *Inscriptions latines d'Algérie*, I–II (Paris 1922–57); A. L. Delattre, *L'épigraphie funéraire chrétienne à Carthage* (Tunis 1926); J. Vives, *Inscripciones cristianas de la España romana y visigoda* (Barcelona 1942, supplement Barcelona 1942); F. X. Kraus, *Die christlichen Inschriften der Rheinlande*, 2 vols. (Freiburg i. Br. 1890–4), now superseded by F. Gose, *Katalog der frühchristlichen Inschriften in Trier* (Berlin 1958); G. Behrens, *Das frühchristliche und merowingische Mainz* (Mainz 1950); J. B. Ward Perkins and J. M. Reynolds, *Inscriptions of Roman Tripolitania* (Rome 1952).

The principal early Christian Latin inscriptions from all areas where discoveries have been made have been collected and explained by E. Diehl in *Inscriptiones latinae christianae veteres*, 3 vols. (Berlin 1925–31).

Greek-Christian inscriptions have been published in: L. Jalabert, R. Mouterde and C. Mondésert, *Inscriptions grecques (et latines) de la Syrie*, 4 vols. (Paris 1929–55); W. H. Buckler, W. M. Calder and W. K. C. Guthrie, *Monuments and Documents from Eastern Asia and Western Galatia, Monumenta Asiae Minoris Antiqua*, IV (Manchester 1933); W. H. Buckler and W. M. Calder, *Monuments and Documents from Phrygia and Caria*, ibid. VI (Manchester 1939); H. Lietzmann, N. A. Bees, and G. Sotiriu, *Die griechisch-christlichen Inschriften des Peloponnes-Isthmos-Korinth* (Athens 1941); J. S. Creaghan and A. E. Raubitschek, *Early Christian Epitaphs from Athens* (Woodstock 1947). New discoveries are reported in the *Supplementum epigraphicum graecum* (Leiden 1923 seqq.).

AIDS to the study of Christian epigraphy: the following articles give a general account of the subject: L. Jalabert and R. Mouterde, "Inscriptions grecques chrétiennes" in *DACL* VII, 623–94; H. Leclerq, "Inscriptions latines chrétiennes", ibid. 694–850. On the growth of the great collections of inscriptions, see 850–1089. Manuals and textbooks: R. Cagnat, *Cours d'épigraphie latine* (Paris, 4th ed. 1914); W. Larfeld, *Griechische Epigraphik* (Munich, 3rd ed. 1914); C. M. Kaufmann, *Handbuch der altchristlichen Epigraphik* (Freiburg i. Br. 1917); P. Testini, "Epigrafia" in *Archeologia cristiana* (Rome 1959), 327–543. Two volumes of the *Tabulae in usum scholarum* ed. by H. Lietzmann, give specimens: No. 4, *Inscriptiones latinae*, compiled by E. Diehl (Bonn 1912), and No. 7, *Inscriptiones graecae*, compiled by O. Kern (Bonn 1913). For the bibliography of the subject, see: *Rivista di archeologia cristiana* (Rome 1924 seqq.); *Fasti archeologici* (Florence 1948 seqq.).

NUMISMATICS

In recent times the ancillary science of numismatics has made a considerable contribution to our understanding of the history of the Church under the Christian emperors. The older bibliography is to be found in H. Leclercq, "Monnaie" in *DACL* XI, 2260–350. Further bibliographies in J. Babelon, "Monnaie" in *DBS* V (1957), 1346–75, and P. Grierson, *Coins and Medals, A Select Bibliography* (London 1954). The coins of imperial times have been collected and described by H. Mattingly and E. A. Sydenham, *The Roman Imperial Coinage* (London 1923 seqq.), of which vol. IX contains the coins of Valentinian I to those of Theodosius I; that containing those of Constantine is in preparation. Until it appears, consult J. Maurice, *Numismatique constantinienne*, 3 vols. (Paris 1906–13). Other important works: A. Alföldi, *Die Kontorniaten* (Budapest 1943); M. Bernhard, *Handbuch zur Münzkunde der römischen Kaiserzeit*, 2 vols. (Halle 1926). For a critical evaluation see V. Schultze, "Christliche Münzprägung unter Constantin" in *ZKG* 44 (1925), 321–7; K. Kraft, "Silbermedaillon Constantins des Großen mit dem Christusmonogramm auf dem Helm" in *Jahrbuch für Numismatik* 5–6 (1954–5), 151–78; G. Bruck, "Die Verwendung christlicher Symbole auf Münzen von Constantin I bis Magnentius" in *Numismatische Zeitschrift* 6 (1955), 26–32.

EARLY CHRISTIAN BURIAL

Early Christian methods of burial are also an important subject of archaeological study, centred largely on Rome. See: J. B. de Rossi, *La Roma sotterranea cristiana*, 3 vols. (Rome 1864–77); P. Styger, *Altchristliche Grabeskunst* (Augsburg 1927); idem, *Die römischen Katakomben* (Berlin 1933); idem, *Römische Märtyrergrüfte* (Berlin 1935); L. Hertling and E. Kirschbaum, *Die römischen Katakomben und ihre Märtyrer* (Vienna, 2nd ed. 1955); J. Wilpert, *Die Malereien der Katakomben Roms*, 2 vols. (Freiburg i. Br. 1903); F. Wirth, *Römische Wandmalerei* (Berlin 1934); S. Bettini, *Frühchristliche Malerei* (Vienna 1942); J. Wilpert, *I sarcofagi cristiani antichi*, 3 vols. (Rome 1929–36); F. Gerke, *Die christlichen Sarkophage der vorkonstantinischen Zeit* (Berlin 1940); G. Bovini, *I sarcofagi paleocristiani* (Rome 1949); C. Cecchelli, *Monumenti cristiano-eretici di Roma* (Rome 1944).

CHRISTIAN ARCHAEOLOGY AND ART

Manuals and periodicals concerning Christian archaeology and accounts of early Christian art: C. M. Kaufmann, *Handbuch der christlichen Archäologie* (Paderborn, 3rd ed. 1922); R. Krautheimer, *Corpus basilicarum christianarum Romae* (Rome 1937 seqq.); C. Cecchelli, *Iconografia dei papi* (Rome 1938 seqq.); B. Ladner, *Papstbildnisse des Altertums und des Mittelalters*, I (Rome 1941); P. Testini, *Archaeologia cristiana* (Rome 1959); O. Wulff, *Altchristliche und byzantinische Kunst* (Berlin, 2nd ed. 1919, supplement Berlin 1939); O. M. Dalton, *Eastern Christian Art* (Oxford 1925); C. R. Morey, *Early Christian Art* (Princeton, 2nd ed. 1953); D. T. Rice, *The Beginnings of Christian Art* (London 1957); W. F. Volbach and M. Hirmer, Eng. tr. *Early Christian Art* (London 1961); F. van der Meer and C. Mohrmann, Eng. tr. *Atlas of the Early Christian World* (London 1958); *Bollettino di archeologia cristiana* (Rome 1863–94) and *Nuovo Bollettino di archeologia cristiana* (Rome 1895–1923); *Rivista di archeologia cristiana* (Rome 1924 seqq.) with bibliography; *Römische Quartalschrift für christliche Altertumskunde und für Kirchengeschichte* (Freiburg i. Br. 1887 seqq.); *Cahiers archéologiques* (Paris 1945 seqq.); *Jahrbuch für Antike und Christentum* (Münster 1958 seqq.); *Atti del III° congresso internazionale di archeologia cristiana* (Rome 1934); *Atti del IV° congresso*, 2 vols. (Rome 1940–8); *Actes du V° congrès* (Paris 1957); F. X. Kraus, *Realencyclopädie der christlichen Altertümer*, 2 vols. (Freiburg i. Br. 1882–6); *Dictionnaire d'archéologie chrétienne et de liturgie*, 15 vols. (Paris 1907–53).

III. HISTORIES OF THE EARLY CHURCH

General

P. Batiffol, *Le catholicisme des origines à s. Léon,* 4 vols. (Paris, 3rd to 5th ed. 1911–30), many times reprinted; B. J. Kidd, *A History of the Church to* A.D. *461* (Oxford 1922); L. Duchesne, *Histoire ancienne de l'église,* 3 vols. (Paris, 3rd to 5th ed. 1923–9), Eng. tr. *Early History of the Christian Church* (New York 1924) from the 1st French edition; idem, *L'église au VIᵉ siècle* (Paris 1925); G. Krüger, *Handbuch der Kirchengeschichte,* I (Tübingen, 2nd ed. 1923); J. Zeiller, *L'empire romain et l'église* (Paris 1928); J. P. Kirsch, *Kirchengeschichte,* I (Freiburg i. Br. 1930); C. Poulet, Eng. tr. *History of the Primitive Church,* 4 vols. (New York 1942–8); A. Ehrhard, *Die Kirche der Märtyrer* (Munich 1932); idem, *Die katholische Kirche im Wandel der Zeiten und Völker,* 2 vols. (Bonn 1935–7); A. Fliche and V. Martin, *Histoire de l'église,* I–V (Paris 1935–8), Eng. tr. *A History of the Catholic Church,* 2 vols. (London – St Louis, 2nd ed. 1956); F. Heiler, *Die katholische Kirche des Ostens und Westens,* I (Munich 1937); H. Lother, *Geschichte des Christentums,* I (Leipzig 1939); J. von Walter, *Die Geschichte des Christentums,* I (Gütersloh, 2nd ed. 1939); K. Müller, *Kirchengeschichte,* I/1 (Tübingen, 3rd ed. 1941); P. Hughes, *A History of the Church,* I (London, 2nd ed. 1948); E. Buonaiuti, *Geschichte des Christentums,* I (Berne 1948); C. Schneider, *Geistesgeschichte des antiken Christentums,* 2 vols. (Munich 1954); P. Carrington, *The Early Church* (1st and 2nd centuries), 2 vols. (Cambridge 1957); H. Lietzmann, *Geschichte der Alten Kirche,* 4 vols. (Berlin, 3rd – 4th edd. 1961), Eng. tr. *A History of the Early Church,* 4 vols. (London 1937–51); K. Bihlmeyer and H. Tüchle, *Kirchengeschichte,* I (Paderborn, 13th ed. 1962), Eng. tr. *Church History,* I (Westminster, Md. 1958); K. D. Schmidt and E. Wolf (ed.). *Die Kirche in ihrer Geschichte* Göttingen 1962 seqq., in parts); *The Christian Centuries,* edd. L. J. Rogier *et alii,* vol. I, J. Daniélou and H. Marrou, *The First Six Hundred Years* (London – New York 1964).

Histories of Dogma

A. von Harnack, *Lehrbuch der Dogmengeschichte,* 3 vols. (Tübingen, 5th ed. 1931, new imp. in preparation), Eng. tr. *History of Dogma,* 7 vols. (New York 1962); idem, *Dogmengeschichte (Grundriß)* (Tübingen, 7th ed. 1931), Eng. tr. *Outline of the History of Dogma* (London 1962); R. Seeberg, *Lehrbuch der Dogmengeschichte,* I–II (Leipzig, 2nd ed. 1922, new imp. Darmstadt 1960), Eng. tr. *Textbook of the History of Doctrines* (Grand Rapids 1956); idem, *Grundriß der Dogmengeschichte* (Leipzig, 7th ed. 1936); J. Tixeront, *Histoire des dogmes dans l'antiquité chrétienne,* 3 vols. (I, 11th ed. Paris 1930, II, 9th ed. 1931; III, 8th ed. 1928), Eng. tr. *History of Dogmas,* from the 5th French ed. (St Louis – London 1928–32); F. Loofs, *Leitfaden zum Studium der Dogmengeschichte* (Tübingen, 6th ed. 1959); K. Prümm, *Der christliche Glaube und die altheidnische Welt,* 2 vols. (Leipzig 1935); idem, *Christentum als Neuheitserlebnis* (Freiburg i. Br. 1939). W. Koehler, *Dogmengeschichte als Geschichte des christlichen Selbstbewußtseins* (Leipzig, 2nd ed. 1951); H. von Campenhausen, *Kirchliches Amt und geistliche Vollmacht in den ersten drei Jahrhunderten* (Tübingen 1953); M. Werner, *Die Entstehung des christlichen Dogmas* (Tübingen, 2nd ed. 1954), Eng. tr. *The Formation of Christian Dogma* (New York 1957); A. E. W. Turner, *The Pattern of Christian Truth* (London 1954); M. Schmaus, J. R. Geiselmann and A. Grillmeier, *Handbuch der Dogmengeschichte* (Freiburg i. Br. 1951 seqq.), Eng. tr. *The Herder History of Dogma:* B. Poschmann, *Penance and the Anointing of the Sick* (Freiburg – London – New York – Montreal 1964) and B. Neunheuser, *Baptism and Confirmation* (Freiburg – London – New York – Montreal 1964); J. N. D. Kelly,

Early Christian Doctrines (London 1958); J. Daniélou, *Histoire des doctrines chrétiennes avant Nicée,* 2 vols. (Tournai 1958–61); A. Grillmeier, "Hellenisierung–Judaisierung des Christentums als Deutungsprinzipien der Geschichte des kirchlichen Dogmas" in *Scholastik* 33 (1958), 321–55 528–58.

SPECIAL SUBJECTS

J. Stelzenberger, *Die Beziehungen der frühchristlichen Sittenlehre zur Ethik der Stoa* (Munich 1933); M. Viller and K. Rahner, *Aszese und Mystik der Väterzeit* (Freiburg i. Br. 1939); P. Pourrat, *La spiritualité chrétienne,* I (Paris, 3rd ed. 1943), Eng. tr. *Christian Spirituality* (Westminster 1954); L. Bouyer, *La spiritualité du Nouveau Testament et des Pères* (Paris 1960), Eng. tr. *The Spirituality of the New Testament and the Fathers* (New York 1963); A. von Harnack, *Die Mission und Ausbreitung des Christentums in den ersten drei Jahrhunderten* (Leipzig, 4th ed. 1924; a new imp. is projected), Eng. tr. *The Mission and Expansion of Christianity in the First Three Centuries* (New York 1937); K. S. Latourette, *A History of the Expansion of Christianity,* I: *The First Five Centuries* (New York 1937); G. Schnürer, *Kirche und Kultur im Mittelalter,* I (Paderborn, 3rd ed. 1936), Eng. tr. *Church and Culture in the Middle Ages* (Patterson 1956); J. H. Waszink *et alii, Het oudste christendom en de antieke cultuur* (down to Irenaeus), 2 vols. (Haarlem 1951); C. N. Cochrane, *Christianity and Classical Culture* (New York, second edition 1944, new impression 1957); W. Durant, *Caesar and Christ. A History of Roman Civilization and of Christianity from the Beginnings to* A.D. *325* (New York 1944); W. Jaeger, *Early Christianity and Greek Paideia* (Cambridge, Mass. 1961); H. Eibl, *Augustin und die Patristik, Geschichte der Philosophie in Einzeldarstellungen,* III, 10/11 (Munich 1923); B. Geyer, *Die patristische und scholastische Philosophie* in F. Ueberweg, *Grundriß der Geschichte der Philosophie,* II (Berlin, 11th ed. 1928, new imp. in preparation); K. Prümm, *Religionsgeschichtliches Handbuch für den Raum der altchristlichen Welt* (Freiburg i. Br. 1943, new imp. Rome 1954); E. Kornemann, *Weltgeschichte des Mittelmeerraumes,* II: *Von Augustus bis zum Sieg der Araber* (Munich 1949); F. Lot, *La fin du monde antique* (Paris 1951), Eng. tr. *The End of the Ancient World* (New York, 2nd ed. 1961); E. Stein, *Histoire du Bas-Empire,* I (A.D. 284–476) (Paris, 2nd ed. 1959), II, (A.D. 475–565) (Paris 1949); L. Bréhier, *Le monde byzantin,* 3 vols. (Paris 1947–50); G. Ostrogorsky, *Geschichte des byzantinischen Staates* (Munich, 3rd ed. 1963), Eng tr. *History of the Byzantine State* (New Brunswick, 2nd ed. 1957).

IV. WORKS OF REFERENCE, PERIODICALS, AND BIBLIOGRAPHIES

WORKS OF REFERENCE

Besides the special lexica already mentioned, the following are important: *The Catholic Encyclopedia,* 15 vols. (New York 1907–12; supplementary volume, 1922), new encyclopedia in preparation; *Catholicisme, Hier–Aujourd'hui–Demain,* ed. by G. Jacquement (Paris 1928 seqq.); *Dictionnaire de la Bible, Supplément,* ed. by L. Pirot and A. Robert (Paris 1928 seqq.); *Dictionnaire de droit canonique,* ed. by R. Naz (Paris 1935 seqq.); *Dictionnaire d'histoire et de géographie ecclésiastique,* ed. by A. Baudrillart, A. de Meyer, E. van Cauwenbergh and R. Aubert (Paris 1912 seqq.); *Dictionnaire de spiritualité ascétique et mystique,* ed. by M. Villier, M. Olphe Gailliard, A. Rayez, and C. Baumgartner (Paris 1932 seqq.); *Dictionnaire de théologie catholique,* ed. by A. Vacant, E. Mangenot, and E. Amann (Paris 1930 seqq.); *Enciclopedia cattolica,* 12 vols. (Vatican City 1949–54); *Evangelisches Kirchenlexikon,* ed. by H. Brunotte and O. Weber (Göttingen 1955 seqq.); *Lexikon für Theologie und Kirche*, ed. by J. Höfer and K. Rahner, (Freiburg, 2nd ed. 1957 seqq.); *Reallexikon für Antike und Christentum*, ed. by T. Klauser (Stuttgart 1950 seqq.); *Die Religion in Geschichte und Gegenwart*, ed. by K. Galling (Tübingen, 3rd. ed. 1957 seqq.); P. Gams, *Series episcoporum ecclesiae catholicae* (Regensburg 1873; supplements 1879–86; new imp. Graz 1957); E. Bayer, *Wörterbuch zur Geschichte* (Stuttgart 1960); *The Oxford Dictionary of the Christian Church*, F. L. Cross ed. (London 1957); K. Pieper, *Atlas orbis antiqui* (Düsseldorf 1931); K. Heussi and H. Mulert, *Atlas zur Kirchengeschichte* (Tübingen, 3rd ed. 1937); B. Llorca, *Atlas y cuadros sincrónicos de historia eclesiástica* (Barcelona 1950); R. S. Dell, *An Atlas of Christian History* (London 1960); J. G. T. Graesse, *Orbis latinus. Verzeichnis der wichtigsten Orts- und Ländernamen* (Berlin, 3rd ed. 1922).

PERIODICALS

Periodicals, most of which contain extensive book reviews, specially devoted to the study of early Christianity: *Antike und Christentum*, by F. J. Dölger, I–VI (Münster 1929–50); *Biblica* (Rome 1920 seqq.) with bibliography of primitive Christianity; *Jahrbuch für Antike und Christentum* (Münster 1958 seqq.); *Jahrbuch für Liturgiewissenschaft*, I–XV (Münster 1921–41); *Archiv für Liturgiewissenschaft* (Regensburg 1950 seqq.); *Liturgisches Jahrbuch* (Münster 1951 seqq.); *Revue des Études Augustiniennes* (Paris 1955 seqq.); *Vigiliae Christianae* (Amsterdam 1947 seqq.); *Zeitschrift für neutestamentliche Wissenschaft und die Kunde der älteren Kirche* (Giessen – Berlin 1900 seqq.).

Among the theological periodicals which give considerable space to matters concerning the early Church, the following are worthy of special mention: *Analecta Sacra Tarragonensia* (Barcelona 1925 seqq.); *Bulletin of the John Rylands Library* (Manchester 1903 seqq.); *Bulletin de littérature ecclésiastique* (Toulouse 1899 seqq.); *Byzantion* (Brussels 1924 seqq.); *Biblische Zeitschrift* (Freiburg 1903–29, Paderborn 1931–39, 1957 seqq.); *Church History* (New York – Chicago 1932 seqq.); *The Catholic Historical Review* (Washington 1915 seqq.); *Dumbarton Oaks Papers* (Cambridge, Mass. 1941 seqq.); *Estudios eclesiásticos* (Madrid 1922–36, 1942 seqq.); *Échos d'Orient* (Paris 1892–1942); *Ephemerides Theologicae Lovanienses* (Bruges 1924 seqq.); *Evangelische Theologie* (Munich 1934 seqq.); *Gregorianum* (Rome 1920 seqq.); *Geist und Leben* (Würzburg 1947 seqq.); *Historisches Jahrbuch* (Cologne 1880 seqq., Munich 1950 seqq.); *The Harvard Theological Review* (Cambridge, Mass. 1908 seqq.); *Irénikon* (Amay – Chevetogne, Belgium 1926 seqq.); *Journal of Ecclesiastical History* (London 1950 seqq.); *Jahrbuch für Liturgik und Hymnologie* (Cassel 1955 seqq.); *Journal of Theological Studies* (London 1899 seqq.); *Mélanges de science religieuse* (Lille 1944 seqq.); *Münchener Theologische Zeitschrift* (Munich 1950 seqq.); *Nouvelle Revue Théologique* (Tournai 1879 seqq.); *Oriens Christianus* (Wiesbaden 1901 seqq.); *Orientalia Christiana Periodica* (Rome 1935 seqq.); *L'Orient syrien* (Paris 1956 seqq.); *Ostkirchliche Studien* (Würzburg 1951 seqq.); *Le Proche-Orient Chrétien* (Jerusalem 1951 seqq.); *Revue d'ascétique et de mystique* (Toulouse 1920 seqq.); *Revue Bénédictine* (Maredsous 1884 seqq.); *Revue des Études byzantines* (Paris 1946 seqq.); *Revue des Études Grecques* (Paris 1888 seqq.); Revue des *Études latines* (Paris 1923 seqq.); *Revue des Sciences Religieuses* (Strasbourg 1921 seqq.); *Revue d'histoire et de philosophie religieuses* (Strasbourg 1921 seqq.); *Revue de l'histoire des religions* (Paris 1880 seqq.); *Revue de l'Orient chrétien* (Paris 1896 seqq.); *Revue de Qumran* (Paris 1958 seqq.); *Revue des sciences philosophiques et théologiques* (Paris 1907 seqq.); *Recherche de science religieuse* (Paris 1910 seqq.); *Rivista di storia della chiesa in Italia* (Rome 1947 seqq.); *Studia Anselmiana* (Rome 1933 seqq.); *Sacris erudiri* (Bruges 1948 seqq.); *Studia Catholica* (Roermond 1924 seqq.); *Theologische Literaturzeitung* (Leipzig – Berlin 1878 seqq.); *Theologische Quartalschrift* (Tübingen 1819 seqq., Stuttgart 1946 seqq.); *Theological Studies*

(Baltimore 1940 seqq.); *Theologische Zeitschrift* (Basle 1945 seqq.); *Traditio* (New York 1943 seqq.); *Trierer Theologische Zeitschrift* (Trier 1888 seqq.); *Zeitschrift für Askese und Mystik* (Innsbruck – Munich 1926 seqq.); *Zeitschrift für Kirchengeschichte* (Stuttgart 1876 seqq.); *Zeitschrift für Katholische Theologie* (Innsbruck – Vienna 1877 seqq.); *Zeitschrift für Theologie und Kirche* (Tübingen 1891 seqq.).

BIBLIOGRAPHIES

The most comprehensive periodical bibliography for the whole field of ecclesiastical history is contained in *Revue d'histoire ecclésiastique* (Louvain 1900 seqq.) Another important publication is *Bulletin de théologie ancienne et médiévale,* which is published in association with *Recherches de théologie ancienne et médiévale* (Louvain 1929 seqq.). The following also contain critical reviews of works on the early history of the Church: *Theologische Rundschau* (Tübingen 1897 seqq.) and *Theologische Revue* (Münster 1902 seqq.), section 5, in the bibliographical appendix.

BIBLIOGRAPHY TO INDIVIDUAL CHAPTERS

Part One: The Beginnings

SECTION ONE

Jewish Christianity

1. Judaism in the Time of Jesus

GENERAL

C. K. Barret, *The New Testament Background: Selected Documents* (London – New York 1957), H. Strack and P. Billerbeck, *Kommentar zum Neuen Testament aus Talmud und Midrasch*, 5 vols. (Munich 1922–56); R. A. Pfeiffer, *History of New Testament Times* (New York 1948); R. Grant, *A Historical Introduction to the New Testament* (London – New York 1963); R. Bultmann, *Primitive Christianity in its Contemporary Setting* (London – New York 1957); W. O. E. Oesterley, *The Jews and Judaism during the Greek Period* (London 1941); J. Parkes, *The Foundations of Judaism and Christianity* (London 1960); H. J. Schoeps, *Theologie und Geschichte des Judenchristentums* (Tübingen 1949); idem, *Aus frühchristlicher Zeit* (Tübingen 1950); idem, *Urgemeinde, Judenchristentum, Gnosis* (Tübingen 1956); J. Daniélou, *The Theology of Jewish Christianity* (London 1964); K. Schubert, *Die Religion des Nachbiblischen Judentums* (Freiburg – Vienna 1955); W. Bousset, *Die Religion des Judentums im späthellenischen Zeitalter* (Tübingen, 3rd ed. 1926); N. Levison, *The Jewish Background of Christianity* (Edinburgh 1932); P. Riessler, *Altjüdisches Schrifttum außerhalb der Bibel* (Augsburg 1928); J. Jeremias, *Jerusalem zur Zeit Jesu* (Göttingen, 2nd ed. 1962); F. Nötscher, *Vom Alten zum Neuen Testament* (Bonn 1962); B. Gerhardsson, *Memory and Manuscript: Oral Tradition in Rabbinic Judaism and Early Christianity* (Uppsala 1961).

PALESTINIAN JUDAISM

E. Schürer, *A History of the Jewish People in the Time of Jesus Christ*, 3 vols. (Edinburgh 1886–90, abridged ed. New York 1961); W. O. E. Oesterley and T. A. Robinson, *A History of Israel*, 2 vols. (Oxford 1932); F.-M. Abel, *Histoire de la Palestine*, 2 vols. (Paris 1952); M. Noth, *The History of Israel* (London, 2nd rev. ed. 1960).
G. F. Moore, *Judaism in the First Centuries of the Christian Era*, 3 vols. (2nd ed. Cambridge, Mass. 1946–8); J. Bonsirven, *Palestinian Judaism in the Time of Christ* (New York 1963); P. Demann, *Judaïsme* (New York 1961); L. Finkelstein, *The Jews, their History, Culture and Religion*, 2 vols. (New York, 3rd ed. 1960); M. Hengel, *Die Zeloten, Untersuchungen zur jüdischen Freiheitsbewegung in der Zeit von Herodes I bis 70 v. Chr.* (Leiden – Cologne 1961); R. Travers Herford, *The Pharisees* (Boston, 2nd ed. 1962); M. Simon, *Die jüdischen Sekten zur Zeit Jesu* (Cologne, 2nd ed. 1962).

QUMRAN

Bibliography in the *Revue de Qumran* (Paris 1958 seqq.), earlier see C. Burchard, *Bibliographie zu den Handschriften vom Toten Meer* (Berlin 1957, vol. II, 1964); W. S. Lasor,

Bibliography of the Dead Sea Scrolls 1948–1957 (Pasadena 1958); H. Bardtke, *Die Hand-schriften vom Toten Meer*, 2 vols. (Berlin 1952–8); idem, *Qumran-Probleme* (Berlin 1963); M. Burrows, *The Dead Sea Scrolls* (New York 1955); idem, *More Light on the Dead Sea Scrolls* (New York 1958); J. T. Milik, *Ten Years of Discovery in the Wilderness of Judaea* (London 1959); F. M. Cross, *The Ancient Library of Qumran* (New York 1958); J. P. M. van der Ploeg, *The Excavations at Qumran* (London 1958); F. Bruce, *Biblical Exegesis in the Qumran Texts* (Grand Rapids 1959); K. H. Rengstorf, *Hirbet Qumran und die Biblio-thek vom Toten Meer* (Stuttgart 1960); J. Schreiden, *Les énigmes des manuscripts de la mer morte* (Wetteren 1961); A. Dupont-Sommer, *The Essene Writings from Qumran* (Oxford 1961); J. Maier, *Die Texte vom Toten Meer*, 2 vols. (Munich 1961); G. Vermes, *The Dead Sea Scrolls in English* (London 1962); J. Carmignac, *Christ and the Teacher of Righteousness* (Baltimore 1962); H. Ringgren, *The Faith of Qumran* (Philadelphia 1963); F. Bruce, *Second Thoughts on the Dead Sea Scrolls* (London, 2nd ed. 1961); L. Mowry, *The Dead Sea Scrolls and the Early Church* (Chicago 1962); A. N. Gilkes, *The Impact of the Dead Sea Scrolls* (London 1963); M. Baillet – J. T. Milik – R. de Vaux, *Les petites grottes de Qumran (2Q, 3Q, 5Q–10Q). Le rouleau de cuivre* (Oxford 1962); E. Lohse, *Die Texte aus Qumran hebräisch und deutsch* (Munich 1964); A. Braun, "Research reports on Qumran and N. T." in *ThR* 28 (1962); 29 (1963); 30 (1964); F. Nötscher, *Zur theo-logischen Terminologie der Qumran-Texte* (Bonn 1956); D. Howlett, *The Essenes and Christianity* (New York 1957); H. Braun, *Spätjüdischer und frühchristlicher Radikalis-mus*, I, *Das Spätjudentum* (Tübingen 1957); K. Schubert, *Die Gemeinde von Qumran* (Munich 1958); H. E. Del Medico, *Le mythe des esséniens* (Paris 1958); H. Kosmala, *Hebräer, Essener, Christen* (Leiden 1959); O. Betz, *Offenbarung und Schriftforschung in den Qumrantexten* (Tübingen 1960); E. F. Sutcliffe, *The Monks of Qumran* (London 1960); K. H. Schelkle, *Die Gemeinde von Qumran und die Kirche des Neuen Testamentes* (Düssel-dorf 1960); A. Adam, *Antike Berichte über die Essener* (Berlin 1961); H. H. Rowley, "The Qumran Sect and Christian Origins" in *BJRL* 44 (1961), 119–56; M. Black, *The Scrolls and Christian Origins* (New York 1961).

THE JEWISH DIASPORA

J. Juster, *Les juifs dans l'empire romain*, 2 vols. (Paris 1914); W. Bousset, *Jüdisch-christ-licher Schulbetrieb in Alexandrien und Rom* (Göttingen 1915); H. J. Bell, *Jews and Christians in Egypt* (Oxford 1924); H. Leon, *The Jews of Ancient Rome* (Philadelphia 1960); J. Leipoldt, *Antisemitismus in der alten Welt* (Leipzig 1933); V. Tscherikover, *Hellenistic Civilization and the Jews* (Philadelphia 1959); W. Maurer, *Kirche und Syn-agoge* (Stuttgart 1953); L. Toombs, *The Threshold of Christianity* (Philadelphia 1960).

PHILO

Critical collected ed. by L. Cohn, P. Wendland, S. Reiter, and J. Leisegang, 8 vols. (Berlin 1896–1930); text with English trans. by F.-H. Colson, G. Whitaker (London 1928–52); text with French trans. by R. Arnaldez, C. Mondésert *et alii* (Paris 1961); general account by H. Leisegang in *Pauly – Wissowa* 19, 1–50; E. Bréhier, *Les idées philosophiques et religieuses de Philon* (Paris, 2nd ed. 1925); E. Stein, *Die allegorische Exegese des Philo aus Alex.* (Gießen 1929); J. Pascher, *Der Königsweg der Wiedergeburt und Vergottung bei Philo von Alex.* (Paderborn 1931); I. Heinemann, *Philons griechische und jüdische Bildung* (Breslau 1932); W. Völker, *Fortschritt und Vollendung bei Philo von Alex.* (Leip-zig 1938); E. R. Goodenough, *The Politics of Philo Judaeus* (New Haven 1938); P. Katz, *Philo's Bible* (Cambridge 1950); H. A. Wolfson, *Philo*, 2 vols. (Cambridge, Mass., 2nd ed. 1948); S. Sandmel, *Philo's Place in Judaism* (Cincinnati – New York 1956); H. Thyen, "Die Probleme der neueren Philoforschung" in *ThR* 23 (1955), 230–46; J. Daniélou,

Philon d'Alexandrie (Paris 1958); S. Jellicose, "Philo and the Septuagint Vorlage" in *JThS* XII (1961), 261–71; R. Marcus, "Philo, Josephus and the Dead See Yahod (meaning community)" in *JBL* 71 (1952), 207–9; S. Lauer, "Philo's Concept of Time" in *Journal of Jewish Studies* 9 (1959), 39–46; H. Wolfson, "Philonic God and his latter-day deniers" in *HThR* 53 (1960), 101–24; J. de Savignac, "Le messianisme de Philon d'Alexandrie" in *NovT* 4 (1960), 318–24.

2. Jesus of Nazareth and the Church

General Accounts by A. Conzelmann in *RGG*, 3rd ed. III, 619–53; and A. Vögtle in *LThK* V, 922–32; A. Schweitzer, *The Quest for the Historical Jesus* (Oxford 1954).

L. de Grandmaison, *Jesus Christ*, 3 vols. (New York 1930–4); J. Lebreton, *The Life and Teaching of Jesus Christ* (New York, new imp. 1957); A. Goodier, *The Public Life of Our Lord Jesus Christ* (New York, new imp. 1950); G. Ricciotti, *Life of Jesus* (Milwaukee 1950); R. Guardini, *The Lord* (London 1956); J. Klausner, *Jesus of Nazareth* (1925); M. Dibelius, *Jesus* (Oxford–Philadelphia 1949); R. Bultmann, *Jesus* (New York 1958); G. Bornkamm, *Jesus of Nazareth* (London 1960, New York 1963); M. Goguel, *Jesus and the Origins of Christianity* (New York 1963); E. Stauffer, *Jesus and his Story* (London 1960).

J. Aufhauser, *Antike Jesus-Zeugnisse* (Berlin, 2nd ed. 1925); J. Moreau, *Les plus anciens témoignages profanes sur Jésus* (Brussels 1944); W. Bousset, *Kyrios Christos* (Göttingen, 4th ed. 1935); R. Bultmann, *History of the Synoptic Tradition* (New York–Oxford 1963); J. M. Robinson, *A New Quest for the Historical Jesus* (1959); H. Zabrut, *The Historical Jesus* (London 1963); F.-M. Braun, *Jésus, histoire et critique* (Paris 1947); B. Rigaux, "Historicité de Jésus devant l'exégèse récente" in *RB* 65 (1958), 482–522; R. Schubert (ed.), *Der historische Jesus und der kerygmatische Christus* (Freiburg i. Br. 1960); J. Blinzler, *The Trial of Jesus* (Westminster, Md., 1959).

R. Schnackenburg, *New Testament Theology Today* (London–New York 1963); R. Bultmann, *The Theology of the New Testament*, 2 vols. (London 1952–6); E. Stauffer, *New Testament Theology* (London 1957); R. Schnackenburg, *God's Rule and Kingdom* (Freiburg–London–New York–Montreal 1963); J. Bonsirven, *Theology of the New Testament* (Westminster, Md. 1964).

3. The Primitive Church at Jerusalem

F. F. Bruce, *The Acts of the Apostles, Greek Text and Commentary* (London 1951); F. J. Foakes-Jackson, *Acts of the Apostles*, 5 vols. (London 1920–33); E. Haenchen, *Die Apostelgeschichte* (Göttingen 1959); A. Wikenhauser, *Die Apostelgeschichte* (Regensburg, 3rd ed. 1956); M. Dibelius, *Studies in the Acts of the Apostles* (New York 1956); J. Dupont, *The Sources of Acts* (New York–London 1962); A. Ehrhardt, "The Construction and Purpose of the Acts of the Apostles" in *StTh* 12 (1958), 45–79.

E. Meyer, *Ursprung und Anfänge des Christentums* (Berlin 1923); A. Loisy, *The Birth of Christian Religion and the Origins of the New Testament* (New York 1962); M. Goguel, *The Primitive Church* (New York–London 1964); O. Cullmann, *The Early Church* (London 1956); P. Carrington, *The Early Christian Church*, 2 vols. (Cambridge 1957); E. Ehrhardt, "Christianity before the Apostles' Creed" in *HThR* 55 (1962) 73–119; O. Cullmann, *Early Christian Worship* (London 1953); W. D. Davies, *Christian Origins and Judaism* (Philadelphia 1962).

The Way into the Pagan World

4. The Religious Situation in the Graeco-Roman World at the Time of its Encounter with Christianity

Sources

A. Fairbanks, *A Handbook of Greek Religion* (New York 1910); M. Nilsson, *Greek Folk Religion* (New York 1961); K. Latte, *Die Religion der Römer und der Synkretismus der Kaiserzeit* (Tübingen 1927); H. Kleinknecht, *Pantheion* (Tübingen 1929); N. Turchi, *Fontes mysteriorum aevi hellenistici* (Rome, 4th ed. 1930); A. D. Nock and A.-J. Festugière, *Corpus Hermeticum*, 4 vols. (Paris 1945–54); F. C. Grant, *Hellenistic Religions*, 2 vols. (New York 1953–4); idem, *Ancient Roman Religion* (New York 1957); H. Haas and J. Leipoldt, *Die Religionen in der Umwelt des Christentums: Bilderatlas zur Religionsgeschichte* (Leipzig 1926–30).

Literature: 1. History of Classical Civilization

See the histories of New Testament times already mentioned in addition to the following: P. Wendland, *Die hellenistisch-römische Kultur in ihren Beziehungen zum Judentum und Christentum* (Tübingen, 3rd ed. 1912); L. Friedlaender, *Roman Life and Manners under the Early Empire*, 4 vols. (London 1928–36); W. R. Halliday, *The Pagan Background of Early Christianity* (Liverpool 1926); R. Heinze, *Die augusteische Kultur* (Leipzig 1930, new imp. Darmstadt 1960); W. Kroll, *Die Kultur der ciceronianischen Zeit*, 2 vols. (Leipzig 1933); A.-J. Festugière and P. Fabre, *Le monde gréco-romain au temps de Notre-Seigneur*, 2 vols. (Paris 1935); J. Carcopino, *Daily Life in Ancient Rome* (New Haven 1945); W. W. Tarn, *Hellenistic Civilization* (London, 3rd ed. 1952); M. Rostovtzeff, *The Social and Economic History of the Hellenistic World*, 2 vols. (Oxford 1941); U. Kahrstedt, *Kulturgeschichte der römischen Kaiserzeit* (Berne, 2nd ed. 1958); U. Paoli, *Rome: its People, Life and Customs …* (London 1963); A. A. M. van der Heyden and H. E. Stier, *Bildatlas der klassischen Welt* (Gütersloh 1960).

2. Religion in Classical Times

A. D. Nock, *Conversion. The Old and New in Religion from Alexander the Great to Augustinus of Hippo* (Oxford 1933); K. Prümm, *Der christliche Glaube und die altheidnische Welt*, 2 vols. (Leipzig 1935); K. Kerényi, *Die Religion der Griechen und Römer* (Munich 1963); R. Bultmann, *Die Religionen im Umkreis des Christentums* (Zürich, 2nd ed. 1954).

(a) Greek religion.

E. Rohde, *Psyche: The Cult of Souls and Belief in Immortality among the Greeks* (New York 1925); O. Kern, *Die Religion der Griechen*, 3 vols. (Berlin, 1926–38); W. Nestle, *Griechische Religiosität*, III (Berlin 1934); M. Nilsson, *A History of Greek Religion* (Oxford 1949); W. Guthrie, *The Greeks and their Gods* (Boston–London 1950); K. Prümm, "Die Religion des Hellenismus" in *König H* II (Freiburg i. Br., 2nd ed. 1961), 169–244; J. Harrison, *Prolegomena to the Study of Greek Religion* (New York 1957); J. Festugière, *Personal Religion Among the Greeks* (Berkeley 1960); U. von Wilamowitz-Moellendorff, *Der Glaube der Hellenen*, 2 vols. (Darmstadt, 3rd ed. 1960).

(b) Roman religion.

J. Geffcken, *Der Ausgang des griechisch-römischen Heidentums* (Heidelberg, 2nd ed. 1929); F. Altheim, *Römische Religionsgeschichte*, III: *Die Kaiserzeit* (Berlin 1933); F. Cumont, *The Oriental Religions in Roman Paganism* (New York 1956); idem, *Lux Perpetua* (Paris 1949); F. Grant (ed.), *Ancient Roman Religion* (New York 1957); H. Rose, *Ancient Roman Religion* (New York 1957); C. Koch, *Religio, Studien zu Kult und Glauben der Römer* (Nuremberg 1960); T. Glover, *Conflict of Religions in the Early Roman Empire* (Boston 1960); K. Latte, *Die Religion der Römer* (Munich 1960); M. Vermaseren, *Mithra, ce dieu mystérieux* (Paris 1960).

(c) The Emperor Cult.

G. Herzog-Hauser, *Pauly–Wissowa*, Suppl. IV 806–853. E. Lohmeyer, *Christuskult und Kaiserkult* (Tübingen 1919); S. Lösch, *Deitas Jesu und antike Apotheose* (Rottenburg 1933); E. Stauffer, *Rom und die Cäsaren* (Hamburg 1952); L. Cerfaux and J. Tondriau, *Un concurrent du Christianisme. Le culte des souverains romains* (Tournai 1957); E. Norden, *Die Geburt des Kindes* (Darmstadt, 3rd ed. 1958); R. Étienne, *Le culte impérial dans la péninsule ibérique d'Auguste à Dioclétien* (Paris 1959); F. Taeger, *Charisma*, 2 vols. (Stuttgart 1960); H. Schlier, *Die Zeit der Kirche* (Freiburg i. Br., 3rd ed. 1962), 14 ff.; M. Nelsson, "The High God and the Mediator" in *HThR* 55 (1963), 101–20; B. Parsi, *Désignation et investiture de l'empereur romain. Ier et IIe siècles après J.-C.* (Paris 1963).

(d) Mystery religions.

F. Cumont, *The Mysteries of Mithra* (New York 1957); R. Reizenstein, *Die hellenistischen Mysterienreligionen* (Leipzig, 3rd ed. 1927); H. Gressmann, *Die orientalischen Religionen im hellenistischen Zeitalter* (Berlin 1930); F. Saxl, *Mithra* (Berlin 1931); B. Heigl, *Antike Mysterienreligionen und das Christentum* (Münster 1932); S. Eitrem, *Orakel und Mysterien am Ausgang der Antike* (Zürich 1947); N. Turchi, *Le religioni misteriche del mondo antico* (Milan 1948); V. Magnien, *Les mystères d'Eleusis* (Paris 1950); H. Idris, *Cults and Creeds in Graeco-Roman Egypt* (Liverpool 1953); E. Wallis, *Osiris: The Egyptian Religion of Resurrection* (New York 1961); A. Schütze, *Mithras-Mysterien und das Urchristentum* (Stuttgart 1948); G. Mylonas, *Eleusis and the Eleunisian Mysteries* (Princeton 1961); B. Metygee, "Considerations of Methodology in the Study of the Mystery Religions and Early Christianity" in *HThR* 48 (1955), 1–20; *Corpus inscriptionum et monumentorum religionis Mithriacae*, I–II (Hagae Comitis 1956–60); M. Vermaseren, *Mithra, ce dieu mystérieux* (Paris 1960); A. Alvarez de Miranda, *Religiones mistéricas* (Madrid 1961); R. Merkelbach, *Isisfeste in griechisch-römischer Zeit* (Meisenheim 1963); H. Hepding, *Attis, seine Mythen und sein Kult* (Berlin, 2nd ed. 1964).

(e) Popular religion.

K. Preisendanz, *Papyri graecae magicae* (Leipzig 1928); F. R. Herzog, *Die Wunderheilungen von Epidaurus* (Leipzig 1931); F. Boll, *Sternglaube und Sterndeutung* (Leipzig, 4th ed. 1931); E. Massonneau, *La magie dans l'Antiquité romaine* (Paris 1934); E. Stemplinger, *Antiker Volksglaube* (Stuttgart 1948); R. Ehnmark, "Religion and Magic" in *Ethnos* 21 (1956), 1 ff.; W. Gundel, "Astrologie" in *RAC* I, 817–31. For a survey of literature on Roman Religion see H. Rose, "Roman Religion 1910–1960" in *JRS* 50 (1960), 161–72.

(f) Philosophy in late Classical times.

P. E. More, *Hellenistic Philosophies* (Princeton 1923); K. Praechter, *Das Altertum* in Ueberweg–Heinze, *Geschichte der Philosophie*, I (Berlin, 12th ed. 1926); L. Robin, *Greek Thought and the Origins of the Scientific Spirit* (New York 1928); E. Zeller, *Grundriß der Geschichte der Philosophie der Griechen* (Leipzig, 13th ed. 1928); K. Reinhardt, *Poseidonios* (Munich 1921); E. Bréhier, *Histoire de la philosophie*, II (Paris 1948);

A.-J. Festugière, *Epicurus and his Gods* (Oxford 1955); M. Pohlenz, *Die Stoa*, 2 vols. (Göttingen 1948–9); M. Spanneut, *Le stoïcisme des pères de l'église de Clément de Rome à Clement d'Alexandrie* (Paris 1957); R. Harder, *Plotin* (Frankfurt 1958).

5. *The Apostle Paul and the Structure of the Pauline Congregations*

SOURCES

The sources are the letters of Paul and the Acts of the Apostles. See also the apocryphal Acts of Paul, L. Vouaux, *Les actes de Paul et ses lettres apocryphes* (Paris 1913); R. A. Lipsius, *Acta apostolorum apocrypha*, I (Darmstadt, new imp. 1959); C. Schmidt, Πράξεις Παύλου.*Acta Pauli* (Hamburg 1936); R. Kasser, "Acta Pauli" in *RHPhR* 40 (1960), 45–7.

LITERATURE

Commentaries on the Acts of the Apostles, cf. above; commentaries on the letters of Paul cf. A. Wikenhauser, *New Testament Introduction* (Freiburg–London–New York 1958). For an extensive survey of Pauline literature see: B. Metzger ed., *Index to Periodical Literature on the Apostle Paul* (Grand Rapids 1960); A. Schweitzer, *Paul and his Interpreters: A Critical History* (Oxford 1948); E. Ellis, *Paul and his Recent Interpreters* (Grand Rapids 1961).

GENERAL ACCOUNTS of Paul's Life: A. Deissmann, *Paul. A Study in Social and Religious History* (New York, new imp. 1963); A. O. Nock, *St Paul* (London 1960); J. S. Stewart, *A Man in Christ* (New York 1944); E.-B. Allo, *Paul, apôtre de Jésus-Christ* (Paris, 2nd ed. 1956); W. von Loewenich, *Paul: His Life and Work* (Edinburgh 1960); M. Dibelius, *Paul*, edited and completed by W. G. Kümmel (London 1953); J. Klausner, *From Jesus to Paul* (Boston 1961); C. Tresmontant, *St Paul and the Mystery of Christ* (New York 1957); S. Sandmel, *The Genius of Paul* (New York 1958).

BIOGRAPHY OF PAUL: H. Böhlig, *Die Geisteskultur von Tarsos* (Göttingen 1913); A. Steinmann, *Der Werdegang des Paulus* (Freiburg i. Br. 1928); O. Kietzig, *Die Bekehrung des Paulus* (Leipzig 1932); E. Kirschbaum, "Das Grab des Völkerapostels" in *Die Gräber der Apostelfürsten* (Frankfurt a. M., 2nd ed. 1959), 166–97; U. Wilckens, "Die Bekehrung des Paulus als religionsgeschichtliches Problem" in *ZThK* 56 (1959), 273–93; J. Dauvillier, "A propos de la venue de S. Paul à Rome" in *BLE* 61 (1960), 3–26.

PAUL'S MISSIONARY ACTIVITY: W. M. Ramsay, *St Paul the Traveller and the Roman Citizen* (London, 7th ed. 1907); A. Oepke, *Die Missionspredigt des Apostels Paulus* (Leipzig 1920); J. Richter, *Die Briefe des Apostels Paulus als missionarische Sendschreiben* (Gütersloh 1929); K. Pieper, *Paulus, seine missionarische Persönlichkeit und Wirksamkeit* (Munster, 3rd ed. 1929); W. L. Knox, *St Paul and the Church of the Gentiles* (Cambridge 1939); M. Dibelius, *Paulus auf dem Areopag* (Heidelberg 1939); R. Liechtenhan, *Die urchristliche Mission* (Zürich 1946); H. Metzger, *Saint Paul's Journeys in the Greek Orient* (New York 1955); C. Maurer, "Paulus als der Apostel der Völker" in *EvTh* 19 (1959), 28–40; J. Cambier, "Paul, apôtre du Christ et prédicateur de l'évangile" in *NRTh* 81 (1959), 1009–28; M. Meinertz, "Zum Ursprung der Heidenmission" in *Biblica* 40 (1959), 762–77.; E. Lerle, *Proselytenwerbung und Urchristentum* (Berlin 1961); F. Maier, *Paulus als Kirchengründer und kirchlicher Organisator* (Würzburg 1961); V. N. Sevenster, *Paul and Seneca* (Leiden 1961).

THEOLOGY AND PIETY: B. Bartmann, *Paulus. Die Grundzüge seiner Lehre* (Paderborn 1914); W. Mundle, *Das religiöse Leben des Apostels Paulus* (Leipzig 1923); J. Schneider,

Die Passionsmystik des Apostels Paulus (Leipzig 1929); H. Windisch, *Paulus und Christus* (Leipzig 1934); W. Schmauch, *In Christus. Eine Untersuchung zur Sprache und Theologie des Paulus* (Gütersloh 1935); J. Leipoldt, *Jesus und Paulus—Jesus oder Paulus* (Leipzig 1936); G. Harder, *Paulus und das Gebet* (Gütersloh 1936); A. Röder, *Die Geschichtstheologie des Apostels Paulus* (Speyer 1938); J. Bonsirven, *Exégèse rabbinique et exégèse paulinienne* (Paris 1939); F. Amiot, *L'enseignement de S. Paul* (Paris, 2 vols. 1946); F. Prat, *The Theology of St Paul*, 2 vols. (Westminster, Md. 1952); J. Dupont, *Gnosis. La connaissance religieuse dans les épîtres de S. Paul* (Louvain 1949); R. Schnackenburg, *Baptism in the Thought of St Paul* (London – New York 1964); G. Bornkamm, *Das Ende des Gesetzes. Paulusstudien* (Munich 1952); A. Schweitzer, *The Mysticism of Paul the Apostle* (New York 1955); A. Wikenhauser, *Pauline Mysticism. Christ in the Mystical Teaching of St Paul* (Freiburg – London – New York 1960); E. Lohmeyer, *Probleme paulinischer Theologie* (Tübingen 1954); W. D. Davies, *Paul and Rabbinic Judaism* (London, 2nd ed. 1955); P. Demann, "Moïse et la Loi dans la pensée de S. Paul" in *Moïse, l'homme de l'alliance* (Paris 1955); K. H. Schelkle, *Paulus, Lehrer der Väter (Rom 1–11)* (Düsseldorf 1956); L. Cerfaux, *Christ in the Theology of St Paul* (Freiburg – London – New York 1959); J. Munck, *Paul and the Salvation of Mankind* (London 1959); O. Kuss, Enthusiasmus und Realismus bei Paulus" in *Festschrift Th. Kampmann* (Paderborn 1959) 23–27; D. Whiteley, *The Theology of St Paul* (Oxford 1964); C. K. Barret, *From First Adam to Last. A Study in Pauline Theology* (London 1962); L. Cerfaux, *Le chrétien dans la théologie paulinienne* (Paris 1962); J. Dupont, *Le discours de Milet. Testament spirituel de Paul* (Paris 1962); O. Kuss, "Die Rolle des Apostels Paulus in der theologischen Entwicklung der Urkirche" in *MThZ* 14 (1963), 1–59, 109–87.

The Pauline Congregations: B. Weiss, *Paulus und seine Gemeinden* (Berlin 1914); W. L. Knox, *St Paul and the Church of Jerusalem* (London 1925); B. Bartmann, *Paulus als Seelsorger* (Paderborn 1921); K. Holl, "Der Kirchenbegriff des Paulus" in *Ges. Aufsätze*, II (Tübingen 1928), 44–67; J. Wagemann, *Die Stellung des Paulus neben den Zwölf* (Giessen 1926); W. Köster, *Die Idee der Kirche beim hl. Paulus* (Freiburg i. Br. 1929); K. Pieper, *Paulus und die Kirche* (Paderborn 1932); A. Wikenhauser, *Die Kirche als der mystische Leib Christi nach dem Apostel Paulus* (Münster, 2nd ed. 1940); L. Cerfaux, *The Church in the Theology of St Paul* (Freiburg – New York – London 1959); H. Greeven, "Propheten, Lehrer, Vorsteher bei Paulus" in *ZNW* 44 (1952), 1–53; J. Colson, *Les fonctions ecclésiales aux deux premiers siècles* (Paris 1956); K. H. Schelkle, "Römische Kirche im Römerbrief" in *ZKTh* 81 (1959) 393–404; R. Schnackenburg, *The Church in the New Testament* (Freiburg – London – NewYork – Montreal 1965); E. Schweizer, *Church Order in the New Testament* (London – Naperville, Ill. 1961); M. Guerra y Gómez, *Diáconos helénicos y bíblicos* (Burgos 1962); G. Dix, *Jew and Greek* (London, 2nd ed. 1955).

Special Studies: E. von Dobschütz, *Der Apostel Paulus. Seine Stellung in der Kunst* (Halle 1937); W. Straub, *Die Bildersprache des Apostels Paulus* (Tübingen 1937); E. Aleith, *Das Paulusverständnis der alten Kirche* (Berlin 1937).

6. Peter's Missionary Activity and his Sojourn and Death in Rome

Extra-Pauline Christianity: F. X. Pölzl, *Die Mitarbeiter des Weltapostels Paulus* (Regensburg 1911); A. Ruegg, *Die Mission in der alten Kirche, ihre Wege und Erfolge* (Basle 1912); K. Pieper, "Etappen und Eigenart der altchristlichen Mission" in *RQ* 34 (1926), 111–27; F. J. Foakes-Jackson, *The Rise of Gentile Christianity* (London 1927); R. Liechtenhan, *Die urchristliche Mission* (Zürich 1946); R. A. Lipsius, *Acta apostolorum apocrypha*, I (Leipzig 1891, new imp. Darmstadt 1959); J. Hervieux, *The New Testament Apocrypha* (New York 1960); *Hennecke-Schneemelcher*, II (Tübingen 1964); R. Söder,

Die apokryphen Apostelgeschichten und die romanhafte Literatur der Antike (Stuttgart 1932); P. M. Peterson, *Andrew, Brother of Simon Peter, his History and his Legend* (Leiden 1958).

MISSION OF THE APOSTLE PETER. Sources: the Acts of the Apostles and the two letters of Peter. Commentaries on the letters of Peter: J. W. C. Wand, *I and II Peter* (London 1934); F. W. Beare, *The First Epistle of Peter* (London 1958); C. Cranfield, *The First Epistle of Peter* (London 1958); idem, *I and II Peter and Jude* (London 1960); K. H. Schelkle, *Die Petrusbriefe. Der Judasbrief* (Freiburg i. Br. 1961), with extensive bibliography on pp. xi–xvi.

On the apocryphal Acts of Peter: L. Vouaux, *Les actes de Pierre* (Paris 1922), and C. Schmidt in *ZKG* 43 (1924), 321–438; 45 (1926), 481–513. See also G. Stuhlfauth, *Die apokryphe Petrusgeschichte in der altchristlichen Kunst* (Berlin 1925); E. Dinkler, *Die ersten Petrusdarstellungen* (Marburg 1937); C. Cecchelli, *Iconografia dei papi*, I: *S. Pietro* (Rome 1938).

F. J. Foakes-Jackson, *Peter Prince of Apostles* (New York 1927); E. T. Robertson, *Epochs in the Life of Simon Peter* (New York 1933). R. Aigrain, *St Pierre* (Paris 1939); O. Cullmann, *Peter: Disciple, Apostle, Martyr* (Philadelphia, 2nd ed. 1962), on which see also P. Gaechter in *ZKTh* 75 (1953), 331–7; J. Schmitt in *RevSR* 28 (1954), 58–71; A. Vögtle in *MThZ* 5 (1954), 1–47; O. Karrer, *Peter and the Church. An Examination of Cullmann's Thesis* (Freiburg–London–New York–Montreal 1963); P. Gaechter, *Petrus und seine Zeit* (Innsbruck 1958); J. Pérez de Urbel, *San Pedro, príncipe de los apóstoles* (Burgos 1959).

SOJOURN AND DEATH IN ROME: For the older literature down to 1934 see U. Holzmeister, *Commentarium in epitulas ss. Petri et Judae* I (Paris 1937), 37–40; H. Lietzmann, *Petrus und Paulus in Rom* (Berlin, 2nd ed. 1927); H. Dannenbauer, "Die römische Petruslegende" in *HZ* 146 (1932), 239–62; 159 (1939), 81–88; H. Lietzmann, *Petrus, römischer Märtyrer* (Berlin 1936); J. Haller, *Das Papsttum*, I (Stuttgart 1950), 475–85; K. Heussi, *Die römische Petrustradition in kritischer Sicht* (Tübingen 1955); K. Aland, "Der Tod des Petrus in Rom", *Kirchengeschichtliche Entwürfe* (Gütersloh 1960), 35 104.

THE TOMB OF PETER: On the problem of the apostles' tombs in S. Sebastiano, see P. Styger, *Römische Märtyrergrüfte* (Berlin 1935); A. Prandi, *La memoria apostolorum in catacumbas* (Rome 1936); C. Mohlberg, "Historisch-kritische Bemerkungen zum Ursprung der sogenannten memoria apostolorum an der Appischen Straße" in *Colligere Fragmenta, Festschrift A. Dold* (Beuron 1952), 52–74; F. Tolotti, *Memorie degli apostoli in Catacumbas* (Vatican City 1953); P. Testini, "Le presunte reliquie dell'apostolo Pietro e la traslazione 'ad catacumbas'" in *Actes du Ve congrès international d'archéologie chrétienne* (Vatican City 1957), 529–38; J. Ruysschaert, "Les documents littéraires de la double tradition romaine des tombes apostoliques" in *RHE* 52 (1957), 791–831.

The excavations under the Basilica of St Peter. The official report on the excavations is *Esplorazioni sotto la confessione di Pietro in Vaticano eseguite negli anni 1940–1949*, 2 vols. (Vatican City 1951). Further discoveries in M. Guarducci, *I graffiti sotto la confessione di S. Pietro in Vaticano*, 3 vols. (Rome 1958); idem, *The Tomb of St Peter: The New Discoveries in the Secret Grottos of the Vatican* (New York 1960). Literature which has appeared since the official report is listed in *Biblica* 34 (1953) 96*f.; and see especially J. Ruysschaert, "Recherches et études autour de la Confession de la basilique Vaticane (1940–58). État de la question et bibliographie" in *Triplice omaggio a S. S. Pio XII*, vol. 2 (Vatican City 1958), 3–47, and E. Dinkler, "Die Petrus-Rom-Frage, ein Forschungsbericht" in *ThR* 25 (1959), 189–230, 289–335; 27 (1961), 33–64, whose standpoint is more critical. Worthy of special mention are: A. M. Schneider, "Das Petrusgrab am Vatikan" in *ThLZ*

77 (1952), 321–6; E. Schäfer, "Das Apostelgrab unter St. Peter in Rom" in *EvTh* 12 (1953), 304–20; J. Carcopino, "Les fouilles de S. Pierre" in *Études d'histoire chrétienne* (Paris, 2nd ed. 1963), 93–286. R. O'Callaghan, "Vatican Excavations and the Tomb of Peter" in *BA* 16 (1953), 70–87; J. Ruysschaert, "Réflexions sur les fouilles Vaticanes, le rapport officiel et la critique" in *RHE* 48 (1953), 573–631, 49 (1954), 5–58; A. von Gerkan, "Kritische Studien zu den Ausgrabungen unter der Peterskirche in Rom" in *Trierische Zeitschrift* 22 (1954), 26–55; J. Fink, "Archäologie des Petrusgrabes" in *ThRv* 50 (1954), 81–102; C. Mohrmann, "A propos de deux mots controversés . . . tropeum–nomen" in *VigChr* 8 (1954), 154–73; J. Toynbee and J. Ward Perkins, *The Shrine of St Peter and the Vatican Excavations* (London 1956); E. Smothers, "The Excavations under St Peter's" in *ThSt* 17 (1956), 293–321; T. Klausner, *Die römische Petrustradition im Lichte der neuen Ausgrabungen unter der Peterskirche* (Cologne–Opladen 1956), on which see also E. Kirschbaum in *RQ* 51 (1956), 247–54; H. Chadwick, "St Peter and St Paul in Rome" in *JThS* 8 (1957), 31–52; E. Kirschbaum, *The Roman Catacombs and Their Martyrs* (Milwaukee 1950); A. von Gerkan, "Basso et Tusco consulibus" in *Bonner Jahrbuch* 158 (1958) 89–105; idem, "Zu den Problemen des Petrusgrabes" in *JbAC* 1 (1959), 79–93; H.-D. Altendorf, "Die römischen Apostelgräber" in *ThLZ* 84 (1959), 731–40; R. Ruysschaert, "Trois campagnes de fouilles au Vatican et la tombe de Pierre" in *Sacra Pagina* II (Paris 1939), 88–97; D. O'Conner, *Peter in Rome* (diss. Columbia University 1960; A. von Gerkan in *JbAC* 5 (1962), 23–32, 39–42; also T. Klauser, ibid. 33–38; R. Eggers, "Zu den neuesten Graffiti des Coemeteriums in Vaticano" in *RQ* 57 (1962), 74–77; E. Kirschbaum, *The Tombs of St Peter and St Paul* (London 1959); J. Carcopino, "Les fouilles de S. Pierre" in *Études d'histoire chrétienne* (Paris 1963), 93–286.

7. The Christianity of the Johannine Writings

COMMENTARIES

General accounts in A. Wikenhauser, *New Testament Indroduction* (Freiburg–London–New York 1958); P.-H. Menoud, "Les études johanniques de Bultmann à Barrett" in *L'évangile de Jean* (Paris 1958), 11–40.

JOHN'S GOSPEL: C. K. Barret, *The Gospel according to St John. A Commentary on the Greek Text* (London 1957); C. H. Dodd, *Interpretation of the Fourth Gospel* (Cambridge 1953); B. F. Westcott, *The Gospel according to St John* (London 1958); R. Bultmann, *Das Evangelium des Johannes* (Göttingen, 4th ed. 1953; supplement 1957); M.-J. Lagrange, *L'évangile de Saint Jean* (Paris, 6th ed. 1936).

REVELATION: E.-B. Allo, *St Jean, L'Apocalypse* (Paris, 3rd ed. 1933); J. Bonsirven, *L'Apocalypse de S. Jean* (Paris 1951); E. Lohmeyer, *Die Offenbarung des Johannes* (Tübingen 2nd ed. 1933); R. A. Charles, *Revelation*, 2 vols. (Edinburgh 1920).

LETTERS OF JOHN: C. A. Dodd, *Johannine Epistles* (London 1946); R. Schnackenburg, *Die Johannesbriefe* (Freiburg i. Br. 1963).

RESEARCH

A. C. Headlam, *The Fourth Gospel as History* (Oxford 1948); C. Dodd, *The Interpretation of the Fourth Gospel* (Cambridge 1955); D. Lamont, *Studies in the Johannine Writings* (London 1956); F. L. Cross, *Studies in the Fourth Gospel* (London 1957); G. Quispel, "L'évangile de Jean et la gnose" in *L'évangile de Jean* (Paris 1958), 197–208;

R. Schnackenburg, "Logos-Hymnus und johanneischer Prolog" in *BZ* 1 (1957), 69–109; idem, "Die Sakramente im Johannesevangelium" in *Sacra Pagina* II (Paris 1959), 235–54; W. C. van Unnik, "The Purpose of St John's Gospel" in *Studia Evangelica* (Berlin 1959), 382–411; E. Schweizer, "Der Kirchenbegriff im Evangelium und den Briefen des Johannes", ibid. 363–81; E. Haenchen, "Johanneische Probleme" in *ZThK* 56 (1959) 19–54; E. M. Sidebottom, *The Christ of the Fourth Gospel in the Light of First-Century Thought* (London 1961); J. N. Sanders, *The Fourth Gospel in the Early Church* (Cambridge 1943); F.-M. Braun, *Jean le théologien et son évangile dans l'église ancienne* (Paris 1959); H. M. Féret, *Die Geheime Offenbarung des hl. Johannes, eine christliche Schau der Geschichte* (Düsseldorf 1955); S. Giet, *L'apocalypse et l'histoire* (Paris 1957); P. K. Smith, "The Apocalypse of St John and the Early Church" in *JBL* 25 (1957), 187–95; A. Feuillet, *L'apocalypse: état de question* (Bruges 1963); J. Bonsirven, *Le témoin du Verbe, le disciple bien-aimé* (Toulouse 1956); K. L. Carroll, "The Fourth Gospel and the Exclusion of Christians from the Synagogue" in *BJRL* 40 (1957), 334–49; E. Käsemann, "Die Johannesjünger in Ephesus" in *ZThK* 49 (1952), 144–54; R. Schnackenburg, "Das vierte Evangelium und die Johannesjünger" in *HJ* 77 (1958), 21–38; G. MacGregor and A. Morton, *The Structure of the Fourth Gospel* (Edinburgh 1961); S. Temple, "A Key to the Composition of the Fourth Gospel" in *JBL* 30 (1961), 220–32; T. Holtz, *Die Christologie der Apokalypse des Johannes* (Berlin 1962); C. Dodd, *Historical Tradition in the Fourth Gospel* (Cambridge 1963); L. Bouyer, *The Fourth Gospel* (Westminster, Md. 1964); J. Sanders, "Saint John on Patmos" in *NTS* 9 (1963), 75–85; M. E. Boismard, "La tradition joannique concernant le baptiste" in *RB* 70 (1963), 5–42; P. Lamarche, "Le prologue de Jean" in *RSR* 52 (1964), 497–538.

SECTION THREE

The Post-Apostolic Age

GENERAL LITERATURE

R. Knopf, *Das nachapostolische Zeitalter* (Tübingen 1905); P. Batiffol, *Primitive Catholicism* (New York – London 1911); W. Bauer, *Rechtgläubigkeit und Ketzerei im ältesten Christentum* (Tübingen 1934); G. Bardy, *La théologie de l'église de S. Clément de Rome à S. Irénée* (Paris 1945); M. Simon, *Verus Israel* (Paris 1948); K. Hörmann, *Leben in Christus. Zusammenhänge zwischen Dogma und Sitte bei den apostolischen Vätern* (Vienna 1952); L. Goppelt, *Christentum und Judentum im 1. und 2. Jahrhundert* (Gütersloh 1954); P. Carrington, *The Early Christian Church*, 2 vols. (Cambridge 1957); J. Daniélou, *La théologie du judéo-christianisme* (Paris 1958), Eng. tr. *The Theology of Jewish Christianity* (London 1964); L. Goppelt, "Die apostolische und nachapostolische Zeit" in *Die Kirche in ihrer Geschichte,* ed. K. D. Schmidt and E. Wolf, vol. I, part A (Göttingen 1962).

8. *The Conflict between Christianity and the Roman State Power*

SOURCES

The writers of the first and second centuries, especially the early apologists; editions: J. C. T. de Otto, *Corpus Apologetarum,* I–IX (Jena, 3rd ed. 1876–81); E. J. Goodspeed, *Die ältesten Apologeten* (Göttingen 1914; omitting Theophilus).

Acts of the Martyrs: general survey in *Altaner* 246–52; G. Lazzati, *Gli sviluppi della letteratura sui martiri nei primi quattro secoli* (Turin 1956); M. Simonetti, "Qualche osservationi a proposito dell'origine degli atti dei martiri" in *RevÉAug* 2 (1956), 39–57; for current bibliography, the reader is referred to *Archivum Historiae Pontificae*, vol. I (Rome 1963).

Texts

Principal editions: *Acta Sanctorum* ed. J. Bolland *et socii* (from 1643, with supplementary matter in the *Analecta Bollandiana* from 1882) (Brussels); also, T. Ruinart, *Acta primorum martyrum* (1689, new imp. Regensburg 1859), with supplementary vol. by E. Blant, *Les actes des martyrs* (Paris 1882); R. Knopf and G. Krüger, *Ausgewählte Märtyrerakten* (Tübingen, 3rd ed. 1929).
Translations: G. Rauschen, *BKV* 14 (Kempten 1913); O. Braun, *BKV* 22 (1915); L. Homo, *Les empereurs romains et le christianisme* (Paris 1931); H. Rahner (Freiburg i. Br. 1941); A. Hamman, *La geste du sang* (Paris 1953); O. Hagemeyer, *Ich bin Christ. Frühchristliche Märtyrerakten* (Düsseldorf 1961).

Literature

General: P. Allard, *Histoire des persécutions* (Paris, 3rd ed. 1903–8); P. Allard, *Dix leçons sur le martyre* (Paris, 8th ed. 1930); Z. Zeiler, *L'empire romain et l'église* (Paris 1928); A. Ehrhard, *Die Kirche der Märtyrer* (Munich 1932); P. Brezzi, *Christianesimo e impero Romano* (Rome, 2nd ed. 1944); H. Grégoire, *Les persécutions dans l'empire romain* (Brussels, 2nd ed. 1963), on which see E. Griffe in *BLE* 53 (1952), 129–60; E. Stauffer, *Christ and the Caesars* (London); G. Ricciotti, *The Age of Martyrs* (Milwaukee 1959); J. Moreau, *La persécution du christianisme dans l'empire romain* (Paris 1956); H. Leclercq, "Persécutions" in *DACL* XIV (1939), 523–94; J. Vogt, "Christenverfolgungen" in *RAC* II (1954), 1159–208; L. Dieu, "La persécution au IIe siècle. Une loi fantôme" in *RHE* 38 (1942), 5–19.

The Trial of Christians: H. Last, "The Study of the Persecutions" in *JRS* 27 (1937), 80–92; E. Griffe, "Le christianisme en face de l'état romain" in *BLE* 50 (1949), 129–45; A. N. Sherwin-White, "The Early Persecutions and Roman Law again" in *JThS NS* 3 (1952), 199–213; J. W. P. Borleffs, "Institutum Neronianum" in *VigChr* 6 (1952), 129–45; E. Griffe, "Les actes du martyr Apollonius et le problème de la base juridique des persécutions" in *BLE* 53 (1952), 65–76; V. Monachino, "Il fondamento giuridico delle persecuzioni nei primi due secoli" in *SC* 81 (1953), 3–32; A. Ehrhardt, "Das corpus Christianorum und die Korporationen im spätrömischen Recht" in *ZSavRGrom* 70 (1953), 299 to 347; 71 (1954), 25–40; H. Last, "Christenverfolgungen" (legal aspect) in *RAC* II (1954), 1208–28; C. Cecchelli, "Il nome e la 'setta' dei cristiani" in *RivAC* 31 (1955), 55–73; P. de Mouxy, "Nomen Christianorum" in *Atti AccadScienze Torino* 91 (1956–7), 204–36; A. Wlosok, "Die Rechtsgrundlagen der Christenverfolgungen der ersten zwei Jahrhunderte" in *Gymnasium* 66 (1959), 14–32; C. Saumagne, "Tertullien et l'Institutum Neronianum" in *ThZ* 17 (1961), 334–57.

The Persecution of Nero: H. Fuchs in *VigChr* 4 (1950), 65–93; H. Hommel, *Theologia Viatorum* 3 (1951), 1–30; E. Griffe in *BLE* 53 (1952), 158–60; B. Doer, *Das Altertum* 2 (1956), 15–28; K. Büchner, *Humanitas Romana* (Heidelberg 1957), 229–39; C. Saumagne, "Les incendiaires de Rome et les lois pénales des Romains" in *RH* 227 (1962), 337–60; J. Beaujeu, *Latomus* (Brussels), 19 (1960), 65–80, 291–311; L. Herrmann, *Latomus* 20

(1961), 817–20; H. Capocci, "Per il testo di Tacito, Annales 15, 44" in *Studia et Documenta hist. et juris* 28 (1962), 65–99; G. Roux, *Néron* (Paris 1962); E. Griffe in *BLE* 65 (1964), 1–16.

DOMITIAN: M. Dibelius, "Rom und die Christen im 1. Jahrhundert" in *SAH* 1941–2, part 2; M. Sordi in *RSTI* 14 (1960), 1–26; L. W. Bernard in *NTSt* 10 (1964), 251–60.

TRAJAN AND HADRIAN: W. Weber, *Festgabe K. Müller* (Tübingen 1922), 24–45; A. Kurfess in *ZNW* 36 (1937), 295–8 and *Mnemosyne* 7 (1939), 237–40; L. Dieu in *RHE* 38 (1942), 5–19; T. Mayer-Maly, *Studia et Documenta Hist. Juris (R)*, 22 (1956), 311–28; W. Schmid in *Maja* 7 (1955), 5–13; M. Sordi in *RSTI* 14 (1960), 344–70; L. Vidman, *Étude sur la correspondance de Pline le Jeune avec Trajan* (Praha 1960), 87–106.

VARIOUS: G. Lopuszanzki, "La police romaine et les chrétiens" in *Antiquité classique* 20 (1951), 5–46; J. Zeiller, "Nouvelles observations sur l'origine des persécutions contre les chrétiens aux deux premiers siècles" in *RHE* 46 (1951), 521–33; S. Giet, "Le témoignage de Clément de Rome sur la cause des persécutions romaines" in *RevSR* 29 (1955), 333–45; V. Grumel, "Du nombre des persécutions païennes dans les anciens chroniques" in *RevÉAug* 2 (1956), 59–66; W. H. Frend, "Some Links between Judaism and the Early Church" in *JEH* 9 (1958), 141–58; H. Meerhing, "Persecution of the Jews and Adherents of the Isis Cult at Rome A.D. 19" in *NovT* 3 (1959), 293–304; A. Fuks, "Aspects of the Jewish Revolt in A.D. 115–17" in *JRS* 51 (1961), 98–104; P. Brown, "Aspects of the Christianization of the Roman Aristocracy" in *JRS* 51 (1961), 1–11.

9. *The Religious World of the Post-Apostolic Age as Mirrored in its Writings*

SOURCES

The writings of the Apostolic Fathers. For the term, see J. A. Fischer in his edition (Munich 1956), IX–XII and G. Jouassard in *MSR* 14 (1957), 129–34. Collected editions: K. Bihlmeyer, *Die apostolischen Väter* (Tübingen 1924, new imp. 1957); J. A. Fischer, *First Epistle of Clement, Letters of Ignatius, Letter of Polycarp* (Munich and Darmstadt 1956). Other editions by K. Lake (London and New York 1930); S. Colombo (Turin 1930); D. Ruiz Bueno (Madrid 1950).

Translations: F. Zeller in *BKV* 35 (Munich 1918); by W. Bauer, M. Dibelius, R. Knopf, H. Windisch (with conmmentary), *Ergänzungsband zum Handbuch zum N.T.;* by J. A. Kleist (English, with commentary) in *ACW* 1 and 6 (Westminster, Md. and London 1946–8). On the language of the Apostolic Fathers: G. J. M. Bartelink, *Lexicologisch-semantische Studië over de Taal van de Apostolische Vaders* (Nijmegen 1952); H. Kraft, *Clavis Patrum Apostolicorum* (Darmstadt 1963).

LITERATURE

General accounts in the textbooks of patrology by *Quasten P* I 29–157; *Altaner* 47–113.

GENERAL INTRODUCTIONS: A. Casamassa, *I padri apostolici* (Rome 1938); J. Lawson, *A Theological and Historical Introduction to the Apostolic Fathers* (New York 1961); K. Aland, "The Problem of Anonymity and Pseudoanonymity in Christian Literature of the First Two Centuries" in *JThS NS* 12 (1961) 39–49.

SPECIAL STUDIES: H. Schumacher, *Kraft der Urkirche* (Freiburg i. Br. 1934); A. Heitmann, *Imitatio Dei* (Rome 1940); I. Giordani, *The Social Message of the Early Church* (Paterson,

N. J. 1944); J. Klevinghaus, *Die theologische Stellung der Apostolischen Väter zur alt-testamentlichen Offenbarung* (Gütersloh 1948); T. F. Torrance, *The Doctrine of Grace in the Apostolic Fathers* (Edinburgh 1948); A. Benoît, *Le baptême au deuxieme siècle* (Paris 1953); M. Spanneut, *Le stoïcisme des pères de l'église de Clément de Rome à Clément d'Alexandrie* (Paris 1957); A. O'Hagan, *The Concept of Material Re-Creation in the Apostolic Fathers* (diss. Munich 1960); E. A. Judge, *The Social Pattern of the Christian Groups in the 1st Century* (London 1960); G. Bruni, *Fonti religiose e riflessione filosofica nella Bibbia e nei Padri Apostolici* (Rome 1960); P. G. Verweijs, *Evangelium und neues Gesetz in der ältesten Christenheit bis auf Marcion* (Utrecht 1961); K. Lake, *The Apostolic Fathers*, 2 vols. (New York 1925); C. Richardson, *Early Christian Fathers* (London 1953), which ist the first volume of a new Protestant collection: *The Library of Christian Classics;* D. Barsotti, *La dottrina dell'amore nei Padri della chiesa fino a Ireneo* (Milan 1963).

SPECIAL EDITIONS and literature on individual texts:

(a) Clement of Rome: K. T. Schäfer in *FlorPatr* 44 (1941); A. Stuiber, "Clemens" in *RAC* III (1957), 188–97; J. Lebreton, "La trinité chez S. Clément de Rome" in *Gr* 6 (1925), 369–404; A. Harnack, *Einführung in die alte Kirchengeschichte* (Leipzig 1929); F. Gerke, *Die Stellung des 1. Klemensbriefs innerhalb der altchristlichen Gemeindever-fassung* (Leipzig 1931); E. Barnikol in *ThJ* 4 (1936), 61–80 (Christology, baptism, and the Lord's supper); P. Meinhold, "Geschehen und Deutung im 1. Klemensbrief" in *ZKG* 58 (1939), 82–126; L. Sanders, *L'hellénisme de S. Clément de Rome et le Paulinisme* (Louvain 1934); M. Smith, "Report about Peter in 1 Clement 5:4" in *NTS* 7 (1960), 86–8; W. C. van Unnik, "1 Clem. 34" in *VigChr* 5 (1951), 204–48; idem, "Le nombre des élus dans la première épître de Clément" in *RHPhR* 42 (1962), 237–46; C. Eggenberger, *Die Quelle der politischen Ethik des 1. Clemensbriefes* (Zürich 1951); A. W. Ziegler, *Neue Studien zum 1. Klemensbrief* (Munich 1958); J. Colson, *Clément de Rome* (Paris 1960); C. Nielsen, "Clement of Rome and Moralism" in *CH* 31 (1962), 131–50.

(b) Ignatius of Antioch: P. G. Crone (Münster, 2nd ed. 1958); T. Camelot in *SourcesChr* 10 (3rd ed. 1958); M. Rackl, *Die Christologie des hl. Ignatius von Antiochien* (Freiburg i. Br. 1914); J. Lebreton, "La théologie de la Trinité d'après S. Ignace d'Antioche" in *RSR* 25 (1925), 97–126, 393–419; H. Schlier, *Religionsgeschichtliche Unter-suchungen zu den Ignatiusbriefen* (Giessen 1929); C. P. S. Clarke, *St Ignatius and St Poly-carp* (London 1930); C. C. Richardson, *The Christianity of Ignatius of Antioch* (New York 1935); J. Moffat, "An Approach to Ignatius" in *HThR* 29 (1936), 1–38; T. Preiss, "La mystique de l'imitation du Christ et l'unité chez Ignace d'Antioche" in *RHPhR* 18 (1938), 197–241; H. B. Bartsch, *Gnostisches Gut und Gemeindetradition bei Ignatius von Antiochien* (Gütersloh 1940); R. Bultmann, "Ignatius und Paulus" in *Festschrift J. de Zwaan* (Haarlem 1952–3), 37–51; W. Bieder, "Zur Deutung des kirchl. Schweigens bei Ignatius" in *ThZ* 12 (1956), 28–43; J. Hannah, "Setting of the Ignatian long recension" in *JBL* 79 (1960), 221–38; V. Corwin, *St Ignatius and Christianity in Antioch* (New Haven 1960); H. Musurillo, "Ignatius of Antioch: Gnostic or Essene" in *ThSt* 22 (1961), 103–9; R. Grant, "Scripture and Tradition in St Ignatius of Antioch" in *CBQ* 25 (1963), 322–35; J. Colson, *Agape chez St Ignace d'Antioche* (Paris 1961).

(c) Polycarp of Smyrna: Letter to the Philippians in T. Camelot, *SourcesChr* 10 (3rd ed. 1958); P. N. Harrison, *Polycarp's Two Epistles to the Philippians* (Cambridge 1936); H. Katzenmayer, "Polykarp" in *IKZ* 59 (1951), 146–56; H. von Campenhausen, *Polykarp von Smyrna und die Pastoralbriefe* (Heidelberg 1951); P. Meinhold, "Polykarp von Smyrna" in *Pauly–Wissowa* 21 (1952), 1662–93; L. Barnard, "Problem of Saint Polycarp's Epistle to the Philippians" in *ChQR* 163 (1962), 421–30.

(d) Didache: H. Lietzmann, *KlT* 6 (Berlin 1936); T. Klausner, *FlorPatr* 1 (1940); J.-P. Audet (Paris 1957) (with commentary), on which see H. de Riedmatten in *Angelicum* 36 (1959), 410–29; J. Schmid, "Didache" in *RAC* III, 1009–13; F. E. Vokes, *The Riddle of the Didache* (London 1938); E. Peterson, "Über einige Probleme der Didache-Überlieferung" in *RivAC* 27 (1952), 37–68; E. Stommel, "Did. 16, 6" in *RQ* 48 (1953), 21–42; A. Adam, "Erwägungen zur Herkunft der Didache" in *ZKG* 68 (1957), 1–47; P. Nautin, "La composition de la Didache et son titre" in *RHR* 155 (1959), 191–214; A. Agnoletto, "Motivi etico-escatologici nella Didache" in *Convivium Dominicum* (Catania 1959), 259–76; B. Butler, "The 'Two Ways' in the Didache" in *JThS* 12 (1961), 27–38.
On the liturgy of the Didache: H. Lietzmann, *Messe und Herrenmahl* (Bonn 1926), 230–8; A. Greiff, *Das älteste Pascharitual der Kirche* (Paderborn 1929); R. H. Connolly in *DR* 55 (1937), 477–89; A. Arnold, *Der Ursprung des christlichen Abendmahls* (Freiburg i. Br 1937); G. Dix in *Theology* 37 (London 1938), 261–83; E. Peterson in *ELit* 58 (1944), 3–13.

(e) Pseudo-Barnabas: T. Klauser in *FlorPatr* 1 (1940); J. Schmid in *RAC* I (1950), 1207–17; A. Williams, "The Date of the Epistle of Barnabas" in *JThS* 34 (1933), 337–46; P. Meinhold, "Geschichte und Exegese im Barnabas-Brief" in *ZKG* 59 (1940), 255–303; K. Thieme, *Kirche und Synagoge* (Olten 1945), on which see *ZKTh* 74 (1952), 63–70; A. Hermans, "Le Ps.-Barnabas est-il millénariste?" in *EThL* 35 (1959), 849–76; L. W. Barnard, "The Epistle of Barnabas — a Paschal Homily?" in *VigChr* 15 (1961), 8–22; P. Prigent, *L'épître de Barnabé et ses sources* (Paris 1961).

(f) Epistula Apostolorum: C. Schmidt, *Gespräche Jesu mit seinen Jüngern* (Leipzig 1919); H. Duensing, *KlT* 152 (Bonn 1925); Hennecke and Schneemelcher, *Neutestamentliche Apokryphen*, I (Tübingen 1959), 126–55.
Its origins: J. Delazer in *Antonianum* 4 (1929), 257–92, 387–430; J. de Zwaan, *Essays presented to R. Harris* (London 1933), 344–55; L. Gry, "La date de la parousie d'après l'epistula apostolorum" in *RB* 49 (1949), 86–97.

(g) Shepherd of Hermas: M. Whittaker, *GCS* 48 (Berlin 1956); English trans. C. Taylor, *The Shepherd of Hermas,* 2 vols. (London 1903–6); R. Joly, *SourcesChr* 53 (1958); Coptic fragments, ed. by T. Lefort in *Muséon* 51 (1938), 239–76; 52 (1939), 223–8; W. J. Wilson, "The Career of the Prophet Hermas" in *HThR* 20 (1927), 21–60; C. Bonner, "A Codex of the Shepherd of Hermas in the Papyri of the University of Michigan" in *HThR* 18 (1925), 115–27; A. V. Ström, *Allegorie und Wirklichkeit im Hirten des Hermas* (Leipzig 1936); E. Peterson, "Beiträge zur Interpretation der Visionen des Hermas" in *OrChrP* 13 (1947), 624–35; idem in *VigChr* 8 (1954), 52–71; A. O'Hagan, "The Great Tribulation to Come in the Pastor of Hermas" in *TU* 79 (1961), 305–11; R. Joly, "Judaïsme, christianisme et hellénisme dans le Pasteur d'Hermas" in *La Nouvelle Clio* 5 (1953), 356–76; S. Giet, *Hermas et les Pasteurs. Les trois auteurs du Pasteur d'Hermas* (Paris 1963). On penance: B. Poschmann, *Poenitentia secunda* (Bonn 1939); R. Mortimer, *The Origins of Private Penance in the Western Church* (Oxford 1939); R. Joly in *RHR* 147 (1955), 32–49; K. Rahner in *ZKTh* 77 (1955), 385–431.

10. *The Development of the Church's Organization*

SOURCES

As for Chapter 9.

LITERATURE

As for Chapter 9 with the addition of the following: H. Bruders, *Die Verfassung der Kirche bis 175 n. Christus* (Mainz 1904); P. Batiffol, *Primitive Catholicism* (New York–London 1911); R. Sohm, *Wesen und Ursprung des Katholizismus* (Leipzig, 2nd ed. 1912); H. Lietzmann, "Zur altchristlichen Verfassungsgeschichte" in *ZWTh* 55 (1913), 97–153; H. Dieckmann, *Die Verfassung der Urkirche* (Berlin 1923); A. J. Maclean, *the Position of Clergy and Laity in the Early Church* (London 1930); O. Linton, "Das Problem der Urkirche in der neuesten Forschung" (diss. Uppsala 1932); N. Lämmle, *Beiträge zum Problem des Kirchenrechtes* (Rottenburg 1933); J. V. Bartlet, *Church Life and Order during the First Four Centuries* (Oxford 1943); K. E. Kirk, *The Apostolic Ministry* (London 1947, new imp. 1957); G. Bardy, *La théologie de l'église de S. Clément de Rome à S. Irénée* (Paris 1947); J. Ebers, *Grundriß des katholischen Kirchenrechts* (Vienna 1950); H. E. Feine, *Kirchliche Rechtsgeschichte* I: *Die katholische Kirche* (Weimar 1950); H. von Campenhausen, *Kirchliches Amt und geistliche Vollmacht* (Tübingen 1952); S. L. Greenslade, *Schism in the Early Church* (London 1953); J. Colson, *Les fonctions ecclésiales aux deux premiers siècles* (Bruges 1956); P. Nautin, *Lettres et écrivains chrétiens des IIe et IIIe siècles* (Paris 1961); A. Ehrhardt, "Christianity Before the Apostles' Creed" in *HThR* 55 (1962), 73–119.

ON THE DIFFERENT OFFICES IN THE CHURCH: G. Sass, *Apostelamt und Kirche* (Munich 1939); G. Saß, "Die Apostel in der Didache" in *Festschrift E. Lohmeyer* (Stuttgart 1951), 233–9; K. H. Rengstorf, ἀπόστολος in *ThW* I, 406–46; A. Michel, "Ordre, Ordination" in *DThC* XI, 1193–1405; L. Maréchal, "Évêque" in *DBS* II, 1297–1333; H. W. Beyer, ἐπίσκοπος in *ThW* II, 604–17; J. Colson, *L'évêque dans les communautés primitives* (Paris 1951); J. Munck, "Presbyters and Disciples of the Lord in Papias. Exegetic Comments on Eusebius, Hist. 3, 39" in *HThR* 52 (1959), 223–43; J. Colson, *La fonction diaconale aux origines de l'église* (Bruges 1960).

ON THE POSITION OF THE ROMAN CONGREGATION: F. R. van Cauwelaert, "L'intervention de l'église de Rome à Corinthe vers l'an 96" in *RHE* 31 (1935), 267–306, 765 f.; O. Perler, "Ignatius von Antiochien und die römische Christengemeinde" in *DTh* 22 (1944), 413–51; H. Katzenmayer, "Zur Frage des Primats und der kirchlichen Verfassungszuständigkeit in der Didache" in *IKZ* 55 (1947), 31–43; K. H. Schelkle, "Römische Kirche im Römerbrief" in *ZKTh* 81 (1959), 393–404; F. Dvornik, *The Idea of the Apostolicity in Byzantium and the Legend of the Apostle Andrew* (Cambridge, Mass. 1959); O. Knoch, "Die Ausführungen des ersten Clemensbriefes über die kirchliche Verfassung im Spiegel der neueren Deutungen" in *TQ* 141 (1961), 385–407; N. Afanassieff *et alii*, *The Primacy of Peter in the Orthodox Church* (Westminster, Md. 1963); B. Hemmerdinger, "La prépondérance de l'église de Rome en 95" in *RSPhTh* 47 (1963), 58–60.

11. *Heterodox Jewish-Christian Currents*

GENERAL: H.-J. Schoeps, *Theologie und Geschichte des Judenchristentums* (Tübingen 1949); B. Reicke, *Diakonie, Festfreude und Zelos* (Uppsala–Wiesbaden 1951); J. Daniélou, *La théologie du Judéo-Christianisme* (Paris 1958), Eng. tr. *The Theology of Jewish Christianity* (London 1964); M. Black, "The Patristic Accounts of Jewish Sectarianism" in *BJRL* 41 (1959), 285–303; J. Munck, "Jewish Christianity in post-Apostolic Times" in *NTS* 6 (1959–60), 103–16.

ON THE EBIONITES: general survey with bibliography by G. Strecker in *RAC* IV (1959), 487–500; H.-J. Schoeps, "Ebionite Christianity" in *JThS NS* 4 (1953), 219–24; L. Goppelt, *Christentum und Judentum im 1. und 2. Jahrhundert* (Gütersloh 1954); J. A. Fitzmyer, "The Qumran Scrolls, the Ebionites and their Literature" in *ThSt* 16 (1955), 335–72; S. G. F. Brandon, *The Fall of Jerusalem and the Christian Church* (London, 2nd ed. 1957); P. Vielhauer, "Judenchristliche Evangelien" in *Hennecke – Schneemelcher* I (Tübingen 1959), 75–108; H.-J. Schoeps, "Apokalyptik im Neuen Testament" in *ZNW* 51 (1960), 101–11; idem, *Das Judenchristentum* (Bern 1964).

ON THE PSEUDO-CLEMENTINES: general survey with bibliography by B. Rehm in *RAC* III (1957), 197–206 and K. Baus in *LThK* VI (1961), 334–5; B. Rehm, *Die Pseudo-Klementinen* I: *Die Homilien*, *GCS* 42 (Berlin 1953), II: *Die Recognitionen*, ed. by B. Rehm and F. Paschke (ibid., in preparation), at present only in *PG* I; W. Frankenberg, "Die syrischen Clementinen mit griechischem Paralleltext" in *TU* 48, 3 (Berlin 1937); H.-J. Schoeps, *Aus frühchristlicher Zeit* (Tübingen 1950), 38–81; idem, *Urgemeinde, Judenchristentum, Gnosis* (Tübingen 1956), 68–86; G. Strecker, *Das Judenchristentum in den Ps.-Klementinen*, *TU* 70 (Berlin 1958); H.-J. Schoeps, "Iranisches in den Ps.-Klementinen" in *ZNW* 51 (1960), 1–10; W. Ullmann, "The Significance of the Epistula Clementis in the Pseudo-Clementines" in *JThS* 11 (1960), 295–317.

ON THE ELCHASAITES: general account by G. Strecker in *RAC* IV (1959), 1171–86 (with bibliography); H. Waitz, "Das Buch des Elchasai" in *Harnack-Ehrung* (Leipzig 1921), 87–104.

ON THE MANDAEANS: general account by C. Colpe in *RGG* 3rd ed. IV, 709–12; K. Rudolf, *Die Mandäer*, 2 vols. (Göttingen 1960–1) (with sources and bibliography); J. Behm, *Die mandäische Religion und das Urchristentum* (Leipzig 1927); R. Reitzenstein, *Die Vorgeschichte der christlichen Taufe* (Leipzig 1929); E. S. Drower, *The Mandaeans of Iraq and Iran* (Oxford 1937); T. Säve-Söderbergh, *Studies in the Gnostic Manichaean Psalm-Book* (Uppsala 1949); W. Baumgartner, "Der heutige Stand der Mandäerfrage" in *ThZ* 6 (1950), 401–10; E. Bammel, "Zur Frühgeschichte der Mandäer" in *Orientalia* 32 (1963), 220–5; M. Simon, *Recherches d'histoire judéo-chrétienne* (Paris 1963).

SECTION FOUR

The Church in the Second Century

12. The Position of the Church under the Emperors Marcus Aurelius and Commodus. Martyrdom of the Congregations of Lyons and Vienne

SOURCES

As for Chapter 9.

LITERATURE

As for Chapter 9, with the following additions: H. Eberlein, *Mark Aurel und die Christen* (Breslau 1914); A. S. L. Ferqharson, *Marcus Aurelius, his Life and his World* (Oxford 1951); W. Görlitz, *Mark Aurel, Kaiser und Philosoph* (Stuttgart 1954); J. Beaujeu, *La politique romaine à l'apogée de l'empire*, I: *La politique religieuse des Antonins* (Paris 1955);

J. Straub, "Commodus und die Christen" in *RAC* III, 262–5; A. Charny, *Les martyrs de Lyon de 177* (Lyons 1936); E. Griffe, *La Gaule chrétienne à l'époque romaine*, I (Paris 1947), 17–33; H. Delehaye, "Les actes des martyrs de Pergame" in *AnBoll* 58 (1940), 142–76; E. Griffe, "Les actes du martyre Apollonius et le problème de la base juridique des persécutions" in *BLE* 53 (1952), 65–76; F. Corsari, "Note sugli Acta martyrum Scillitanorum" in *Nuovo Didaskaleion* 6 (Catania 1956), 5–51; H. Karpp, "Die Zahl der scilitanischen Märtyrer" in *VigChr* 15 (1961), 165–72; M. Sordi, "I 'nuovi decreti' di Marco Aurelio contro i cristiani" in *Studi Romani* 9 (1961), 365–78; J. Colin, *L'empire des Antonins et les martyrs Gaulois de 177* (Bonn 1964).

13. *Literary Polemic against Christianity*

GENERAL: J. Geffcken, *Das Christentum im Kampf und Ausgleich mit der griechisch-römischen Welt* (Berlin, 3rd ed. 1920); J. Geffcken, *Der Ausgang des griechisch-römischen Heidentums* (Heidelberg, 2nd ed. 1929); P. de Labriolle, *La réaction païenne* (Paris 1934); W. Nestle, "Die Haupteinwände des antiken Denkens gegen das Christentum" in *ARW* 37 (1941), 51–100; M. Sordi in *RSCI* 16 (1962), 1–28; J. Jungkuntz, "Christian Approval of Epicurism" in *CH* (1962) 279–93.

ON FRONTO: Labriolle, *op. cit.* 87–94; M. Brock, *Studies in Fronto and his Age* (Cambridge 1911).

ON LUCIAN: K. Mras, in *Pauly-Wissowa* XIII 2, 1725—77; A. Lesky, *Griechische Literaturgeschichte* (Bern 1958), 759–63, 765. Editions of *De morte Peregrini:* C. Jacobitz, *Luciani Opera*, III (Leipzig 1904), 271–87; K. Mras, *Die Hauptwerke des Lukian griechisch-deutsch* (Munich 1954), 470–505. Other works: J. Schwartz, *Lucien de Samosate. Philopseudès et De morte Peregrini* (Paris 1951, with commentary); M. Caster, *Lucien et la pensée religieuse de son temps* (Paris 1936); C. Curti, "Luciano di Samosata ed i cristiani" in *Misc. di Studi di letteratura cristiana antica* (Catania 1954), 86–109; G. Bagnani, "Peregrinus Proteus and the Christians" in *Historia* 4 (1955), 107–12; H. D. Betz, "Lukian von Samosata und das Christentum" in *NovT* 3 (1959) 226–37; idem, *Lukian von Samosata und das Neue Testament* (Berlin 1961).

ON CELSUS: P. Merlan, "Celsus" in *RAC* II, 954–65 (bibliography to 1953). Editions of the fragments of Ἀληθὴς λόγος: O. Glöckner in *KlT* 151 (Bonn 1924); R. Bader (Tübingen 1940); English translation with commentary by H. Chadwick, *Origen, Contra Celsum* (Cambridge 1953); W. de Boer, *Scripta paganorum I–IV saec. de Christianis testimonia* (Leiden 1948); A. Miura-Stange, *Celsus und Origenes* (Giessen 1926); W. Völker, *Das Bild vom nichtgnostischen Christentum bei Celsus* (Halle 1928); A. Wifstrand, *Die wahre Lehre des Kelsos* (Lund 1942); W. de Boer, *De eerste bestrijder van het christendom* (Groningen 1950); C. Andresen, *Logos u. Nomos. Polemik des Kelsos wider das Christentum* (Berlin 1955, with bibliography); H. O. Schroeder, "Celsus und Porphyrius als Christengegner" in *Die Welt als Geschichte* 17 (1957), 190–202.

14. *The Early Christian Apologists of the Second Century*

COLLECTED EDITIONS of the apologists: J. C. T. de Otto, *Corpus apologetarum* (Jena, 3rd ed. 1876–81); E. J. Goodspeed, *Die ältesten Apologeten* (omitting Theophilus) (Göttingen 1914) with idem, *Index apologeticus* (Leipzig 1912). A new edition for the *GCS* is planned.

GENERAL LITERATURE: see *Bardenhewer* I, 181 ff. and *Quasten P*, I, 189 f.; J. Geffcken, *Zwei griechische Apologeten* (Leipzig 1907), IX–XLIII and 239–322; A. Puech, *Les apologistes grecs du deuxième siècle de notre ère* (Paris 1912); A. Hauck, *Apologetik in der alten Kirche* (Leipzig 1918); I. Giordani, *La prima polemica cristiana, gli apologetici del II° secolo* (Turin 1930; Brescia, 2nd ed. 1943); M. Pellegrino, *Gli apologetici greci* (Rome 1947); idem, *Studi sull'antica apologetica* (Rome 1947); E. Benz, "Christus und Sokrates in der alten Kirche" in *ZNW* 43 (1950–1), 195–224.

V. Monachino, "Intento pratico e propagandistico nell'apologetica greca del secondo secolo" in *Gr* 32 (1951), 5–49, 187–222; R. M. Grant, "The Chronology of the Greek Apologists" in *VigChr* 9 (1955), 25–33; idem, "The Fragments of the Greek Apologists and Irenaeus" in *Festschrift R. P. Casey* (Freiburg i. Br. 1963), 179–218.

SPECIAL STUDIES: F. Andres, *Die Engellehre der griechischen Apologeten des 2. Jahrhunderts* (Paderborn 1914); K. Gronau, *Das Theodizeeproblem in der altchristlichen Auffassung* (Tübingen 1922); J. Lortz, "Das Christentum als Monotheismus in den Apologien des 2. Jahrhunderts" in *Festschrift A. Ehrhard* (Bonn 1922), 301–27; V. A. S. Little, *The Christology of the Apologists* (London 1934); F. J. Dölger, "Sacramentum Infanticidii" in *AuC*, IV (1934), 188–228; H. Rossbacher, *Die Apologeten als politisch-wissenschaftliche Schriftsteller* (Halberstadt 1937); M. Pellegrino, *Il cristianesimo di fronte alla cultura classica* (Turin 1954); H. Hommel, *Schöpfer und Erhalter, Studien zum Problem Christentum und Antike* (Berlin 1956); H. Wey, *Die Funktionen der bösen Geister bei den griechischen Apologeten des 2. Jahrhunderts* (Winterthur 1957); J. Daniélou, *Message évangélique et culture hellénistique aux II° et III° siècles* (Tournai 1961), 11–80; A. Wifstrand, *L'église ancienne et la culture grecque* (Paris 1962); J. H. Waszink, "Some Observations on the appreciation of the Philosophy of the Barbarians" in *Mélanges Chr. Mohsmann* (Utrecht 1963), 41–56.

ARISTIDES: Syrian and Greek text in R. Harris and J. A. Robinson, *The Apology of Aristides* (Cambridge 1893); Greek text in J. Geffcken, *op. cit.* 3–27, with commentary, ibid. 28–96; Goodspeed, *op. cit.* 3–23.

JUSTIN: *The Apologies*, ed. by A. W. F. Blunt (Cambridge 1911); G. Rauschen (Bonn, 2nd ed. 1911); G. Krüger (Tübingen 1915); M. Pfättisch (Münster 1933); S. Frasca (Turin 1938); *Dialogus cum Tryphone*, ed. by G. Archambauld (Paris 1909) and Goodspeed, *op. cit.* 90–265. A new fragment of the *Dialogus* may be found in G. Mercati, *Biblica* 22 (1941), 339–66. On the text of the Apology see W. Schmid in *ZNW* 40 (1941), 87–138. General appreciation in M.-J. Lagrange, *S. Justin* (Paris, 3rd ed. 1914); G. Bardy in *DThC* VIII, 2228–77; M. S. Enslin in *JQR* 34 (1943), 179–205. See also: E. R. Goodenough, *The Theology of Justinus Martyr* (Jena 1923); K. Thieme, *Kirche und Synagoge* (Olten 1945); W. H. Shotwell, *The Exegesis of Justin* (Chicago 1955); R. Holte, "Logos Spermatikos: Christianity and Ancient Philosophy according to St Justin's Apologies" in *StTh* 12 (1958), 106–68; O. Piper, "The Nature of the Gospel according to Justin Martyr" in *The Journal of Religion* 41 (1961), 155–68; J. Romanides, "Justin Martyr and the Fourth Gospel" in *The Greek Orthodox Theological Review* 4 (1959), 115–34. Cullen, "I. K. Story" in *VigChr* 16 (1962), 172–8 (Justin on baptism); O. Giordano, "S. Giustino e il millenarismo" in *Asprenas* 10 (1963), 155–71. On the influence of Justin on Irenaeus, see F. Loofs, *Theophilus von Antiochien adversus Marcionem* (Leipzig 1930), 339–74.

TATIAN: E. Schwartz (Leipzig 1888), *TU* 4, 1; translation, *BKV* 12 (1913), 177–257. On the dating, see R. M. Grant in *HThR* 46 (1953), 99–101. Earlier literature in *Quasten P*, I, 220–8. The basic work at present is M. Elze, *Tatian und seine Theologie* (Göttingen 1960), with full bibliography, 130–4.

ATHENAGORAS: E. Schwartz (Leipzig 1891), *TU* 4, 2; P. Ubaldi and M. Pellegrino (Turin 1947); Geffcken, *op. cit.* 120–54, with commentary 155–238; English translation with commentary in *ACW* 23 (London 1956); H. A. Lucks, *The Philosophy of Athenagoras*

(Washington 1936); R. M. Grant, "Athenagoras or Pseudo-Athenagoras" in *HThR* 47 (1954), 121–9; idem, "Some Errors in the Legatio of Athenagoras" in *VigChr* (1958), 145–56.

THEOPHILUS: ed. by S. Frasca (Turin 1938); G. Bardy and J. Sender in *SourcesChr* 20 (1948); history of the text, R. M. Grant in *VigChr* 6 (1952), 146–59. General appreciation: E. Rapisarda, *Studi Ubaldi* (Milan 1937), 381–400; F. Loofs, *Theophilus von Antiochien adversus Marcionem* (Leipzig 1930), *TU* 46, 2, on which see J. Lebon, in *RHE* 26 (1930), 675–9, and R. M. Grant in *HThR* 40 (1947), 227–56; idem, "The Problem of Theophilus" in *HThR* 43 (1950), 179–96; A. Ziegler, *Festschrift G. Söhngen* (Freiburg i. Br. 1962), 332–6.

MELITO OF SARDES: the Fragments are in Routh, *Reliquiae Sacrae* (Oxford 1846), 111–53. Editions of the Homily: C. Bonner (London 1940); B. Lohse (Leiden 1958); M. Testuz (Cologne – Geneva 1960). On the text of the Homily see A. Wifstrand in *VigChr* 2 (1948), 211–23 and P. Nautin, in *RHE* 44 (1949), 429–38 (also against the authenticity); for its authenticity see esp. E. Peterson in *VigChr* 6 (1952), 33–43, and B. Lohse in the foreword to his edition; H. Chadwick, "A Latin Epitome of Melito's Homily on the Pascha" in *JThS NS* 11 (1960), 76–82. On his theology see A. Grillmeier in *ZKTh* 71 (1948), 5–14; idem in *Scholastik* 20–24 (1949), 481–502 (*Descensus Christi* and doctrine of original sin). On his doctrine of baptism see R. M. Grant in *VigChr* 4 (1950), 733–6. On his christology see R. Cantalamessa in *RSR* 37 (1963), 1–26.

LETTER TO DIOGNETUS: ed. by J. Geffcken (Heidelberg 1928); H.-I. Marrou in *SourcesChr* 33 (1951); English translation with commentary by A. Kleist in *ACW* 6 (1948); literature on the question of authorship in *Altaner* 136. On the contents see J. G. O'Neill in *IER* 85 (1956), 92–106.

HERMIAS: Text in *PG* 6, 1169–80, and H. Diels, *Doxographi graeci* (Berlin, 2nd ed. 1929); A. di Pauli, *Die Irrisio des Hermias* (Paderborn 1907); L. Alfonsi, *Ermia filosofo* (Brescia 1947).

15. *The Dispute with Gnosticism*

SOURCES

W. Völker, *Quellen zur Geschichte der christlichen Gnosis* (Tübingen 1932); H. Leisegang, *Die Gnosis* (Stuttgart, 4th ed. 1955); F. Sagnard, "Extraits de Théodote" in *SourcesChr* 23 (1948); G. Quispel, "Lettre de Ptolémée à Flora", ibid. 24 (1949); *Coptic Gnostic Writings*, I, ed. by C. Schmidt, *GCS* 13 (1905), new ed. by W. Till, *GCS* 45 (1959) (Contents: *Pistis Sophia*, the *2 Books of Jeû*, the *Apocryphon of John*); W. Till, *Die Gnostischen Schriften des Papyrus Berolinensis 8502, TU,* 60 (Berlin 1955) (Contents: *Gospel according to Mary, Apocryphon of John, Sophia Jesu Christi*); P. Labib, *Coptic Gnostic Papyri in the Coptic Museum at Old Cairo* I (Cairo 1950) (Photocopies of *Sermon on the Resurrection, Apocryphon of John, Gospel of Thomas, Gospel of Philip, On the Nature of Archons*); M. Malinine, H.-C. Puech, and G. Quispel, *Evangelium veritatis* (Zürich 1956); A. Guillaumont, H.-C. Puech . . ., *L'Évangile selon Thomas* (Leiden 1959) (Coptic text); J. Doresse, *L'évangile selon Thomas ou les paroles secrètes de Jésus* (Paris 1959); W. C. van Unnik, *Newly Discovered Gnostic Writings* (Naperville, Ill. 1960); J. Leipoldt and H. M. Schenke, *Koptisch-gnostische Schriften aus den Papyruscodices von Nag Hammadi* (Hamburg-Bergstadt 1960) (*Gospel of Thomas, Gospel of Philip, On the Nature of Archons*, with commentary); R. M. Grant and D. N. Freedman, *The Secret Sayings of Jesus* (London, 2nd ed. 1960); R. Grant, *Gnosticism: A Source Book of Heretical*

Writings from the Early Christian Period (New York 1961); K. Grobel, *The Gospel of Truth. A Valentinian Meditation on the Gospel*, trans. from the Coptic (Nashville 1960); A. Klijn, *The Acts of Thomas* (Leiden 1962); W. C. Till, *Das Evangelium nach Philippos* (Berlin 1963).

LITERATURE: 1. GENERAL

General accounts in *RGG* 3rd. ed. III, 1652–61; *LThK* IV, 1021–30; and *Altaner* 138–147. See further E. de Faye, *Gnostiques et Gnosticisme* (Paris, 2nd ed. 1925); F. C. Burkitt, *Church and Gnosis* (Cambridge 1932); G. Quispel, *Gnosis als Weltreligion* (Zürich 1951); H. Leisegang, *Die Gnosis* (Stuttgart 1955); H. Jonas, *Gnosis und spätantiker Geist*, I (Göttingen, 2nd ed. 1954), II/1 (Göttingen 1954); A.-J. Festugière, *La révélation d'Hermas Trismégiste*, IV: *Le Dieu inconnu et la gnose* (Paris 1954); G. van Moorsel, *The Mysteries of Hermas Trismegistus* (Utrecht 1955); H.-J. Schoeps, *Urgemeinde, Judenchristentum, Gnosis* (Tübingen 1956); W. Schmithals, *Die Gnosis in Korinth* (Göttingen 1956); W. Frei, *Geschichte und Idee der Gnosis* (Bern 1958); R. McL. Wilson, *The Gnostic Problem* (London 1958); R. Ambelais, *La notion gnostique du démiurge dans les écritures et les traditions judéo-chrétiennes* (Paris 1959); R. M. Grant, *Gnosticism and Early Christianity* (New York–London 1959); E. Peterson, *Frühkirche, Judentum und Gnosis* (Freiburg i. Br. 1959); C. Colpe, *Die religionsgeschichtliche Schule* I (Göttingen 1961).

2. THE DISCOVERIES AT NAG HAMMADI

H.-C. Puech, "Les nouveaux écrits gnostiques découverts en Haute-Égypte" in *Coptic Studies in Honour of W. E. Crum* (Boston 1950), 91–154; M. Schenke in *ZRGG* 14 (1962). On the Jung Codex: H. C. Puech and G. Quispel in *VigChr* 8 (1954), 1–51; 9 (1955), 65–102; F. L. Cross, *The Codex Jung* (London 1955); J. Doresse, *The Secret Books of the Egyptian Gnostics* (New York 1960). On the Gospel of Thomas: G. Quispel, "L'évangile selon Thomas et les Clémentines" in *VigChr* 12 (1958), 181–96; R. M. Grant, ibid. 13 (1959), 170–80; G. Quispel, "L'évangile selon Thomas et le Diatessaron", ibid. 13 (1959), 87–117; J. A. Fitzmyer, "The Oxyrhynchos Logoi of Jesus and the Coptic Gospel according to Thomas" in *ThSt* 20 (1959), 505–60; K. T. Schäfer, *Bibel und Leben*, 1 (1960), 62–74; O. Cullmann in *ThLZ* 85 (1960), 321–34; H. Montefiore, "A Comparison of the Parables of the Gospel according to Thomas and the Synoptic Gospels" in *NTS* 7 (1960), 220–48; C. H. Hunziger in *ZNW* suppl. 26 (1960), 209–30; R. Roques in *RHR* 157 (1960), 187–218; G. Scholem, *Jewish Gnosticism* (New York 1960); B. Gärtner, *The Theology of the Gospel of Thomas* (London 1961); R. Kasser, *L'évangile selon Thomas* (Neuchâtel 1961); R. Wilson, *The Gospel of Philip* (London 1962).

3. SPECIAL STUDIES

W. C. Till, "Die Gnosis in Ägypten" in *Parola del passato* 4 (1949), 230–49; G. Widengren, "Der iranische Hintergrund der Gnosis" in *ZRGG* 4 (1952), 97–114; E. Haenchen, "Gab es eine vorchristliche Gnosis?" in *ZThK* 49 (1952), 316–49; H. C. Puech, "La gnose et le temps" in *Eranos* 20 (1952), 57–113; W. H. C. Frend, "The Gnostic-Manichaean Tradition in Roman North Africa" in *JEH* 4 (1953), 13–26; idem, "The Gnostic Sects and the Roman Empire", ibid. 5 (1954), 25–37; R. McL. Wilson, "Gnostic Origins" in *VigChr* 9 (1955), 193–211; 11 (1957), 93–110; E. Segelberg, "The Coptic-Gnostic Gospel according to Philip and its Sacramental System" in *Numen* 7 (1960) 182–200; W. C. van Unnik, "Die jüdische Komponente in der Entstehung der Gnosis", ibid. 15 (1961), 65–82; G. Mead, *Fragments of Faith Forgotten* (Toronto 1960); J. G. Davies, "The Origins of Docetism" in *Studia Patristica* 6 (*TU* 81, Berlin 1962), 13–35; J. Maier, "Judentum und Gnosis" in *Kairos* 5 (1963), 18–40.

The Principal Manifestations of Gnosticism

1. BASILIDES: H. Waszink, "Basilides" in *RAC* I, 1217–25; G. Quispel, "L'homme gnostique. La doctrine de Basilide" in *Eranos* 16 (1948), 89–139; R. M. Grant, "Gnostic Origins and the Basilidians of Irenaeus" in *VigChr* 13 (1959), 121–5; W. Foerster, "Das System des Basilides" in *NTS* 9 (1962–3), 233–55.

2. VALENTINIAN GNOSIS: F.-M.-M. Sagnard, *La gnose Valentinienne et le témoignage de s. Irénée* (Paris 1947); G. Quispel, "La conception de l'homme dans la gnose Valentinienne" in *Eranos* 15 (1947), 249–86; idem, "The Original Doctrine of Valentine" in *VigChr* 1 (1947), 48–73; idem, "Neue Funde zur Valentinianischen Gnosis" in *ZRGG* 6 (1954), 289–305; O. Reimhers, "Irenaeus and the Valentinians" in *The Lutheran Quarterly* 12 (1960), 55–59; A. Orbe, "Estudios Valentinianos" in *AnGr* (1955), 113 (1961).

3. MARCION: A. von Harnack, *Marcion* (Leipzig, 2nd ed. 1924; new imp. Darmstadt 1961); E. Barnikol, *Die Entstehung der Kirche im 2. Jahrhundert und die Zeit Marcions* (Kiel, 2nd ed. 1933); R. S. Wilson, *Marcion* (London 1933); J. Knox, *Marcion and the New Testament* (Chicago 1942); E. C. Blackman, *Marcion and his Influence* (London 1949); F. M. Braun, "Marcion et la gnose Simonienne" in *Byz(B)* 25–7 (1955–7), 631–48; A. Salles, "Simon le magicien ou Marcion?" in *VigChr* 12 (1958), 197–224.

4. CHRISTIAN GNOSIS: E. Haenchen, "Das Buch Baruch und die christliche Gnosis" in *ZThK* 48 (1953), 123–58; C. Grant, "Earliest Christian Gnosticism" in *CH* 22 (1953), 81–98; L. Bouyer, "Gnosis, le sens orthodoxe de l'expression jusqu'aux pères Alexandrins" in *JThS NS* 4 (1953), 188–203; G. Quispel, "Christliche Gnosis und jüdische Heterodoxie" in *EvTh* 14 (1954), 474–84; H. Schlier, "Das Denken der frühchristlichen Gnosis" in *Neutestamentliche Studien für R. Bultmann* (Berlin 1954), 67–82.

The Church's Self-Defence and the Importance of the Christian Victory

TRADITION: J. Ranft, *Der Ursprung des katholischen Traditionsbegriffes* (Würzburg 1931); A. Deneffe, *Der Traditionsbegriff* (Münster 1931); B. Reynders, "Paradosis" in *RThAM* 5 (1933), 155–91; O. Cullmann, *Tradition* (Zürich 1954). For Irenaeus's idea of tradition, see the following articles: H. Holstein in *RSR* 36 (1949), 229–70; 41 (1953), 410–20; E. Molland in *JEH* 1 (1950), 12–28; E. Lanne in *Irénikon* 25 (1952), 113–41; A. Benoît in *RHPhR* 40 (1960), 32–43; M. Thurian, "La tradition" in *Verbum Caro* 57 (1961), 49–98. — Y. Congar, *La tradition et les traditions* (Paris 1960); G. Hanson, *Tradition in the Early Church* (London 1962); G. Widengren, "Tradition and Literature in Early Judaism and the Early Church" in *Numen* 10 (1963), 42–83.

APOSTOLIC SUCCESSION: C. H. Turner, *Apostolic Succession: Essays on the Early History of the Church and the Ministry*, ed. H. B. Swete (London, 2nd ed. 1921), 93–214; A. Ehrhardt, *The Apostolic Succession in the First Two Centuries of the Church* (London 1953); H. von Campenhausen, *Kirchliches Amt und geistliche Vollmacht in den ersten drei Jahrhunderten* (Tübingen 1953); H. E. W. Turner, *The Pattern of Truth* (London 1954); G. Dix, "The Ministry in the Early Church" in K. E. Kirk, *The Apostolic Ministry* (London, 2nd ed. 1957) 183–303; J. Colson, "La succession apostolique au niveau du Ier siècle" in *Verbum Caro* 54 (1960), 138–72; E. Schlink, "Die apostolische Sukzession" in *KuD* 7 (1961), 79–114; A. Benoît, "L'apostolicité au second siècle" in *Verbum Caro* 58 (1961), 173–84; G. Blum, *Tradition and Sukzession* (Berlin 1963).

THE ESTABLISHMENT OF THE CANON: A. Wikenhauser, *New Testament Introduction* (Freiburg–London–New York, 4th imp. 1963), 18–35; M.-J. Lagrange, *Histoire ancienne du canon du N.T.* (Paris 1933); R. M. Grant, "The Bible of Theophilus of Antioch" in *JBL* 66

(1947), 173–96. For Marcion, see the works by J. Knox and E. C. Blackman mentioned at the beginning of the bibliography to this chapter. W. L. Dulière, "Le canon néotestamentaire et les écrits chrétiens approuvés par Irénée" in *NC* 6 (1954), 199–234; R. Harris, *Inspiration and Canonicity of the Bible* (Grand Rapids 1957); H. Bacht, "Die Rolle der Tradition in der Kanonbildung" in *Catholica* 12 (1958), 16–37; W. Marxsen and C. H. Ratschow in *NZSTh* 2 (1960), 137–50, 150–60; Y. Congar, "Inspiration des écritures canoniques et apostolicité de l'église" in *RSPhTh* 45 (1961), 32–42; W. van Unnik, Ἡ καινὴ διαθήκη, *TU* 79 (1961), 212–27; K. Aland, *The Problem of the N.T. Canon* (London 1962).

THE CREED: H. Lietzmann, "Symbolstudien" in *ZNW* 2 (1922); 26 (1927) repr. in *Kleine Schriften* III (Berlin 1962), 189–281; J. Lebreton, *Histoire du dogme de la trinité*, I (Paris 1928), 141–73; J. de Ghellinck, "Les recherches sur l'origine du symbole" in *RHE* 38 (1942), 91–142, 361–410; O. Cullmann, *Les premières confessions de la foi chrétienne* (Paris, 2nd ed. 1948); J. N. D. Kelly, *Early Christian Creeds* (London 1950); W. Trillhaas, *Die apostolischen Glaubensbekenntnisse* (Witten 1953).

HEGESIPPUS: K. Mras, "Die Hegesippfrage" in *AnzAW* 95 (1958), 143–53; W. Telfer, "Was Hegesippus a Jew?" in *HThR* 53 (1960), 134–53; N. Hyldahl, "Hegesipps Hypomnemoneumata" in *StTh* 14 (1960), 70–113.

IRENAEUS: W. W. Harvey's ed. (Cambridge 1857) was reprinted unaltered in 1949; J. Keble, *Five Books of St Irenaeus, Bishop of Lyons, Against Heresies* (Oxford 1872). A new critical ed. by F. Sagnard is appearing in *SourcesChr*.; Book III has already been published, 34 (Paris 1952), on this see P. Nautin *RThAM* 20 (1953), 185–202, B. Botte, ibid. 21 (1954), 165–78 and *ACW* 16 (1952), *Proof of the Apostolic Preaching*. A new French translation of the *Demonstratio evangelica* with commentary by L.-M. Froidevaux in *SourcesChr* 62 (Paris 1959). Other works on Irenaeus: A. Benoît, *S. Irénée. Introduction à l'étude de sa théologie* (Paris 1960; with bibliography 257–62); J. Lawson, *The Biblical Theology of Saint Irenaeus* (London 1948); W. Leuthold, *Das Wesen der Häresie nach Irenäus* (diss. Zürich 1954); L. Thornton, "St Irenaeus and Contemporary Theology", *TU* 64 (1957), 317–30. G. Wingren, *Man and the Incarnation* (Philadelphia 1959); E. Lanne, "La vision de Dieu dans l'Œuvre de s. Irénée" in *Irenikon* 33 (1960), 311–20; V. Hahn, "Schrift, Tradition und Primat bei Irenaeus", in *TThZ* 70 (1961), 233–43, 292–302; B. Reynders, "Premières réactions de l'église devant les falsifications du dépot apostolique" in *L'infallibilité de l'église* (Chevetogne 1963), 27–52; H. Dörries, "Urteil und Verurteilung – Ein Beitrag zum Umgang der alten Kirche mit Häretikern" in *ZNW* 55 (1964), 78–94.

16. *The Rise of Montanism and the Church's Defence*

SOURCES

P. de Labriolle, *Les sources de l'histoire du Montanisme* (Paris 1913); N. Bonwetsch, *Texte zur Geschichte des Montanismus* (Bonn 1914), *KlT* 129.

LITERATURE

P. de Labriolle, *La crise Montaniste* (Paris 1913); W. M. Calder, "Philadelphia and Montanism" in *BJRL* 7 (1923), 309–54; W. M. Ramsey, "Phrygian Orthodox and Heretics" in *ByZ* 6 (1931), 1–35; J. Zeiller, "Le Montanisme a-t-il pénétré en Illyricum?" in *RHE* 30 (1934), 847–51; H. Bacht, "Die prophetische Inspiration in der kirchlichen

Reflexion der vormontanistischen Zeit" in *ThQ* 125 (1944), 1–18; G. Freeman, "Montanism and the Phrygian cults" in *DomSt* 3 (1950), 297–316; S. S. P. Freeman-Grenville, "The Date of the Outbreak of Montanism" in *JEH* 5 (1954), 7–15; K. Aland, "Der Montanismus und die kleinasiatische Theologie" in *ZNW* 46 (1955), 109–16, *Kirchengeschichtliche Entwürfe* (Gütersloh 1960), 105–11; idem, "Augustin und der Montanismus"; ibidem, 149–64.

17. The Expansion of Christianity down to the End of the Second Century

GENERAL

W. M. Ramsey, *The Church in the Roman Empire before 170* (London, 13th ed. 1913); A. von Harnack, *Die Mission und Ausbreitung des Christentums in den ersten drei Jahrhunderten* (2 vols. Leipzig, 4th ed. 1924), Eng. tr. *The Mission and Expansion of Christianity in the First Three Centuries*, I (New York, 2nd ed. 1962); F. J. Foakes-Jackson, *The Rise of Gentile Christianity (to 150)* (London 1927); K. S. Latourette, *A History of the Expansion of Christianity*, I (New York 1937); G. Bardy, *La conversion au christianisme durant les premiers siècles* (Paris 1949); B. Kötting, "Christentum (Ausbreitung)" in *RAC* II (1954), 1138–59; P. Carrington, *The Early Christian Church*, II: *The Second Century* (Cambridge 1957); F. van der Meer and C. Mohrmann, *Atlas of the Early Christian World* (London 1958).

SPECIAL STUDIES

K. Pieper, *Die Kirche Palästinas bis zum Jahre 135* (Cologne 1938); C. Korolevsky, "Antioche" in *DHGE* III, 563–72; V. Schultze, *Altchristliche Städte und Landschaften*, III: *Antiochien* (Gütersloh 1930); J. Kollwitz, "Antiochien" in *RAC* I, 461–9; I. Ortiz de Urbina, "Le origini del cristianesimo in Edessa" in *Gr* 15 (1934), 82–91; H. Leclercq, "Edesse" in *DACL* IV, 2055–110; E. Kirsten, "Edessa" in *RAC* IV, 568–72; M. Höfner, "Arabien" in *RAC* I, 579–85; R. Devreesse, "Le christianisme dans la province d'Arabie" in *Vivre et Penser* 2 (1942), 110–46; N. Edelby, "La Transjordanie chrétienne des origines aux croisades" in *PrOrChr* 6 (1956), 97–117; A. Böhlig, "Ägypten" in *RAC* I, 128–38; E. R. Hardy, *Christian Egypt* (New York 1952); H. I. Bell, *Cults and Creeds in Greco-Roman Egypt* (Liverpool 1954); H. Leclercq, "Rome" in *DACL* XIV/2, 2546–67; G. de la Piana, "The Roman Church at the End of the Second Century" in *HThR* 18 (1925), 201 ff.; A. Audollent, "Afrique" *DHGE* I, 706–12; A. M. Schneider, "Afrika" in *RAC* I, 173–9; J. Mesnage, *L'Afrique chrétienne* (Paris 1912); C. Cecchelli, *Africa Christiana — Africa Romana* (Rome 1936); J. Ferron, "Carthage chrétienne" in *DHGE* XI, 1178–87; W. H. C. Frend, "The 'seniores Laici' and the Origins of the Church of North Africa" in *JThS NS* 12 (1961), 280–4; E. Griffe, *La Gaule chrétienne*, I (Paris 1947), 7–50; R. Kasser, "Les origines du christianisme égyptien" in *RThPh* 12 (1962), 11–28; L. W. Barnard, "The Background of Early Egyptian Christianity" in *ChQR* 164 (1963), 300–10, 428–41; W. H. C. Frend, "A Note on the Influence of Greek Immigrants on the Spread of Christianity in the West" in *Festschrift T. Klauser* (Münster 1964), 125–9.

Part Two:

The Great Church of Early Christian Times

(c. A.D. 180–324)

GENERAL LITERATURE

A. Ehrhard, *Die Kirche der Märtyrer* (Munich 1932); *Fliche–Martin* II; *Lietzmann* II, 219–329, III, 1–67.

ON THE ROMAN EMPIRE IN THE THIRD CENTURY: M. Besnier, *L'empire romain de l'avènement des Sévères au concile de Nicée* (Paris 1937); *The Cambridge Ancient History*, XII (Cambridge 1939); E. Kornemann, *Weltgeschichte des Mittelmeerraumes*, II (Munich 1949), 174–288; F. Altheim, *Niedergang der alten Welt*, II: *Imperium Romanum* (Frankfurt a. M. 1952); J. Geffcken, *Der Ausgang des griechisch-römischen Heidentums* (Heidelberg, 2nd ed. 1929); L. Pareti, *Storia di Roma e del mondo Romano*, vol. VI: *Da Decio a Costantino* (Turin 1961).

SECTION ONE

The Inner Consolidation of the Church in the Third Century

18. *The Attack of the Pagan State on the Church*

SOURCES

As for Chapter 9 above. The *acta* of the martyrs are referred to in the footnotes. New critical edition of Tertullian's *Ad martyras* by A. Quacquarelli (Rome 1963).

LITERATURE

K. Bihlmeyer, *Die syrischen Kaiser zu Rom und das Christentum* (Rottenburg 1916); L. Homo, *Les empereurs romains et le christianisme* (Paris 1931); A. Quacquarelli, "La persecuzione secondo Tertulliano" in *Gr* 31 (1950), 562–89; L. Koep, "Antikes" Kaisertum und Christusbekenntnis im Widerspruch" in *JbAC* 4 (1961) 58–76; G. de Ste Croix, "Why were the Early Christians Persecuted?" in *Past and Present* (1963), 6–38.

SEPTIMIUS SEVERUS: A. Calderini, *I Severi* (Bologna 1949); M. Fluss in *Pauly–Wissowa* A 2 (1923), 1940–2002; M. Platnauer, *Life and Reign of Septimius Severus* (Oxford

1918); U. Instinsky, "Studien zu Septimius Severus" in *Klio* 35 (1942), 200–19; J. Straub, "Caracalla" in *RAC* II, 893–901 (with bibliography); K. Gross, "Elagabal" in *RAC* IV, 998–1000; J. Straub, "Alexander Severus" in *LThK* I, 312 ff.; A. Alföldi, "Der Rechtsstreit zwischen der römischen Kirche und dem Verein der popinarii" in *Klio* 31 (1938), 249–53; A. A. Schwarte, "Das angebliche Christengesetz des Septimius Severus" in *Historia* 12 (1963), 185–208.

DECIUS: K. Gross in *RAC* III, 611–29. As sources the following are important: Cyprian, *De lapsis,* and *Epist.* 5–43, 55–6, 65–7; Dionysius of Alexandria in *Euseb. HE* 6, 39 to 42, and cf. H. Delehaye in *AnBoll* 40 (1922), 9–17.
E. Liesering, *Untersuchungen zur Christenverfolgung des Kaisers Decius* (diss. Würzburg 1933); A. Alföldi in *Klio* 31 (1938), 323–48; C. Saumagne, "La persécution de Dèce à Carthage d'après la correspondance de s. Cyprien" in *Bulletin soc. nat. antiquaires de France* (1957), 23–42; idem, "La persécution de Dèce en Afrique" in *Byz* 32 (1962), 1–29.
Texts of the *libelli: POr* IV, 2; XVIII, 3; *RB* 54 (1947), 365–9, and cf. R. Knipfing in *HThR* 16 (1923), 345–90; also *DACL* 9 (1930), 81–5; A. Bludau in *RQ* Supplement 27 (1927).

THE VALERIAN PERSECUTION: P. Franchi de' Cavalieri in *SteT* 9 (1902), 39–51; 27 (1915), 65–82; 33 (1920), 147–78; 65 (1935), 129–99; P. Healy, *The Valerian Persecution* (Boston 1905); P. Paschini, "La persecuzione di Valeriano" in *Studi Romani* 6 (Rome 1958), 130–7.

19. *Further Development of Christian Literature in the East in the Third Century*

GENERAL LITERATURE

Bardenhewer II; *Quasten P,* II; *Altaner* 212 ff.; D. van den Eynde, *Les normes de l'enseignement chrétien dans la littérature patristique des trois premiers siècles* (Gembloux 1933); J. Daniélou, *Message évangélique et culture hellénistique aux II* et *III* siècles (Tournai 1961); P. Nautin, *Lettres et écrivains chrétiens des II* et *III* siècles (Paris 1961).

SCHOOL OF ALEXANDRIA

W. Bousset, *Jüdisch-christlicher Schulbetrieb in Alexandrien und Rom* (Göttingen 1915); G. Bardy, "Les écoles romaines au second siècle" in *RHE* 28 (1932), 501–32; idem, "L'église et l'enseignement pendant les trois premiers siècles" in *RevSR* 12 (1932), 1–28; L. Allevi, *Ellenismo e cristianesimo* (Milan 1934); G. Bardy, "Pour l'histoire de l'école d'Alexandrie" in *Vivre et penser* 2 (Paris 1942), 80–109; L. López Oreja, "Alejandría, su escueala, un maestro" in *Helmantica* I (1950), 402–52; A. Knauber, "Katechetenschule oder Schulkatechumetat? Um die rechte Deutung des 'Unternehmens' der ersten großen Alexandriner" in *TThZ* 60 (1951), 243–66; P. Brezzi, *La gnosi cristiana e le antiche scuole cristiane* (Rome 1950); E. A. Parsons, *The Alexandrian Library, Glory of the Hellenic World* (London 1952).
R. Cadiou, *La jeunesse d'Origène. Histoire de l'école d'Alessandrie au début du III* siècle (Paris 1936); G. Bardy, "Aux origines de l'école d'Alexandrie" in *RSR* 27 (1937), 65–90; M. Hornschuh, "Das Leben des Origenes und die Entstehung der alexandrinischen Schule" in *ZKG* 71 (1960), 1–25, 193–214; R. B. Tollinton, *Alexandrian*

Teaching on the Universe (New York 1932); E. Molland, *The Conception of the Gospel in the Alexandrian Theology* (Oslo 1938); J. Guillet, "Les exégèses d'Alexandrie et d'Antioche: Conflit ou malentendu?" in *RSR* 34 (1947), 247–302; H. de Lubac, "Typologie et allégorisme" in *RSR* 34 (1947), 180–226; ibid. 47 (1959), 5–43; W. Gruber, *Die pneumatische Exegese bei den Alexandrinern* (Graz 1957); R. Cadiou, "La bibliothèque de Césarée et la formation des Chaînes" in *RevSR* 16 (1936) 474–83; G. Lattey, "The Antiochene Text" in *Scripture* 4 (1951), 273–77; F. Pericoli Ridolfini, "Le origini della scuola di Alessandria" in *RSO* 37 (1962), 211–30.

PANTAINUS: G. Gnolfo in *PrOrChr* 1 (1951), 295–304; P. Nautin in *Tome commémoratif du millénaire de la Bibliothèque d'Alexandrie* (Alexandria 1953), 145–52; A. Parsons, "A Family of Philosophers at Athens and Alexandria" in *Hesperia Suppl.* VIII (1950).

CLEMENT

WORKS in *GCS*, 4 vols. (1905–36, 2nd ed. 1936–60), edited by O. Stählin; also *SourcesChr* 2 (2nd ed. 1949): *Protrepticus;* 30 (1951): *Stromata* I; 38 (1954): *Stromata* II; 70 (1960): *Paidagogus* I; 23 (1948): *Excerpta ex Theodoto.* This latter work also edited by R. P. Casey (London 1934). Eng. *ANF* 2 (New York 1905).

LITERATURE: J. Munck, *Untersuchungen über Klemens von Alexandrien* (Stuttgart 1933); G. Lazzati, *Introduzione allo studio di Clem. Alex.* (Milan 1939); C. Mondésert, *Clément d'Alexandrie. Introduction à l'étude de sa pensée religieuse* (Paris 1944); M. S. Enslin, "A Gentleman among the Fathers" in *HThR* 47 (1954), 213–41; M. Pohlenz, *Klemens von Alexandrien und sein hellenistisches Christentum* (Göttingen 1943); T. Camelot, *Foi et gnose. Introduction à l'étude de la connaissance mystique chez Clément d'Alexandrie* (Paris 1945); F. Quatember, *Die christliche Lebenshaltung des Klemens von Alexandrien nach seinem Pädagogus* (Vienna 1946); T. Rüther, *Die sittliche Forderung der Apatheia bei Klemens von Alexandrien* (Freiburg i. Br. 1949); W. Völker, *Der wahre Gnostiker nach Klemens von Alexandrien* (Berlin 1952); E. F. Osborne, *The Philosophy of Clement of Alexandria* (Cambridge 1957); K. Prümm, "Glaube und Erkenntnis nach Klemens von Alexandrien" in *Scholastik* 12 (1937), 17–57; J. Lebreton, "La théologie de la Trinité chez Clément d'Alexandrie" in *RSR* 34 (1947), 55–76, 142–79; J. Moingt, "La gnose de Clément d'Alexandrie dans ses rapports avec la foi et la philosophie" in *RSR* 37 (1950), 195–241, 381–421, 537–64; ibid. 38 (1951), 82–118; A. Orbe, "Teología bautismal de Clem. Alex." in *Gr* 36 (1955), 410–48; F. Hofmann, "Die Kirche bei Klemens von Alexandrien" in *Festgabe K. Adam* (1956), 11–57; J. Wytzes, "The Twofold Way: Platonic Influences in the Work of Clement of Alexandria" in *VigChr* II (1957), 226–45; ibid. 14 (1960), 129–53; E. Fascher, *Der Logos-Christus als göttlicher Lehrer bei Clemens von Alexandrien, Studien zum NT und zur Patristik, TU* 77 (Berlin 1961), 193–207; T. Finan, "Hellenism and Judeo–Christian History in Clement of Alexandria" in *ITQ* 28 (1961), 83–114; G. W. Butterworth, *Clement of Alexandria with an English Translation (Loeb Classical Library)* (London – New York 1919); *Christ the Educator, FC* 23 (1954).

ORIGEN

WORKS in *GCS*, 12 volumes so far (Berlin 1899–1959), edited by P. Koetschau, E. Klostermann, E. Preuschen, W. A. Baehrens, M. Rauer; Engl. *ANF* 10 (New York 1903), Commentary on John and Matthew; *ACW* 19 (1954): *Exhortation to Martyrdom;* 26 (1957): *The Song of Songs; SourcesChr* 7 (1944): *Homilies on Genesis* (French translation only); 16 (1947): *Homilies on Exodus* (French translation only); 29 (1951): *Homilies on Numbers* (French translation only); 37 (1954): *Homilies on the Canticle*

484

of Canticles; 67 (1960): *Dialogue with Heracleides;* 71 (1960): *Homilies on Josue;* 87 (1962): *Homilies on Luke; Philocalia,* ed. J. A. Robinson (Cambridge 1893); *Hexapla Fragments,* ed. F. Field, 2 vols. (Oxford 1871-5); R. Cadiou, *Commentaires inédits des Psaumes* (Paris 1935); J. Scherer, *Le commentaire d'Origène sur Rom. 3:5-5:7* (Cairo 1955); idem, *Extraits des livres I et II du Contra Celsum d'Origène* (Cairo 1956). German translation *BKV (De orat.; exhort. mart.); 52-53 (Contra Celsum); Commentary on St John's Gospel* (Selections), R. Gögler (Einsiedeln 1959). Selections from the works as a whole, Hans Urs von Balthasar (Salzburg, 2nd ed. 1954).

GENERAL SURVEYS: G. Bardy: *DThC* XI, 1489-1565; H. Koch: *Pauly—Wissowa* 18/1, 1036-56; F. H. Kettler: *RGG,* 3rd ed. IV, 1692-1701; E. de Faye, *Origène,* 3 vols. (Paris 1923-30); R. Cadiou, *Introduction au système d'Origène* (Paris 1932); J. Daniélou, *Origen* (New York 1955), H. Musurillo, "The recent revival of Origen studies" in *ThSt* 24 (1963), 250-63; J. Daniélou, "Origène comme Exégète de la Bible" in *Stud. patrist.* 1 (*TU* 63, Berlin 1957), 280-90, H. Crouzel, "Origène est-il un systématique?" in *BLE* 60 (1959), 81-116.

SPECIAL STUDIES: W. Völker, *Die Vollkommenheitslehre des Origenes* (Tübingen 1931); H. Koch, *Pronoia und Paideusis* (Leipzig 1932); A. Lieske, *Die Theologie der Logos-mystik bei Origenes* (Münster 1938); C. Vagaggini, *Maria nelle opere di Orig.* (Rome 1942); S. Bettencourt, *Doctrina ascetica Orig.* (Rome 1945); E. Latko, *Origen's Concept of Penance* (Quebec 1949); H. de Lubac, *Histoire et esprit. L'intelligence de l'Écriture d'après Origène* (Paris 1950); J. Daniélou, *From Shadows to Reality* (London 1960); F. Bertrand, *Mystique de Jésus chez Origène* (Paris 1951); R. P. C. Hanson, *Origen's Doctrine on Tradition* (London 1954); E. C. Jay, *Origen's Treatise on Prayer* (London 1954); H. Crouzel, *Théologie de l'image de Dieu chez Origène* (Paris 1956); M. Harl, *Origène et la fonction révélatrice du verbe incarné* (Paris 1958, with comprehensive bibliography); G. Teichweier, *Die Sündenlehre des Origenes* (Regensburg 1958); F. Faessler, *Der Hagiosbegriff bei Origenes* (Fribourg 1958); R. P. C. Hanson, *Allegory and Event. A Study of the Sources and Significance of Origen's Interpretation of Scripture* (London 1959); H. Crouzel, *Origène et la philosophie* (Paris, 2nd ed. 1962); B. Drewery, *Origen and the Doctrine of Grace* (London 1960); P. Nemeshegyi, *La paternité de Dieu chez Origène* (Tournai 1960); H. Crouzel, *Origène et 'la connaissance mystique'* (Bruges 1961); G. Gruber, *Ζωή. Wesen, Stufen und Mitteilungen des Lebens bei Origenes* (Munich 1961).

ARTICLES ON THE THEOLOGY OF ORIGEN: Hans Urs von Balthasar, "Le mystère d'Origène" in *RSR* 26 (1936), 513-62; 27 (1937), 38-64; H. Rahner, "Das Menschenbild des Origenes" in *Eranos* 15 (1947), 197-248; J.-F. Bonnefoy, "Origène, théoricien de la méthode théologique" in *Mélanges Cavallera* (Toulouse 1948), 87-145; K. Rahner, "La doctrine d'Origène sur la pénitence" in *RSR* 37 (1950), 47-97, 252-86, 422-56; C. Vagaggini, "La natura della sintesi Origeniana e l'ortodossia e l'eterodossia della dogmatica di Origene" in *SC* 82 (1954), 169-200; A. Méhat, "Apocatastase" in *VigChr* 10 (1956), 196-214; G. Müller, "Origenes und die Apokatastasis" in *ThZ* 14 (1958), 161-90; E. von Ivánka, "Der geistige Ort von Περὶ ἀρχῶν zwischen Neuplatonismus, Gnosis und der christlichen Rechtgläubigkeit" in *Scholastik* 35 (1960), 481-502; V. Peri, "I passi sulla trinità nelle omelie origeniane" in *Studia Patristica* 6 (*TU* 81 [1962]), 155-80; M. Simonetti, "Due note sull'angelologia origeniana" in *Rivista di cultura classica mediaevale* 4 (1962), 165-208.

ARTICLES ON ORIGEN'S SPIRITUAL DOCTRINE: K. Rahner "Les débuts d'une doctrine des cinq sens spirituels chez Origène" in *RAM* 13 (1932), 113-145; J. Daniélou, "Les sources bibliques de la mystique d'Origène" in *RAM* 23 (1947), 126-141; H. Jonas,

"Die origenistische Spekulation und Mystik" in *ThZ* 5 (1949), 24–45, and in the contrary sense J. Lebreton in *AnBoll* 67 (1949), 542–76; K. Baus, "Das Nachwirken des Origenes in der Christusfrömmigkeit des heiligen Ambrosius" in *RQ* 49 (1954), 21–55; H. Crouzel, *Virginité et Mariage selon Origène* (Paris 1963).

Dionysius of Alexandria: Engl. *ANF* 6 (New York 1903); C. L. Feltoe, *The Letters and Other Remains* (Cambridge 1904); P. S. Miller, *Studies in Dionysius the Great of Alexandria* (diss. Erlangen 1933); H. G. Opitz, "Dionys und die Libyer" in *Studies K. Lake* (London 1937), 41–53.

Peter of Alexandria: Fragments: *PG* 18, 449–522; *POR* I, 383–400; 3, 353–61. F. H. Kettler in *Pauly–Wissowa*, 19/2, 1281–8; E. W. Kemp, "Bishops and Presbyters at Alexandria" in *JEH* 6 (1955), 125–42.

Gregory Thaumaturgus: Works: *PG* 10, 963–1232; Engl. *ANF* 6 (1903); "On Origen" ed. by P. Koetschau (Leipzig 1894). L. Froidevaux, "Le symbole de s. Grégoire le Thaumaturge" in *RSR* 19 (1929), 193–247; W. Telfer, "The Cultus of St Gregory Thaumaturgus" in *HThR* 29 (1936), 225–344; A. Soloview, "S. Grégoire, patron de Bosnie" in *Byz* (B) 19 (1949), 263–79.

Methodius: Works, edited by N. Bonwetsch in *GCS* (Berlin 1917); *De autexusio* in *POR* 22, 5; Engl. *ACW* 27 (Westminster 1958): *The Symposium; ANF* 6 (New York 1903).
J. Farges, *Les idées morales et religieuses de Méthode d'Olympe* (Paris 1929); K. Quensell, *Die wahre Stellung und Tätigkeit des Methodius von Olymp* (diss. Heidelberg 1952); V. Buchheit, *Studien zu Methodius von Olymp* (Berlin 1958); M. Pellegrino, *L'inno di simposio di s. Metodio* (Turin 1958, with text and commentary).

Lucian and the School of Antioch: G. Bardy, *Recherches sur Lucien d'Antioche et son école* (Paris 1936); H. Dörries, "Zur Geschichte der Septuaginta" in *ZNW* 39 (1940), 57–110; A. Vaccari, "La 'teoria' della scuola antiochena" in *Scritti di erudizione* (Rome 1942), 101–42; G. Mercati, "Di alcune testimonianze antiche sulle cure bibliche di San Luciano" in *Biblica* 24 (1943), 1–17; F. Alvarez Seisdedos, "La teoría antioquena" in *EstB* II (1952), 31–67; P. Ternant, "La θεωρία d'Antioche dans le cadre de l'Écriture" in *Biblica* 34 (1953), 135–58, 354–83, 456–86.

20. The Development of Christian Literature in the West in the Third Century

P. de Labriolle, *History and Literature of Christianity* (London–New York, 2nd ed. 1947).

Early Christian Latin: F. Stummer, *Einführung in die lateinische Bibel* (Paderborn 1928); J. Schrijnen, *Charakteristik des altchristlichen Latein* (Nijmegen 1932); W. Süss, *Studien zur lateinischen Bibel* (Tartu 1932); M. A. Sainio, *Semasiologische Untersuchungen über die Entstehung der christlichen Latinität* (Hamburg 1940); M. Müller, *Der Übergang von der griechischen zur lateinischen Sprache in der abendländischen Kirche von Hermas bis Novatian* (Rome 1943); T. Klauser, "Der Übergang der römischen Kirche von der griechischen zur lateinischen Liturgiesprache" in *MiscMercati* I, 467–82; G. Bardy, *La question des langues dans l'église ancienne*, I (Paris 1948); K. Baus in *TThZ* 61 (1952), 192–205; ibid. 68 (1959), 306–15 (with bibliography); C. Mohrmann, "Les origines de la latinité chrétienne à Rome" in *VigChr* 3 (1949), 67–106, 163–185. Further works of Mohrmann in the collected volumes: *Le latin des chrétiens*, I (Rome 1958); II (Rome 1961); *Liturgical Latin* (London 1959); E. Löfstedt,

Late Latin (Oslo 1959); M. Dilworth, "The Morphology of Christian Latin" in *The Clergy Review* 45 (1960) 88–97; E. Franceschini, "Latino dei Cristiani e Latino della Chiesa" in *Mélanges C. Mohrmann* (Utrecht 1963), 152–64.

MINUCIUS FELIX: Editions of the Works: J. P. Waltzing (Leipzig 1926); J. Martin (Bonn 1930); G. Quispel (Leyden 1949); M. Pellegrino (Turin 1950); Engl. *ANF* 4 (New York 1905); *FC* 10 (New York 1950). H. J. Baylis, *Minucius Felix and his Place among the Early Fathers of the Latin Church* (London 1928); R. Beutler, *Philosophie und Apologetik bei Minucius Felix* (Diss. Marburg 1936); M. Pellegrino, *Studi sull'antica apologetica* (Rome 1947). On the problem of the priority of Minucius Felix or Tertullian, and on the language of the *Octavius,* see *Quasten P,* II, 160–2.

HIPPOLYTUS: Works, edited by G. N. Bonwetsch, H. Achelis, P. Wendland, A. Bauer, R. Helm, in *GCS* 1, 26, 46 (Berlin 1916–55); Engl. *ANF* 5 (New York 1903). P. Nautin, *Hippolyte, Contre les hérésies* (Paris 1949); M. Brière–L. Mariès–B. C. Mercier, *Hippolyte, Les bénédictions d'Isaac, de Jacob et de Moïse, POR* 27 (1954), B. Botte, *La tradition apostolique de s. Hippolyte. Essai de reconstruction* (Münster 1963). Separate editions: *Commentary on Daniel* ed. by G. Bardy in *SourcesChr* 14 (1947); *Traditio Apostolica,* edited B. Botte in *SourcesChr* 11 (1946); Funk 2, 97–119; G. Dix (London 1937); Ethiopian text edited by H. Duensing in *AAG* 32 (1946); Coptic text, edited W. Till–J. Leipoldt in *TU* 58 (1954). Literature on the most recent discussion regarding the authorship of the *Philosophoumena,* the *Chronicle* and the *De universo:* P. Nautin, *Hippolyte et Josipe* (Paris 1947); idem, *Le dossier d'Hippolyte et de Méliton* (Paris 1953); idem, *Lettres et écrivains chrétiens des IIᵉ et IIIᵉ siècles* (Paris 1961), 177 to 207; for a contrary view see G. Bardy, M. Richard, B. Capelle, B. Botte, G. Oggioni in *MSR* 1948, 1950–1, 1953–4; *RThAM* 1949–50, 1952; *RSR* 1947, 1954–5; *RHE* 1952; *SC* 1950–52; A. de Alès, *La théologie de s. Hippolyte* (Paris, 2nd ed. 1929); B. Capelle, "Le logos, fils de Dieu, dans la théologie d'Hippolyte" in *RThAM* 9 (1937), 109–24; K. Prümm, "Mysterion bei Hippolyt" in *ZKTh* 63 (1939), 207–25; E. Lengling, *Die Heilstat des Logos-Christos bei Hippolyt* (Rome 1947); A. Hamel, *Die Kirche bei Hippolyt von Rom* (Gütersloh 1952); J. Lecuyer, "Épiscopat et presbytérat dans les écrits d'Hippolyte" in *RSR* 41 (1953), 30–50; A. Amore, "Note su s. Ippolito martire" in *RivAC* 30 (1954), 63–97; C. Edsman, "A Typology of Baptism in Hippolytus" in *TU* 64 (1957), 35–40; J.-M. Hanssens, *La liturgie d'Hippolyte* (Rome 1959), criticized by T. G. Davies in *JTS* 11 (1960), 163–6; B. Botte in *BThAM* 8 (1960), 575–7; A. Amore, "La personalità dello scrittore Ippolito" in *Antonianum* 36 (1961), 3–28. A. Walls, "The Latin Version of Hippolytus' Apostolic Tradition" in *TU* 78 (1961), 155–62; G. Ogg, "Hippolytus and the Introduction of the Christian Era" in *VigChr* 16 (1962), 2–18; B. Botte, *La tradition apostolique de S. Hippolyte* (Münster 1963), on this C. Lambert in *RBén* 74 (1964), 144–7.

NOVATIAN: No collected edition exists. Works: *De trinitate,* ed. W. Y. Fausset (Cambridge 1909); with German translation, and commentary by H. Weyer (Düsseldorf 1962); Engl. *ANF* 5 (New York 1903); *Concerning the Trinity, On the Jewish Meats, De cibis iud.* edited by A. Landgraf–C. Weymann in *Archlat Lexikogr.,* 11 (1898 to 1900) 221–49; *De spect.,* edited by A. Boulenger (Paris 1933), and see on this H. Koch in *Religio* 12 (1936), 245–65. On language and style, A. Boulenger in *Religio* 13 (1937), 278–94; B. Melin, *Studia in corpus Cyprianeum* (Uppsala 1946).

A. d'Alès, *Novatien* (Paris 1924); M. Kriebel, *Studien zur älteren Entwicklung der abendländischen Trinitätslehre bei Tertullian und Novatian* (diss. Marburg 1932); M. Simonetti, "Alcune osservazioni sul De trinitate di Novaziano" in *Studi in onore di A. Monteverdi* 2 (Modena 1959), 771–83. On the Logos doctrine: G. Keilbach in *Bogoslovska Smotra* 21 (1933), 193–224. On the *communicatio idiomatum:* R. Favre in *BLE*

37 (1936), 130–45. On angel Christology: F. Scheidweiler in *ZKG* 66 (1955), 126–39, and J. Barbel in *TThZ* 67 (1958) 96–105. On Novatian's biography: F. J. Dölger in *AuC* II (1930), 258–67; C. Mohlberg in *ELit* 51 (1937), 242–9; A. Ferrua in *CivCatt* (1944) 4, 232–9.

TERTULLIAN: Works in a collected edition, in *CSEL*, edited by A. Reifferscheid – G. Wissowa, A. Kroymann, H. Hoppe, V. Bulhart, P. Borleffs 20 (1890), 47 (1906), 69 (1939), 70 (1942), 76 (1957); and in *CChr* 1 and 2 (1954). For editions of individual works see *Altaner* 166–82, and *CChr* 1, XII–XIV. Engl. *ANF* 3 and 4 (1905); *Treatises on Marriage and Remarriage*, *ACW* 13 (1951); *The Treatise against Hermogenes* 24 (1956); *Treatises on Penance*, 28 (1959); apologetical works, *FC* 10 (1951); disciplinary, moral and ascetical works, *FC* 40 (1959); *On baptism*, ed. E. Evans (London 1964); *Against the Jews*, ed. H. Tränkle (Wiesbaden 1964).

On Language and Style: T. W. Teuwen, *Sprachlicher Bedeutungswandel bei Tertullian* (Paderborn 1926); E. Löfstedt, *Zur Sprache Tertullians* (Lund 1920); H. Hoppe, *Beiträge zu Sprache und Kritik Tertullians* (Lund 1932); A. d'Alès, "Tertullian helléniste" in *RÉG* (1937), 320–62; H. Janssen, *Kultur und Sprache bei Tertullian* (Nijmegen 1938); V. Morel, "Disciplina" in *RHE* 40 (1944–5), 5–46; J. H. Waszink, "Pompa diaboli" in *VigChr* 1 (1947), 13–41; A. Kolping, *Sacramentum Tertullianeum* (Münster 1948); C. Mohrmann, *Tertull. Apologeticum* (Utrecht 1951), LXXXVI–CII. A *Lexicon Tertullianeum* is in preparation by G. Claesson. P. Guilloux, "L'évolution religieuse de Tertullien" in *RHE* 19 (1923), 5–24, 141–56; B. Nisters, *Tertullian, seine Persönlichkeit und sein Schicksal* (Münster 1950); M. Bévenot, *The Tradition of Manuscripts* (Oxford 1961).

Tertullian's Theology: A. d'Alès, *La théologie de Tertullien* (Paris 1905); R. E. Roberts, *The Theology of Tertullian* (London 1924); J. Morgan, *The Importance of Tertullian in the Development of Christian Dogma* (London 1928); J. Lortz, *Tertullian als Apologet*, 2 vols. (Paderborn 1927–8); C. Becker, *Tertullians Apologeticum, Werden und Leistung* (Munich, 2nd ed. 1961); A. Quacquarelli, *Tertullianus ad Scapulam* (Rome 1957); G. Zimmermann, *Die hermeneutischen Prinzipien Tertullians* (diss. Leipzig 1937); J. Stirnimann, *Die Praescriptio Tertullians* (Fribourg 1949); K. Adam, *Der Kirchenbegriff Tertullians* (Paderborn 1907); H. Koch, *Callist und Tertullian* (Heidelberg 1920); W. Köhler, *Omnis ecclesia Petri propinqua* (Heidelberg 1938); V. Morel, *De ontwikkeling van de christl. overlevering volgens Tertullian* (Bruges 1946); T. Brandt, *Tertullians Ethik* (Gütersloh 1929); J. Büchner, *Tert. de spectaculis, Kommentar* (Würzburg 1935); the same work with commentary by E. Castorina (Florence 1961); J. Klein, *Tertullians christliches Bewußtsein* (Bonn 1940); K. Baus, *Der Kranz in Antike und Christentum (Kommentar zu De corona)* (Bonn 1940); R. Franco, *El final del reino de Cristo en Tertuliano* (Granada 1955); G. Säflund, *De pallio und die stilistische Entwicklung Tertullians* (Lund 1955); G. Calloni, *Tertulliano, Vita, Opere, Pensiero* (Modena 1957).

Tertullian's Doctrine of Penance: K. Rahner in *ZKTh* 60 (1936), 471–510; *Festschrift K. Adam* (Düsseldorf 1952), 139–67; B. Poschmann, *Poenitentia secunda* (Bonn 1940), 270–348; H. Karpp, *Schrift und Geist bei Tertullian* (Gütersloh 1955); E. Langstadt, "Tertullian's Doctrine of Sin and the Power of Absolution in 'de pudicitia'" in *TU* 64 (1957), 251–7; H. Finé, *Die Terminologie der Jenseitsvorstellungen bei Tertullian* (Bonn 1958); S. Otto, *Natura und dispositio, Untersuchungen zum Naturbegriff und zur Denkform Tertullians* (Munich 1960); K. Wöllfl, *Das Heilswirken Gottes durch den Sohn nach Tertullian*, *AnGr* 112 (Rome 1960); V. Décarie, "Le paradoxe de Tertullien" in *VigChr* 15 (1961), 23–31; W. Bender, *Die Lehre über den Heiligen Geist bei Tertullian* (Munich 1961); E. Dekkers, *Tertullian en de geschiedenis der liturgie* (Brussels 1947);

R. Cantalamessa, *La cristologia di Tertulliano* (Fribourg 1962); G. G. Blum, "Der Begriff des Apostolischen im theologischen Denken Tertullians" in *KuD* 9 (1963) 102 to 121; G. C. Stead, "Divine Substance in Tertullian" in *TThS* 14 (1963), 46–66; B. Piault, "Tertullien a-t-il été subordinatien?" in *RSPhTh* 46 (1936), 181–204. On *De idol.* and *De cultu fem.* see P. G. Van der Nat in *VigChr* 17 (1963), 71–84.

CYPRIAN: Works, edited by W. Hartel in *CSEL* 3, 1–3 (1868–71); *Tractatus*, edited S. Colombo (Turin 1935); *Epistulae*, edited L. Bayard, 2 vols. (Paris, 2nd ed. 1945); Engl. *Epistles and Treatises ANF* 5 (1903); *Treatises FC* 36 (1958). On Textual Criticism and Language: H. Koch, *Cyprianische Untersuchungen* (Bonn 1926); B. Melin, *Studia in corpus Cyprianeum* (Uppsala 1946). The *Vita* of Cyprian by Pontius, and the *Acta proconsularia* in *CSEL* 3, 3; the *Vita* separately, edited by M. Pellegrino (Alba 1955). On the *Vita* see R. Reitzenstein in *AGG* (1919), 177–219; J. Martin in *HJ* (1919), 674–712; *Delehaye PM* 82–104.

Special Studies: P. Monceaux, *S. Cyprien* (Paris 1902 and, without notes, 1914); S. Colombo, "S. Cipriano, l'uomo e lo scrittore" in *Didaskaleion* 6 (Turin 1928), 1–80; A. A. Ehrhardt, "Cyprian, Father of Western Christianity" in *ChQR* 133 (1941), 178–96; E. Hummel, *The Concept of Martyrdom according to St Cyprian* (Washington 1946); J. Ludwig, *Der heilige Märtyrerbischof Cyprian von Karthago* (Munich 1951); M. Jourjon, *Cyprien de Carthage* (Paris 1957).

Cyprian's Theology: A. d'Alès, *La théologie de S. Cyprien* (Paris 1922). Doctrine of Baptism: G. Bardy in *RSR* 14 (1924), 255–72, 385–99; N. Zernov in *ChQR* 117 (1934), 304–36; A. Stenzel in *Scholastik* 30 (1955), 372–85. Doctrine of the Eucharist: P. Batiffol, *L'eucharistie* (Paris, 9th ed. 1930), 226–47; G. Bardy in *VS Suppl.* 60 (1939), 87–119; S. Salaville in *ÉO* 39 (1941–42), 268–82. On the question of penance: H. Koch, *Cyprianische Untersuchungen* (Bonn 1926); M. C. Chartier in *Antonianum* 14 (1939), 17–42, 135–56; B. Poschmann, *Poenitentia secunda* (Bonn 1940), 368–424; K. Rahner in *ZKTh* 74 (1952), 252–76, 381–438; M. Bévenot in *ThSt* 16 (1955), 175–273; C. Daly, *TU* 64 (1957) 202–7; M. F. Wiles, "The Theological legacy of St Cyprian" in *JEH* 14 (1963), 139–49.

On Cyprian's Conception of the Church: H. Koch, *Cathedra Petri* (Giessen 1930); E. Altendorf, *Einheit und Heiligkeit der Kirche* (Berlin 1932), 44–116; B. Poschmann, *Ecclesia principalis* (Breslau 1933); J. Plumpe, *Mater ecclesia* (Washington 1943), 81–108; G. Bardy, *La théologie de l'église*, II (Paris 1947), 171–251; J. Ludwig, *Die Primatsworte in der altkirchlichen Exegese* (Münster 1952); M. Bévenot in *RSR* 39–40 (1951–2), 397–415. G. Klein in *ZKG* 68 (1957), 48–68; J. Colson, *L'évêque, lieu d'unité et de charité chez saint Cyprien de Carthage* (Paris 1961).

21. The First Christological and Trinitarian Controversies

J. Tixeront, *History of Dogmas* (St Louis–London 1928–32). A. von Harnack, *History of Dogma* (New York 1958); R. Seeberg, *Textbook of the History of Doctrines* (Grand Rapids 1956); F. Loofs, *Leitfaden zum Studium der Dogmengeschichte*, ed. K. Aland (Tübingen, 6th ed. 1959); W. Koehler, *Dogmengeschichte als Geschichte des christlichen Selbstbewußtseins*, I (Leipzig, 2nd ed. 1951); M. Werner, *Die Entstehung des christlichen Dogmas problemgeschichtlich dargestellt* (Tübingen, 2nd ed. 1954), abridged English edition: *The Formation of Christian Dogma* (London 1957); J. N. D. Kelly, *Early Christian Doctrines* (London 1958); P. Meinhold, "Zur Grundlegung der Dogmengeschichte" in *Saeculum* 10 (1959), 1–20; W. Bauer, *Rechtgläubigkeit und Ketzerei im ältesten Christentum* (Tübingen 1934); J. Brosch, *Das Wesen der Häresie* (Bonn 1936);

G. L. Prestige, *God in Patristic Thought* (London, 2nd ed. 1952); S. L. Greenslade, *Schism in the Early Church* (London 1953); H. E. W. Turner, *The Pattern of Christian Truth* (London 1954); W. Doskocil, *Der Bann in der Urkirche* (Munich 1958); G. L. Prestige, *Fathers and Heretics* (London, 4th ed. 1958); J. Lebreton, Eng. tr. *History of the Dogma of the Trinity* I (New York 1939); F. L. Dölger, "Sonne und Sonnenstrahl als Gleichnis der Logostheologie des christlichen Altertums" in *AuC* 1 (1929), 271–90; M. Kreibel, *Studien zur ältesten Entwicklung der abendländischen Trinitätslehre bei Tertullian und Novatian* (diss. Marburg 1932); J. Barbel, *Christos Angelos* (Bonn 1941); E. Peterson, "Der Monotheismus als politisches Problem" in *Theologische Traktate* (Munich 1951), 45–147; A. Gilg, *Weg und Bedeutung der altkirchlichen Christologie* (Munich 1955); G. Kretschmar, *Studien zur frühchristlichen Trinitätslehre* (Tübingen 1956); W. Marcus, *Der Subordinationismus als historiologisches Phänomen* (Munich 1963).

G. Bardy, "Monarchianisme" in *DThC* X, 2193–209; idem, "Les écoles romaines au second siècle" in *RHE* 28 (1932), 501–32; G. La Piana, "The Roman Church at the End of the Second Century" in *HThR* 18 (1925), 201–77; H. Stork, *Die sogenannten Melchisedekianer (Theodotianer)* (Leipzig 1928); H. Schöne, "Ein Einbruch der antiken Logik in die altchristliche Theologie" in *Pisciculi, Festschrift F. J. Dölger* (Münster 1939), 252–65; V. Macchioro, *L'eresi Noëtiana* (Naples 1921); A. d'Alès, "Le désaccord de la foi populaire et de la théologie savante dans l'église du IIIe siècle" in *RHE* 19 (1923), 481–506, 20 (1924), 5–37. E. Hatch, *The Influence of Greek Ideas on Christianity* (New York 1957); R. Williams, *Guide to the Teachings of the Early Church Fathers* (Grand Rapids 1960); H. Hoppenbrouwers, *Recherches sur la terminologie du martyre de Tertullien à Lactance* (Nijmegen 1961); B. Schultze, *Teología latina y teología oriental* (Madrid 1961); J. Daniélou, *Message évangelique et culture hellénistique aux IIe et IIIe siècles* (Tournai 1961); R. Cantalamessa, "Prassea e l'eresia monarchiana" in *SC* 90 (1962), 28–50.

On Zephyrinus: A. von Harnack in *SAB* (1923), 51–7; B. Capelle in *RBén* 38 (1926), 321–30; E. Evans, *Tertullian's Treatise against Praxeas* (London 1948); A. d'Alès, *La théologie de s. Hippolyte* (Paris, 2nd ed. 1929); B. Capelle, "Le logos, fils de Dieu, dans la théologie d'Hippolyte" in *RThAM* 9 (1937), 109–24; C. L. Feltoe, *The Letters of Dionys of Alexandria* (Cambridge 1904); K. Müller, "Dionys von Alexandrien im Kampf mit den libyschen Sabellianern" in *ZNW* 24 (1925), 278–85; H. G. Opitz, "Dionys und die Libyer" in *Studies K. Lake* (London 1937), 41–53.

On Paul of Samosata: F. Loofs, *Paul von Samosata* (Leipzig 1924), and cf. A. von Harnack in *SAB* (1924), 130–51; É. Amann in *RevSR* 5 (1925), 328–42; H. de Riedmatten, *Les actes du procès de Paul de Samosate* (Fribourg 1952), and on this, see H. Scheidweiler in *ZNW* 46 (1955), 116–29; M. Richard, "Malchion et Paul de Samosate. Le témoignage d'Eusèbe de Césarée" in *EThL* 35 (1959), 325–38; J. M. Dalmau, "El 'homousios' y el concilio de Antioquía de 268" in *MCom* 34–35 (1960) 323–40.

22. Manichaeism

Sources

P. Alfaric, *Les écritures manichéennes*, 2 vols. (Paris 1918–19); A. Adam, *Texte zum Manichäismus*, selected texts (*KlT* 175) (Berlin 1954), vi–ix.

1) Direct Sources
The *Fragments* of Turfân, published by F. W. Müller in *SAB* (1904–5); *AAB* (1904), II, and (1912), V; by A. von Le Coq in *SAB* (1907; *AAB* (1910–11; 1919; 1922); by

W. Bang in *Muséon* 38 (1925), 1–55; by W. Bang and A. von Gabain in *SAB* (1929–30); by F. C. Andreas and W. Henning in *SAB* (1932–34) and *Bulletin of the School of Oriental and African Studies* 10–12 (1942–47–8). The Chinese *Treatise*, edited by E. Chavannes and P. Pelliot in *JA* 1 (1911), 499–617. The Chinese *Hymnarium* of London, edited by E. Waldschmidt and W. Lentz in *SAB* (1933); the Latin *Fragment* of Tebessa, edited by P. Alfaric in *RHLR NS* 6 (1920), 62–98.

The Coptic Texts from Fayyum: *Homilies*, edited by H. Polotzsky (Stuttgart 1934); *Cephalaia* I, edited C. Schmidt (Stuttgart 1940); *A Manichaean Psalm-Book*, part II, C. R. C. Allberry (Stuttgart 1938). A selection of direct sources may be found in A. Adam, *op. cit.* nos. 1–34; there are a few texts also in G. Widengren, *Iranische Geisteswelt* (Baden-Baden 1961).

2) Indirect Sources

Papyrus J. Rylands n. 469 in *BJRL* 3 (1938), 38–46; Alexander Lycop., *Contra Manichaei opiniones*, edited A. Brinkmann (Leipzig 1895); *Acta Archelai*, edited C. H. Beeson (Leipzig 1906); *Serapion of Thmuis, Adversus Manichaeos*, edited R. P. Casey (Cambridge, Mass. 1931); *Titus of Bostra, Contra Manichaeos*, edited P. de Lagarde (Berlin 1895); Epiphanius, *Panarion, Haer.* 66, edited K. Holl (Leipzig 1931); the anti-Manichaean writings of Augustine in *CSEL* 25, edited J. Zycha (Vienna 1891); a selection is given in A. Adam, *op. cit.* nos. 35–64. J. Ries, "La Bible chez Saint Augustin et chez les Manichéens" in *RevÉAug* 7 (1961), 231–43.

Literature

Survey of researches: H. S. Nyberg in *ZNW* 34 (1935), 70–91, and J. Ries in *EThL* 33 (1957), 453–82, 35 (1959), 362–409. General studies: H. J. Polotzsky in *Pauly–Wissowa* Suppl. VI (1935), 240–71; G. von Selle, "Der Manichaeismus" in *Festschrift H. Kraus* (Kitzingen 1953), 422–35; C. Colpe in *RGG*, 3rd ed. IV, 714–22. H.-C. Puech, *Le Manichéisme. Son fondateur, sa doctrine* (Paris 1949); H.-C. Puech, "Die Religion des Mani" in *König H*, II (Freiburg, 2nd ed. 1961), 499–563; G. Widengren, *Mani und der Manichäismus* (Stuttgart 1961); F. C. Burkitt, *The Religion of the Manichees* (Cambridge 1925); H. H. Schaeder, "Urform und Fortbildungen des manichäischen Systems" in *Vorträge Bibliothek Warburg* 4 (Leipzig 1927), 65–157; H.-C. Puech, "Der Begriff der Erlösung im Manichäismus" in *Eranos* 5 (1937), 183–286; T. Säve-Söderbergh, *Studies in the Coptic Manichaean Psalm-Book* (Uppsala 1949).

Spread and Influence of Manichaeism: E. de Stoop, *Essai sur la diffusion du manichéisme dans l'Empire romain* (Ghent 1909); É. Chavannes–P. Pelliot in *JA* 2 (1913), 99–199, 261–394 (for China); W. Henning in *ZDMG* 90 (1936), 1–18; H. H. Schaeder, "Manichäismus und spätantike Religion" in *Zeitschrift MkRel* 50 (1935), 65–85; H. H. Schaeder, "Der Manichäismus und sein Weg nach Osten" in *Festschrift F. Gogarten* (Giessen 1948), 236–54; W. H. C. Frend, "The Gnostic-Manichaean Tradition in Roman North Africa" in *JEH* 4 (1953), 13–26. Stephen Runciman, *The Medieval Manichee* (Cambridge 1936); D. Obolensky, *The Bogomils. A Study in Balkan Neo-Manichaeism* (Cambridge 1948).

Manichaeism and Christianity: H. Leclercq, "Manichéisme" in *DACL* X, 1395–400; G. Bardy in *DThC* IX, 1841–95; E. Waldschmidt–W. Lentz, "Die Stellung Jesu im Manichäismus" in *AAB* (1926), 4; G. Messina, "La dottrina manichea e le origini del cristianesimo" in *Biblica* 10 (1929), 313–31; F. J. Dölger, "Konstantin der Große und der Manichäismus; Sonne und Christus im Manichäismus" in *AuC* II (1930), 301–14; E. Rose, *Christologie des Manichäismus* (diss. Marburg 1942); A. Böhlig, *Die Bibel bei den Manichäern* (diss. Marburg 1947); G. Messina, *Cristianesimo, Buddhismo, Mani-cheismo nell'Asia antica* (Rome 1947); O. Stegmüller, "Das manichäische Fundamentum in einem Sakramentar der frühen Karolingerzeit" in *ZKTh* 74 (1952), 450–63; A. Adam, "Das Fortwirken des Manichäismus bei Augustin" in *ZKG* 69 (1958), 1–25; A. Böhlig, "Christliche Wurzeln im Manichäismus" in *BullSocArchéolcopte* 15 (1960), 41–61.

23. Further Development of the Liturgy

Sources

C. del Grande, *Liturgiae preces hymni christianorum e papyris collecti* (Naples 1934); J. Quasten, *Monumenta eucharistica et liturgica vetustissima* in *FlorPatr* 7 (1935); A. Adam, "Zur Geschichte der orientalischen Taufe und Messe im 2. und 4. Jahrhundert" in *KlT* 5 (3rd ed. 1960); Tertullian, *De baptismo*, edited J. W. P. Borleffs in *SCpr* 4 (1948); edited R. F. Refoulé in *SourcesChr* 35 (1952); Hippolytus, *Traditio apostolica*, edited G. Dix (London 1937); edited B. Botte in *SourcesChr* 11 (1946); *Didascalia*, edited F. X. Funk, *Didascalia et Constitutiones apostolorum*, I (Paderborn 1905), 1–384 (Latin translation); edited H. Achelis – J. Fleming in *TU* 25, 2 (Leipzig 1904, German translation). Asterius Sophistes, *Commentarii in psalmos*, edited M. Richard in *Symbolae Osloenses* Suppl. 16 (Oslo 1956). H. Follieri, *Initia Hymnorum Ecclesiae Graecae* (Vatican City 1960); P. Radó, *Enchiridion Liturgicum*, 2 vols. (Barcelona 1961).

Literature

L. Duchesne, *Christian Worship. Its Origin and Evolution* (London, 5th ed. 1949); A. Baumstark, *Vom geschichtlichen Werden der Liturgie* (Freiburg i. Br. 1923); F. L. Dölger, *Sol salutis* (Münster, 2nd ed. 1925); J. H. Srawley, *The Early History of the Liturgy* (Cambridge, 2nd ed.); H. Schmidt, *Introductio in Liturgiam Occidentalem* (Freiburg i. Br. 1959); T. Klauser, *Abendländische Liturgiegeschichte* (Bonn 1949); A. Baumstark, *Comparative Liturgy* (Westminster 1958); B. Steuart, *The Development of Christian Worship* (London 1953); A. A. King, *The Liturgy of the Roman Church* (London 1957); idem, *Liturgies of the Primatial Sees* (London 1957); J. A. Jungmann, *The Early Liturgy to the Time of Gregory the Great* (Notre Dame 1957); E. Werner, *The Sacred Bridge* (New York 1959); A. Quacquarelli, *Retorica e liturgia antenicena* (Rome 1960); B. Thompson, *Liturgies of the Western Church* (Cleveland – New York 1961); E. Dekkers, *Tertullianus en de geschiedenis der liturgie* (Brussels – Amsterdam 1947); J.-M. Hanssens, *La liturgie d'Hippolyte* (Rome 1959); W. Nagel, *Geschichte des christlichen Gottesdienstes* (Berlin 1962); A. G. Martimort (ed.), *L'église en prières: Introduction à la liturgie* (Paris 1961).

Easter and the Dispute about the Date of Easter: H. Kellner, *Heortologie* (Freiburg i. Br., 3rd ed. 1911); F. Cabrol, "Fêtes" in *DACL* V, 1403–14; A. Hollard, *Les origines des fêtes chrétiennes* (Paris 1936); A. A. McArthur, *The Evolution of the Christian Year* (London 1953); H. Leclercq, "Pâques" in *DACL* XIII, 1521–74; J. Jeremias, Πάσχα in *ThW* V, 895–903; O. Casel, "Art und Sinn der ältesten christlichen Osterfeier" in *JLW* 14 (1938), 1–78; J. Daniélou, "Le symbolisme du jour de Pâques" in *Dieu Vivant* 18 (1951), 45–56; H. Vorgrimler, "War die altchristliche Osternacht eine ununterbrochene Feier?" in *ZKTh* 74 (1952), 464–72; C. Mohrmann, "Pascha, passio, transitus" in *ELit* 66 (1952), 37–52, *Études sur le latin des chrétiens* (Rome 1958), 205–22; A. W. Watts, *Easter, its Story and Meaning* (London 1959); C. Marcora, *La vigilia nella liturgia (sec. I–VI)* (Milan 1954); A. Baumstark–O. Heiming,

Nocturna laus, Typen frühchristlicher Vigilfeier (Münster 1957); P. Jounel, "La nuit pascale. Le dimanche et le temps de Pâques: La tradition de l'église" in *MD* 67 (1961), 123–44, 163–82; B. Lohse, *Das Passafest der Quartadecimaner* (Gütersloh 1953) (pages 143–8 for the older literature on the subject); B. Botte, "La question pascale" in *MD* 41 (1955), 84–95; M. Shepherd, *The Paschal Liturgy and the Apocalypse* (Richmond 1960); M. Richard, "La question pascale au II⁰ siècle" in *OrSyr* 6 (1961), 179–212; P. Nautin, *Lettres et écrivains chrétiens au II⁰ et III⁰ siècles* (Paris 1961), 65–89; C. Mohrmann, "Le conflit pascal au II⁰ siècle" in *VigChr* 16 (1962), 154–71; W. Cadman, "The Christian Pascha and the Day of the Crucifixion" in *TU* 80 (1962), 8–16; B. J. Van der Veken in *SE* 14 (1963), 5–33.

CATECHUMENATE AND BAPTISM: P. de Puniet, "Catéchuménat" in *DACL* II, 2579–90; F. J. Dölger, "Tertullian und die Bluttaufe" in *AuC* II (1930), 117–41; H. Rahner, "Pompa diaboli" in *ZKTh* 55 (1931), 239–73; B. Capelle, "L'introduction du catéchuménat à Rome" in *RThAM* 5 (1933), 129–54; G. Bardy, "L'enseignement religieux aux premiers siècles in *RAP* 66 (1938), 641–55; 67 (1938), 5–18; E. Dick, "Das Pateninstitut im altchristlichen Katechumenat" in *ZKTh* 63 (1939), 1–49; B. Welte, *Die postbaptismale Salbung* (Freiburg i. Br. 1939); O. Cullmann, *Le baptême des enfants* (Neuchâtel 1949); G. W. H. Lampe, *The Seal of the Spirit. A Study in the Doctrine on Baptism and Confirmation in the New Testament and the Fathers* (London 1951); J. Lupi, "Catechetical Instruction in the First Two Centuries" in *Melita Theologica* 9 (1956), 61–71; R. J. Zwi Werblowsky, "On the Baptismal Rite according to St Hippolytus" in *Studia Patristica* II (Berlin 1957), 93–105; J. Fisher, "The Consecration of Water in the Early Rite of Baptism" in *TU* 64 (1957), 41–46; A. Stenzel, *Die Taufe, eine genetische Erklärung der Taufliturgie* (Innsbruck 1958); J. Jeremias, *Infant Baptism in the First Four Centuries* (London 1960); T. Torrance, "The Origins of Baptism" in *Scottish Journal of Theology* 11 (1958), 158–71; W. A. Be Vier, "Water Baptism in the Ancient Church" in *Bibliotheca sacra* 116 (1959), 136–44, 230–40; J. A. Jungmann, "Aufbauelemente im römischen Taufritus" in *LJ* 9 (1959), 1–15; E. Stommel, "Christliche Taufriten und antike Taufsitten" in *JAC* 2 (1959), 5–14; K. Kirsten, *Die Taufabsage* (Berlin 1960); A. Aland, *Die Säuglingstaufe im Neuen Testament und in der alten Kirche* (Munich 1961); T. Ysebaert, *Greek Baptismal Terminology* (Nijmegen 1962); G. Kretschmer, "Baptismal Liturgy in Egypt" in *JLH* 8 (1963), 1–54.

THE BAPTISMAL CREED: Texts, *Denzinger* 1–14; *KlT* 17–18 (2nd ed. 1931). Studies: F. Kattenbusch, *Das apostolische Symbolum*, 2 vols. (Leipzig 1894–1900, reprinted Darmstadt 1961); B. Dörholt, *Das Taufsymbol in der alten Kirche* (Paderborn 1898); J. Brinktrine in *ThQ* 102 (1921), 156–90; J. Lebreton in *RSR* 20 (1930), 97–124; F. J. Dölger in *AuC* IV (1933), 138–46; F. Badcock, *The History of the Creeds* (London 1938); O. Cullmann, *The Earliest Christian Confessions* (London 1949); J. H. Crehan, *Early Christian Baptism and the Creed* (London 1950); E. Lichtenstein in *ZKG* 63 (1950), 1–74; B. Botte, *Mélanges J. de Ghellinck*, I (Brussels–Paris 1951), 181–200; T. Camelot in *Lumière et Vie*, I (1952), 61–80.

EUCHARIST: G. Rauschen, *Eucharistie und Bußsakrament in den ersten sechs Jahrhunderten* (Freiburg i. Br., 2nd ed. 1910); T. Schermann, *Ägyptische Abendmahlsliturgien* (Paderborn 1912); J. A. Jungmann, *Die Stellung Christi im liturgischen Gebet* (Münster 1925); P. Batiffol, *L'Eucharistie* (Paris, 7th ed. 1930); G. Dix, *The Shape of the Liturgy* (London 1954); H. Lietzmann, *Messe und Herrenmahl* (Berlin, 2nd ed. 1955); J. Betz, *Die Eucharistie in der Zeit der griechischen Väter*, I (Freiburg i. Br. 1955); J. A. Jungmann, *The Mass of the Roman Rite*, 2 vols. (New York 1951–5); W. Dürig, *Pietas liturgica* (Regensburg 1958); L. C. Mohlberg, "Carmen Christo quasi deo" (on

Pliny the Younger, *Ep.* 10, 96) in *RivAC* 14 (1937), 93–123; A. W. Ziegler, "Das Brot von unsern Feldern, ein Beitrag zur Eucharistielehre des Irenäus" in *Festschrift zum Eucharistischen Kongreß* (Munich 1960), 21–43.

On Hippolytus' liturgy: R. H. Connolly in *JThS* 39 (1938), 350–69; H. Engberding in *MiscMohlberg*, I (1948), 47–71; E. Dekkers, "L'église ancienne a-t-elle connu la Messe du soir?" in *MiscMohlberg*, I (1948), 231–57. R. Hanson, "The Liberty of the Bishop to Improvise Prayer in the Eucharist" in *VigChr* 15 (1961), 173–6; G. Dollar, "The Lord's Supper in the Second Century" in *Bibliotheca Sacra* 117 (1960), 249–57; A. Adam in *TLZ* 88 (1963), 9–20.

DISCIPLINE OF THE SECRET: E. Vacandard in *DHGE* III, 1497–513; O. Perler in *RAC* I, 667–79 (with very full bibliography); H. Clasen, *Die Arkandisziplin in der alten Kirche* (diss. Heidelberg 1956); A. Stenzel, *Die Taufe, eine genetische Erklärung der Taufliturgie* (Innsbruck 1958), 147–53.

THE BEGINNINGS OF CHRISTIAN ART: In addition to the works listed above, page 454, see: W. Neuss, *Die Kunst der alten Christen* (Augsburg 1926); D. T. Rice, *The Beginnings of Christian Art* (London 1957); E. Syndikus, *Die frühchristliche Kunst* (Aschaffenburg 1960); F. van der Meer, *Early Christian Art* (London 1961); J. Daniélou, *Primitive Christian Symbols* (Baltimore 1964).
J.-R. Laurin, "Le lieu du culte chrétien d'après les documents littéraires primitifs" in *Studi sulla chiesa antica* (Rome 1954), 39–57; C. Hopkins–P. V. C. Baur, *Christian Church at Dura-Europos* (New Haven 1934); O. Eissfeldt, "Dura-Europos" in *RAC* IV, 362–70; E. Kirschbaum, *The Roman Catacombs and their Martyrs* (Milwaukee 1957); J. Kollwitz, *Das Christusbild des 3. Jahrhunderts* (Münster 1953); W. Schöne–J. Kollwitz–H. von Campenhausen, *Das Gottesbild im Abendland* (Berlin 1957); T. Kemp, *Christus der Hirt* (Rome 1943); A. M. Schneider, "Die ältesten Denkmäler der römischen Kirche" in *Festschrift der Akademie der Wissenschaften, Göttingen*, II (Göttingen 1951), 166–98. On the historical origins of ancient Christian art see T. Klauser, "Zur Entstehungsgeschichte der altchristlichen Kunst" in *JbAC* I (1958), 20–51; 2 (1959), 115–45; 3 (1960), 112–33; 4 (1961), 128–45; 5 (1962), 113–24; P. Thoby, *Histoire du Crucifix, des origines au concile de Trente* (Nantes 1959); A. von Gerkan in *Mullus, Festschrift T. Klauser* (Münster 1964), 144–9 (Dura-Europos).

24. *Spiritual Life and Morality in the Communities of the Third Century*

SOURCES

F. Cabrol–H. Leclercq, *Monumenta ecclesiae liturgica*, vol. 1b (Paris 1913); M.-J. Rouët de Journel, *Enchiridion asceticum* (Freiburg i. Br., 5th ed. 1958); H. Koch, *Quellen zur Geschichte der Askese und des Mönchtums* (Tübingen 1933).
Translations: F. Cabrol, *Le livre de la prière antique* (Paris, 5th ed. 1913); G. Bardy, *La vie spirituelle d'après les pères des trois premiers siècles* (Paris 1935); L. A. Winterswyl, *Gebete der Urkirche* (Freiburg i. Br., 2nd ed. 1952); A. Hamman, *Early Christian Prayers* (Chicago 1961); idem, *Le pater expliqué par les pères* (Paris 1952); idem, *Prières eucharistiques des premiers siècles* (Paris 1957); idem, *Le baptême d'après les pères de l'église* (Paris 1962).

Literature

F. Martinez, *L'ascétisme chrétien pendant les trois premiers siècles* (Paris 1913); H. Strathmann, *Geschichte der frühchristlichen Askese*, I (Leipzig 1914); E. Buonaiuti, *Le origini dell'ascetismo cristiano* (Pinerolo 1928); M. Viller–K. Rahner, *Askese und Mystik in der Väterzeit* (Freiburg i. Br. 1939); P. Pourrat, *Christian Spirituality* (Westminster 1955); F. Cayré, *Spirituels et mystiques des premiers temps* (Paris 1956); L. Bouyer, *The Spirituality of the New Testament and the Fathers* (New York 1963); W. Völker, *Das Vollkommenheitsideal des Origenes* (Tübingen 1931); J. Stelzenberger, *Die Beziehungen der frühchristlichen Sittenlehre zur Ethik der Stoa* (Munich 1933); J. Klein, *Tertullians christliches Bewußtsein und sittliche Forderungen* (Bonn 1941); F. Bertrand, *Mystique de Jésus chez Origène* (Paris 1951); W. Völker, *Der wahre Gnostiker nach Clemens Alexandrinus* (Berlin 1952).

Baptismal Spirituality: H. Windisch, *Taufe und Sünde im ältesten Christentum* (Tübingen 1908). A. von Harnack, *Die Terminologie der Wiedergeburt* (Leipzig 1920) (*TU* 42, 2); H. Rahner, "Taufe und geistliches Leben bei Origenes" in *ZAM* 7 (1932), 205–23; P. Lundberg, *La typologie baptismale de l'ancienne église* (Uppsala 1942); J. Daniélou, "Le symbolisme des rites baptismaux" in *Dieu vivant* 1 (1945), 17–43; W. M. Bedard, *The Symbolism of the Baptismal Font in Early Christian Thought* (Washington 1951); G. H. W. Lampe, *The Seal of the Spirit. A Study in the Doctrine of Baptism and Confirmation in the New Testament and the Fathers* (London 1951); T. Camelot, *Spiritualité du baptême* (Paris 1960); T. Ysebaert, *Greek Baptismal Terminology* (Nijmegen 1962).

Devotion to Martyrdom: H. Delehaye, "Martyr et confesseur" in *AnBoll* 39 (1921), 20–49; H. Delehaye, *Sanctus* (Brussels 1927); O. Michel, *Prophet und Martyrer* (Gütersloh 1932); H. von Campenhausen, *Die Idee des Martyriums in der alten Kirche* (Göttingen, 2nd ed. 1964); E. Peterson, *Zeuge der Wahrheit* (Leipzig 1937); E. Günter, Μάρτυς (Gütersloh 1941); M. Lods, *Confesseurs et martyrs, successeurs des prophètes dans l'église des trois premiers siècles* (Neuchâtel 1958); R. Krautheimer, "Mensa-Coemeterium-Martyrium" in *Cahiers Archéologiques* 11 (1960), 93–119; N. Brox, *Zeuge und Martyrer, Untersuchungen zur frühchristlichen Zeugnis-Terminologie* (Munich 1961); H. A. M. Hoppenbrouwers, *Recherches sur la terminologie du martyre de Tertullien à Lactance* (Nijmegen 1962); M. Pellegrino in *RevSR* 35 (1961), 151–75.

Asceticism: H. Strathmann–P. Keseling, "Askese" II in *RAC* I, 758–95; M. Viller–M. Olphe-Galliard, "Ascèse, Ascétisme" in *DSAM* I, 960–77; H. Leclercq, "Cénobitisme" in *DACL* II, 3058–90; H. Chadwick "Enkrateia" in *RAC* V, 343–65; E. Peterson, "Einige Beobachtungen zu den Anfängen der christlichen Askese" in *Frühkirche, Judentum und Gnosis* (Freiburg i. Br. 1959), 209–22; P. de Labriolle, "Le 'mariage spirituel' dans l'antiquité chrétienne" in *RH* 137 (1921), 204–25; J. Schmid, "Brautschaft, heilige" in *RAC* II, 546–64; H. Koch, *Virgines Christi* (Leipzig 1907) (*TU* 31–2); K. Müller, *Die Forderung der Ehelosigkeit in der alten Kirche* (Tübingen 1927); M. R. Nugent, *Portrait of the Consecrated Woman in Greek Christian Literature of the First Four Centuries* (Washington 1941); T. Camelot, *Virgines Christi* (Paris 1944); F. de B. Vizmanos, *Las vírgenas cristianas en la Iglesia primitiva* (Madrid 1949); K. Heussi, *Der Ursprung des Mönchtums* (Tübingen 1937); F. Quatember, *Die christliche Lebenshaltung des Klemens von Alexandrien nach seinem Pädagogus* (Vienna 1946). A. Vööbus, *History of Asceticism in the Syrian Orient* (Louvain 1960).

Prayer: E. von der Goltz, *Das Gebet in der ältesten Christenheit* (Leipzig 1901) (328–53, texts of prayers); O. Dibelius, *Das Vaterunser, Umrisse zu einer Geschichte des Gebetes in der alten und mittleren Kirche* (Giessen 1903); G. Walther, *Untersuchungen zur*

Geschichte der griechischen Vaterunser-Exegese (Leipzig 1914) (*TU* 40, 3); F. Heiler, *Das Gebet* (Munich, 5th ed. 1923); F. L. Dölger, *Sol salutis, Gebet und Gesang im christlichen Altertum* (Münster, 2nd ed. 1925); J. A. Jungmann, *Die Stellung Christi im liturgischen Gebet* (Münster, 2nd ed. 1962); F. Cabrol, *The Prayer of the Early Christians* (London 1930); T. Ohm, *Die Gebetsgebärden der Völker und das Christentum* (Leyden 1948); B. Fischer, *Die Psalmenfrömmigkeit der Märtyrerkirche* (Freiburg i. Br. 1949); K. Baus, "Das Gebet der Märtyrer" in *TThZ* 62 (1953), 19–32; L. Vischer, "Das Gebet der alten Kirche" in *EvTh* 17 (1957), 531–46; A. Stuiber, *Refrigerium interim* (Bonn 1957); E. Peterson, "Das Kreuz und das Gebet nach Osten" in *Frühkirche, Judentum und Gnosis* (Freiburg i. Br. 1959), 15–35; A. Hamman, *Early Christian Prayers* (Chicago 1961); J. P. T. Deroy, *Bernardus en Origenes* (Haarlem 1963).

FASTING: F. Cabrol, "Jeûnes" in *DACL* VII, 2481–501; J. Svennung, "Statio-Fasten" in *ZNW* 32 (1933), 294–308; J. Schümmer, *Die altchristliche Fastenpraxis* (Münster 1933); R. Arbesmann, "Fasting and Prophecy in Pagan and Christian Antiquity" in *Tr* 7 (1949–51), 1–71; A. Guillaume, *Jeûne et charité dans l'église latine des origines au XIIe siècle, en particulier chez Léon le Grand* (Paris 1954); P. Gerlitz, *Das Fasten im religionsgeschichtlichen Vergleich* (diss. Erlangen 1954); article by the same author under the same title in *ZRGG* 7 (1955), 116–26; H. Musurillo, "The Problem of Ascetical Fasting in the Greek Patristic Writers" in *Tr* 12 (1956), 1–64.

WORKS OF CHARITY: H. Leclercq, "Charité" in *DACL* III, 598–653; G. Marsot, "Bienfaisance" in *Dict. de Sociol.* III, 864–83; G. Uhlhorn, *Die christliche Liebestätigkeit*, I (Stuttgart, 2nd ed. 1895, reprinted Darmstadt 1959); W. Liese, *Geschichte der Caritas* (Freiburg i. Br. 1922); G. Meffert, *Caritas und Krankenwesen bis zum Ausgang des Mittelalters* (Freiburg i. Br. 1927); H. Bolkestein, *Wohltätigkeit und Armenpflege im vorchristlichen Altertum* (Utrecht 1939); F. Lovsky, *L'église et les malades depuis le IIe siècle jusqu'au début du XXe siècle* (Thonon Les Bains 1958); J. von dem Driesch, *Geschichte der Wohltätigkeit*, volume I: *Die Wohltätigkeit im Altertum* (Paderborn 1959).

AGAPE: "Agape" in *DACL* I, 775–848; P. Batiffol, *Études d'histoire et de théologie positive* (Paris, 7th ed. 1926); K. Völker, *Mysterium und Agape* (Gotha 1927); Bo Reicke, *Diakonie, Festfreude und Zelos in Verbindung mit der altchristlichen Agapenfeier* (Uppsala 1951); C. Donahue, "The ἀγάπη of the Eremites of Scete" in *Studia Monastica* 1 (1959), 97–120; A. Armstrong, "Platonic *eros* and Christian *agape*" in *Downside Review* 79 (1960–1), 105–2; J. Colson, *Agapè chez S. Ignace d'Antioche* (Paris 1961); C. Spicq, *Agape in the New Testament* (St Louis 1963).

EARLY CHRISTIAN MORAL LIFE: A. Baudrillart, *Moeurs païennes, moeurs chrétiennes*, 2 vols. (Paris, 2nd ed. 1936); J. Leipoldt, *Der soziale Gedanke in der altchristlichen Kirche* (Leipzig 1952); W. Schwer, "Almosen" in *RAC* I, 302–7; A. Kalsbach, "Armut I" in *RAC* I, 702–5; A. Bigelmair, "Armut II", ibid. 705–9; H. Greeven, *Das Hauptproblem der Sozialethik in der neueren Stoa und im Urchristentum* (Gütersloh 1935); H. Larmann, *Christliche Wirtschaftsethik in der spätrömischen Antike* (Berlin 1935); H. Holzapfel, *Die sittliche Wertung der körperlichen Arbeit im christlichen Altertum* (Würzburg 1941); A. T. Geoghegan, *The Attitude towards Labour in Early Christianity and Ancient Culture* (Washington 1945); J.-P. Brisson, "Les origines du danger social dans l'Afrique chrétienne du IIIe siècle" in *RSR* 33 (1946), 280–316; M. Maeder, *La liberté et l'esclavage dans l'église primitive* (1951); G. Kehnscherper, *Die Stellung der Bibel und der alten Kirche zur Sklaverei* (Halle 1957), and on this see *ZKG* 69 (1958), 328 ff.; E. K. Jonkers, "Das Verhalten der alten Kirche hinsichtlich der Ernennung zum Priester" in *Mnemosyne* 10 (1942), 286–302; N. H. Baynes, "Idolatry in the Early

Church" in *Byzantine Studies* (London 1955); J. Alameda, *Como era la vida de los primeros cristianos* (Bilbao 1957).

MARRIAGE AND FAMILY: H. Preisker, *Christentum und Ehe in den ersten drei Jahrhunderten* (Berlin 1928); J. Köhne, *Die Ehen zwischen Christen und Heiden in den ersten christlichen Jahrhunderten* (Paderborn 1931); F. Blanke – F. J. Leenhard, *Die Stellung der Frau im Neuen Testament und in der alten Kirche* (Zürich 1949); J. Leipoldt, *Die Frau in der Antike und im Urchristentum* (Gütersloh 1962); J. Mayer, *Monumenta de viduis diaconissis virginibusque tractantia* (Bonn 1938) (*FlorPatr* 42); A. Kalsbach, *Die altkirchliche Einrichtung der Diakonissen* (Freiburg i. Br. 1926); A. Kalsbach, "Diakonisse" in *RAC* III, 917–28; C. C. Ryrie, *The Place of Women in the Church* (New York 1958); J. Daniélou, "Le ministère des femmes dans l'église ancienne" in *MD* 61 (1960), 70–96.

CHURCH AND CIVILIZATION AND CULTURE; CHURCH AND STATE: J. H. Waszink, *Het oudste Christendom en de antieke Cultuur*, 2 vols. (Haarlem 1951); C. J. Cadoux, *The Early Church and the World* (Edinburgh, 2nd ed. 1955); O. Cullmann, "Early Christianity and Civilization" in *The Early Church* (London 1956), 195–209; C. N. Cochrane, *Christianity and Classical Culture* (New York, 3rd 1957); W. Krause, *Die Stellung der frühchristlichen Autoren zur heidnischen Literatur* (Vienna 1958); W. Durant, *Caesar and Christ* (New York 1944). A. Decker, *Kenntnis und Pflege des Körpers bei Klemens von Alexandrien* (Innsbruck 1936); K. Baus, *Der Kranz in Antike und Christentum, eine religionsgeschichtliche Untersuchung mit besonderer Berücksichtigung Tertullians* (Bonn 1940); C. Andresen, "Altchristliche Kritik am Tanz, ein Ausschnitt aus dem Kampf der alten Kirche gegen heidnische Sitte" in *ZKG* 72 (1961), 217–62; W. Bieder, *Ekklesia und Polis im Neuen Testament und in der alten Kirche* (diss. Basle) (Zürich 1941); R. Petry, *Christian Eschatology and Social Thought* (Nashville 1956); F. Stratmann, *Die Heiligen und der Staat*, II (Frankfurt a. M. 1949); J. Ferguson, "The Nature of Early Christian Pacifism" in *The Hibbert Journal* 55 (1956–7), 340–9; E. Peterson, "Der Monotheismus als politisches Problem" in *Theologische Traktate* (Munich 1961), 45–147. A. von Harnack, *Militia Christi* (Tübingen 1905, reprinted Darmstadt 1963); R. H. Bainton, "The Early Church and War" in *HThR* 39 (1946), 189–212; E. A. Ryan, "The Rejection of Military Service by the Early Christians" in *ThSt* 13 (1952), 1–32; H. Karpp, "Die Stellung der alten Kirche zu Krieg und Kriegsdienst" in *EvTh* 17 (1957), 496–515; H. von Campenhausen, "Der Kriegsdienst der Christen in der Kirche des Altertums" in *Tradition und Leben* (Tübingen 1960), 203–15; J. Leipoldt, *Griechische Philosophie und frühchristliche Aszese* (Berlin 1961); W. Jaeger, *Early Christianity and Greek Paideia* (Cambridge, Mass. 1961); A. Wifstrand, *L'église ancienne et la culture grecque* (Paris 1942); S. Perowne, *Caesars and Saints. The Evolution of the Christian State A.D. 180–313* (London 1962); J.-M. Hornus, *Politische Entscheidung in der alten Kirche* (Munich 1963).

25. The Holiness of the Christian and his Church

GENERAL SURVEYS: É. Amann, "Pénitence" in *DThC* XII, 748–845; B. Poschmann, "Buße, Bußkleid, Bußstufen" in *RAC* II, 805–12, 813–16; K. Rahner, "Bußdisziplin" in *LThK* II, 805–9; W. Teller, *The Forgiveness of Sins* (Philadelphia 1960); P. Palmer, *Sacraments and Forgiveness* (London 1960); B. Poschmann, *Penance and the Anointing of the Sick* (Freiburg – London – New York – Montreal 1963).

SPECIAL STUDIES OF PENITENTIAL DISCIPLINE: H. Windisch, *Taufe und Sünde im ältesten Christentum bis auf Origenes* (Tübingen 1908); P. Batiffol, "Les origines de la pénitence" in *Études d'histoire et de théologie positive* (Paris 1902), 45–302; G. Rauschen,

Eucharistie und Bußsakrament (Freiburg i. Br., 2nd ed. 1910); K. Adam, *Das sogenannte Bußedikt des Kallistus* (Munich 1917); J. Hoh, *Die kirchliche Buße im 2. Jahrhundert* (Breslau 1932); P. Galtier, *L'église et la remission des péchés aux premiers siècles* (Paris 1932); B. Poschmann, *Poenitentia secunda* (Bonn 1940); B. Poschmann, "Die altchristliche Buße" in *HDG* IV/3 (Freiburg i. Br. 1951), 18–41; P. Galtier, *Aux origines du sacrement de la pénitence* (Rome 1951) (*AnGr* 54); H. von Campenhausen, *Kirchliches Amt und geistliche Vollmacht in den drei ersten Jahrhunderten* (Tübingen 1953); J. Grotz, *Die Entwicklung des Bußstufenwesens in der vornicänischen Kirche* (Freiburg i. Br. 1955).

OTHER SPECIAL STUDIES: P. Galtier, "A propos de la pénitence primitive. Méthodes et conclusions" in *RHE* 30 (1934), 517–57, 797–846; H. von Campenhausen, "Die Schlüsselgewalt der Kirche" in *EvTh* 4 (1937), 143–69; R. Joly, "La doctrine pénitentielle du Pasteur d'Hermas et l'exégèse récente" in *RHR* 147 (1955), 32–49; K. Rahner, "Die Bußlehre im Hirten des Hermas" in *ZKTh* 77 (1955), 385–431; K. Rahner, "Die Sündenvergebung nach der Taufe in der Regula fidei des Irenaeus" in *ZKTh* 70 (1948), 450–5; K. Rahner, "Zur Theologie der Buße bei Tertullian" in *Festschrift K. Adam* (Düsseldorf 1952), 139–67; H. Koch, "Die Bußfrage bei Cyprian" in *Cyprianische Untersuchungen* (Bonn 1926), 211–85; P. Chartier, "La discipline pénitentielle d'après les écrits de s. Cyprien" in *Antonianum* 6 (1939), 17–42, 135–56; K. Rahner, "Die Bußlehre des heiligen Cyprian" in *ZKTh* 74 (1952), 257–76, 381–438; M. Bévenot, "The Sacrament of Penance and St Cyprian's De lapsis" in *ThSt* 16 (1955), 175–213; S. Hübner, "Kirchenbuße und Exkommunikation bei Cyprian" in *ZKTh* 84 (1962), 49–84, 171–215; A. Méhat, "'Pénitence seconde' et péché involontaire chez Clément d'Alexandrie" in *VigChr* 8 (1954), 225–33; H. Karpp, "Die Bußlehre des Klemens von Alexandrien" in *ZNW* 43 (1950–1), 224–42; K. Rahner, "La doctrine d'Origène sur la pénitence" in *RSR* 37 (1950), 47–97, 252–86, 422–56; K. Rahner, "Bußlehre und Bußpraxis der Didascalia apostolorum" in *ZKTh* 72 (1950), 257–81. A. d'Alès, *Novatien* (Paris 1924); C. B. Daly, "Novatian and Tertullian. A Chapter in the History of Puritanism" in *IThQ* 19 (1952), 33–43. E. H. Röttgers, "Marcellinus–Marcellus. Zur Papstgeschichte der diokletianischen Verfolgungszeit" in *ZKTh* 78 (1956), 385–420; A. Amore, "È esistito Papa Marcello?" in *Antonianum* 33 (1958), 57–75.

26. The Development of the Church's Constitution in the Third Century

GENERAL TREATMENT

See the bibliography to Chapter 10 above, as well as: K. Müller, "Die Kirchenverfassung im christlichen Altertum" in *RGG* 2nd ed. III, 986–88; K. Müller, *Aus der akademischen Arbeit* (Tübingen 1930), 101–34; A. Adam, "Kirchenverfassung II" in *RGG* 3rd ed. III, 1533–945; H. Lietzmann, "Zur altchristlichen Verfassungsgeschichte" in *Kleine Schriften*, I (Berlin 1958), 141–85; E. Rösser, *Göttliches und menschliches, unveränderliches und veränderliches Kirchenrecht von der Entstehung der Kirche bis zur Mitte des 9. Jahrhunderts* (Paderborn 1934); G. Krüger, *Die Rechtsstellung der vorkonstantinischen Kirchen* (Stuttgart 1935, reprinted Amsterdam 1961); G. Bardy, *La théologie de l'Église de s. Irénée au concile de Nicée* (Paris 1947); E. Kohlmeyer, "Charisma oder Recht? Vom Wesen des ältesten Kirchenrechts" in *ZSavRGkan* 38 (1952), 1–36; H. Chadwick, *The Circle and the Ellipse. Rival Concepts of Authority in the Early Church* (Oxford 1959).

The Clergy

M. Andrieu, *Les ordres mineurs* (Paris 1925); H. Leclercq, "Célibat" in *DACL* II, 2802–32; G. Dix, "The Ministry of the Early Church" in K. E. Kirk, *The Apostolic Ministry* (London, 2nd ed. 1947), 183–303; E. Lanne, "Le ministère apostolique dans l'œuvre de s. Irénée" in *Irénikon* 25 (1952), 113–41; J. Lecuyer, "Épiscopat et presbytérat dans les écrits d'Hippolyte de Rome" in *RSR* 41 (1953), 30–50; A. Adam, "Die Entstehung des Bischofsamtes" in *Wort und Dienst* (Bethel) 5 (1957), 1–16; J. Colson, *La fonction diaconale aux origines de l'Église* (Bruges–Paris 1960); H. von Campenhausen, "Die Anfänge des Priesterbegriffes in der alten Kirche" in *Tradition und Leben* (Tübingen 1960), 272–89; L. Ryan, "Patristic Teaching on the Priesthood of the Faithful" in *IThQ* 29 (1962), 25–51; J. G. Davies, "Deacons, Deaconesses, and Minor Orders in the Patristic Period" in *JEH* 14 (1963), 1–15; O. Perler, "L'évêque, représentant du Christ" in *L'épiscopat et l'Église universelle* (Paris 1962), 31–66; J. Colson, *L'épiscopat catholique. Collegialité et primauté dans les trois premiers siècles* (Paris 1963).

Local Churches and Synods

P. de Labriolle, "Paroecia" in *RSR* 18 (1928), 60–72; K. Müller, "Rom, Arelate und spanische Kirchen um 250" in *ZNW* 28 (1929), 296–305; J. P. Kirsch, *Die römischen Titelkirchen im Altertum* (Paderborn 1918); F. Lanzoni, "I titoli presbiterali di Roma antica" in *RivAC* 2 (1925), 195–257; E. Kirsten, "Chorbischof" in *RAC* II, 1105–14; P. Batiffol, "Le règlement des premiers conciles africains et le règlement du sénat romain" in *Bulletin d'ancienne lit. et archéol. chrétiennes* 3 (Paris 1913), 3–19; G. Roethe, *Zur Geschichte der römischen Synoden im 3. und 4. Jahrhundert* (Stuttgart 1937); W. de Vries, "Der Episkopat auf den Synoden von Nicäa" in *Theologisch-praktische Quartalschrift* (1963), 263–77.

The Roman Primacy

H. J. Vogels, *Textus antenicaeni ad primatum Romanum spectantes* (Bonn 1937) (*FlorPatr* 9); K. Adam, "Neue Untersuchungen über die Ursprünge der kirchlichen Primatslehre" in *ThQ* 109 (1928), 161–256, and *Gesammelte Aufsätze zur Dogmengeschichte* (Augsburg 1936), 123–85; K. J. Kidd, *The Roman Primacy to A.D. 461* (London 1936); P. Batiffol, *Cathedra Petri* (Paris 1938); E. Stauffer, "Zur Vor- und Frühgeschichte des Primats" in *ZKG* 61 (1943–44), 3–34; L. Hertling, "Communio und Primat" in *Misc. hist. pontif.* 7 (1943), 1–48, and also *Una Sancta* 17 (1962), 91–125; A. Rimoldi, *L'apostolo San Pietro fondamento della Chiesa ... dalle origini al Concilio di Calcedonia* (Rome 1958).

Hegesippus: T. Klauser, "Die Anfänge der römischen Bischofsliste" in *BZThS* 8 (1931), 193–213; H. von Campenhausen, "Lehrerreihen und Bischofsreihen im 2. Jh." in *Festschrift E. Lohmeyer* (Stuttgart 1951); N. Hydahl, "Hegesipps Hypomnemata" in *StTh* 14 (1960), 70–113.

Irenaeus: L. Spikowski, *La doctrine de l'église dans s. Irénée* (Strasbourg 1926) (lists older literature on the subject); H. Holstein, "Propter potentiorem principalitatem" in *RSR* 36 (1949), 122–35; R. Jacquin, "Ab his qui sunt undique dans s. Irénée" in *RevSR* 24 (1950), 72–87; D. J. Unger, "St Irenaeus and the Roman Primacy" in *ThSt* 13 (1952), 359–418; P. Nautin, "Irénée, Adv. Haer. III 3, 2. Église de Rome ou Église universelle?" in *RHR* 151 (1957), 37–78, and on this B. Botte in *Irénikon* 30 (1957), 156–63.

CYPRIAN AND THE CONTROVERSY ON HERETICAL BAPTISM: G. Bardy, "Cyprien" in DHGE XIII, 1152–54, 1158–60; A. d'Alès, La théologie de s. Cyprien (Paris 1922), 380–8; H. Koch, Cathedra Petri, Neue Untersuchungen über die Anfänge der Primatslehre (Giessen 1930), and on this K. Adam, Gesammelte Aufsätze zur Dogmengeschichte (Augsburg 1936), 186 95); B. Poschmann, Ecclesia principalis (Breslau 1933); T. Zapelena, "Petrus origo unitatis apud s. Cyprianum" in Gr 15 (1934), 500–23; F. de St Palais d'Aussac, La réconciliation des hérétiques dans l'église latine (Paris 1943); B. Neunheuser in HDG IV/2 (Freiburg i. Br. 1956), 44–47; G. Klein, "Die hermeneutische Struktur des Kirchengedankens bei Cyprian" in ZKG 68 (1957), 48–68; P. Camelot, "Saint Cyprien et la Primauté" in Istina 4 (1947) 421–34; G. Mongelli, "La chiesa di Cartagine contro Roma durante l'episcopato di s. Cipriano (249–258)" in MF 59 (1959), 104–201.

DEVOTION TO THE CHURCH IN THE THIRD CENTURY: J. C. Plumpe, Mater Ecclesia. An Inquiry into the Concept of the Church as Mother in Early Christianity (Washington 1943); H. Rahner, Mater Ecclesia. Lobpreis der Kirche aus dem 1. Jahrtausend (Einsiedeln 1944); J. Daniélou, "Die Kirche, Pflanzung des Vaters. Zur Kirchenfrömmigkeit der frühen Christenheit" in Sentire ecclesiam, Festschrift H. Rahner (Freiburg i. Br. 1961), 92–103; L. Bouyer, "Zur Kirchenfrömmigkeit der griechischen Väter", ibid. 104–12; H. Rahner, "Navicula Petri" in ZKTh 69 (1947), 1–35.

27. The Extent of Christianity prior to the Diocletian Persecution

GENERAL TREATMENT: In addition to the works given in the bibliography to Chapter 17 above, the following may be consulted: A. Bigelmair, "Der Missionsgedanke bei den vorkonstantinischen Vätern" in ZMR 4 (1914), 264–77; L. Hertling, "Die Zahl der Christen zu Beginn des 4. Jahrhunderts" in ZKTh 62 (1934), 243–53; K. Prümm, Christentum als Neuheitserlebnis (Freiburg i. Br. 1939); J. Zeiller, "Observations sur la diffusion du christianisme en Occident" in ATh 5 (1944), 193–208; F. Altheim, Die Krise der alten Welt, III: Götter und Kaiser (Berlin 1943); Niedergang der alten Welt, II (Frankfurt a. M. 1952), 198–383; A. Ehrhardt, "The Adoption of Christianity in the Roman Empire" in BJRL 45 (1962–3), 97–114.

EGYPT: J. Faivre, "Alexandrie" in DHGE II, 289–369; H. Leclercq, "Égypte" in DACL IV, 2457–571; A. Heckel, Die Kirche von Ägypten bis zur Zeit des Nicänums (diss. Strasbourg 1918); H. Delehaye, Les martyrs d'Égypte (Brussels 1923); G. Bardy, "Les premiers temps du christianisme de langue copte en Égypte" in Mémorial Lagrange (Paris 1940), 203–16; J. M. Creed–De Lacy O'Leary, The Legacy of Egypt (London 1942), 300–31; R. Remondon, "L'Égypte de la suprême résistance au christianisme" in BIFAO 51 (1952), 63–78.

ARABIA: R. Aigrain, "Arabie" in DHGE III, 1158–339; H. Charles, Le christianisme des Arabes nomades (Paris 1936); P. K. Hitti, History of the Arabs (London–New York 1940); D. S. Attema, Het oudste christendom en Zuid-Arabie (Amsterdam 1949); G. Kretzschmer, "Origenes und die Araber" in ZThK 50 (1953), 250–79.

PALESTINE: R. Devreesse, "Les anciens évêchés de Palestine" in Mémorial Lagrange (Paris 1940), 217–27.

SYRIA: E. R. Hayes, L'école d'Édesse (Paris 1930); P. V. C. Baur, Christian Church at Doura-Europos (New Haven 1934); G. Watzinger, "Die Christen in Dura" in ThBl 17 (1938), 113–19; O. Eissfeldt, "Dura-Europos" in RAC IV, 362–70; A. F. J. Klijn, Edessa. Het Oudste Christendum in Syrie (Baam 1963).

PERSIA: J. Labourt, Le christianisme dans l'empire perse (224–632) (Paris 1904); A. Allgeier, "Untersuchungen zur ältesten Kirchengeschichte von Persien" in *Katholik* 98, II (1918), 224–41, 289–300; K. Lübeck, *Die altpersische Missionskirche* (Aachen 1919).

INDIA: M. D'Sa, *History of the Catholic Church in India* (Bombay, 2nd ed. 1924); A. Väth, *Der heilige Thomas, der Apostel Indiens* (Aachen, 2nd ed. 1925); A. Mingana, "The Early Spread of Christianity in India" in *BJRL* 10 (1926), 435–95; L. W. Brown, *The Indian Christians of St Thomas* (Cambridge 1955); E. Tisserant, "Nestorienne" and "Syro-Malabare (Église)" in *DThC* 11, 157–66; 14, 3089–93.

ARMENIA: G. Klinge, "Armenien" in *RAC* I, 678–89; S. Weber, *Die katholische Kirche in Armenien* (Freiburg i. Br. 1903); F. Tournebize, *Histoire politique et religieuse de l'Arménie* (Paris 1910); L. Arpee, *A History of Armenian Christianity* (New York 1946); M. Ormanian, *The Church of Armenia* (London 1955).

GEORGIA: K. Lübeck, *Georgien und die katholische Kirche* (Aachen 1918); K. Kekelidse, *Die Bekehrung Georgiens* (Leipzig 1928); W. Allen, *A History of the Georgian People* (London 1932); P. Peeters, "Les débuts du christianisme en Géorgie d'après les sources hagiographiques" in *AnBoll* 50 (1932), 5–58.

BALKANS: A. Lippold–E. Kirsten, "Donauprovinzen" in *RAC* IV, 166–89; J. Zeiller, *Les origines chrétiennes dans les provinces danubiennes* (Paris 1918); R. Noll, *Frühes Christentum in Österreich* (Vienna 1954); I. Zibermayr, *Noricum, Bayern und Österreich* (Horn, 2nd ed. 1956).

ITALY: H. Leclercq, "Italie" in *DACL* VII, 1612–841; *ECatt* VII, 386–9; F. Lanzoni, *Le diocesi d'Italia dalle origini al principio del sec. VII* (Faenza, 2nd ed. 1927); J. P. Kirsch, *Die römischen Titelkirchen im Altertum* (Paderborn 1918); U. Stutz, "Die römischen Titelkirchen und die Verfassung der stadtrömischen Kirche unter Papst Fabian" in *ZSavRGkan* 40 (1920), 288–312; E. Josi, "Titoli della chiesa Romana" in *ECatt* XII, 152–8; P. Styger, *Die römischen Katakomben* (Berlin 1933); H. Leclercq, "Ravenne" in *DACL* XIV, 2070–146; M. Mazzotti, "Ravenna" in *ECatt* X, 558–73.

AFRICA: J. Mesnage, *Le christianisme en Afrique. Origine, développement, extension* (Paris 1914); J. P. Brisson, *Gloire et misère de l'Afrique chrétienne* (Paris 1949), 32–141; A. Berthier–F. Logeart–M. Martin, *Les vestiges du christianisme antique dans la Numidie centrale* (Paris 1951); C. Courtois, *Les Vandales et l'Afrique* (Paris 1955); C. Speel, "The Disappearance of Christianity from North Africa in the Wake of the Rise of Islam" in *CH* 29 (1960), 379–97; W. Telfer, "The Origins of Christianity in Africa" in *Stud. patrist.* 4 (Berlin 1961), 512–17; W. H. C. Frend in *JThS* 12 (1961), 280–4.

SPAIN: H. Leclercq, *L'Espagne chrétienne* (Paris, 2nd ed. 1916); *García–Villada*, I (Madrid 1929); S. McKenna, *Paganism and Pagan Survivals in Spain up to the Fall of the Visogothic Kingdom* (Washington 1938); A. Ferrua, "Agli albori del cristianesimo nella Spagna" in *CivCatt* (1940), IV, 421–31; T. Fernández Alonso, "Espagne" in *DHGE* 15 (1963), 892–901 (bibl.).

GAUL AND BELGIUM: L. Duchesne, *Fastes épiscopaux de l'ancienne Gaule,* I (Paris, 2nd ed. 1907); E. Griffe, *La Gaule chrétienne,* I (Paris 1949), 51–116; M. Schuler, "Über die Anfänge des Christentums in Gallien und Trier" in *Trierer Zeitschrift* 6 (1931), 80–103; A. de Moreau, *Histoire de l'Église en Belgique,* I (Brussels, 2nd ed. 1947).

GERMANY: Hauck, I (4th ed. 1922), 3–33; W. Neuss, *Die Anfänge des Christentums im Rheinland* (Bonn, 2nd ed. 1933); *Tüchle,* I (1950); *Bauerreiss,* I (2nd ed. 1958); H. Lehner–W. Bader, "Baugeschichtliche Untersuchungen am Bonner Münster" in *Bonner Jahrbücher* 136–7 (1932), 1–216; W. Neuss, "Eine altchristliche Märtyrerkirche unter dem

Chor der St.-Viktor-Kirche in Xanten" in *RQ* 42 (1934), 177–82; H. Leclercq, "Xanten et Bonn" in *DACL* XV, 3271–6 (with bibliography).

BRITAIN: E. Kirsten in *RAC* II, 603 ff.; J. Chevalier, "Angleterre" in *DHGE* III, 145–9; L. Gougaud, *Christianity in Celtic Lands* (London 1932); G. Sheldon, *The Transition from Roman Britain to Christian England* (London 1932); W. Levison, "St Alban and St Alban's" in *Antiquity* 15 (1941), 337–59; N. Chadwick, *Studies in the Early British Church* (Cambridge 1958).

SECTION TWO

The Last Attack of Paganism and the Final Victory of the Church

28. *The Intellectual Struggle against Christianity at the End of the Third Century*

SOURCES

Porphyry, Περὶ Χριστιανῶν Fragments, edited A. von Harnack in *AAB* 1916/1 (97 fragments); addenda in *SAB* 1921–14 (five additional fragments); P. Nautin, "Trois autres fragments du livre de Porphyre 'Contre les chrétiens'" in *RB* 57 (1950), 409–16; Eusebius, *Contra Hieroclem*, *PG* 22, 795–868; also in C. L. Kayser, *Philostratus opera*, I (Leipzig 1870), 369–413, reprinted, F. C. Conybeare, *Philostratus, The Life of Apollonius of Tyana* (London 1912).

LITERATURE

See the works listed in Chapter 13 by J. Geffcken, P. de Labriolle and W. Nestle, and in addition the following:
On neo-Platonism in general, *Ueberweg* I, 590–612. On Porphyry, *Ueberweg* I, 609–12 and 190* f. Articles on Porphyry by L. Vaganay in *DThC* XII, 2555–90, and R. Beutler in *Pauly–Wissowa* XXII, 278–313; J. Bidez, *Vie de Porphyre* (Ghent 1913); A. von Harnack, "Griechische und Christliche Frömmigkeit am Ende des 3. Jahrhunderts", in *Aus der Friedens- und Kriegszeit* (Berlin 1916), 47–65; A. B. Hulen, *Porphyry's Work against the Christians* (New Haven 1933); W. Theiler, *Porphyrios und Augustin* (Halle 1933); H. O. Schroeder, "Celsus und Porphyrius als Christengegner" in *Die Welt als Geschichte* 17 (1957), 190–202; J. J. O'Meara, *Porphyry's 'Philosophy from Oracles' in Augustine* (Paris 1959); J.-B. Laurin, *Orientations maîtresses des apologists chrétiens de 270 à 361* (Rome 1954).

29. *Outbreak and Course of the Diocletian Persecution down to Galerius' Edict of Toleration in 311*

SOURCES

Lactantius, *De mortibus persecutorum*, edited J. Moreau in *SourcesChr* 39 (Paris 1954), I: Text and translation, II: Commentary; Eng. Trans. in *ANF* 7; *Euseb. HE* Book VIII and *De martyribus Palaestinae*; *Panegyrici latini*, edited E. Galletier, 2 volumes (Paris 1949–52). Various accounts of individual martyrs are indicated in the footnotes. On

Eusebius, cf. R. Laqueur, *Eusebius als Historiker seiner Zeit* (Berlin 1929); D. Wallace-Hadrill, *Eusebius of Caesarea* (London 1960); J. Sirinelli, *Les vues historiques d'Eusèbe de Césarée durant la période prénicéenne* (Dakar 1961).

LITERATURE

See above Chapter 8, bibliography, in particular the works on the persecutions by H. Grégoire, J. Moreau, and J. Vogt. In addition: L. Pareti, *Storia di Roma e del mondo romano*, VI; *Da Decio a Constantino (251–337)* (Turin 1962); J. Vogt, *Constantin der Große und sein Jahrhundert* (Munich, 2nd ed. 1960); J. Vogt, *Zur Religiosität der Christenverfolger* (Heidelberg 1962); G. Ricciotti, *The Age of Martyrs, Christianity from Diocletian to Constantine* (London 1960); G. E. M. de Ste Croix, "Why were the Early Christians Persecuted?" in *Past and Present* 26 (1963), 6–38; H. U. Instinsky, *Die alte Kirche und das Heil des Staates* (Munich 1963).

ON DIOCLETIAN: W. Ensslin in *Pauly–Wissowa* VII A, 2418–95; W. Seston in *RAC*, III 1036–53, and on this, cf. J. Straub, *Historia* I (Baden-Baden 1950) 487–99; W. Seston, *Dioclétien et la Tétrarchie*, I (Paris 1946); W. Seston, "A propos de la 'passio Marcelli centurionis'. Remarques sur les origines de la persécution de Dioclétien" in *Mélanges M. Goguel* (Paris 1950), 239–46; K. Stade, *Der Politiker Diokletian und die letzte große Christenverfolgung* (Wiesbaden 1927); N. H. Baynes, "The Great Persecution" in *Cambridge Ancient History*, 12 (London 1929), 646–77; A. Rehm, "Kaiser Diokletian und das Heiligtum von Didyma" in *Philologus* 93 (1938), 74–84; J. Straub, *Vom Herrscherideal der Spätantike* (Stuttgart 1939), 84–89, and J. Moreau in *Annales Univ. Sarav.* 2 (1953), 97 ff. Both these works deal with Diocletian's abdication.

ON MAXIMIANUS HERCULIUS: W. Ensslin in *Pauly–Wissowa* XIV, 2486–16.

ON GALERIUS: W. Ensslin in *Pauly–Wissowa* XIV, 2516–28; J. Vogt in *RAC* II, 1192–99; *Fliche–Martin* II, 457–77; M. Gelzer, "Vom Wesen und Wandel der Kirche" in *Festschrift E. Vischer* (Basle 1935), 35 ff.

ON MAXIMINUS DAIA: O. Seeck in *Pauly–Wissowa* IV, 1986–90; H. Grégoire, "La religion de Maximin Daia" in *Byz (B)* 8 (1933), 49–56.

ON MAXENTIUS: E. Groag in *Pauly–Wissowa* XIV, 2417–87; H. Leclercq in *DACL* X, 2752–69.

30. The Definitive Turning-Point under Constantine the Great

SOURCES

As in the previous chapter, together with Eusebius, *Vita Constantini*, edited by I. A. Heikel, *GCS* Eusebius I (Leipzig 1902). On the question of authenticity: I. Daniele, *I documenti Constantiniani della 'Vita Constantini' di Eusebio di Cesarea* (Rome 1938); J. Vogt, "Die Vita Constantini des Eusebius und der Konflikt zwischen Constantin und Licinius" in *Historia* 2 (1953), 463–71; P. Franchi de Cavalieri, *Constantiniana* (Rome 1953), 51–65; F. Vittinghoff, "Eusebius als Verfasser der Vita Constantini" in *RhMus* 96 (1953), 330–73; A. Jones "Notes on the Genuineness of the Constantinian Documents in Eusebius' Life of Constantine" in *JEH* 5 (1954), 196–200; H. Grégoire, "L'authenticité et l'historicité de la Vita Constantini attribuée à Eusèbe de Césarée" in *Bulletin Acad. Royale Belg.* 39 (1953), 466–83; J. Moreau, "Zum Problem der Vita Constantini" in *Historia* 4 (1955), 234–45; F. Scheidweiler, "Die Kirchengeschichte des Gelasios und die Vita Constantini" in *ByZ* 46 (1953), 293–301, and by the same author "Nochmals die Vita Constantini" in *ByZ* 49 (1955), 1–32.

The Letters, Decrees, and Laws of Constantine with religious content are dealt with by H. Dörries, *Das Selbstzeugnis Kaiser Konstantins* (Göttingen 1954), and by H. Kraft, *Kaiser Konstantins religiöse Entwicklung* (Tübingen 1955) (with abundant bibliography 273–82). A. Bolhuis, "Die Rede Konstantins an die Versammlung der Heiligen und Lactantius' 'Divinae Institutiones'" in *VigChr* 10 (1956), 25–32.

On Eusebius as a historian, as well as J. Lacqueur (cf. bibliography to Chapter 29 above), I. Sirinelli, *Les vues historiques d'Eusèbe de Césarée durant la période prénicéenne* (Dakar 1961); G. Downey, "The Builder of the Original Church of the Apostles at Constantinople: A Contribution to the Criticism of the Vita Constantini Attributed to Eusebius" in *DOP* 6 (1951), 53–80.

LITERATURE

Only a selection can be made from more recent writings; the literature available is immense. Surveys of this in: N. H. Baynes, *Constantine the Great and the Christian Church* (London 1929); J. Miller in *BJ* 246 (1935), 42–130, 279 (1942), 237–365; E. Gerland, *Konstantin der Große in Geschichte und Sage* (Athens 1937); F. Staehelin, "Konstantin der Große und das Christentum" in *ZSKG* (1937), 385–417; 19 (1939), 396–403; A. Piganiol in *Historia* I (1950), 82–96; H. Karpp in *ThR* 19 (1950), 1–21; K. F. Strohecker in *Saeculum* 3 (1952), 654–80; E. Delaruelle in *BLE* 54 (1953), 37–54, 84–100.

GENERAL TREATMENT OF CONSTANTINE: J. Vogt in *RAC* III, 306–79 gives the best summary and survey of the problems of research regarding Constantine. J. Burckhardt, *Die Zeit Constantins des Großen* (1853, Stuttgart, 6th ed. 1949); A. Piganiol, *L'empereur Constantin* (Paris 1932); E. Schwarz, *Kaiser Konstantin und die christliche Kirche* (Leipzig, 2nd ed. 1936); K. Hönn, *Konstantin der Große* (Leipzig, 2nd ed. 1945); A. H. Jones, *Constantine the Great and the Conversion of Europe* (London 1948); L. Voelkl, *Der Kaiser Konstantin* (Munich 1957); H. Dörries, *Konstantin der Große* (Stuttgart 1958); H. Dörries, *Constantine and Religious Liberty* (New Haven 1960); J. Vogt, *Constantin der Große und sein Jahrhundert* (Munich, 2nd ed. 1960).

CONSTANTINE'S CONVERSION: An account of research in J. Vogt, *Relazioni del X° Congresso internazionale di Scienze stor.* II (Florence 1955), 375–423; H. Grégoire, "La conversion' de Constantin" in *Rev. univ. Bruxelles* 36 (1930–1) 231–72; H. Grégoire, "La statue de Constantin et le signe de la croix" in *Antiquité classique* I (1932), 135–42; W. Seston, "La vision païenne de Constantin et les origines du christianisme constantinien" in *Mélanges Cumont* (Brussels 1936), 373–95; H. Grégoire, "La vision de Constantin 'liquidée'" in *Byz (B)* 14 (1939), 341–51; A. Alföldi, "In hoc signo victor eris" in *Pisciculi, Festschrift F. J. Dölger* (Münster 1939); J. Vogt, "Die Bedeutung des Jahres 312 für die Religionspolitik Konstantins des Großen" in *ZKG* 61 (1942), 171–90; J. Moreau, "Sur la vision de Constantin" in *RevÉAug* 55 (1953), 307–33; C. Martin, "L'Empereur Constantin fut-il un chrétien sincère?" in *NRTh* 78 (1956), 952–4; F. Altheim, "Konstantins Triumph von 312" in *ZRGG* 9 (1957), 221–331; H.-I. Marrou, "Autor du monogramme Constantinien" in *Mélanges Étienne Gilson* (Paris 1959), 403 to 414. On Constantine's attitude towards the *Sol invictus* see J. Karayannopulos in *Historia* 5 (1956), 341–57 and S. Kyriakidis in *Hellenika* 17 (1962), 219–46.

CONSTANTINE'S RELATION TO CHRISTIANITY: H. Koch, *Konstantin der Große und das Christentum* (Munich 1913); P. Batiffol, *La paix Constantinienne et le Catholicisme* (Paris, 4th ed. 1929); J. Straub, "Christliches Sendungsbewußtsein Konstantins" in *Das neue Bild der Antike* 2 (Leipzig 1942), 374–94; H. Lietzmann, "Der Glaube Konstantins" in *SAB* 1937, 29; H. von Schoenebeck, *Beiträge zur Religionspolitik des Maxentius und Constantin* (Leipzig 1939), new imp. Aalen 1962); J. Vogt, "Zur Frage des christlichen Einflusses auf die Gesetzgebung Konstantins des Großen" in *Festschrift L. Wenger*, II (Munich 1945), 118–48; J. Gaudemet, "La législation religieuse de Constantin" in *RHEF* 33 (1947), 25–61; H. Berkhof, *Kirche und Kaiser* (Zürich 1947); A. Al-földi, *The Conversion of Constantine and Pagan Rome* (London 1948); W. H. C. Frend, *The Donatist Church* (Oxford 1952); C. Cecchelli, *Il trionfo della Croce* (Rome 1954); K. Kraft, "Das Silbermedaillon Constantins des Großen mit Christusmonogramm auf dem Helm" in *Jahrbuch für Numismatik* 5–6 (1954–5), 151–78; J.-J. Van de Casteele, "Indices d'une mentalité chrétienne dans la législation civile de Constantin" in *Bulletin Assoc. Guillaume Budé* 14 (1955), 65–90; A. Ehrhardt, "Constantins Verzicht auf den Gang zum Kapitol" in *Historia* 4 (1955), 297–313; H. U. Instinsky, *Bischofsstuhl und Kaiserthron* (Munich 1955); I. Karayannopulos, "Konstantin der Große und der Kaiserkult" in *Historia* 5 (1956), 341–57; R. Carson, "The Emperor Constantine and Christianity" in *History Today* (1956), 12–20; H. Kraft, "Kaiser Konstantin und das Bischofsamt" in *Saeculum* 8 (1957), 32–42; K. Aland, "Die religiöse Haltung Kaiser Konstantins" in *Kirchengeschichtliche Entwürfe* (Gütersloh 1960), 202 to 239, and by the same author "Der Abbau des Herrscherkultes im Zeitalter Konstantins" ibid. 240–56; J. Vogt, "Heiden und Christen in der Familie Constantins des Großen" in *Eranion, Festschrift H. Hommel* (Tübingen 1961), 148–68; I. Gillmann, "Some Reflections on Constantine's 'Apostolic Consciousness'" in *Studia patristica* 4 (Berlin 1961), 422–8; S. Calderone, *Costantino e il Cattolicesimo* (Florence 1962); E. L. Grasmück, *Coercitio. Staat und Kirche im Donatistenstreit* (Bonn 1964).

31. The Causes of the Victory of the Christian Religion. The Scope and Import of the Turning-Point under Constantine

SECTION ONE: M. Sdralek, *Über die Ursachen, welche den Sieg des Christentums im römischen Reich erklären* (Breslau 1907); K. S. Latourette, *History of the Expansion of Christianity*, I (New York 1937), 160–70: "Reasons for Ultimate Success"; K. Prümm, *Das Christentum als Neuheitserlebnis* (Freiburg i. Br. 1939); W. Eltester, "Die Krisis der alten Welt und das Christentum" in *ZNW* 42 (1949), 1–19; G. E. M. de Ste Croix, "Aspects of the Great Persecution" in *HThR* 47 (1954), 75–113; W. H. Frend, "The Failure of the Persecutions in the Roman Empire" in *Past and Present* 16 (London 1959) 10–30.

SECTION TWO: In addition to the Literature on Constantine in the bibliography to Chapter 30, see: K. Voigt, *Staat und Kirche von Konstantin dem Großen bis zum Ende der Karolingerzeit* (Stuttgart 1936); K. Setton, *Christian Attitude Towards the Emperor in the Fourth Century, Especially as Shown in Address to the Emperor* (New York 1941); H. Berkhof, *Kirche und Kaiser. Eine Untersuchung der byzantinischen und theokratischen Staatsauffassung im 4. Jahrhundert* (Zürich 1947); F. E. Cranz, "Kingdom and Polity in Eusebius of Caesarea" in *HThR* 45 (1952), 47–66; S. L. Greenslade, *Church and State from Constantine to Theodosius* (London 1954); G. Downey, *Philanthropia* in Religion and Statecraft in the Fourth Century after Christ in *Historia* 4 (1955), 199–208; J.-P. Brisson, *Autonomisme et christianisme dans l'Afrique romaine de Septime Sévère à l'invasion arabe* (Paris 1958); K. Aland, "Das Konstantinische Zeitalter" in *Kirchengeschichtliche Entwürfe* (Gütersloh 1960), 165–201; ibid. "Kirche und Kaiser von Konstantin bis Byzanz", 257–79; B. Lohse, "Kaiser und Papst im Donatistenstreit" in *Ecclesia und Res Publica: Festschrift für K. D. Schmidt* (Göttingen 1961), 76–88; H. Rahner, "Konstantinische Wende?" in *Stimmen der Zeit* 167 (1960–1), 419–28; A. Momigliano (ed.), *The Conflict between Paganism and Christianity in the Fourth Century* (Oxford 1963); R. Hornegger, *Macht ohne Auftrag* (Olten – Freiburg i. Br. 1963); P. Stockmeier, "Konstantinische Wende und kirchengeschichtliche Kontinuität" in *HJ* 82 (1963), 1–21; G. Brunner, "Zur Konstantinischen Frage" in *OstKSt* 11 (1962), 43–51.

GENERAL INDEX

Figures in italics denote pages where the subject receives more intensive treatment.

507